EVENTS THAT FORMED
THE MODERN WORLD

EVENTS THAT FORMED THE MODERN WORLD

FROM THE EUROPEAN RENAISSANCE
THROUGH THE WAR ON TERROR

VOLUME 5: FROM 1900 THROUGH THE WAR ON TERROR

Frank W. Thackeray
and John E. Findling, Editors

ABC-CLIO

Santa Barbara, California • Denver, Colorado • Oxford, England

Library of Congress Cataloging-in-Publication Data

Events that formed the modern world : from the European Renaissance through the war on terror / Frank W. Thackeray and John E. Findling, editors.
     p. cm.
   Includes bibliographical references and index.
   ISBN 978-1-59884-901-1 (hardback : alk. paper) — ISBN 978-1-59884-902-8 (ebook)
   1. History, Modern—Encyclopedias.   I. Thackeray, Frank W.   II. Findling, John E.
   D209.E98 2012
   909.08—dc23   2012008325

ISBN: 978-1-59884-901-1
EISBN: 978-1-59884-902-8

16 15 14 13 12   1 2 3 4 5

This book is also available on the World Wide Web as an eBook.
Visit www.abc-clio.com for details.

ABC-CLIO, LLC
130 Cremona Drive, P.O. Box 1911
Santa Barbara, California 93116-1911

This book is printed on acid-free paper ∞
Manufactured in the United States of America

CONTENTS

1

The Chinese Revolution, 1911–1949

INTRODUCTION

China, the world's most populous country, spent much of the twentieth century in a state of almost continual revolutionary upheaval. The origins of China's turmoil date to the nineteenth century, when the antiquated Chinese Empire came under relentless pressure from a technologically more advanced Western world. These pressures eventually shattered the Chinese status quo and ushered in the era of revolution.

By 1839, the Qing dynasty had ruled China for almost 300 years. However, it had grown old and brittle, and in the nineteenth century, it showed clear signs of exhaustion. The Qing faced increasing discontent, manifesting itself in open rebellions that the rulers had difficulty repressing. Even more ominous for the Qing, aggressive European states had turned their attention to China.

In 1839, China and Great Britain went to war over the issue of free trade. Great Britain demanded that China accommodate British trading interests, especially the continued importation into China of opium from India. When the Chinese refused, war broke out. This First Opium War ended in 1842 with the Treaty of Nanjing, but it was soon followed by a Second Opium War that ended in 1858 with the Treaty of Tianjin. In both conflicts, the Europeans (France had joined Great Britain in the Second Opium War) administered humiliating defeats to the Chinese. The result of the European victories was the so-called treaty system, a series of agreements that reduced Chinese sovereignty and extended to the Europeans and Americans special privileges such as extraterritoriality, a quasi-legal device that exempted foreigners in China from Chinese legal jurisdiction. The message of China's weakness was driven home in 1860 when an Anglo-French expedition marched to Beijing (then known as Peking), the Chinese capital, and burned the emperor's summer palace to the ground.

Simultaneously, the Qing faced a major domestic crisis. The Taiping Rebellion began in 1850 and dragged on for 14 years. It drained the central government of what meager resources it possessed and contributed greatly to the breakdown of central authority. It was only with the help of foreigners that the Qing ended the Taiping Rebellion, but the dynasty now found itself more beholden to those foreigners than ever, while at home its authority in many regions had virtually disappeared.

Taking advantage of China's weakness, other powers enriched themselves at its expense. For example, Great Britain claimed Hong Kong, France encroached in what was to become French Indochina, and, in 1860, Russia forced China to surrender its claims to the lands north of the Amur River and east of the Ussuri River. This huge area became Russia's Maritime province, where the Russians then founded the city of Vladivostok.

During the latter part of the nineteenth century, the Qing grip on power continued to weaken. Toward the end of the century, the dynasty experimented with reform in an effort to revitalize its decrepit state. Copying their Japanese neighbors (whom they despised), the Chinese hoped to foster both Western technology and efficiency to defeat those very same Westerners and to restore Chinese pride and sovereignty. Although these efforts never really got off the ground, they did alarm the imperialists, who feared that a revived China would thwart their ambitions. The result was a wild scramble for control over bits and pieces of China.

War with Japan in 1894–1895 ended in yet another humiliating defeat for the Chinese, all the more galling this time because of their hatred of the Japanese and the fact that Japan, an Oriental state, had successfully copied the Western model to defeat China, another Oriental state. Although Japan was forced to relinquish many of its gains from the 1895 Treaty of Shimonoseki that ended the war, the defeat revealed China's utter helplessness. In a short time, Germany, Russia, France, and Great Britain staked out claims for themselves on China's prosperous east coast.

In their rush to fill the vacuum created by China's disintegration, the imperial powers sometimes collided with each other. The most spectacular collision resulted in the Russo-Japanese War of 1904–1905. The Japanese were victorious once again, and Japan's sphere of influence in East Asia expanded accordingly; however, Japan's victory held additional significance. For the first time in modern history, a nonwhite country had defeated a major European state. This event's significance was not lost on the other victims of European imperialism, including China. Although these victims condemned Japan's imitation of European imperialism, they could not help but notice that Japan had made itself a formidable power by copying the West.

Among educated Chinese, the spectacle of their proud empire being devoured piecemeal intensified their desire for change. Not only did they passionately hate the imperialists, they also despised the Qing dynasty, which they viewed as either incompetent or traitorous or a combination of both. Secret societies proliferated and, in the case of the Boxers, launched deadly attacks on foreigners that prompted further Western intervention in China.

In 1911, the dam of pent-up frustration burst. Revolution broke out, and the Qing dynasty was quickly overthrown. Dr. Sun Yat-sen, a leading opponent of the old regime, proclaimed a Chinese Republic. However, the revolution was only a partial success. Although the Qing had been toppled, a stable national government did not emerge. Sun's republic was stillborn, and the country plunged into acute anarchy characterized by the rise of warlords, individuals who commanded military detachments and who ruled in regions or provinces without any recourse to a national government. Eventually, a nominal government formed in the north at Peking while Sun remained strong in the south; but in fact central authority had disappeared, and the bulk of China was dominated by freebooting warlords.

In January 1915, Japan took advantage of Western preoccupation with World War I to expand its influence in China once again. Japan presented to the Peking government its Twenty-One Demands, a set of proposals that would have given Japan even greater sway over China's land and commerce than it already enjoyed. China at first resisted these demands, receiving support from the United States, which sought to safeguard its own interests. However, China eventually acquiesced to most of what Japan wanted, and Japan replaced Germany as the dominant foreign power in Shandong province and gained virtual control over Manchuria.

In 1917, China entered World War I on the side of the Allies. As was the case with many other exploited peoples, Chinese intellectuals were stirred by the ideals and ideas of U.S. president Woodrow Wilson, and they looked forward to the Paris Peace Conference with great anticipation in the hopes of ending the treaty system and regaining full sovereignty. However, their hopes were shattered when the Paris conferees ignored China and instead confirmed Japan in its possession of Germany's former concession at Shandong, thereby validating Japan's increasing domination of China.

The shabby treatment accorded the Chinese gave rise to the May Fourth Movement, named for the date in 1919 of the first of many demonstrations against the decisions of the Paris Peace Conference. The May Fourth Movement galvanized the country; Chinese from all walks of life protested against foreign, but especially Japanese, interference in China. They pledged themselves to a course of revitalization and national unity. So significant was the May Fourth Movement that noted historian Theodore Von Laue refers to it as "the first stirring of patriotic mass politics in China."

In the course of the 1911 Revolution and the turmoil that followed, Sun Yat-sen, who strongly supported the May Fourth Movement, emerged as the most important Chinese leader. Although Sun's movement, the Kuomintang (KMT) or Chinese nationalists, failed to supplant the Qing dynasty, he worked to extend its authority from its stronghold in the south and to bring the entire country under KMT control. Sun saw this as a first step toward achieving his twin goals of modernizing China and terminating all special privileges for foreigners. Sun's prescription for China's success was spelled out in his most important writing, *The Three People's Principles.*

Disappointed by China's treatment at the Paris Peace Conference, Sun turned to the new Marxist state in Russia. Lenin and the Bolsheviks were only too happy to encourage Sun, if for no other reason than to strike a blow at their capitalist enemies. Early in the 1920s, the Soviets began to send equipment and advisors to Sun. The Soviet advisors did a particularly good job of reorganizing the Kuomintang, turning it into an effective political force, and establishing a credible army capable of launching a military offensive. Furthermore, the ranks of the nationalists were augmented in 1923 when the tiny Chinese Communist Party, founded two years earlier, allied itself with the KMT under pressure from the Soviet-dominated Communist International, or Comintern.

In 1925, Sun Yat-sen died. He was succeeded as head of the Kuomintang by Chiang Kai-shek, a young general who had received training in the Soviet Union. Chiang resumed the Northern Expedition, a military and political offensive designed to unify the nation and to bring all China under Kuomintang rule. In 1927, in the middle of this successful campaign, Chiang, who was considerably more conservative than Sun, unexpectedly turned on his communist allies and massacred them. What was left of the Chinese Communist Party retreated to a remote area of southern China, where it tried to reconstitute itself. Meanwhile, in 1928, Chiang occupied Peking and declared the

KMT to be the official government of a unified and sovereign Chinese state. Although the KMT was clearly the strongest Chinese force, its authority in many regions remained nominal at best. Warlords and renegades continued to enjoy considerable strength.

Chiang's success alarmed an increasingly militaristic Japan, which wanted a weak and pliable China and feared that the KMT success would undermine its position. In 1931, Japan began to tighten its grip over the important province of Manchuria. In the following year, despite Chinese protests, Japan converted Manchuria into Manchukuo, a Japanese puppet state. For the next several years, Japan systematically bullied China; then, in 1937, it launched a full-scale invasion. Chiang and the increasingly corrupt nationalists put up ineffective resistance, and Japan overran much of eastern China. In response, Chiang moved his capital inland to the city of Chongqing.

Throughout the 1930s, as Japan devoured China, Chiang and the KMT continued to battle the Chinese communists. The communists, having regrouped in southern Jiangxi province after Chiang initially turned on them, in 1931 proclaimed the "Chinese Soviet Republic." However, despite some initial military success, they were too weak to ward off the nationalists, who attacked relentlessly. Finally, in October 1934, a ragtag band of communists took flight to avoid annihilation. This was the start of the legendary Long March, a journey of some 6,000 miles undertaken by perhaps 100,000 hard-core communists that lasted more than a year. During the course of the Long March, Mao Zedong (then known as Mao Tse-Tung), a former teacher and librarian, outmaneuvered his rivals to emerge as the leading figure of Chinese communism, a position he held until his death in 1976. When the fleeing communists finally came to rest in the caves of Yenan in northwestern China's remote Shaanxi province, only a handful of the original marchers remained.

In 1937, the nationalists and the communists formed a united front to oppose the Japanese. But this was an artificial concoction, and it soon fell apart. For the rest of World War II, the nationalists and communists spent as much time competing against each other as they did fighting the Japanese. Consequently, after the deaths of perhaps 2.2 million Chinese during World War II and the surrender of Japan in 1945, it was not surprising that civil war engulfed China. Despite significant aid from the United States, the KMT was defeated by the communists, who received considerably less aid and encouragement from the Soviet Union. On October 1, 1949, having driven Chiang and his forces from the mainland onto the offshore island of Taiwan, Mao Zedong and the communists proclaimed the People's Republic of China with its capital at Beijing.

However, revolution in China did not end with the communist victory. Rather, during the past several decades, the communists themselves have initiated a number of revolutionary programs. Some, such as the Great Leap Forward and the Cultural Revolution, have failed ignominiously; others, such as the economic reforms of Deng Xiaoping, Mao's successor, have shown great promise. In any event, all these programs represent a radical departure from Chinese tradition. Equally important, they have been carried out in a China free from foreign domination. No one today questions that China is both a unified and sovereign state.

INTERPRETIVE ESSAY

JEFFREY N. WASSERSTROM

Throughout most of this century, the words "China" and "revolution" have been closely linked in the American mind. From the Wuchang Uprising of 1911 that led to Sun Yat-sen's inauguration as the first president of a Chinese republic, to the protest movement that broke out in Beijing and other cities in 1989, the Chinese events that have made headlines in the West have often been revolutionary struggles. The relatively few Chinese names Americans have come to know during this century have typically been those of revolutionary leaders. And when American pundits have discussed China's international position in recent decades, they have often highlighted the tendency of revolutionary groups in other developing nations (ranging from Vietnam to Peru) to look to the Chinese Communist Party (CCP) for inspiration and practical assistance. Over the course of the twentieth century, in sum, we grew accustomed to thinking of China as a country in flux, a land of revolutions.

A century and a half ago, the Western view of East Asia's largest nation was very different indeed. Foreign observers of that time typically portrayed China as a once great country that had proved unable to keep pace with the modern world, a "changeless" land whose state ideology of Confucianism inhibited all forms of social evolution. The Chinese government's efforts to circumscribe the actions of Western traders and missionaries were dismissed as a despotic regime's futile efforts to block the natural course of "progress," and Western military victories in the Opium Wars of the 1830s through the 1860s were hailed as proof of the inferiority of Confucian beliefs and practices.

One explanation for China's inability to compete with the West was that the Chinese had gone for millennia without participating in a "revolution" worthy of the name. Some Westerners insisted that China's lack of revolutionary potential was at the root of its problems. One thing that nineteenth-century foreign observers found particularly striking about the stability of China's imperial system was its vulnerability to invasion as well as domestic rebellion. The Chinese historical record contained several examples of dynasties falling to armies that had come from beyond the nation's borders and been led by people who were not members of the Han ethnic group to which most people within China proper belong. It seemed, however, that even in these cases, the political status quo remained fundamentally unchanged. The case of the Qing dynasty (1644–1912) was often cited to illustrate this point.

Most China specialists now agree that nineteenth-century writers overstated the extent to which foreign dynasties adopted Chinese ways after taking power and had a tendency to go too far in contrasting the supposed stagnation of imperial China with the alleged dynamism of the industrializing West. There is good reason to think that, despite their adoption of Confucian principles and trappings, Manchu emperors of the Qing ruled the country in a significantly different way from many of their Han predecessors. There is also evidence that patterns of social and diplomatic relations were in a state of flux throughout the final centuries of imperial rule, as merchants began to gain power in certain regions and officials in frontier areas experimented with new strategies for dealing with the rulers of neighboring states. Finally, and probably most significantly, demographic changes of enormous proportions were taking place during the century preceding the First Opium War. Even by the most conservative estimates, the Chinese population doubled during this period, from roughly 200 million to about 400 million. This demographic explosion was both the result and the cause of a whole range of economic, technological, cultural, and political changes.

This said, it remains true that although a series of new dynasties had indeed been founded by rebel leaders during earlier periods, once in power, these former insurgents had tended to make only minor adjustments to the basic bureaucratic structure of the state. Chinese philosophers had, moreover, developed a sophisticated political cosmology, centered on the concept of the Tianming (Heavenly Mandate) and a vision of dynastic cycle, that provided justification for rebellious acts (providing only that the emperor against whom one rebelled could be shown to have failed to behave benevolently) but left no room for revolutionary ones.

The concept of the Tianming, as articulated by Confucian philosophers such as Mencius, provided the clearest legitimization for righteous rebellion. The Confucian argument was that no dynasty could come to power without Heaven (Tian) bestowing a special mandate to rule (ming) upon that ruling house but that the deity remained free to revoke its blessing at any time if the heirs of a founding emperor proved unworthy. In other words, unlike the European notion of the divine right of kings, the Tianming was not granted in perpetuity. Because Mencius claimed that Heaven "sees with the eyes and hears with the ears" of the people, any sign of popular discontent could be interpreted as an indication that the dynasty had lost or was in danger of losing its mandate. The ultimate proof lay in the rebellion's outcome: because Heaven was seen as having the power to determine the fate of human battles, whichever side won on the battlefield was considered the rightful possessor of the Tianming. The notion of dynastic cycles reinforced the motivation to rebel, by implying that no family could expect to retain its mandate forever and that the virtuous founders of new ruling houses played a crucial role in an organic process of decay and rejuvenation.

How did China go from being a land of rebellion to a land of revolutions? Why did the fall of the Qing lead to the founding of a republic rather than the establishment of yet another dynasty? How has China's vision of its own place in the world changed as Confucianism has been replaced by other state ideologies? And does the Chinese word *geming*, which is routinely translated as "revolution" but literally means "stripping of the mandate," have the same connotations as its English-language equivalent? Before attempting to answer these questions, it is worth taking some time to ask a more basic question: Does it make sense to talk about the Chinese Revolution as if it were a single coherent event, or is it more appropriate to think of modern China as having undergone a series of revolutions?

The authors of general surveys of world history and books on the revolutionary process tend to take for granted the idea that the Chinese Revolution is best treated as a single event, which began with the uprisings of 1911 and ended with the founding of the People's Republic of China (PRC) in 1949. They typically argue, moreover, that this 38-year event should be seen as one of the relatively few "Great Revolutions" of modern times, and should be placed in the same category as the considerably shorter revolutions that began in France in 1789 and in Russia in 1917. What is thought to make these and other Great Revolutions unusual is that, far from simply affecting who was in power or even how a country was governed, they also triggered basic transformations in general patterns of social and political life.

Western scholars who specialize in the history of modern China also view the first half of the twentieth century as a time of profound changes but tend to approach the notion of a Chinese Revolution in a somewhat different fashion. Some Chinese specialists use the term "Chinese Revolution" to refer to a long process of transformation that began in the late Qing and has continued into the communist era. However, other specialists reject the idea of viewing the Chinese Revolution as a single coherent event. Instead of speaking of an uppercase Revolution, these scholars prefer to present China's recent past as a series of interconnected but separable lowercase revolutions.

Similarly, when politicians and historians linked to the CCP and the Nationalist Party (Kuomintang; KMT) speak of China's *geming* (which can be translated with equal validity as either its "Revolution" or its "revolutions"), they often have in mind periods that are either much shorter or considerably longer than the standard 1911–1949 time frame. In some contexts, leaders of both parties still refer to the *geming* as a single struggle, which began approximately a century ago and continues to this day. CCP and KMT versions of this Revolution differ from each other markedly in certain ways: most notably, they diverge on the question of whether communist leaders should be seen as heroes or villains. Their viewpoints often converge on key points, however, such as the notion that the Revolution's glorious legacy should be preserved for each new generation of youths and that these youths have a sacred duty to fight for revolutionary goals that remain unfulfilled.

The CCP and KMT history textbooks written for these youths typically begin by echoing the sentiments described earlier but then proceed to divide the past century and a half into several distinctive eras, each of which is described as having been shaped by the outbreak of separate revolutions or revolutionary movements. For obvious reasons, the two types of textbooks differ considerably on countless specific issues relating to interpretation and terminology. Furthermore, both CCP and KMT textbooks offer equally ambiguous answers to the question of whether China's *geming* should be treated as a single long-term quest or a series of separable struggles.

The ongoing debates relating to periodization and definition sketched out above are so important and complex that it would be foolish to attempt to resolve them in a short essay. Rather, it is better simply to draw attention to the strengths and weaknesses of various approaches to the issue, so that readers will be in a better position to make up their own minds. One way to break up Chinese revolutionary history into component parts is to differentiate between a Republican Revolution led by Sun Yat-sen, a Nationalist Revolution led by Chiang Kai-shek, and a Communist Revolution led by Mao Zedong. This self-explanatory schema puts emphasis on three clear-cut chronological turning points: the birth of the republic in 1912, the establishment of KMT rule in 1927, and the founding of the PRC in 1949. Implicit in this approach is a vision of the world in which the formal ideologies espoused by political parties and the activities of charismatic leaders are viewed as centrally important. Its great strength is its simplicity and the attention it draws to the different agendas pursued by key political groups.

A second, more complex way to divide up China's recent past is to think in terms of a series of four revolutions, each of which transformed a different sphere of activity. Because no major event ever affects only one aspect of a nation's life and because some kinds of revolutions occur rapidly whereas others unfold gradually over long periods of time, one needs to allow for considerable overlap when distinguishing between, say, a country's "socioeconomic" and "political" revolutions. If this is kept in mind, a potentially useful way to conceptualize China's modern transformation is to differentiate between the *political revolution* that precipitated the transition from imperial to republican institutions; the *intellectual and cultural revolution,* the high point of which came in the late teens and early twenties; the *diplomatic revolution* that began in the late 1920s and peaked in the late 1940s; and the *socioeconomic revolution* that began early in the century but reached national proportions only in the 1950s.

The political revolution is the only one of the four that is easy to link to a specific starting date: October 10, 1911. The Wuchang Uprising, which broke out on that day, was not the first important challenge to the Qing dynasty. Throughout the nineteenth and early twentieth centuries, a wide range of revolts, ranging from large-scale peasant rebellions to attempted coups organized by secret organizations, had threatened Qing rule. None of these efforts was successful, however, until the mutiny at Wuchang inspired military units and local authorities around the country to issue the declarations of provincial autonomy that undermined the imperial regime's authority and set the stage for the founding of the republic.

The fact that these actions ultimately brought about the end of the imperial system does not mean that participants in the 1911 Revolution were all committed republicans. Philosophical critiques of the imperial system had appeared in various intellectual journals during the first decade of the century, to be sure, but so had vitriolic polemics deriding the Manchus as "barbarians" who had no right to control the fate of "real" (i.e., Han) Chinese, and appeals to racial pride were at least as important as appeals to republican ideals when it came to inspiring people to take action in 1911.

It is also worth noting that the most skillful political figures of the day, including Sun Yat-sen, were so adept at combining ethnic themes with political ones that it was often hard to tell where the former ended and the latter began. In their writings, the despotic nature of imperial institutions was frequently linked to the alien origins and purported inborn inferiority of the Manchu emperors. At times, the desire for a *geming* was presented as driven by a kind of filial piety toward China's last Han rulers, the last emperors of the Ming dynasty. This meant that, until the events of 1911 actually unfolded, it was not clear that if a "revolution" came, it would be anything more than an effort to *ge* (strip) the Manchus of their *ming* (mandate). Even when the military mutinies swept the nation, there was no guarantee that they would end up changing anything other than the identity and ethnicity of the person who occupied the Dragon Throne.

The complex motivations of the individuals who took part in the events of 1911 made this a very real possibility. Nationalist Party historians have tried to present the Wuchang Uprising as part of a complicated master plan that was crafted by Sun Yat-sen and carried out primarily by members of his Revolutionary Alliance, the organization that later evolved into the KMT. The reality is much more complex: many participants in the 1911 mutinies had no contact whatever with the Revolutionary Alliance and knew little of Sun Yat-sen (who, incidentally, was in Denver when the Wuchang Uprising took place). Some of those involved in the revolts were indeed members of radical groups who were committed to the idea that China needed to adopt a republican form of government, but others had less explicitly political reasons for taking part in the uprisings. Some participants were motivated to act by their general distrust of the Qing "barbarians," others by anger at the way particular officials had behaved toward them in the past, and still others by an opportunistic desire to advance their careers by being on the winning side when the mandate shifted.

This diversity of grievances and the lack of a unifying ideology notwithstanding, the uprisings ended up leading to changes that were much more profound than those that typically come in the wake of coups and rebellions. The uprisings of 1911 extinguished not just a particular dynasty but a whole tradition of imperial rule. The National Assembly and the other institutions of the new republic quickly proved ineffectual, to say the least, and as a result the country descended into a chaotic period of warlordism. The complete failure of two attempts by warlords to found new dynasties demonstrated, however, that the rules of political life had indeed undergone a profound transformation in the early 1910s.

Unlike the political revolution described earlier, the attempts Chinese revolutionaries have made to transform their nation's traditional belief structures and patterns of behavior are difficult to link to a particular date. The roots of this intellectual and cultural revolution can be traced back at least as far as the First Opium War (1839–1842) because the Chinese military defeats of the 1840s led many within the dominant scholar-official class to begin questioning long-standing assumptions about the inferiority of foreign cultures. The first generations of intellectuals to rethink these issues, although interested in what the West had to offer in terms of specific kinds of scientific knowledge and technological know-how, were seldom revolutionary in their approach. Their belief in the basic superiority of traditional moral codes and Confucian ideals remained unshaken, and their concern was with finding a reformist path that would allow them to hold firm to a Chinese essence *(ti)* while adapting the best that the West had to offer in terms of useful *(yong)* techniques.

The ti–yong distinction remained at the heart of intellectual debate within China for decades, until the New Culture Movement of 1915–1923 ushered in a period of genuinely revolutionary challenges to the traditional intellectual and cultural order. Most of the participants in this multifaceted event were professors and students who had either studied abroad or been exposed to foreign ideas at one of the Western-style academic institutions founded in China during the late Qing and Warlord (1912–1927) eras. They disagreed among themselves about many things, but they tended to share several basic convictions. First, they attributed much of the blame for China's current weakness to the enduring power of certain entrenched beliefs (e.g., that people should strive to recapture the glories of a past golden age rather than work to create a new kind of world) and practices (including arranged marriages and rituals associated with filial piety and ancestor worship) that they considered "Confucian" and "feudal." Second, they welcomed the best that the West had to offer in terms of moral codes and methods of critical inquiry as well as practical techniques. Finally, they felt that intellectuals needed to reach out to ordinary people and find a way to include them in the struggle for cultural renewal.

One of the key practical aspects of the New Culture Movement was the publication of a host of new periodicals filled with articles that introduced readers to the various Western ideologies (Social Darwinism, Dewey's pragmatism, anarchism, Marxism) that seemed to offer a means for explaining and resolving China's contemporary crises. Some of these new periodicals also served another purpose: written in a mode the intellectuals termed "plain speech" *(baihua),* as opposed to the less vernacular "classic style" *(wenyen)* of traditional scholarship, they were designed to inform and mobilize people outside of the academy. This literary move to break down the barriers between intellectuals and members of other classes was reinforced by public speaking campaigns intended to educate the illiterate about everything from Western ideas relating to disease to the humiliating nature of the Treaty of Versailles, under which Japan was given rights to govern parts of China that had been under German control prior to World War I.

This interest in breaking down barriers between intellectuals and the masses took an important new turn with the May Fourth Movement of 1919. This event began with students taking to the streets to protest the Versailles Treaty and to call for the resignation of three "traitorous officials" of the warlord regime then in power, who the demonstrators claimed had sold out the nation's interests to line their pockets with Japanese gold. The struggle soon broadened into a general fight against imperialist threats from abroad and oppression at home and grew from a student movement into one that involved members of many social groups.

The May Fourth Movement, although originally inspired by a diplomatic dispute, did not lead to a radical change in the way China related to the outside world. May Fourth activists proved much more successful when it came to achieving domestic goals. Most notably, although the protests of 1919 did lead to the dismissal of the "traitorous officials," they did not prevent Japan from taking charge of the port city of Qingdao in the Shandong province and other northern territories formerly under German control.

No diplomatic revolution could take place as long as the country lacked a strong central government committed to overturning the unequal treaties and defending China's national sovereignty. The Northern Expedition of 1925–1927, in which the KMT formed a united front with the CCP and the two parties called on the people of China to join them in a fight to the death against warlordism and imperialism, is perhaps the most logical place to start the story of China's diplomatic revolution. Major changes in China's international position did not follow directly in the wake of the KMT's victories of the late 1920s, however, for during the years immediately following his establishment of a new central government in Nanjing, Chiang Kai-shek decided that the spread of communism was more dangerous than the continuation of imperialism. This meant that throughout the Nanjing Decade (1927–1937), the generalissimo spent a great deal of energy fighting domestic threats to his power, which came from both the CCP and from groups headed by members of the KMT who claimed that Chiang was not the most fitting successor to Sun Yat-sen. Chiang was a much more outspoken critic of the unequal treaties and Japan's increasingly aggressive brand of imperialism than any of his warlord predecessors had been, but like many of them, he argued that China could not regain its place in the world until it got its own house in order.

World War II, which Chinese scholars claim (with considerable justification) began with the outbreak of Sino-Japanese hostilities in 1937, precipitated a sea change in China's diplomatic situation. China's position as one of the Allies gave Chiang Kai-shek new leverage in pushing for an end to the system of unequal relations with industrialized nations created by the treaties of the nineteenth century. In 1943, the Western powers formally renounced all claims to the concessions they had controlled for roughly a century in Shanghai and other cities on the Chinese mainland. Thanks to this decision and Japan's withdrawal from northern China in 1945, when World War II ended, the Chinese state was freer of foreign influence than it had been since the outbreak of the First Opium War.

CCP historians argue, however, that even then the diplomatic revolution was not complete. These writers claim that even though the formal structures of imperialism had disappeared, the KMT regime remained too economically and diplomatically dependent on the United States and other Western powers to be seen as a truly independent entity. The political motivations for making this claim are obvious because CCP historians have a clear stake in making their party's rise to power appear a patriotic act. Even though this argument is often overstated and used for political purposes, it has some validity. If credit for starting the diplomatic revolution should rightly go to Chiang Kai-shek's regime, it remains true that China did not fully regain its status as an independent nation able to negotiate with other countries on its own terms until the CCP took power.

The socioeconomic revolution also needs to be seen as something that began before 1949 but did not reach fruition until the founding of the PRC. Each of the revolutions described in this essay was both affected by and in turn triggered changes in patterns of social and economic life. To take but one example, a close look at the backgrounds of the leaders of the political revolution of the 1910s reveals that a disproportionate number belonged to newly created or newly ascendant social groups, the members of which enjoyed a relatively high status within society but felt dissatisfied with the way power was allocated within the imperial system. Managers of new industrial enterprises such as Western-style steamship companies; local gentry involved in the provincial assemblies that the last Manchu rulers sanctioned, as part of a last-ditch effort to save their dynasty by introducing a broad program of reforms; officers in the permanent regional armies originally created in the nineteenth century as temporary units whose sole function was to help the central government suppress peasant rebellions; and intellectuals who had studied in Japan or the West—members of these groups had little in common except a shared sense that they deserved to rise higher than they were able to under the existing system.

The rise and disaffection of these ascendant occupational groups between the 1860s and the 1930s was an important phenomenon because theorists of revolution often stress the leading role that "marginal elites" play in bringing about political change. Neither the development of new alignments near the top of the social ladder nor other associated socioeconomic shifts (such as the dramatic increase in the number of factory jobs available in bustling coastal cities around the turn of the century) had much effect, however, on the lives of the vast majority of Chinese, who resided in inland villages and either worked as tenant farmers or owned small plots of land. For these villagers, a socioeconomic revolution worthy of the name did not take place until the CCP launched its ambitious land reform campaigns in the late 1940s and early 1950s, during which poor peasants were called on to denounce publicly and at times even physically assault rich peasants within their villages as well as absentee landlords. Designed to redistribute land in a way that minimized social inequality and to pave the way for ambitious forms of agricultural collectivization, these campaigns radically changed the basic structure of Chinese social and economic life.

The two schema described here both provide plausible methods for dividing up the Chinese Revolution, but there are at least three strong arguments for thinking of the *geming* as a single event. One of these has already been alluded to: participants in this struggle have often insisted that the Revolution be seen as an ongoing quest for national salvation and transformation. Chinese leaders on both sides of the Taiwan Strait have continually, if at times inconsistently, argued that their legitimacy stems from their status as revolutionaries. The CCP and the KMT have very different visions of what exactly the *geming* is, and leaders of the two parties have blamed different kinds of factors (Soviet conspiracies, capitalist conspiracies, China's economic backwardness) for their inability to bring the Revolution to a close. What they share, however, is a vision of the revolutionary quest as a single enduring struggle, which will not be complete until Taiwan and the mainland are both ruled by the same government and China regains its proper place in the world as a leading cultural and political power. Party leaders are not the only ones, moreover, who think of the Revolution as an ongoing quest: some of the wall posters put up by protesters in 1989 chastised the heads of the CCP for allowing the *geming* to veer off its proper course.

A second important reason to think of the Revolution as a single event is that it forces us to focus on the continuities running through all of the various revolutions described in this essay. For example, dividing the *geming* into republican, nationalist, and communist revolutions obscures the fact that revolutionaries of all three eras shared certain basic convictions about China's predicament and the way to solve it. All three groups of revolutionaries were convinced that China could only be saved by an approach that might best be called nationalist cosmopolitanism. That is, each sought to identify internal sources of strength and combine them with powerful new ideologies and practices associated with the West and Japan. This common thread can be seen running through the policies and proclamations of Sun Yat-sen (who combined appeals to racial pride with flourishes of republican rhetoric), Chiang Kai-shek (who flirted with ideas associated with American-style democracy, German-style fascism, and Confucianism, while simultaneously presenting himself as Sun's most devoted follower), Mao Zedong (who argued that the CCP was using Marxist principles to carry a distinctively Chinese tradition of peasant rebellion to new heights), and even Deng Xiaoping (who justified recent experiments with market economy forces as part of an ongoing revolutionary effort to develop a form of "socialism with Chinese characteristics").

The third reason to think of China's *geming* as a single ongoing event is that it forces us to pay attention to those features of Chinese life that have remained relatively constant throughout the last century. Again, to take but one example, even though writings by various revolutionaries (including both noncommunist participants in the New Culture Movement and CCP leaders such as Mao Zedong) insist that one of the greatest evils of the Confucian order was its celebration of a patriarchal family system that gave men a disproportionate amount of power within the home, Chinese women continue to suffer from many of the same kinds of discrimination as their predecessors of earlier eras. Patterns of gender-based inequality exist today that are uncomfortably similar to those that New Culture Movement activists decried in their critiques of the Confucian order several decades ago. Phenomena such as these raise important questions about the appropriateness of describing China's "social" and "cultural" revolutions as completed events.

In conclusion, there are strong arguments to be made both for viewing the Chinese Revolution as a single cohesive event and for treating it as a series of overlapping but distinctively different struggles for transformation. If the definition and periodization of this (or these) *geming* remain open to a variety of interpretations, at least one thing about this event or set of events is clear: it (or they) unquestionably did change both China and the world in important ways.

Perhaps the most striking of these changes can be linked to the strengthening of the Chinese state. Although China specialists debate whether the 1911–1949 period was one in which the state was strengthened or weakened, there is a general consensus that the party-state of the CCP that emerged in the 1950s was a much more powerful and intrusive one than any of its immediate predecessors.

The process of strengthening the state has affected the lives of ordinary Chinese people in myriad ways, and it has also transformed the basic character of China's relations with other countries. Domestically, the changes have reshaped nearly every aspect of social, economic, cultural, and political life. For example, the Old Regime state tended to play only an indirect role in agricultural production, which was done primarily by families. Aside from paying taxes to government officials and appealing to these same bureaucrats for help when famine hit or disputes arose with other groups of farmers, these families tended to operate as largely autonomous economic units, which either worked their own land or (in the case of poorer households) negotiated directly with landlords to obtain the right to plant crops on particular fields.

The CCP party-state has adopted a host of policies relating to rural land ownership and agricultural production, ranging from redistributing private plots, to forcing villagers to join large-scale cooperatives, to introducing reforms that reemphasize the importance of families as economic units. All these policies, however, have at least one thing in common—each assumes that the state and its representatives should be intimately involved in deciding how the land is worked and how agricultural products are distributed. Similarly, in the case of industry, the CCP has always assumed that the party-state should take an active role in matters relating to work, including not only the setting of quotas but also the supervision of unions.

On the positive side, the development of an intrusive, powerful, and ideologically driven state apparatus has gone hand-in-hand with a host of improvements relating to education and health care. The party-state's commitment to social welfare programs has also helped mitigate the effects of the demographic crises that have plagued China throughout the past few centuries, which can all be traced back to overpopulation.

On the negative side, many Chinese have paid a high price for the kinds of material and cultural gains described in this essay. Not only has the regime periodically launched campaigns against intellectuals and discriminated against members of ethnic and religious minorities in a more systematic fashion, but people from all walks of life have consistently had to bow to the whims of corrupt members of the new privileged class composed of party officials and those with powerful connections. Worst of all, perhaps, the population as a whole has suffered from a series of ideologically inspired policy blunders, such as the Great Leap Forward (in which farmers were encouraged to forget their crops and concentrate on producing iron so that China could catch up to the West) and Mao Zedong's flirtation with pro-natalist ideas (during which he claimed that the larger China's population became, the stronger the nation would be), which have exacerbated the already precarious demographic situation.

State-strengthening has had a much more positive effect, at least for China and its allies, where international relations are concerned. China entered the twentieth century a weak nation at the mercy of Western and Japanese imperialists, desperately looking to other lands for answers to its internal crises. The past several decades, by contrast, have seen China consistently try (usually with considerable success) to deal with the world's most powerful nations on its own terms. It has even served at times as a model for developing nations seeking to defend or achieve a comparable political independence.

Although important transformations have occurred, it is also worth remembering that not everything about China has changed over the course of the past century. Rather, there has been a good deal of continuity even in those aspects of life that the *geming* was intended to transform. One indication of this is that many of the specific demands voiced by revolutionaries of earlier generations continue to be heard within the PRC. The China we see today is unquestionably a very different and much stronger country than it was at the beginning of the twentieth century, but it is worth closing with a reminder that when the protesters of 1989 called for an end to bureaucratic corruption and the creation of more responsive political institutions, they were asking for the very things for which some of their revolutionary predecessors of the Late Imperial, Warlord, and Nationalist eras had given their lives.

SELECTED BIBLIOGRAPHY

Bergere, Marie-Claire. *Sun Yat-sen.* Stanford, CA: Stanford University Press, 2000. A recent biography of modern China's founding father, Bergere's well-executed portrait of Sun is even handed, scholarly, and accessible.

Bianco, Lucien. *The Origins of the Chinese Revolution, 1915–1949.* Stanford, CA: Stanford University Press, 1966. Still in many ways the best short overview of the topic.

Chow Tse-tung. *The May Fourth Movement: Intellectual Revolution in Modern China.* Cambridge, MA: Harvard University Press, 1960. A comprehensive study of a major turning point in modern Chinese history.

Eastman, Lloyd E. *The Abortive Revolution: China under Nationalist Rule, 1927–1937.* Cambridge, MA: Harvard University Press, 1974. An eclectic collection of essays by a leading scholar of KMT politics.

Fairbank, John K. *The United States and China.* Cambridge, MA: Harvard University Press, 1983. A seminal survey of China's modern history and its diplomatic relations with the United States by the century's most influential American China specialist.

Hinton, William. *Fanshen: A Documentary of Revolution in a Chinese Village.* New York: Random House, 1966. A seminal study of a village undergoing land reform.

Huang, Philip C. C. *The Peasant Economy and Social Change in North China.* Stanford, CA: Stanford University Press, 1985. A detailed and sophisticated examination of local economic patterns.

Johnson, Chalmers. *Peasant Nationalism and Communist Power: The Emergence of Revolutionary China 1937–1945.* Stanford, CA: Stanford University Press, 1962. A classic study that puts forth the thesis that the CCP's rise to power had less to do with its social programs and ideology than with its ability to capitalize on nationalist sentiment triggered by the Japanese invasion.

Meisner, Maurice. *Mao's China and After: A History of the People's Republic.* New York: Free Press, 1986. A thoughtful general introduction to a complex era.

Ono Kazuko. *Chinese Women in a Century of Revolution, 1850–1950.* Edited by Joshua A. Fogel. Stanford, CA: Stanford University Press, 1989. The best single-volume history of the topic.

Pepper, Suzanne. *Civil War in China: The Political Struggle, 1945–1949.* Berkeley: University of California Press, 1978. The best single-volume overview of this complex and chaotic period.

Perry, Elizabeth J. *Rebels and Revolutionaries in North China, 1845–1945.* Stanford, CA: Stanford University Press, 1980. This impressive work highlights the difficulties communist organizers faced when trying to force a rebellious tradition to serve a specific type of revolutionary purpose.

Schwarcz, Vera. *The Chinese Enlightenment: Intellectuals and the Legacy of the May Fourth Movement of 1919.* Berkeley: University of California Press, 1986. A superb study of the predicament of intellectuals in twentieth-century China.

Selden, Mark. *The Yenan Way in Revolutionary China.* Cambridge, MA: Harvard University Press, 1971. A seminal though controversial account of the CCP's rise to power.

Snow, Edgar. *Red Star over China.* Rev. ed. New York: Grove Press, 1968. A fascinating firsthand account of the lives and views of CCP leaders.

Spence, Jonathan. *The Gate of Heavenly Peace: The Chinese and Their Revolution, 1900–1985.* New York: Viking Press, 1981. A beautifully written survey of the Chinese Revolution, this work is centered around the life histories of several key intellectual figures.

Spence, Jonathan. *Mao Zedong: A Life.* New York: Penguin, 2006. Probably the most accessible short biography of the man who climbed from nothingness to lead the world's most populous nation.

Taylor, Jay. *The Generalissimo: Chiang Kai-shek and the Struggle for Modern China.* Cambridge, MA: Harvard University Press, 2009. A revisionist author of sorts, Taylor portrays Chiang as relatively competent and successful if exceptionally brutal. That he "lost" China has more to do with its ungovernability than Chiang's effectiveness.

Twitchett, Denis, and John K. Fairbank, general eds. *The Cambridge History of China.* Vols. 1–15. New York: Cambridge University Press, 1978–[1991]. Volumes 10 through 15 provide a comprehensive introduction to Western scholarship on the political, social, intellectual, and diplomatic history of late imperial and revolutionary China.

Wakeman, Frederic E., Jr. *The Fall of Imperial China.* New York: Free Press, 1975. A superb introduction to the social and political processes that led up to the 1911 Revolution.

Wasserstrom, Jeffrey N., and Elizabeth J. Perry, eds. *Popular Protest and Political Culture in Modern China.* 2nd ed. Boulder, CO: Westview Press, 1994. A collection of essays by leading specialists from several disciplines who attempt to put China's current crises into historical perspective.

Wolfe, Margery. *Revolution Postponed: Women in Contemporary China.* Stanford, CA: Stanford University Press, 1985. An engaging study of one of the more problematic legacies of the Chinese Revolution.

Wright, Mary C., ed. *China in Revolution: The First Phase.* New Haven, CT: Yale University Press, 1968. The most important single work on events leading up to and following the Wuchang Uprising.

CHIANG KAI-SHEK (1887–1975)

In pursuit of a unified China, Chiang Kai-shek followed in the footsteps of Sun Yat-sen, the father of modern China and the creator of the Kuomintang (Nationalist Party). Chiang, however, was unwilling to build the nation in a way that took the needs of

China's peasant majority into account. His strident belief in his military invincibility eventually led to his defeat.

Chiang was born on October 31, 1887, in Zhejiang Province. His father, a moderately prosperous salt merchant, died in 1896. In the time of Chiang's boyhood, China underwent enormous upheaval as the ruling Qing dynasty had been disgraced and weakened by foreign encroachments on Chinese sovereignty. Many Chinese blamed this on Qing traditionalism and backwardness and believed China had to become more modern to expel the foreigners and regain its power and dignity.

Chiang agreed with this. When he traveled to Japan in 1907 to train for a military career at the Shikan Gakko Military Academy, he came into contact with other Chinese students who advocated reform. Chiang even joined the revolutionary group founded by Sun, the Revolutionary Alliance, committed to overthrowing the Qing dynasty and establishing a republican form of government.

Chiang served in the Japanese army from 1909 to 1911. When on October 10, 1911, revolution erupted in the Chinese province of Wuhan, Chiang returned home to fight under General Chen Qimei against the Qing government. The revolutionaries overthrew the dynasty, and on January 1, 1912, Sun proclaimed the Republic of China. Sun, however, did not have the military power necessary to unite China. Yuan Shikai, a political boss based in the north, possessed the most military might, and so Sun agreed to his becoming president. Yuan quickly ignored the national legislature controlled by Sun's political party, the Kuomintang. Instead, Yuan developed a dictatorship and moved militarily against the Nationalists. In 1913, this aggression produced a "second revolution" in which Sun and Chiang fought against Yuan's forces, but by the end of the year, Sun had lost, and Chiang was forced to flee to Japan.

Chiang led a secretive existence from 1916 to 1917, during which time he apparently involved himself with the Shanghai underworld and associated with a group called the Green Gang. In 1918, he returned to China and rejoined Sun's movement, developing a close relationship with the Nationalist hero. By this time, Yuan had died, and his government had disintegrated, ushering in a chaotic period in which warlords exerted power in various territories. Sun led a Kuomintang government that existed only in name, as he still struggled to unite China under his banner. In the early 1920s, Sun reorganized the Kuomintang along the lines of the communist revolutionaries in Russia. In 1923, Sun sent Chiang to Moscow to study Soviet military methods and the close political arrangement between the army and the Communist Party.

Chiang returned to China late in 1923 and directed the Whampoa Military Academy, established near Canton with the help of Soviet advisers. Such talented Communists as Zhou Enlai headed its political department, and Lin Biao enrolled as a cadet. The organizational skills and nationalist enthusiasm of the Communists convinced Sun to create alliances and admit them into the Kuomintang.

Sun died in March 1925, and Chiang, for some time considered Sun's heir apparent, used the support of the Whampoa army in a political struggle with his main rival in the Kuomintang, Wang Jingwei, to emerge as the new Nationalist leader. The Communists, however, still posed a threat to his power. In 1927, Chiang took the Nationalist army into northern China, where he gained control of the lower Yangzi Valley. He then moved on Shanghai and captured that city after a Communist-led uprising of workers paved the way for his entry. In a surprise move on April 12, 1927, Chiang attacked the labor unions and captured the Communists, killing several hundred of them. Having betrayed the Communists and the leftist faction in the Nationalist movement, Chiang increasingly allied himself with the right.

In December 1927, Chiang married Soong Mei-ling (he had earlier divorced his second wife, to whom he was still married when he first courted Soong), whose Westernized family convinced him to become a Christian. The marriage drew him closer to the conservatives in Chinese society, and Soong subsequently played a dominant role in Chiang's Nationalist government.

Chiang had feared that the Communists would undermine his power, particularly because many Nationalist troops sympathized with them. He also believed that the Communists were more concerned with promoting the interests of the international communist movement than the interests of China. More pragmatically, Chiang needed the support of warlords who disdained the Communists. It was for these reasons that Chiang broke with the increasingly popular Communists and forced two leading competitors in the Kuomintang to retire: Wang Jingwei, sympathetic to the left wing, and Mao Zedong, Communist head of the propaganda department. After additional military assaults, by October 1928, Chiang's forces had control of nearly all of China.

Chiang claimed he supported economic reform, but he never initiated any major changes. His Nationalist government sided with the business interests and the landed gentry. In a country where most people were peasants who were suffering great hardship, his policies won little popular support. At the same time, his rule became known for its widespread corruption.

Chiang committed a serious blunder in his policy toward Japan. The Japanese captured Manchuria in 1931 and showed every intention of invading northern China and beyond. Rather than prepare his army primarily for this invasion, Chiang decided to concentrate on the Communists and eliminate them from the scene. However, the Communists, led by Mao, eluded Chiang and won a substantial following by focusing their attention on ousting the despised Japanese. Although General Zhang Xueliang captured Chiang and attempted to force him to accept that the Nationalists and Communists should form a common front against Japan, Chiang went back on his word once he was released, and Zhang was imprisoned. Only after the Japanese occupied half the country in 1937 would Chiang submit to the Communist offers of concerted action against the common enemy.

In 1934, Chiang began the New Life movement (Soong played a central role in its creation), trying to get the Chinese to adopt Confucian values mixed with puritanical Protestantism. This ideology paled in appeal next to the radicalism, particularly the land reform, offered by the Marxists.

When Japan finally did invade China in 1937, the Communists rallied the countryside, and the Red Army grew enormously. Millions of Chinese who had little understanding of Marxism found in Mao a hero who would protect China. Chiang worsened his situation by withholding his army from much of the fighting. He let the Communists and later the Allies bear the brunt during World War II, thinking he would save his men for the postwar struggle against Mao. In the meantime, his army grew indolent and overconfident. Chiang was mortified when in 1944, the Japanese attacked Nationalist forces with devastating results: 700,000 men lost, along with 100,000 square miles of territory in seven months.

In 1946, the Nationalists and Communists engaged in fierce fighting, ignited when Chiang blocked Mao's troops, who sought to move from central China to the north, where they could reinforce communist units in Manchuria. For three years, the so-called Chinese Communist Revolution continued, and Chiang made serious military mistakes, the most damaging being his decision to move his army into Manchuria, thus overextending his supply lines. Furthermore, he blundered when he outlawed reform movements and consequently convinced many liberals to support the Communists.

Even Mao expressed surprise at how fast the Nationalists disintegrated. In 1949, Chiang fled to Taiwan, an island near China's southeast coast, where with U.S. backing, he founded the Republic of China. While Mao and the Chinese Communist Party ruled the People's Republic of China on the mainland and developed a cultlike Maoist ideology, Chiang insisted that his Kuomintang constituted the legitimate Chinese government—a claim only the United States took seriously—and for more than twenty years, Taiwan held the Chinese seat in the United Nations.

Under Chiang, Taiwan developed a prosperous capitalist economy, helped greatly by massive infusions of U.S. aid and military protection. Although Taiwan had a representative assembly, Chiang ruled the island as his personal domain.

Chiang claimed he would recapture the mainland, but it never came about, and he grew more isolated. In 1972, the People's Republic of China regained the Chinese seat in the UN, and throughout the 1970s, the United States normalized its contacts with the mainland. Chiang did not live to see the United States sever its formal ties with Taiwan in 1979, when it established diplomatic relations with mainland China. He died on April 5, 1975, and was succeeded as Taiwan's leader by his son, Chiang Ching-kuo.

NEIL HAMILTON

MAO ZEDONG (1893–1976)

Mao Zedong was the leader of the People's Republic of China. A great visionary, Mao Zedong was also one of history's deadliest tyrants. A rebel from childhood, Mao helped found the Chinese Communist Party in 1921, took command of the revolution 14 years later in the midst of the Red Army's epic Long March, fought another 14 years before the Communists' final victory, and then remained China's supreme ruler for more than a quarter-century until his death at age 82.

The leader of the Chinese Communist Revolution was born on December 26, 1893, in a peasant home in Hunan Province. He was educated at his village primary school and subsequently entered high school in Changsha, the provincial capital. Mao was in Changsha when, on October 10, 1911, revolution broke out against the last of the Qing dynasty emperors. Mao joined the revolutionary army but saw no fighting and returned to his studies after six months as a soldier.

After graduating from the provincial teacher-training college, Mao went to Beijing, where he worked as an assistant librarian at Peking University and began to learn about Marxism. In July 1921, he attended the Chinese Communist Party's founding congress in Shanghai. Seeing Marxist theories through a Chinese prism, unlike many of his more orthodox comrades, Mao believed that revolution in China had to begin among peas-

In this idealized representation, a young Mao Zedong is portrayed on his way to organize a workers' strike in 1921. During his rule in China, Mao proved exceptionally adept at using propaganda to reinforce his image as a strong, progressive leader. (Stefan Landsberger/Liu Chunhua)

ants, rather than in an embryonic industrial working class. During the 1920s, he spent much of his time organizing peasant unions in his native Hunan Province.

At the end of the decade, with the Communists fighting for survival against Chiang Kai-shek's Nationalist (Kuomintang) government, Mao retreated farther into the countryside instead of joining other Communist leaders in suicidal urban uprisings. By 1934, Mao's base in Jiangxi province was under heavy pressure from Nationalist troops. That October, some 86,000 Communists slipped through the Nationalist blockade and began a 6,000-mile retreat that became known as the Long March. Mao, in political eclipse when the march began, became the party's supreme leader during the trek, a role he never relinquished. At the end of the Long March, with only about 4,000 left from the original force, Mao and his comrades established a new base in Yenan in northern China.

Between 1937 and 1945, Mao and his army fought a new enemy: Japan. In the Sino-Japanese War of 1937–1945, Mao and his commanders refined the art of "people's war." Mao summed up the strategy in only 16 Chinese characters: "The enemy advances, we retreat; the enemy camps, we harass; the enemy tires, we attack; the enemy retreats, we pursue."

The Red Army became a political as well as military organization. Instead of victimizing the peasantry, as Chinese soldiers had done from time immemorial, Mao's troops sought to win over the population to their cause. Instead of looting, raping, and destroying, Communist soldiers were ordered to pay for food, respect women, and help repair war damage. The ideal, and to an extent the reality, was an army that commanded public support and could, in Mao's most famous simile, swim among the people as fish swim in the sea.

Following Japan's defeat, the struggle between Communists and Nationalists resumed, but by now the tide was running strongly in Mao's favor. By the fall of 1949, the Nationalist government and what remained of its army had fled to the island of Taiwan. On October 1, Mao stood under China's new flag, red with five gold stars, and proclaimed the People's Republic of China.

The Communists were not gentle in establishing their regime. "A revolution is not the same thing as inviting people to dinner or writing an essay or painting a picture or embroidering a flower," Mao once wrote. "It cannot be anything so refined, so calm and gentle." In the first years of the People's Republic, hundreds of thousands, perhaps millions, were executed as landlords or capitalist exploiters. Millions more were imprisoned or tortured for real or imaginary crimes against the revolution, or simply for having a privileged background. Rigid ideological controls were imposed on educators, artists, and the press.

Less than a year after he came to power, the outbreak of the Korean War presented Mao with difficult choices. His priority was on consolidating his new government and rebuilding China. But a North Korean defeat would bring hostile foreign forces to China's northeastern border and, Mao feared, might encourage Chiang to send his forces back across the Taiwan Strait to reopen the civil war on the mainland. The key issue for China was whether counterattacking U.S. forces would halt at the 38th parallel in the fall of 1950 or continue their advance into North Korea. If the latter, Mao decided, China had no choice but to enter the war.

On October 8, the day after the first U.S. troops moved onto North Korean territory, Mao issued the official directive: "It has been ordered that the Northeast Border Defense army be turned into the Chinese People's Volunteers" (the name was a fig leaf, a transparent device for China to go to war with the United States without formally avowing it) "and that the Chinese People's Volunteers move immediately into the territory of Korea to assist the Korean comrades in their struggle."

Mao's decision to intervene in Korea cost the life of his oldest son. Mao Anying, age 28, was killed in a U.S. air strike on a Chinese People's Volunteer army command post in November 1950, just weeks after the intervention began.

For many ordinary Chinese, life gradually improved in the years following 1949. But Mao was impatient for faster progress. Uninformed about economics and technology and convinced that the sheer muscle power of China's huge population could accomplish any goal if it were just mobilized properly, he began dreaming of a "Great Leap Forward" that would hurl China out of poverty and backwardness and create a modern, prosperous state virtually overnight.

The Great Leap produced numerous follies, but the worst calamity occurred in agriculture. Intoxicated by his own visions and seduced by crackpot theorists (at one point, Chinese "scientists" claimed to have crossed a cotton plant and a tomato plant to produce red cotton!), Mao decreed an overnight transition from family or small cooperative farms to vast People's Communes, while also calling for absurdly high increases in grain production. The results were devastating. From 1959 to 1961, as many as 30 million Chinese died as a direct or indirect result of Great Leap policies.

In the wake of the disaster, Mao withdrew from day-to-day administrative details. But he nursed a deep grievance against those who he imagined had sabotaged his plan. In 1966, Mao struck back with the Great Proletarian Cultural Revolution, an event so irrational and bizarre that recorded history shows nothing else quite like it. Proclaiming "rebellion is justified," Mao urged China's youth to rise up against the party bureaucracy and against the "Four Olds": old habits, old customs, old culture, and old thinking.

At Mao's call, brigades of youthful Red Guards waving the little red book of Mao's thoughts spread out to "make revolution" in schools, factories, and offices throughout China. Within months, the country was in chaos. Red Guard groups splintered into rival mobs, each determined to outdo the other in rooting out enemies and tearing down everything that symbolized incorrect thoughts or China's past. Teachers, managers, intellectuals, and anyone suspected of insufficient revolutionary purity were paraded before howling mobs and forced to confess their misdeeds. Savage beatings were common. Many victims died under torture; constant physical and mental harassment drove many others to commit suicide.

Among those persecuted were almost all of the old cadres—party workers and Red Army soldiers whose struggle and sacrifice had brought the Communists to power. Meanwhile, the glorification of Mao reached extraordinary heights. His face, with its high-domed forehead, backswept hair tufting over each ear, and the celebrated mole just to the left of the center line of the chin, gazed out from virtually every wall in China. Badges with his image became part of the national dress. Schoolchildren and office workers began every day with bows before Mao's picture.

Not even the frenzy of leader worship could stem a growing sense that something was wrong, however. In the torrent of slogans and accusations, the movement's goals grew steadily more inexplicable. "The whole nation slid into doublespeak," Jung Chang, then a teenager, recalled in her memoir, *Wild Swans*. "Words became divorced from reality, responsibility, and people's real thoughts. Lies were told with ease because words had lost their meanings—and had ceased to be taken seriously by others."

China paid a heavy price for Mao's mad fantasies: the educational system was shattered for years; economic losses were ruinous; much of China's rich artistic legacy was destroyed; society was fractured; and ideals crumbled. After two years of chaos, order was gradually restored, often at gunpoint by People's Liberation army units, but a mood of fear and uncertainty persisted through the remaining years of Mao's rule.

The Red Guards were disbanded and millions of young people were sent from towns and cities to work as farm laborers. Out loud, nearly all of them obediently vowed willingness to "serve the people" wherever they were sent. But inwardly, many were confused, disillusioned, and hurt.

On July 28, 1976, the disastrous Tangshan earthquake struck north China. Nearly 250,000 people were killed, and physical destruction was immense, even in Beijing, 100 miles from the epicenter. In Chinese tradition, such disasters were thought to signal the end of a dynasty. The Communist regime officially scorned such superstitions, but to many Chinese the old beliefs were vindicated when, at 10 minutes past midnight on September 9, Mao died.

Believing that sheer willpower and human muscle could overcome any obstacle, Mao had turned China into a gigantic laboratory for his experiments in transforming human society. But when his grandiose dreams failed, instead of recognizing that his policies were flawed, Mao tore China apart in mad witch-hunts for the "demons and monsters" who had frustrated his efforts.

Mao's career was rich in contradictions. He proclaimed Marxism his lifelong faith, but his revolutionary ideas owed little to Marx and much more to ancient Chinese sagas of bandits and peasant rebellions. He preached simplicity and egalitarianism, but had himself glorified as a virtual god-king. He declared war against China's feudal past and its oppressive traditions, but his reign, rife with arbitrary cruelties and constant intrigues, mirrored many of the worst aspects of imperial despotism.

Mao's remains were given a place of high honor in an enormous mausoleum on Tiananmen Square, but his ideas were entombed with him. Less than a month after his death, his widow Jiang Qing and her three closest associates, the Gang of Four who had been the chief zealots of the Cultural Revolution, were imprisoned. Deng Xiaoping, whom Mao had twice expelled from the leadership, regained power and within a few years reversed nearly all of Mao's policies. In the end, it was the pragmatic Deng rather than the visionary Mao who laid the groundwork for economic reforms that transformed China in the 1980s and 1990s.

SPENCER C. TUCKER

SUN YAT-SEN (1866–1925)

In the early twentieth century, Sun Yat-sen was China's most important revolutionary leader during the fall of the Qing dynasty and the following decade when the nation's political turmoil inspired many Chinese to examine and debate the possibilities for progress. Determined to oust foreigners from China but at the same time attracted to many Western ideas, Sun is widely considered to have been the father of modern China. He led nationalists into an alliance with communists based on their shared hopes for the lasting reunification and reform of their vast nation.

Sun was born into a poor peasant family on November 12, 1866, in Guandong Province, near Canton. At first he obtained a traditional Confucian education, but in 1879, his brother brought him to Honolulu, Hawaii. There, he attended a British missionary school and then the U.S.-run Oahu College. Western science and philosophy attracted him, as did Christianity.

In 1883, Sun returned to Canton, where he was heavily criticized for his Westernization. He then moved to Hong Kong, where Western influences were more accepted. In 1884, he began studying at the Diocesan Home before transferring the next year to the Government Central School. Around that time, a U.S. missionary baptized him, and he married Lu Mu-chen, who had been chosen by his parents to be his wife. He enrolled in the Canton Hospital Medical School, followed by the College of Medicine for Chinese, located in Hong Kong. Graduating in 1892, he tried to begin his medical practice at Macau, a Portuguese colony. However, the Portuguese denied him a license, and Sun returned to Hong Kong, where he began a brief career as a doctor.

China was then ruled by the Qing dynasty. Along with many Chinese, especially the younger, educated groups, Sun condemned his country's technological backwardness that allowed outside powers to dominate. He criticized the foreign nations that had humiliated the dynasty and the nation by carving China into spheres of influence. He tried to get the Chinese authorities to listen to his pleas for reform, but when he got only rejection, he gave up his medical practice and dedicated himself to radical revolutionary change.

In 1894, he went back to Hawaii and formed the Revive China Society, a secret revolutionary organization. After China suffered more humiliation with its loss to Japan in the Sino-Japanese War of 1894–1895, Sun journeyed to Hong Kong, where he plotted an uprising to be staged in Canton. The Chinese government uncovered his revolutionary group, however, and executed several of its members. Sun fled to Japan, where he found new stimuli, for many Chinese exiles gathered there to discuss and plan great changes.

Sun traveled extensively and to spread his belief that revolution must ensue and sought monetary contributions from Chinese living overseas. He visited the United States and then the United Kingdom. In July 1897, Sun arrived back in Japan and obtained financial assistance from several influential Japanese. Sun's ideology never assumed the importance of his actions, which he himself considered the marrow of revolutionary activity. In 1900, he sponsored an uprising in Huizhou, but it collapsed after just 12 days. Then Sun received assistance from Liang Qichao, a Qing official who had fled to Japan and that attacked the various Qing practices and praised Sun. These published essays widely read publications boosted Sun's following. In 1905, he and several other radicals formed the Tongmenghui (Revolutionary Alliance) in Tokyo. Sun then went to Hanoi, where he put together several uprisings in southern China. Those revolts also failed, and Sun lost supporters and financial backing.

The Qing dynasty continued to struggle, however, as its attempts at reform pleased nobody. On October 10, 1911, a rebellion that Chinese call the Double Tenth, broke out in Wu-han, and the rebels, led by army units sympathetic to the Tongmenghui, overthrew the provincial government. Several provinces in central, south, and northwest China declared their independence from the Qing. At the time, Sun was traveling in the United States to raise money. He departed quickly for China, and revolutionary delegates gathered in Nanjing elected him president of a provisional government. On January 1, 1912, Sun proclaimed a new nation: the Republic of China. He also formed a new political party, the Kuomintang (the Chinese Nationalist Party).

Sun, however, lacked the military support he needed to extend his power throughout China, where local leaders had always tested the control of central government. In Beijing, Yuan Shikai, an official in the Qing government and a political boss in northern China with military backing, stepped in and expressed his support for Sun and his desire to mediate a settlement between Sun and the government. In February 1912, the Qing dynasty agreed to abdicate, and as part of the arrangement, Sun relinquished his presidency in favor of Yuan, who was inaugurated at Beijing, the new capital of the provisional government. Sun became director of railroad development and formulated plans to modernize China's transportation. At the same time, Yuan amassed power for himself and undermined the Kuomintang-dominated legislature.

Sun benefited from events during World War I, when Japanese incursions spurred Chinese nationalism. Amid those developments, Sun rebelled against Yuan, but he was forced to flee in failure to Japan. Sun then took a series of actions that alienated many revolutionaries: he promised concessions to the Japanese in a fruitless attempt to get their backing; he required his supporters to take an oath of allegiance to him personally; and he married his secretary without officially divorcing his first wife. Meanwhile, Yuan died in June 1916.

As strong local leaders began to compete for power, China entered into the Warlord period. In 1917, Sun formed a military government in Canton allied with a southern warlord. That government collapsed in 1918. By that time, many factions of Chinese society were increasingly aware of the need for unification and reform in order for the nation to become strong. In 1919, the May Fourth movement developed in Beijing as students held a mass demonstration at the Tiananmen gate to protest Japan's intrusions and call for nationalist and socialist goals. That movement stirred an intellectual ferment that strengthened the Marxist beliefs of many educated Chinese.

Sun supported the student movement and continued his fight for power. In 1921, he headed a new regime based in Canton. Once again, however, he was frustrated in his attempts to create a nationwide movement. When he allied with northern Chinese warlords to expand his power, he met resistance from his major military supporter in the south, Chen Jiongming. Sun then took his struggle into a new phase and accepted help from the Soviet communists. Sun admired the Russians for having led a successful revolution in their own country, and he joined with a Russian agent, Adolf Joffe, to collaborate in China. In 1923, Sun sent his chief lieutenant and brother-in-law, Chiang Kai-shek, to Moscow for training. Later that year and into 1924, the Kuomintang allied itself with the Chinese Communist Party, which helped Sun to develop a tighter party organization, centralize it, and put it in control of all civilian and military activities. Sun gained a lifetime appointment as party director, but his alliance with the Communists alienated some conservatives within the Kuomintang.

During 1923, Sun maneuvered himself to gain control of a military government in Canton and renewed his drive to link with the north and unite China. In 1924, he went to Beijing and met with the warlord who controlled that city, but the negotiations failed. While Sun was still in Beijing, cancer overtook him, and he died on March 12, 1925.

NEIL HAMILTON

ZHOU ENLAI (1898–1976)

Zhou Enlai was a senior Communist Party leader and prime minister of the People's Republic of China (PRC). In a career spanning nearly six turbulent decades, Zhou Enlai became known as the "indispensable man" of China's Communist regime. A superhuman administrator, master diplomat, and supremely skilled political tactician, Zhou was a key party leader during the Communists' long struggle for power. Named China's prime minister on the day the People's Republic was founded, he remained in that post for more than 26 years until his death. For the first eight years of that period, he served concurrently as foreign minister as well.

Born March 5, 1898, in Jiangsu Province, although his family's ancestral home was in Zhejiang on the East China Sea coast south of the Yangtze River, Zhou distinguished himself in school as a talented actor in student plays. At 19, he went to Japan to study but returned two years later to join the ferment of the May Fourth movement, named for the date of massive student demonstrations in 1919 calling for modernization and democracy (the same slogans would be revived 70 years later by student protesters in Tiananmen Square).

After being imprisoned briefly for his political activities, Zhou left China in late 1920 for France, where he helped organize a branch of the new Chinese Communist Party. Returning after four years abroad, Zhou embarked on his revolutionary career, partici-

Zhou Enlai was a senior Communist Party leader and prime minister of the People's Republic of China from 1949 to 1975. (Getty Images)

pating in the Shanghai uprising at the start of the Chinese Civil War, the Long March, the Sino-Japanese War of 1937–1945, and the Chinese Communist Revolution against Chiang Kai-shek's Nationalists. In his early years in the party, Zhou outranked Mao Zedong in the leadership. But when Mao took command during the Long March, Zhou willingly assumed a subordinate role in their partnership. For more than 40 years, he would be the movement's supreme survivor—the only one of Mao's inner circle never to fall victim to the incessant purges, intrigues, power struggles, and policy shifts that characterized Mao's long reign.

When the Korean War broke out in June 1950, less than a year after the PRC was founded, Zhou played a key role in carrying out Mao's decisions and in orchestrating Chinese diplomacy. In early July, Zhou presided over the initial deliberations that led to the creation of the Northeast Border Defense army and the Chinese military buildup in the border region. Thereafter, Zhou supervised the military preparations, chairing a series of crucial meetings to decide on the structure, strategy, deployment, and logistical needs of the border force.

Meanwhile, Zhou was also responsible for managing China's relations with both its allies and prospective enemy. Zhou personally instructed Indian ambassador in Beijing Sardar K. M. Panikkar to warn the United States that China would enter the war if U.S. forces crossed the 38th parallel into the Democratic People's Republic of Korea (North Korea). It was also Zhou who led a Chinese delegation to Moscow to redeem a Soviet promise of military support, including air strikes, for Chinese troops in Korea. However, neither move achieved the desired result. U.S. leaders dismissed Zhou's warning as a bluff; in Moscow, Joseph Stalin reneged on providing air cover.

As the Korean peace negotiations entered their climactic phase following Stalin's death on March 5, 1953, it was Zhou, again, who signaled that China was ready to end the conflict. Shortly after returning from Stalin's funeral, Zhou offered a compromise on the prisoner of war (POW) issue that had knotted the truce talks for many months. Although the wording was oblique, Zhou in effect withdrew Beijing's demand for the forced repatriation of Chinese POWs who did not wish to return to China. The concession cleared the way for the signing of the Korean armistice four months later.

The following year, Zhou headed China's delegation to the Geneva Conference of 1954 negotiations on settling the French Indochina War. Soon after arriving, he unexpectedly encountered U.S. secretary of state John Foster Dulles in an anteroom. Zhou offered his hand, but Dulles coldly turned his back and walked out of the room. The incident symbolized the deep-frozen U.S.-Chinese hostility that would endure for nearly two more decades. Despite Dulles's snub, Zhou became the crucial conciliator in the Geneva talks, personally persuading the Vietnamese Nationalist leader Ho Chi Minh to make substantial concessions in return for a settlement.

During his long tenure as prime minister, working in enigmatic partnership with the mercurial Mao, Zhou used his extraordinary organizational talent to keep China's vast administrative and economic bureaucracy functioning through the constant upheavals of Mao's policies. As the party's most skilled, supple, and polished negotiator, he continued to serve as China's chief emissary to the outside world, seldom failing to charm even the most wary foreigners. He also played a crucial role as mediator and conciliator in disputes inside the party leadership.

In 1971, Zhou received President Richard Nixon's emissary Henry Kissinger in Beijing, paving the way for the restoration of U.S.-Chinese relations and erasing, at last, the memory of Dulles's rebuff in Geneva 17 years before.

Zhou died on January 8, 1976, leaving behind a widely accepted image of a wise, flexible, humane statesman.

SPENCER C. TUCKER

DOCUMENT: EXCERPT FROM QUOTATIONS FROM CHAIRMAN MAO ZEDONG (1964)

Also known as the **Little Red Book,** **Quotations from Chairman Mao Ze-dong** *was published in China in 1964. The book was a series of statements made by Mao Zedong at various points in his career about different aspects of Chinese society and communism. Following is an excerpt that looks specifically at his thoughts regarding the Chinese Communist Party. The book played a large role in fostering China's Cultural Revolution and became particularly popular among the Red Guards, whose main duty was to enforce the principles of the Cultural Revolution on China's large population. The guards were often seen waving copies of the* **Little Red Book** *while marching through the streets.*

Chapter 1. The Communist Party

The force at the core leading our cause forward is the Chinese Communist Party. The theoretical basis guiding our thinking is Marxism-Leninism. —Opening address at the First Session of the First National People's Congress of the People's Republic of China (September 15, 1954).

If there is to be revolution, there must be a revolutionary party. Without a revolutionary party, without a party built on the Marxist-Leninist revolutionary theory and in the Marxist-Leninist revolutionary style, it is impossible to lead the working class and the broad masses of the people in defeating imperialism and its running dogs. —"Revolutionary Forces of the World Unite, Fight Against Imperialist Aggression!" (November 1948), Selected Works, Vol. IV, p. 284.

Without the efforts of the Chinese Communist Party, without the Chinese Communists as the mainstay of the Chinese people, China can never achieve independence and liberation, or industrialization and the modernization of her agriculture. —"On Coalition Government" (April 24, 1945), Selected Works, Vol. III, p. 318.

The Chinese Communist Party is the core of leadership of the whole Chinese people. Without this core, the cause of socialism cannot be victorious. —Talk at the general reception for the delegates to the Third National Congress of the New Democratic Youth League of China (May 25, 1957).

A well-disciplined Party armed with the theory of Marxism-Leninism, using the method of self-criticism and linked with the masses of the people; an army under the leadership of such a Party; a united front of all revolutionary classes and all revolutionary groups under the leadership of such a Party—these are the three main weapons with which we have defeated the enemy. —"On the People's Democratic Dictatorship" (June 30, 1949), Selected Works, Vol. IV, p. 422.

We must have faith in the masses and we must have faith in the Party. These are two cardinal principles. If we doubt these principles, we shall accomplish nothing. —On the Question of Agricultural Co-operation (July 31, 1955), 3rd ed., p. 7.

Armed with Marxist-Leninist theory and ideology, the Communist Party of China has brought a new style of work to the Chinese people. A style of work which essentially entails integrating theory with practice, forging close links with the masses and practicing self-criticism. —"On Coalition Government" (April 24, 1945), Selected Works, Vol. III, p. 314.

No political party can possibly lead a great revolutionary movement to victory unless it possesses revolutionary theory and knowledge of history and has a profound grasp of the practical movement. —"The Role of the Chinese Communist Party in the National War" (October 1938), Selected Works, Vol. II, p. 208.

As we used to say, the rectification movement is "a widespread movement of Marxist education." Rectification means the whole Party studying Marxism through criticism and self-criticism. We can certainly learn more about Marxism in the course of the rectification movement. —Speech at the Chinese Communist Party's National Conference on Propaganda Work (March 12, l957), 1st pocket ed., p. 14.

It is an arduous task to ensure a better life for the several hundred million people of China and to build our economically and culturally backward country into a prosperous and powerful one with a high level of culture. And it is precisely in order to be able to shoulder this task more competently and work better together with all non-Party people who are actuated by high ideals and determined to institute reforms that we must conduct rectification movements both now and in the future, and constantly rid ourselves of whatever is wrong. —Ibid., pp. 15–16.

Policy is the starting-point of all the practical actions of a revolutionary party and manifests itself in the process and the end-result of that party's actions. A revolutionary party is carrying out a policy whenever it takes any action. If it is not carrying out a correct policy, it is carrying out a wrong policy; if it is not carrying out a given policy consciously, it is doing so blindly. What we call experience is the process and the end-result of carrying out a policy. Only through the practice of the people, that is, through experience, can we verify whether a policy is correct or wrong and determine to what extent it is correct or wrong. However, people's practice, especially the practice of a revolutionary party and the revolutionary masses, cannot but be bound up with one policy or another. Therefore, before any action is taken, we must explain the policy, which we have formulated in the light of the given circumstances, to Party members and to the masses. Otherwise, Party members and the masses will depart from the guidance of our policy, act blindly and carry out a wrong policy. —"On the Policy Concerning Industry and Commerce" (February 27, 1948), Selected Works, Vol. IV, pp. 204–205.

Our Party has laid down the general line and general policy of the Chinese revolution as well as various specific lines for work and specific policies. However, while many comrades remember our Party's specific lines for work and specific policies, they often forget its general line and general policy. If we actually forget the Party's general line and general policy, then we shall be blind, half-baked, muddle-headed revolutionaries, and when we carry out a specific line for work and a specific policy, we shall lose our bearings and vacillate now to the left and now to the right, and the work will suffer. —"Speech at a Conference of Cadres in the Shansi-Suiyuan Liberated Area" (April 1, 1948), Selected Works, Vol. IV, p. 238.

Policy and tactics are the life of the Party; leading comrades at all levels must give them full attention and must never on any account be negligent. —"A Circular on the Situation" (March 20, 1948), Selected Works, Vol. IV, p. 220.

2

World War I, 1914–1918

INTRODUCTION

In 1914, Europe stumbled into a catastrophic war that lasted for more than four years and claimed the lives of millions of soldiers and civilians. The causes of World War I are complex and multifaceted. They have stirred debate among historians and laymen alike ever since the war ground to a halt in 1918. It seems clear, however, that the outbreak of war was an unintended consequence of an extremely tense international order in which the Great Powers of Europe eyed each other with varying degrees of hatred, envy, fear, and suspicion.

The event that detonated this powder keg was the assassination of Archduke Franz Ferdinand, the heir to the throne of Austria-Hungary, at Sarajevo on June 28,1914. This act of political terror infuriated Austria, which concluded that Serbia, a small Balkan country, was behind the assassination. When Austria threatened Serbia, the Serb government appealed for protection to its ally, Russia. Meanwhile, Austria received strong encouragement for its confrontational stance from its ally, Germany. As the crisis deepened, Russia consulted with its ally, France; France, in turn, entered into discussions with its friend, Great Britain. When Austria sent an ultimatum to Serbia and the antiquated Russian army began to mobilize, the dominoes fell. By early August 1914, World War I had begun.

In light of the terrible destruction that followed, it is interesting to note that not only the European governments but also their populations went to war with great enthusiasm. Huge crowds filled the streets of Europe's capital cities, wildly cheering the declarations of war. Not only was this first general war since Napoleon's campaigns of one hundred years earlier greeted with enthusiasm, there was also a universal conviction that the war would be a short one and that "the boys would be home by Christmas."

As the war progressed, more and more countries became involved. At the start, however, the major combatants were, on one side, Germany and Austria-Hungary, which, together with their allies, would be known as the Central Powers; and, on the other side, Great Britain, France, and Russia, which, together with their allies, would be known as the Allied Powers or Allies.

From the start, the Central Powers found themselves fighting a two-front war—that is, they were forced to fight simultaneously in both the west and the east. Aware of the grave dangers inherent in a two-front war, the German general staff had drawn up the Schlieffen Plan, which called for Germany, in the event of war, to mass the bulk of its army in the west to deliver a quick and devastating knockout blow to the French. After defeating the French, the German army could turn its attention to the east and destroy the Russian army at its leisure.

Employing the Schlieffen Plan, the Germans came very close to capturing Paris in the first month of the war. They were barely stopped at the First Battle of the Marne, when the French took advantage of gaps in the German lines caused in part by the transfer of some German units from the Western Front to the Eastern Front, where the Russians had unexpectedly mounted an offensive. Ironically, these German troops were not crucial to the outcome in the east. Although the Russians, under Generals Alexander Samsonov and Pavel Rennenkampf, had moved westward into the German territory of East Prussia, their attack was so confused and poorly coordinated that a smaller German force defeated both Russian armies at the twin battles of Tannenberg and the Masurian Lakes. These huge German victories in the east focused the spotlight on Generals Erich Ludendorff and Paul von Hindenburg, two of the most effective military commanders in a war notable for undistinguished if not abominable military leadership.

The failure of the German offensive in the west and of the Russian offensive in the east shattered all illusions about the war being a short one. Instead, both sides settled in for a protracted struggle featuring trench warfare. Trench warfare called for each side to concentrate great numbers of men in a series of parallel fortified ditches, or trenches, and to attack in massed formations in the hope of breaching the enemy's lines. Those on the defensive would exploit their dug-in positions to repel the offensive. The nature of trench warfare, with its massed assaults into the teeth of entrenched defensive positions, resulted in truly appalling casualty figures. World War I quickly became a war of attrition in which each side readily sacrificed incredible numbers of its own men to exhaust the enemy, "bleed them white," and thus achieve victory.

During 1915, the war on the Western Front witnessed wave after wave of British, French, and German soldiers attacking across barren "no man's land" into the face of entrenched machine-gun nests. Although the casualty figures skyrocketed, the front barely moved. Much of the military action in that year took place on the Eastern Front. Having failed to destroy France in 1914, the Central Powers in 1915 sought to drive Russia from the war. In a series of coordinated attacks, the Central Powers regained Galicia, expelled Russia from Poland and Lithuania, and invaded Russia proper. However, victory proved elusive. Although the Russian army was poorly led, poorly equipped, poorly fed, and beaten on the battlefield, it nevertheless relied on its seemingly unlimited supply of men and the vast expanses of the Russian countryside to remain in the field as a viable foe.

During the first months of hostilities in the east, it became obvious that Austria-Hungary was not up to the military task at hand. Austria-Hungary's offensives, even against tiny Serbia, failed, and often Germany had to come to its rescue when the Russians pummeled its army. Consequently, by 1916, Austria-Hungary had virtually surrendered its freedom of action to Germany, and it was relegated to this inferior position until the end of the war.

In 1915, the western allies (France and Great Britain) invaded Turkey, which had entered the war on the side of the Central Powers in October 1914. This attack, known as the Gallipoli campaign and fought chiefly by soldiers from the British Empire, ended in defeat for the Allies. Nevertheless, the Allies now determined to destroy the Ottoman Empire. By virtue of a secret treaty concluded in 1915, Russia was granted the right to

U.S. troops advance against entrenched German positions in the Battle of Belleau Wood in June 1918. (National Archives)

fulfill its long-standing desire to annex Constantinople and thereby gain control over the straits leading from the Black Sea to the Aegean Sea and the Mediterranean. Subsequently, the British, led by Colonel T. E. Lawrence, successfully incited the Turkish Empire's Arab populations. In 1917, the British issued the Balfour Declaration, pledging themselves to support the establishment of a Jewish homeland in Palestine.

As the British were becoming bogged down at Gallipoli, Italy, having been promised territorial gains at the expense of Austria-Hungary, entered the war on the side of the Allies in May 1915. Also during the early stages of the war, the Allies, especially Great Britain, moved against Germany's African colonies. Japan, Britain's Pacific ally, grabbed Germany's colonies in Asia and the South Pacific.

In 1916, while the armies of the Central Powers slowly chewed up the fading Russian army, the military spotlight shifted to the west once again. In particular, two battles on the Western Front that year came to symbolize the futility and mindless bloodletting that were hallmarks of World War I. In February, the Germans launched a massive attack against French positions in and around the fortress town of Verdun. The objective was to bleed the French and hasten their surrender. However, the French determined to hang on, and under the tenacious leadership of General Henri-Philippe Pétain, whose pledge "they shall not pass" lifted French morale, France withstood the German attack, but at a terrible price. By the end of the battle, the Germans and the French had each lost 350,000 men. Later that same year, the British launched a massive attack against

German positions along the Somme River. After several weeks of intense combat, the Allies had gained a mere 15 square miles at the cost of 410,000 British dead and 190,000 French dead. The Germans lost 500,000 men.

The staggering number of casualties can be attributed not only to incredibly stupid strategic planning and leadership but also to the perfection of already existing weapons of mass destruction and the introduction of new ones. During World War I, the machine gun and heavy artillery were employed with devastating effect. Weapons used for the first time included aircraft, tanks, poison gas, and submarines. Their effect was no less devastating.

In particular, the submarine and its effects transcended the battlefield. At the onset of the war, both sets of belligerents declared a blockade in the belief that they could starve their opponent into submission. Whereas the Allies relied chiefly on Britain's fleet to maintain their blockade, the Central Powers placed their hopes in Germany's submarines. The German submarines were quite effective, but the type of campaign they waged was flawed because, unlike surface vessels, they could not stop and board their intended target. Rather, they could only sink their targets in an indiscriminate fashion, demonstrated quite dramatically in May 1915 with the sinking of the passenger ship *Lusitania* with the loss of 1,200 lives, including 118 Americans. The United States, a neutral country that had protested the blockade actions of the belligerents, erupted in anger at the sinking of the *Lusitania*. The United States threatened war against Germany, a prospect that caused German leaders to modify their submarine campaign. However, at the start of 1917 Germany once again decided to wage unrestricted submarine warfare. This decision played an important part in the American determination to enter the war on the side of the Allies in April 1917.

The only major conventional clash at sea occurred in spring 1916 when the German fleet ventured from its harbors and fought the British fleet at the Battle of Jutland. The clash was essentially an accidental one, and although the German fleet probably gained a slight victory (German guns proved better than English ones, and the Germans sank twice the tonnage that the British did), it retreated to port and never again sallied forth to challenge the British.

While millions of men slaughtered each other at the front, important changes occurred at home. World War I introduced the concept of "total war." Subjected to the requirements of a war effort of unprecedented scope and size, each belligerent government eventually adopted policies that interfered profoundly with normal civilian activity in order to marshal all available human and material resources for the conflict. Perhaps the best example of this development is found in the policy of national conscription that placed all able-bodied young and middle-aged men at the state's disposal.

The now regimented populations were also the target of incessant campaigns of state-sponsored but often distorted propaganda designed to boost civilian morale and generate support for the war. Meanwhile, the war effort drained the financial resources of the state and eventually bankrupted almost every belligerent. Standards of living also declined, and each state struggled to find substitutes for items that were no longer available, including labor, as women performed heretofore exclusively male tasks.

Germany, under the organizational genius Walter Rathenau, practiced total war most effectively. Rathenau successfully organized Germany's productive capacity and directed German scientists in the production of many ersatz, or artificial, items that served to mitigate the effects of the Allied blockade. Such steps enabled a resource-strapped Germany to fight effectively for more than four years. Those countries least successful in waging total war (Russia and Austria-Hungary) found their chances for success, even survival, rapidly diminishing.

In fact, the failure to shoulder the crushing burdens of modern warfare led to the collapse of Russia in 1917. In March of that year, revolution broke out in the capital, St. Petersburg, which had been renamed Petrograd at the beginning of the war. Nicholas II, the Russian tsar, or emperor, quickly abdicated; but the chaos intensified. While the situation at home continued to deteriorate, the Russian army mounted a summer offensive under General Alexis Brusilov. As had been the case in 1916, when Brusilov launched a similar campaign, he was defeated.

With Brusilov's defeat, the Russian army began to disintegrate. At home a power struggle was under way to see who would fill the vacuum created by the collapse of the tsarist state. In November 1917, the Bolsheviks, a small, radical group espousing Marxism and led by Vladimir Ilyich Lenin, seized power. Believing in the inevitability of a global, working-class revolution, the Bolsheviks sought to withdraw Russia from the war. Negotiations ensued during which the Germans drove a hard bargain. These negotiations resulted in the March 3, 1918, Treaty of Brest-Litovsk, which validated the German victory in the east. The Germans could now devote their full attention to the Western Front. There, however, circumstances had changed dramatically.

Russia's departure from the war roughly coincided with the U.S. entry into the war. In early 1917, an increasingly desperate Germany, now fully under the control of Generals Ludendorff and Hindenburg, decided to resume unrestricted submarine warfare in an effort to starve Great Britain into submission once and for all. This decision infuriated the United States, which declared war on Germany on April 6, 1917. Several months later, in January 1918, U.S. president Woodrow Wilson issued the Fourteen Points, which for the first time clearly set out Allied war aims.

Both the American entry into the war and the Fourteen Points, following closely upon the triumph of Bolshevism in Russia, gave the Allies a huge boost in morale. Moreover, the prospect of unlimited American men, money, and material seemed to ensure that the Allies would eventually win the stalemated conflict. However, the United States would take about a year to move to a war footing, and the bloodletting on the Western Front continued unabated throughout 1917.

The French, under a new commander, General Robert Nivelle, determined to continue the failed tactic of the massed assault. This time, however, French troops mutinied, refusing to go on the offensive. Unbeknownst to the Germans, the French army was on the verge of collapse. That catastrophe was avoided when Pétain, the hero of Verdun, replaced Nivelle and restored discipline. To save his army, Pétain abandoned the doctrine of attack and took up a defensive posture awaiting the arrival of the Americans. The British, however, continued to press forward. Fighting in "Flanders' Fields" at Passchendaele and Ypres, the British army absorbed staggering casualties at the hands of dug-in German forces. In October, the Southern Front flared when the Austrians routed the Italian army at Caporetto. Approximately 300,000 Italians surrendered, and more than 400,000 deserted.

The failures of 1917 might have been enough to break the Allies had it not been for the entry of the United States into the war and the coming to power of Georges

Clemenceau in France and David Lloyd George in Britain. These hard-nosed leaders, who sometimes rode roughshod over both their political opponents and prevailing legal standards, were determined to achieve victory.

Their determination proved helpful as the war reached its climax in 1918. Freed of major military responsibilities in the east, the Germans now transferred the bulk of their forces to the Western Front as they prepared for an all-out onslaught against the British and the French before the Americans could arrive to tip the scales in favor of the Allies. Launching their massive attack in March 1918, the Germans came perilously close to success until they were defeated in July at the gates of Paris in the Second Battle of the Marne. The failure of the German offensive foreshadowed the end of the war. With American troops pouring into France at the rate of 250,000 a month, the German armies lost all chance of victory.

In September 1918, the German generals informed a shocked Kaiser William II that Germany was defeated and dumped further responsibility for the conduct of the war in his lap. In Austria-Hungary, the empire itself was disintegrating as each of its component national parts started to go its own way. On November 11, 1918, an armistice took effect. After more than four years of the bloodiest fighting the world had ever seen, the guns stopped firing.

In January 1919, peace negotiations opened at Paris. The Paris Peace Conference, as the negotiations were called, tried to deal with the many consequences of the war. However, Soviet Russia, already a pariah among nations, was not invited to the conference, and defeated Germany was effectively barred from participating in the discussions. As for the victorious Allies, they tended to squabble among themselves and could never agree on whether to impose a truly Draconian peace or a generous peace. The main product of this flawed effort to bring peace to Europe was the Treaty of Versailles, signed on June 28, 1919, five years to the day after the assassination of Franz Ferdinand at Sarajevo.

INTERPRETIVE ESSAY

MARILYN SHEVIN-COETZEE AND FRANS COETZEE

In 1914, as temperatures soared during one of the hottest summers on record in Europe, tempers flared as well. Lacking conveniences such as air-conditioning that twenty-first century readers take for granted and bound by heavy conventional fashions, the peoples of Europe were challenged by both the weather and events. The heat was an irritation, possibly a catalyst rather than a direct cause of World War I, the origins of which can be traced to deep-seated economic, military, diplomatic, and political developments. Ironically, the very technology that brought the Continent closer together, such as the telegraph and the telephone, helped to tear it asunder. Eventually, a combination of long-term causes and short-term accidents combined to precipitate the first total war.

The most serious of these crises was triggered—literally—by the assassination in Sarajevo of the heir to the Austro-Hungarian throne, Archduke Franz Ferdinand, and his wife, Sophie, on June 28, 1914. The assassin was Gavrilo Princip, a teenaged Serbian nationalist. On July 23, 1914, Austria-Hungary issued an ultimatum to Serbia; Serbia's response, although conciliatory, failed to prevent Austria-Hungary from declaring war on Serbia five days later. Russia responded by mobilizing its military, prompting Germany to do the same and eventually to declare war on Russia on August 1 and on France two days later. On August 4, after German troops violated the Belgian frontier, Britain honored its treaty obligation to protect Belgian neutrality and entered the conflict on the side of France and Russia. As the Continent plunged into war that evening, British foreign secretary Sir Edward Grey observed: "The lamps are going out all over Europe. We shall not see them lit again in our lifetime."

Grey's somber assessment was at odds with the prevailing orthodoxy, which depicted the process of mobilization as one greeted everywhere with enthusiasm and nationalistic fervor. War as Christmas, as a holiday to be celebrated, not a calamity to be mourned, a spiritual release from the mundane banalities of everyday life, a transformation of the degeneracy inherent in modern culture by means of the elevating impact of a higher, common moral purpose—these were among the sentiments with which Europeans anticipated the conflict. In part, these suppositions were sustained by the mistaken presumption, shared by participants in all countries, that the war would be something of a sporting match, brief and glorious, concluded by Christmas. Propaganda posters in Germany of young, beautiful maidens handing flowers or beverages to soldiers departing by train to the front, and of men, young and older, rushing to volunteer before they missed out on the fun, further emphasized the refreshing sense of unity and camaraderie that bore a welcome contrast to the domestic discord of the prewar years. A British poster appropriately titled "Are you in this picture?" depicted Britons from all social classes waiting in a long line to enlist in the army. The *Burgfrieden* (Fortress under Siege) or the *Union sacrée* (Sacred Union) expressed the sentiment that under external pressure the nation would come together and rally around the flag.

Yet this picture was incomplete and in some ways misleading. If some Europeans looked to the war optimistically, others viewed it through less rosy spectacles. The grounds for a more guarded response to the outbreak of hostilities would become apparent as the combatants' lack of preparation was revealed repeatedly. In underestimating the conflict's duration, the opposing nations failed to take requisite measures to ensure the uninterrupted flow of food for both soldiers and civilians and the stockpiling of raw materials for weapons and munitions. The British presumption that they could continue to conduct "business as usual" typified the initial response.

European expectations of a brief conflict were conditioned by the short and decisive Prussian campaigns against Austria and later France in 1866 and 1870–1871, which suggested that one Great Power could defeat another with relative ease. In retrospect, military planners should have taken their cue from the American Civil War, which dragged on for four years with staggering casualties. Of course, the first few weeks of campaigning in August 1914 conformed to expectations as the various armies jockeyed for position. An observer from the Napoleonic Wars would have recognized much. Cavalry still cantered at the head of columns, soldiers trudged on foot, horse-drawn carts laboriously pulled supplies. But once the German advance into France was stymied at the Battle of the Marne (September 1914), war on the Western Front settled into a prolonged and bloody stalemate.

That stalemate reflected the fact that technological advances favored the defensive. Barbed wire, which had confined cattle on America's Great Plains, proved even more effective in impeding the advance of men. Machine guns employed to deadly effect by imperialists in Africa and Asia were now turned with equal success against the soldiers of the European powers themselves. And the devastating bombardments of heavy artillery forced troops to burrow ever deeper merely to survive. By early 1915, parallel lines of German and Allied trenches stretched virtually from the Belgian coast to the Swiss frontier. The constant shellfire tore up the once pristine countryside, and the pitted terrain between the trenches, a morass of mud, corpses, shell craters, and tangled wire, appropriately became known as no man's land.

The contradiction between the initial dreams of a brief, glorious, and inexpensive victory and the seemingly ineffectual efforts of soldiers to win more than a few yards of blood-soaked ground at tremendous cost fostered disillusion, apathy, cynicism, and disgust. Like the myriad faces of war, the literature produced in response to the conflict was both varied and prodigious, ranging from outright nationalistic propaganda to realistic portrayals of battle to pacifistic appeals. Clergymen, physicians, and workers at the front became journalists, recording their personal experiences for posterity. In France, Dr. Georges Duhamel, a respected physician who voluntarily served for four years as a medical officer (his novels being translated into English as *The New Book of Martyrs* and *Civilization*), and Henri Barbusse, whose *Under Fire* detailed the miseries of war, were among the controversial and thought-provoking authors active during the war.

The main wave of famous war novels, however, began to appear a decade or so after the Armistice, by which time many authors felt that they had achieved the distance necessary to write about so painful an experience. Those publications (such as Robert Graves's *Goodbye to All That* and Erich Maria Remarque's *All Quiet on the Western Front*) testified to the profound sense of irony through which soldiers sought to comprehend their ghastly experiences, to the loyalty they felt to the comrades for whom they fought (rather than for the grandiose war aims trumpeted by the governments), and to the feeling of isolation they sensed when they returned on leave to civilians who had no comprehension of the realities of the front.

And yet these very civilians were essential to the war effort. Given the unprecedented scale of the war and the military leadership's inability to secure a decisive knockout blow, it gradually became apparent that victory would be secured through a slow process of attrition. This situation ensured that civilian production, whether of weapons, munitions, or foodstuffs, would be critical to the outcome. Accordingly, considerations of civilian morale on this second or "home front" took on additional importance, and governments devoted themselves to cultivating enthusiasm for the war. Perhaps never before had the visual arts been conscripted to such a degree to stimulate enlistment, to promote female employment, and to vilify the enemy as lacking in human decency and respect. Indeed, the pen proved as mighty as the sword, and art no longer existed for its own sake. Along with literature and film, it had become politicized, manipulated by supporters and opponents of the conflict alike to deliver a specific message.

The benefits of propaganda were already known to nineteenth-century figures such as France's Louis Napoleon (Napoleon III), whose successful presidential campaign was aided by an impressive array of placards, buttons, and other such paraphernalia. As Europe's electorate expanded and politics took on greater significance, the use of propaganda increased. Posters not only carried easily remembered slogans or catchphrases, but their visual graphics also served to reinforce a particular message. One need only recall what might well be the most famous of all American war posters—that of Uncle Sam as a recruiter for the war. Dressed in patriotic red, white, and blue, this fatherly figure beckoned males of enlistment age to answer the call to arms and thereby protect their country and its values, threatened by Germany and its allies. European governments commissioned posters that glorified the act of recruitment as well: on the one hand, young men were pictured in uniform, showered with the adulation of beautiful young women and adoring crowds; on the other, prospective soldiers were reminded, even if indirectly, of the horrors of war that could befall their innocent mothers, wives, and children should they fail to heed the call to arms. Images of the bestial Hun or the animalistic Cossack were invoked as barbarous threats to one's own humane and civilized existence.

In view of food shortages and other hardships caused by inevitable disruptions in supply and demand and to ensure the continued cooperation of civilians and soldiers alike, Europe's governments increasingly disseminated propaganda that often contained only a small modicum of truth, but the impact of which proved devastating for their opponents. Above all, Germany's invasion of neutral, defenseless Belgium and its ruthless destruction of cathedrals, libraries, and other historical buildings served the Allied propaganda machine extraordinarily well. Claims of German barbarism against property and women not only enabled Germany's enemies to justify their participation in the war, but also served to reinforce the idea of a holy Christian war waged against the German barbarians.

While governments churned out propaganda posters and literature directed at their nemeses, peace advocates and disillusioned soldier-writers also used literature and the visual arts to express their version of the war, although state-imposed censorship often tempered their impact. These works all revealed uneasiness with the pursuit of war and its brutal character. Some were written during the war, but much of the war literature was published as a postscript to the authors' experiences and memories, whether of the conflict itself or of life on the home front.

Artists, too, created a visual testimony to the war with their paintings. Cubism remained the style of choice of many artists at the front. Dissonant, irreverent, and dissociated from the past, cubist paintings portrayed the helter-skelter nature of modern warfare, one that departed from traditional conventions and whose impact was more destructive than its predecessors. But on the home front in France, for example, artists preferred a more traditional approach to their works. This classicist revival, which began in earnest after 1917, was due in part to Italy's entry into the war in 1915 on the Allied side. Italy's association with classical civilization, humanism, and Christianity served as a counterpoise to Germany's barbarism; thus, the Allies could justify their war against Germany as one waged to preserve Western Civilization. And since France was part of the Latin tradition, French artists in particular responded to the call with portraits of Roman ruins, protective antique goddesses hovering above wounded soldiers, and well-known figures such as Dante urging combatants to continue their struggle against the barbaric enemy. In an effort to reinforce the bonds between classical Rome and twentieth-century France and to uplift the French national spirit, artistic figures like that of Marianne took on classical qualities. Indeed, posters, portraits, picture cards, and paintings evoked special symbolism, some carrying overwhelmingly nationalistic messages, others evoking pacifistic images.

But propaganda, whether persuasive or not, was by itself insufficient to mobilize societies effectively for the conduct of total war. Each combatant nation's leadership faced the same dilemma: how to fill the ranks with hundreds of thousands of recruits while simultaneously maintaining (or even accelerating) industrial production in the face of the inevitable disruption that the transfer of so many men would entail. This dilemma was the driving force behind the significant extension of state intervention throughout Europe. One common response was for the state to "militarize" the labor process and civilian war production, imposing military-style discipline and penalties for disruptions in the factories. Likewise, private enterprise might be subordinated to governmental regulation, as in the case of the British railroads under the Defense of the Realm Act, or that of French munitions workers, who were forbidden to strike. Governments soon found, however, that the unregulated departure of manpower to the front, although applauded by generals seeking replacements for the escalating casualties, proved counterproductive by denuding key industries of skilled workers. For without the requisite shells, no number of soldiers alone would suffice. With the passage in 1916 of the Auxiliary Service Act, German workers were transferred from less crucial civilian jobs to military industries. Agriculture, too, was susceptible to the same difficulties, especially given the degree to which it still relied on manual labor.

The longer the stalemate at the front persisted, the more acute these problems became. As a result, some skilled workers were actually withdrawn from front-line service or prohibited from joining as members of reserved occupations. But the principal solution lay in reconstituting the work force itself. By simplifying job tasks, semiskilled workers could substitute for skilled men departed to the front; even more dramatically, by tapping pools of potential female labor, employers could maintain production. In the process, of course, women gained access to occupations from which they had often been excluded, and they also became accustomed to earning regular wages. In France, women accounted for one-quarter of the personnel in war factories, numbering some 1.6 million workers. Russian women assumed greater prominence in the transport and utility industries; German women engaged in engineering, metallurgy, and chemical production in numbers six times greater than on the eve of the war; British women were a mainstay of munitions production. Some scholars have suggested that by permitting greater access to paid employment and, to some extent, to occupational choice, the war proved a liberating experience for women. In this way, women gained an added measure of satisfaction from their contribution to the war effort, whereas men were forced to concede, however grudgingly, that many tasks once segregated by gender could now be performed with equal facility by female workers. One could also point to the concession of female suffrage in Britain and Germany as evidence of the newfound roles for women.

Did gender lines blur so rapidly and completely? One reason for doubting that they did is, first, that the rapid upsurge in female employment in war-related industries proved a transitory phenomenon; women workers were displaced as economies readjusted to a peacetime footing and soldiers returned to the jobs they had left. Second, female suffrage remained a contentious issue, denied in France and implemented in Britain on terms more restrictive than for male voters. Third, during the war itself, whether employed in the industrial or agricultural sector or engaged in domestic service, women still bore principal responsibility in the traditional female sphere, the home front, and for enduring the rigors of domestic life, such as the seemingly interminable lines for food, often in short supply.

The shortage of critical foodstuffs, exacerbated by the absence of plans to govern distribution and prevent price inflation, led eventually in Germany (beginning in January 1915), France (selectively in 1917), and England (in 1918) to rationing. Although intended to provide a basic minimum caloric intake for citizens, in reality the system often did not alleviate the food shortages. Many, including working-class children and pensioners on fixed incomes, still found food difficult to obtain, especially in view of the prevailing practice of allocating the best food to male workers. England and France appear to have suffered the least, while privation was more severe in Russia, Austria-Hungary, and blockaded Germany. In Austria, for example, in 1916 some 40 percent of all strikes were prompted by food shortages, and by 1917 the figure had climbed to 70 percent. Beginning in the spring of 1915, Russian women agitated against shortages and inflated prices.

In these circumstances, frugality and thrift, not to mention ingenuity, were preached as the best way to endure the hardships of the home front. It is no surprise, therefore, that the conflict witnessed the cultivation of numerous small "war gardens" and the publication of many cookbooks designed to instruct working-class wives on the principles of nutrition and the more practical matter of stretching inadequate and even unappetizing ingredients into each day's breakfast, lunch, and modest supper. State intervention to limit the wartime pressure on standards of living also included the introduction of rent controls, but such action was not universal. In France, for example, the price of housing escalated to new heights and led to serious overcrowding.

Given the repetitive slaughter on the battlefields, the accelerating pressures of labor in the factories, and the accumulating tensions of civilian life, it is perhaps surprising that authority was maintained for so long. But the sense of common sacrifice implied by the *Burgfrieden* and the *Union sacrée* could persist for only so long in such an environment. The most obvious breakdown of authority occurred in Russia in 1917, followed by Germany and Austria-Hungary the following year. The various combatant nations' efforts to mobilize their societies for total war implied that the rewards of the conflict would be commensurate with the great effort expended. For nations that could not secure victory, however, the prospect of defeat implied the likelihood of revolution. Although one cannot ignore the deep-seated social and political antagonisms that fragmented all three nations before 1914, it was the experience of the war itself that brought about a collapse of authority.

However, it would be a mistake to regard revolution as the sole wartime challenge to authority. Dissent emerged in a variety of ways—on the factory floor, in the food lines, and in the trenches. The later years of the war saw an upsurge in strike activity throughout Europe that continued to escalate as the war dragged on (it is worth recalling that even early in 1918, there were few signs that the war's conclusion was imminent). The expansion of trade unions suggested that a stronger working-class presence in economic and political life would be a permanent feature of the European landscape and a potential challenge to the status quo. Nearly a century before, in England, a Chartist radical had defied anyone "to agitate on a full stomach," and by 1917, there were growing numbers of restive citizens to confirm his dictum on the relationship between hunger and protest.

Dissent emerged not just among civilians but also among the men in uniform. In 1917 substantial sections of the French army were wracked by mutiny, ending only with an understanding that the French military leadership would avoid needless or ill-conceived offensives. The German navy in Kiel mutinied in 1918 when official orders for a suicide mission to atone for the fleet's inactivity infuriated crews tired of their officers' incompetence and their own idleness. In Russia, the situation was more complex, and after a first revolution in March 1917 that resulted in the abdication of Tsar Nicholas II and the formation of the Provisional Government, the Russian army continued to fight, seeking victory to validate the previous three years of extensive sacrifice. A quantitative superiority, however, was no substitute for the qualitative edge enjoyed by the Germans; and in the wake of further defeats, the Bolshevik platform of peace, land, and bread grew more attractive. A second revolution in November 1917 led to a Bolshevik take-over and eventually to a prolonged civil war.

Even Britain was not immune to upheaval. In the spring of 1917, a massive series of strikes disrupted the vital engineering and shipbuilding region of the Clyde in western Scotland, and similar outbreaks in Wales and Lancashire took their toll as well. Most spectacularly, Dublin echoed to the sound of gunfire in April 1916 when Irish national-ists in the so-called Easter Rising proclaimed an independent Irish Republic, only to be forcibly repressed by British troops and hanging judges.

Socialist principles also persisted during the conflict. Initially, of course, such ideo-logical considerations were largely, although not completely, submerged in the wide-spread support for the war from socialist parties. Germany's Social Democratic Party (SPD) approved war credits, many members of Britain's Labour Party rejected pacifistic appeals to abstain from the war, and French socialists supported the sacred union. But as the war progressed, socialist parties suffered a decline in membership, for the move-ment was divided, not just in its attitude toward capitalism but also over whether to continue the conflict in the face of mounting casualties or to sue for peace. In France socialist membership dropped by two-thirds to some 30,000 by the war's end, whereas in Germany SPD membership plummeted by three-quarters to 243,000 in 1917.

However, the critical role of organized labor in wartime production strengthened the hand of trade unions. In France, union membership rose from 355,000 in 1913 to 600,000 by 1918, and in Britain the comparable gain was from 4 million in 1914 to 8 million by 1920. Germany was the exception here, partly from the departure of union members to the front and partly from the severe restrictions placed on unions by the government, especially the so-called silent dictatorship of Generals Paul von Hinden-burg and Erich Ludendorff in the war's later stages. Absolute numbers, however, do not convey the degree to which the terms of debate over the role of labor had shifted. In some measure, the wartime extension of state influence could be regarded as an experiment in "war socialism," and thereby a partial vindication of labor ideology (in Britain, for ex-ample, the Labour Party, encouraged by its wartime experience, adopted a more explic-itly socialist constitution in 1918). By the war's end, Germany and Russia had socialist governments, and five years later, Britain experienced its first Labour administration.

In November 1918, the guns fell silent (although Russia would be wracked by civil war), but despite the widespread desire for a "return to normalcy," in U.S. president

Warren G. Harding's famous phrase, restoring domestic stability proved problematic. No aspect of the war received greater attention (or condemnation) than efforts to fashion a lasting peace settlement. Part of the problem lay in the fact that Germany's military collapse occurred rapidly in 1918, by which time the battles had still largely been waged on other countries' terrain. In fact, despite its victory over Russia, the German war machine was as exhausted as those of France or Britain and unable to resist the weight of American numbers as fresh doughboys poured into Europe (the United States having entered the conflict against Germany in April 1917).

The peacemakers—or rather the victorious powers, for Germany was not represented but only summoned to sign a treaty—met at Versailles to establish a framework for postwar Europe. In doing so, they were guided by their interpretation of the war's origins. In practice, this meant recognizing the rights of subject nationalities to self-determination and stripping defeated Germany of its colonial empire as well as severely restricting the size and equipment of its military. Accordingly, the peacemakers redrew the map of Europe, erasing the collapsed Austro-Hungarian and Ottoman Empires, and creating a series of new states in eastern Europe, which, it was also thought, could provide a buffer to protect democratic Europe from Bolshevik contamination from the east. In retrospect, many of these states proved too small to withstand either German or Soviet expansion in the 1930s. Furthermore, many were badly splintered by ethnic rivalries.

Yet the limitations of the Versailles settlement were not confined to geographic issues. The enormous financial and human cost of the conflict, and the prospect of tangible rewards for persistent sacrifice, encouraged discussion of reparations to be paid to the victors by the defeated nations. Germany, widely regarded as the aggressor, was assigned full and sole responsibility for the war's outbreak and, therefore, for the damages incurred in its conduct (the famous Article 231, or War Guilt Clause, of the Versailles Treaty). Such a posture only assisted extremists within Germany who contended that the Allies, so careful to recognize the rights of nations in other cases, were determined to trample on those of Germany. Making Germany bear the burden of the war was unrealistic (especially given the fluctuating estimates of both the total cost and Germany's capacity to pay) and unwise, burdening that nation's first democratic government, the Weimar Republic, with an economic and emotional albatross.

In the end, Sir Edward Grey's prophecy proved correct, for World War I was a watershed in history. In some respects, it accelerated existing trends (such as the growth of state intervention), and in others (such as the position of women), it failed to produce a decisive shift. But in many other respects, European life was very different after the war. Most countries' economies had been dealt harsh blows from which they did not fully recover, as was evidenced in the prolonged fiscal crisis beginning in 1929. Liquidated investments, accumulated debts, and disrupted trade all bore witness to the conflict's impact. Liberalism, which had seemed so confident of progress during the nineteenth century, appeared out of touch with postwar realities. Promoting the rational mediation of disputes had not forestalled war, and the claims of the sovereign, respectable individual withered in the face of state authority and the slaughter. After 1918, ideologies extolling the group and collective action, such as fascism and communism, and urging physical violence as a liberating experience, proved more attractive than the old liberal ideals. Indeed, it is difficult to imagine the success of either the Russian Revolution or the Nazi seizure of power without the groundwork laid by the war itself. Moreover, U.S. military involvement in the conflict, and its crucial financial role in postwar economic life, ensured that, despite strong isolationist sentiment, the United States was now tied to European affairs. Therefore, the principal trends of twentieth-century European history are all tied to the experience of the first total war.

SELECTED BIBLIOGRAPHY

Audoin-Rouzeau, Stephan. *Men at War, 1914–1918*. Providence, RI: Berg Press, 1992. An investigation of the ordinary soldier's experience as reflected in trench journalism.

Becker, Jean-Jacques. *The Great War and the French People*. Leamington Spa, England: Berg Press, 1985. The best account of civilian life in France during the conflict.

Bourne, John. *Britain and the Great War, 1914–1918*. London: Edward Arnold, 1989. A helpful synthesis of recent scholarship on both the home front and military campaigns.

Braybon, Gail. *Women Workers in the First World War*. London: Croom Helm, 1981. Still a standard account of its subject.

Ekstein, Modris. *Rites of Spring: The Great War and the Birth of the Modern Age*. Boston: Houghton Mifflin, 1989. An imaginative and wide-ranging cultural study.

Feldman, Gerald D. *Army, Industry and Labor in Germany 1914–1918*. Princeton, NJ: Princeton University Press, 1966; reprinted 1992 by Berg Press. The pioneering study of civil-military relations.

Ferro, Marc. *The Great War 1914–1918*. London: Routledge, 1973. A good starting point.

Fischer, Fritz. *Germany's Aims in the First World War*. New York: Norton, 1967. Originally published in German in 1961, this is a fundamental but controversial study of the expansionist aims of German elites.

Fussell, Paul. *The Great War and Modern Memory*. New York: Oxford University Press, 1975. Sensitive exploration of the aesthetic side of the war, based on British sources.

Hardach, Gerd. *The First World War, 1914–1918*. Berkeley: University of California Press, 1977. The best brief introduction to the economic aspects of the conflict.

Joll, James. *The Origins of the First World War*. London: Longmans, 1981; 2nd ed., 1991. A wonderfully lucid and balanced introduction to a complex and controversial topic.

Kocka, Jürgen. *Facing Total War: German Society, 1914–1918*. Leamington Spa, England: Berg Press, 1984. The only substantial study in English of German class relations during the war.

Marwick, Arthur. *The Deluge*. London: Macmillan, 1965; 2nd ed., 1991. A pioneering book arguing that the war produced profound social change in Britain.

Neiberg, Michael S. *Fighting the Great War: A Global History*. Cambridge, MA: Harvard University Press, 2006. A scholarly yet very readable account of the seemingly never-ending war. Although Neiberg breaks no new ground, his book is a good starting point for the serious student.

Offer, Avner. *The First World War: An Agrarian Interpretation*. Oxford: Clarendon Press, 1989. Unconventional and uneven, but often brilliant.

Robbins, Keith. *The First World War*. Oxford: Clarendon Press, 1984. Thematic rather than narrative approach.

Stevenson, David. *Cataclysm: The First World War as Political Tragedy*. New York: Basic Books, 2004. Stevenson lays blame for the coming of the war and its murderous conduct at the feet of every government. Every combatant played with fire and got burned—badly. The United States is not spared, especially President Wilson, whose naiveté and self-assuredness helped to lay the groundwork for problems that continue to plague the world today.

Stevenson, David. *The First World War and International Politics.* Oxford: Clarendon Press, 1988. A persuasive study of the various countries' war aims and the obstacles to a satisfactory peace settlement.

Stone, Norman. *The Eastern Front 1914–1917.* London: Hodder and Stoughton, 1975. A standard account.

Storey, William Kelleher. *The First World War.* New York: Rowman and Littlefield, 2009. A recent short survey of the war notable for the emphasis that it places on technological and environmental factors. Concentrates on the Western Front at the expense of the war's other theaters.

Turner, John. *British Politics and the Great War.* New Haven, CT: Yale University Press, 1992. The best detailed study of coalition governments and the collapse of Britain's last Liberal administration.

Wohl, Robert. *The Generation of 1914.* Cambridge, MA: Harvard University Press, 1979. Elegant comparative analysis of the hopes and eventual disillusion of the younger, university-educated generation.

BATTLE OF AMIENS (1918)

The Battle of Amiens marked the turning point of World War I on the Western Front. For the first time, German units began to collapse and surrender to the attacking British. All the territory gained in Germany's spring offensive was lost. Amiens was also the scene of the most advanced combined arms tactics used in World War I.

By August 1918, the German advance begun in March during the Second Battle of the Marne had been halted. The most dangerous salient on the Marne had been reduced. Ferdinand Foch, commander of all Allied forces, had convinced the national commanders of the Allies that coordinated offensives were the best way to defeat the Germans. The first of the coordinated offensives was at Amiens. The initial objective was clearing the Paris-Châlons railroad. The overall British commander was Douglas Haig, but the chief striking force was the British Fourth army under Sir Henry Rawlinson. Rawlinson had 17 divisions, including one American, four Canadian, and five Australian. Four hundred tanks would support the attack as well. The planners intended to use all the hard-earned lessons of the past four years. The primary element was surprise, with a sudden artillery barrage and an effort to hide the buildup of units. The attack also emphasized the close cooperation between armor and infantry. They would lead the assault, with a heavy rolling barrage of artillery. Aircraft would play an important role by attacking antiarmor weapons, dropping supplies, and keeping contact between advanced units and commanders.

The German defenders consisted of 20 worn divisions divided between the 2nd and 18th Armies. They were surprised on August 8 when the British attacked on a 10-mile front. Within two hours, the British took 16,000 prisoners. By nightfall, they had penetrated nine miles into German territory. German general Erich Ludendorff later referred to this as the "Black Day" for the German army. Morale among the defenders collapsed, and whole units surrendered or ran away. The French 1st army to the south also attacked on August 8 and made considerable progress. On August 10, the French 3rd army attacked farther south and captured some territory. The British continued to attack, although their progress was slower on following days. By August 12, they had reached the old Somme battlefield. The British 1st and 3rd Armies launched an attack on August 21 and put further pressure on the defenders. The advances ground to a halt by September 3, and Haig suspended further attacks, arguing that the gains would not outweigh the casualties.

The defeat at Amiens convinced German leaders that peace was a necessity as soon as possible. On August 14, Kaiser Wilhelm II authorized the foreign minister to initiate peace negotiations through the Netherlands. The Germans also fell back along a 30-mile front to the Hindenburg Line. German losses totaled 75,000, including 30,000 captured. French casualties were 24,000, whereas the British, who had gained the most territory, lost only 22,000.

TIM WATTS

FRANZ FERDINAND, ARCHDUKE OF AUSTRIA (1863–1914)

Franz Ferdinand, Archduke of Austria-Este, was the heir to the throne of the Austro-Hungarian Empire in the late 1800s and early 1900s. As nephew of Emperor Franz Joseph I, he became heir to the throne after the deaths of his father and Franz Joseph's son. His assassination in Sarajevo in 1914 was the immediate cause of World War I.

Franz Ferdinand was born on December 18, 1863, in Graz, Austria. His full name in German was Franz Ferdinand, Erzherzog von Österreich-Este. His father was Archduke Charles Louis, the brother of Austrian emperor Franz Joseph. His mother, Princess Maria Annunciata, daughter of Ferdinand II, the Bourbon king of the Two Sicilies, had tuberculosis and died when Franz Ferdinand was a small child. As a boy, Franz Ferdinand was delicate, and it was thought that he might not survive.

When he was 14, Franz Ferdinand became a second lieutenant in the army. Soon after, he was promoted to first lieutenant and sent to Enns to join the Dragoons. He did not enjoy his first military experiences but liked the life better after he became a major in 1888 and moved to Prague.

When Franz Joseph's son, the archduke Rudolf, committed suicide in 1889, Franz Ferdinand's father became the next in line for the Austro-Hungarian throne. When his father died in 1896, Franz Ferdinand found himself the heir to the throne. Franz Ferdinand was strong, intelligent, and very religious. He had few close friends. When he comprehended what his future might hold, he concentrated on the study of political science and the various languages of the empire. He also went on a world tour to give his studies some practical grounding.

Austro-Hungarian officials did not expect Franz Ferdinand to survive long enough to take over the empire because his health was poor. Instead, they focused on his younger brother Otto as a more likely prospect for the succession. This was a source of great bitterness to Franz Ferdinand. He also wanted to marry a lady-in-waiting, Sophie, Countess von Chotek, but Emperor Franz Joseph and the royal court disapproved of the match. He finally was allowed to marry Sophie in 1900 after agreeing to give up his children's possible claim to the throne.

Hopeful of succeeding Franz Joseph, Franz Ferdinand concentrated on diplomacy and foreign relations. In Austria and Hungary, he encouraged reforms to strengthen the throne and suggested innovative policies to deal with the fractious and potentially dangerous multinational nature of the empire. In 1906, he started involving himself with

Archduke Franz Ferdinand and his wife in Sarajevo on June 28, 1914, shortly before they were killed by an assassin working with the Black Hand terrorist group. The assassination set off a chain of events leading to the outbreak of World War I. (The Illustrated London News Picture Library)

the military and increasing his influence there, and in 1913 became inspector general of the Austro-Hungarian army.

Franz Ferdinand and Franz Joseph did not have a close, amicable relationship. Franz Joseph in his later years displayed less and less interest in handling state matters himself but resented any interference, and Franz Ferdinand's constant pressure on foreign and domestic matters was not welcome.

On the morning of June 28, 1914, Franz Ferdinand and his wife were traveling in a motorcade through Sarajevo. Franz Ferdinand had been warned of a possible assassination plot but decided to tour the city to celebrate the anniversary of the 1389 Battle of Kosovo, in which the Serbs were defeated by the Turks and Serbia lost its independence. Serbia had regained its independence from the Ottoman Empire in 1878 and laid claim to Bosnia and Herzegovina. Austria-Hungary, however, citing the Congress of Berlin, believed that it had the right to occupy that area and officially annexed Bosnia and Herzegovina in 1908. This annexation outraged the Serbs since they regarded Bosnia and Herzegovina as integral parts of the Serbian lands. Consequently, Austria-Hungary's relations with Serbia became quite strained, and plots against Austria sprang to life in Belgrade, the Serbian capital. One such plot featured the Black Hand, a group of Serbian conspirators who trained several Serbian youths to infiltrate Bosnia and assassinate

Franz Ferdinand. It is quite possible that the Serbian government had a hand in this plot.

As Franz Ferdinand's motorcade traveled through the streets of Sarajevo, one of the terrorists tossed a bomb at his car. Neither Franz Ferdinand nor Sophie was injured; however, the archduke, who was known for his temper, was incensed. After a luncheon reception, the royal couple set off to the nearby military installation where they were staying. However, Franz Ferdinand decided to deviate from the established route to visit those who had been wounded in the morning attack. The imperial couple's driver was unfamiliar with Sarajevo and became lost. Unintentionally, he entered a cul-de-sac where another Black Hand member, Gavrilo Princip, happened to be walking. Princip took advantage of his good luck to walk up to the stationary automobile and shoot both Sophie and Franz Ferdinand with a pistol. Sophie died instantly, and Franz Ferdinand followed a few minutes later. Princip tried to kill himself but was captured before he could. Escaping the death penalty because of his youth, Princip was sent to an Austrian prison where he died in 1918 of tuberculosis.

One month after the Sarajevo assassination, on July 28, 1914, Austria declared war on Serbia, starting World War I.

AMY BLACKWELL

JOSEPH JOFFRE (1852–1931)

General Joseph Jacques Césaire Joffre headed the French army when World War I broke out in 1914. He was not a brilliant or innovative leader, but his calm demeanor and professionalism did a great deal to help France weather the first difficult stages of the conflict.

Joffre was born on January 12, 1852, at Rivesaltes, in the French department of Pyrénées-Orientales, one of 11 children of an artisan father. An excellent student, he attended the prestigious École Polytechnique, but his studies were interrupted by the Franco-Prussian War in 1870. He worked on the defense of Paris as an engineer and finished his studies after France was defeated in 1871. He then entered the army full time, becoming a captain in 1876. In 1885, distraught over the death of his wife, he applied for a transfer to colonial service, beginning the overseas career that would make his reputation and propel him to the pinnacle of the army hierarchy.

Joffre's first assignment was in Formosa (present-day Taiwan), where he saw service in the final stages of the Sino-French War of 1883–1885. He then moved on to Indochina (Vietnam), where he organized the defense of Hanoi. Later he served in west Africa with General Joseph Galliéni, cementing a relationship that would help Joffre's career at several vital stages. During 1900–1905, he served under Galliéni in Madagascar and was promoted to general of division and director of engineers at the War Ministry in Paris in 1905. Joffre was a member of the Supreme War Council in 1911 when Galliéni was offered appointment as head of the army. The old general turned down the offer, suggesting instead his former subordinate in the colonies. Joffre thus became chief of the General Staff and vice president of the Supreme War Council.

Under Joffre's direction, the General Staff drew up a general strategic plan to be implemented in case of war with Germany. The result, the infamous Plan XVII, went into effect when World War I broke out in August 1914. Plan XVII assumed that the Germans would not invade through Belgium, thus violating that nation's neutrality. The plan thus expected the main German force to move into France further south and called for an aggressive French offensive into German territory. The precise location of the French effort was to be in the area of Alsace and Lorraine, two territories that the French had lost to Germany in the Franco-Prussian War more than 40 years earlier. The plan was in accordance with the predominant strategic and tactical mentality of the time, the "Doctrine of the Offensive," which denigrated the value of the defense in warfare and exalted the power of offensive power and élan.

Unfortunately for the French, the Germans did in fact cross through Belgium, thus bypassing completely the French forces that had been stationed further south and that might have stopped them. In a very short time, as the French were still seeking to make headway in Alsace and Lorraine, the German army was threatening Paris. Moreover, the doctrine of unconditional offensive warfare was disastrous at the tactical level as well, as the higher rates, volume, and accuracy of machine gun, rifle, and artillery fire made massed frontal assaults literally suicidal and futile. The French suffered appalling casualties in the first weeks of the fighting, and by the beginning of September, it seemed that they would lose the war.

Joffre's old colleague Galliéni was in Paris directing the defense of the city when he saw that the German line of advance exposed them to a French flanking attack from the direction of the city. Joffre and the General Staff had been desperately redeploying their forces in the area of Paris to prepare a defense, and now they acted on Galliéni's recommendation, ordering a counterattack in the area of the Marne River outside the capital. The result was the "Miracle of the Marne." In five days of dramatic fighting during September 5–10, the French stopped, then reversed the German advance, saving Paris and keeping France in the war in the dramatic First Battle of the Marne.

To be sure, Joffre deserves a fair share of the blame for the disastrous Plan XVII and the losses in the first weeks of the war, but his calmness under pressure and decisive action during the Battle of the Marne literally saved France. Even during the worst of the fighting, "Papa" Joffre—a large, grandfatherly figure who never allowed his duties to interfere with regular mealtimes—provided the French army and people with the reassurance they needed to withstand the pressures of near-defeat. A comment he made after the war, responding to the controversy over who really deserved credit for the victory at the Marne, summed up his resigned, imperturbable character: "I don't really know; but I know who would have been responsible had it been a defeat."

The Battle of the Marne was Joffre's finest hour, and the rest of his war service was disappointing. Once the fighting settled down to a stalemate in the trenches of the Western Front, he and the other commanders on both sides were at a loss about how to gain a decisive advantage. Two offensives in 1915, in Champagne and Artois, resulted in heavy casualties and had to be called off. In 1916, the Germans launched a massive attack on the fortified city of Verdun, catching Joffre and the French completely by surprise. Although little territory was lost, the Battle of Verdun raged for 10 months and was one of the bloodiest conflicts in the history of warfare. The slaughter at Verdun became a symbol of the futility of the French war effort. Despite the protection of his old mentor Galliéni, who was minister of war when the Battle of Verdun began in early 1916, Joffre could not survive the criticism that this battle evoked, criticism made all the more bitter by Joffre's secretive behavior. He refused to keep politicians informed about the progress of the war, and he did not allow them to visit the front to see for themselves. This kind of behavior might have been acceptable from a successful general but quickly became intolerable in the face of continued stalemate.

Joffre's public stature, however, was still sufficient to necessitate circumspection, so the government removed him from direct command at the front while elevating him to the rank of marshal of France, the highest military honor in the French army. For the last two years of the war, he exercised no direct control over the fighting, but in 1917, he was appointed head of a French military mission to the United States. After the war ended, Joffre retired, living quietly and writing his memoirs. He died in Paris on January 3, 1931.

ABC-CLIO

T. E. LAWRENCE (1888–1935)

In a daring guerrilla campaign during World War I, T. E. Lawrence placed himself at the head of several Arab tribes and successfully neutralized the Turkish army on the Arabian Peninsula. Proceeding northward, he helped Great Britain's forces defeat the Turks in the Holy Land. Although he may have embellished his actions in his war memoir, *The Seven Pillars of Wisdom,* and contemporaries have inflated the importance of his activities, Lawrence's romantic campaign captured the public's imagination, providing it some relief from the unmitigated horror of the Western Front, and earned for the man the now-famous sobriquet of "Lawrence of Arabia."

Born on August 15, 1888, in Tremadoc, Caernarvonshire, Wales, Thomas Edward Lawrence was the illegitimate son of Sir Thomas Chapman, a member of the Anglo-Irish gentry who had abandoned his wife, and Sarah Maden, the governess of Chapman's daughters. Under the assumed surname of Lawrence, Chapman and Maden lived openly as man and wife. The family moved to Oxford in 1896, where Lawrence attended Oxford High School and compiled a good academic record. He obtained a scholarship to attend Jesus College at Oxford University, choosing to study Crusader military architecture in the Holy Land. Lawrence traveled to France, Syria, Palestine, and Turkey to study medieval castles. After completing his thesis, he obtained a degree with honors in history in 1910.

In the same year, Lawrence won a traveling fellowship from Magdalen College at Oxford University to work on the British Museum's excavation of the ancient Hittite city of Carchemish (Barak). From 1911 to 1914, he worked at the site on the Euphrates, picking up the local language and learning about Arab culture. In the latter year, Lawrence joined an expedition supported by the Palestine Exploration Fund (but with ties to the British War Office) that surveyed the strategic area between Gaza and Al Aqabah, otherwise known as the Negev.

Just before the outbreak of World War I, Lawrence found employment with the British army, working in the Geographical Section of the General Staff. When Turkey entered the war against Britain in October 1914, Lawrence was transferred to Cairo to work in the Arab Bureau, which gathered and analyzed military intelligence. As months

In a daring guerrilla campaign during World War I, T. E. Lawrence placed himself at the head of several Arab tribes and successfully neutralized the Turkish army on the Arabian peninsula, earning him the now-famous sobriquet of "Lawrence of Arabia." (Library of Congress)

passed, he became increasingly convinced that a British-supported Arab revolt could undermine the Turkish position in the Middle East.

Lawrence saw an important opportunity emerge in June 1916, when Hussein ibn Ali, the emir of Mecca, rose in rebellion against the Turks. In October 1916, Lawrence accompanied Ronald Storrs's mission to Jeddah, where the British established contact with Hussein's Arab Uprising. During his stay in the Hejaz, Lawrence formed a close relationship with Hussein's son, Faisal I, who commanded Arab forces against the Turks near Medina. Back in Cairo, Lawrence advised his superiors to aid the rebellion. Appointed as Britain's political and military liaison officer to Faisal's forces, Lawrence returned to the Hejaz shortly thereafter.

Helping rally Arab forces around Faisal by providing magnetic leadership, Lawrence launched a daring guerrilla campaign against the Turks on the western side of the Arabian Peninsula. Engaging in hit-and-run attacks and blowing up trains, Arab forces directed by Lawrence wreaked havoc on the Turks. Lawrence and Faisal slid up the coast of the Red Sea, hoping to disrupt the railway between Medina and Amman, thus cutting off supplies to the Turkish garrison in the former town. To that end, they captured Al Wajh on January 24, 1917.

Pushing even deeper into Turkish territory, Lawrence and Faisal captured Al Aqabah on July 6, 1917. Leaving Faisal behind, Lawrence advanced still farther, meeting up with other Arab tribes led by Auda Abu Tayi. With those, he destroyed a Turkish force at Ma'an. Heading northward alone on reconnaissance, Lawrence reached Dar'a in November. At that latter town, it appears the Turks may have captured Lawrence and raped him. A variety of sources offer conflicting accounts of that incident, including Lawrence himself. Lawrence escaped (or returned) southward to join his forces near Al Aqabah and coordinate his movements with the offensive of General Edmund Allenby in Palestine.

Shortly after Allenby captured Jerusalem, Lawrence defeated a Turkish force at Al Tafilah in January 1918. That victory, along with Lawrence's raids on Turkish supply lines, isolated Turkish forces in Medina, rendering them helpless. Henceforth, Lawrence conducted operations on Allenby's right flank, to the east of the River Jordan, pushing northward toward Amman and then Damascus. In late September 1918, Lawrence captured Dar'a. Only several days later, after Allenby had successfully destroyed the Turkish army in Palestine, Lawrence captured Damascus on October 1. A lieutenant colonel by that point, Lawrence resigned his commission and refused all recognition of his services.

Exhausted by his efforts, Lawrence nevertheless attempted to defend Arab interests at the peace conference that produced the Treaty of Versailles (1919), hoping to prevent the French from obtaining Lebanon and Syria as mandates of the League of Nations. His efforts proved futile, but his story, just then emerging, captured the public imagination. The tale of this hero—now known as "Lawrence of Arabia"—who had led a small band of Arab tribesmen against the Turks in a romantic crusade made him a national hero. Returning to Britain, he obtained a fellowship from All Souls' College at Oxford University, which he used to write his memoirs of the Arab campaign.

In 1921, Secretary of State for the Colonies Winston Churchill asked Lawrence to join the Middle Eastern Division of the Colonial Office. Lawrence accepted but quickly grew disillusioned with British colonial policy (although Faisal did become king of Iraq). He resigned in 1922. Emotionally drained from writing his memoir and seeking anonymity, he joined the British Royal Air Force (RAF) as a private. Nevertheless, a newspaper discovered his subterfuge, and the RAF discharged him in early 1923. Only months later, Lawrence enlisted in the Royal Tank Corps, again as a private, under the name of T. E. Shaw (which he assumed legally in 1927).

For the rest of his life, Lawrence continued to tinker with his heroic memoir (*The Seven Pillars of Wisdom*) and write other works. Most did not see wide circulation until after his death. Transferred to the RAF in 1925, he served in India on the Northwest frontier. Soviet allegations that he was a spy led to his return to Britain in 1929. For the next six years, he worked on RAF seaplane design. Discharged from the RAF in 1935, he was fatally injured in a motorcycle accident several months later, dying on May 19, 1935.

ABC-CLIO

ERICH LUDENDORFF (1865–1937)

Erich Ludendorff was a career soldier who commanded the German army during World War I. He was a skillful military leader and strategist, although his political judgment was often questionable. He and his colleague, General Paul von Hindenburg, ruled Germany as virtual military dictators during the last years of World War I as Kaiser Wilhelm II's government crumbled.

Ludendorff was born on April 9, 1865, at Kruszewnia, near Posen (Poznań). His family was not well-off, so his prospects as a military officer seemed limited. Nonetheless, he entered the army at the age of 18, and his intellectual brilliance and appetite for hard work won him admission to the prestigious Kriegsakademie in 1893. Upon his graduation in 1894, he joined the General Staff, rising rapidly under the patronage of the highly placed General Alfred von Schlieffen and the younger General Helmuth von Moltke Jr. From 1908 to 1913, Ludendorff headed the mobilization section of the General Staff, but he unwisely involved himself in political lobbying to increase the size of the army. This effort caused the war minister to assign him to an obscure regimental command, where he was serving when World War I broke out in 1914.

The war quickly propelled Ludendorff back into favor. In August, during the initial weeks of the conflict, the main German effort was directed against defeating France quickly under the provisions of the Schlieffen Plan. As a consequence, only a small defensive force was left in the east to guard against an attack by France's ally Russia. Tsar Nicholas II mobilized his forces much more quickly than the Germans had expected, and the enormous Russian army entered East Prussia by the third week of August.

The German High Command immediately turned to Ludendorff, who had distinguished himself in operations at Liège in Belgium during the previous weeks, to serve as Hindenburg's chief of staff in the eastern defense. This combination proved to be perfect, as Ludendorff complemented Hindenburg's sagacity and emotional stability with his own brilliance and appetite for action. Together, the two men smashed the poorly led and underequipped Russian army at the Battle of Tannenberg between August 26 and August 31. This operation was what can only be described as a battle of annihilation, and they followed it with another Russian defeat at the Battle of Masurian Lakes, which ran from September 9 to September 14. The Russians were driven from East Prussia completely, and Hindenburg and Ludendorff became national heroes, retaining overall command on the Eastern Front for the next several years.

The two men remained paired together for the rest of the war, and they continued to be quite successful in the east. Under their command, German armies handed the Russians defeat after defeat, and the Germans began to acquire Russian territory. On August 29, 1916, Hindenburg was made chief of the General Staff, taking Ludendorff with him to Berlin to assume command of the entire German army. Although technically subordinate to Hindenburg, Ludendorff was the brains behind the successful offensives undertaken in both men's names, and Ludendorff became the more popular of the two. Regarding Russia as the weakest enemy in the alliance against them, they fortified the defensive positions on the Western Front against the French and the British and undertook an offensive in the East that broke the back of the Russian war effort. The tsarist regime collapsed into defeat with the eruption of the Russian Revolution of 1917. In March 1918, the Germans eventually negotiated the Treaty of Brest-Litovsk with the new Soviet regime. This treaty ceded to Germany huge areas of Russian territory.

Hindenburg and Ludendorff now became, by virtue of their dramatic successes and great popularity, de facto dictators of Germany in both military and political affairs. After the defeat of Russia, they turned their attention to the West. In 1917, they gambled that German military might, unhindered now by a two-front war, could achieve a decisive victory over the French and British before the United States could bring its considerable human and material resources to bear on the Western Front.

The generals removed any potential opposition to their plans by insisting on the dismissal of Prime Minister Theobald von Bethmann-Holweg, whom they considered to be a defeatist. At Ludendorff's insistence, Germany resumed unrestricted submarine warfare against any ships, including ones flying the U.S. flag, supplying Germany's enemies. The United States did declare war on Germany, but a spectacular offensive in the spring and summer of 1918, planned by Ludendorff, broke the stalemate that had prevailed on the Western Front since 1914 and brought the German army within easy striking distance of Paris. However, the German army was exhausted by the effort and the French and British turned them back. It was only a matter of time before American power tipped the balance decisively in the Allies' favor.

By the autumn of 1918, the German army was being driven back on all fronts. Hindenburg and Ludendorff informed Wilhelm II that the war was lost and suggested that he abdicate the throne. They then handed responsibility for ending hostilities to the new civilian government, ensuring that the army evaded any responsibility for the ultimate surrender. This political maneuver, and the fact that the war was ended before the Allies invaded Germany and while the German army was still technically intact in the field, was one of the legacies most damaging to the new Weimar Republic that ruled Germany after the war. Critics found it easy to blame Germany's defeat not on the "unconquered army" but on the democratic regime that capitulated on November 11, 1918, and negotiated the humiliating Treaty of Versailles. After the war, Ludendorff would work with other right-wing political figures, including Nazi leader Adolf Hitler, to exploit this issue and discredit the new democratic regime.

As soon as he and Hindenburg handed power over to the new government, Ludendorff fled to Sweden. There, he wrote his memoirs, returning to Germany in 1919. He immediately plunged himself into ultra right-wing political agitation and an obscure Nordic mystic religion. He consorted with several figures on the fringe of the right-wing, ultimately becoming involved in Hitler's Beer Hall Putsch in Munich on November 8 and 9, 1923. This attempt to overthrow the government and erect a reactionary and ultranationalist dictatorship was a miserable and embarrassing failure. Despite his acquittal on charges of treason at the subsequent trial, the fact that Ludendorff—one-time supreme military authority in Germany—would participate in such a plot spoke volumes about how far he had fallen. Many questioned his sanity, and his actions over the next years of his life did nothing to quiet them. He continued to associate himself with extremists, entering Parliament as a member of the Nazi Party. When he ran for president of the republic in April 1925, he polled only 1 percent of the vote. He lived out the remaining years of his life in obscure retirement, his grip on reality getting steadily more questionable. Ludendorff died on December 20, 1937, in Munich.

ABC-CLIO

DOCUMENT: SCHLIEFFEN PLAN (1905)

German general Alfred von Schlieffen devised the Schlieffen Plan in response to the threat of a joint attack on Germany by France and Russia. Schlieffen's plan anticipated a quick German victory through the use of a large flanking movement to crush the French, followed by a redeployment of troops toward Russia via railroad. As World War I opened in 1914, a modified version of the Schlieffen Plan was put into action, but French forces stalled the Germans at the Marne River, and the Russians mobilized faster than expected. Ultimately, the plan failed, and Germany was forced to fight enemies on both the Western Front and Eastern Front.

Berlin, December 1905
War against France

In a war against Germany, France will probably at first restrict herself to defence, particularly as long as she cannot count on effective Russian support. With this in view she has long prepared a position which is for the greater part permanent, of which the great fortresses of Belfort, Epinal, Toul and Verdun are the main strong points. This position can be adequately occupied by the large French army and presents great difficulties to the attacker.

The attack will not be directed on the great fortresses, whose conquest requires a great siege apparatus, much time and large forces, especially as encirclement is impossible and the siege can only be conducted from one side. The attacker will prefer to advance on the intervening gaps. Two of them (Belfort-Epinal and Toul-Verdun) are filled with barrier forts, but these are of no considerable importance. It matters more that the gaps are already strong natural positions in which sector lies behind sector, and which, by the great fortresses on their wings, impede their envelopment by the enemy, while threatening him with the same fate himself. The greatest promise of success is offered by an attack on the right wing of the Moselle forts (Fort Ballon de Servance). But we are not sufficiently prepared to overcome the difficult terrain here. Even when that has been attended to, one will hardly wish to open a campaign with a siege of "Ballon de Servance." In a later period of the war, however, the reduction of this fort may be of importance.

Another promise of success is offered by an attack on Nancy, which is protected by field-works and is open to easy envelopment and bombardment. But after the town and the heights beyond are taken (Foret de Haye) we are faced with the fortifications of Toul. Almost the only advantage of an attack on Nancy is that in order to save the capital of Lorraine the French might perhaps be induced to come out of their fortresses and accept open battle. But they would then have their defence lines so close in their rear that a defeat would not bring them great damage, nor the victor great success. It would be a repulsed sortie from a fortress, involving besieger and defender in about the same number of casualties and leaving the situation of both unchanged.

Therefore a frontal attack on the position Belfort-Verdun offers little promise of success. An envelopment from the south would have to be preceded by a victorious campaign against Switzerland and by the capture of the Jura forts—time-consuming enterprises during which the French would not remain idle.

Against a northern envelopment the French intend to occupy the Meuse between Verdun and Mézières, but the real resistance, it is said, is not to be offered here but behind the Aisne, roughly between St. Menehould and Rethel. An intermediate position beyond the Aire seems also to be under consideration. If the German envelopment reaches even further, it will run into a strong mountain position whose strongpoints are the fortresses of Rheims, Laon and La Fère.

The Germans are therefore confronted with the following:

(1) The position Belfort, Epinal, Toul, Verdun with a continuation along the Meuse at Mézières. Screening troops are pushed out to the Vosges, the Meurthe, Nancy and the Cotes Lorraines between Toul and Verdun.

(2) The intermediate position on the Aire.

(3) The position on the Aisne.

(4) The position Rheims–La Fère.

One cannot have great confidence in an attack on all these strong positions. More promising than the frontal attack with an envelopment by the left wing seems to be an attack from the north-west, directed on the flanks at Mézières, Rethel, La Fère, and across the Oise on the rear of the position.

To make this possible, the Franco-Belgian frontier left of the Meuse must be taken, together with the fortified towns of Mézières, Hirson and Maubeuge, three small barrier forts, Lille and Dunkirk; and to reach thus far the neutrality of Luxembourg, Belgium and the Netherlands must be violated.

The violation of Luxembourg neutrality will have no important consequences other than protests. The Netherlands regard England, allied to France, no less as an enemy than does Germany. It will be possible to come to an agreement with them.

[Belgium will probably offer resistance.] In face of the German advance north of the Meuse, her army, according to plan, will retreat to Antwerp and must be contained there; this might be effected in the north by means of a blockade of the Scheldt which would cut communications with England and the sea. For Liège and Namur, which are intended to have only a weak garrison, observation will suffice. It will be possible to take the citadel of Huy, or to neutralise it.

Making a covered advance against Antwerp, Liège, and Namur, the Germans will find a fortified frontier, but not a frontier as thoroughly and extensively fortified as that opposite Germany. If the French wish to defend it, they will be obliged to move corps and armies from the original front and replace them by reserves from the rear, for instance by the corps on the Alpine frontier. But it is to be hoped that they will not be fully successful in this. Therefore they may perhaps give up the attempt to man such an overextended line and instead take the offensive against the threatening invasion with all the troops they can scrape together. Whether they attack or defend, it is not unlikely that battle will be joined near the frontier.

DOCUMENT: WOODROW WILSON'S FOURTEEN POINTS (1918)

On January 8, 1918, U.S. president Woodrow Wilson explained to a special joint session of Congress his dream of maintaining world peace after the end of World War I in 14 points. Following is an excerpt of Wilson's speech. Known now as simply the Fourteen Points, Wilson's aims manifested themselves in the League of Nations, an international organization created to settle disputes between countries, which was founded during the Paris Peace Conference in the spring of 1919. Ironically, the U.S. Senate failed to either ratify the Treaty of Versailles or join the League of Nations, hoping instead to remain isolated from world affairs.

1. Open covenants of peace, openly arrived at, after which there shall be no private international understandings of any kind but diplomacy shall proceed always frankly and in the public view.

2. Absolute freedom of navigation upon the seas, outside territorial waters, alike in peace and in war, except as the seas may be closed in whole or in part by international action for the enforcement of international covenants.

3. The removal, so far as possible, of all economic barriers and the establishment of an equality of trade conditions among all the nations consenting to the peace and associating themselves for its maintenance.

4. Adequate guarantees given and taken that national armaments will be reduced to the lowest point consistent with domestic safety.

5. A free, open-minded, and absolutely impartial adjustment of all colonial claims, based upon a strict observance of the principle that in determining all such questions of sovereignty the interests of the populations concerned must have equal weight with the equitable claims of the government whose title is to be determined.

6. The evacuation of all Russian territory and such a settlement of all questions affecting Russia as will secure the best and freest cooperation of the other nations of the world in obtaining for her an unhampered and unembarrassed opportunity for the independent determination of her own political development and national policy and assure her of a sincere welcome into the society of free nations under institutions of her own choosing; and, more than a welcome, assistance also of every kind that she may need and may herself desire. The treatment accorded Russia by her sister nations in the months to come will be the acid test of their good will, of their comprehension of her needs as distinguished from their own interests, and of their intelligent and unselfish sympathy.

7. Belgium, the whole world will agree, must be evacuated and restored, without any attempt to limit the sovereignty which she enjoys in common with all other free nations. No other single act will serve as this will serve to restore confidence among the nations in the laws which they have themselves set and determined for the government of their relations with one another. Without this healing act the whole structure and validity of international law is forever impaired.

8. All French territory should be freed and the invaded portions restored, and the wrong done to France by Prussia in 1871 in the matter of Alsace-Lorraine, which has unsettled the peace of the world for nearly fifty years, should be righted, in order that peace may once more be made secure in the interest of all.

9. A readjustment of the frontiers of Italy should be effected along clearly recognizable lines of nationality.

10. The peoples of Austria-Hungary, whose place among the nations we wish to see safeguarded and assured, should be accorded the freest opportunity of autonomous development.

11. Rumania, Serbia, and Montenegro should be evacuated; occupied territories restored; Serbia accorded free and secure access to the sea; and the relations of the several Balkan states to one another determined by friendly counsel along historically established lines of allegiance and nationality; and international guarantees of the political and economic independence and territorial integrity of the several Balkan states should be entered into.

12. The Turkish portions of the present Ottoman Empire should be assured a secure sovereignty, but the other nationalities which are now under Turkish rule should be assured an undoubted security of life and an absolutely unmolested opportunity of

autonomous development, and the Dardanelles should be permanently opened as a free passage to the ships and commerce of all nations under international guarantees.

13. An independent Polish state should be erected which should include the territories inhabited by indisputably Polish populations, which should be assured a free and secure access to the sea, and whose political and economic independence and territorial integrity should be guaranteed by international covenant.

14. A general association of nations must be formed under specific covenants for the purpose of affording mutual guarantees of political independence and territorial integrity to great and small states alike.

3

The Russian Revolution, 1917–1921

INTRODUCTION

In March 1917, the imperial Russian state, staggering under the blows inflicted by the German army during the course of World War I, collapsed. (Before the Bolshevik Revolution, Russia followed the Julian rather than the Gregorian Calendar. Consequently, depending on which calendar is being followed, the collapse of imperial Russia occurred in either February or March 1917, and the Bolshevik Revolution occurred in either October or November 1917.) Nicholas II, the weak-willed and indecisive tsar, or emperor, abdicated the throne. When no other member of the Romanov family chose to succeed him, 300 years of rule by the Romanovs came to an end and Russia found itself adrift in a revolutionary sea.

Almost immediately, two rival bodies began to compete for control of Russia. One was the Provisional Government, which claimed to be the legitimate successor to the tsarist state. Until 1905, the Russian Empire had been an autocracy, in which all legal power had been concentrated in the hands of the tsar. However, despite energetic attempts to crush any sign of political activity, underground opposition to the regime had flourished in Russia during the nineteenth century. When revolution came in 1905, the tsar reluctantly surrendered a portion of his authority, allowing for the creation of the Duma, or parliament, which exercised some legislative powers. Russian moderates were satisfied with this concession, but radicals rejected the Duma and demanded renewal of revolutionary activity. Although the tsar circumscribed its powers after 1907, the Duma remained in existence and in March 1917 was transformed into the Provisional Government.

The Provisional Government's great rival for power in revolutionary Russia was the Petrograd Soviet (Council) of Workers' and Soldiers' Deputies, which inspired imitators throughout the country. (The Russian capital St. Petersburg had been renamed Petrograd at the start of the war.) Formed in March 1917, the Soviet featured representatives from Russia's most radical political parties, including the Social Revolutionaries, the Mensheviks, and the Bolsheviks. The Soviet also included a fair number of indigenous leaders from military units and the factories who did not formally belong to any radical faction.

The Soviet favored an undefined form of socialism for Russia and demanded more radical action than the Provisional Government was willing to undertake. By virtue of its revolutionary stance, the Soviet more closely reflected the desires of the common people than did the Provisional Government. However, in its early days the Soviet lacked unity of purpose and clear leadership. In fact, its component parts often clashed with each other. Furthermore, the Soviet had no experience at governing. Consequently, the Soviet shied away from seizing power from the Provisional Government, preferring to act as a parallel but competing force. In sum, the Soviet enjoyed considerable popular support but had no clear vision of the future, whereas the Provisional Government had a marginally better idea of what it wished to accomplish but lacked popular support.

During the spring and early summer of 1917, the Provisional Government of Prime Minister Prince Georgy Lvov failed to establish control over the deteriorating situation. The Russian economy continued to collapse, the war dragged on, and the poverty-stricken Russian peasants, who constituted the overwhelming bulk of the population, pressed their demands for land. Slowly the composition of the Provisional Government moved leftward until Alexander Kerensky, the only socialist member of the original Provisional Government, was named prime minister on July 20.

While elements of the moderate, non-revolutionary left gained power in the Provisional Government, the Bolsheviks, the most revolutionary of the socialist parties, increased their strength in the Soviet. This development was directly attributable to the return to Russia from exile of the Bolshevik leader, Vladimir Ilyich Lenin, who gave renewed direction and purpose to his small and divided party. Arriving in Petrograd on April 16, Lenin issued his "April Theses," which called for the Bolsheviks to reject cooperation with the Provisional Government and instead to prepare for the seizure of power. Lenin urged the Bolsheviks to gain control of the Soviet, which would then serve as the vehicle for the socialist revolution they sought. He also demanded that the Bolsheviks provide leadership for the disgruntled workers and peasants, and use the discontent of the masses to propel themselves to power.

Lenin's return to Russia and his call for more radical measures took place against a backdrop of increasing chaos and confusion that undermined what little authority the Provisional Government commanded. Ironically, in many respects the Provisional Government was its own worst enemy. Not only did it fail to meet the demands of the peasants for land, but it kept Russia in the war. Astonishingly enough, in spring 1917, it even ordered the beaten and demoralized Russian army to go on the offensive; this act of gross stupidity resulted in a major Russian defeat that shattered what remained of the army's cohesion.

In July, disturbances broke out in Petrograd. Enraged civilians and disaffected soldiers, frustrated by the deepening crisis, joined forces to attack the Provisional Government. These riots, known as the July Days, were unanticipated, spontaneous, and, for a while, leaderless. The July Days placed the Bolsheviks in a dilemma. Lenin scorned the rioters, characterizing them as "playing at revolution," and wished to hold his Bolsheviks aloof from what he considered to be a lost if not downright stupid cause. Lenin felt that if the Bolsheviks were to join the rioters, they might very well be subjected to significant retribution once the July Days failed. However, Lenin realized that if the Bolsheviks stood aside they would appear to be less than the revolutionary firebrands they claimed to be and could lose hard-earned support among the Petrograd masses.

Reluctantly, Lenin threw the Bolsheviks into the fray, aligning them with the radicalized mobs. As envisioned, however, the Provisional Government retained enough strength to quell the riots and to restore order in Petrograd. With the failure of the July

Bolshevik (Communist) supporters—including soldiers pictured here—overthrew the Russian Provisional Government on November 7, 1917. This brought V. I. Lenin to power and inaugurated 75 years of Soviet rule in Russia. (The Illustrated London News Picture Library)

Days, the Bolshevik Party was banned, Lenin fled Petrograd and went into hiding, and several important Bolshevik leaders were arrested. However, the Provisional Government proved too weak to exploit its victory by moving decisively against the Bolsheviks.

A few weeks after putting down this threat from the left, the Provisional Government faced a serious challenge from the right. Alarmed at the dismal showing of the increasingly socialist-dominated Provisional Government, conservatives and some moderate elements rallied behind General Lavr Kornilov, a popular military figure reputed to have "the heart of a lion and the brain of a sheep." In early September, Kornilov drew close to Petrograd. In response, Kerensky's Provisional Government called on the Soviet to defend the revolution. It also lifted the ban on the Bolshevik Party and released imprisoned Bolsheviks. In a moment of panic, the Provisional Government also distributed tens of thousands of rifles to the masses to repel Kornilov. Most of these weapons fell into the hands of the Bolshevik militia, the Red Guards.

Meanwhile, the Kornilov threat evaporated. The general failed to launch his expected attack, a victim of his own muddled thinking and the unwillingness of troops under his command to follow his orders. However, the Bolsheviks profited greatly from the Kornilov Affair. Having won the sympathy of many in the mob for their stand during the July Days, they now found themselves relegalized and armed.

In the wake of the Kornilov Affair, the Bolsheviks gained control over both the Petrograd and Moscow Soviets. This allowed them to speak in the name of the Soviets, a much broader and popular organization than the Bolshevik Party. A few weeks later, Lenin returned to Petrograd and began to urge an armed insurrection against the Provisional Government.

As Bolshevik power waxed, the authority of the Provisional Government waned. Confused, unpopular, and divided in its own councils, the Provisional Government drifted. Gauging the weakness of the Provisional Government correctly, Lenin, aided by veteran maverick Marxist Leon Trotsky, convinced the Bolsheviks to strike. On November 7, 1917, Bolshevik forces seized most of Petrograd and stormed the Winter Palace, home of the Provisional Government. Few rallied to the side of the beleaguered Provisional Government, and by nightfall the Bolsheviks proclaimed victory. The course of the Russian Revolution had taken a new turn.

Many, especially in the West, expected the new Soviet government to fail quickly. The Russia that the Bolsheviks now ruled was virtually a corpse. More than three years of intense fighting in World War I had bled it white, and despite the Bolshevik seizure of power, the war continued its relentless pace, with the German army bearing down on Petrograd. Russia was bankrupt. Its transportation and communication systems, inadequate to begin with, now lay in ruin. Industrial production shrank almost daily, and anarchy prevailed in the countryside. Finally, the ethnic minorities of western Russia, such as the Poles and the Ukrainians, who had been forcibly brought into the Russian Empire, now demanded their independence.

Facing such a bleak prospect, Lenin and his followers concluded that their first priority must be to strengthen their grasp on the levers of power while simultaneously keeping faith with the Marxist ideology that had sustained them for so long. To that end, they began their rule with a flurry of decrees, including the Decree on Land, which sanctioned peasant seizure of estates belonging to the well-to-do, and the Decree on Peace, which called on all belligerents to enter into negotiations designed to achieve a just peace. In December, they followed up on the peace decree when they concluded an armistice and opened peace negotiations with the Central Powers.

In addition to issuing popular decrees, the Bolsheviks tightened their grip on power when in December they established the Cheka, or secret police, and ordered it to ferret out and destroy all real or potential opposition to Bolshevik rule. Then, in January 1918, the Bolsheviks forcibly dissolved the democratically elected Constituent Assembly that had been expected to create a new set of governmental institutions for Russia. The Bolsheviks, who had done poorly in the fall 1917 elections, winning only 170 of 707 seats, regarded the Constituent Assembly as a threat to their power, and shut it down after allowing it to meet for only one day.

Meanwhile, the peace negotiations proved difficult. Meeting with German representatives at the small Polish town of Brest-Litovsk, the Bolsheviks discovered that their adversaries intended to extract major concessions from the fledgling regime. Bolshevik efforts to evade the German demands failed, and on March 3, 1918, the new Soviet state was forced to sign the humiliating Treaty of Brest-Litovsk. By the terms of the treaty, Soviet Russia gave up control over Poland, Finland, Estonia, Latvia, Lithuania, and Ukraine. It lost 60 million people, or more than one-quarter of its total population. It also surrendered more than one-quarter of its arable land, railways, and factories and three-quarters of its iron and coal production. Only Germany's ultimate defeat in World War I enabled the weak Soviet state to recover some of its losses at Brest-Litovsk.

Many Bolshevik leaders balked at signing the Draconian peace, but Lenin carried the day when he argued that peace was absolutely essential for the retention of Soviet power in Russia, even if it meant that the war had to be concluded at virtually any price. Lenin maintained that peace would give the Bolsheviks a "breathing space" in which to build socialism in Russia. However, his optimism proved unfounded because civil war broke out only weeks after the treaty was signed.

As with most civil wars, the Russian one was a bloody and brutal conflict. Emotions ran high, and both sides committed numerous indescribable atrocities. The Bolsheviks relied on their newly created Red Army, the product of Leon Trotsky's prodigious organizational skills. Their opponents were the Whites, an unlikely mixture of liberals, moderate socialists, radical but anti-Bolshevik socialists, army officers, monarchists, and conservatives. Ultimately, mindless reactionaries and fanatical Russian nationalists gained the upper hand and directed most White operations.

During the course of the civil war, the Bolsheviks instituted a policy known as War Communism. War Communism was designed to achieve two goals simultaneously: the marshalling of all available resources to prosecute the civil war and the rapid transformation of Russia into a model Marxist state. To that end, the Bolsheviks under War Communism nationalized both land and industry, outlawed private trade, implemented a system of rationing and government distribution, and introduced the forced requisitioning of food and labor.

Although War Communism seriously disrupted Russia's already chaotic economy and earned for the Bolsheviks the enmity of millions, it probably helped the Reds to win their war against the Whites. Even more decisive for the Red victory, however, was the ineptitude of the White forces. Despite receiving help in the form of intervention and a blockade from several countries, including France, Great Britain, Japan, and the United States, the Whites failed to dislodge the Reds.

Basic to the White failure was their inability to coordinate their forces. Rather than a single, unified unit, the White army really consisted of several different armies, each under independent command, each following its own course of action, and each pursuing its own goals. Furthermore, the ultra-nationalistic Whites alienated the various minorities located on the periphery of the old Russian Empire, that is, the very places where the White forces had congregated to launch their attacks on the Bolsheviks. Finally, the Whites failed to win the hearts and minds of the vast peasant population. In fact, their behavior during the conflict as well as their stated desire to return to a pre-revolutionary form of land tenure frightened and angered the peasants, without whose support the Whites' chances of success were slim.

The Russian Civil War dragged on for almost three years and, together with the famine it caused, resulted in the death of several million Russians. When the Bolsheviks finally emerged victorious in early 1921, their Russian state was a complete shambles. Nevertheless, the Bolsheviks had triumphed. The revolution was over, Lenin and the Bolsheviks had won, and the future of Russia was theirs to command.

INTERPRETIVE ESSAY

BRUCE F. ADAMS

In 1917, Vladimir Lenin, leader of the Bolshevik Party, which would soon seize control of Russia, was living in Zurich, Switzerland. For most of the previous 16 years, he had lived in self-imposed exile from tsarist Russia, watching intently events in the country whose government he had worked all his adult life to destroy. Once, when revolution had broken out in 1905, he had returned to St. Petersburg, hoping to help topple the tsar, but he had had to flee again when Nicholas II's forces crushed that revolution. Yet for more than 20 years, he had sustained his faith that a socialist revolution would soon occur in Russia. Now in January 1917, he was heard to say, "We of the older generation"—Lenin was forty-six—"may not see the decisive battles of this coming revolution."

He was wrong, of course. Nicholas II was forced to abdicate less than two months later. One of the critical questions of recent history, endlessly debated by historians and taken up with renewed vigor since the collapse of the Soviet Union, is why this revolution occurred. Did the forces of worker discontent and revolutionary organization, which the Bolsheviks watched and tried to mold, make it inevitable, as Marxist-Leninist theory held? Or was the revolution an accident, a product of the economic collapse and suffering caused by World War I in Russia? Was the nature of the Bolshevik government also foreordained, or was it, too, the product of local and temporary circumstances?

To understand the impact the revolution had, both within and outside Russia, we must understand the contradictory answers to these questions. The people who made this history acted as they did in large part because they believed one version or the other. And history is after all not so much the story of the past as a continuing argument about how to tell that story.

We must also understand the long-term trends of Russian history. The revolution that convulsed Russia in the 1990s resembled the 1917 revolution in many ways. In both, the empire ruled by the Russians disintegrated and large numbers of refugees fled from war-torn lands. But in one important way, these two revolutions are very different. After the 1917 revolution, the Bolsheviks began to construct wholly new forms of government and society that were threatening to their neighbors. In the Gorbachev and Yeltsin years, however, the Russians tried to develop a more democratic government and a more open market economy, both of which were welcomed and supported by Russia's developed and powerful neighbors.

Despite his momentary doubt in 1917, Lenin would later insist that the revolution was the inevitable product of historical forces. And for the next 70 years, until the era of *glasnost* (openness), Soviet historians almost unanimously supported this view. In the West, however, most historians adopted a different interpretation. As they understood Russia's history up to 1917, Russia was evolving in the direction of Western constitutional monarchies and democracies, and not only was the revolution not inevitable, it violently contravened the general direction of Russian development. Revisionist historians have been challenging and modifying this so-called liberal view since the 1960s. But since the breakup of the Soviet Union and the subsequent democratic developments in Russia, liberal historians have retorted that the revolution and the following 70 years of communist domination were but an interruption in this general trend.

The Russian Revolution was, as practically all revolutions are, not so much an event as a process, a long period of instability that proceeded through several stages. It began in February 1917 in the midst of the third bleak winter of war. Almost 8 million Russians had died by that time, more than in the rest of the combatant nations combined. Enemy armies occupied much of western Russia, territory including more than a quarter of its industry and about a fourth of the prewar population. In unoccupied Russia, much of the rest of the population suffered from unemployment, inflation, hunger, and cold. Most Russians had lost confidence in their army, in the tsar's government, and, most important, in Nicholas II himself. This was particularly true in St. Petersburg, Russia's capital. When yet another strike broke out there in late February, it quickly turned into an enormous antiwar demonstration, with tens of thousands of marchers calling for the tsar's ouster. This time the police were unable to suppress the demonstrators, and the army was unwilling to do so. The demonstration had become a revolution.

Russia's other leaders, including elected representatives to the Duma (a legislature established during the Revolution of 1905), generals in command of the armies, captains of industry, and leaders of other public institutions, agreed that the only way to restore order was to ask Nicholas II to abdicate. When they insisted, he did so reluctantly, and they formed a new interim government called the Provisional Government. They did not mean to seize power and keep it. Rather, they intended to hold elections for a Constituent Assembly, which would write a constitution and oversee the election of a permanent government. The leaders of the Provisional Government believed above all else in the rule of law. And although it would lead to their destruction, they also believed that Russia must continue fighting alongside democratic France and England against the kaiser's Germany.

Reaction in Russia and in the Western democracies to this first revolution was immensely enthusiastic. The rapid growth of industrialization, urbanization, and higher education in Russia had by 1917 created a powerful middle class with liberal aspirations and a large working class that shared at least its distrust of the tsar. The former group dominated the tsarist-era public institutions, such as the Duma, and provided the foundation for the first Provisional Government. The interests and aspirations of the latter group were represented by the Soviet (Council) of Workers' and Soldiers' Deputies, which was established in St. Petersburg on the same day as the Provisional Government and which gave its conditional support to the new government. Both groups welcomed Nicholas II's fall and the opportunity to restructure their country.

European and American leaders shared their enthusiasm. The U.S. government recognized the Provisional Government within a week of its formation. (It would take it 16 years to recognize the Bolsheviks.) In his first speech after the event, President Woodrow Wilson welcomed Russia to the "partnership of democratic nations" and spoke of "the wonderful and heartening things that have been happening within the last few weeks in Russia." Like Russia's European allies, Americans were pleased to see democracy developing in Russia. Having recently decided to commit the U.S. military to the war, they were probably even more pleased that the revolution might strengthen Russia's resolve and ability to fight Germany.

But the honeymoon for the Provisional Government was short. Continuing the war drained industry, finances, and manpower, thereby diminishing the people's loyalty and goodwill. All the problems that had led to Nicholas's ouster only got worse, and left-wing opposition to the war and the Provisional Government that now waged it grew rapidly. In just six months, three Provisional Governments fell as each failed to deal with shortages and the suffering they caused. Each new coalition government included more socialist ministers, and each was more torn by conflict than its predecessor. Ministers who proposed a solution to one of the problems found their way blocked by others who found it too radical—or too retrograde. The only real solution to Russia's problems was probably to make a separate peace with the Germans, but that was unacceptable to the government.

In June 1917, at the request of its allies, the Provisional Government launched a major offensive against Austria and Germany. The Allies hoped that a simultaneous offensive on both fronts would break the stalemate that World War I had become and push Germany to surrender. The Russians hoped also that a successful offensive would restore order to their army, whose morale had been sapped by earlier defeats and high losses, and thereby shore up support for the government. The European allies were not disappointed. Drawing more German troops east allowed them a measure of success in the west. But the Russians were more than disappointed. Early victories in the new offensive were quickly followed by defeats; the German counterattack turned into a rout. Whole units often refused orders to attack after this, and the desertion rate soared. The Russian army did not recover.

From July to October, the Provisional Government continued to decay, tearing itself apart with internal squabbles while an ever-stronger Soviet organization and the growing Bolshevik Party picked at it from outside. By October, of all the major political parties from the center to the far left, only the Bolsheviks had remained outside the Provisional Government and consistently called for its ouster and an end to the war. While every other group was tarred by the common brush of failure, the Bolsheviks alone stood against the war and remained unblamed for its disaster. When they revolted on October 25, they overthrew a government that was barely standing.

The new Soviet government, which was essentially identical to the leadership of the Bolshevik Party, was not greeted with the same enthusiasm that the first Provisional Government had been. Most Russians were probably uncertain what the Bolsheviks intended to do. It would have been strange if they were not, because the Bolsheviks themselves did not know what they intended. On some major issues they did not hesitate. The night they took power, Lenin announced to the Congress of Soviets that henceforth all land belonged to the peasants and the factories belonged to the workers. Exactly what that meant or how it would work was not immediately clear, but it placated large segments of the angry population. On the issue of the war, the Bolsheviks equivocated. The Allies were fearful that the Bolsheviks would follow through on their repeated promises to leave the war. But the Bolsheviks feared German conquest, and a majority thought that they could mount a "revolutionary war" to defend the socialist revolution and inspire German troops to turn on their officers. A minority, led by Lenin, feared that they would not survive the Russian people's anger if they did not pull out. They played in the middle ground on this issue from October 1917 to March 1918, much of that time following a policy they called "neither peace nor war."

What seems to have saved the Bolsheviks at this point was their determination and the relative weakness of their enemies. Only one other party, the Socialist Revolutionaries (SR), enjoyed widespread popularity. Most of them were too close to the Bolsheviks doctrinally to oppose them with force, and the Bolsheviks had stolen much of the SR thunder with the Decree on Land. No other group, including the army, had the following or even sufficient confidence in itself to mount resistance. The Bolsheviks, on the other hand, were dedicated revolutionaries and true believers in the historical inevitability and justice of their cause. They were prepared to destroy their opponents with force and violence.

The election to and the meeting of the Constituent Assembly illuminate this point. The Provisional Government had waited until September to set a November date for the election to the assembly. It had been in constant crisis since March and wanted to postpone so important and potentially divisive a meeting until the war was over. Finally, however, the Provisional Government could no longer avoid it. When the Bolsheviks came to power, they debated whether they should allow the election to take place, fearing they would not win; but they did not want to appear undemocratic and dictatorial. In fact, when the election took place, the Bolsheviks won only 24 percent of the national vote, whereas the SR factions polled 57 percent. The assembly met for one day in January 1918 and elected an SR chairman. When the delegates attempted to reassemble the second day, they found their way barred by Bolshevik guards and were disbanded. There were much grumbling and some editorializing against the Bolsheviks' high-handedness, but no armed resistance.

The work of the Cheka illustrates the point more clearly. Shortly after the October revolution, Lenin authorized Felix Dzerzhinsky to establish the Extraordinary Commission to Combat Counterrevolution, Sabotage, and Speculation. Its ostensible purpose was to restore civic and economic order by arresting speculators, saboteurs, and other criminals. Very quickly, however, it became a political police. Unrestrained by the rules of procedure that had controlled the tsarist police, the Cheka quickly arrested many thousands of people. Often ignoring its own rules, it dispensed quick "revolutionary justice," imprisoning, interrogating, trying (or not), and executing prisoners without turning them over to the courts. In 1918, the Cheka executed more prisoners than the tsarist regime had put to death in the previous 300 years. It did so again in 1919.

Opposition to the Bolsheviks was slow to organize. After the Bolsheviks disbanded the Constituent Assembly in January and pulled out of the war with Germany in March, however, opponents started to gather. Military opposition began in several areas, led by former officers of the tsarist army and politicians from a wide range of parties. By mid-1918, while large parts of Russia were still occupied by the Germans (the war was not over until November), civil war had begun. It would rage for almost three years. Although it was much shorter than the World War, and for the most part fought with weapons far less destructive, it was bitterly contested and vicious. Five million more Russians died in this war. All of the problems begun by the world war—industrial dislocation, unemployment, and inflation—intensified. In 1921, Russian industry produced less than one-fifth of what it had produced in 1914. Because both sides fed themselves by ravaging peasant villages and took reprisals against villagers who had "helped" their enemies, very little was planted in spring 1921, and the harvest that fall was too small to feed the country. Another million Russians died in the subsequent famine of 1921–1922.

Another form of opposition to the Bolsheviks ineffectually organized in 1918–1919. The Allies were afraid that the Bolshevik withdrawal from the war would allow Germany to concentrate its forces in the west. They were also concerned about social unrest in their own countries. If they allowed communism to be established in Russia, it could encourage labor and social democratic organizations in the West to revolt. The Bolsheviks believed that world revolution was about to begin and, beyond that, that their revolution could not survive unless it did. In March 1919 they had established the Communist International, or Comintern, whose raison d'être was to "export" revolution. Calling their intervention an effort to reopen a second front against Germany, near the end of the war the Allies landed small British, French, and American forces at Archangel and Murmansk, Vladivostok, and the Crimea. The Japanese, who were not part of the alliance but who took advantage of the Russian Empire's collapse to do the same, occupied parts of Russia's eastern maritime provinces and eastern Siberia. These foreign troops had few serious engagements with Bolshevik forces and rendered only insignificant assistance to the White forces in the civil war. They did little to affect the outcome of the civil war and less to affect the course of the world war. The fact that the intervention continued beyond the end of the world war showed, however, that Western leaders were worried about the threat of international communist revolution.

As well they should have been. No sooner had the war ended than communist revolutions broke out in several parts of Europe. Like the Russian Revolution, these all stemmed from local movements and problems, but undoubtedly the Bolshevik revolution inspired their leaders. Communists took power briefly in both Bavaria and Hungary. Demonstrations, riots, and terrorist activity occurred in many other countries. In free elections shortly after the war, communist, social democratic, and labor parties made large gains. In several European nations, legislation establishing parts of the modern welfare state was soon passed. This was more a consequence of the world war than of the Russian Revolution, but the Bolsheviks' apparent success increased the need to placate radical political forces.

In some countries, including the United States, postwar radicalism and fear of communism brought on a backlash, called the Red Scare. In the United States many radicals in unions and other labor and political movements were foreign born, often recent emigres who had not yet become citizens. The decades around the turn of the century had seen a huge wave of immigrants come to America, many from eastern Europe and Russia. When several large strikes and a few anarchist bombings occurred in 1919, many Americans saw in them a communist revolution brewing and pressured the government to act. In August 1919, Attorney General A. Mitchell Palmer established in the Department of Justice a General Intelligence Division, headed by J. Edgar Hoover. In November 1919 and January 1920, it raided suspected radical organizations all over the country, including one called the Union of Russian Workers, and arrested almost 7,000 people. Although the police and federal agents violated the civil rights of many of these people in their investigations and interrogations, few turned out to have committed offenses for which they might be deported. The Red Scare petered out quickly in mid-1920.

One of the major consequences of the revolutions cannot be separated from the war and the peace settlement. By the end of 1918, the tsarist empire had been torn apart. In the Treaty of Brest-Litovsk, which the Bolsheviks signed with the Germans in March 1918, Russia lost western and southern territory, including more than a fourth of its population. Germany's subsequent surrender nullified this treaty, but the treaties signed in Paris in 1919 ratified most of the territorial losses. Finland, Estonia, Latvia, and Lithuania became independent states. Taking territory principally from Russia, Poland also became independent. Romania received former Bessarabia. As happened again in the 1990s, many other areas populated by non-Russian peoples took advantage of the disorder to claim their independence also. This was particularly true on the periphery of the country in areas that had been joined to Russia relatively recently. Georgians, Armenians, Uzbeks, and others experienced a few years of independence before reconquest and reabsorption into the Soviet Union.

The most important consequences of the revolutions, in Russia and outside it, were changes in the nature of Russian government and society. The Bolsheviks did not know in 1917 what sort of government was suitable for "building socialism," and they argued bitterly about it until Joseph Stalin ended all discussion. Initially, in part because their first several years in power were passed in continual crisis and insecurity, the Bolshevik leadership agreed that they would need to be a "dictatorship of the proletariat." The Bolsheviks shared power with no other party. As a matter of fact, they suppressed rival parties, often violently. Within their own party, however, for the first 10 years they tolerated wide-ranging discussion and dissent. In theory this dictatorship was meant to be temporary and would "wither away" as socialism made government almost unnecessary. But by 1928, four years after Lenin died, Joseph Stalin had maneuvered his way to preeminence, silenced his critics, taken control of the levers of power, and established a personal dictatorship. In 1929, he began to collectivize agriculture and to industrialize rapidly. Employing great violence and brutality, Stalin achieved his twin goals; however, more than 20 million Soviet citizens died in the process.

Russia's neighbors feared this dictatorship, which abetted revolution abroad and which mobilized its people and its industrial forces in part by proclaiming (and often believing) that war with the capitalist states was inevitable. Because of this mutual fear and distrust, Russia remained a pariah, an outcast among the European nations. Even before Lenin's death, this outcast status drew Russia closer to Germany, the other European pariah of the 1920s, which was blamed for causing World War I. These fears and relationships helped create the European alliance system that led into World War II and helped shape the period of postwar tensions that we call the Cold War.

The origins of this dictatorship form the other major historiographical issue of the Russian revolutions. One camp claims that Stalinism, as the whole system came to be called, was the product of Stalin's personal character. Proponents like to claim that had Lenin lived longer, such a brutal dictatorship would not have developed, a proposition that cannot, of course, be tested. Since the collapse of the Communist Party of the Soviet Union and of the Soviet Union itself in 1991, many communists have preferred to blame Stalin personally for the great tragedies of his era, thereby preserving the belief that the revolution could have evolved very differently. These sentiments first surfaced (albeit quietly) after Stalin's death in 1953.

Historians on the other side of this argument find Stalinism to be a logical development of the earlier dictatorship. Writers in the West have been as divided on this issue as on the question of the causes of the revolution. Most research, however, seems to suggest that the nature of the Bolsheviks (most of whom were professional revolutionaries), their experience in the very bitter civil war, and their dedication to the idea of building socialism led logically, if not inevitably, to a Stalinist sort of dictatorship. The ruthlessness with which enemies were eradicated from 1917 to 1921 and the frustrations experienced in building socialism by 1928 came together in Stalin's violent dictatorship.

Russian society was also changed radically by the revolutions. Not only did the Bolsheviks not know in 1917 what sort of government they needed to create, they were not at all certain what socialism looked like. What did it mean that the workers owned the factories and the peasants owned the land? Was it private ownership or collective ownership? Did it allow for some farms and factories to flourish and others to fail? What would become of former owners and specialists, members of the upper class against whom the proletariat had presumably revolted? Were the products of labor to be redistributed? What role did the state play in all this?

In the civil war years, the Bolsheviks nationalized all large-scale industry, banks, and the means of communication—what they called the "commanding heights" of the national economy. They took from everyone else whatever they needed to feed the Red Army and fight the war, particularly food from the peasants. Altogether this policy was called War Communism. Like practically everything else in these first years, it was considered a temporary expedient.

The real problems surfaced again when the Bolsheviks controlled the country and had the freedom to decide what they really wanted to do. They could not agree. Until the so-called Stalin revolution at the end of the 1920s, they dithered and argued bitterly over policy. The New Economic Policy (NEP) that was begun in 1921 allowed for a mixed economy. The "commanding heights" remained in the hands of the government, but farming, small-scale industry, retail sales, and services were left to the private sector. And the private sector flourished as the state sector did not, reproducing the very inequalities that socialism was meant to end. Radical Bolsheviks, veterans of the civil war, and poor workers and peasants resented the successful NEPmen (those who profited from the NEP) and wondered why they had suffered through the revolution and war. When Stalin acted to build his version of socialism, he crushed all independent economic activity (and essentially all intellectual activity) and brought everything within the state sector. The state did not wither away but came to dominate people's lives by means of an enormous and pervasive bureaucracy.

The Russian Revolution deeply affected life in Russia, much of the rest of Europe, and eventually the entire world. What it ultimately produced bore little resemblance to the dreams of most of the people who made it, but that is true of all revolutions. Until 1949, when the Chinese communists won their civil war, the Soviet Union stood as the world's only socialist society. Its reputation was tarnished and its international following diminished after the horrors of the Stalin years came to light, some in the 1930s and many more after 1953. But until at least 1989, it continued to provide hope and an example for some communist parties around the world who wished to make their own revolutions.

SELECTED BIBLIOGRAPHY

Acton, Edward. *Rethinking the Russian Revolution.* London: Edward Arnold, 1990. This survey of literature on the revolution concentrates on histories written since the 1960s.

Brooks, Jeffrey, and Georgiy Chernyavskiy, eds. *Lenin and the Making of the Soviet State.* Boston: Bedford/St.Martin's, 2007. After a short introductory essay, the editors assemble almost 60 documents outlining the Bolshevik seizure of power and the steps subsequently taken by Lenin and his followers to hang on to power.

Carrère d'Encausse, Hélène. *Lenin.* Teaneck, NJ: Holmes and Meier, 2001. One of the few "experts" who foresaw the collapse of the Soviet Union well before it happened, the author finds Lenin to be one of the most influential—if not the most influential—figures in the twentieth-century. His lasting influence proved unmatched, even though he died in 1924.

Daniels, Robert V. *Red October: The Bolshevik Revolution of 1917.* New York: Charles Scribner's Sons, 1967. Concentrating on events in the capital, Daniels concludes that the Bolsheviks struck when the Provisional Government was on the point of collapse and came to power largely by default.

Deutscher, Isaac. *The Prophet Armed: Trotsky, 1879–1921.* New York: Vintage Books, 1965. This is the first volume of the classic three-volume biography of Trotsky.

Fischer, Louis. *The Life of Lenin.* New York: Harper Colophon Books, 1964. Probably still the most readable, thorough biography of Lenin.

Fitzpatrick, Sheila. *The Russian Revolution.* Oxford: Oxford University Press, 2001. Of the thousands of books written about the Russian Revolution, this is one of the best. Fitzpatrick sees the revolution not as a single seizure of power but, rather, as a long drawn-out event covering at least the first 40 years of the twentieth century. She pays particular attention to the social transformations brought by the revolution.

Keep, John L. H. *The Russian Revolution: A Study in Mass Mobilization.* New York: W. W. Norton, 1976. An important history of the revolution concentrating on events outside Petrograd.

Leggett, George. *The Cheka: Lenin's Political Police.* Oxford: Oxford University Press, 1981. Appendices include biographical sketches of Cheka leaders and statistics on arrests and executions.

Lincoln, W. Bruce. *Passage through Armageddon: The Russians in War and Revolution, 1914–1918.* New York: Simon & Schuster, 1986. A well-written scholarly account of Russia's collapse in World War I, the complexities of the 1917 revolutions, and the establishment of Bolshevik power.

Lincoln, W. Bruce. *Red Victory: A History of the Russian Civil War.* New York: Touchstone, 1989. A thorough account of the politics, personalities, and battles of the civil war.

Pipes, Richard. *The Russian Revolution.* New York: Vintage Books, 1991. A huge (944-page) narrative and analysis of the revolution by a leading conservative thinker.

Rabinowitch, Alexander. *The Bolsheviks Come to Power: The Revolution of 1917 in Petrograd.* New York: W. W. Norton, 1978. This work focuses on the Bolsheviks in Petrograd and finds spontaneous activity by soldiers and workers to be a major cause of the revolution.

Reed, John. *Ten Days That Shook the World.* New York: New American Library, 1967. A colorful, not always accurate look by an American sympathetic to the Bolsheviks.

Rosenberg, William. *Liberals in the Russian Revolution: The Constitutional Democratic Party, 1917–1921.* Princeton, NJ: Princeton University Press, 1974. A history of liberalism and of the leading liberal party in the revolutionary years.

Shulgin, V. V. *Days of the Russian Revolution: Memoirs from the Right, 1905–1907.* Translated and edited by Bruce F. Adams. Gulf Breeze, FL: Academic International Press, 1990. The only memoir in English by a major conservative figure of the revolutionary period.

Stites, Richard. *Feminism, Nihilism, and Bolshevism, 1860–1930.* Princeton, NJ: Princeton University Press, 1990. The best history of radical women before and during the revolutionary period.

Trotsky, Leon. *The History of the Russian Revolution.* New York: Monad Press, 1980. An insider's look at events by one of the Bolshevik leaders.

Tucker, Robert C. *Stalin as Revolutionary, 1879–1929: A Study of History and Personality.* New York: W. W. Norton, 1973. A biography of Joseph Stalin, a minor figure in the 1917 revolution who became the leader of the Party and the nation by 1928.

Von Hagen, Mark. *Soldiers in the Proletarian Dictatorship: The Red Army and the Soviet Socialist State, 1917–1930.* Ithaca, NY: Cornell University Press, 1990. The formation of the Red Army, the civil war, and the years following to 1930.

Von Laue, Theodore H. *Why Lenin? Why Stalin? A Reappraisal of the Russian Revolution, 1905–1930.* Philadelphia: J. B. Lippincott, 1964. An attempt to explain the sources of the revolution and the Soviet dictatorship.

Wildman, Allan K. *The End of the Russian Imperial Army: The Old Army and the Soldiers' Revolt (March–April* 1917). Princeton, NJ: Princeton University Press, 1980. The collapse of the tsarist army in World War I and how it helped lead to the revolution.

ALEKSANDR KERENSKY (1881–1970)

Aleksandr Kerensky was a charismatic speaker and ardent socialist who provided the link between the people and the Russian Provisional Government during the Russian Revolution of 1917.

Aleksandr Fyodorovich Kerensky was born on May 2, 1881, in Simbirsk, Russia (now Ulyanovsk, named after Vladimir Lenin, who was born and attended school there; Ulyanov was Lenin's surname at birth). His father was Fyodor Mikhailovich Kerensky, the director of the local grammar school who married his student Nadezhda Adler. Kerensky had three sisters and one brother. A lengthy childhood illness led to extensive bed rest during which he read extensively.

Kerensky studied law at St. Petersburg University and graduated in 1904. Shortly after his graduation, he married Olga Baranovskaya, the daughter of an army officer. They had two sons. The unhappy marriage led to Kerensky's several affairs, and one produced a child. In 1939, he divorced his wife and married Lydia Ellen Tritten. She died in 1946.

As a student, Kerensky read the journals of Peter Struve, the author of *Osvobozhdeniye (Liberation).* He then joined the Union of Liberation student movement. In 1905, Kerensky became editor of the radical newspaper *Burevestnik* and joined the Socialist Revolutionary Party, thereby leading to his arrest and exile. In 1906, he returned to St. Petersburg and earned his living as a successful lawyer. His outstanding speaking skills and well-chosen political trials earned him a solid reputation. In 1912, Kerensky won election to the fourth Duma as a member of the Russian Labor Party representing Volsk.

On March 15, 1917, after Tsar Nicholas II's abdication, the Duma established the Provisional Government until elections for a Constituent Assembly could be held later in the year. The first cabinet consisted of Russian prince Georgy Lvov serving as prime minister, Paul Miliukov as foreign minister, and Kerensky as minister of justice. Kerensky was the only Socialist Party member. The Provisional Government was quickly recognized by the United States and subsequently by the United Kingdom, Italy, and France.

Civil liberties were proclaimed for the first time in Russian history: police were replaced by militia, amnesty was granted to political prisoners, and equal rights were granted to women. Freedom of assembly, speech, religion, and the press were also instituted in Russia for the first time, and Kerensky became extremely popular as a result of his reforms.

Kerensky was responsible for dealing with the affairs of Nicholas and his family during the Russian Revolution. He initially allowed them to stay at their palace just outside

Aleksandr Kerensky, a moderate socialist, led Russia's Provisional Government that ruled Russia after the overthrow of Tsar Nicholas II. His ineptitude paved the way for the Bolshevik takeover in November 1917. (*The Great War in Gravure: The New York Times Portfolio of the War,* The New York Times Co., 1917)

St. Petersburg. As agitation increased, he moved them to Ekaterinburg for their safety. Kerensky was not involved in the execution of the royal family. Meanwhile, the Central Executive Committee of the Soviets had been formed in St. Petersburg alongside the Provisional Government. The committee was commanded by leaders of various socialist parties but governed by a presidium. The Central Executive Committee of the Soviets competed directly with the Provisional Government.

The abdication of the tsar did not resolve Russia's unmanageable problems, and World War I was the biggest problem that faced the Provisional Government. Kerensky and the moderates insisted on remaining involved in World War I. Miliukov told the Allies that he believed Russia should honor its military obligations and continue the war; as a result, the Provisional Government asked him to resign and appointed Kerensky as minister of war and the navy. He also was appointed as vice chairman of the Petrograd Soviet of Workers' and Soldiers' Deputies and acted as the liaison between both governments.

Kerensky toured the front to revitalize the demoralized Russian soldiers; there his speaking skills came to good use as he attempted to rally the soldiers to continue fighting. On July 17, 1917, he became prime minister. The Kerensky Offensive of July 1–19,

1917, at the Eastern Front was a dismal failure; entire regiments mutinied, and General Lavr Kornilov called for extreme military discipline. Kornilov was made commander in chief on July 30, 1917. However, he appeared to be a counterrevolutionary threat; he resented Soviet influence and disobeyed Kerensky's orders. On September 10, 1917, Kornilov's clumsy and ill-conceived attempt at revolt failed.

Economically, Kerensky failed to act on the needs of the peasants, who preferred to believe in the communist message advocated by Vladimir Lenin and Leon Trotsky. Russian peasants had wanted land reform, which Kerensky neglected. Industrial production dropped nearly 50 percent, in part because the workers had taken control but lacked sound management skills. Also, significant price increases led Kerensky to devalue the currency and issue emergency "Kerensky bills," which contributed heavily to inflation.

On September 2, 1917, Kerensky declared Russia a democratic republic. He acted alone and without the approval of the Constituent Assembly which had yet to be elected. By that time, Kerensky had alienated a large portion of the Russian population. Even the Allies were provoked by his demeanor.

The Provisional Government also had to struggle against the Bolshevik Party agitation of Lenin and Trotsky. On November 7, 1917, the country's discontent with Kerensky's governing style had reached its end. The Bolsheviks, commanded by Trotsky, seized the Winter Palace where the Provisional Government had its headquarters. Kerensky escaped and fled to France.

In 1940, Nazi Germany's invasion of France prompted Kerensky to relocate to the United States, where he joined the Hoover Institute at Stanford University. Kerensky led a Russian Revolution project at the institute and spent much of his time writing about those events. He died on June 11, 1970, in New York City.

ABC-CLIO

VLADIMIR ILYICH LENIN (1870–1924)

The revolutionary leader of the Bolshevik Party and chief theoretician of Russian communism, Vladimir Lenin was one of the most charismatic political leaders of the early twentieth century and a guiding force behind the emergence of the Soviet Union.

Lenin was born Vladimir Ilyich Ulyanov on April 22, 1870, in Simbirsk, Russia. (The name Lenin was one of many pseudonyms he used throughout his life.) His father held the coveted position of school inspector, which made him a member of the local intelligentsia and elevated the family to the upper middle class. Lenin's elder brother Aleksandr exerted a tremendous influence on his childhood and became a hero to the young boy. Aleksandr's execution in 1887 for planning an attempt on Tsar Alexander III's life devastated Lenin and encouraged him to follow in his brother's footsteps as a proponent of social change. Russia during this period churned with discontented groups, most of which advocated drastic changes in the government and society. Government authorities were quick to repress all agitation, but their vigilance only seemed to spawn new revolutionaries and harden the people's attitudes against maintaining the status quo.

Russian universities fostered the advocacy of social change. Although he was interested in politics, Lenin opted not to study in the politically volatile climate of Moscow or St. Petersburg and instead attended the provincial Kazan University in 1887. Here, he

Vladimir Lenin led the 1917 Russian Revolution that brought his Bolshevik (Communist) movement to power. Highly intelligent but ruthless and driven, Lenin established a model Marxist state that was to last for 75 years. (Library of Congress)

hoped to study law, but after only three months, school authorities expelled him for subversive activity. In 1891, almost four years after his expulsion, school officials at St. Petersburg University allowed him to take his exams as an external student. He earned high marks, thus proving that he had worked hard to educate himself during these years.

In the course of his studies, Lenin discovered the communist theories of Karl Marx in his masterpiece of economic theory, *Das Kapital.* In addition to his economic analysis of the flaws of capitalism, Marx devised a theory of history that proposed that the progress of man through the ages was determined by a series of class conflicts. Just as the bourgeoisie had overthrown the aristocracy to establish capitalism, the proletariat would ultimately overthrow the bourgeoisie in a massive revolution to establish socialism. Once in control, the proletariat would forbid anyone from owning capital (i.e., property), thus creating a communal society. In such a society, where everyone's interests were aligned and there were no classes to conflict with one another, the need for government (or the state) would eventually disappear.

Having become an avid devotee of Marx's theories, Lenin moved to St. Petersburg in the fall of 1893, where he practiced law and became active in the emerging socialist movement, helping to organize the Union of Struggle for the Emancipation of the Working Class. Lenin wrote political pieces for this group, which attempted to focus labor discontent through propaganda literature. As a result, he was arrested in 1895 and spent 14 months in prison. Upon his release in February 1897, he was exiled to Siberia for three years. In 1898, he married fellow revolutionary and educator Nadezhda Krupskaya, who transferred from her own place of exile to live with him in Siberia. Lenin used this period of exile to write political tracts. He also secretly engaged in an extensive correspondence with other revolutionaries in exile and planned for future political disturbances.

After his return from Siberia in February 1900, Lenin decided that he could best organize opposition to the government from abroad through the publication of a newspaper that would be clandestinely sent all over Russia and form the "scaffolding" of the Communist Party. To avoid trouble from local authorities, Lenin moved his operation around Europe, residing first in Munich, then London, and finally Geneva. He returned to Russia after the onset of the 1905 Revolution, but by 1907, he realized the revolution had utterly failed and fled back to Switzerland.

For the next 10 years, Lenin remained active in the organization of underground organizations and the production of communist literature. He continued to move around Europe, living in Paris, Cracow, and Vienna during these years as he maneuvered within the Russian Social-Democratic Workers' Party (RSDWP) to enlist support for his faction, known as the Bolsheviks. He returned to Switzerland shortly after the outbreak of World War I. The war placed a great strain on the Russian government, reducing the Russian people to near-famine conditions and imposing significant wartime sacrifices. These deprivations, combined with massive losses on the battlefield and general incompetence in the government, caused the Russian people to lose all faith in Tsar Nicholas II and his autocratic regime. In February 1917, the Russian Revolution erupted, compelling the tsar to abdicate and resulting in the establishment of a provisional government. In April 1917, the Germans, hoping to foster more instability within Russia, secretly arranged for Lenin to return home in a sealed train.

The Provisional Government proved unpopular with the Russian people because it refused to end Russia's involvement in World War I or to promote such agrarian reforms as redistributing land to peasants. Severe hardship continued to devastate Russia. The Bolsheviks did not see the revolution they had hoped for with the downfall of the tsar, and therefore, in October 1917, they planned their own revolution and overthrew the Provisional Government on November 7. Even after the Bolsheviks assumed power, they continued to squabble with other radical factions. More important, various anticommunist forces joined together to oppose the communist regime. This loosely aligned anti-Bolshevik force became known as the Whites and in spring 1918 civil war broke out in Russia. Leon Trotsky led the Bolshevik Red Army and eventually managed to defeat the Whites in 1921 after three years of conflict.

During the civil war, Lenin brought the government under his control and struggled to organize the country. Although Marx had been an insightful analyst of events that had already occurred, his predictions for socialist government were very vague and provided no guide to setting up a government. Lenin's most important differences with Marxist theory had already become obvious during his prerevolutionary struggles with other Russian socialists. Most important, he believed that the revolution must be controlled by a group of highly trained and dedicated revolutionaries (not a large mass of workers) who would not trade short-term gains for long-term goals or sell out the revolution before it was completed. The need for the so-called vanguard party justified the authoritarian control of Lenin himself. Such leadership was particularly necessary in a setting like Russia, where capitalism was far from advanced and there was hardly any bourgeoisie. Thus, the development of capitalism that Marx had posed as the necessary precondition for socialism was ignored by Lenin as was the possibility of peaceful, social-democratic reformism. By March 1918, Lenin and the Bolsheviks officially changed the RSDWP into the All-Russian Communist Party (later renamed the Communist Party of the Soviet Union).

Lenin led the faction that believed peace with Germany and withdrawal from World War I should be accomplished at any sacrifice. In 1918, the Treaty of Brest-Litovsk accomplished this goal with the loss of much territory. In 1919, Lenin organized the Communist International (or Comintern) to coordinate the efforts of European communist parties to spread the revolution. As head of Russia's communist government, Lenin embarked on programs to encourage trade unions and workers' control over industries, nationalize land holdings and private finances (such as joint-stock companies), disband the imperial army, and wipe out all political opposition. Not all of these policies had support in Russia, however, and protests, riots, and political splinter groups began to emerge. In addition to the Red Army, a secret police force was organized to deal with dissidents within as well as external threats to the revolution.

In 1921, after three years of civil war, and with the failure of economic prosperity to return to the country, Lenin revised his original policies. To revitalize the economy, he instituted the New Economic Policy, which allowed more innovation and freedom in agriculture, industry, and trade. This revision accompanied other experimentation with socialist society. Throughout the early 1920s, Lenin grew fearful at the number of elements threatening to undermine socialism. The growth of a massive Communist Party bureaucracy to manage all aspects of life in the Soviet Union worried Lenin, as did the Russian chauvinism with which many high party officials regarded the national minorities of the Soviet Union. An even graver danger appeared to Lenin in the personalities of divisive and ambitious leaders such as Joseph Stalin, who had been elected to the powerful position of general secretary in 1922. With his health failing rapidly, however, Lenin was no longer in a position to require the party's compliance with his wishes.

Lenin's health never fully recovered from a failed assassination attempt in 1918, although he continued to hold the reins of power for several more years. No doubt, the stress of his position contributed to his health problems. He suffered a series of strokes beginning on May 25, 1922, that slowly forced him to relinquish power. He died on January 21, 1924, leaving both Trotsky and Stalin fighting to succeed him. His body, now embalmed, lies in a mausoleum in Red Square, where it is visited by thousands every year, although he specifically left instructions asking that no such tributes be performed.

NEIL HAMILTON

NICHOLAS II, TSAR OF RUSSIA (1868–1918)

Nicholas II was emperor of Russia from 1894 to 1917. A symbol of the tremendous wealth of the Russian aristocracy and the source of the monarchy's autocratic rule in the country, Nicholas was plagued throughout much of his reign by social and political unrest. His determination to maintain the undiminished power of the throne convinced many Russians that much needed reforms could only come through revolution. With the Russian people in turmoil, he led the country into World War I, only to have his dynasty violently overthrown by the Russian Revolution of 1917.

Born Nikolay Aleksandrovich on May 6, 1868, in St. Petersburg, Russia, Nicholas was part of the Romanov dynasty, a powerful and autocratic family that had ruled the country for more than 250 years at the time of his birth. His father, Aleksandr Aleksandrovich, was the heir to the throne, and his mother, Maria Fyodorovna, was the daughter of King Christian IX of Denmark. In 1881, when his father ascended the throne and became Tsar Alexander III, Nicholas became the tsarevich, the son and heir of the emperor.

As a child, Nicholas was frail and sickly, but he revered his strong and domineering father. Nicholas received a well-rounded private education but did not enjoy formal schooling. He showed the greatest aptitude in foreign languages and military training. Between 1887 and 1893, Nicholas served as an officer in the Russian army during summer military maneuvers.

In 1889, Nicholas was appointed to the State Council and the Committee of Ministers in order to begin his training in public affairs. Two years later, he was appointed to the Siberian Committee (responsible for constructing the Trans-Siberian Railroad) and the Special Committee on Famine Relief (focused on alleviating suffering from drought and crop failure in the central provinces). Although Nicholas served these committees in a conscientious manner, he was young and still inexperienced.

Between 1890 and 1891, Nicholas began an extensive tour of the Near East and Asia, visiting Greece, Egypt, India, Ceylon, Singapore, Siam, Java, Indochina, and Japan. The visits were ceremonial in nature, and Nicholas was regularly received by cheering crowds and elaborate banquets. However, while in Japan, he was attacked by a fanatic who believed him to be part of a Russian plot against his country. Nicholas's wounds were not serious, but they did cause him to end his visit ahead of schedule.

Only a few years later, when Nicholas was 26 years old and still politically immature, Alexander III died suddenly of kidney disease on November 1, 1894. His father had kept him out of most affairs of state, but the ill-prepared Nicholas nevertheless became the tsar. Acutely aware of his limitations, he was initially overwhelmed by the responsibility of ruling Russia. However, his fatalistic attitude and his resolution to fulfill his duty helped him survive this initial crisis. Nicholas married the German princess Alix Victoria of Hesse-Darmstadt, who changed her name to Alexandra Fyodorovna after converting to Russian Orthodoxy.

Nicholas believed absolute power should remain with the Russian monarchy, and he opposed any democratic reforms. He proved to have little talent for leadership, however, which is an essential ingredient for a successful monarchy. In 1895, he publicly rejected the idea that *zemstvos*, or public assemblies, should participate in the process of social change. He called these democratic aspirations "senseless dreams," a condemnation that shocked and angered many of his subjects. Furthermore, Nicholas seemed insensitive to the increasing hardships faced by the Russian people at this time. Unrest was high as the largely agricultural country struggled to industrialize and urbanize. As economic hardship worsened for the Russian people, the tsar seemed unconcerned with their needs.

Ten years after ascending the throne, Nicholas was faced with his first truly national crisis. In 1904, Russia's Pacific Squadron, based in Port Arthur, was suddenly attacked by Japan, beginning the Russo-Japanese War. After a series of defeats at the hands of the small island nation, Russia finally reached a negotiated peace that ended the conflict. However, the Russian people were left with little confidence in Nicholas's leadership.

In addition, the war had put intense pressure on Russia's workers. In January 1905, St. Petersburg was paralyzed by strikes. Workers and their families marched on Nicholas's palace to present their grievances, only to be fired on by Russian soldiers. The date was thereafter referred to as Bloody Sunday, and strikes, violence, and rioting continued throughout the country. With his authority and prestige severely diminished, Nicholas appointed Sergei Witte to control the government.

Nicholas also agreed to change the Russian government from an absolute monarchy to a constitutional monarchy, with an elected assembly known as the Duma. However, still believing that he was responsible only to God (rather than to the Russian people), Nicholas minimized the power and effectiveness of the Duma. These efforts to undermine the Duma caused many in Russia's middle and upper classes to question further his ability to rule. Those who favored a continuance of Russia's autocratic government believed that he looked foolish for ever having agreed to the creation of the Duma, whereas those who advocated the establishment of a constitutional monarchy resented Nicholas's treachery in creating the Duma and then ensuring that it remained ineffective.

The monarchy's prestige suffered further as the entire royal family was subjected to harsh criticism. Alexandra had never been popular with the Russian people. Her cold and austere manner had alienated even many aristocrats. Nicholas and Alexandra's four daughters and one son were held in higher regard, but they had little if any interaction with Russian society. The tsarevich Alexis was also a hemophiliac, a condition that Nicholas and Alexandra carefully hid from all but their closest companions. Between 1905 and 1917, the royal family came into further disrepute through their association with an alleged holy man and mystic known as Grigori Rasputin. On several occasions, Rasputin appeared to help heal Alexis when he was in real physical danger from his hemophilia. In gratitude, Alexandra made Rasputin the most influential member of her entourage, a move that infuriated much of the aristocracy and brought her scorn from the public. Although less impressed with Rasputin, Nicholas relied on his advice to some degree and defended him despite claims that he was a fraud and led a bizarre and debauched life. The monarchy's connection to Rasputin further alienated the Russian people.

When World War I broke out in 1914, Russia was unprepared. It soon became clear that there were shortages of ammunition and officers, as well as immense difficulties in transporting food. In 1915, Nicholas assumed personal command of the army. The country subsequently blamed him for all military failures. The public was also convinced that Rasputin controlled Russia's internal affairs in the tsar's absence, a conviction that deepened resentment against the Crown. Fears regarding Rasputin's power and influence ended on December 29, 1916, when a group of highly placed officials and royal family members murdered him. Although there was a general sense of relief following Rasputin's death, public support for the tsar, his family, and his government continued to wane.

As the war dragged on, Nicholas ignored pleas from advisers, relatives, and courtiers, and refused to address the concerns of his people. He remained oblivious to the disorganized state of his government and the high public dissatisfaction with the war. On March 8, 1917, street demonstrations broke out in the capital, Petrograd (formerly St. Petersburg). Over the next several days, there was large-scale violence, and most of the local garrisons mutinied. Nicholas finally recognized the severity of the situation, and in a desperate attempt to save the monarchy he abdicated power to his brother, the

Grand Duke Mikhail Aleksandrovich. The Grand Duke declined to serve, recognizing that the people of Petrograd were no longer willing to accept a tsar at all and that the monarchy had come to an end.

The Provisional Government, primarily made up of liberal Duma leaders, placed Nicholas and his family under house arrest at their palace in Tsarskoe Selo. The Romanovs were treated well until the more revolutionary Bolsheviks overthrew the Provisional Government. In April 1918, the royal family was moved to Ekaterinburg in the Ural Mountains where they no longer enjoyed the amenities of house arrest in a royal palace. Plans for a public trial of the Romanovs were abandoned when civil war threatened Bolshevik rule. The new Soviet government authorized the execution of the family before anticommunists could rescue them and possibly attempt to restore Nicholas to the throne.

On July 17, 1918, Nicholas, Alexandra, their five children, the family physician, and three servants were all executed in the basement of their living quarters. Their remains were burned and thrown down a mine shaft. Although rumors spread that Nicholas's daughter Anastasia escaped, these claims have never been substantiated.

ABC-CLIO

GRIGORI RASPUTIN (1871–1916)

Grigori Efimovich Rasputin was a mystic whose influence on the imperial court of Russia is often cited as contributing to the downfall of the Romanov dynasty during the Russian Revolution of 1917.

Rasputin was born in Pokrovskoye, Siberia, in 1871 or 1872 (the date of his birth continues to be disputed by historians). Although most scholars place his birth in 1872, his daughter's biography asserts that Rasputin's birth coincided with a brilliant meteor that went over his Siberian village on January 23, 1871. Although an uneducated peasant, Rasputin was fascinated by and eventually consumed with religion. As a youth, he would commit to memory the biblical passages he heard in church (he did not learn to read or write until late in life). At the age of 18, Rasputin claims to have experienced a visitation by the Holy Virgin of Kazan. He subsequently became convinced that God had chosen him for some special purpose that had not yet been revealed.

At age 19, Rasputin married Praskovia Feodorovna, a local woman with whom he eventually had two sons and two daughters. For six years, he was a devoted husband, but he continued to be troubled by what he believed was a genuine encounter with the Holy Virgin. He finally sought spiritual guidance at the monastery of Verkhoture. Although he received no answers there, Rasputin was led to the revered hermit Father Makarii, who confirmed that Rasputin had been chosen by God. Makarii recommended that Rasputin abandon his family and his worldly possessions and become a *strannik*, or wanderer. The hermit instructed him to continue his pilgrimage until he heard "the earth speak" and learned "to understand its words." Then he could return and "proclaim to men what the voice of our holy Russian earth says to them." Rasputin left his family and headed to the West Siberian steppe. His journey lasted six years. During that time, he was allegedly converted to Khlystovshchina, the oldest Russian religious sect.

Grigori Rasputin was a mystic whose influence on the imperial court of Russia is often cited as contributing to the downfall of the Romanov Dynasty during the Russian Revolution of 1917. (The Illustrated London News Picture Library)

The erotic spiritualism that Rasputin eventually practiced did not follow true Khlysty doctrine but rather the misrepresentations of it that permeated propaganda from the Russian Orthodox Church. The true Khlysty practiced a severe asceticism, including total abstinence from alcohol, tobacco, medicine, drugs, and sexual relations (even between husband and wife). However, there was a Khlysty rite that required marathon singing and frenzied dancing, all of which was intended to create an ecstatic state that would prompt the faithful to speak in tongues before collapsing in exhaustion. Those practices gave rise to the general misconception that senseless bliss occurred only after an orgiastic rite.

Rasputin clearly found the lies and rumors about the Khlysty more appealing than the truth. He began preaching a heretical doctrine that espoused rebirth through sin. He believed communion with God occurred only in the state of "holy passionlessness" brought on by sexual exhaustion. Thus, his teachings followed neither the Orthodox nor Khlyst beliefs.

By the time Rasputin ended his travels in approximately 1902, he had gained a reputation as an exorcist and healer and was recognized as a holy man or *starets*. He was called Father Grigori and returned to Pokrovskoye, where he enjoyed a large following until he was accused of heresy by a local priest, charges that were later dropped. After the investigation, Rasputin left Pokrovskoye and made his first visit to St. Petersburg in 1903.

Shortly after arriving in the capital, Rasputin was recognized as a man of God by John of Kronstadt, the greatest preacher of the day. That legitimization of Rasputin led to his entrée into fashionable society. Militsa, the daughter of Prince Nicholas I of Serbia, introduced Rasputin to the Tsarina Alexandra, who regularly consulted with soothsayers and mediums. She was impressed with Rasputin, as were many learned ecclesiastics. They found his simple wisdom and ability to explain arcane religious texts appealing. At the urgings of his wife, Tsar Nicholas II also came to believe that Rasputin was a man of God and the true voice of Russia.

Rasputin soon became a friend and confidant to members of the royal family. He was told their dark secret: that Alexis Nikolaevich, heir to the throne, was a hemophiliac. Amazingly, Rasputin seemed to have an ability to lessen Alexis's sufferings (probably because he calmed the boy by gently hypnotizing him). Increasingly dependent on Rasputin to preserve the health of Alexis, Alexandra made Rasputin an extremely influential member of her entourage.

Alexandra came to believe that Rasputin had mystical powers; that God listened when Rasputin prayed on her behalf. The tsar had a somewhat more down-to-earth view of Rasputin. Nicholas believed that Rasputin was an important link to his people and claimed that he was "just a good, religious, simple-minded Russian." Nicholas still kept doctors on hand, despite Rasputin's seemingly miraculous ability to help his son. He also found some of Rasputin's advice very strange.

Although Nicholas was apprised of Rasputin's lecherous behavior when he was away from the palace, he chose to ignore it. Possibly Nicholas feared that if he sent Rasputin away and his son died, Alexandra would blame him. However, Nicholas could not defend Rasputin publicly without divulging the family's secret. Therefore, Nicholas's approach was simply to try to silence those who criticized Rasputin.

Enjoying tremendous royal patronage, Rasputin's clientele grew quickly. However, many of his patrons were not interested in rewards in the afterlife as much as rewards in the present. They asked him to use his influence to gain a promotion, a contract, dismissal of a legal case, or some other assistance. Furthermore, despite Nicholas's efforts, word of Rasputin's numerous sexual liaisons and affairs became common knowledge among court society. Religious leaders attacked Rasputin, and the tsar's advisers feared that his presence at court decreased public confidence and distracted the government.

By 1911, the public condemnation of Rasputin had grown so substantial that Nicholas asked him to leave St. Petersburg for a time. Rasputin left for the Middle East in March 1911. When he returned at Alexandra's request, the public outcry against him continued. Consequently, he was sent back to Pokrovskoye. Although Rasputin's influence decreased during that period, his fortune changed in August 1915. World War I had erupted in Europe the previous year, and after months of fighting, Nicholas decided to assume command of Russia's military efforts at the front. Alexandra remained at the home front and assumed control of the government in her husband's absence, allegedly relying heavily on Rasputin's advice. Many at the time claimed that Rasputin destabilized the government and brought on its collapse by convincing Alexandra—who in turn convinced the tsar—to replace ministers with incompetent friends of Rasputin. Only six of the 13 nominees who gained posts during that period were supported by Rasputin, however, and many historians question whether Rasputin really had a significant impact on civil or military policy.

The public perception, however, was quite different. The myth of Rasputin's unbounded influence on affairs of state was believed at the time, prompting several members of the nobility to plot his assassination. The conspirators included many members of the tsar's own family, as well as representatives from the Duma (Russia's Parliament). On the night of December 29, 1916, Rasputin was invited to the home of Prince Yusupov (the husband of the tsar's niece), where he was served poisoned tea cakes and wine. Remarkably, Rasputin did not die, although he ate several of the cakes and drank a good deal of wine. Yusupov panicked and shot the mystic, but Rasputin managed to stagger out into the courtyard, where Yusupov shot him again. Still not dead, the conspirators bound Rasputin in a rug and threw him through a hole in the ice into the Neva River. When his body was later recovered, the autopsy revealed that he had died by drowning.

Shortly before his assassination, Rasputin composed a final prophecy. He foretold his own murder before the end of the year, warning, "Tsar of the Russian land, if you hear the sound of the bell which will tell you that Grigori has been killed, you must know this: if it was your relations who have wrought my death, then no one of your family, that is to say, none of your children or relations will remain alive for more than two years. They will be killed by the Russian people." The prophecy proved to be chillingly accurate as the tsar, his wife, and children were murdered by Russian revolutionaries less than a year and a half later.

ABC-CLIO

DOCUMENT: NICHOLAS II'S ABDICATION PROCLAMATION (1917)

Forced by a general uprising to relinquish his claims to the throne at the beginning of the Russian Revolution of 1917, Tsar Nicholas II issued this proclamation of abdication under duress on March 15, 1917, both on his behalf and on behalf of his young son, Alexis. Tsarist rule thus officially came to an end in Russia and was replaced by the Provisional Government. Nicholas and his family were held under house arrest until July 1918, when they were executed by communist forces.

By the Grace of God, We, Nikolai II, Emperor of All the Russias, Tsar of Poland, Grand Duke of Finland, and so forth, to all our faithful subjects be it known:

In the days of a great struggle against a foreign enemy who has been endeavouring for three years to enslave our country, it pleased God to send Russia a further painful trial.

Internal troubles threatened to have a fatal effect on the further progress of this obstinate war. The destinies of Russia, the honour of her heroic army, the happiness of the people, and the whole future of our beloved country demand that the war should be conducted at all costs to a victorious end.

The cruel enemy is making his last efforts and the moment is near when our valiant army, in concert with our glorious Allies, will finally overthrow the enemy.

In these decisive days in the life of Russia we have thought that we owed to our people the close union and organisation of all its forces for the realisation of a rapid victory; for which reason, in agreement with the Imperial Duma, we have recognized that it is for the good of the country that we should abdicate the Crown of the Russian State and lay down the Supreme Power.

Not wishing to separate ourselves from our beloved son, we bequeath our heritage to our brother, the Grand Duke Mikhail Alexandrovich, with our blessing for the future of the Throne of the Russian State.

We bequeath it our brother to govern in full union with the national representatives sitting in the Legislative Institutions, and to take his inviolable oath to them in the name of our well-beloved country.

We call upon all faithful sons of our native land to fulfil their sacred and patriotic duty of obeying the Tsar at the painful moment of national trial and to aid them, together with the representatives of the nation, to conduct the Russian State in the way of prosperity and glory.

May God help Russia.

DOCUMENT: LENIN'S DECLARATION OF THE RIGHTS OF THE TOILING AND EXPLOITED PEOPLES (1918)

Published in the Russian newspaper **Pravda** *on January 17, 1918, the Declaration of the Rights of the Toiling and Exploited Peoples was written by communist leader Vladimir Lenin in conjunction with Joseph Stalin, Nikolai Bukharin, and Yakov Sverdlov and read before the Russian Constituent Assembly on January 18. The Constituent Assembly had been called to forge a constitution for Russia following the fall of the tsarist government in March 1917. The declaration declared the need for the Constituent Assembly to dissolve and called for the acceptance of the communist Bolsheviks as the ruling power in the land. Although the assembly rejected the declaration, Lenin and his supporters continued to push for its ratification in the months ahead. The disagreement over the declaration was, in effect, the opening volley of the Russian Civil War, which Lenin and his followers ultimately won.*

Chapter One

1. Russia is proclaimed a Republic of Soviets of Workers', Soldiers', and Peasants' Deputies. All central and local authority is vested in these Soviets.

2. The Russian Soviet Republic is established on the basis of a free union of free nations, a federation of National Soviet Republics.

Chapter Two

The Constituent Assembly sets for itself as a fundamental task the suppression of all forms of exploitation of man by man and the complete abolition of class distinctions in society. It aims to crush unmercifully the exploiter, to reorganize society on a socialistic basis, and to bring about the triumph of Socialism throughout the world. It further resolves:

1. In order to bring about the socialization of land, private ownership of land is abolished. The entire land fund is declared the property of the nation and turned over free of cost to the toilers on the basis of equal right to its use. All forests, subsoil resources,

and waters of national importance as well as all live stock and machinery, model farms, and agricultural enterprises are declared to be national property.

2. As a first step to the complete transfer of the factories, shops, mines, railways, and other means of production and transportation to the Soviet Republic of Workers and Peasants, and in order to ensure the supremacy of the toiling masses over the exploiters, the Constituent Assembly ratifies the Soviet law on workers' control and that on the Supreme Council of National Economy.

3. The Constituent Assembly ratifies the transfer of all banks to the ownership of the workers' and peasants' government as one of the conditions for the emancipation of the toiling masses from the yoke of capitalism.

4. In order to do away with the parasitic classes of society and organize the economic life of the country, universal labor duty is introduced.

5. In order to give all the power to the toiling masses and to make impossible the restoration of the power of the exploiters, it is decreed to arm the toilers, to establish a Socialist Red Army, and to disarm completely the propertied classes.

Chapter Three

1. The Constituent Assembly expresses its firm determination to snatch mankind from the claws of capitalism and imperialism which have brought on this most criminal of all wars and have drenched the world with blood. It approves whole-heartedly the policy of the Soviet Government in breaking with the secret treaties, in organizing extensive fraternization between the workers and peasants in the ranks of the opposing armies and in its efforts to bring about, at all costs, by revolutionary means, a democratic peace between nations on the principle of no annexation, no indemnity, and free self-determination of nations.

2. With the same purpose in mind the Constituent Assembly demands a complete break with the barbarous policy of bourgeois civilization which enriches the exploiters in a few chosen nations at the expense of hundreds of millions of the toiling population in Asia, in the colonies, and in the small countries. The Constituent Assembly welcomes the policy of the Soviet of People's Commissars in granting complete independence to Finland, of removing the troops from Persia and allowing Armenia the right of self-determination. The Constituent Assembly considers the Soviet law repudiating the debts contracted by the government of the Tsar, landholders, and the bourgeoisie a first blow to international banking and finance-capital. The Constituent Assembly expresses its confidence that the Soviet Government will follow this course firmly until the complete victory of the international labour revolt against the yoke of capital.

Chapter Four

1. Having been elected on party lists made up before the November Revolution, when the people were not yet in a position to rebel against the exploiters whose powers of opposition in defense of their class privileges were not yet known, and when the people had not yet done anything practical to organize a socialistic society, the Constituent Assembly feels that it would be quite wrong even technically to set itself up in opposition to the Soviet.

2. The Constituent Assembly believes that at this present moment of decisive struggle of the proletariat against the exploiters there is no place for the exploiters in any organ of government. The government belongs wholly to the toiling masses and their fully empowered representatives, the Soviets of Workers', Soldiers', and Peasants' Deputies.

3. In supporting the Soviet and the decrees of the Soviet of People's Commissars, the Constituent Assembly admits that it has no power beyond working out some of the fundamental problems of reorganizing society on a socialistic basis.

4. At the same time, desiring to bring about a really free and voluntary, and consequently more complete and lasting, union of the toiling classes of all nations in Russia, the Constituent Assembly confines itself to the formulation of the fundamental principles of a federation of the Soviet Republics of Russia, leaving to the workers and peasants of each nation to decide independently at their own plenipotentiary Soviet Congresses whether or not they desire, and if so on what conditions, to take part in the federated government and other federal Soviet institutions.

4

The Rise of Fascism, 1919–1945

INTRODUCTION

Fascism is defined as a system of government characterized by a rigid one-party dictatorship, forcible suppression of the opposition, the retention of private ownership of the means of production under centralized governmental control, belligerent nationalism and racism, and glorification of war. Although fascism's intellectual antecedents are rooted in the nineteenth century, it is universally regarded as one of the most important twentieth-century movements. Fascist regimes under Benito Mussolini in Italy and Adolf Hitler in Germany not only spawned numerous imitators but also introduced unique political, economic, and social forms. Eventually, fascist aggression plunged the world into the cataclysmic World War II.

Mussolini (1883–1945), the son of a poor blacksmith, led Italian fascism. A socialist like his father, Mussolini abandoned a teaching career, joined the Socialist Party, and became editor of its official newspaper, *Avanti!* (Forward). When Mussolini shockingly rejected the socialist commitment to neutrality and urged Italian entry into World War I on the side of the Entente, the socialists expelled him from their party.

Mussolini founded the Fascio di Combattimento, or Fascists, in Milan in March 1919. With no clear goal in mind other than self-advancement, Mussolini led his fascists on an ultranationalistic course. He also condemned the capitalist socioeconomic system. With time, the nationalistic stance hardened; but strident attacks on socialism, especially Marxism, replaced the criticism of capitalism. Mussolini, who depended on contributions from Italian businessmen, converted his party into a staunch champion of property rights and the existing social order. Thanks to his attacks on socialism and his nationalistic demagoguery, Mussolini also gathered support among the middle class. Nevertheless, the Fascists remained on the political periphery. In the 1921 parliamentary elections, they managed to win just 35 of the more than 500 seats contested.

To give his party the muscle it lacked at the ballot box, Mussolini created the *squadristi,* black-shirted paramilitary street gangs that brawled incessantly with Fascism's opponents. In October 1922, the *squadristi* responded to Mussolini's command to "march on Rome" and seize power. Although the legitimate government possessed the resources to crush the Fascist threat, it lacked the necessary leadership and willpower. Consequently, Mussolini's bold gamble succeeded, and the Fascist leader was named prime minister.

Although Mussolini headed only a coalition government, it was quite apparent that he was in charge. In a matter of months, he easily converted Italy's parliamentary democracy into a fascist dictatorship. However, because he never fully controlled several independent institutions, including the monarchy, the military, and the Roman Catholic Church, he had to proceed cautiously when dealing with them.

In practice, Italian fascism was often inefficient if not chaotic. Overlapping and competing layers of bureaucracy created numerous opportunities for corruption. The chain of command was unclear, and so were the regime's ultimate goals.

By the end of 1926, Mussolini had many essential elements of his dictatorship in place. A stringent censorship muzzled the press, and the Fascist Party wrested control over local government from elective bodies. The Fascists also dominated the educational establishment. With the exception of the Fascist Party, all political organizations were abolished. Labor, considered the bastion of socialism, attracted special attention. Fascist labor unions replaced independent ones, and labor lost the right to strike.

Mussolini continued his cozy relationship with Italian big business, which delightedly applauded his rough treatment of the unions. He subsequently developed the concept of corporativism, which divided all Italian economic life into a number of units, or corporations. The corporations allegedly represented all the concerned parties, including business and labor, but in fact they were dominated by Fascists, who nevertheless were careful not to antagonize factory owners. Attempts to coordinate the national economy to achieve autarky, or self-sufficiency, failed in the face of inefficiency, corruption, and Italy's dependence on imported raw materials.

The Fascists also fashioned government-like institutions that gradually superseded the state apparatus. To enforce their rule, the Fascists created a secret police, the OVRA (Organizzazione per la Vigilanza e la Repressione dell'Antifascismo, or Organization for Vigilance and Repression of Antifacism), and arrested a number of opponents, who were incarcerated in political prisons. However, it was not until 1938, after Mussolini had moved close to Hitler, that the Italian fascists began to discriminate against and harass Jews and other racial minorities.

Mussolini initiated the "leader" principle, which subsequent fascist chieftains eagerly copied. Mussolini, supported by his sprawling propaganda apparatus, claimed for himself the title Duce, or leader, and increasingly portrayed himself as infallible. One of the regime's most important slogans was "Mussolini is always right."

This same propaganda apparatus denigrated liberalism and democracy, and glorified brute strength and mindless violence. "Action," often with no particular purpose, became a way of life. Mussolini tried to dress his people in a dizzying array of uniforms, and the government proclaimed numerous causes for battle, including a battle for grain and one for population, the so-called battle for births. Italian nationalism was virtually sanctified, and a cult of male virility took on such proportions that Mussolini himself was shown engaging in the most ludicrous physical activity, including leaping through burning hoops.

In foreign affairs, the fascist credo of "action" assumed a bombastic and often expansionistic form. Mussolini began his foreign policy adventures with a bang—literally—when in 1923 he bombarded the Greek island of Corfu. For a number of years afterward, he occupied himself with domestic matters, including the 1929 Lateran Accords, which regularized relations with the Roman Catholic Church. However, by the mid-1930s, Italian fascism was on the move. In 1934, Mussolini rallied behind Austria's archconservative government to prevent that state from succumbing to the Nazis. The following

The 1938 Munich Conference, also known as the Four Powers Conference, involved representatives from Great Britain, France, Germany, and Italy. Hermann Goering, Benito Mussolini, Adolf Hitler, and Count Ciano (front, from left to right) exit the conference among several other representatives on September 30, 1938. Western capitulation at Munich not only awarded Czechoslovakia's Sudetenland to Nazi Germany but also convinced Hitler that he could move aggressively without fear of retaliation. (The Illustrated London News Picture Library)

year, Italy attacked Abyssinia (Ethiopia) in northeast Africa in a bid to revive Italy's colonial empire. In rapid succession, Mussolini reversed his course and teamed up with Adolf Hitler, intervened in the Spanish Civil War on the side of General Francisco Franco and the Spanish Falangists or fascists, acquiesced to Hitler's 1938 annexation of Austria, and finally joined the Germans in World War II, a decision that ultimately led to the destruction of both Mussolini and Italian fascism.

Mussolini's counterpart in Germany was Adolf Hitler (1889–1945). German fascism, called National Socialism or Nazism, was considerably more virulent than Mussolini's Italian version. Hitler was the son of a minor Austrian customs official. As a young man, the lazy and untalented Hitler failed to gain entry to art school and drifted first to Vienna and then to Munich, where he joined the German army at the outbreak of World War I. Hitler enjoyed his military experience and was decorated for bravery.

At the close of the war, Hitler returned to Munich, where he immersed himself in radical politics. In 1919, he joined the National Socialist German Workers' (Nazi) Party, and two years later he emerged as its leader. The Nazis, a fringe party at best, adopted an ultranationalistic program that denounced both the Treaty of Versailles and the Weimar Republic, the democratic state formed in the wake of Germany's defeat in the war. The Nazis originally flirted with socialism but later came to condemn it. Hitler added a unique racial element to German fascism, proclaiming the superiority of the Aryan, or German, race and calling for the subjugation of "inferior" races, especially the Jews, whom he blamed for all of Germany's problems.

In 1923, Hitler led a failed coup d'état, the so-called Beer Hall Putsch, and was sentenced to jail, where he wrote his autobiography, *Mein Kampf* (*My Struggle*). Released from jail in late 1924, Hitler resumed his leadership of the Nazi Party, which continued to be politically inconsequential. In the 1928 elections, the Nazis garnered only 2.6 percent of the popular vote and elected only 12 deputies in the 491-seat German Reichstag, or parliament.

Nazi fortunes improved dramatically when the Great Depression struck Germany in late 1929. When the economy collapsed, the German voters, who were never entirely satisfied with the democratic republic, turned to the political extremes. In the 1930 elections, the Nazis increased their popular vote by more than 700 percent and elected 107 deputies, which made them the second largest party in the Reichstag.

The economic collapse provoked a political crisis, and another round of elections in 1932 served to confirm the Nazis' popularity. Consequently, it was not at all remarkable that Hitler, as leader of the largest political party in Germany, was named chancellor in January 1933. Like Mussolini, Hitler originally headed up a coalition government, and like Mussolini he soon dispensed with his partners in favor of dictatorial rule.

Immediately after the Reichstag building burned to the ground in a suspicious February fire, Hitler issued a decree suspending civil rights in Germany and began to arrest his opponents. A week later, new but less than totally free elections resulted in a Nazi landslide, with Hitler's party capturing almost 44 percent of the vote and electing 288 deputies. At the end of March 1933, a now docile Reichstag passed the Enabling Act, which gave Hitler's government the right to enact laws at will. Democracy in Germany was dead; the fascists now ruled.

Before the year was out, the Nazis had opened their first concentration camp at Dachau and were busy filling it with political prisoners. All political parties other than the Nazis were outlawed as the fascists imposed a one-party state. Independent trade unions were dissolved as well, replaced by the Labor Front, a Nazi organization officially dedicated to the well-being of the German working class but in fact charged with keeping German labor quiet. The first of numerous book-burning spectacles during which Nazi thugs torched millions of volumes deemed to be subversive, decadent, authored by Jews or communists, or in some way unfit for the master race, also occurred in 1933. The racial side of German fascism made itself felt in April 1933 when the Nazis organized a nationwide boycott of Jewish shops.

German fascism continued to consolidate its grip on power in 1934. The Law on the Reconstruction of the Reich destroyed the independence of the German *Länder*, or provinces, and a system of Nazi-controlled People's Courts replaced the existing German judicial structure. Hitler also secured his personal position. On June 30, he carried out a bloody purge of the Nazi Party. This purge, known as the Night of the Long Knives, eliminated Hitler's real and potential rivals, such as Ernst Röhm, head of the party's SA (Sturm Abteilungen), a paramilitary organization comprised of Nazi hoodlums.

A few weeks later, German president Paul von Hindenburg, the antiquated World War I general, died. Hitler seized the occasion to unite the offices of chancellor and president in himself, thereby institutionalizing the concept of the infallible leader, or Führer. As with the Duce in Italy, the German Führer could do no wrong.

Hitler also followed the Italian example when he promoted the absorption of the state by the party. However, in the German case the Nazis went much further. The Nazi Party gradually expanded its authority to perform functions normally carried out by the state, and the state's traditional governing institutions either disappeared or became superfluous. The Nazis energetically encouraged *Gleichschaltung*, or coordination, which aimed to invade every nook and cranny of German life to Nazify all human activity. With *Gleichschaltung*, the Nazis planned first to atomize German society and then to rebuild it according to Nazi specifications.

That *Gleichschaltung* was never fully realized is at least partially attributable to the rampant inefficiency and corruption of German fascism. Nazi party bosses frequently behaved like feudal barons, jealously guarding their fiefdoms, ceaselessly squabbling over minor details, and slavishly competing for the Führer's favor. Nevertheless, German fascism clearly affected society more profoundly than did its Italian counterpart. Hitler developed more effective means of control, especially the brutal and omnipresent secret police, or Gestapo, under the command of Heinrich Himmler. Joseph Goebbels, Hitler's chief propagandist, orchestrated a constant stream of nationalistic propaganda that further buttressed the repressive Nazi regime. Romanticizing the past, glorifying Hitler and the present, and promising a triumphant future, Goebbels's propaganda machine enveloped Germany in a cloud of hallucinatory smoke.

Hitler was more successful than Mussolini in bringing independent institutions under his control. After first allying himself with big business, Hitler came to dominate it. By the late 1930s, German businessmen and their factories were virtually subject to the Führer's command. German industrialists quietly accepted their reduced status because they retained ownership of their property and enjoyed the profits that their businesses generated. In the case of the German army, a proud bastion of traditional conservatism and the Prussian aristocracy, Hitler managed by 1938 to discredit its leadership and to fill its command ranks with loyal Nazis.

German fascism clearly reflected Hitler's obsessive racial hatred. It turned its full force against society's "outsiders," especially the Jews. In 1935, the Nazis imposed the Nuremberg Laws, which deprived Jews of their German citizenship, forbade Jews to marry non-Jews, and set quotas for Jews in the professions. In November 1938, Hitler unleashed his Nazi hordes in an orgy of violence directed against the tiny (about 1 percent of the population) German Jewish community. This pogrom, called *Kristallnacht* (or Night of Broken Glass), resulted in the deaths of more than 1,000 Jews and the arrest of another 30,000. German fascism's violent, anti-Semitic outbursts proved to be merely a prelude to the concentration camps and the systematic extermination of Europe's Jews during World War II.

Nazi foreign policy was an active one, seeking two goals: the destruction of the Treaty of Versailles and the expansion of Germany's boundaries, or the quest for living space *(Lebensraum),* as Hitler characterized it. With much of Europe deeply mired in the Depression and paralyzed by memories of World War I, Hitler achieved a series of diplomatic triumphs that seemed to confirm his self-proclaimed infallibility. In rapid succession, he withdrew Germany from the League of Nations (1933), commenced rearmament (1935), remilitarized the Rhineland (1936), intervened in the Spanish Civil War (1936–1939), annexed Austria (the Anschluss) (1938), and destroyed Czechoslovakia with the acquiescence of the western democracies at the Munich Conference (1938). Only when he invaded Poland in September 1939 did he overreach himself. The error proved to be fatal. In inaugurating the European phase of World War II, Hitler set in motion forces that eventually brought him down and destroyed fascist Germany in the process.

INTERPRETIVE ESSAY

GEORGE P. BLUM

Fascism as a dominant force burst quite suddenly on the European scene in the aftermath of World War I. Next to communism, fascism has been one of the most problematic phenomena of the modern era, and historians have offered various explanations of its origins and its political, economic, social, cultural, and international impact. Originally the term "fascism" referred to the movement that Benito Mussolini organized in 1919 and turned into Italy's ruling regime three years later. Since the 1930s, the term has also been applied to other extreme nationalist authoritarian movements and regimes such as National Socialism or Nazism in Germany, the Falange in Francisco Franco's Spain, the Arrow Cross in Hungary, and the Iron Guard in Romania.

Fascist movements promoted intense nationalism with expansionistic territorial aspirations. They were vehemently antisocialist and anti-Marxist, and they aimed to destroy working-class parties and organizations. They rejected liberalism and democracy, and once in power, they eliminated nonfascist political parties and emasculated parliamentary institutions. In their place, they established an authoritarian regime, the center of which was a political party embracing fascist ideology, led by a single charismatic leader and legitimized by plebiscites. Ruthless repression and terror without respect for the law crushed any opposition. Militarism, war, and conquests were glorified, and uniforms, military rituals, and parades were used to generate a spirit of unity among the fascist militants and the people. Controlled mass propaganda imparted the aims of the movement to the people and kept them psychologically attuned to the leader's designs. Racism and anti-Semitism were primarily characteristic of the National Socialist movement. Italian fascism embraced anti-Semitism only after Italy became an ally of Nazi Germany on the eve of World War II.

Italian Fascism had its formal beginning in Milan, when Benito Mussolini formed the first Fasci di Combattimento (fighting units) in March 1919. Made up of dissident socialists, syndicalists, and nationalist war veterans, the Fascists were united in their patriotism and their demand for social and political change. Fascist participation in electoral politics brought at first nothing but disappointment. However, new opportunities arose when Fascist *squadristi* (armed bands dressed in black shirts) fanned out into the countryside and offered their services to large landowners as a private police force against peasants. This alliance between landed wealth and Fascist bands came about when landowners felt threatened by peasant leagues organized on socialist lines. Similar cooperation between property and Fascism occurred in some urban areas, where industrialists paid *squadristi* to raid the offices of left-wing newspapers, socialist headquarters, and even Catholic trade unions.

Mussolini's propaganda skillfully used patriotic and anti-Bolshevik themes, playing on the fears of the broader populace. The Fascist movement attracted support from the lower middle class, small shopkeepers, clerical workers, artisans, and also intellectuals and professionals who faced a chronic shortage of white-collar jobs. Lastly, Mussolini gained the respect of the middle class, which was becoming more and more insecure.

The economic and social disarray following the war, including the return to a civilian economy that threw 2.5 million demobilized soldiers onto the labor market, greatly exacerbated Italy's political problems. The physical hardship of unemployment and inflation was added to the Italian public's psychological disappointment over the peace settlement. The legend arose that the arrogant allied peacemakers and the unassertive liberal Italian politicians at the peace conference had "mutilated" Italy's victory by denying Italy promised annexations.

By the summer of 1922, many Italian politicians had determined that Mussolini and his Fascists had to be taken into the government if stability was to be restored in the country. It was hoped that once the Fascists shared governmental responsibilities, they would be tamed and desist from violence. Mussolini encouraged this view by softening his earlier antirepublican stance and by showing receptiveness to liberal economic policies and to a possible accommodation with the Catholic Church. However, he also threatened an insurrectionary "march on Rome."

Although Mussolini gathered 17,000 or so *squadristi* ready to descend on Rome, the government had more than enough military force to suppress a Fascist insurrection. But neither the government nor the king nor the army leadership mustered the will to resist the Fascists. King Victor Emmanuel III backed off from declaring martial law and on October 30, 1922, appointed Mussolini prime minister. Mussolini formed a fourteen-member coalition government consisting of Fascists, nationalists, liberals, democrats, and Catholic Popolari. He reserved the most important ministerial posts for his party, adding the foreign and interior ministries to his prime ministership. The Italian strongman then received a vote of confidence from the parliament and was given temporary authority to rule by decree. In the words of historian Alan Cassels, Mussolini's takeover of government "could hardly be called a coup d'état because the authorities surrendered before a blow could be struck."

The Fascists held less than 10 percent of the seats in the Chamber of Deputies. Even a formal union with the Nationalists in 1923 increased their representation only minimally. To improve their position, the Fascists initiated a new electoral law to give the party that received the most votes in a national election two-thirds of the seats in parliament so long as that party attained at least a quarter of the total votes cast. In the 1924 election, Mussolini's list received 65 percent of the votes, giving him a secure parliamentary majority even without the new law.

Mussolini faced a major crisis in 1924 when several Fascists murdered Giacomo Matteotti, a socialist leader who had protested Fascist violence during the elections. Despite public and parliamentary outcry, Mussolini retained the support of the king who, together with conservatives and the Church, feared the socialists if Mussolini were removed. After months of wavering, early in 1925 the Fascist leader assumed moral responsibility for Matteotti's death but also ominously declared, "Italy wants peace and quiet . . . this we shall give her, by love if possible, by force if need be."

Within two years, the coalition government was ended and the cabinet made fully Fascist. The Socialist Party, the Catholic Popolari, and labor unions were banned. The parliament was further weakened when Mussolini obtained virtual permanent authority to rule by decree and the principle of ministerial responsibility to parliament was abolished. The suppression of the press silenced all public opposition, and a newly formed secret police combatted antifascist activity. A Special Tribunal for the Defense of the State passed arbitrary and sometimes secret sentences, although never on a scale equal to the Nazi or Soviet abuse of justice. Only a small number of death sentences were passed and no more than 10,000 persons imprisoned. To be sure, Fascist jails were often wretched places for political prisoners, and penal colonies were notoriously brutal, claiming the lives of unknown numbers. However, Mussolini's rule never became an absolute dictatorship comparable to Hitler's or Stalin's regimes. Hannah Arendt, in *The Origins of Totalitarianism*, characterizes Fascist Italy as "not totalitarian, but just an ordinary national dictatorship."

Mussolini had to work within a governmental structure that retained an independent monarchy and military. Even though in 1928 the legislative authority to nominate a premier was transferred from the king to the Grand Council of Fascism, the ruling committee of the party, the king remained the legal commander in chief until Italy's entry into World War II in 1940. Many Italian aristocrats, civil servants, and military officers continued to give their first allegiance to the monarchy. The Catholic Church also asserted an independent role in Italian life, which was strengthened rather than weakened by the Lateran Accords of 1929 with the Fascist government. The Duce, Mussolini's favored title as party leader, managed to control the bureaucracy, but not the army or the Church. It was striking how in the face of military defeat the king, the army leadership, and even the Grand Council of Fascism turned against Mussolini and deposed him in 1943.

Nazism, the German version of fascism, seemed to have a better prepared base in the antidemocratic traditions of the authoritarian German Empire than did fascism in the nineteenth-century Italian movement for unity and liberalism. Germany acquired democracy in the wake of military defeat, and many Germans viewed it as a foreign imposition. Throughout much of its life, the Weimar Republic remained a political system supported by a minority of people, struggling in the aftermath of World War I with an economic slump, foreign occupation, unprecedented hyperinflation, and reparations. Yet the first German republic managed to weather these crises and the persistent challenges to parliamentary democracy by opponents from the right and the left 10 years longer than Italy under its constitutional monarchy. As German economic conditions improved after the mid-1920s, in part with foreign credits, so did the prospects of parliamentary democracy. Quite likely, it would have survived in Germany and Nazism would have remained but a noisy fringe movement if the Great Depression had not cut short prosperity.

The early traces of National Socialism can be found in various small pan-German and anti-Semitic political associations that appeared in the Austro-Hungarian Empire around the turn of the century. It was an offshoot of these fringe organizations, the recently organized German Workers' Party in Munich, that Adolf Hitler joined in 1919. A product of an Austrian lower-middle-class family, Hitler drifted aimlessly before volunteering for the German army at the outset of World War I. Hitler found comradeship and direction for his life in the trenches on the Western Front, where he served bravely throughout the war. Bitterly disappointed by Germany's defeat, he decided to become a politician. Because of his oratorical talent, he became the principal propagandist of the fledgling Munich party and, by 1921, the dictatorial leader, the Führer, of the newly named National Socialist German Workers' (Nazi) Party.

The tenets of the Nazi Party reflected many of the prejudices and ideas that Hitler had embraced in prewar Vienna: vehement German racial nationalism, including imperial aspirations for *Lebensraum,* anti-Semitism, hostility to liberal democracy, and, especially, hatred of Marxism. Nazi propaganda attacked the "November criminals," that is, Jews, socialists, communists, and liberals who allegedly had brought down the imperial government in the revolution of 1918. It condemned the "dictate" of the Versailles Treaty and perpetuated the legend that the German front-line soldiers had held off the enemy, but had been "stabbed in the back" by the home front. At first the Nazi Party remained concentrated in Bavaria. In 1923, Hitler felt confident enough to stage the Beer Hall Putsch, trying to seize power in Munich, the capital of Bavaria, in preparation for a march on Berlin in imitation of Mussolini; but he failed ingloriously. He was arrested and his party temporarily outlawed.

In due time, however, the Nazi movement recovered. When tried on charges of treason, Hitler turned the proceedings into a propaganda triumph, charging that the socialist president of the Weimar Republic and those in government were the real traitors. After his release from prison in 1924, he showed considerable organizational talent in the reconstruction of his party. By the end of the decade, worsening socioeconomic conditions gave him and his party the opportunity to gain wide support among the masses.

One major effect of the severe economic conditions of the Great Depression, with its attendant social hardships, was deep political polarization of the German electorate. When unemployment reached three million in 1930, many of the workers began to support the communists. Members of the middle and lower middle class, many of whom had suffered in the hyperinflation of 1923, saw this trend as a threat to the established order. They flocked to the Nazis, who claimed to be a bulwark against revolution. In the 1930 Reichstag election, the Nazis increased their representation from 12 to 107 seats and became the largest party in Germany next to the Social Democrats. Increasingly, the Weimar president had to use constitutional emergency provisions to govern the country, which meant that the democratically elected parliamentary-based cabinet was replaced with a presidentially appointed cabinet. In short, democracy ceased to function in Germany several years before Hitler came to power.

In 1932, when unemployment peaked at 6.5 million, three successive national elections gave Hitler a unique opportunity to engage in mass agitation. His bitter attacks on political opponents and his emotional appeals for the restoration of Germany's greatness impressed voters of all social classes. He was also the first to use the airplane to reach more cities and audiences, thereby revolutionizing the style of campaigning. The Nazi Party emerged as Germany's largest party with 37 percent of the vote in July 1932. As the leader of the largest party, Hitler held out for the office of chancellor. Intrigue by conservative nationalist politicians like Franz von Papen and Kurt von Schleicher as well as Hitler's shrewd calculations brought his appointment as chancellor by a reluctant President Paul von Hindenburg on January 30, 1933.

Hitler presided over a coalition cabinet containing only a handful of Nazis, but they held important positions. He moved quickly to consolidate his dictatorial powers. A Reichstag fire, which allegedly portended a communist uprising, was used as a pretext to suspend constitutional guarantees. Communists and some Social Democrats were arrested and soon incarcerated in permanent concentration camps. After gaining an increased plurality of 43.9 percent—but not a majority—in the March Reichstag election, Hitler masterminded the adoption of the Enabling Act, which gave him dictatorial powers. Between May and July, he dissolved the trade unions and political parties, replacing them with Nazi-directed mass organizations in a process called *Gleichschaltung*, or coordination. One year later, in June 1934, he violently purged the leadership of the paramilitary Storm Troopers (SA) under Ernst Röhm to mollify the army leadership, the only force that might have challenged him on his road to absolute dictatorship. When President von Hindenburg died in August, the army leaders accepted the merger of the offices of president and chancellor, with Hitler taking the titles of Führer and Reichskanzler. He thereby became the supreme commander of all the Reich's armed forces, and officers and soldiers were required to swear an oath of personal allegiance to Hitler.

Whereas Mussolini's regime retained aspects of a semipluralistic state based on law, the Nazi Führerstaat was a complex, one-man dictatorship over the state administration, army, big business, and industry. In the Hitler regime, the party or its affiliated organizations, such as the elite SS (Schutzstaffel or guard echelon), which carried out police, state security, intelligence, and in World War II also military functions, commanded a prominent and powerful place. This was in contrast to Mussolini's Italy, where the party enjoyed little autonomy and was subordinate to the state bureaucracy.

The rise of fascism in Italy and Germany stimulated radical national politics in many European countries and resulted in the formation of sometimes competing fascist parties. None of them produced a lasting strong leader. The absence of a charismatic personality and the presence of authoritarian and nationalist movements and parties inhibited—if not prevented—the establishment of fascist regimes. Although most European states developed some totalitarian groups or parties, it will be helpful to look briefly at the particular experience of Spain, Hungary, and Romania, all of which showed significant variations of fascism.

Spanish fascism emerged from several radical right-wing factions in the late 1920s and early 1930s, and became consolidated with the establishment of the Falange Española in 1933 under the leadership of José Antonio de Rivera. He and his Falangists were antiliberal, antiparliamentary, and authoritarian. They also evinced an interest in socialism. After General Francisco Franco, a conservative military commander, rebelled against the Spanish Republic, he merged the reactionary Catholic Carlists, the Requetés, with the Falange in 1937. As Falange leader, Franco, now also the head of state, kept the revolutionary aspirations of the Old Falangists in check and manipulated the party to his own ends. Franco was never a fascist, neither during the Civil War nor during his long rule as Caudillo (leader), but he based his conservative dictatorship on the army, the Catholic Church, the upper class, and segments of the middle class.

In Hungary and Romania, fascism and reactionary politics were intertwined. Between 1920 and 1944, Hungary was under the regency of Admiral Miklós Horthy, a reactionary who hoped to see the large Hungarian realm of earlier centuries restored. Fascist movements, inspired by German National Socialism, appeared in the early 1930s. They flourished under the pro-fascist, anti-Semitic prime minister Gyula Gömbös. In 1935, most fascist factions were united in the Arrow Cross Party under the leadership of Ferenc Szálasi, a former general staff officer. During World War II, the Arrow Cross leader plotted to overthrow the reactionary Horthy regime. He succeeded only in 1944, after Horthy had fallen out of favor with Hitler, and presided over a short-lived fascist regime that collaborated with the Nazis in the killing of Hungary's Jews.

A peculiar form of fascism appeared in Romania in 1927 with the formation of the Legion of the Archangel Michael, soon better known as the Romanian Iron Guard. C. Z. Codreanu, the founder of this movement, was a religious mystic, and the Legionaries advanced their own interpretation of Romanian Orthodoxy, aspiring to attain national salvation for the Romanian people or "race." They appealed to radical nationalist youth and the peasantry, professed a strident anti-Semitism, engaged in violence and murder at times, and maintained a rigidly hierarchical internal organization with a paramilitary external form. In 1940, General Ion Antonescu, a conservative favorite of the fascists, formed a right-wing coalition government that included the Iron Guard. When the latter staged a coup against him in the following year, Antonescu liquidated the Iron Guard with the encouragement of Hitler, who wanted to preserve stability in Romania to protect his oil supplies.

Fascist regimes, intent on exercising utmost power, subordinated economic policies to their domestic and external objectives. Private property was not abolished, as under communism, but it was subjected to regulatory or racial restrictions and occasional political meddling. Economic planning was instituted haphazardly during peacetime and more rigorously during war. Fascists attacked economic liberalism because it advocated individual self-interest, and socialism because it caused conflicts between labor and capital that undermined national unity. To eliminate antagonism between workers and employers, the fascists prohibited labor unions and strikes, and formed associations or corporations that included both workers and employers.

In Fascist Italy, much attention was devoted to the idea of corporativism. Mussolini's propaganda touted it as an alternative "third way" between capitalism and socialism. Corporativism aimed to restore social cohesion by encompassing labor and capital in corporations. The basis for the Fascist corporative state was laid in 1925, when the Italian General Confederation of Industry (Confindustria) and the Confederation of Fascist Trade Unions recognized each other as respective spokesmen of capital and labor. Soon a law designated several branches of economic activity, for example, industry, agriculture, banking, and commerce, as appropriate for corporations. However, it was not until 1934 that mixed corporations of employers and employees were actually established. The capstone of the corporate structure was put in place in 1939 when the Chamber of Fasces and Corporations, consisting of elected and appointed members of corporations, replaced the Italian parliament.

Fascist corporative theory had the potential of innovation in economic life, but in practice corporativism failed to effect convincing results. It was difficult to establish a workable relationship among business, labor, the Fascist Party, and the Duce's dictatorship. Overall, Fascist economic policies favored the interests of commerce and industry. They increased national income only modestly at best, ballooned the public debt, and thanks to falling wages and rising prices, left the poor poorer and the rich richer.

In contrast to less developed Italy, Germany boasted rich natural and industrial resources. Hitler understood that Germany's recovery from the Depression was a prerequisite for rearmament and the attainment of economic self-sufficiency, or autarky. He enacted pragmatic policies that poured larger and larger funds into public works projects: roads, canals, public buildings, bridges, and the popular program of constructing motor highways, the *Autobahnen.* In addition, tax breaks allowed industries to expand. These dynamic economic activities absorbed many unemployed; other young men were taken into the voluntary, later compulsory, labor service and the expanding army. The unemployment figures fell from 6 million in 1932, to 4.5 million in 1933, 1.7 million in 1935, and less than half a million in 1937. At the same time, rearmament expenditures rose dramatically from 1 billion Reichsmarks in 1933 to 30 billion in 1939, requiring enormous deficit spending in addition to ordinary tax levies. The condition of workers improved moderately, although real wages began to decline toward the end of the decade with the production of more guns and less butter.

Quite early the German government faced an unfavorable balance of payments, because it lacked foreign exchange to pay for increasing imports of raw materials to feed rearmament. Greater state control was imposed, and in 1936, the Four-Year Plan was instituted to spur German production of raw materials to achieve autarky. In pursuing its economic policies, Nazi Germany did not adopt the tortuous process of corporativism but instead operated with programs that were partial to big business and industry. From the start, Hitler intended to solve most of Germany's economic problems by *Lebensraum,* or the acquisition of territory, which of course required gearing the German economic engine for eventual war.

For dictators such as Mussolini and Hitler, the control of government and coordination of economic life were only some of the prerequisites for the achievement of absolute power. Another very major objective was the creation of a national community in which every member internalized the aims of fascist ideology. Both regimes tried to silence prestigious intellectual, scientific, and artistic figures who were known to reject fascism. In Italy this forced the historian Gaetano Salvemini, the physicist Enrico Fermi, and the conductor Arturo Toscanini to become expatriates. In Nazi Germany, the novelist Thomas Mann and the physicist Albert Einstein, together with many other luminaries, suffered the same fate. Joseph Goebbels, the Nazi minister of public enlightenment and propaganda, publicly burned the works of Karl Marx, Sigmund Freud, and many others. In Mussolini's Italy, where repression was less brutal and arbitrary, such incidents did not occur, but intellectuals and artists either had to remain silent on political matters or compromise with the regime.

Radio, film, newspapers, and publications were controlled in both fascist societies. Goebbels, who was in charge of all the media and the arts, showed considerable ingenuity in the effort to keep the German populace attuned to Nazi aims and psychologically receptive to the regime's message. He saw to it that newspaper editors followed his ministry's daily guidelines and received foreign news only from the German Press Agency. Keenly aware of popular culture's effectiveness, the Third Reich's propaganda master particularly promoted films. Because he realized that continuous Nazi propaganda films would turn audiences off, he encouraged the production of entertaining films to provide viewers with plenty of escapist experience, especially during the war.

The fascist regimes regulated public education from elementary to university levels. However, they placed their major hope for shaping the attitudes and character of the youth along ideological lines in youth organizations: the Fascist youth cadres, which encompassed Italian boys from age 8 to 21, and the Hitler Youth, which included 10- to eighteen-year-olds. Comparable but separate formations reached girls. Males in their late teens were inducted into the Italian army or into the Wehrmacht, or German army, after spending a short term in the labor service.

Adults in both societies belonged to organizations directly affiliated with the party or under party control. In Italy the largest and most active organization for working adults was the Dopolavoro, through which the Fascist regime influenced the social and leisure-time activities of the urban masses. These activities emphasized uplift and self-improvement less than the comparable Nazi organization Strength Through Joy, an arm of the German Labor Front designed to coordinate the free time of the working class. In addition to the SS for the elite and the SA for many other males, the Nazis maintained a great variety of party-affiliated professional organizations as control mechanisms, ranging from the National Socialist Physicians' League to the National Socialist Stenographers' League. Women and mothers especially were urged to belong to the National Socialist Women's League. Both Fascist Italy and Nazi Germany emphasized a traditional role for women that placed them in the home, divided between the kitchen and the bedroom. Official policies and differential wages discriminated against women in the professions and in the ordinary workplace.

In retrospect, it is evident that social policies failed to transform Italian society in the image of the fascist personality and community. The collapse of the regime during World War II allowed reconstruction to proceed along lines indicated before the advent of Mussolini. In Germany the consequences of Nazi social policies were more complex. The intention of primarily transforming the belief systems rather than effecting a social revolution miscarried. What Hitler and the Nazis achieved in their blind pursuit of rearmament, war, and racial empire was, however, the destruction of some major pillars of the old order: the German aristocracy and the Prussian army leadership. They also significantly weakened the rigidity of the traditional social structure. These developments made possible the remodeling of western Germany and, since the reunification, of eastern Germany as well, in the image of a revised capitalist socioeconomic system with liberal democratic values.

Fascist efforts to unite the nation through sociopsychological changes were not ends in themselves; rather, they were designed to ready the people for the achievement of greatness through imperial expansion. A basic principle in Italian Fascism and German Nazism was the idea that nations (and races, according to Nazism) were engaged in a perpetual struggle for self-assertion and survival. The early Fascist movement was boosted in the public's eye when Mussolini promised that he would end the submission of Italy to the stronger powers, which was evident in the peace settlement of World War I that supposedly denied Italy its justly earned territorial rewards. Similarly, Hitler's party capitalized on the German perception of the harshness of the "dictate" of Versailles and pledged to restore Germany's greatness as a nation. Even under the Weimar Republic, Germany pressed for a revision of the peace settlement by negotiation. Under the domination of ideologically aggressive regimes, Italy and Germany became a perpetual threat to international peace because they were prepared to go to war.

Within a year after becoming prime minister, Mussolini found a pretext to seize the Greek island of Corfu and soon thereafter to occupy Fiume, whose status was under dispute with Yugoslavia. He was rebuffed on Corfu but won a compromise settlement on Fiume largely because Britain and France, Italy's wartime allies, raised no serious objections. Until the mid-1930s, Fascist foreign policy balanced precariously between Italy's alliance with Britain and France, and a rapprochement with Germany. After Hitler's advent to power, the Duce wanted both to ensure continuous revisionism and to check excessive pan-German aspirations. In July 1934, the Austrian Nazis attempted to seize power in Vienna in preparation for Austria's unification with Germany. However, the effort collapsed when Mussolini announced that he was sending Italian forces to the Brenner Pass.

What changed the cool relationship with Hitler to an alliance was Mussolini's decision to pursue colonial schemes in Africa. His attempt to gain control of the Mediterranean—the *mare nostrum* reminiscent of ancient Roman days—and the acquisition of Ethiopia were but the first steps in his ambitious plan for expansion. It seems to have been undertaken, in part, as an alternative to domestic social reform. The British and French governments appeared at first ready to make territorial concessions to Italy in Ethiopia, but public opinion induced them to back weak League of Nations sanctions against Italy. Mussolini now moved closer to an alliance with Hitler, establishing the Rome-Berlin Axis in 1936. He acquiesced to Hitler's annexation of Austria in 1938 and became a junior partner in what Hitler later called "the brutal friendship" with Italy.

Many scholars believe that Nazi foreign objectives were outlined in Hitler's *Mein Kampf* (My Struggle), which he wrote in the mid-1920s. In implementing his decisions, however, Hitler demonstrated singular opportunism in the means and timing of his actions and remarkable skill in exploiting the weaknesses of the democracies. In 1935 and 1936, he ostentatiously violated the Treaty of Versailles and the Locarno Pact by announcing full rearmament of Germany and occupying the demilitarized Rhineland. British and French appeasement encouraged Hitler to make even bolder moves, convinced that the Allies would not fight. The annexation of Austria was followed by the destruction of Czechoslovakia as an independent state and finally an attack on Poland in September 1939, which unleashed World War II in Europe. A nonaggression pact with the Soviet Union, concluded only days before the strike against Poland, was envisaged as a temporary maneuver by Hitler.

After blitzkrieg strikes brought unprecedented German military successes in Poland, Norway, and France, Hitler was ready to invade Soviet Russia in 1941, even though Britain, by refusing to give in, presented him with his first strategic deadlock. Hitler's decision to attack the USSR was his fatal error. The lure of living space and the attainment of territorial hegemony in Europe from the Atlantic to the depths of Russia blinded him to the military and political realities that thwarted the realization of these aims. Germany's (and Italy's) unilateral declaration of war on the United States after Japan attacked Pearl Harbor in December 1941 (a step not necessitated by the alliance with

Italy and Japan) pointed to Hitler's increasing irrationality in the pursuit of his all-or-nothing designs and in time brought disaster and ultimate defeat.

A good idea of the nature of the Nazi New Order can be gained from the occupation regime that the Germans imposed on European territories under their control during the war. Whereas the Italian Fascist conquerors followed a fairly typical military occupation policy in France and in the Balkans, the Nazi treatment of occupied people was largely based on ideological principles. In addition to exploiting the economic and human resources of conquered areas for Germany's war effort, Nazi authorities applied racial criteria to occupied populaces. For vast numbers of Europeans, especially from eastern Europe, this brought enslavement as "racially inferior" masses. Millions of them were deported to different areas of Europe or brought to Germany and used as slave labor. The persecution of Jews in prewar Germany was but a harsh prelude to the destruction of millions of Jews and others as "parasitic subhumans" under Hitler's Final Solution. Hitler's New Order in Europe was composed of an empire of concentration camps under the infamous head of the SS, Heinrich Himmler, and, after 1941, extermination camps in Poland as well. Mechanized racial genocide became the very last end of Nazi policy.

Fascism in Europe came to an abrupt end in spring 1945 with the total defeat of Nazi Germany by the Allies and Adolf Hitler's suicide on April 30. Shortly before that, Benito Mussolini had been captured by antifascist Italian partisans and summarily shot. After the collapse of Fascist Italy in 1943, he had been ordered by Hitler to head a new Fascist regime in German-occupied northern Italy.

Being closely tied to the personalities of Hitler and Mussolini, fascism as an ideology and a political system was a European phenomenon, if not principally a German and Italian phenomenon. Outside Germany and Italy, it made only a limited impact on countries such as Spain, Hungary, and Romania, becoming submerged in the political ambitions of fairly traditional military dictators. The legacy of fascism, especially vehement Nazism, was a vast sea of material destruction, the loss of tens of millions of human lives, and the horror of unprecedented dehumanization. Until recently, Germany and Europe remained deeply divided and dominated by two ideologically antagonistic powers as a stark reminder of fascism's defeat. Today it is fairly easy to discern fascist elements in other political regimes—both right-wing authoritarian and left-wing socialist or communist. However, it is not likely that another fascist regime of the magnitude of Nazi Germany or Fascist Italy will arise in Europe. For that to happen would require a unique combination of a seductive nationalist ideology, a mass party led by a charismatic leader, and a society under severe socioeconomic stress, making its populace receptive to the all-or-nothing solutions of a future ruthless dictator.

SELECTED BIBLIOGRAPHY

Allen, William S. *The Nazi Seizure of Power: The Experience of a Single Town, 1922–1945*. Rev. ed. New York: Franklin Watts, 1984. Classic study of the takeover of a town by the Nazis and their impact on the community.

Arendt, Hannah. *The Origins of Totalitarianism*. Rev. ed. New York: Harcourt, Brace and World, 1966. An important study of totalitarianism's antecedents and its significance for the twentieth century.

Bracher, Karl Dietrich. *The German Dictatorship: The Origins, Structure, and Effects of National Socialism.* Translated by Jean Steinberg. New York: Praeger, 1970. The best scholarly account of the Nazi regime by a distinguished German historian.

Bullock, Alan. *Hitler: A Study in Tyranny.* Rev. ed. New York: Harper and Row, 1964. This remains the best scholarly account of Hitler as the man and historical actor.

Carsten, F. L. *The Rise of Fascism.* Berkeley: University of California Press, 1967. A very good overview of the formative period of fascism in Italy, Germany, and other European countries.

Cassels, Alan. *Fascism.* New York: Thomas Crowell, 1974. A lucid comparative study of Italian Fascism, German National Socialism, and other European fascist movements.

Deakin, Frederick William. *The Brutal Friendship: Mussolini, Hitler, and the Fall of Italian Fascism.* New York: Harper and Row, 1962. An interesting study of the decline of Mussolini's power and regime.

Fest, Joachim C. *The Face of the Third Reich: Portraits of the Nazi Leadership.* Translated by Michael Bullock. New York: Pantheon, 1977. Good short biographies of Hitler's close associates.

Fleming, Gerald. *Hitler and the Final Solution.* Berkeley: University of California Press, 1984. Elucidates Hitler's role in instigating the destruction of the European Jews.

Haffner, Sebastian. *The Meaning of Hitler.* Translated by Ewald Osers. Cambridge, MA: Harvard University Press, 1979. A very readable account of Hitler as a modern dictator with a relentless penchant for all-or-nothing actions.

Kershaw, Ian. *Hitler.* New York: Longman, 1991. Excellent short account of how Hitler acquired, maintained, and expanded his power.

Kirkpatrick, Ivone. *Mussolini: A Study in Power.* New York: Hawthorne Books, 1964. One of the best biographies in English of the Duce.

Kitchen, Martin. *Fascism.* London: Macmillan, 1976. A brief introduction to the major theories of fascism before the 1970s.

Mack Smith, Denis. *Mussolini.* New York: Alfred A. Knopf, 1982. An authoritative, concise biography of the Italian dictator.

Mann, Michael. *Fascists.* Cambridge: Cambridge University Press, 2004. Among the welter of books about Hitler and the Third Reich, Mann's work reminds us that Fascism was a pan-European movement stretching from the Iberian Peninsula to the boundaries of Soviet Russia. Mann, a sociologist, writes clearly and free of jargon. Of interest, he notes that Europe's youth culture of the 1920s and 1930s was a receptive breeding ground for Fascist ideas.

Paxton, Robert O. *The Anatomy of Fascism.* New York: Vintage, 2005. Paxton, a celebrated scholar of the Vichy regime in wartime France, attempts the monumental task of defining what exactly fascism is, and, to a large extent, he succeeds. He emphasizes that fascism is neither a leader nor an ideology. Rather, it is defined by what its adherents do.

Payne, Stanley G. *Falange.* Stanford, CA: Stanford University Press, 1961. Standard work on the subject.

Payne, Stanley G. *Fascism: Comparison and Definition.* Madison: University of Wisconsin Press, 1980. An excellent comparative survey of fascist movements and regimes in Europe and a brief consideration outside Europe, offering a typology of fascism.

Redles, David. *Hitler's Millennial Reich.* New York: New York University Press, 2005. This fascinating book advances the thesis that Hitler and the Nazis were successful in Germany because they catered to the desires of a defeated and despairing population that yearned for a messianic leader who would cure all their ills, restore a mythical past, and defeat their antagonists in something resembling Armageddon.

Schoenbaum, David. *Hitler's Social Revolution: Class and Status in Nazi Germany, 1933–1939.* Garden City, NY: Doubleday, 1966. A study of the impact of Nazism on German society before World War II.

Sugar, Peter, ed. *Native Fascism in the Successor States.* Santa Barbara, CA: ABC-CLIO, 1971. Short accounts of fascist fronts and movements in central and eastern Europe.

Tannenbaum, Edward R. *The Fascist Experience: Italian Society and Culture, 1922–1945.* New York: Basic Books, 1972. An informative examination of popular culture, literature, and intellectual and cultural life concentrating on the 1920s and 1930s.

Woolf, S. J., ed. *Fascism in Europe.* New York: Methuen, 1981. First published in 1968, this expanded edition analyzes the political, economic, and social conditions that produced fascist movements.

NEVILLE CHAMBERLAIN (1869–1940)

One of the most prominent British politicians of the interwar period, Neville Chamberlain served as prime minister of the United Kingdom in the years preceding World War II. Chamberlain initially achieved prominence because of his attempts to grapple with the social issues spawned by the economic difficulties of the 1920s and 1930s. Nevertheless, he is best remembered for his failed attempt to appease Nazi Germany in the years leading up to World War II.

The son of Joseph Chamberlain (a British Conservative statesman) and his second wife, Florence Kenrick, Arthur Neville Chamberlain was born on March 18, 1869, in Edgbaston, Birmingham. In 1875, his mother died. His father's sisters, Caroline and Clara, took up the task of acting as hostess to the statesman and foster parents to the six Chamberlain children.

As a youth, Chamberlain loved music and nature. He entered school in Southport, but in 1880, the Chamberlain family moved to Highbury Hall in Birmingham, which remained his home for 30 years. There, he attended Mason College, a business school. In 1889, he undertook a short-lived apprenticeship with a firm of public accountants and traveled abroad for the first time. While his brother Austen carried on the family's political tradition by serving in the British Parliament, Chamberlain took care of the family business in Birmingham.

During a visit to the United States, Joseph became convinced that he could expand the family's fortune by growing sisal hemp in the Bahamas. He bought an estate on Andros, 35 miles from Nassau, the capital of the Bahamas. Only 22 years old, Neville Chamberlain left Birmingham for Andros and lived there from 1891 until 1896. He felt lonely and overworked, and the adventure proved a failure. Abandoning the enterprise, Chamberlain returned to Highbury. He acquired a manufacturing concern, Hoskins and Son, and became a public-spirited businessman. A Conservative Unionist like the rest of his family, he became increasingly drawn to politics. By 1904, Chamberlain had joined 14 Birmingham city committees, taking a particular interest in the city's hospitals and Birmingham University. Despite his civic activities, he continued to travel and visited India in 1904.

In 1911, Chamberlain married Annie Vere Cole. They eventually had two children, Dorothy and Frank. Also in 1911, he was elected to Birmingham's city council. The following year, he chaired the town planning committee in Birmingham. Two years later, Chamberlain was elected alderman in Birmingham. In 1915, he became lord mayor of Birmingham and was reelected the following year. During this same period, he helped establish the Birmingham Municipal Bank. In 1917, he spent eight months in London as director of the Department of National Service, which oversaw conscription and the allocation of manpower during World War I. In the following year, he was elected to Parliament from the Ladywood division of Birmingham.

Chamberlain served on a number of important parliamentary committees and in 1922 became postmaster general. After a brief stint as minister of health, he became chancellor of the exchequer in Prime Minister Stanley Baldwin's Conservative government. He returned to the Ministry of Health in 1924 during the second Baldwin government and stayed there until 1929. Throughout the 1920s, Chamberlain compiled an outstanding record and gradually emerged as an important influence in the British Conservative Party. His Housing Act of 1923 sought to ameliorate Britain's great housing shortage by providing subsidies to builders. At the same time, he fought to keep the costs of benefits down. A 1926 act gave the minister of health the power to supersede local authorities who paid higher rates of relief than those approved by the central authority. In 1928, he rationalized and streamlined local government by concentrating all local authority in counties and county boroughs.

After the Conservatives' defeat in the general election of 1929, Chamberlain participated in the rejuvenation of the party. From 1930 until 1931, first as chairman of the Conservative Party's Research Department, then as party chairman, he devoted his efforts to party reorganization and reconstruction.

Chamberlain once again became chancellor of the exchequer in 1931. He remained at this post until 1937. In 1932, he ended Britain's 80-year-old policy of free trade, reintroducing a tariff system to protect British domestic manufacturers. He was also responsible for the Unemployment Act of 1934, which created an autonomous system of unemployment relief, independent of both the central and local authorities.

In 1937, Chamberlain became prime minister after Baldwin's retirement. For the next two years, he found his agenda dominated by foreign policy questions. The most serious consisted of finding some peaceful means of containing German dictator Adolf Hitler's expansionism. Chamberlain's policies operated on two assumptions. First, he felt the Treaty of Versailles (1919) that ended World War I had dealt with Germany too harshly. Second, he believed that Hitler's ambitions were limited to uniting all ethnically German areas in Europe under the Third Reich. Believing that the principle of national self-determination sanctioned such ambitions, Chamberlain sought to satisfy Hitler's demands for territories outside of Germany when the population of these areas consisted mainly of Germans. This policy became known as appeasement. By satisfying what he saw as Germany's legitimate grievances, Chamberlain, who was haunted by the prospect of a second world war, hoped to avert conflict in Europe.

Chamberlain initially sought to forge a European-wide agreement that would take care of all European diplomatic difficulties. When this policy failed and Hitler seized Austria in March 1938, Chamberlain only redoubled his efforts on behalf of peace. When Hitler demanded that Czechoslovakia cede the Sudetenland (an area in the westernmost portion of Czechoslovakia that was home to three million Germans), Chamberlain engaged in a desperate diplomacy to resolve the dispute peacefully. Flying to Germany on September 15, 1938, Chamberlain met Hitler in Berchtesgaden. He offered to give the Sudetenland to Germany, and Hitler agreed. The French followed the British lead, and Czechoslovakia, without support from the big powers, felt compelled to yield.

In order to finalize the details of the arrangement between Germany and Czechoslovakia, Chamberlain flew to Germany again on September 22. Hitler confronted him with the demand that the Czechs yield the Sudetenland immediately, without further negotiation. War with Germany appeared imminent, with Britain mobilizing its fleet while France and Czechoslovakia called up reservists. Nevertheless, Italian dictator Benito Mussolini intervened, offering his services as mediator. On September 29, Chamberlain flew to Germany once again to meet with Hitler, Mussolini, and Edouard Daladier, the French premier. At Munich, the four powers reached an agreement that conveyed the Sudetenland to Germany. At the same time, Hitler and Chamberlain signed a resolution forsaking war as a means of settling disputes between their two countries.

Relieved at the outcome of this crisis, the British public gave a rapturous welcome to Chamberlain upon his return, when he waved the piece of paper on which the agreement was written to a crowd of spectators and proclaimed that the document secured "peace for our time." Nevertheless, this relief overlay a sense of shame at having capitulated to German bullying. Chamberlain sought to rearm Britain so that in the future it would not negotiate from a position of weakness. He stepped up production of fighter aircraft, expedited the installation of the British radar defense system, and laid the foundations for the enlargement of the British army.

British shame over Czechoslovakia turned to outrage when Hitler annexed the rest of Czechoslovakia in March 1939. Hitler's aggressiveness precipitated a general crisis of allegiances in Europe as the smaller powers looked to Britain and France for protection. Britain and France extended guarantees to Poland, Greece, and Romania, while pursuing negotiations for an alliance with the Soviet Union, which proved unsuccessful. Hitler, undaunted by the big powers' apparent attempts to contain him, invaded Poland just six months later. Britain and France, already embarrassed by their failure to come to the aid of Czechoslovakia, declared war on Germany. Chamberlain's last-ditch efforts to preserve peace had failed, as war once again engulfed Europe.

In 1940, Chamberlain's government fell following the German invasion of Norway. Chamberlain became lord president in Winston Churchill's cabinet, although his tenure would be brief. As the war escalated, many criticized Chamberlain's policy of appeasement. On September 30 of that same year, Churchill accepted Chamberlain's resignation from the cabinet.

Public displeasure over his policies was not the only reason that Chamberlain retired from politics. His health failed rapidly during this period, as he was first stricken with cancer and then an abdominal pain that sent him to exploratory surgery, which revealed an intestinal stricture. He underwent a major operation in late July, after which he was informed that his cancer was incurable. Chamberlain died in London on November 9, 1940. His ashes are interred at Westminster Abbey.

ABC-CLIO

FRANCISCO FRANCO (1892–1975)

Considered by many to be the most dominant figure in Spanish history since the sixteenth century, Francisco Franco was the generalissimo of the Spanish armed forces and the authoritarian leader of Spain from 1936 until his death in 1975.

Francisco Franco Bahamonde was born in El Ferrol, in the province of Galicia, on December 4, 1892. He was descended from a long line of naval officers but was unable to enter the naval academy, so he entered the infantry academy in Toledo and subsequently volunteered for service in Morocco. This campaign was the beginning of a distinguished military career as the young Franco showed great courage, leadership ability, and professionalism. He gained rapid promotions through combat duty and became a brigadier general at age 33, the youngest general in Europe at that time.

In the 1920s, Spain was divided between supporters of the traditional monarchy and those who wished for a modern, republican form of government. Franco was clearly identified with the monarchy and the nationalist conservatives, so when the Republicans came to power in 1931, they closed the General Military Academy that Franco had headed since 1928. His brother-in-law was a leader of the Spanish Confederation of Autonomous Rights, a Catholic nationalist party that gained a majority in the government in 1933 and restored Franco to high position in the military.

Franco became a specialist in suppressing worker demonstrations and rebellions in Morocco as he countered the influence of liberals and leftists in the armed forces. When the Popular Front, a coalition of left and center parties, was returned to the government in 1936, Franco was posted to the Canary Islands. He moved to Morocco, however, to command rightist forces as political polarization worsened and Spain descended into civil war. From Morocco, he contacted the fascist governments in Germany and Italy to request military assistance.

By late 1936, the Nationalist factions in the Spanish Civil War had designated Franco commander in chief of the army and then chief of state of the insurgent regime. He responded by saying that "his hand would not tremble" until he had achieved victory, not only in the civil war but also in restoring Spain to the social structure of previous centuries. To accomplish his program—the elimination of political parties of the liberals and the left, the development of prosperous industry, and the re-Catholicization of all Spain—Franco organized a new party called the Falange that united previous rightist groups. All other parties were outlawed or dissolved and their members invited to join the Falange.

With the assistance of Italy and Germany, Franco led the Nationalists to victory in the civil war against the Republicans by 1939. Although Soviet leader Joseph Stalin sought influence over the forces of the left, their situation was ignored by the governments of western Europe. Franco secured his position by dealing harshly with his foes and setting up a tightly controlled corporate state. Franco kept Spain out of World War II despite his previous alliance with Germany and Italy, even going so far as barring German chancellor Adolf Hitler from using Spanish territory to launch an attack on British-held Gibraltar. His inactivity put him in a better position to promote good relations with the United States and other Western nations after the war. The development of the Cold War furthered this trend, as Western regimes overlooked Franco's excesses at home to secure his cooperation in the struggle against communism. In 1953, he signed an official concordat with the Vatican and a 10-year pact with the United States.

The decade of the 1950s was quiet politically, but Spain was facing a severe financial crisis by 1957, forcing Franco to open the economy to more interaction with other European countries, as stipulated in a Stabilization Plan in 1959. The new policy was very successful in promoting the growth of the economy, but this very growth began to undermine Franco's social goals. Franco encouraged material achievement in the hopes that more prosperous people would not question political restrictions so much. Exchange with other countries, however, led many toward the secularism and cultural modernism of the rest of Europe. By the time of Franco's death, the old rural, conservative, Catholic society that had brought him to power was largely gone.

Franco is considered one of the more successful dictators of the twentieth century for his nearly 40 years in power. Although his plans to reinstitute traditional cultural and spiritual values ended in failure, his attempts to modernize the economy were a success. The majority of Spanish people recognized that there would be no political change until he died, and they waited patiently for the end of the regime. Franco died on November 20, 1975, after a series of illnesses and surgeries.

ABC-CLIO

SIR OSWALD MOSLEY (1896–1980)

Sir Oswald Mosley is best remembered for his support of Nazi Germany and his leadership of the British Union of Fascists during the 1930s. Before his fascist career began, he was active in British politics from an early age, supporting in turn the Conservative, Liberal, and Labour parties.

Oswald Ernald Mosley was born on November 16, 1896, in London. He was the oldest of three children born to Katherine Mead Heathcote and Oswald Mosley. As a member of the landed British aristocracy, Mosley attended prep school and then became a "gentleman cadet" at 17. In early 1915, he served on the front at the Battle of Ypres during World War I. As an old injury grew worse as he sat in the trenches, he was soon sent home on permanent injury leave. Mosley's lasting impression of the army was of discipline and sacrifice, as well as the possibility of a collective triumph over selfishness and the individual.

In July 1918, Mosley ran for the British Parliament as a member of the British Conservative Party. He stressed the need to win the war and for new ideas by new men. He soon discovered that the old guard, mostly those who had benefited financially from the war, still dominated Parliament. This disillusionment, combined with his criticism of the government's handling of the situation in Ireland, led Mosley to the British Liberal Party in 1920. By 1923, Mosley had broken with the Liberals but continued to hold his seat as an independent. In 1924, Mosley joined the Independent Labour Party, an organization to the left of the rapidly growing British Labour Party.

After losing the next election in 1924, Mosley focused on a plan for economic reform, rejecting laissez-faire economics and the free market. Instead, he argued that the state, not the market, should solve the problems of the world economy, mass unemployment, and poor housing. In 1927, Mosley returned to Parliament, but his ideas for solving unemployment received little attention within the Labour Party or by other members of Parliament. He resigned his seat in 1930 and left the Labour Party.

In 1931, Mosley founded the New Party. He combined a coherent economic plan with an appeal to the young, postwar generation. He argued that the British Empire should be protected against unfair competition and foreign labor to create full employment and that a strong executive who used quick action to solve problems should run

During the 1930s, Sir Oswald Mosley (shown here with his wife Cynthia) established the British Union of Fascists. Modeled after Benito Mussolini's Italy, Mosley's brand of fascism enjoyed a degree of popularity among Great Britain's wealthy prior to the outbreak of World War II. (Library of Congress)

the British government. After a disastrous showing in the 1931 elections, Mosley disbanded the New Party in 1932.

The New Party was seen as a young man's folly rather than an unforgivable political mistake. All of the major parties were still interested in Mosley because of his appeal to the young. Mosley himself felt alienated from parliamentary politics and was convinced that the liberal economic system was doomed. An alternative party was needed to oppose communism when the system collapsed.

Mosley founded the British Union of Fascists in October 1932. The fascist party was the means for bringing about "managed capitalism," where the state would direct resources for maximum efficiency. The British Union of Fascists was similar to the early German Nazi Party in that it had a dual nature: it was a political party seeking power through elections, and it was a paramilitary force fighting communism and ethnic minorities. The party was organized along military lines; its members wore gray uniforms and black shirts. Mosley's following was largely middle class, although he attracted the young of all classes. In 1935, Mosley gained members from among small-business owners and nonindustrial workers by promising tariffs and protection against low-paid foreign workers.

Throughout the 1930s, Mosley and the British Union (the name was shortened in 1936) moved to the right, prompting communist groups to regularly disrupt fascist marches and public meetings. Mosley lost the propaganda war as the press blamed his followers for all the resulting violence, which drew parallels to the violent clashes in Italy and Germany. By the late 1930s, anti-Semitism was more prevalent in Mosley's writings and speeches, but his primary concern remained unemployment and the defense of Britain against communism. Mosley thus opposed Britain's entry into World War II.

When war broke out in September 1939, Mosley was considered a traitor to Britain for being a fascist and opposing the war. He was jailed in May 1940 and held without trial until November 1943, when he was released due to illness. He was never tried for treason after the war. He returned to politics in 1948, when he founded the Union Movement. He ran for Parliament in 1959 and 1966 on the Union Movement platform of a unified and protected Europe. Although he gave up leadership of the Union Movement in 1966, he appeared on television and wrote articles on these same issues into the early 1970s.

Mosley and his British Union of Fascists shared characteristics of fascism found elsewhere: a focus on the young, quick action, a strong executive, emphasis on military structure, a rejection of parliamentary politics, and a society composed of functional groups rather than classes or individuals. Despite his calls for the protection of Britain against foreigners, Mosley never completely embraced the anti-Semitism, overt racism, and eagerness for war displayed by Nazi Germany. Mosley died on December 3, 1980, in Paris, France.

ABC-CLIO

BENITO MUSSOLINI (1883–1945)

The bombastic Benito Mussolini sought to rule Italy like a modern-day Caesar and even went so far as to attempt to recreate a new Roman Empire in his own image. However, military adventures abroad and an alliance with Adolf Hitler's Third Reich in Germany led to Italy's defeat and Mussolini's eventual downfall.

Benito Amilcare Andrea Mussolini was born in Dovis, Italy, on July 29, 1883, and was the son of a blacksmith and a schoolteacher. He inherited from his father an abiding interest in the socialist movement and a taste for political extremism. Having briefly worked as a school teacher, Mussolini fled to Switzerland to escape compulsory military service but subsequently returned to fulfill it. Afterward, he worked as a manual laborer, a left-wing agitator, and an effective editor of the official Italian Socialist Party newspaper, *Avanti!*, in 1912. He broke ranks with the party and was expelled, however, over the issue of Italian intervention in World War I and his desire for Italy to take a more active role. That rejection angered Mussolini, who rejoined the military, was wounded in 1917, and returned to civilian life committed to a new right-wing ideology—fascism.

Mussolini's concept of fascism was his own unique blend of nationalism, imperialism, corporatism, and a political alliance with large business interests. The resulting corporate state that he envisioned was to be organized by groups, rather than by individuals as in a democracy. Thus, the state would deal with such corporate groups of workers

Italian dictator Benito Mussolini (left) sits next to German dictator Adolf Hitler in this June 1940 photo. The Axis military alliance between their two nations enjoyed success during the early years of World War II; however, by May 1945 both leaders were dead and their countries conquered. (National Archives)

and industrialists together, or small farmers and large landowners together, rather than with individuals or class divisions. That new structure of the state was designed to carry Italy into the future, even as it recaptured the glory of ancient Rome. To that end, Mussolini adopted as the party logo an ax bound in wooden rods or *fascia*—the Roman symbol for authority. In 1919, his Italian Fascist Party was founded officially and began its quest for political conquest in Italy.

As Italy slipped deeper into the postwar economic depression, Mussolini's agitation and effective rabble-rousing attracted a large following. His call for strong central authority to restore order was especially well heeded at the polls, and by 1922, that seemingly upstart politician was on the verge of taking control of the government. In October of that year, King Victor Emmanuel III appointed him prime minister in the wake of the fascist coup known as the March on Rome, and Mussolini took command of a large, right-wing coalition. He celebrated his "conquest" with a carefully orchestrated parade in which he led paramilitary fascist cadres known as *squadristi* through the streets of Rome.

Once installed as "Il Duce" (The Leader), Mussolini cracked down on dissent and laid the foundations for an authoritarian state. He also reorganized the economy on a wartime footing, which created badly needed jobs, and began a series of military adventures abroad. In 1935, he launched an attack on the African country of Ethiopia, which he conquered successfully despite an outburst of world condemnation. The following year, he introduced land and air units into the Spanish Civil War in concert with Hitler, another aggressive nationalist whom Mussolini initially disliked and distrusted. Although the ideologies of fascism and Nazism were not exactly identical, the two men saw a need to align themselves against the Western democracies, and in 1936, they signed the Rome-Berlin Axis pact. To placate Hitler, Mussolini also instituted his own brand of anti-Semitism, which was something Italy had been spared thus far. Mussolini anticipated in the event of war that additional conquests and the Caesar-like image that he cultivated would enable him to abolish the Italian monarchy and establish a totalitarian state.

Over the next few years, the conquests of Libya, Ethiopia, and Albania made Italy the dominant Mediterranean power. However, Mussolini's tottering military establishment, beset by poor morale and obsolete equipment, had been stretched to the breaking point. When Hitler began World War II in September 1939, the Italian economy was still feeble and unable to sustain any moves toward world domination. Mussolini realized that weakness and delayed declaring war on France until 1940, after the German conquest of western Europe was nearly complete. For that act, British Prime Minister Winston Churchill branded him "a jackal," as Mussolini appeared to be trying to secure the spoils of war without doing any actual fighting. Italian armies subsequently fared poorly, which underscored the façade of fascist rhetoric. They had to be rescued by Germany from a near disaster in the Balkans in 1941 and also met with embarrassing defeats in North Africa at the hands of the British that same year. Italy sustained further losses through its significant commitment of units to Operation Barbarossa, the German-led invasion of the Soviet Union, in June 1941.

By the middle of 1943, many Italians had had enough of Mussolini. When the Allied invasion of Sicily began in July 1943, both King Victor Emmanuel and the Fascist Grand Council voted to strip Mussolini of his powers, and he was deposed. Mussolini remained under house arrest until that September, when a special German commando operation rescued him. He spent the last days of World War II as the puppet head of a tiny fascist state in northeastern Italy, where his only notable accomplishment was the trial and execution of five council members, including his own son-in-law, who had voted to oust him. When the German defenses finally collapsed, Mussolini and his mistress tried to flee but were caught and executed by Italian partisans on April 28, 1945. Two decades of ideological pretension had finally been shattered, and as a final token of disrespect, Il Duce's body was hung upside down in a public square and interred in an unmarked grave.

JOHN C. FREDRIKSEN

SPANISH CIVIL WAR (1936–1939)

The Spanish Civil War was fought from 1936 to 1939 between the government of the Second Republic and insurgent army officers who wanted to overthrow it. Its ferocity was due in part to the fears and frustrations of recent Spanish history. The extreme

The Spanish Civil War began in 1936 and ended three years later with the triumph of the nationalists under the leadership of General Francisco Franco, who established a fascist regime similar to that of Benito Mussolini in Italy. The conflict was exceptionally brutal and the fighters also drew support from other governments including Mussolini's Italy, Hitler's Germany, and Stalin's Russia. The photo shows Foreign Legion troops fighting at Navalcarnero in 1936. (The Illustrated London News Picture Library)

ideological positions that polarized Spain, however, mirrored those of the rest of Europe in the 1930s. The conflict pitted fascists against an array of leftist forces, presaging the events of World War II as it destroyed Spain.

The army officers who conspired to overthrow the government in 1936 wanted only to unseat the Popular Front that had come to power in recent elections. They did not intend to begin a war. General Emilio Mola, the main strategist, knew that working-class organizations would try to defend the government, but he believed these could be quickly crushed by the army. The insurrection began in the Spanish colony of Morocco and spread quickly throughout many areas of Spain as the German Air Force transported Spanish troops across the Mediterranean. Mola's predictions for a short conflict were proved wrong when workers' confederations joined with loyalist troops (known as Republicans) and police in Madrid, Valencia, and Barcelona to stop the advance of the rebels (known as Nationalists).

Early victories led by workers, however, inspired them to carry out more revolutionary actions, which made it difficult for the republican government to coordinate its defenses. Because the Nationalist army was very well organized, it had the tactical advantage. Another advantage was the assistance of the German Condor Legion, which served as the Nationalist air force, and a steady supply of munitions from Germany and Italy.

The Popular Front government of France was sympathetic to the Spanish republic but provided only minimal assistance. Britain was so dedicated to its policy of nonconfrontation that it organized a Non-Intervention Commission to persuade all European governments to avoid involvement in the Spanish conflict. Germany and Italy ignored this commission. In response to their intervention on the side of the fascist Nationalists, the Soviet Union provided arms to the republic. The democratic and socialist ideals of the republican government aroused such passion during this period, however, that many individuals from the Allied nations ignored their cautious governments and came to fight for the Spanish republic, forming the International Brigades. The Abraham Lincoln Brigade was formed by similarly motivated volunteers from the United States.

After the successful defense of Madrid in 1936, the first great republican victory, Nationalist forces commanded by Francisco Franco headed into the northern part of the country. The difficulty of the terrain made for slow going, and Franco's impatience led to the famous Guernica bombing, the first saturation bombardment of a civilian target in world history.

Although the government of the republic worked to unify its forces under a centralized command increasingly controlled by communists, it was ultimately defeated by the fascist Nationalists in the most decisive and traumatic event in modern Spanish history.

ABC-CLIO

DOCUMENT: MUSSOLINI'S DEFINITION OF FASCISM (1932)

The leader of Italian fascism, Benito Mussolini, wrote a definition of fascism, an excerpt of which appears here, for an Italian encyclopedia in 1932. Along with Germany's fascist leader Adolf Hitler, Mussolini emerged as one of the most fierce dictators in the world during the 1930s and led Italy through the early years of World War II, when the country was allied with Nazi Germany.

Fascism, the more it considers and observes the future and the development of humanity quite apart from political considerations of the moment, believes neither in the possibility nor the utility of perpetual peace. It thus repudiates the doctrine of Pacifism—born of a renunciation of the struggle and an act of cowardice in the face of sacrifice. War alone brings up to its highest tension all human energy and puts the stamp of nobility upon the peoples who have courage to meet it. All other trials are substitutes, which never really put men into the position where they have to make the great decision—the alternative of life or death. . . .

The Fascist accepts life and loves it, knowing nothing of and despising suicide: he rather conceives of life as duty and struggle and conquest, but above all for others—those who are at hand and those who are far distant, contemporaries, and those who will come after. . . .

Fascism [is] the complete opposite of . . . Marxian Socialism, the materialist conception that the history of human civilization can be explained simply through the conflict of interests among the various social groups and by the change and development in the means and instruments of production. . . . Fascism, now and always, believes in holiness and in heroism; that is to say, in actions influenced by no economic motive, direct or indirect. And if the economic conception of history be denied, according to which theory men are no more than puppets, carried to and fro by the waves of chance, while the real directing forces are quite out of their control, it follows that the existence of an unchangeable and unchanging class-war is also denied—the natural progeny of the economic conception of history. And above all Fascism denies that class-war can be the preponderant force in the transformation of society. . . .

After Socialism, Fascism combats the whole complex system of democratic ideology, and repudiates it, whether in its theoretical premises or in its practical application. Fascism denies that the majority, by the simple fact that it is a majority, can direct human society; it denies that numbers alone can govern by means of a periodical consultation, and it affirms the immutable, beneficial, and fruitful inequality of mankind, which can never be permanently leveled through the mere operation of a mechanical process such as universal suffrage. . . .

Fascism denies, in democracy, the absur[d] conventional untruth of political equality dressed out in the garb of collective irresponsibility, and the myth of "happiness" and indefinite progress. . . .

Given that the nineteenth century was the century of Socialism, of Liberalism, and of Democracy, it does not necessarily follow that the twentieth century must also be a century of Socialism, Liberalism and Democracy: political doctrines pass, but humanity remains, and it may rather be expected that this will be a century of authority . . . a century of Fascism. For if the nineteenth century was a century of individualism it may be expected that this will be the century of collectivism and hence the century of the State. . . .

The foundation of Fascism is the conception of the State, its character, its duty, and its aim. Fascism conceives of the State as an absolute, in comparison with which all individuals or groups are relative, only to be conceived of in their relation to the State. The conception of the Liberal State is not that of a directing force, guiding the play and development, both material and spiritual, of a collective body, but merely a force limited to the function of recording results: on the other hand, the Fascist State is itself conscious and has itself a will and a personality—thus it may be called the "ethic" State. . . .

The Fascist State organizes the nation, but leaves a sufficient margin of liberty to the individual; the latter is deprived of all useless and possibly harmful freedom, but retains what is essential; the deciding power in this question cannot be the individual, but the State alone. . . .

For Fascism, the growth of empire, that is to say the expansion of the nation, is an essential manifestation of vitality, and its opposite a sign of decadence. Peoples which are rising, or rising again after a period of decadence, are always imperialist; and renunciation is a sign of decay and of death. Fascism is the doctrine best adapted to represent the tendencies and the aspirations of a people, like the people of Italy, who are rising again after many centuries of abasement and foreign servitude. But empire demands discipline, the coordination of all forces and a deeply felt sense of duty and sacrifice: this fact explains many aspects of the practical working of the regime, the character of many forces in the State, and the necessarily severe measures which must be taken against those who would oppose this spontaneous and inevitable movement of Italy in the twentieth century, and would oppose it by recalling the outworn ideology of the nineteenth century—repudiated whereseever there has been the courage to undertake great experiments of social and political transformation; for never before has the nation stood more in need of authority, of direction and order. If every age has its own characteristic doctrine, there are a thousand signs which point to Fascism as the characteristic doctrine of our time. For if a doctrine must be a living thing, this is proved by the fact that Fascism has created a living faith; and that this faith is very powerful in the minds of men is demonstrated by those who have suffered and died for it.

DOCUMENT: MUNICH PACT (1938)

On September 29, 1938, the leaders of Germany, Italy, France, and Great Britain signed this agreement while attending a conference in Munich, Germany, called to decide the fate of Czechoslovakia. Essentially, it granted German dictator Adolf Hitler a large section of Czechoslovakia known as the Sudetenland, which he insisted was ethnically German anyway and therefore rightly belonged to the German nation. Although the British and French leaders declared that the agreement had preserved the fragile peace of Europe for their generation, many condemned the Munich Pact as the height of appeasement policy in the years leading up to World War II. A few months later, Hitler seized all of Czechoslovakia.

Germany, the United Kingdom, France and Italy, taking into consideration the agreement, which has been already reached in principle for the cession to Germany of the Sudeten German territory, have agreed on the following terms and conditions governing the said cession and the measures consequent thereon, and by this agreement they each hold themselves responsible for the steps necessary to secure its fulfillment:

1. The evacuation will begin on 1st October.

2. The United Kingdom, France and Italy agree that the evacuation of the territory shall be completed by the 10th October, without any existing installations having been destroyed, and that the Czechoslovak Government will be held responsible for carrying out the evacuation without damage to the said installations.

3. The conditions governing the evacuation will be laid down in detail by an international commission composed of representatives of Germany, the United Kingdom, France, Italy and Czechoslovakia.

4. The occupation by stages of the predominantly German territory by German troops will begin on 1st October. The four territories marked on the attached map will be occupied by German troops in the following order: The territory marked No. I on the 1st and 2nd of October; the territory marked No. II on the 2nd and 3rd of October; the

territory marked No. III on the 3rd, 4th and 5th of October; the territory marked No. IV on the 6th and 7th of October. The remaining territory of preponderantly German character will be ascertained by the aforesaid international commission forthwith and be occupied by German troops by the 10th of October.

5. The international commission referred to in paragraph 3 will determine the territories in which a plebiscite is to be held. These territories will be occupied by international bodies until the plebiscite has been completed. The same commission will fix the conditions in which the plebiscite is to be held, taking as a basis the conditions of the Saar plebiscite. The commission will also fix a date, not later than the end of November, on which the plebiscite will be held.

6. The final determination of the frontiers will be carried out by the international commission. The commission will also be entitled to recommend to the four Powers, Germany, the United Kingdom, France and Italy, in certain exceptional cases, minor modifications in the strictly ethnographical determination of the zones which are to be transferred without plebiscite.

7. There will be a right of option into and out of the transferred territories, the option to be exercised within six months from the date of this agreement. A German-Czechoslovak commission shall determine the details of the option, consider ways of facilitating the transfer of population and settle questions of principle arising out of the said transfer.

8. The Czechoslovak Government will within a period of four weeks from the date of this agreement release from their military and police forces any Sudeten Germans who may wish to be released, and the Czechoslovak Government will within the same period release Sudeten German prisoners who are serving terms of imprisonment for political offences.

Annex to the Agreement:

His Majesty's Government in the United Kingdom and the French Government have entered into the above agreement on the basis that they stand by the offer, contained in paragraph 6 of the Anglo-French proposals of the 19th September, relating to an international guarantee of the new boundaries of the Czechoslovak State against unprovoked aggression.

When the question of the Polish and Hungarian minorities in Czechoslovakia has been settled, Germany and Italy for their part will give a guarantee to Czechoslovakia.

Declaration:

The heads of the Governments of the four Powers declare that the problems of the Polish and Hungarian minorities in Czechoslovakia, if not settled within three months by agreement between the respective Governments, shall form the subject of another meeting of the Heads of the Governments of the four Powers here present.

Supplementary Declaration:

All questions which may arise out of the transfer of the territory shall be considered as coming within the terms of reference to the International Commission.

Composition of the International Commission:

The four Heads of Governments here present agree that the international commission provided for in the agreement signed by them to-day shall consist of the Secretary of State in the German Foreign Office, the British, French and Italian Ambassadors accredited in Berlin, and a representative to be nominated by the Government of Czechoslovakia.

Munich, September 29, 1938.

Adolf Hitler
Neville Chamberlain
Edouard Daladier
Benito Mussolini

5

The Great Depression, 1929–c. 1939

INTRODUCTION

An economic depression is a period of substantially decreased business activity usually accompanied by high unemployment, falling wages, and declining prices. Although depressions are historically not an uncommon occurrence (there were major depressions in 1873–1878 and 1893–1897), the one that began in 1929 was so severe, long-lasting, and global in nature that it earned the name the Great Depression.

After the debilitating economic upheaval caused by World War I, the world warmly welcomed the return of prosperity in the early 1920s. However, the glow of prosperity, which lasted until 1929, masked some significant economic problems. For a start, not all the world shared in this prosperity. During the 1920s, global agriculture underwent a profound crisis. Encouraged by increased demand during World War I, when much of Europe's agricultural capacity was in limbo, farmers in such countries as the United States, Canada, Argentina, and Australia had gone deeply into debt to expand their operations. It is estimated that during the war, 33 million new acres were put under plow. With the war's end and the resumption of normal agricultural activity in Europe, demand slumped and production grew. Above average global harvests from 1925 to 1928 aggravated the resultant overproduction. By the late 1920s, debt-ridden farmers everywhere were going bankrupt, agrarian purchasing power had virtually disappeared, the world agricultural price index, which registered 226 in 1919, now stood at 134, and the price of a bushel of wheat in terms of gold was the lowest it had been in 400 years.

Furthermore, the prosperity of the late 1920s clearly rested on the export of U.S. capital and the strength of U.S. import markets. Europe was especially dependent on the United States. Beginning in 1924, a huge infusion of U.S. capital jump-started the German economy, the improvement of which subsequently sparked a general European economic upturn. Nevertheless, even before 1929, the European economy showed signs of weakening as U.S. investors shifted their resources from Europe back to the United States to take advantage of the unprecedented boom in the American stock market. However, the stock market surge was not a permanent one and, in fact, it ended abruptly. On Thursday, October 24, 1929, the U.S. stock market collapsed, setting off a spectacular panic that ultimately brought about the Great Depression.

By the end of November 1929, the average share of stock had lost 40 percent of its precrash value; over the next few years the average share would lose another 40 percent of its value. Between 1929 and 1932, the Dow Jones Industrial Average plunged from a high of 381 to a low of 41. Five thousand American banks were forced to close.

Shaken by the stock market's collapse, U.S. investors who had overextended themselves now called in their loans and liquidated their investments. Germany, more dependent on American capital than any other country, suffered accordingly. As the German economy slowed to a standstill, the rest of Europe, itself heavily dependent on German reparations payments from World War I and closely integrated with the German economy as a whole, started to grind to a halt. Furthermore, as the downturn in the United States spread to the industrial sector of the economy, American markets—which the rest of the world had relied on for the export of their goods—began to dry up. The 1930 Smoot-Hawley Tariff, which raised already high protective duties on imported goods, aggravated matters by making U.S. markets even less accessible. Unemployment rose dramatically. In this fashion, the collapse of the U.S. stock market created a ripple effect that swept over the world economy with devastating consequences.

The crisis deepened perceptibly when the most important bank in Vienna, the Credit-Anstalt, collapsed on May 11, 1931. The failure of the Credit-Anstalt caused a major financial panic. Worried investors withdrew funds from banks everywhere and moved them about in a desperate attempt to find a haven for their wealth. Numerous banks simply failed, leaving depositors in the lurch. The world banking system teetered on the brink of collapse.

Many investors made their way to London, where they sought to exchange pounds sterling for gold. This "flight from the pound" reached gigantic proportions, and on September 19, 1931, it forced the British government to abandon the gold standard. Henceforth, the Bank of England would no longer sell gold for pounds. This decision, which spelled the end of the post–World War I attempt to recreate an international banking system based on gold, brought chaos to international trade and further intensified the Depression.

The worst of the Depression came in 1932. It is estimated that world production declined by 38 percent between 1929 and 1932 and that world trade dropped by more than 66 percent. Reported global unemployment reached 30 million, and millions of others, especially in the non-Western world, worked only sporadically. With so many people unemployed or underemployed, demand plummeted, causing additional layoffs and business closings. A vicious downward economic spiral gripped the globe.

Quite naturally, the universal misery spawned by the Great Depression sparked calls for action. However, most governments refused to implement radical policies and confined themselves to modest relief measures designed to alleviate human suffering. The principle of classical, or liberal, economics dictated this essentially passive response. According to classical economic theory, which prevailed at that time, business activity is cyclical. Periods of prosperity will inevitably be followed by slumps, which in turn will inevitably be followed by periods of prosperity. When slumps come, as they must, the government response should be to refrain from action and wait for the business cycle to run its course. If governments wish to speed up the cycle, they should adopt deflationary measures such as balanced budgets and reduced governmental expenditures to restore business confidence more rapidly. Although these steps may hurt some people, the pain will be temporary. Once business confidence is restored, investment and economic expansion will resume, unemployment will decline, demand will increase, and prosperity will return.

Even though the ideas of classical economics dominated conventional wisdom at the time, the cataclysmic nature of the Great Depression motivated others to seek different solutions. A handful of socialists turned for inspiration to the Soviet Union, where Karl Marx's dictum about the collective ownership of the means of production was being implemented and Joseph Stalin was introducing his planned economy. However, most people recoiled from the Soviet model because it was too radical.

The concept of corporatism, which predated the Great Depression, found some enthusiastic adherents, especially in the business community. Under corporatism, each branch of a nation's economy would be organized into corporations resembling cartels or trusts. The corporations would be dominated by business leaders with, perhaps, representatives of the government and labor sitting in. These units would then regulate and manage the economy to the presumed benefit of all. Among other things, the corporations would set prices, control wages, and determine production and distribution.

The British economist John Maynard Keynes offered a different solution. For Keynes, the fundamental cause of the Great Depression was inadequate demand rather than excessive supply. Deflationary steps only aggravated the problem. In his 1936 book, *General Theory of Employment, Interest, and Money,* Keynes advised governments to step in and stimulate the economy by increasing the money supply, undertaking public works, and redistributing income through tax policy. He argued that government intervention designed to put the unemployed back to work and to put more money in the pockets of more people would bring increased demand and a general revival of economic activity. This would be a much-desired result, even if it required the government to run a deficit rather than balance its budget. Although Keynes's ideas would become popular after World War II, during the Depression most governments followed the dictates of classical economics.

Typical of the commitment to classical economics were the actions of successive British governments. The Labour Party, led by Prime Minister Ramsay MacDonald, held power when the Depression began. After tepid and unsuccessful attempts to stimulate the economy, MacDonald's wing of the Labour Party broke away in 1931 and formed a coalition government with the Conservatives under Stanley Baldwin. Dominated by the Conservatives, the so-called National Government initiated deflationary policies. Government expenditures were reduced, welfare payments were cut, protectionist tariffs were introduced, and business leaders were left to their own devices. The results were disappointing. Great Britain, which had never really shared in the prosperity of the 1920s, recovered from the Depression only gradually, if at all. Unemployment, which stood at 1.2 million in 1929, soared to 2.7 million (or 22 percent of the work force) in 1932, and remained above 2 million until 1936. In 1938, the unemployment figure was 1.8 million.

The Great Depression arrived in France later and less suddenly than in other countries. As late as 1930, France continued to exceed its pre–World War I industrial production level by at least 40 percent. However, when the slump hit, it lasted longer in France than elsewhere. By 1938, recovery was nowhere in sight. Industrial production remained below 1930 and 1931 figures, and unemployment stood at historically high levels. Reacting to the economic downturn, a series of unstable coalition governments applied deflationary measures, including a reduction of civil servants' salaries. French governments vigorously resisted any proposals to stimulate the economy. In 1936, a coalition socialist government under the leadership of Léon Blum attempted to reinflate the French economy. The Blum experiment was short-lived, due in part to French conservatives' implacable hostility to any program devised by socialists.

In the United States, the Great Depression took a heavy toll. By 1932, U.S. industrial production was just barely half of what it had been in 1929, more than 12 million Americans were unemployed, and national income had dropped by more than 50 percent. President Herbert Hoover refused to depart significantly from traditional classical economic doctrine and consequently was defeated in the election of 1932. Although the new president, Franklin D. Roosevelt, had run on the promise of further deflationary policies, once in office he instituted a number of measures designed to reinflate the American economy. In this manner, Roosevelt's New Deal somewhat resembled Keynes's ideas. However, despite this flurry of government activity and Roosevelt's immense personal popularity, the U.S. economy remained in the doldrums. Although national income rose dramatically from its low point in 1932, by 1938 it still fell short of the 1929 level.

The Great Depression in Germany not only wrecked that country's economy, it also destroyed Germany's fragile republic and cleared the way for the Nazi dictatorship. Devastated by the loss of American capital in the wake of the stock market crash, Germany experienced a precipitous economic slide that by 1932 resulted in more than 6 million unemployed (about 35 percent of the workforce) and a decrease in industrial production of about 50 percent. After the collapse of the ruling socialist government in 1930, a shaky conservative coalition under the leadership of Heinrich Brüning governed Germany. Following classical economic precepts, the Brüning government strove to balance the budget by reducing state expenditures, cutting wages, and slashing unemployment benefits. This course of action simply exacerbated an impossible situation, increasing economic misery for millions of Germans and causing the electorate to seek solace in the political extremes.

A major beneficiary of this misguided policy was Adolf Hitler, who came to power on January 30, 1933, and quickly turned Germany into a Nazi dictatorship. Following the advice of financial wizard Hjalmar Schacht, the Nazi state actively intervened in Germany's economic life. It made huge investments in public works, especially road building and arms production. This policy, combined with strong government controls over both business and labor, and a determination to achieve autarky, or economic self-sufficiency, helped to pull Germany out of the Depression. By 1936, German unemployment had dropped markedly, and a miraculous economic recovery appeared to be under way. By 1938, Germany's economy was booming, and German purchasing power had regained its 1929 level.

It is hard to gauge the effects of the Great Depression in Italy because that country's economy was—even by 1929—not fully developed. As a result, unemployment levels and the amount that national income decreased are difficult to determine. Furthermore, Benito Mussolini's fascist dictatorship set up a smoke screen of propaganda about its grandiose development projects to obscure the effects of the Depression. Nevertheless, there can be no doubt that Italy suffered an economic decline.

In response to the Great Depression, Mussolini's regime, which had already experimented with corporatism, developed its version of that concept more fully. In practice this meant turning essential control of the country's economy over to the Italian business community, although the government intervened when necessary to bail out enterprises that appeared ready to go bankrupt. As a consequence, the Italian government sometimes found itself owning a controlling interest in a business or industry. Nevertheless, the government usually left decision making for those industries in the hands of the industrialists, preferring the support of the Italian business community to the exercise of absolute power over the Italian economy.

The course of the Great Depression varied from country to country. By 1938, some countries had virtually recovered their economic vitality, whereas others continued to lag behind or languished in economic disarray. Nevertheless, as important as the Great Depression was, the outbreak of World War II was about to overshadow it.

INTERPRETIVE ESSAY

LOWELL J. SATRE

The Great Depression is historically overshadowed by other traumatic events of the twentieth century, particularly the two World Wars and the savage brutality of the Nazi and Stalinist regimes. The Great Depression itself, however, proved to be the longest sustained economic depression of the modern world and helped to create feelings of utter despair that destroyed what appeared to be the orderly and prosperous world of the late 1920s. Indeed, the collapse of the industrialized economies of the Western world not only led to long-term mass unemployment but also transformed social relationships, destroyed established governments, brought the Nazis to power, and helped to cause international diplomatic complications that led to World War II. Moreover, the impact of the Great Depression was truly worldwide, as the peoples of the non-European world also found their economies and societies transformed.

By the 1920s, the United States had become the dominant economic force in the world. American manufactured goods, along with coal and oil, serviced much of the world, and U.S. loans to Europe helped to restore a modicum of material and political stability to an area still recovering from the ravages of the Great War. Just as the world prospered with the United States, so it also suffered as the U.S. economy plunged into its greatest crisis. Although the crisis began dramatically with the New York stock market crash of October 1929, the economies of the United States and European nations had begun slowing down earlier. Prices of agricultural products had collapsed, and wages for large numbers of the labor force, so important as consumers of manufactured goods, were exceptionally low.

The Great Depression was effectively two interrelated problems: a financial crisis with international consequences and a downturn in production that caused massive unemployment and accompanying social and political problems. Governments generally focused initially on overcoming the financial crisis; unfortunately, steps taken to deal with that crisis all too often created even greater unemployment.

The collapse of stock prices in the United States forced American banks, which had overinvested in the heady atmosphere of the stock market bonanza of the late 1920s, to raise money to cover their investments, which were often only partially paid for. Banks refused to extend short-term loans as they became due. Banking houses in Germany and Austria were especially harmed, because they had been major recipients of American loans. This massive movement of dollars and gold from Europe to the United States, which had commenced in the 1920s as investors were attracted by the promise of high or quick financial gain in the U.S. stock market, would continue well into the 1930s. In fact, U.S. prosperity in the 1920s created international economic problems. The United States, with its massive production base, imported relatively few finished goods and maintained a healthy balance of payments. Other nations, because they were unable to sell goods to the United States, were also unable to purchase U.S. goods. A shortage of capital in Europe in turn curtailed capital investment in manufacturing facilities, which led to the laying off of workers.

The financial crisis peaked in 1931. Credit-Anstalt, the largest Vienna bank and a major holder of foreign funds, went broke in May. This failure precipitated a crisis of confidence in German banks. President Herbert Hoover's call for a moratorium on the payment of war debts and reparations failed to stop the hemorrhaging of funds. Investors, looking for security, turned to the British pound sterling, which in turn came under pressure. The culminating event occurred on September 19, 1931, when the British government announced that it was pulling the pound from the gold standard. Britain's Commonwealth associates followed Britain off the gold standard, as did several other European nations. The United States followed suit in 1933. The international exchange mechanism, so painfully rebuilt following World War I, had effectively ceased to exist.

While the financial and stock markets were collapsing, consumption of goods fell off, manufacturing dramatically slowed down, and unemployment mounted. By 1932, unemployment in Europe, excluding the Soviet Union, amounted to 15 million, with 6 million in Germany alone. How did the governments react? All of them, to a greater or lesser degree, took steps to cope with the economic crisis. Ultimately, government intervention in the economy became a significant hallmark of the Great Depression.

Compared with many other European nations, Britain's relatively weak economy of the 1920s meant that it did not suffer from overproduction. British banks and stock exchanges were not as severely affected, and although unemployment was high in older industries such as coal, cotton textiles, and shipbuilding, newer industries were relatively healthy, as was home construction. Britain shed its free trade policy and instituted protective tariffs in 1931. Orthodox financial responses called for curtailing government spending as revenue decreased; as a result, relief payments were reduced. Despite the suffering of the unemployed, extremist political ideologies gained relatively little support in Britain.

The Scandinavian countries were more successful than other nations at dealing with the Depression. Although these northern states suffered high unemployment because their economies were tied to foreign trade, reformist Social Democratic parties took steps to alleviate the problems and to direct the economy toward recovery. The Swedish government, unlike other European governments, increased expenditures via deficit spending to encourage economic recovery. The government also aided in the expansion of consumer and production cooperatives, expanded social services, and early on provided relief work for the unemployed and developed an extensive public works program.

France, which did not significantly feel the effects of the Depression until 1932, was ultimately one of the hardest hit. Until 1936, the French government, rent by political divisions, remained wedded to orthodox economic policy and did not attempt to aid the economy with government spending. In 1936, Léon Blum led a left-of-center coalition, the Popular Front, in a New Deal–style program providing for wage increases, labor union recognition for collective bargaining, a 40-hour workweek and paid vacation, increased public spending, and devaluation of the franc, making French products more competitive in the world market. Blum's government, however, lasted but a short time, and the politically and socially divided nation had not recovered from the ravages of the Depression when World War II erupted in 1939.

In Germany, the conservative governments of the Weimar Republic bowed to the enormous pressure of the industrialists and large landowning interests to curtail government spending, especially on social measures, and to reduce the taxes on employers and increase them on laborers. When the Reichstag refused to approve this program, the government resorted to emergency executive powers and ruled by decree. Government policy only worsened the Depression, and the inability of the government to deal meaningfully with the crisis was a key ingredient in Adolf Hitler's attaining power in January 1933.

Hitler's government wielded more control over the economy than that of any other European nation except the Soviet Union. On the whole, Hitler did not curtail the power of large companies, and businesses remained under private ownership; a hybrid system of planning was imposed on a capitalist economic structure. Hitler's initial program called for large public works projects to provide relief for the huge numbers of unemployed. In November 1934, the government oriented the economy to rearmament and military preparation. This was paid for by increased taxes and deficit spending and by restricting private investment in the manufacture of consumer goods. The policy brought a quick end to unemployment.

Benito Mussolini's fascist Italian government attempted to direct the economy through corporations of employers and workers, but in fact real power was increasingly concentrated in the hands of industrialists and Fascist Party officials. The government did come to the rescue of several basic industries by investing in them, thus bringing about limited government ownership.

The government of the Soviet Union exercised the greatest control over any one nation's economy; this had begun before the onset of the Depression with the massive movement for the collectivization of agriculture and the forced development of a huge industrial base. Although the Soviet Union could satisfy most of its own needs internally, it continued to trade with the noncommunist world throughout the 1930s, exporting grain—despite a shortage of it in the nation and a deliberately planned famine that took the lives of millions—at a greater rate than at any time since the 1917 Russian Revolution to procure goods needed for manufacturing.

Nations of eastern Europe, already struggling for survival, were particularly hard hit by the Great Depression. These nations had recently emerged from the ruins of World War I and the disintegration of the Habsburg, Romanov, and Ottoman Empires. The new nations were saddled with long-standing nationality conflicts while struggling to develop their political institutions and their economies, which generally lacked diversity or natural resources. With some exceptions, these nations exported agricultural products or raw materials. Unfortunately, the price on the world market for foodstuffs and raw materials had dropped more than 50 percent by 1938. Many of these nations were unable to generate the funds needed to import manufactured articles or to repay international loans contracted in the 1920s, not only because of the price collapse of their chief export items, also because neighboring trading partners had taken steps to protect their own agricultural interests, as in the case of Germany's powerful Prussian landholding Junkers.

Even before Hitler's rise to power, however, some Germans had advocated economic integration and cooperation between Germany and nations in the Danube River basin. But these economies were not sufficiently complementary to make economic union a reality, because all had a strong agricultural component. The German state, under the Nazi regime, did successfully negotiate goods-exchange agreements with these nations. Most of the foreign trade of Bulgaria, Turkey, Yugoslavia, and Hungary was with Germany, making them economically dependent on their more powerful neighbor.

In addition, east-central European nations faced major domestic economic and social crises. Both large and small landholding farmers were destroyed; peasants were unable to purchase manufactured goods. Members of the middle class and civil servants were thrown out of work. Anti-Semitism, long present in the area, intensified as people sought an explanation for their collapsed material world and focused on those from whom they held loans—often Jews. Nationalities, artificially merged after the war in states such as Yugoslavia and Czechoslovakia, blamed each other for the crisis. Home-bred right-wing political movements, loosely patterned after the Fascist and Nazi parties, emerged.

Although the impact of the Great Depression on politics and financial policy is relatively easy to follow, the tremendous upheaval the prolonged economic crisis caused in society is less easy to measure. Millions became unemployed and found their standard of living greatly reduced; as a result, many suffered acute physical and social problems. Family employment patterns altered, as women and occasionally young adults replaced the elder male as the chief breadwinner. Class hatred was often exacerbated, as those at the bottom of the economic ladder despised the wealthy, who, despite their own occasionally reduced incomes, continued to enjoy an exceptionally comfortable material life.

In Germany, as in many other countries, young people completing school were faced with little or no chance of employment. These German students were often supporters of National Socialism, which attracted them by its promises of dynamic change and by criticism of the prevailing economic order. Yet one must not assume that despair was all-encompassing. In Great Britain, for example, great numbers of people continued to enjoy leisure activities such as the incredibly popular cinema halls or other venues to which they could drive their automobiles. Disillusionment with the breakdown of normal or anticipated lifestyles was especially noticeable in the literature of the period, in which writers graphically questioned and criticized the prevailing social order and political structure, and called for a more just society. In Great Britain, George Orwell in particular expressed this despair in several works, including *The Road to Wigan Pier* (1937), in which he examined the desperate plight of the English coal miners. Walter Greenwood, in his novel *Love on the Dole* (1933), followed the trials of the young in England's industrial north, who were unable to find meaningful employment and all too often attached themselves to the corrupt elements in society to gain social recognition or economic support. A similar German novel, Hans Fallada's *Little Man, What Now?* (1933), portrayed a young married couple and their baby struggling to survive in the vicious atmosphere of Berlin in the early 1930s.

The fiscal crisis caused by the Great Depression initiated a series of international meetings to attempt to solve the monetary problems facing the United States and Europe. The matter was particularly complex because it involved not only economic issues but also very sensitive political considerations. World War I had left in its wake the complicated issue of war debts and reparations. Germany, deemed the primary guilty party in the war, was required to make substantial payments toward the rebuilding of war-ravaged Europe, particularly to France and Belgium, the scene of much fighting on the Western Front. At the same time, the victorious nations were expected to repay their loans to the United States, from which they had borrowed heavily during the war. The Dawes Plan of 1924 had established a workable reparations plan for Germany, aided by substantial loans from the United States. The Young Plan made further modifications in 1929. French and British debt repayment to the United States depended at least partially on the receipt of reparations payments from Germany. The Great Depression curtailed loans from the United States to Europe and put these repayment schemes in jeopardy. European nations approved President Herbert Hoover's call for a one-year moratorium on payments of war debts and other international obligations on July 6, 1931, but it was too late to stem the German financial crisis. In June 1932, a conference in Lausanne, Switzerland, effectively ended war debt payments almost by default.

While governments met to attempt to solve some aspects of the Great Depression, they individually took steps that ultimately hindered economic recovery. Economic nationalism was a common response to mounting unemployment and sagging sales. The already high U.S. tariffs were significantly raised in 1930 with the passage of the Smoot-Hawley Tariff Act. This in turn led to a series of retaliatory tariffs by other nations. One of the problems with the Smoot-Hawley Tariff, in addition to its direct economic impact, was that it gave the impression that the United States was providing no leadership in the crisis. The World Economic Conference held in London in 1933 failed to resolve the gold currency issue or to reduce tariffs, partly because of steps taken by Franklin D. Roosevelt, recently elected president of the United States.

This conference marked the last major collective attempt to solve the problems of the Great Depression; thereafter economic nationalism was in the forefront. Although the Great Depression was not the only factor in bringing Hitler to power, it was certainly a key ingredient. With Hitler in power, the diplomatic affairs of Europe were dramatically altered and Europe drifted toward World War II. Preoccupation with Depression-induced economic or fiscal problems detracted from England and France's willingness to concentrate on the dangers of aggressive nations such as Germany or Japan. Great Britain, for example, was struggling politically over its budget and the gold standard when Japan invaded Manchuria in September 1931. France's fractured economy caused turmoil in its political life, resulting in a series of weak governments when Hitler illegally remilitarized the Rhineland in March 1936.

The Great Depression caused a crisis in politics, especially in east-central Europe, where governments still recovering from the terrible disruptions of the Great War were unable to solve the economic crisis. International cooperation, long preached as a means of resolving issues, had failed. These nations not only turned toward their own internal resources but also began arming themselves in an attempt to solve the crisis by aggressive international action. Ironically, preparation for war through the expansion of military forces and the manufacturing of weapons was to a great extent responsible for significantly reducing unemployment and pulling nations, including Germany, Britain, and the United States, out of the Depression.

The impact of the Great Depression on the world outside of the United States and Europe varied rather considerably. Generally, those areas with close economic ties to the Western trading nations found that their international trade collapsed, whereas countries with peasant-based or subsistence-level economies were less affected. One key factor in the response of the various countries to the Depression was their own political power; colonies had no choice but to follow the dictates of their mother country, whereas independent nations had a greater possibility of shaping their own economy.

Most primary producing countries—that is, those producing basic agricultural goods such as rice, coffee, sugar, and cotton, and raw materials such as minerals, ores, and rubber, all normally important trading items—were very adversely affected by the Depression. In fact, many of these producers faced major economic problems in the 1920s, long before the onset of the Great Depression. A. J. H. Latham, in *The Depression and the Developing World* (1981), argues that developing countries helped cause the Depression by expanding production of basic goods, especially foodstuffs, during the 1920s. An overabundance of grains from Canada, the United States, Australia, and Argentina, combined with a restored European agricultural base, coincided with overproduction in the East, especially in the rice culture of Asia. These surpluses dramatically depressed agricultural prices worldwide, which remained low throughout much of the 1930s. Economic recovery throughout the world was slow partly because the income of farmers, who were a very large portion of the spending public, remained low.

Primary producing countries found their economies hurt in several ways. Income from exports dropped dramatically, but the cost of imports, although also declining, remained relatively high. Because nations could not afford to continue importing these goods—often manufactured—they either went without or began producing them themselves. But these countries were also affected by the startling drop in foreign investment, especially by the largest investors, the United States and Great Britain. New foreign investment by the United States declined from $1.15 billion in 1929 to $2.4 million in 1937, and British foreign investment for the same period fell from $720 million to $96.4 million. As examples, United States investment in Asia and Oceania plummeted from $137 million in 1928 to nil in 1932; that in Latin America dropped from $331 million to nil for the same period.

Chile and Brazil were two Latin American nations with economies that shifted from commodities toward industrial goods. Chile's cotton fabric production increased more than fivefold between 1929 and 1937, providing for 50 percent of the domestic market by the latter year. In Brazil, production of steel and cement showed large increases. As a result, neither nation was as dependent on its primary commodities, coffee for Brazil and nitrates for Chile. Latin American governments—playing a growing role in directing the economy and in the process transforming society—took various steps to develop domestic manufacturing. Argentina and Brazil had both begun industrialization during World War I when they were unable to purchase manufactured goods from foreign sources. These nations, often imposing protective tariffs in the 1930s, were thus able to expand on a manufacturing base that had been established earlier. Politics in many of these nations, and specifically in Argentina and Brazil, followed a worldwide trend toward more authoritarian governments. Despite a more diversified economy, life for the poor in Latin America remained extremely difficult.

Latin American nations, as a whole, probably took more decisive steps than any other group of countries to reorient their economies. But some other countries showed similar moves, including Egypt, which suffered initially from a sharp drop in the price of exported raw cotton. Employment in manufacturing increased 66 percent between 1927 and 1937, and production mushroomed in many sectors, including cement, petroleum goods, and especially mechanically woven cloth.

The shift from a rural to an urban economy could be seen in parts of India, as in the southern area of Madras, with implications for the social order. Peasants there traditionally borrowed money from the large landowners, who not only had the financial resources but also could hold grain off the market until prices rose. The seemingly permanent drop in the price of grain was hard not only on the peasants but also on the large landowners, who could not sustain the traditional loans and often found themselves in bankruptcy. Members of some landholding families, to survive, had to find work outside the traditional family occupation. When some landowners/creditors attempted to manipulate the market to drive up prices, food riots ensued. Peasants also successfully organized against payment of unreasonable rent to the *zamindari*, or estate owners, whose privileged social and economic positions in the community were permanently altered during the Depression.

As southern Madras's agricultural economy deteriorated, its urban economy developed more fully. Those who had financial interests in both rural and urban areas shifted their focus to the latter, partly because industrial prices in India declined less than agricultural prices. In urban areas, capital was increasingly invested in agricultural processing, heavy industries such as electricity and cement, and financial institutions such as banking and insurance. Despite these economic shifts, India's economy and society remained predominantly agricultural. Although it is true that peasant India was far more directly affected by the famine of 1918 than by the Great Depression, the country's overall economic growth was particularly slow throughout the 1930s.

China, like India, had a primarily agricultural economy. Although China's foreign trade, including silk and silk-related products, cotton cloth, tea, tobacco, and handicraft goods, was markedly reduced by the Depression, factories—Chinese or foreign-owned— located on the coast and tied to international markets were the most directly affected. Peasants often responded to the drop in prices for cash crops by returning to the cultivation of more traditional grains. Probably no more than 3 percent of the peasants were involved in export-based commodities; peasants consumed most of their own agricultural products, and those marketed were sold locally. A case can be made that the Chinese economy was not adversely affected by the Great Depression. Although poverty, even famine, occurred in some provinces, these were a part of the normal Chinese economy and resulted from natural catastrophes as well as banditry and the rule of warlords. In 1931, for example, the great Yangtze flood took as many as two million lives and left a trail of destruction and disease in its wake. One historian estimates that China's economy, both agricultural and manufacturing, continued to expand throughout the period, even excluding development in Manchuria. A primary cause of this was that China's huge domestic market dictated the direction and production of the economy. External trade, which did decline, was a small and relatively unimportant part of the economy.

Japan suffered more initially from the Depression than most nations. Farmers were hardest hit because the already weak international markets for raw silk and rice collapsed. Unemployment in Japan's export-oriented manufacturing sector skyrocketed, as companies cut back sharply on production. The initial government reaction to the Depression was to do nothing and wait for the economy to right itself. Government inaction and growing distress led to social unrest and violence, including the assassination of the prime minister.

Yet Japan was the first nation to recover from the Depression, and government policy was to a great extent responsible. Under Finance Minister Takahashi Korekiyo, Japan undertook an aggressive investment plan to increase demand. While spending on the military expanded, even more important to recovery were the public works relief programs for rural areas, in which farmers switched from working in silk production to growing wheat and potatoes. Certain home industries were protected by tariffs, and incentives and subsidies were provided for industries such as shipbuilding and automobiles, all aided by a devalued yen. Industry became even more efficient by reducing already low labor costs and by developing better machines. The *zaibatsu,* or financial combines, which had sufficient capital to survive the Depression, especially benefited from government policy. By 1931, recovery was under way in Japan.

Despite Japan's early economic recovery, the Depression played an important role in the antidemocratic, authoritarian military gaining control over the government. Japanese politics during the 1920s had been a contest between civilian political parties and military leaders. After 1929, this balance tilted decisively to the military elite and helped lead to policies that culminated in World War II. Blame for Japan's economic ills fell especially on the political parties and the bureaucracy that had sought prosperity through cooperation and trade with other nations. Some military leaders believed that the military could better deal with economic problems, especially in view of the tariff barriers raised by other nations to stem the influx of Japanese goods. It was believed that military expansion and the creation of an empire would help provide the needed raw materials and markets. The success of the Japanese military in Manchuria beginning in 1931 and the open warfare in China after 1937 helped to point Japan in the direction of a military-dominated government. The rise of authoritarian regimes in Germany and Italy, as well as the frustrations and problems associated with the Depression and a weak civilian government, reinforced the movement toward authoritarian government.

The Philippines did not suffer particularly from the Depression, mainly because its sugar-producing sector, which employed about six million workers, enjoyed a protected market in the United States. In contrast to the situation in many other primary producing countries, industrialization did not accelerate in the Philippines during the 1930s. The landholding elite, whose livelihood appeared safeguarded by the guaranteed sugar market in the United States, was not interested in reorienting the economy. Moreover, because the United States controlled the colony, its government did not have the power to institute tariffs that would protect industry from manufactured goods flowing in from the United States and Japan.

Africa was unique in that virtually all of the countries were under the control of various European nations. However, the Union of South Africa, although formally under British rule, was essentially self-governing by this time. Except for the early part of the Depression, South Africa's economy expanded considerably during the 1930s as capital flowed in to help expand the gold-mining industry, which benefited from a substantial rise in the price of gold during the decade. Iron and steel were also produced for the first time in Pretoria, and farming remained viable because of the need to feed the growing urban population. Not all mining in Africa flourished; markets for copper and diamonds, for example, were depressed, and unemployment mounted. Although native labor was needed in the gold mines, especially in South Africa, Southern Rhodesia, and the Gold Coast, wages remained depressed, and few benefits such as education were extended. Not only was there a huge pool of available native labor but colonial governments, working hard to strengthen export-based companies, helped to discipline workers who went on strike over low wages or poor working conditions. Although natives often gained little from the healthy mining industry, skilled whites such as engineers thrived as mining districts bid for their services. The white-black earnings ratio in Northern Rhodesia was about 30 to 1.

Farmers producing goods destined for export, such as coffee, were hard hit by the Depression. Many were European settlers whose monoculture estates were particularly vulnerable. Although the government aided them by reducing taxes and by loans, many could not survive; in Kenya about one in five went bankrupt. Revenues for many African colonies, based on foreign trade, shrank. British colonial governments found themselves increasingly dependent on the natives for their tax base and they maintained taxes on households and individuals as much as possible. In fact, colonial governments such as Kenya's found that native farmers were often more efficient and adaptable than their European settler counterparts. The British colonial governments were expected to balance their budgets, and payments had to be made to overseas creditors who had lent substantial funds for work on infrastructure such as roads in the 1920s. In the case of the Gold Coast, import duties on certain goods were raised, some officials were required to retire early, and spending on public works was slashed. Generally, the British were not effective at providing public works for relief measures. The French government, attempting to develop an economically self-sufficient empire, was more inclined to aid colonies through loans and protective tariffs.

Some colonial-based European companies did very well during the Depression. In West Africa, many small exporting businesses went under, but huge ones such as Unilever, with greater capital bases, were able to thrive because they could cut expenses and buy out weaker competitors. Aided by friendly governments, large companies could also control competition and reduce prices for basic commodities by establishing a commodities pool from which all large purchases would be made.

How did the native Africans respond to the Depression, which so often altered their lives and brought economic deprivation? In certain parts of British West Africa, some Africans took their wealth out of the increasingly insecure land and invested it in education and urban institutions. In French West Africa, peasants drifted to towns, where few opportunities existed, and became part of the urban poor. Workers occasionally attempted to unionize and to strike. Riots in several colonies helped to reduce taxes. In places the Depression also led to the radicalization of native politics, as was the case with the Kikuyu in central Kenya. The Kikuyu proved relatively successful at overcoming the Depression, some becoming shopkeepers and others independent farmers who competed successfully with European settlers. The Kikuyu Central Association protested government and settler activities that discriminated against the indigenous people, aided a series of strikes in the late 1930s, and gained political support outside its own tribe. The economic success and political involvement of the Kikuyu would lead them onto a collision course with the European community in the post–World War II era.

Government leaders were not prepared politically or intellectually to cope with the all-pervading crisis caused by the Great Depression. Governments did respond, however. After a flurry of ineffective international meetings to try to solve the currency and gold standard problems, nations turned increasingly to national responses. They abandoned gold, raised tariffs, and created monopolies. This was ironic, for over the previous several decades trade had become far more international and interdependent, even though that trend had been temporarily interrupted by the Great War. This nationalistic response was eventually accompanied—worldwide and not simply in the better-known cases of Nazi Germany and Fascist Italy—by increasingly authoritarian regimes that acted as activist governments pledged to solve economic and social problems. The Great Depression caused enormous personal suffering through the loss of jobs and self-esteem, decline in income, and deprivation of material goods, and led to greater class friction. The Depression, by encouraging the rise of vicious nationalism exemplified by a rapid growth in racialism and anti-Semitism and by aggressive military action, was a major cause of the catastrophic World War II.

SELECTED BIBLIOGRAPHY

Baker, Christopher J. "Debt and Depression in Madras, 1929–1936." In *The Imperial Impact: Studies in the Economic History of Africa and India,* edited by Clive Dewey and A. G. Hopkins, pp. 233–242. London: Athlone Press, 1978. Examines impact of the Depression on the Indian agricultural sector and its society.

Beyan, Amos. "The Development of Kikuyu Politics During the Depression, 1930–1939." *Journal of Third World Politics* 6 (Spring 1989): 29–47. Shows how the Depression helped radicalize African politics.

Brown, Ian, ed. *The Economies of Africa and Asia in the Inter-war Depression.* New York: Routledge, 1989. Revisionist writers question some of the accepted interpretations of the Depression.

Davis, Joseph. *The World Between the Wars, 1919–39: An Economist's View.* Baltimore: Johns Hopkins University Press, 1975. Detailed economy-oriented account of the interwar period.

Fallada, Hans. *Little Man, What Now?* New York: Simon & Schuster, 1933. Novel set in Germany during the Depression.

Galbraith, John Kenneth. *The Great Crash, 1929.* 3rd ed. Boston: Houghton Mifflin, 1972; first published 1954. Brief classic account oriented toward the United States.

Garraty, John A. *The Great Depression.* New York: Harcourt Brace Jovanovich, 1986. Excellent on social impact of the Depression in the United States and Europe, includes an interesting chapter comparing the New Deal and Nazi responses to the Depression.

Gray, Nigel. *The Worst of Times.* Totowa, NJ: Barnes and Noble, 1985. An oral history of British working-class life during the Depression.

"The Great Depression." *Journal of Contemporary History* 4 (October 1969). Outstanding resource; entire issue devoted to the Depression, with separate articles on each of the major European nations, on east-central Europe, and on the primary producing countries.

Greenwood, Walter. *Love on the Dole.* London: Penguin, 1969; first published 1933. Depression-era novel set in England.

Jewsiewicki, B. "The Great Depression and the Making of the Colonial Economic System in the Belgian Congo." *African Economic History* 4 (Fall 1977): 153–176. Sees the Great Depression as leading to the development of a highly controlled, exploiting, European-dominated economic system.

Kindleberger, Charles P. *The World in Depression 1929–1939.* London: Penguin Press, 1973. Scholarly account of causes and course of the Depression, especially governments' fiscal policies.

Klein, Maury. *Rainbow's End: The Crash of 1929.* Oxford: Oxford University Press, 2001. A straightforward account of the Wall Street collapse of October 1929 and the economic disaster that followed. The author, a noted economic historian, also catalogues the various unusual social phenomena that accompanied economic downfall.

Latham, A. J. H. *The Depression and the Developing World, 1914–1939.* Totowa, NJ: Croom Helm, 1981. Sees overproduction of commodities in the developing world as an important cause of the Depression.

Markwell, Donald John. *John Maynard Keynes and International Relations: Economic Paths to War and Peace.* Oxford: Oxford University Press, 2006. Markwell, a University of Melbourne professor, turns his attention to the great economist's take on the interaction of economics and international relations.

Orwell, George. *The Road to Wigan Pier.* New York: Harcourt, Brace, 1958; first published 1937. Classic study of the unemployed in industrial England during the early years of the Depression.

Rees, Goronwy. *The Great Slump: Capitalism in Crisis, 1929–1933.* New York: Harper and Row, 1970. A study of the United States and Europe during the crisis; especially good on politics.

Roberts, A. D., ed. *The Cambridge History of Africa.* Volume 7: *From 1905 to 1940.* Cambridge, England: Cambridge University Press, 1986. Decent coverage of the Depression, especially in regard to policies of the European nations over their colonies.

Taylor, David A. *Soul of a People: The WPA Writers' Project Uncovers Depression America.* Hoboken, NJ: Wiley and Sons, 2009. An entertaining and informative look at the U.S. writers who participated in this Depression era government project. Revealing about both the writers and the condition of the United States at that time.

Thorp, Rosemary, ed. *Latin America in the 1930s: The Role of the Periphery in World Crisis.* London: Macmillan, 1984. Specialist-oriented; includes formulas, statistics, and excellent case studies of various economies.

Tomlinson, B. R. *The Political Economy of the Raj 1914–1947.* London: Macmillan, 1979. A scholarly study of the impact of the Depression on India and on the economic relationship between India and Britain.

Van der Wee, Herman. *The Great Depression Revisited.* The Hague, the Netherlands: Martinus Nijhoff, 1972. This interesting collection contains both broad and specific articles on a variety of Depression-related issues.

CREDIT-ANSTALT FAILURE (1931)

Credit-Anstalt, Austria's largest private bank, declared its impending insolvency in May 1931. The failure of Credit-Anstalt and the failure of the Austrian government to secure a complicated political and diplomatic solution to the crisis contributed to deepening the Great Depression on the European continent and hastened the rise of authoritarian power in Austria before World War II.

In 1931, the Austrian government was aware that the failure of Credit-Anstalt would cause massive dislocation in the economy and throughout southeastern Europe. Many of the Balkan states and their larger investors had their holdings with Credit-Anstalt. The Austrian government quickly stepped in to guarantee the deposits to prevent a nationwide economic collapse.

Because Austria adhered to the gold standard, the Austrian Central Bank did not have the available funds to prevent the collapse of Credit-Anstalt. The most feasible solution required the transfer of large amounts of money into Austria from abroad, most likely in the form of a loan. Thus, the Austrian bank crisis became an international incident. Austria appealed to Great Britain and France for help.

Investors, fearing that Austria would not be able to raise the gold and might devalue its currency, began to pull their investments from Austria and to reinvest abroad. Those actions deepened the crisis and made it imperative that a solution be implemented as quickly as possible.

The nationalist government of France blocked the arrangement of a major loan to Austria; it refused to allow French money to aid a former enemy while France also suffered from the effects of the Depression. The delay forced Austria to pursue its only remaining option: it abandoned the gold standard and devalued its currency to pay for the support of Credit-Anstalt.

In the aftermath of the devaluation, a massive recession swept the Austrian economy. A major result of the crisis was the defeat of the Social Democratic leadership in the elections of 1931. Conservatives, led by Engelbert Dollfuss, assumed power and disbanded the Austrian Parliament. Austria began a steady move toward authoritarian rule that culminated with the Anschluss with Nazi Germany in 1938.

ABC-CLIO

WOODY GUTHRIE (1912–1967)

The legendary Woody Guthrie of the United States is best remembered for such songs as "This Land Is Your Land" and "Reuben James." His belief that music could change social conditions influenced a younger generation of American singer-songwriters that included Bob Dylan and Joan Baez. Coming of age in the migrant labor camps of California during the Great Depression, Guthrie's songs honored working people and called attention to the social inequities that they faced.

Woodrow Wilson Guthrie was born on July 14, 1912, in Okemah, Oklahoma, the third of five children. His father, Charley, a real estate speculator with political ambitions, supported the family comfortably until Guthrie was seven. Then, his father's prosperity—undermined by alcoholism and threatened by the oil boom—foundered.

Things went from bad to worse for the family. In 1919, his oldest sibling, Clara, died in a fire. In 1927, his father was badly burned in another blaze. Thereafter, Charley left Okemah to join his two younger children, who lived with his sister Maude in Texas, and recuperate. Meanwhile, Guthrie's mother, Nora, was afflicted with Huntington's disease, a degenerative neurological disease, and was consigned to a mental institution. Left on his own at 15, Guthrie drifted and was sporadically taken in by friends and relatives.

A restless loner, Guthrie spent his days reading in the public library and went to school infrequently until he dropped out at 16. He taught himself to play the harmonica

In 1939 Woody Guthrie toured the Imperial Valley with John Steinbeck, whose *Grapes of Wrath* sold 420,000 copies in its first year of publication. He sang at Communist party rallies and union-organizing meetings, but was unimpressed by doctrine and never joined the party. (Library of Congress)

and the guitar and performed at barn dances and revival meetings, and in pool halls and bars. In 1929, he rejoined his family in Pampa, Texas. Six years later, Guthrie headed for California, one of thousands of "Okies" who fled the Dust Bowl in the 1930s. That hobo life, punctuated by menial jobs and occasional street singing, shaped his convictions and heightened his sense of mission.

In 1937, Guthrie's radio program, *Here Come Woody and Lefty Lou*, was heard over KFVD in Los Angeles. Guthrie went on to broadcast in New York with *Cavalcade of America* and *Pipe Smoking Time*. By 1938, he was on the West Coast again singing in migrant camps and on radio shows with Will Geer and Cisco Houston. A mimeographed songbook he put together, *On a Slow Train through California*, found its way to the famous folk singer Pete Seeger. Guthrie and Seeger met at a concert for migrant workers in 1940. That year, ethnomusicologist Alan Lomax, the son and collaborator of folklorist John Lomax, recorded Guthrie's *Dust Bowl Ballads* for the Library of Congress Archive of Folk Song. Following Guthrie's relocation to New York, Lomax introduced Guthrie to the city's liberal café society and helped him search out publishers and sponsors for his works.

In 1941, the Almanac Singers formed in New York with Guthrie, Seeger, and others. The group toured the country, then settled in Greenwich Village later that year. Guthrie founded and worked briefly with the Headline Singers (Huddie Ledbetter, Sonny Terry, and Brownie McGhee) and wrote an article for the magazine *Common Ground.* The piece led to an autobiography, *Bound for Glory,* published in 1943. Early writings, spurred by his sympathy for the underdog, were published in *The Daily Worker* and *People's Daily World.*

In 1943, Guthrie joined the U.S. Merchant Marine with Houston. In the course of his travels during World War II, he collected musical instruments; sang in North Africa, the United Kingdom, and Sicily; and survived dangerous torpedo attacks. After Guthrie's discharge in 1945, he recorded hundreds of songs for the Folkways label.

The more than 1,000 songs written or adapted by Guthrie (he often put new words to old tunes) were nearly all inspired by his life on the road. He sang of hard times in the Great Depression, the Dust Bowl drought, unions, and the New Deal. He performed frequently at protest meetings, on picket lines, and on marches, and his lyrics urged action as they underlined his beliefs. "This Land Is Your Land" and "Union Maid" are especially well known, as are "So Long, It's Been Good to Know Ya," "Goin' Down the Road," "Roll on Columbia," "Reuben James," and "Pastures of Plenty." Guthrie also wrote songs like "My Car" and "Why Oh Why" for children.

Guthrie's column for the communist paper *People's Daily World* made him a target during the McCarthy era. By the mid-1950s, he was seriously ill, struck down by Huntington's disease. By the 1960s, he was bedridden, and his son, Arlo, began to perform his songs. It was at that time that the young Dylan began to visit him regularly.

Guthrie died in Brooklyn, New York, on October 3, 1967. After his death, *Tribute to Woody Guthrie* concerts were held at Carnegie Hall in January 1968 and the Hollywood Bowl in September 1970. A year later, he was inducted into the Songwriters' Hall of Fame. A film, *Bound for Glory,* starring David Carradine as Guthrie, was released in 1976. He was inducted into the Rock and Roll Hall of Fame in 1988. In 1998, Guthrie's daughter Nora asked British folk singer Billy Bragg and American rock band Wilco to put music to the hundreds of unpublished song lyrics discovered after Guthrie's death. The resulting *Mermaid Avenue* and *Mermaid Avenue II* were critically praised and spurred new interest in Guthrie's work.

ABC-CLIO

HERBERT HOOVER (1874–1964)

Brilliantly successful as an engineer and humanitarian, Herbert Hoover failed as a president to lead the United States effectively during the Great Depression because, in the words of the historian Arthur Schlesinger Jr., he was "a man of high ideals whose intelligence froze into inflexibility and whose dedication was smitten by self-righteousness."

Born on August 10, 1874, in West Branch, Iowa, to devout Quaker parents, Herbert Clark Hoover was orphaned at age nine. He worked his way through Stanford University, graduating in 1895 with a degree in engineering. By 1914, he was a well-known international engineer. He had discovered major gold and coal deposits in Australia and China and had accumulated a substantial fortune. He wrote, "To feel great works grow under one's feet and to have more men constantly getting good jobs is to be the master of contentment."

During World War I, Hoover, living in London, headed the Commission for Relief in Belgium, which managed to save millions of people from starvation. When the United States entered the war, President Woodrow Wilson asked Hoover to return to the United States to serve as director of the Food Administration. While at the bureau, Hoover introduced the concept of standardized sizes for packages to prevent waste; to "Hooverize" meant to save food. At the end of the war, Hoover returned to Europe, first to head the Inter-Allied Food Council and then to become the director of the American Relief Administration. He also served as an adviser to President Wilson at the Paris Peace Conference, where the Versailles Treaty (1919) that officially ended the war was drafted. His relief work significantly eased the threat of famine in war-torn Austria and Germany in 1919.

After his return to the United States in September 1919, Hoover conducted an unofficial and unsuccessful campaign for the Republican nomination for president. When Warren Harding was nominated instead and elected in 1920, Hoover accepted an appointment as secretary of commerce.

At the Commerce Department, the frugal and energetic Hoover worked to reduce waste and eliminate bureaucratic inefficiencies. He counseled moderation in dealing with the new communist government in the Soviet Union and secured the shipment of food to that country with no political strings attached. Hoover believed in a doctrine of "associationalism," by which he meant the voluntary association of bankers with bankers, farmers with farmers, manufacturers with manufacturers, and so on, regardless of such factors as nationality or religion. Such economic associations, he was convinced, would spur economic growth, encourage a wholesome spirit of cooperation and commonwealth in economic activity, and preclude the need for direct government interference in economic affairs. These views, along with his international relief work and his good performance as commerce secretary, made him an attractive Republican candidate for president in 1928.

With peace and prosperity on his side, Hoover felt confident that he would defeat anti-Prohibition and Catholic Democratic candidate Alfred E. Smith. During the campaign, the stock market soared, and that August, Hoover said in a speech, "We are nearer to the final triumph over poverty than ever before in the history of any land. The poorhouse is vanishing from among us. We have not yet reached the goal, but we shall soon with the help of God be in sight of the day when poverty will be banished from this nation." "The Great Engineer and Humanitarian" won 444 electoral votes to Smith's 87.

In October 1929, less than a year after Hoover took office, the stock market crashed and killed Hoover's dream of presiding over a period of increasing prosperity. At first, through a tax cut and in meetings with business leaders, Hoover tried to encourage expansion of public and private construction—"the greatest tool which our economic system affords for the establishment of stability"—to deal with what he viewed as a temporary economic collapse. He was convinced that the cause of the depression lay not in domestic affairs but in the structure of international finance.

With what appeared to be a ruthless disregard for human suffering, Hoover remarked, "The sole function of government is to bring about a condition of affairs favorable to the beneficial development of private enterprise." When he vetoed a proposal to have the government build a huge electrical project in the Tennessee Valley at Muscle Shoals, he said, "I am firmly opposed to the Government entering into any business the major purpose of which is competition with our citizens." Relief activities belonged, he believed, to state and local governments. To tamper with that principle would "have struck at the roots of self-government." From the perspective of those in need of immediate relief, it appeared as though Hoover was helping the rich instead of the poor. Hoover's name became associated with the misery of the Great Depression. Shantytowns of the homeless and unemployed were called Hoovervilles, and the newspapers people used to keep warm were known as Hoover blankets.

As the economic depression deepened, however, the dynamic Hoover, who was genuinely interested in resolving economic tensions, actually started many of the innovative programs the New Deal later received credit for. In 1932, for example, he supported the creation of the Reconstruction Finance Corporation (RFC), through which the government lent money directly to companies and banks. This innovation shifted the financial power from private institutions to the federal government.

Still, as the election of 1932 approached, Hoover appeared to cling to his worn-out, "mean-spirited" convictions. He authorized the RFC to grant money to state governments for direct relief programs, but it was too late. The RFC had $500 million available for local relief but had spent only $37 million before the end of Hoover's presidency.

Renominated in 1932 by the Republican Party, Hoover, appalled at the dangers the election of Franklin D. Roosevelt portended, vigorously campaigned across the nation against "changes and so-called new deals which would destroy the very foundations of the American system." The American people rejected his arguments and elected Roosevelt, 472 electoral votes to 59.

A gloomy and depressed Hoover retired to Palo Alto, California, in 1933 to work at the Hoover Institute for War, Revolution, and Peace at Stanford University. After World War II, Hoover returned to Europe at President Harry Truman's request to help organize food relief programs. In 1947, again at the request of Truman, and in 1953, at the request of President Dwight D. Eisenhower, Hoover headed commissions that studied ways to improve the efficiency of the executive branch of the federal government.

Hoover lived an active life until his death at age 90 on October 20, 1964. By the time of his death, the image of Hoover as inflexible and out of touch with the feelings of the people had been modified by a growing appreciation of his more dynamic and innovative efforts to cope with the overwhelming economic problems of the Great Depression, as well as his useful post-presidential work in food relief and government efficiency. Even New Dealer Rexford Tugwell conceded, "We didn't admit it at the time, . . . but practically the whole New Deal was extrapolated from programs Hoover started." A combination of Hoover's deeply held principles and a crisis of unprecedented magnitude made it impossible for Hoover to carry his reform impulses far enough.

ABC-CLIO

FRANKLIN D. ROOSEVELT (1882–1945)

The only president ever to serve more than two terms, Franklin Delano Roosevelt was elected to office in 1932 and was reelected three more times before he died near the end of World War II. During the 12 years of his presidency, Roosevelt aroused both intense loyalty and opposition. His critics and supporters agree, however, that more than any other president, Roosevelt was the architect of the American welfare state and established government responsibility for individual social welfare. Roosevelt's impact on the United States through his social and economic legislation was huge and lasting.

No other president in the twentieth century has enjoyed the adulation of the masses to the degree conferred on Roosevelt. He was the first president to use mass communication (the radio) to its full advantage. Through his speeches and famous "fireside chats," Roosevelt sounded like a kind uncle or grandfather to millions of Americans who had never heard a president speak before. Hundreds of thousands sent him letters detailing their plight, asking for his assistance, and thanking him for his help.

Born on January 30, 1882, Roosevelt spent his early years at his family estate in Hyde Park, New York, and attended the exclusive Groton School before going on to Harvard University and Columbia University Law School. In 1905, he married Eleanor Roosevelt, his distant cousin and the niece of Theodore Roosevelt. He ran for the New York Senate in 1910. Although a Democrat in an overwhelmingly Republican district, Roosevelt won an impressive victory. He quickly made a name for himself by challenging the Tammany Hall political machine's control over the Democratic Party. In 1913, Josephus Daniels, President Woodrow Wilson's new secretary of the navy, appointed Roosevelt assistant secretary of the navy, the same post his distant cousin Theodore Roosevelt had once held. In 1920, Roosevelt ran as the vice presidential candidate with James M. Cox. Although the Democratic Party lost the election, Roosevelt used the opportunity to establish a national reputation. His political future seemed assured when, in 1921, he was stricken with polio (infantile paralysis) and almost completely paralyzed.

For two years, he struggled to teach himself how to cope with the disease and the loss of the use of his legs. Many people thought paralysis would be an insurmountable obstacle to a political career, but with the help of his wife, Roosevelt developed a bold, active personal style that more than compensated for his inability to stand without assistance. Before his illness, Roosevelt had appeared to many of his contemporaries as a spoiled rich man dabbling in politics. Little of his liberalism or political seriousness was apparent before his bout with polio. Once, when asked how he could be so patient with a political opponent, he said, "If you had spent two years in bed trying to wiggle your big toe, after that anything else would seem easy."

In 1928, with the encouragement of outgoing Governor Alfred E. Smith, Roosevelt managed to win the race for governor of New York. With the onset of the Great Depression, Roosevelt became known for his willingness to use the state government to relieve widespread misery and established a reputation as a compassionate, reform-oriented chief executive. He was reelected in 1930.

In many respects, Roosevelt seemed the ideal candidate to recapture the White House for the Democrats in 1932. Still, it wasn't until after John Nance Garner withdrew from the race at the Democratic convention and instructed his Texas and California delegates to vote for Roosevelt that Roosevelt was able to win the nomination on the fourth ballot.

Then he captured the attention of the nation by flying to Chicago to become the first candidate to directly address a convention immediately after nomination. He said, "You have nominated me and I know it, and I am here to thank you for the honor. Let it . . . be symbolic that in so doing I broke traditions. Let it be from now on the task of our Party to break foolish traditions. . . . I pledge you, I pledge myself, to a new deal for the American people."

During the campaign, Roosevelt promised to balance the federal budget and to provide direct aid to the needy. Although vague on exactly how he would accomplish this, he exuded tremendous confidence that he could do what was necessary to end the depression: "The country needs, and, unless I mistake its temper, the country demands bold, persistent experimentation. It is common sense to take a method and try it. If it fails, admit it frankly and try another. But above all, try something."

Roosevelt carried all but six states and defeated Herbert Hoover by more than 7 million votes: 22,821,857 to 15,761,841. Roosevelt also stymied the efforts of the Socialist and Communist parties to capitalize on the economic turmoil gripping the nation. Socialist candidate Norman Thomas obtained less than a million votes, and the Communist Party's representative, William Foster, managed to win only 100,000 votes.

Roosevelt, confident of victory, had begun preparing for the presidency months before his campaign and election. Besides a core of loyal political assistants, he had enlisted the aid of a number of college professors, Rexford Tugwell, Adolph Berle Jr., and Raymond Moley—nicknamed the brain trust—to assist him so that once in office he could move swiftly to deal with the national crisis.

In his inaugural address, Roosevelt announced that he would call Congress into an immediate special session to obtain the legislation necessary to deal with the banking crisis and the collapse of the economy. He told the nation that if Congress hesitated, he would ask it "for broad executive power to wage a war against the emergency, as great as the power that would be given to me if we were in fact invaded by a foreign foe. This great Nation will endure as it has endured, will revive and prosper. So, first of all, let me assert my firm belief that the only thing we have to fear is fear itself."

The special session of Congress Roosevelt called convened on March 9, 1933, and adjourned on June 16. During that hundred days, more important legislation was passed than in any other comparable period in U.S. history. The three aims of the New Deal were recovery, relief, and reform. The first New Deal legislation concentrated on recovery and relief. To accomplish these goals, Roosevelt had to overcome deep-seated American prejudices against a strong federal government.

Two days after assuming office, Roosevelt issued a proclamation closing all of the nation's banks. The special session of Congress passed an emergency banking bill just three days later that gave the president broad powers over the nation's banks, currency, and foreign exchange. Roosevelt went on radio to talk informally to the public about what he had authorized the U.S. Federal Reserve Board and Treasury Department to do and to promise: "I can assure you that it is safer to keep your money in a reopened bank than under the mattress." The combination of decisive action and personal persuasion worked. Public confidence in reopened banks was restored.

Roosevelt also took the nation off the gold standard and devalued the currency by 40 percent to make American goods more competitive abroad, raise prices of goods at home, and reduce individual debt. As one would anticipate, those in debt applauded, but creditors, such as those holding bonds and long-term mortgages, were enraged.

The most popular New Deal measures were those that tried to relieve the suffering of the approximately 25 percent of the labor force who were unemployed. Roosevelt knew local and state agencies had run out of funds, so he created the Federal Emergency Relief Administration, headed by Harry Hopkins, to give money to local relief agencies. The Civil Works Administration (CWA, 1933), the Civilian Conservation Corps (CCC, 1933), the Public Works Administration (PWA, 1933), and later the Works Progress Administration (WPA, 1935) were also created to provide temporary relief jobs. Among the other innovative programs were the Agricultural Adjustment Administration (AAA, 1933), which attempted to buoy farm prices by limiting production; the Home Owners' Loan Corporation (HOLC, 1933), which worked to protect people from mortgage foreclosures; the National Recovery Administration (NRA, 1933), which was designed to regulate business competition; the National Labor Relations Board (NLRB, 1935), which was established to guarantee the right of labor to organize; the Social Security Act, which set up an old-age pension system; and the Tennessee Valley Authority project, which brought low-cost power and jobs to millions of people in the Tennessee River Valley area.

Although these efforts failed to end the Great Depression, they did provide a sense of the government's commitment to alleviating the suffering and led to Roosevelt's landslide reelection in 1936. They also marked the first extensive use of government's fiscal powers—what would later be termed Keynesian (after English economist John Maynard Keynes) policies—to stimulate mass purchasing and thereby promote economic recovery. Then in 1937, after the U.S. Supreme Court angered Roosevelt by declaring (in 1935) the NRA and AAA unconstitutional, Roosevelt made a costly political blunder by launching a plan to increase the size of the court by 6 more judges, to 15, so that he could appoint enough new justices to overcome the existing 5-member conservative majority. Public reverence for the court and Roosevelt's miscalculation that he could orchestrate the election defeat of congressional opponents in 1938 resulted in his first major congressional setback. This "court-packing" plan, combined with the 1937 recession and his apparent unwillingness to curb a wave of sit-down strikes, sharply limited his political power. The Republicans and conservative Democrats won enough seats in the 1938 congressional elections to halt further substantial New Deal legislation, although Roosevelt did put through the Executive Reorganization Act in 1939, which enlarged and strengthened the executive branch of the government. World War II, not innovative New Deal legislation, returned the nation to prosperity.

By the time he won reelection in 1936, it was clear to Roosevelt that ominous dictatorial regimes in Japan, Germany, and Italy were going to solve their economic problems through military expansion. Roosevelt hoped to keep the United States out of war, but as World War II began in 1939, he worked to bring about the repeal of the Neutrality Act of 1935 so that he could provide aid to Great Britain. In 1940, he decided to run for an unprecedented third term. Promising to keep Americans out of any foreign wars, Roosevelt easily defeated his Republican rival, Wendell Willkie, 449 electoral votes to 82.

After his reelection, Roosevelt obtained congressional approval to provide lend-lease aid to Great Britain and, in 1941, to the Soviet Union. The Lend-Lease Act, passed mainly to allow the British more credit to buy war supplies, provided for the sale, transfer, exchange, or lease of arms or equipment to any country whose defense was vital to the United States. (Total lend-lease aid by the end of the war would amount to nearly $50 billion.) American ships and planes also began convoying supply ships far out into the North Atlantic and reporting German submarine locations to the British Royal Navy. In the Far East, the United States attempted in 1941 to halt Japan's military expansion by announcing a potentially crippling embargo of vital war materiel and oil to Japan. Instead of backing down, Japan launched a surprise attack on December 7, 1941 designed to wipe out the U.S. Pacific fleet stationed at Pearl Harbor in Hawaii. In asking Congress for a declaration of war against Japan, the president declared December 7 as "a date which will live in infamy." Germany and Italy then declared war, and the United States found itself fighting adversaries in both Asia and Europe.

During the war, congressional conservatives managed to dismantle some of the New Deal's innovative programs and forced Roosevelt to orchestrate economic mobilization in a manner that gave considerable authority and profit opportunities to corporate elites. Although severely criticized for various aspects of his direction of the war effort, Roosevelt behaved in his characteristically pragmatic fashion. His goal was to win the war with as few American casualties as possible. To do this, he needed to keep the wartime alliance of Great Britain, the Soviet Union, and the United States together until after Germany and Japan were defeated, and he did. At the same time, war-induced prosperity in combination with a widespread belief among Americans that they were fighting "the Good War" sustained national unity and enough of Roosevelt's popularity to gain him reelection to a fourth term in 1944.

Roosevelt did not live to see the end of World War II. At the Allied Yalta Conference in 1945, he had been unable to secure a Poland free of Soviet domination, but he did manage to obtain a Soviet promise to join the war against Japan and to participate in the United Nations. Critics attack his refusal to challenge Soviet domination of east-central Europe, but supporters point out that it was merely an acceptance of political reality—Soviet troops occupied the region. Ordered by his doctors to rest after his return from Yalta, Roosevelt traveled to his favorite retreat at Warm Springs, Georgia, where he suffered a massive cerebral hemorrhage and died on April 12, 1945.

Perspectives on Roosevelt over the years have varied widely. In the 1930s, his Republican opponents saw him as a virtual socialist. Liberal historians of the 1940s and 1950s lionized him for leading a popular crusade to restore prosperity and justice in America. The radical historians of the 1960s viewed him as a servant of capital, seeking mainly to restore capitalism to health and not truly interested in helping the downtrodden. Still others have stressed the pragmatic, nonideological nature of his approach—his willingness to try policies that promised to work and that seemed feasible. None of these interpretations, however, has sought to deny the centrality of Roosevelt and his New Deal in the shaping of modern America.

ABC-CLIO

STOCK MARKET CRASH (1929)

The stock market crash in New York City on Black Tuesday, October 29, 1929, devastated the U.S. economy and wiped out the fortunes and life savings of many investors. The event marked the end of the securities boom of the 1920s and the beginning of the Great Depression.

The United States had been riding high on the economic growth of the 1920s. The economy remained strong after World War I, and the widespread availability of credit

Distressed investors and speculators mobbed the New York Stock Exchange in 1929 in the wake of the great stock market crash. (Library of Congress)

brought luxurious modern conveniences to average American families. A few wealthy, powerful investors dominated the stock market, and stock price manipulation through insider information was not uncommon. Successful stock speculators led rich and glamorous lives, and more and more ordinary people were trading securities. Brokerages allowed customers to play the stock market with mostly borrowed money: customers would pay cash for just a small fraction of the value of a security and borrow the balance from the brokerage. If the stock price fell, the broker would make a "margin call" on the investor, which would require the investor either to pay more cash or sell other securities to cover further losses.

On September 3, 1929, stock prices reached a 10-year high. After that, they began a slow and steady decline, marked by tumbles followed by small rallies. That pattern continued through October, and fear, pessimism, apprehension, confusion, and uncertainty began to take grip among both big and small investors. Many investors scrambled to cover their losses as the market continued its decline and more and more margin calls went out. On October 18, stock prices fell precipitately, alarming many investors, although overall confidence in the market remained.

On the morning of October 24, nervous investors began selling off their stocks quickly; the volume of sales triggered a further fall in stock prices that sent the market heading for a crash. The day quickly became known as Black Thursday and marked the first day of real panic regarding the soundness of the market. A record 12,894,650 shares of stock were traded as many investors tried to unload their stock, regardless of the price, in an attempt to cut their losses. The stock market was saved from collapse, however, when many major banks and investment companies bought large blocks of stock and successfully stemmed the panic.

When the market opened on Monday, October 28, prices again began to plummet, but the rich, powerful bankers did not extend their support this time. The panic continued through Black Tuesday, the day the great bull market completely collapsed. From the moment of the October 29 opening bell, stock prices dropped in a furious selling frenzy that ended with a record 16 million shares traded. That record stood for 40 years.

Many investors lost their life savings, and many businesses and banks failed because of their losses. Few people saw the crash coming. One economist, Roger W. Babson, was the first to predict the crash: he drew on evidence that consumers' credit burdens were increasing, steel production was dropping, auto sales were falling, and some stocks were showing signs of price inflation. Other economists, such as Irving Fisher, dismissed the market's downward trend as a shaking-out of speculators that would ultimately bring stability.

Ultimately, the crash triggered the reform of laws regulating the securities market and led to the establishment of the Securities and Exchange Commission, which acted to enforce new reporting and listing requirements and other laws that aimed to end corrupt practices in securities trading.

ABC-CLIO

DOCUMENT: JOHN MAYNARD KEYNES'S "THE ECONOMIC CONSEQUENCES OF THE PEACE" (1919)

In 1919, British economist John Maynard Keynes attended the Paris Peace Conference as a representative of the British treasury. Later that same year, Keynes resigned his position in disgust over the course of the negotiations and the way the Treaty of Versailles (1919) was shaping up. When he returned to England, he wrote an article, "The Economic Consequences of Peace," an excerpt of which appears here. In it, he condemned the treaty for levying excessive reparation demands against Germany that virtually guaranteed that Germany could not recover economically and correctly predicted that such economic dislocation would have serious effects on the rest of Europe. Furthermore, he criticized the British government's laissez-faire economic position and suggested instead that government should play a far more active role in managing the economy, a view that later met with great acceptance during the Great Depression and during the aftermath of World War II.

This chapter must be one of pessimism. The Treaty includes no provisions for the economic rehabilitation of Europe,—nothing to make the defeated Central Empires into good neighbors, nothing to stabilize the new States of Europe, nothing to reclaim Russia; nor does it promote in any way a compact of economic solidarity amongst the Allies themselves; no arrangement was reached at Paris for restoring the disordered finances of France and Italy, or to adjust the systems of the Old World and the New.

The Council of Four paid no attention to these issues, being preoccupied with others,—Clemenceau to crush the economic life of his enemy, Lloyd George to do a deal and bring home something which would pass muster for a week, the President to do nothing that was not just and right. It is an extraordinary fact that the fundamental economic problems of a Europe starving and disintegrating before their eyes, was the one question in which it was impossible to arouse the interest of the Four. Reparation was their main excursion into the economic field, and they settled it as a problem of theology, of politics, of electoral chicane, from every point of view except that of the economic future of the States whose destiny they were handling. . . .

The essential facts of the situation, as I see them, are expressed simply. Europe consists of the densest aggregation of population in the history of the world. This population is accustomed to a relatively high standard of life, in which, even now, some sections of it anticipate improvement rather than deterioration. In relation to other continents Europe is not self-sufficient; in particular it cannot feed itself. Internally the population is not evenly distributed, but much of it is crowded into a relatively small number of dense industrial centers. This population secured for itself a livelihood before the war, without much margin of surplus, by means of a delicate and immensely complicated organization, of which the foundations were supported by coal, iron, transport, and an unbroken supply of imported food and raw materials from other continents. By the destruction of this organization and the interruption of the stream of supplies, a part of this population is deprived of its means of livelihood. Emigration is not open to the redundant surplus. For it would take years to transport them overseas, even, which is not the case, if countries could be found which were ready to receive them. The danger confronting us, therefore, is the rapid depression of the standard of life of the European populations to a point which will mean actual starvation for some (a point already reached in Russia and approximately reached in Austria). Men will not always die quietly. For starvation, which brings to some lethargy and a helpless despair, drives other temperaments to the nervous instability of hysteria and to a mad despair. And these in their distress may overturn the remnants of organization, and submerge civilization itself in their attempts to satisfy desperately the overwhelming needs of the individual. This is the danger against which all our resources and courage and idealism must now co-operate.

On the 13th May, 1919, Count Brockdorff-Rantzau addressed to the Peace Conference of the Allied and Associated Powers the Report of the German Economic Commission charged with the study of the effect of the conditions of Peace on the situation of the German population. "In the course of the last two generations," they reported, "Germany has become transformed from an agricultural State to an industrial State. So long as she was an agricultural State, Germany could feed forty million inhabitants. As an industrial State she could insure the means of subsistence for a population of sixty-seven millions; and in 1913 the importation of foodstuffs amounted, in round figures, to twelve million tons. Before the war a total of fifteen million persons in Germany provided for their existence by foreign trade, navigation, and the use, directly or indirectly, of foreign raw material." After rehearsing the main relevant provisions of the Peace Treaty the report continues: "After this diminution of her products, after the economic depression resulting from the loss of her colonies, her merchant fleet and her foreign investments, Germany will not be in a position to import from abroad an adequate quantity of raw material. An enormous part of German industry will, therefore, be condemned inevitably to destruction. The need of importing foodstuffs will increase considerably at the same time that the possibility of satisfying this demand is as greatly diminished. In a very short time, therefore, Germany will not be in a position to give bread and work to her numerous millions of inhabitants, who are prevented from earning their livelihood by navigation and trade. These persons should emigrate, but this is a material impossibility, all the more because many countries and the most important ones will oppose any German immigration. To put the Peace conditions into execution would logically involve, therefore, the loss of several millions of persons in Germany. This catastrophe would not be long in coming about, seeing that the health of the population has been broken down during the War by the Blockade, and during the Armistice by the aggravation of the Blockade of famine. No help however great, or over however long a period it were continued, could prevent these deaths en masse." "We do not know, and indeed we doubt," the report concludes, "whether the Delegates of the Allied and Associated Powers realize the inevitable consequences which will take place if Germany, an industrial State, very thickly populated, closely bound up with the economic system of the world, and under the necessity of importing enormous quantities of raw material and foodstuffs, suddenly finds herself pushed back to the phase of her development, which corresponds to her economic condition and the numbers of her population as they were half a century ago. Those who sign this Treaty will sign the death sentence of many millions of German men, women and children."

I know of no adequate answer to these words. The indictment is at least as true of the Austrian, as of the German, settlement. This is the fundamental problem in front of us, before which questions of territorial adjustment and the balance of European power are insignificant. Some of the catastrophes of past history, which have thrown back human progress for centuries, have been due to the reactions following on the sudden termination, whether in the course of nature or by the act of man, of temporarily favorable conditions which have permitted the growth of population beyond what could be provided for when the favorable conditions were at an end.

6

World War II, 1939–1945

INTRODUCTION

The origins of World War II are rooted in such causes as aggressive nationalism, expansionistic imperialism, virulent Social Darwinism, bitter resentment of the Treaty of Versailles that concluded World War I, and the global power vacuum that World War I helped to create. The first instance of violence associated with World War II occurred in 1931, when a belligerent, militaristic Japan seized the Chinese province of Manchuria. Despite condemnation by the League of Nations, the international body created after World War I to maintain global peace and security, Japan continued to press China throughout the 1930s. Finally, in 1937 Japan launched a full-scale attack on China. During their offensive, the Japanese captured the city of Nanking, setting off a seven-week-long orgy of looting, rape, and murder that took the lives of perhaps 200,000 Chinese.

In Europe, Adolf Hitler's rise to power in Germany in 1933 foreshadowed the end of what proved to be a precarious peace. Intent on solidifying his hold on Germany, Hitler at first moved slowly in international affairs. Nevertheless, by early 1936, he had withdrawn Germany from the League of Nations, sponsored a failed coup d'état in Austria, and announced the rearmament of Germany in violation of the Treaty of Versailles.

Beginning in 1936, Hitler increasingly turned his attention to foreign affairs. In March of that year, he remilitarized the Rhineland in defiance of the Treaty of Versailles. He also intervened on the side of the Spanish fascists in the Spanish Civil War, which began in 1936. In March 1938, again in defiance of the Treaty of Versailles, he annexed the independent Austrian state to his Third Reich.

The Anschluss, as the annexation of Austria was called, brought scant response from Great Britain and France, the chief guarantors of Versailles. Mired in the depth of the Great Depression and haunted by gruesome memories of World War I, the French and especially the British had determined to follow a policy of appeasement in their relations with Hitler's Germany. According to the architects of appeasement such as British prime minister Neville Chamberlain, war could be avoided by giving in to legitimate and limited German demands. Unfortunately, Hitler's demands were both illegitimate and unlimited, although for a long time Western statesmen refused to acknowledge this.

The height of appeasement occurred in September 1938 at the Munich Conference. There France and Great Britain disgracefully reneged on their real and implied commitments to Czechoslovakia and permitted Hitler to annex the Sudetenland, or the part of Czechoslovakia that bordered Germany. Appeasement waned only in 1939 when Hitler broke his solemn promise and absorbed what was left of the Czech state. Shortly thereafter, Hitler began to threaten Poland. The Poles, relying nervously on promises of support from Great Britain and France, resisted.

World War II in Europe began on September 1, 1939, when Nazi Germany invaded Poland. Using a tactic called blitzkrieg, or "lightning war," the Germans soon overwhelmed the hapless Poles. Blitzkrieg called for massed mobile units having enormous firepower to punch a hole in the enemy lines and then race to the enemy's rear, cutting lines of communication and creating chaos. Two days after the invasion, Poland's allies, Great Britain and France, declared war on Germany. Meanwhile, Joseph Stalin's Soviet Union, which had signed a nonaggression pact with Germany on August 23, 1939, also attacked Poland and annexed the eastern portion of that country. This proved to be the prelude to the Soviet seizure of Estonia, Latvia, and Lithuania in the summer of 1940. During 1939–1940, the USSR also fought a short war with Finland, the so-called Winter War, bringing the Soviets additional territory. After the conquest of Poland, military activity virtually ceased until the following spring, when Hitler turned his attention to western Europe.

Beginning with the invasion and conquest of Denmark and Norway, Hitler moved against the Netherlands, Belgium, and Luxembourg, and attacked the important nation of France on May 10, 1940. Hitler's victory over France was unexpectedly easy. France, suing for peace on June 22, 1940, was divided between an army of German occupation in the north and a puppet regime called Vichy France in the south. Henri Pétain, a French World War I war hero, and Pierre Laval, a prewar politician, administered Vichy France. These two collaborators were often referred to as "quislings," a term of scorn derived from Vidkun Quisling, the Nazi puppet who oversaw conquered Norway. Eventually, a vigorous resistance movement called the Free French, led by Charles de Gaulle, a French officer who had fled the Nazis, challenged both Vichy France's legitimacy and the Nazi occupation. As France fell, the British army, which had helped to defend France, barely escaped to Britain from encirclement on the French beaches at Dunkirk. Benito Mussolini, fascist dictator of Italy, had also joined his ally Hitler in the attack on France and was preparing an attack on Greece. Germany and Italy, the Axis Powers, were experiencing great success.

Having defeated France, Hitler now turned his attention to Britain, where he faced a new leader, the resolute Winston Churchill, who had been named prime minister in May 1940. During the Battle of Britain in the fall of 1940, Hitler unsuccessfully tried to bomb the British into submission by striking at civilian as well as military targets.

In 1941, the course of the war in Europe entered a new phase when Hitler launched a surprise attack on his erstwhile ally, the Soviet Union, after having achieved additional military success in the Balkans. In December 1941, the German armies reached the gates of Leningrad and Moscow before their offensive bogged down and Soviet resistance stiffened.

Meanwhile, on the other side of the globe, Germany's ally Japan pursued a policy of conquest. Having occupied much of China as well as the French colony of Indochina, Japan now challenged the United States. In response to a surprise attack on its fleet at Pearl Harbor in December 1941, the United States declared war on Japan. In a matter of days, Germany and Italy declared war on the United States. Great Britain, the USSR, and the United States now found themselves aligned against Germany, Italy, and Japan. The former countries soon formed what came to be known as the Grand Alliance and

U.S. soldiers landing on the Normandy coast of France under heavy German machine-gun fire, D-Day, June 6, 1944. (National Archives)

made the strategic decision to dedicate the bulk of their resources to achieving victory in Europe.

The high-water mark for the Axis Powers came in December 1941, but the next three and a half years witnessed a slow but steady erosion of their position. During 1942, the British, under General Bernard Montgomery, first stopped the Axis advance in North Africa at the Battle of El Alamein and then successfully counterattacked. By the spring of 1943, British and American units had cleared North Africa of Axis forces.

The African victories set the stage for the invasion of Sicily and then the Italian mainland, which occurred later in 1943. The Allied triumph in Sicily led to the overthrow of Mussolini and the opening of armistice negotiations between the Italian army and the Allies in July 1943. However, the Germans intervened, rescued the captured Mussolini, reestablished his dictatorship and, most important, occupied Rome and proceeded to mount a staunch defense of their position on the Italian Peninsula.

Perhaps the most consequential battle of the war took place on the Eastern Front during the winter of 1942–1943. At the city of Stalingrad (now Volgograd) on the banks of the Volga, Russia's most important river, the Soviet army, or Red Army, under the leadership of Generals Vasily Chuikov and Georgi Zhukov, surrounded and annihilated its German opponents. The victorious Soviet army lost more men at Stalingrad than the United States lost in combat during the entire war. In July 1943, the Soviets followed up their victory at Stalingrad by defeating the Germans at the Battle of Kursk, World War II's largest tank battle. These two crushing defeats broke the back of the German army and forced it to commence its slow and bitter retreat to Berlin.

Meanwhile, during 1942 the United States, with help from its British allies, stopped the Japanese onslaught in the Pacific theater of operations. After defeating the Japanese navy at the battles of Midway and the Coral Sea, the United States adopted a strategy of "island hopping," which called for Allied forces to move toward the Japanese heartland one island at a time. Repulsing the Japanese at Guadalcanal and ousting them from the Gilbert, Marshall, Caroline, and Mariana Islands, U.S. forces under General Douglas MacArthur and Admiral Chester Nimitz moved steadily closer to Japan's home islands. In October 1944, the United States destroyed the remnants of Japan's fleet at the Battle of Leyte Gulf and liberated the Philippines.

During the latter part of 1943, Anglo-American units became bogged down in Italy while the Red Army gradually but decisively defeated the Germans on the Eastern Front. It was not until June 6, 1944, that the Western allies finally launched a much anticipated cross-channel invasion when they went ashore at Normandy in France and opened the long-awaited "second front." D-day, as the invasion was known, proved to be a great success. Under the leadership of the American general Dwight D. Eisenhower, the Western allies cleared the Nazis from France. Paris was liberated on August 24, 1944.

By the start of 1944, the Red Army had expelled the Germans from Soviet soil and was beginning to move against Germany's allies in eastern Europe and the Balkans. The Soviets defeated Romania and Bulgaria, invaded Hungary and Slovakia, and liberated parts of Yugoslavia, including the capital, Belgrade. By late 1944, the Red Army had crossed into East Prussia, thereby bringing the war to German soil.

The Soviet triumphs in eastern Europe alarmed some Westerners who had never trusted Joseph Stalin and who regarded his communist regime almost as distastefully as they regarded Hitler's Nazi state. However, the Western leaders, Winston Churchill and the U.S. president, Franklin D. Roosevelt, early on had agreed not to ask Stalin tough questions about the nature of a postwar Europe for fear that Stalin might abandon the alliance and seek a separate peace with the Germans. Consequently, Allied wartime diplomacy tended to focus on other issues.

Even before American entry into the war, Churchill and Roosevelt met at sea off the coast of Newfoundland in August 1941 and signed the Atlantic Charter, which set forth a series of liberal principles to guide the postwar world. Almost a year earlier, Roosevelt defied isolationist sentiment at home and gave the hard-pressed British 50 aged but serviceable destroyers in return for 99-year leases on several British bases in the western Atlantic and the Caribbean. In March 1941, Roosevelt persuaded the U.S. Congress to approve his policy of Lend-Lease, in which the United States lent or leased to its allies billions of dollars worth of supplies with the understanding that they would be returned or paid for after the war. Originally designed to supply Great Britain, Lend-Lease was extended to include the Soviet Union once it entered the war.

Roosevelt and Churchill met again at Casablanca in January 1943. The Casablanca Conference resulted in a pledge to continue hostilities until Germany surrendered unconditionally. The next meeting took place at Teheran, Iran, in December 1943. With Stalin participating for the first time, the three allies discussed the occupation and demilitarization of a conquered Germany. They also discussed Roosevelt's proposal to create an international body designed to maintain global peace.

In October 1944, Churchill, ignoring Roosevelt's belief that Stalin was manageable and growing ever more worried about the expanding Soviet presence in eastern Europe, traveled to Moscow. The British leader sought to determine Stalin's intentions for the lands liberated by the Red Army. The result of Churchill's trip was an old-fashioned division of eastern Europe into well-defined spheres of influence. However, postwar events rendered this agreement virtually worthless.

The last major wartime diplomatic conference convened in February 1945 at Yalta in the Soviet Union. Topics on the agenda included the disposition of Poland and, by extension, the rest of eastern Europe, the future of Germany, Soviet participation in the war against Japan, and Roosevelt's international organization, the United Nations.

Yalta took place against a backdrop of stunning Allied victories. After a December 1944 setback at the Battle of the Bulge, the British and the Americans, now joined by units of liberated France's army, pushed forward into Germany, crossing the Rhine River in March 1945. At the same time, Soviet forces captured Warsaw, Budapest, Vienna, Danzig, and Königsberg, expelled the Germans from Poland, and pushed farther into Germany proper from the east.

In the course of reclaiming captured territory from the Germans, the Allies discovered a number of concentration camps where the Nazis had interned Jews, "undesirables" such as communists and homosexuals, and prisoners of war. At infamous camps such as Auschwitz, Treblinka, and Maidanek, millions of innocent people were put to death. Especially horrendous was the systematic murder of Europe's Jews, the "Final Solution" that Hitler applied to what he termed the "Jewish Question." Of the approximately 12 million who died in the camps, 6 million were Jews.

In late April 1945, with the war's end drawing near, Mussolini was captured and executed by Italian partisans. A few days later, on April 30, 1945, Hitler committed suicide in his besieged bunker in Berlin. On May 7, 1945, representatives of the German military surrendered to Eisenhower. One day later, the act of surrender was repeated at Russian headquarters in the fallen German capital.

All that remained was to wrap up the war in the Pacific. Japan, which had lost Saipan in 1944, and Iwo Jima and Okinawa early in 1945, now faced a horrible new weapon of mass destruction. On August 6, 1945, the United States dropped the world's first atomic bomb on Hiroshima; three days later Nagasaki suffered the same fate. Meanwhile, on August 8, 1945, in keeping with agreements reached at Yalta, the USSR entered the war against Japan. A formal announcement of surrender by the emperor was read to the Japanese people on August 15, 1945; on September 2 formal surrender ceremonies took place on the U.S. battleship *Missouri*, anchored in Tokyo Bay. World War II had finally ended.

INTERPRETIVE ESSAY

LARRY THORNTON

More destructive than any other conflict, World War II dominates twentieth-century world history. The forces that produced the war occupied center stage for much of the preceding 20 years, and the ramifications of the changes wrought by this war continue to affect the world today. For an entire generation—as well as the following generations influenced by that generation—World War II was and remains the defining mark by which all subsequent conflicts are measured.

Strictly speaking, World War II was two separate but coterminous wars that had little relationship to each other. In Asia, Japan waged a war of conquest against China and the British, French, Dutch, and American empires. The European war pitted Germany, Italy, and their junior allies—Bulgaria, Hungary, and Romania—against the Soviet Union and several of the same states Japan was battling. Nominally allies, Germany and Japan made little pretense of coordinating their military plans.

Thus, for example, when Germany launched Operation Barbarossa (the 1941 invasion of the Soviet Union), no corresponding Japanese campaign was launched from Asia, even though Soviet and Japanese forces had repeatedly clashed along the Soviet-Manchurian frontier since 1937. German and Japanese imperial interests went in completely different directions. The enemies of Germany and Japan did a better job of coordinating their efforts in the two theaters simply because they had to determine priorities (Europe had the higher priority) to allocate resources.

Each major power had an ideological rationale to support its war efforts. The Japanese proclaimed a Greater East Asia Co-Prosperity Sphere, which promised Asia for the Asians under Japanese leadership. The Nazis believed that Germany needed *Lebensraum,* or "living space," to survive the Darwinian struggle among the races. Germany would conquer substantial sections of eastern Europe and make room for future generations of Germans by reducing the indigenous populations.

In June 1941, the states aligned against Germany signed the Inter-Allied Declaration, pledging to work for "a world in which, relieved of the menace of aggression, all may enjoy economic and social security." In August 1941, the British and the Americans announced their war aims in the Atlantic Charter, which promised a postwar world safe and secure for all people. These sentiments were reiterated on January 1, 1942, in the United Nations Declaration.

The contrast between war aims is quite manifest. The Germans and the Japanese sought conquest, plain and simple. Despite their claims of liberating the oppressed from Stalinism or Western domination, the brutal occupation policies followed by the Germans and the Japanese convinced the conquered peoples of just the opposite. These unfortunates had simply changed masters, and the new ones were, in many ways, more ruthless and demanding. On the other hand, the idealistic war aims espoused by the Allies were frequently unattainable, which at times made the Allies appear deceitful.

At its peak, World War II involved military forces from 56 nations (not including colonies or imperial territories). The war raged throughout Asia, Africa, and Europe as well as above, on, and beneath the surface of the Atlantic and Pacific oceans. World War II was also total war. Although the term "total war" had been used during the French revolutionary wars and during World War I, there is no comparison between these efforts and World War II.

Waging total war required mobilizing a society's human and technical resources. Just as a nation drafts its young men, so it must also organize its economy for the war effort. Inherent in thoroughgoing mobilization is the tendency toward compulsion. Total war conscripts every resource; it utilizes the entire society.

Governments requisitioned property, registered and directed labor, controlled industry, allocated the distribution of raw materials, rationed or cut production of consumer goods, and limited civilian consumption. Germany was slower to mobilize its economy fully, striving to supply both guns and butter. When Albert Speer became minister for armaments and production in 1942, Germany successfully moved to a total war economy, thereby prolonging the war by one to two years. Germany and Japan never grasped the inherent contradiction between their efforts to wage unlimited war and their limited resources and production capacity. In this sense, their campaigns were doomed to fail when they engaged opponents with superior economies.

In addition to mobilizing their economies earlier, the Allies had greater industrial capacity and capital resources than the Axis powers. Claiming to be the "Arsenal of Democracy," the United States alone supplied $50 billion worth of arms and equipment to its allies. In contrast to Germany and Japan, the combined American, British, and Soviet industrial capacity could support total war.

Nations also mobilized their human resources. Obviously, military conscription became the order of the day, but total war required more than uniformed warriors. Civilians also had to be enlisted in the war effort. In most countries men between the ages of 18 and 60 carried out work considered vital to the war effort. Most societies also recruited women to replace the men who had marched off to the front. Great Britain decreed the compulsory employment in war work of women between the ages of 19 and 40, while "Rosie the Riveter" and her counterparts became war heroines working to build tanks or other vital goods for the United States, the Soviet Union, and other states.

World War II also fostered the roots of what Dwight D. Eisenhower, in the 1950s, called the military-industrial complex through the mobilization of the scientific, academic, and technical communities. More than 30,000 scientists and engineers were part of the war effort in the United States alone. Governments financed research projects and sought expert advice on the adaptation of inventions and discoveries for military purposes. Although the United States' Manhattan Project (the development of the atomic bomb) is the most dramatic example of this mobilization of science and technology, the list of new or improved weapons is long and impressive, including radar, sonar, magnetic mines, proximity fuses, rockets, missiles, and jet planes. In addition to the development of new weapons, war-related research also led to new products and procedures with nonmilitary applications, such as quinine, DDT, the cyclotron, and the first blue baby operation.

Research and development was one of several areas where the Allies had a distinct advantage over the Axis powers. Virtually all nonmilitary achievements were the prerogatives of the Allies, who had the industrial, financial, intellectual, and moral resources to engage in major research and development beyond the immediate demands of the war. By comparison, the Axis states realized no significant nonmilitary achievements because they could not spare the resources and their values did not impel them in this direction.

Beyond compulsion or coercion, every state found propaganda quite useful to instill commitment, to maintain morale, and to promote sacrifice. German propaganda, which Joseph Goebbels, Germany's minister of propaganda, considered as important as the army in the field, appealed to patriotism, stressed elements of Nazi ideology and, to a lesser extent, used racist images to diminish the humanity of the supposedly inferior peoples. Japanese propaganda also stressed inherent differences between the purity of its cause and the tainted qualities of its opponents.

The Soviet propaganda effort evolved from early emphasis on vigorous defense of the revolution and socialism to the defense of Mother Russia; the conflict became the Great Patriotic War as the Nazis joined the evil pantheon that included the Mongols, the Tartars, the Turks, and Napoleon. To reinforce this theme, Soviet propaganda emphasized elements of both classic and popular culture. With themes of perseverance and victory, Sergei Eisenstein's film *Alexander Nevsky*, Leo Tolstoy's *War and Peace*, and Dmitri Shostakovich's *Leningrad Symphony* received considerable attention. Popular arts also joined the war effort. In the first four days of the war, more than 100 songs were composed in Moscow. During the war, professionals and amateurs alike composed thousands of songs for state- or party-sponsored contests and festivals, or for their own amusement and expression. Soviet propaganda also stressed vengeance against the "gray-green slugs" and promised to shed a pool of blood for every drop of Soviet blood, or to blind two eyes for every blinded Soviet eye.

In the United States, Hollywood joined the war effort, producing the "Why We Fight" series, seven films initially made to educate servicemen and women and subsequently shown to the general population. Even Bugs Bunny, Daffy Duck, and other cartoon characters went to war, and Spike Jones and His City Slickers mocked the Nazis in their hit song "Der Fuehrer's Face." American propaganda was not always so lighthearted, though, as evidenced by the regular portrayal of Japanese leaders and soldiers as monkeys or apes.

In many ways, one can argue that World War II as total war represented the logical application of modern rationality to war. After defining victory as the desired end or goal, officials set out to devise the most efficient means to realize that goal. The extent of organization and technological sophistication required to produce the desired goal was unparalleled. It may seem odd to characterize destruction of this magnitude as the culmination of rationality, but lucid men and women, for the most part, made the organizational and operational decisions and formulated the tactics and strategies. Without advanced industrialized, technical, mechanical societies, which require rational officials, total war is not possible.

The human toll remains the most obvious measure of the success of modern rationality—the cold, mechanical harnessing of vast amounts of talent, energy, and resources resulting in the most destructive war in history. Statistics overwhelm one's capacity to comprehend. Estimates of the total death toll reach as high as 57 million. In the Soviet Union, which bore the brunt of the European war, perhaps one out of every eight or nine people died. Fifteen percent of the Polish population was killed. About four million Germans and at least two million Japanese perished.

War consciously and intentionally waged against civilians distinguished the violence of World War II. Civilian deaths accounted for approximately 50 percent of the total casualties (compared with 5 percent in World War I). Civilians were constantly targeted, as bombs fell on cities like Shanghai and Warsaw at the start of the war and on Berlin and Tokyo at the very end. The Japanese conquest of Nanking, late in 1937, set off an unprecedented seven-week wave of mass murder, rape, torture, and pillage in which more than 200,000 Chinese died. Despite his public statements that Germany did not wage war against women and children, Hitler's forces everywhere attacked civilian populations. The Allies also carried the war to their opponents' homelands.

However, the Axis powers engaged in unparalleled atrocities. Rooted in the desire to exploit fully their conquered territories and in assumptions of inherent racial superiority, these states imposed occupation policies that brooked no opposition and harshly retaliated against manifestations of resistance. Although the Japanese viciously retaliated against their opponents, attempted to cow the conquered peoples, mistreated and starved prisoners of war, conducted brutal experiments of dubious medical value, and forcibly recruited Korean and other women to serve as prostitutes or "comfort girls," they never matched Germany's systematic violence.

Germany established new standards of violence and horror as Nazis sought to rearrange Europe's demographic composition. The Nazis were ruthlessly determined to apply Darwin's principle of natural selection, as they understood it, to human society. This meant that "races," or ethnic groups, were considered superior or inferior organisms shaped by nature through a struggle in which only the fittest survived. Because nature's law was kill or die, no moral or humanitarian constraints could sway the Nazis from their self-appointed task to build up the superior Germanic or Aryan "race" in its war against the inferior peoples. Bolstered by this ideology, the Nazis had few qualms about administering their conquered territories with ruthless abandon. The Nazis focused their primary efforts against what they perceived as the most immediate threats: the Jews and the Soviet Union.

In what was euphemistically called the "Final Solution to the Jewish Question," the Nazis attempted to kill every Jew in Europe, and they were more successful at this than at any other endeavor. About two-thirds of Europe's Jews died at the hands of the Nazis; this amounted to some 5.8 million people. In the Soviet Union, more than 7 million soldiers died, almost half as a result of starvation after surrender. Nazi administrators ruthlessly went about reducing the population of the occupied Soviet territory by about two-thirds; this accounted for a significant portion of the estimated 15 million Soviet civilian casualties. Orders were issued to kill immediately all members of the Communist Party, and the Nazis executed hundreds more in retaliation for each act of sabotage, resistance, or assassination.

Other Nazi programs operated on a smaller scale but were less murderous only by degree. An effort was made to eliminate every vestige of Polish leadership by killing priests, trade union leaders, professors, and other prominent people. The infamous Nacht und Nebel order provided for the disappearance without any explanation into the "night and fog" of anyone considered a threat to the Nazi Reich. Concentration camp inmates were subjected to brutal medical and pseudoscientific experiments in which no consideration was given to their willingness or to their well-being before, during, or after the procedures. In addition, many people across Europe starved as a result of the Nazi policy of exporting foodstuffs to Germany.

All across Europe and Asia people suffered because of forced labor. Workers were forcibly recruited and sent off to work in factories supplying the German or Japanese war efforts. Tens of thousands of forced laborers perished because of long hours, starvation diets, unmerciful discipline, and inhumane living conditions. This policy was counterproductive because output was low and replacement difficult, at the very time that

German and Japanese industrial production increasingly lagged behind that of the United States and the Soviet Union.

The most serious charges of systematic brutality leveled against any of the Allies pale by comparison, although some Soviet policies provoked considerable embarrassment. To many, the 1939 Nazi-Soviet Pact and subsequent occupation of eastern Poland, the 1939–1940 Winter War against Finland, and the occupation of the Baltic states and the Romanian province of Bessarabia challenged the ideals of the Atlantic Charter and the United Nations Declaration. Worse still, approximately 10,000 Polish army officers perished at the hands of Stalin's NKVD (The People's Commissariat for Internal Affairs) security forces (ironically, in 1943 the Germans discovered and exposed their graves in Katyn Forest near Smolensk). Many observers were also shocked by the disorderly behavior of the Red Army once it entered Germany and by interference in the internal affairs of the states occupied by the Red Army.

The incarceration of Japanese Americans and Japanese Canadians was another noteworthy manifestation of Allied brutality. Out of fear and racism in the aftermath of the Japanese attack on Pearl Harbor, the U.S. and Canadian governments authorized the forcible removal of more than 110,000 citizens of Japanese descent from the western states and provinces. Placed in isolated, prison-like internment camps for the duration of the war, these people, who had displayed no disloyalty, suffered considerable deprivation and humiliation as well as the loss of their homes, farms, and businesses.

In terms of horror or scale of violence, one must look back hundreds of years to find other periods that, although lacking modern means of destruction, might match World War II in reckless and shameless abandon: to the Thirty Years' War (1618–1648), which depopulated entire regions of the German states through the ravages of war and the accompanying blights of starvation, disease, and economic disruption, or to the thirteenth-century Mongol invasion. However, these examples, once standards, dim by comparison. Nothing in history matches World War II.

Beyond this, the end of World War II presented immediate problems and altered the shape of the world over the next two generations. Much as when a child knocks down a pile of building blocks, one of the most immediate and vexing problems was how to put it all back together again. However, the war so altered the countries, cultures, and societies it touched that restoration of the status quo ante bellum was not feasible in many cases. New power relationships emerged from the war, bringing new perspectives to world politics and complicating the process of drawing new maps and making the peace. Unfortunately, in many places the end of the war did not bring peace or even an end to the shooting.

Foremost among the immediate problems presented by the end of the war was the human problem. In one way or another, the war had uprooted millions of people: forced laborers, concentration camp inmates, refugees, collaborators, and others labeled displaced persons (DPs). Many wanted to return home, but for others home no longer existed; and most of the survivors of concentration camps or forced labor were so physically debilitated that they were incapable of setting off for home. The war's destructiveness in Europe made moving people around very difficult because few trains ran, few bridges stood, and little road transportation existed.

In addition to the DPs, all of whom faced immediate problems, three other groups experienced unique difficulties. Many Soviets who found themselves in regions controlled by the Western Allies did not want to return to the Soviet Union, where the security forces assumed that anyone who survived Nazi captivity had betrayed the Soviet state and deserved punishment. Unfortunately, the Western Allies had earlier agreed to Stalin's demand that all Soviets be repatriated, which meant, in some cases, that fixed bayonets and pointed guns were used to force people onto trains headed east.

Another great tragedy befell many Jews who outlasted the Nazis. It became abundantly clear to many that they were not welcome in their old communities and even in their old homes. After the Jews had been deported, their possessions were often seized by their former neighbors, who were not eager to see the rightful owners return. In the seven months after the war, at least 350 Polish Jews who tried to return home were murdered. The worst incident took place in Kielce on July 4, 1946. After a Polish boy claimed to have escaped imminent death at the hands of two Jews, a mob killed forty-two Jews. Following this pogrom, about 100,000 Polish Jews, more than half of those who survived the Nazis, left Poland. Prompted by the Nazi effort to slaughter all of them and by postwar anti-Semitism, many Jews left for Palestine, soon to become Israel, or for the Western Hemisphere.

Germans living outside the postwar boundaries of Germany also suffered. As former German territory was absorbed into the Soviet Union or Poland, the Allies agreed to the expulsion to Germany of those residents who were ethnic Germans. Following this precedent, Czechoslovakia and Hungary also deported the German minorities living within their frontiers. Altogether, between 12 and 13 million expelled ethnic Germans arrived in Germany, most penniless and competing with other Germans for shelter, food, and jobs, all of which were in short supply. Frequently those expelling the Germans took advantage of the opportunity for vengeance or profit and robbed, raped, harassed, and murdered them (some estimates put this death toll near 2 million). The process of expulsion often marked the end of German communities that had flourished for centuries in eastern Europe.

For millions of people in both Asia and Europe, the end of the war did not mean the end of suffering. The populations in the defeated states and in many other devastated regions faced an ongoing struggle to survive. Economies collapsed, money ceased to have value, jobs and materials did not exist, food and fuel were scarce. In many places, cigarettes became the only functioning currency and the occupying armies the only source for cigarettes. Without the black market, basic goods such as soap or glass or coffee were impossible to get. Recovery and reconstruction appeared improbable in the foreseeable future. The victorious armies found themselves responsible for the populations that had recently been their enemies. No other agencies existed that could provide basic maintenance or reconstruction assistance.

The victors also attempted to do away with those forces they thought had caused the war and to punish responsible individuals. In Germany, the powers conducted denazification campaigns in their respective zones of occupation. The campaigns differed and reflected each state's emphasis on the roots of Nazi ideology. The Soviets took swift and drastic action against some 45,000 individuals who had occupied prominent positions in the pre-1945 economy or politics. Industrialists, landowners, military officers, civil servants, and Nazi Party officials were punished as active Nazis, which meant that they lost their positions and property; in addition, many were sent to Soviet labor camps. The Americans distributed about 12 million questionnaires that, when completed, would identify Nazis who could then be subjected to judicial proceedings. Initial estimates called for trials for about three million Germans, but the demands of reconstruction and the pressures of the Cold War meant lenient treatment for many offenders whose skills were needed in the new Germanies. In all four occupation zones, reeducation campaigns were instituted to instill antifascist values as a foundation for new political and social systems.

In both Germany and Japan, the Allies also indicted individuals and organizations for crimes against peace, conspiracy to wage aggressive war, war crimes, and crimes against humanity. Using captured documents and witnesses, the prosecution argued that the atrocities were so offensive that civilization demanded accountability. After months of testimony, most of the defendants were found guilty and given sentences ranging from death to imprisonment. Subsequently, thousands of Nazis and Japanese were tried in international tribunals as well as in the courts of Germany, the United States, the Soviet Union, Poland, Czechoslovakia, Israel, Hong Kong, Singapore, and Borneo. Even so, many people accused of committing horrific atrocities managed to escape prosecution.

Continuing the fighting long past the time when the military outcome was determined significantly shaped the politics of a postwar world in ways that none of the combatants had anticipated. The United States and the Soviet Union imposed a peace on Europe that preserved the postwar status quo for more than 40 years. No dominating force imposed its will on Asia. Because the Japanese had driven out the Westerners and then withdrawn after their defeat, a vacuum existed. With the door open, many nationalist conflicts and revolutions followed.

Germany ceased to exist for all practical purposes until the occupying powers returned sovereignty to the defeated Germans (Germany did not reappear in a complete sense until its stunning reunification in 1990). Similarly, Poland did not regain its national independence, lost first to the Germans and then to the Soviets, until the end of the 1980s. The crushing German victory over France in 1940 meant that the restoration of French power and prominence depended on states more powerful than France. Acknowledged as one of the so-called Big Four and given a permanent seat on the United Nations Security Council and an occupation zone in Germany, France assumed these perquisites of rank less from its own efforts than through the beneficence of its allies. Great Britain, still weakened from World War I, suffered apparently irreversible national exhaustion. As a primary result of Germany's destruction, the diminution of both France and Britain, and the overshadowing power of the United States and the Soviet Union, Europe could no longer politically dominate the world as it had for centuries.

Japan also ceased to exist for all practical purposes. However, in 1947 the United States imposed a new constitution on Japan, and in 1951, a formal peace treaty was signed. Meanwhile, civil war resumed in China. Waging a type of "undeclared peace" during World War II, Chiang Kai-shek's China had attempted to spend as few of its resources as possible against Japan in anticipation of the postwar resumption of hostilities with Chinese communist forces. With this strategy, China retained enough of its nominal Great Power status to warrant a permanent seat on the UN's Security Council; but Chiang's government did not survive the battle with Mao Zedong's communist forces. In 1949 Mao's army drove Chiang's Kuomintang army from the mainland to the island of Taiwan.

When the imperial powers attempted to reassert authority over their prewar colonies, many of which were in Asia, they faced increased opposition, growing expectations for independence, and, in some cases, armed resistance. U.S. support of decolonization added further impetus to this drive and, starting with the Philippines in 1946, the ranks of independent states expanded over the next two decades. Although the former imperial powers managed to restore their economic power in the decade after the war, their political influence never returned to prewar levels.

After World War II, new conflicts, wars, and revolutions broke out around the world. In addition to China, Greece fought a civil war that pitted Greek royalists, who had fled before the Nazis, against Greek communists, who had played a significant role in the anti-Nazi resistance.

Ho Chi Minh declared Vietnamese independence and led forces that had battled against the Japanese against the returning French colonials. From 1948 to 1959 the British fought a communist-led insurrection in Malaya. Other serious conflicts in the late 1940s pitted the Dutch against Indonesian nationalists, Arabs against Israelis, and Indians against Pakistanis. In the aftermath of a war that disrupted the status quo for much of the world, the process of shaping a new global status quo was long, contentious, and frequently bloody.

Perhaps the postwar changes most affected the status of the two clearest victors, the Soviet Union and the United States. For the Soviet Union, the victory over Hitler's Germany allowed—at a devastating cost—the projection of Soviet influence and power into eastern and central Europe, and gave Stalin's communism legitimacy as a viable alternative to liberal democracy. In addition, the success of the Chinese communist revolution and the turmoil throughout the Third World offered opportunities for further expansion of Soviet influence. Nevertheless, as impressive as it seemed at the time, Soviet success proved temporary.

For the United States, the only power to emerge largely unscathed and considerably stronger than before the war, victory brought increased postwar responsibilities that could not be ignored. In many ways, the decision to locate the headquarters of the United Nations in New York City reflected the recognition of the United States' dominant position and U.S. acceptance of its leading economic and political role in the world. American policy makers faced the dilemma of deciding what part of the prewar status quo to preserve, what to rebuild, and what to change. The United States also shouldered the burden of supporting reconstruction through loans, grants, investments, and security costs. Of course, this increased economic role also meant an increased political role because the United States expected a voice in shaping the processes it funded.

Reflecting the heightened power and prestige of both the Soviet Union and the United States and the diminished stature of several of the traditional Great Powers, the postwar political system developed into a kind of bipolarity. The two superpowers, each with its own distinct ideological foundation, struggled to promote their own security and political agenda while limiting the other's successes. This struggle came to be known as the Cold War. Each superpower emphasized the self-evidence of its own ideology and attempted to persuade any who would listen that the other's efforts amounted to malevolence. In the late 1950s, bipolarity gave way to multipolarity through the Non-Aligned Movement, an organization of smaller states that sought to avoid exclusive association with either superpower in an effort to chart their own courses and exert influence on political and economic questions before the United Nations or other forums. After the mid-1960s, global power was more diffuse than it had ever been.

Efforts were made to achieve collective security in the postwar world through the auspices of the United Nations. Even before the war ended, Allied representatives met to discuss the new UN organization. In 1945, the UN Charter was drafted and ratified, taking effect on October 24 of that year. Specific powers to investigate any situation that might lead to conflict between members were vested in the Security Council. Since the war, the United Nations has sponsored peacekeeping forces, negotiations, and wide-ranging humanitarian programs. Although its record has been spotty, the organization has developed an effectiveness that its predecessor, the League of Nations, never had.

Although the guns have been silent for nearly 70 years, the legacy of World War II is still very much with us. Both academic and popular culture attest to its continuing fascination. With the dissolution of the Soviet Empire and of the Soviet Union itself, the world may see the war's last chapters being written as a new century begins. Ironically, Asia, the site of substantial nationalist and revolutionary turmoil in the decade after the war, appears to have attained a semblance of stability. Meanwhile, Europe, so long locked into the stability imposed by the Cold War, faces new challenges, especially of a financial and economic nature. Perhaps most unsettling, it appears as though many forces held in check by the postwar settlement, including virulent nationalism and neo-Nazism, may be resurfacing. No matter how these ramifications of World War II play out, the world has never seen anything like it before or since.

SELECTED BIBLIOGRAPHY

Barnhart, Michael. *Japan Prepares for Total War: The Search for Economic Security, 1919–1941*. Ithaca, NY: Cornell University Press, 1987. An account of the outbreak of the war in Asia, this work focuses on Japan's efforts to overcome its economic vulnerabilities.

Bell, P. M. H. *The Origins of the Second World War in Europe*. 3rd ed. New York: Longman, 2007. Bell's study is the most thorough and balanced of the complex issues and actions leading to the outbreak of war in Europe. He writes in a lucid manner and, unlike some other histories of this period, is more judicious in his conclusions.

Calder, Angus. *The People's War: Britain, 1939–1945*. New York: Pantheon, 1969. A good discussion of the British home front during the war.

Clausen, Henry C., and Bruce Lee. *Pearl Harbor: Final Judgement*. New York: Crown, 1992. A thorough account of who was responsible for this debacle.

Dallin, Alexander. *German Rule in Russia, 1941–1945*. London: Macmillan, 1957. This is the standard account of Nazi occupation policies in the USSR.

Dower, John W. *War Without Mercy: Race and Power in the Pacific War*. New York: Pantheon Books, 1986. In one of the most important books on the war, the author compares how race was invoked by the Japanese and the Americans.

Dziewanowski, M. K. *War at Any Price: World War II in Europe, 1939–1945*. Englewood Cliffs, NJ: Prentice-Hall, 1987. A concise survey of the war in Europe.

Fussell, Paul. *Wartime: Understanding and Behavior in the Second World War*. New York: Oxford University Press, 1989. In this follow-up to his highly acclaimed study on World War I, Fussell continues his examination of the culture of war.

Gilbert, Martin. *The Second World War; A Complete History*. Rev. ed. New York: Henry Holt, 2004. Possibly the best available volume on the war. Gilbert adroitly interweaves the story of the military campaigns with home front anecdotes to give one a sense of both the breadth and depth of the conflict.

Hilberg, Raul. *The Destruction of the European Jews.* Chicago: Quadrangle, 1967. One of the standard studies of the Holocaust.

Hough, Richard. *The Longest Battle: The War at Sea, 1939–1945.* New York: Morrow, 1986. A general survey of the naval aspects of the war, with some excellent battle maps.

Ienaga, Saburo. *The Pacific War, 1931–1945: A Critical Perspective of Japan's Role in World War II.* New York: Pantheon Books, 1978. Ienaga has written a penetrating analysis of the war against Japan.

Jones, F. C. *Japan's New Order in East Asia, 1937–1945.* London: Oxford University Press, 1954. This is one of the best accounts of the way Japan governed its empire.

Merridale, Catherine. *Ivan's War: Life and Death in the Red Army, 1939–1945.* New York: Henry Holt, 2006. Merridale, University of London, provides a valuable service by turning her attention to the long-neglected story of the Red Army's wartime soldiers. Based on numerous interviews as well as archival research, she shows that "G.I. Ivan" was not only brave and resourceful but also hopeful of a better post-wartime life that—thanks to Stalin—never materialized.

Presseisen, E. L. *Germany and Japan: A Study in Totalitarian Diplomacy.* The Hague, the Netherlands: Martinus Nijhoff, 1958. Presseisen has written a clear description of the relationship between these two powers.

Taylor, A. J. P. *The Origins of the Second World War.* New York: Atheneum, 1961. Taylor's controversial study attacks the standard view that Hitler was solely responsible for the coming of war.

Terkel, Studs. *"The Good War": An Oral History of World War II.* New York: Pantheon, 1984. Terkel invites a variety of Americans to tell stories of their experiences at the battlefront as well as the home front.

Toland, John. *The Rising Sun: The Decline and Fall of the Japanese Empire, 1936–1945.* New York: Random House, 1970. A fine popular history.

Trunk, Isaiah. *Judenrat: The Jewish Councils in Eastern Europe under Nazi Occupation.* New York: Macmillan, 1972. Trunk examines the validity of the accusation that Jewish officials collaborated, willingly or unwillingly, with the Nazis.

Werth, Alexander. *Russia at War, 1941–1945.* New York: Dutton, 1964. Werth's book is the standard account of World War II on Europe's Eastern Front.

Willmott, H. P. *The Great Crusade: A New Complete History of the Second World War.* London: M. Joseph, 1989. One of the best single-volume accounts of the war, with considerable interpretation as well as narrative.

Wright, Gordon. *The Ordeal of Total War, 1939–1945.* New York: Harper and Row, 1968. Part of the magnificent Rise of Modern Europe series, Wright's book focuses on the war's economic and social aspects as well as its military and political ones.

WINSTON CHURCHILL (1874–1965)

In a versatile career that spanned four decades, Winston Churchill served the United Kingdom as a war correspondent, soldier, politician, member of the British Parliament, first lord of the Admiralty, and prime minister. A prolific writer and an eloquent orator as well, he inspired Britons with his writings and speeches during the dark days of World War II. A man of action as well as a man of words, he was an inspiring and decisive military and political leader during both World Wars.

In a versatile career that spanned four decades, Winston Churchill served Great Britain as a war correspondent, soldier, politician, member of the British Parliament, First Lord of the Admiralty, and Prime Minister. (Library of Congress)

Winston Leonard Spencer Churchill was born at Blenheim Palace, Woodstock, Oxfordshire, on November 30, 1874. He was the eldest son of Lord Randolph Churchill, chancellor of the exchequer, and Jennie Churchill, the beautiful daughter of a New York businessman. At age seven, Churchill was sent to St. George's Ascot, a preparatory school. Rough and rebellious, he learned to read quickly but showed little interest in other areas of study. In 1888, he transferred to Harrow, another prestigious preparatory school, where he excelled at swimming, fencing, history, and writing. Impertinent to his instructors, Churchill was nonetheless fascinated by all things military, taking a particular interest in toy soldiers and mock warfare. In 1893, he qualified with difficulty to attend Sandhurst Royal Military College as a cavalry cadet. His conduct improved through strict military discipline, and he became an avid equestrian. After graduating in 1894, he was commissioned in the British army and joined the Fourth Hussars.

In 1895, Churchill obtained a brief leave of absence from his military duties to visit war-torn Cuba, which was then fighting for independence from Spain. Churchill observed the course of the war and then informally embarked on a career as a war correspondent by writing his first newspaper article on the fighting.

After Churchill returned to Britain that same year, his father died at age 45. Although Randolph had spent little time with his son, he had a tremendous impact on the young Churchill's character. Randolph had been one of Britain's foremost politicians during the late nineteenth century, but through a series of political blunders and suffering from the increasingly debilitating effects of syphilis, he slowly lost his prominence in politics. His brief political success and hard-hearted efforts to instill in his son a sense of responsibility compelled Churchill to strive for his father's approval as long as Randolph was alive. His death, therefore, came as quite a blow to Churchill, who sincerely mourned his father and regretted that he had never lived up to Randolph's expectations.

In an effort to assuage his grief, Churchill threw himself into his military career at the same time that Britain was fighting a series of conflicts to consolidate its hold on the country's various colonies around the globe. From 1896 until 1897, he was on active service in India with the Malakand Field Force, about which he published a book, *The Malakand Field Force*. Joining the Nile expeditionary force in 1898, he fought hand-to-hand against the Dervishes in the Battle of Omdurman and served in the cavalry during the reconquest of the Sudan, writing his second book, *The River War*.

After running unsuccessfully for political office in 1899, Churchill went to South Africa as a war correspondent for the *Morning Post* to cover the Boer War. He was captured in an ambush in November and held prisoner until he staged a dramatic escape one month later, returning to England a hero and publishing two books on the war, as well as a novel, *Savrola*.

In 1900, Churchill became a member of Parliament for Oldham, standing with the British Conservative Party. When fellow conservative Joseph Chamberlain launched his campaign for higher tariffs in 1904, however, Churchill joined the British Liberal Party in support of the free trade issue and bitterly attacked the conservatives. The following year, he became parliamentary undersecretary for the colonies. In 1906, Churchill became a member of Parliament for North West Manchester. That same year, he published a biography of his father.

After being appointed president of the Board of Trade in 1908, Churchill introduced the labor exchanges, a national employment service that he hoped would reduce unemployment in the country. In September of that same year, he married Clementine Ogilvy Hozier, daughter of Sir Henry and Lady Blanche Hozier. They enjoyed life-long domestic happiness and eventually had three daughters and one son.

In 1910, Churchill became home secretary, one of the most powerful positions in the government, where he consistently worked for social reform. He asked for troops to keep order during the prolonged miners' strike and played a prominent role in quelling the "Siege of Sidney Street," a famous London street shoot-out that took place in 1911.

In 1911, Churchill was appointed first lord of the Admiralty, a position that seemed a perfect match for Churchill's talents and interests. During his four-year tenure at the Admiralty, he methodically prepared Britain for the major war that he felt sure would come. He developed an experienced and well-trained war staff and reorganized the Royal Navy, modernizing it and securing its position as the finest fleet in the world. When World War I erupted in 1914, Britain's command of the seas was unrivaled, despite Germany's efforts to win the naval arms race that the two countries had been engaged in since the turn of the century. Throughout the course of the war, Churchill also showed his foresight by investing in the development of military aviation and the armored car (the precursor of the tank).

British forces suffered a series of setbacks during the first two years of the war that caused many to question Churchill's abilities, particularly as he was the most aggressive and active member of an otherwise slow-moving cabinet. Supremely confident in the Royal Navy, Churchill convinced the cabinet to countenance several maneuvers that proved disastrous to British forces. Foremost among these was the 1915 attack on the Dardanelles. Churchill proposed that the Royal Navy could come to the aid of the Russians (who were fighting the Turks) by launching a massive naval campaign against the Dardanelles while the British army landed at Gallipoli and launched a ground campaign. The controversial operation began in February 1915 but turned sour when the fleet encountered a row of undetected mines that destroyed a large portion of the British and French naval force. The Gallipoli campaign in April of that same year proved just as disastrous for British forces and ended in their total withdrawal from the region.

In the aftermath of public criticism over the Dardanelles and Gallipoli campaigns, Churchill was removed as first lord of the Admiralty, although he briefly remained a member of the cabinet. In November, he resigned from the cabinet as well and went to the Western Front, serving as colonel of the Sixth Battalion Scots Fusiliers. In July 1917, he returned to politics with his appointment as minister of munitions, where he concentrated on the production of tanks and ammunition.

After the war ended in November 1918, Churchill held a series of government positions, first as secretary of state for war and air from 1919 to 1921, from which position he supervised demobilization. In 1921, he became colonial secretary, helping to negotiate the treaty that resulted in Irish Home Rule in a large portion of Ireland. He was defeated in his bid for parliamentary office in 1922, but in October 1924, he was elected for Epping. He changed political parties once again by realigning himself with the Conservatives and was subsequently appointed chancellor of the exchequer under Prime Minister Stanley Baldwin. His tenure as chancellor, however, was marked by national unrest and economic instability. In 1925, he returned Britain to the gold standard, a move that he believed promised long-term benefits but resulted in severe short-term hardships for the country, particularly as Britain struggled to reestablish a firm economic footing during the postwar depression. The General Strike of 1926, in which thousands of workers in all industries in Britain walked out of their jobs in support of a miners strike, inspired Churchill's wrath, as he pushed the government to break the strikers' will. The strike marked the most dramatic episode in Churchill's lifelong battle against labor unions.

Out of office in 1929, Churchill decided to visit Canada and the United States. He embarked on a lecture tour and published his memoirs, *A Roving Commission*. While visiting New York in December 1932, he was knocked down by a taxi and badly hurt. Suffering from 15 broken bones and an internal hemorrhage, doctors feared for his life, but with characteristic tenacity, he recovered from his injuries with remarkable speed.

Throughout the 1930s, Churchill became increasingly angry at the government's unwillingness to recognize the threat posed by the rise of fascism in Europe in general and the establishment of the Nazi Party in Germany in particular. Believing that peace could not be maintained for long in Europe in the light of these related threats, he urged Britain to rearm and to establish a defensive alliance of democracies. He remained an outspoken opponent of Prime Minister Neville Chamberlain's policy of appeasement toward German dictator Adolf Hitler, whereby Britain acceded to Germany's territorial demands in an effort to stave off war. During this period, he continued to write, publishing a volume of essays, *Amid These Storms* (the first book of a four-volume life of his ancestor, John Churchill) and two more volumes of speeches and articles.

When World War II began in September 1939, Churchill returned to politics once again as first lord of the Admiralty. In May 1940, after Chamberlain resigned the premiership, Churchill formed a coalition government and became prime minister. At that point, Britain was facing what many believed was the country's darkest hour. Paris had been captured by the Nazis, and all of France was on the point of capitulation to the Germans. Few doubted that Hitler would turn his attention to Britain next. Churchill appeared to meet the German threat without fear, and he rallied the British people to what he called the ultimate fight for survival. His leadership would prove vital to the British war effort, as he forcefully denounced proposals to negotiate with the Germans for some kind of settlement or conditional peace. Such submission to what he saw as the forces of evil was unthinkable.

Although Churchill offered the British people nothing but "blood, toil, tears and sweat," they rallied behind him, inspired by his eloquent, patriotic speeches that cited the noblest aspects of Britain's cultural heritage to stave off the threat of invasion and conquest. Britain faced incredible odds, as the German war machine appeared to be unstoppable. Nevertheless, Churchill vowed publicly that the British people would "never surrender." He faced his first serious challenge when France fell to the Germans in June 1940. In a last-ditch effort to rescue what was left of the British Expeditionary Force and part of the French army (which were trapped on a beachhead at Dunkirk in northern France), Churchill called on privately owned British vessels to assist the Royal Navy with evacuation efforts, in what many proclaim as one of the most dramatic rescues in history.

Churchill's next challenge came in preparing Britain for the inevitable attack from German forces. With steely determination, Churchill braced the country for the German onslaught, stepping up efforts to mobilize the home guard and preparing the Royal Navy and Royal Air Force (RAF) to defend the island nation. In one of his most impassioned speeches during the summer of 1940, Churchill inspired the British people with the words:

> What General Weygand called the Battle of France is over. I expect that the Battle of Britain is about to begin. Upon this battle depends the survival of Christian civilization. Upon it depends our own British life and the long continuity of our institutions and our empire.
>
> The whole fury and might of the enemy must very soon be turned on us. Hitler knows that he will have to break us in the island or lose the war. If we can stand up to him, all Europe may be free and the life of the world may move forward into broad, sunlit uplands. But if we fail, then the whole world, including the United States, including all that we have known and cared for, will sink into the abyss of a new dark age made more sinister and perhaps more protracted by the lights of perverted science.
>
> Let us, therefore, brace ourselves to our duties and so bear ourselves that if the British empire and its commonwealth last for a thousand years men will still say, "*This* was their finest hour."

In September 1940, the German Luftwaffe (air force) attacked, hoping to bomb the British into submission and ease the way for German ground troops in a subsequent land invasion. Hitler even optimistically hoped that the British would negotiate a surrender after the Luftwaffe finished with them. Much to Hitler's anger and disappointment, the British people, particularly those living in London and other major industrial cities, refused to break under the pressure of nightly bombings that killed hundreds and destroyed large segments of the city. In addition, the RAF launched a decisive defense that stymied the Luftwaffe, refusing to yield control of the skies over Britain. The Battle of Britain was the Germans' first significant defeat of the war and convinced Hitler that he should turn his attention to weaker parts of Europe before attempting to conquer Britain again.

Churchill was widely proclaimed a hero for his role in leading the British through this period. After staving off the Germans, he turned his attention to rebuilding Britain's military forces. He actively solicited financial and material help from the United States, although it was a neutral country in the conflict. His close friend, U.S. president Franklin D. Roosevelt, obliged by initiating the Lend-Lease program, which supplied Britain with much-needed military supplies and equipment. Churchill doggedly encouraged Roosevelt to bring the United States into the war, reminding him repeatedly that Britain was "standing alone" against the Nazis. After the United States entered the war in December 1941 (in the aftermath of the Japanese attack against the U.S. Navy at Pearl Harbor, Hawaii, rather than Churchill's urgings), Churchill and Roosevelt quickly allied their efforts to form a powerful coalition against the Axis powers. He also welcomed the Soviet Union to the alliance, albeit somewhat reluctantly as he despised communism and distrusted Soviet premier Joseph Stalin. Nevertheless, Churchill recognized the Soviet Union's massive military potential and set aside his misgivings to devote all of his efforts to winning the war.

Throughout the war, Churchill advocated a controversial military strategy that centered around attacking what he called the "soft underbelly of Europe"—the Mediterranean—rather than launching a costly offensive against well-defended France. Stalin openly objected to this policy, believing that Churchill's plan meant that Soviet troops would end up doing most of the actual fighting. Roosevelt, too, had misgivings, but the Allies launched a series of successful, but hard-fought, campaigns in North Africa and the Mediterranean between 1941 and 1943. More Allied victories in the Balkans and Italy seemed to confirm the wisdom of Churchill's plan.

By 1944, the Allies had built up their own strength and weakened the Germans enough that Churchill gave his support to an invasion of France. He played an instrumental role in organizing the resulting D-Day operation in June of that year, which ultimately led to the liberation of western Europe and the defeat of Germany.

With victory for the Allies in sight, Churchill turned his attention increasingly to the shape of the postwar world. Through a series of conferences, Churchill, Roosevelt, and Stalin hammered out tentative agreements for dealing with a defeated Germany and restoring order to the world. Earlier than his colleagues, Churchill perceived the great struggle between communism and democracy that emerged as the Cold War in 1945 and would dominate world affairs for the next 45 years. Following the surrender of Germany in May 1945, Churchill was alarmed and disheartened by the amount of territory the Soviets held in Europe.

Churchill received another blow in July 1945, when the conservatives were defeated in the general election. He became the leader of the opposition in Parliament, a cruel disappointment after his wartime prestige. He remained, however, an international hero and proved himself an astute observer of worldwide affairs. In a 1946 speech that he delivered in Fulton, Missouri, he warned of the developing East-West rift, stating that an "iron curtain" was dividing Europe, behind which (in the countries controlled by the Soviet Union) tyranny reigned.

In 1948, Churchill published the first volume of a six-volume history of World War II. In August 1949, he attended the first session of the Council of Europe at Strasbourg, fostering the conception of a European and Atlantic unity, later to bear fruit in several supranational organizations. In 1951, he returned to the premiership at the age of 77. This second tenure in office was considerably less dramatic than his first but resulted in a number of honors for the elder statesman, including a knighthood and a Nobel Prize for literature. By this time, he had become almost a legend in his own time, known for his political career, his writing abilities, his irascible personality, and his sharp wit. One of the more famous Churchill anecdotes concerns a dinner party where he was seated next to Lady Nancy Astor. At one point, Astor quipped to Churchill, "Sir, if you were my husband, I'd poison your coffee." To which Churchill replied, "Madam, if you were my wife, I'd drink it."

For years, Churchill had suffered from a series of strokes, with the first actually occurring during the war. In 1953, he suffered his third and most serious stroke. He continued in office for two more years, however, resigning on April 5, 1955. Shortly after leaving office, he published the first volume of a four-volume *History of the English-Speaking Peoples*. In July 1964, he formally retired from the House of Commons.

Although Churchill's detractors saw in him a man of political expediency and of grating temperament, at the end of his life he was looked upon with veneration, enjoying a world reputation as an all-seeing strategist, an inspiring war leader, and the last of the classic orators. Churchill died in London on January 24, 1965. After one of the largest state funerals in British history attended by thousands and viewed on television throughout the world, he was buried beside his parents in Bladon Churchyard, near Blenheim Palace.

ABC-CLIO

ADOLF HITLER (1889–1945)

Adolf Hitler was the charismatic, forceful leader of Germany who led his nation to bloody ruin. In a failed bid for world conquest, his Third Reich overran more land in Europe, Asia, and North Africa than any European leader and led to the deaths of tens of million people. Even today, many years after the end of World War II, he remains the personification of evil.

Hitler was born at Brannau, Austria, on April 20, 1889, the son of a German customs clerk and an Austrian peasant woman. An indifferent, sullen student, he dropped out of high school to work as an aspiring artist but failed to gain entrance into the Vienna Academy of Fine Arts. He subsequently migrated to Munich where he enlisted in the 16th Bavarian Infantry Regiment at the onset of World War I. For four years, Hitler served chiefly as a messenger, and he received four decorations for bravery, including the prestigious Iron Cross, First Class. At one point, he sustained serious injuries in a gas attack and spent several months recuperating. Hitler finally mustered out of the German army in 1919 with a rank of corporal.

The German surrender that ended World War I in November 1918 led to the 1919 Treaty of Versailles, which imposed severe penalties on Germany. Among other consequences,

Adolf Hitler at a Nazi Party rally in Nuremberg, Germany, ca. 1928. The economic crisis that began in Germany after World War I and escalated with the U.S. stock market crash of 1929 created a climate of fear and anger that Hitler and the Nazi Party manipulated to gain political power. (National Archives)

these penalties brought much hardship to the German people and increased their resentment of the democratic German government that signed the treaty. The angry and disenchanted Hitler joined the German Worker's Party, which he later helped expand into the National Socialist German Workers' Party, better known as the Nazis. Hitler proved himself a master of oratory and political intrigue and became intent on seizing the national political agenda. However, when his attempted coup against the Bavarian government (later known as the Beer Hall Putsch) was crushed by police and military units on November 8–9, 1923, Hitler was sentenced to five years in Landsberg Prison. He only served nine months before a general amnesty was proclaimed, and he used the interval to outline his political philosophy in the book *Mein Kampf* (*My Struggle*). In it, he openly flaunted his anti-Semitism and emphasized his belief that German success required territorial expansion in the east. However, the book was never taken seriously by critics, and its warning signs went unheeded.

Hitler's trial and subsequent imprisonment gained him and the Nazis some notoriety, and he resolved to overthrow the established Weimar Republic by working within the system. Despite his eloquence and nationalist fervor, as well as the country's general discontent with the republican form of government, the Nazis remained an insignificant force during most of the 1920s. However, Hitler's ambitions received a tremendous boost during the global depression that began in 1929. More and more desperate Germans turned to him for leadership in this national economic crisis. By 1932, the Nazis had become Germany's most popular party. Hitler's promises of jobs, security, and a revitalized and respected if not feared Germany resonated with the electorate. On January 30, 1933, president Paul von Hindenburg appointed Hitler chancellor of Germany.

When Hindenburg died the following year, Hitler combined the offices of chancellor and president to become the "uncontested leader" (*Der Führer*) of the German nation.

Once in power, Hitler ruthlessly suppressed civil rights, murdered his political opponents within the Nazi Party during the infamous Night of the Long Knives on June 30, 1934, and began to reinvigorate the emaciated German economy. He accomplished an economic revival for the country by expanding the military-industrial sector in clear violation of the Versailles Treaty. As a military leader, Hitler was well versed in military tactics and had a working grasp of military technology. He took a special interest in developing fast tanks and airplanes that would eventually form the basis for the extremely mobile "blitzkrieg" warfare of World War II.

As Germany grew stronger militarily, Hitler grew bolder on the international stage. He also routinely disregarded sound military advice from his senior generals, whose perceived timidity he regarded with open contempt. In 1936, he marched troops into the demilitarized Rhineland and also formed an alliance with Benito Mussolini's fascist Italy. Two years later, Hitler annexed Austria to Germany. At the Munich Conference of September 1938, Hitler convinced Britain and France to allow him to annex the Sudetenland (an area of western Czechoslovakia containing mostly ethnic Germans). Hitler, however, decided after the conference to annex all of Czechoslovakia, embarrassing Britain and France and making all of Europe increasingly wary of his expansionist ambitions. He then stunned the world in August 1939 by signing a nonaggression pact with Soviet Union leader Joseph Stalin, which not only divided eastern Europe between the two dictatorships but also ensured that if war came Germany would not have to fight on two fronts. The lack of decisive leadership and resistance to his plans evidenced by the Western democracies did little to discourage Hitler, who by the end of the 1930s was finally ready to gain new territories by force.

In September 1939, German forces attacked Poland thereby precipitating World War II in Europe. Britain and France quickly declared war on Germany in defense of their Polish ally. The newly developed blitzkrieg tactics worked brilliantly, and Poland was crushed in a matter of weeks. Despite the declaration of war, however, France and Britain took no offensive action on their own. Hitler used the impasse to shift his forces westward, and by June 1940, France had been conquered, and English troops chased off the Continent from their vulnerable beachhead at Dunkirk, in northern France. During the Battle of Britain which followed, Germany failed to bomb the British into submission and an invasion of England had to be postponed.

Hitler turned his attention to other parts of Europe. Greece and Yugoslavia were subdued, along with most of North Africa, before Hitler committed his single biggest mistake of the war. In June 1941, German forces launched an all-out offensive against the Soviet Union, in open disregard of the nonaggression pact. Initial Russian casualties were colossal, and the Soviet army was driven back deep into Russia's interior. When Hitler refused to allow his men to retreat from Russia for the winter, the Soviets counterattacked at Moscow, inflicting the first real defeat on Hitler's army.

Hitler was so enraged that he sacked most of his leading generals, remained contemptuous of the rest, and appointed himself as commander in chief of the armed forces. For the next four years, Germany waged a losing war in the east against superior numbers of Russian forces, and in late 1941, Hitler compounded his mistakes by declaring war on the United States after the Japanese attack on Pearl Harbor in December 1941. As a sign of his growing degeneration, he began relying more on astrology than the opinions of his senior military leadership when making major decisions.

In addition to waging a war of aggression, Hitler embarked on one of the greatest crimes against humanity ever committed. Having espoused the notion of a racially pure (or Aryan) nation, he turned his hatred of Jews into a national policy of mass extermination through creation of numerous death camps. An estimated 6 million Jews died in this process that the Nazis called the "Final Solution," and is perhaps better known as the Holocaust. An equal number of "undesirables" including communists, prisoners of war, Gypsies, intellectuals, and handicapped people were either murdered or worked to death as forced labor. Many of these unfortunates were deported from occupied countries.

By 1944 the Third Reich's days were clearly numbered, but Hitler embarked on several desperate gambits to stave off defeat. He directed construction of numerous "super weapons" including jet fighters and guided missiles in a futile attempt to turn the tide of the war back to Germany's favor. After surviving a July 1944 assassination attempt, he squandered Germany's final military reserves in the ill-fated Battle of the Bulge in December of that year but failed to defeat the western Allies. By April 1945, the vengeful Soviet army had all but surrounded Berlin, and Hitler was a virtual captive in his command bunker. He had always declared that Germany would fight "until five past midnight," but on April 30, 1945, Hitler and his longtime mistress, Eva Braun, committed suicide rather than face capture. Thus the vaunted Third Reich, which the Nazis boasted would last 1,000 years, collapsed in utter ruin after only 12 years.

JOHN C. FREDRIKSEN

JOSEPH STALIN (1879–1953)

An important member of the Bolshevik Party during the Russian Revolution of 1917, Joseph Stalin rose to become the successor to Vladimir Lenin as the leader of the Soviet Union. Stalin shaped the early Soviet Union without regard for the consequences of his actions among the Soviet population and achieved prodigious growth and a police state of unrivaled proportions. He also led his country to victory in World War II as Russian soldiers and civilians absorbed the vast majority of casualties suffered by the Allied forces. Finally, he was one of the primary architects of the postwar world and its bipolar division between East and West.

Stalin (which means "steel" in Russian) was born Iosif Vissarionovich Dzhugashvili on December 21, 1879, in Gori, Georgia. Stalin's parents were simple peasants, and his father supported the family as a cobbler. He had several childhood aliments including smallpox (which left scarring marks on his face), and a carriage accident that caused his left arm to be permanently shortened and stiffened. Despite his physical aliments, however, Stalin was reported to be in good shape and very strong for his size.

Like the majority of the population in the Georgian countryside, Stalin grew up in poverty and uncertainty. He did receive a good education, however, and he did especially well in history and geography. He began to learn Russian at age nine, adding it to his native Georgian. In 1894, he graduated near the top of his class from a local church school in his hometown and received a scholarship to attend Tiflis Theological Seminary,

An important if rather inconspicuous member of the Bolshevik Party during the Russian Revolution, Joseph Stalin succeeded Vladimir Lenin as leader of the Soviet Union. Stalin steered his country through the formative years of its existence, rallied his people to victory during World War II, and led the USSR through the early years of the Cold War. He was a defining figure of the Soviet state and of twentieth-century totalitarianism. As dictator, he carried out a ruthless series of purges in which he imprisoned and killed millions of Soviets including his chief political rivals as well as anyone else not deemed sufficiently loyal to him. (Library of Congress)

a leading school in Georgian society. At the seminary, Stalin was exposed to Marxism and became involved in revolutionary circles that caused his interest in school to wane. He was expelled from the seminary in 1899.

By 1900, Stalin was deeply involved in the Marxist revolutionary movement in Georgia. Following several conflicts with authorities, he was exiled to Siberia. Following his escape from Siberia, Stalin grew involved with the Bolshevik Party and became a member in 1905. In 1912, he was nominated by Lenin to the party's highest governing body, the Central Committee. In the next few years, Stalin's tasks within the party were primarily operational and theoretical. Stalin wrote about how to integrate the various ethnic groups of the Russian Empire into the future Bolshevik state. He would retain this role of a behind-the-scenes operator through the Russian Revolution of 1917 and the Russian Civil War that followed.

Stalin's chief role during most of the revolution was that of propagandist and supporter of Lenin, especially when the latter was out of the country. Although he remained in the background, Stalin's work was critical to the success of the revolution, and in Lenin's eyes, Stalin showed capable leadership. It was mainly because of Lenin's favor that Stalin gained additional power in the Communist Party. However, other prominent revolutionaries like Leon Trotsky and Nikolai Bukharin had doubts about Stalin's personality and abilities. They believed that he was not fit for a leadership role in the new All-Russian Communist Party (later renamed the Communist Party of the Soviet Union [CPSU]).

On April 3, 1922, Stalin was nevertheless granted the post that would eventually catapult him to the leadership of the Soviet Union: he was made general secretary of the

Central Committee of the CPSU. From that position, Stalin was able to wield enormous power. In the month after Stalin's appointment, Lenin had a stroke that would ultimately lead to his death less than two years later. Lenin's poor health during that time led to uncertainty among the party leadership. Lenin wrote what came to be known as his *Testament,* in which he alleged that Stalin was too "rude" and "coarse" to be an effective leader of the party. In contrast, Lenin praised Trotsky for his leadership and called him "perhaps the most capable man in the present Central Committee." Lenin's comments came too late and were somewhat ambiguous on the question of succession. Because of the power he already wielded, Stalin was able to block the *Testament* from being used against him.

Stalin moved carefully to solidify his authority. He ruled the country along with Lev Kamenev and Grigory Zinoviev, two of Lenin's closest compatriots, following Lenin's death on January 21, 1924. By 1928, Stalin had solidified his grip on power by first moving against Trotsky, whom he saw as his fiercest rival, and then moving against Kamenev, Zinoviev, and Bukharin.

From that point on, Stalin ruled without significant obstacles to his authority. His first priority was to create the communist state that Lenin and the Bolsheviks had once envisioned. In 1929, he ordered the first of many Five-Year Plans to modernize and industrialize the Soviet Union. He also ordered the collectivization of agriculture and essentially created large agricultural communities that would feed the growing industrial state. The Soviet Union's economy and industry did grow, but collectivization was achieved only with the dramatic sacrifice of the Russian people. The CPSU, although it ran the government, did not have a large membership compared with the population of the entire country. Many people resisted the efforts of the government to take their land from them for the purposes of the state. Famines resulted in 1931 and in 1932. Some historians estimate that as many as 10 million people died as a result of collectivization and the resulting famines.

Soon after the revolution, Lenin had organized a system of secret police, and that apparatus was greatly expanded under Stalin. In addition, beginning in 1934, Stalin began to move against the old Bolsheviks, whom he viewed as potential enemies. In the resulting chaos of trials and upheaval, millions of people died in what became known as the Great Purge. In 1938, the terror subsided, but not before millions were sent to the Gulag (a system of Soviet prison camps in the northern reaches of Russia or in Siberia), and all of Stalin's potential or imagined enemies were eliminated. Many of those who were sent to the camps died, in addition to the millions who were killed by execution or famine. In their absence, Stalin was free to develop a cult of personality around himself as loyal party members wrote songs of praise to him and rewrote history texts for school children.

In 1939, a new danger threatened the Soviet Union: Nazi leader Adolf Hitler and his Third Reich. Hitler wanted the lands east of Germany as *Lebensraum* (living space) for the German people. Stalin secured a temporary peace for the Soviet Union by signing the Nazi-Soviet Pact (also known as the nonaggression pact) with Hitler in that year. The pact divided Poland between Germany and the Soviet Union. Stalin hoped that this would appease Hitler's appetite for land, but it did not.

In the summer of 1941, a year after the Germans conquered France, Hitler attacked the Soviet Union. The attack caught Stalin and the Soviet Union unprepared. Initially, the attack went very well for the Germans, who made it all the way to Moscow before winter. The harsh Russian winter trapped the Germans, however, and they suffered severe losses from disease and starvation during early 1942.

Seizing his chance to turn the tide of the war, Stalin rallied the Russian people by putting aside communist rhetoric and calling on Russian patriotism to save the country from the German invaders. Stalin also drew on the military and economic resources created by the industrialization of the Soviet Union and the assistance of the Allies. Soviet (and Allied) fortunes began to change in 1943 with victory at the Battle of Stalingrad, and by the spring of 1945, the Germans were beaten. The Soviet Union had advanced far into Central Europe during the final months of the war, and Stalin emerged victorious.

Through a series of conferences with Allied leaders both during and immediately after the war, Stalin secured for the Soviet Union all territory in eastern Europe occupied by the Red Army at the time of the German surrender. Stalin saw those lands not only as territory that could be exploited for the benefit of the Soviet Union (much of this territory had been surrendered during World War I when the Bolsheviks withdrew from the war) but also as a buffer zone between the Soviet Union and future attacks from the West. By the late 1940s, the boundary between the Soviet sphere and the nations of western Europe had been christened the "iron curtain" by Winston Churchill, and the Cold War was setting in.

During the early 1950s, Stalin's health began to wane. As his mind and body decayed, his suspicion and paranoia of others (which had always been strong) were further amplified. On his death on March 5, 1953, there is evidence that Stalin was planning another purge against his supposed enemies. He died as a result of a brain hemorrhage at age 73.

ABC-CLIO

DOCUMENT: NAZI-SOVIET NON-AGGRESSION PACT (1939)

In 1939, Adolf Hitler and Joseph Stalin signed the Nazi-Soviet Nonaggression Pact, also known as the Molotov-Ribbentrop Pact, in which they agreed to solve conflict between their countries in a peaceful manner. A secret protocol to the pact clarified the borders between Germany and the Soviet Union. Poland was divided between the two and the Baltic states were assigned to the Soviet sphere of influence. Although Stalin hoped that the pact would satisfy Hitler's desire to control lands east of Germany, he was sorely disappointed. After less than two years, the agreement ended when Germany invaded the Soviet Union in June 1941.

The Government of the German Reich and the Government of the Union of Soviet Socialist Republics desirous of strengthening the cause of peace between Germany and the USSR, and proceeding from the fundamental provisions of the Neutrality Agreement concluded in April, 1926 between Germany and the USSR, have reached the following Agreement:

Article I. Both High Contracting Parties obligate themselves to desist from any act of violence, any aggressive action, and any attack on each other, either individually or jointly with other Powers.

Article II. Should one of the High Contracting Parties become the object of belligerent action by a third Power, the other High Contracting Party shall in no manner lend its support to this third Power.

Article III. The Governments of the two High Contracting Parties shall in the future maintain continual contact with one another for the purpose of consultation in order to exchange information on problems affecting their common interests.

Article IV. Neither of the two High Contracting Parties shall participate in any grouping of Powers whatsoever that is directly or indirectly aimed at the other party.

Article V. Should disputes or conflicts arise between the High Contracting Parties over problems of one kind or another, both parties shall settle these disputes or conflicts exclusively through friendly exchange of opinion or, if necessary, through the establishment of arbitration commissions.

Article VI. The present Treaty is concluded for a period of ten years, with the proviso that, in so far as one of the High Contracting Parties does not advance it one year prior to the expiration of this period, the validity of this Treaty shall automatically be extended for another five years.

Article VII. The present treaty shall be ratified within the shortest possible time. The ratifications shall be exchanged in Berlin. The Agreement shall enter into force as soon as it is signed.

Secret Additional Protocol

Article I. In the event of a territorial and political rearrangement in the areas belonging to the Baltic States (Finland, Estonia, Latvia, Lithuania), the northern boundary of Lithuania shall represent the boundary of the spheres of influence of Germany and the USSR. In this connection the interest of Lithuania in the Vilnius area is recognized by each party.

Article II. In the event of a territorial and political rearrangement of the areas belonging to the Polish state, the spheres of influence of Germany and the USSR shall be bounded approximately by the line of the rivers Narev, Vistula and San.

The question of whether the interests of both parties make desirable the maintenance of an independent Polish State and how such a state should be bounded can only be definitely determined in the course of further political developments.

In any event both Governments will resolve this question by means of a friendly agreement.

Article III. With regard to Southeastern Europe attention is called by the Soviet side to its interest in Bessarabia. The German side declares its complete political disinterestedness in these areas.

Article IV. This protocol shall be treated by both parties as strictly secret.

Moscow, August 23, 1939.
For the Government of the German Reich: V. Ribbentrop
Plenipotentiary of the Government of the USSR: V. Molotov

7

The End of Colonialism, c. 1945–Present

INTRODUCTION

On the eve of World War I (1914), Western nations controlled virtually the entire globe. Beginning with the explorations of the fifteenth century and continuing through the middle of the eighteenth century, Europeans extended their domination over vast reaches. After a hiatus of about 100 years during which the Western world focused on domestic developments, the process of swallowing up the globe began again. Over the next few decades, the Western nations completed their conquest of the world.

The triumphant march of colonial conquerors did not go unopposed; however, the native peoples simply lacked the requisite technology, particularly military hardware, to resist successfully. Nevertheless, those who found themselves oppressed by colonial masters deeply resented the inferior status imposed on them. In the years before 1914, in the Ottoman Empire, China, and India, indigenous leaders began to rebel against the racial bigotry, economic exploitation, cultural imperialism, and political subjugation that were imperialism's hallmarks.

World War I hastened this process. Many colonial soldiers fought for the mother country, and at least a few came away from this experience convinced that their sacrifice entitled their people to autonomy if not independence. Furthermore, although U.S. president Woodrow Wilson had not intended to stimulate anti-imperialist sentiment in Asia and Africa, his Fourteen Points (1918), which outlined an idealistic vision of the future, fired the imagination of subject peoples everywhere. More important, the 1917 Russian Revolution—a direct consequence of the war—brought to power the Communists, who provided both encouragement for liberation movements among the colonial peoples (as a way of attacking their capitalist foes) and an alternative to the hated capitalism that many colonial peoples viewed as an exploitative and inhuman system imposed by their imperial masters.

Between the end of World War I and the start of World War II, Persia (which in 1935 began to call itself Iran), Turkey, and China achieved greater control of their own destiny, while India laid the groundwork for its future independence. In 1921, revolution in Persia brought to power Reza Khan, who was less inclined to do the bidding of the Western world. Mustafa Kemal, who later renamed himself Ataturk, dominated Turkey and instituted a series of reforms designed in part to free his country from subservience to the Western states. In China, the imperialists lost power as the nationalistic Kuomintang, under the leadership of first Sun Yat-sen and then Chiang Kai-shek, and a strong Communist movement under Mao Zedong competed for power. Both the Kuomintang and the communists despised the Westerners who had manipulated China for much of the nineteenth century. In India, the English-educated lawyer Mohandas Gandhi led an increasingly popular struggle against the British rulers. Relying on a campaign of non-violence and passive resistance, Gandhi undercut British authority and forced a number of concessions from the reluctant imperialists. However, Great Britain refused to capitulate on his principal demand—independence for India.

World War II greatly accelerated the drive for independence among non-Western peoples. As was the case in World War I, colonial peoples supplied the war effort with necessary raw materials and finished products as well as soldiers. A strong feeling emerged among both the colonial peoples and some important segments of Western public opinion that the sacrifices of the native populations should not go unrewarded. This sentiment was further reinforced by the nature of the war, which seemed to pit the forces of good against the forces of evil. If the victory of the Allies over Nazi Germany represented the triumph of a liberal, humane, egalitarian, and democratic philosophy, how could the winners possibly continue to maintain an imperial system resting on racism, brutality, exploitation, and inequality? The professed ideals of the Western world were clearly at variance with imperialism.

Most significant, perhaps, was the destruction of the old relationship between the colonies and their imperial masters. For many in Asia, Japan's military victories reinforced the notion already born of Japan's success against Russia in the Russo-Japanese War (1904–1905) that the white man was not militarily invulnerable. Furthermore, when the Japanese, who were as imperialistic as the Europeans, supplanted white colonial rule in the colonies of Asia, indigenous leaders who had opposed colonial rule before the war formed guerrilla units to resist them. Leaders such as Ho Chi Minh in French Indochina and Achmed Sukarno in the Dutch East Indies not only established effective fighting forces but also gained a large popular following. With the end of the war, independence movements led by figures who enjoyed the support of their people and commanded well-organized and experienced fighting units confronted the returning imperialists. Restoration of the prewar colonial status quo now became unlikely, especially as the cost to the Europeans in terms of men and precious resources desperately needed to rebuild the mother country was simply too great.

Some imperial countries, such as Great Britain and the United States, quickly grasped the lessons of World War II. Others, such as France and the Netherlands, attempted to regain control of their colonies and became embroiled in costly and exhausting warfare. The largest and most populous colony was India, where the movement for independence from Great Britain was already significant before the war. In 1947, Great Britain vacated the great Indian subcontinent; however, religious and ethnic rivalry, an all too common curse among the colonial peoples, not only led to the assassination of Gandhi in 1948 but also prevented the formation of a single state. Instead, two states were created: India, with a Hindu majority, and Pakistan, with a Muslim majority. India, under the leadership of Gandhi's disciple Jawaharlal Nehru, who served as prime minister from 1947 until his death in 1964, developed an enduring constitutional democracy, a rare occurrence in the former colonial world, where dictatorship tended to be the norm.

Nehru also guided India toward a socialist economy that became the model for several newly independent countries. Except for brief periods, Pakistan has been dominated by its military. The rivalry that divided India and Pakistan at the start has continued, resulting in several wars and a seemingly permanent state of tension between the two countries.

In 1948, Britain also granted independence to Ceylon (Sri Lanka) and to Burma, which renamed itself Myanmar in 1989. The Burmese refused to join the Commonwealth of Nations, a consultative organization of 50 former British colonies sponsored by Great Britain, preferring to follow a path of rigid isolation that has led to major human rights abuses and great poverty. Nine years later, in 1957, Britain granted independence to the peoples of the Malayan Peninsula after putting down a communist insurgency.

In contrast to the bloodless emancipation of the former British colonies in Asia, the Dutch fought a debilitating colonial war from 1945 to 1949 in a futile attempt to retain the Dutch East Indies, or Indonesia. The Indonesian national liberation movement, led by Sukarno and including a large Communist contingent, had resisted the Japanese during World War II and, consequently, was prepared to oppose the return of the Dutch.

France also tried to reclaim its empire in Asia. In Indochina Ho Chi Minh led a popular, well-organized national liberation movement that administered a series of military setbacks to the French, culminating in the 1954 Battle of Dien Bien Phu. Depicting the struggle as a communist-inspired and -led rebellion rather than a national liberation movement, the French interested the United States in Indochina, with devastating results for the Americans. This was a curious turn in U.S. policy, clearly reflecting the prevailing tensions of the Cold War, as evidenced by the fact that a few years earlier (1946) the United States had willingly granted independence to the Philippines, the principal U.S. colony in Asia.

The end of colonialism in sub-Saharan, or black, Africa came rapidly and unexpectedly. Unlike Asia, where organized anti-colonialism had existed for decades, black Africa had been quiescent until the end of World War II. Then, beginning in the 1950s, imperialism in sub-Saharan African collapsed in the space of about two decades, and more than thirty independent, black-ruled countries emerged.

The process of African decolonization began with the British Empire. In 1957, the Gold Coast (Ghana) gained independence under its charismatic leader Kwame Nkrumah. Six years later, in 1963, Great Britain granted independence to Nigeria, its largest colony in Africa and the continent's most populous country. Britain was able to surrender its West African colonies with relative ease because so few whites lived there; however, the British were not so fortunate in East Africa, where white settlers had taken advantage of a moderate climate and good soil to settle permanently. These whites strongly resisted any suggestion of black rule. However, the unsuccessful Mau Mau uprising in Kenya in the 1950s gave Great Britain a glimpse of how costly it would be to retain its colonies. Sobered by this experience and burdened by many problems at home, Great Britain granted independence to Tanganyika and Zanzibar in 1961 (in 1964 they merged to become Tanzania under the leadership of Julius Nyerere), to Uganda in 1962, and to Kenya under the popular Jomo Kenyatta in 1963.

In shedding its black African empire, Britain faced great difficulties in southern Africa, where a substantial number of whites had settled. Northern Rhodesia (Zambia–1964), Nyasaland (Malawi–1964), and Bechuanaland (Botswana–1966) achieved independence without undue strife, but the white settlers of Southern Rhodesia resisted national liberation until 1980, when Zimbabwe was born under the rule of black nationalist leader Robert Mugabe. The Republic of South Africa, where some whites have lived for centuries, abandoned its policy of apartheid (racial segregation) in 1994 and accepted black majority rule under the leadership of the wise and charismatic Nelson Mandela. Nevertheless, even today the Republic of South Africa continues to grope its way toward a stable compromise acceptable to black, colored (East Asian), and white alike.

In comparison to its misguided colonial policies in Asia and North Africa, France's approach to its sub-Saharan empire was positively enlightened. Not only did the French freely release their black colonies, they consciously fostered a sense of "Frenchness" among the emerging black elite and willingly gave economic assistance to the newly independent states. As a result, French influence remains strong in sub-Saharan Africa.

The authoritarian Portuguese state, whose empire dated back to the late Middle Ages, determined to hold its possessions in black Africa at all costs. Consequently, Portugal found itself mired in a seemingly endless guerrilla war with national liberation movements in both Angola and Mozambique. The war had a corrosive effect on Portuguese life and was a major contributory factor to the 1974 coup that eventually brought democracy to Portugal. In the wake of the coup, Portugal gave up the fight and liberated its African empire.

In 1960, Belgium relinquished the Belgian Congo (Zaire), its large African colony. However, because of Belgium's utter disdain for the Congolese, few if any natives had been prepared for independence. Furthermore, the colony was fractured by tribal disputes, regional differences, and rivalry among its would-be leaders. With Belgium's departure, the Congo suffered a series of armed rebellions, secessionist movements, and civil war, all aggravated by Soviet and U.S. meddling in the affairs of the hapless Congo as part of their Cold War rivalry. The end result for the mineral-rich and potentially wealthy Congo was an independent but devastated and impoverished state ruled by Mobutu Sese Seko, an extravagant and brutal military dictator who was propped up by the United States.

The third great area where colonial empires disappeared was the Arab world, stretching from Morocco on the Atlantic to the Persian Gulf. At the end of World War II, France's empire included much of North Africa. However, as was the case in Indochina, indigenous national liberation movements that predated the war worked to drive out the French. After failing to either cajole or repress the native populations, France granted independence to Morocco and Tunisia in 1956.

For France, however, its Algerian colony held special significance. France had governed it since 1830, and with at least one million Frenchmen living there, Algeria was considered an integral part of metropolitan France. When France categorically refused to consider independence for Algeria, the FLN (Front de Liberation Nationale) rebelled in 1954. The ensuing Algerian War lasted for more than seven years, involving 500,000 French troops and causing perhaps one million deaths. The war shook France to its very core, bringing that nation to the brink of civil war. In 1958, the Fourth French Republic collapsed, and World War II hero Charles de Gaulle was summoned from retirement to save the nation. De Gaulle instituted the Fifth Republic, and over the objections of the French settlers and many French military men, he conceded independence to Algeria in 1962.

Decolonization in the Middle East was not so rancorous for the Europeans, but it was made complicated and violent by the Israeli question. At the close of World War I, the defeated Ottoman Empire (Turkey) ceded its Middle Eastern possessions to the League of Nations, which in turn assigned them to Great Britain and France as mandates. Beginning with Egypt in 1922 and continuing into the post–World War II era, several Middle Eastern countries, including Iraq, Syria, Jordan, Lebanon, Saudi Arabia, Yemen, and Kuwait, gained their independence without much opposition from the mandate powers.

However, difficulties arose when European Jews took steps to establish a state of their own in the Middle East. Relying on the Balfour Declaration of 1917, which promised British support for a Jewish homeland in Palestine, and fleeing European anti-Semitism, which had culminated in Hitler and the Holocaust, Jewish settlers proclaimed the state of Israel in 1948. The indigenous Arab population reacted violently to the Jewish state, and war ensued on several occasions (1948–1949; 1956—the Suez War; 1967—the Six-Day War; 1973—the Yom Kippur War; 1982—the Lebanese War; 2006—the Second Lebanese War). Complicating matters was the interest both the United States and the Soviet Union showed in the region. Because of the Middle East's strategic location and its massive oil reserves, both superpowers became deeply involved in its disputes.

While the end of the Cold War put a stop to Soviet-American rivalry in the Middle East, the situation remains quite precarious. Continued Arab-Israeli hostility, the rise of a violent Islamic fundamentalism, and, beginning in December 2010, demonstrations in several countries demanding basic political and economic reform, threaten the region's already dubious stability. Obviously, the end of colonialism has been less than auspicious for the peoples of the Middle East.

Nevertheless, the dismantling of the colonial empires remains a principal development. Perhaps the best indication of its importance can be found in the composition of the United Nations. When the UN was established in 1945, it consisted of 51 member states. Today it has 192 member states, the vast majority of which were colonies when the United Nations came into existence.

INTERPRETIVE ESSAY

MARIJAN SALOPEK

Since World War II, interest in the Third World has grown, largely because these nations represent nearly two-thirds of the world's population. However, the majority of Third World citizens live on the edge of subsistence. The predicament of the Third World has piqued the world's conscience. Its plight must be examined not only in the context of the damage—real or imagined—the imperial powers inflicted on these lands, but also in terms of the optimism that Third World leaders displayed on the eve of decolonization. The Third World, it should be noted, is as much a state of mind as an economic and political fact. Furthermore, the term "Third World" suggests a degree of homogeneity that does not exist and masks the cultural, linguistic, and political diversity of the nations it characterizes.

One response to the condition of the Third World has been to denigrate imperialism in terms such as "World Revolution of Westernization," the title of historian Theodore H. von Laue's 1987 study of the Western world's impact on the globe in the twentieth century. Von Laue claims that this revolution "produced a worldwide association of peoples compressed against their will into an inescapable but highly unstable interdependence laced with explosive tensions." This interpretation reinforced the long-standing thinking of some Third World leaders and their Western allies who believed that former colonies would experience dramatic economic growth once the imperialists were displaced and an indigenous commercial and political elite assumed the reins of power.

However, these proponents of decolonization were clearly too optimistic. Their self-confidence was greater than the tools available to them to take politically and economically underdeveloped territories into the realm of the Second or First World. In short, the anti-colonialists had set themselves up for a psychological fall, as their level of expectation was too high to be realized in the time frame that they had established for themselves. They arrogantly asserted that the Third World could match the industrially and economically advanced former imperial powers in a relatively short period of time, possibly a single generation. However, to be fair, their expectations had been shaped by the experience of other nations, principally the Soviet Union, which had attained Great Power status in the space of a few decades. Third World leaders expressed faith in their ability to apply the Soviet model to their circumstances. However, they totally ignored the long political and economic development of the former Russian Empire.

Imperialism reflected the institutional development of the First and Second Worlds; these nations enjoyed human and material assets, a sense of unity, nationalism, and political maturity born of war and internal struggle. The Third World's political elite ignored these points and concentrated exclusively on the wealth that the imperial powers had extracted from the colonies; this skewed perspective blinded them to the economic and political realities of the lands they managed.

Although the decolonization era is generally thought to have begun after World War II, decolonization began in the eighteenth and nineteenth centuries with the emancipation of the North and South American colonies. The second wave of imperialism in the late nineteenth century led to the creation of new empires. The peoples affected—Africans, Chinese, Japanese, and other Southeast Asians—often reacted strongly, seeking to affirm their cultural and political sovereignty. The Taiping Rebellion (1850–1864), the Boxer Revolt (1898–1901), the Chinese Revolution (1911), and the Meiji Restoration in Japan (1868–1912) were reactions to foreign intervention as much as responses to internal social and political problems. A striking feature of the decolonization movement in this period before World War II was the total lack of interaction or even contact among nationalist leaders in Asia and Africa. Although aware of the events taking shape around them, the nationalists campaigned for independence in isolation.

Except for the active nationalist clubs and societies that proliferated in the former colonies, few in the industrialized world had any understanding or concern for the peoples or nations beyond western Europe or the United States. Development of the colonies was hardly a popular topic, even at the height of the imperial era before World War I. It was even less so during the interwar years and World War II. The imperial powers, faced with domestic economic and political problems, had little surplus energy to devote to the concerns of nations on the verge of development. In fact, the terms "development" and "underdevelopment" were conspicuously absent from the vocabulary of the Europeans or Americans until the 1950s.

In the years immediately after World War II, the victorious powers understandably concentrated on rebuilding war-ravaged Europe and Japan. The Europeans, the Americans, and, later, the Japanese were the world's international players. For years they had managed the bulk of the world's trade, and it was generally assumed that the world's future prosperity depended on the revival of Europe's and Japan's economies. The needs of former and existing colonies were generally ignored.

The world's attention shifted to the nations soon to be known as the Third World as relations between the Western powers and the Soviet Union deteriorated. Thus, decolonization and the rise of the Third World must be considered in the context of the Cold War. By 1947, the world had divided into clearly identifiable political blocs, referred to by commentators of the day as the First World and the Second World. In the First World were the states of western Europe, the United States, Canada, and the other British Dominions; in the Second World, the Soviet Union and its allies in east-central Europe.

The term "Third World" was devised to identify the nations outside the first two blocs. Originally it had a political rather than an economic meaning, referring to the nonaligned nations of Yugoslavia, Egypt, India, Ghana, and Indonesia. Later, it was applied in an economic sense to the impoverished nations of the world. However, the Third World as a concept was open to interpretation. This is exemplified by Mao Zedong's remarks in February 1974: "In my view, the United States and the Soviet Union form the First World. Japan, Europe and Canada, the middle section, belong to the Second World. The Third World has a huge population. With the exception of Japan, Asia belongs to the Third World, and Latin America too." By Mao's definition, Africa would not even fall within the limits of the Third World because its economic and political development lagged far behind that of Asia and Latin America.

The Soviet Union's moral and political support for nationalist and communist movements in east central Europe, Southeast Asia, and China gave the West's leaders considerable reason for concern, and they responded with a political and humanitarian campaign that highlighted the West's commitment to the underdeveloped nations of Asia and Africa. During the 1950s, the former imperial powers often presented themselves as economic saviors, and the Third World's misfortunes were ascribed to technical and structural faults in the economies of these nations. The consensus was that the poorer nations could attain prosperity with the financial assistance of the West. In essence, it was expected that the breach separating the wealthy and poor regions of the world could be narrowed easily and in a short period of time.

To some degree, the Western powers fueled the expectations of the Third World. International conventions, like the 1950 Colombo Plan, emerged from the West's suspicion and fear of Communism. Confronted with the prospect of Communist regimes in Asia and elsewhere, Western leaders congregated at Colombo, Ceylon (now Sri Lanka), to discuss the political and economic health of the Asian and African world. This conference marks the beginning of the West's fascination with the Third World. The expectation of the participants was that Communism could be averted with a generous deployment of aid.

Undoubtedly, the imperial powers faced a dilemma about emancipating their colonies, similar to the dilemma that nineteenth-century governments faced about emancipating their slaves. Material interests aside, the humanitarian impulse cannot be ignored in any assessment of imperialism's decline. Moral arguments were advanced throughout the interwar years to justify retreat from the colonies. Furthermore, Italian and German military action in Africa and Europe highlighted the moral bankruptcy of the imperialist argument, and Europeans and Americans emerged from World War II expressing an idealistic view of a better and just world.

The Atlantic Charter, devised and interpreted by the United States, prepared the ground for the decolonization process. Led by President Franklin D. Roosevelt, the United States advanced a positive interpretation of self-determination and regarded independence as a fitting reward for colonial peoples who furthered Allied interests during World War II. As during World War I, the United States, by words and actions, whetted the colonial world's appetite for freedom.

The Soviets, avowed anti-colonialists, seized the opportunity and inspired nationalists throughout the world. Thus the world's two superpowers accelerated the imperialist retreat. Each brought the issue of decolonization before the United Nations and consequently gave colonial peoples a forum to present their concerns. From this point on, Third World nationalists no longer functioned in isolation. They voiced their views on the international stage, formed political alliances, and capitalized on the conflict between the West and the Soviet Union. Special United Nations agencies were formed specifically to investigate conditions in the undeveloped world, and the reports emanating from commissions such as the United Nations Economic Committee for Latin America identified global capitalism as the principal cause of poverty.

The Declaration on the Granting of Independence to Colonial Countries and Peoples, adopted by the General Assembly on December 14, 1960, is characteristic of the response to the subject. Articles 1 and 2 of the declaration provide the foundation for the anti-imperialist view. Article 1 condemns the subjugation, domination, and exploitation of peoples as a denial of fundamental human rights. Such actions not only constitute a violation of the Charter of the United Nations, but also impede the promotion of world peace and cooperation. Article 2 declares that "all peoples have the right to self-determination." Consequently, they should have political independence and be free to choose their own form of government. Likewise, they should have the right to determine their own economic system and to develop their social and cultural life as they see fit. Armed with this declaration, the anti-colonialists could justly argue that imperialism was immoral, unjust, and contrary to the welfare of the world community. Since the adoption of the declaration, more than 50 new states have gained independence and subsequent inclusion in the ranks of the Third World bloc.

Left-wing, socialist, and Marxist writers boosted the cause of the Third World. These intellectuals formulated the anti-imperialist interpretation that the Third World was in a desperate state because of the policies pursued by the former colonial powers. Third World writers and thinkers like Frantz Fanon widely disseminated this point of view. Fanon, a black French West Indian psychoanalyst turned author whose most famous work was *The Wretched of the Earth,* became a major spokesman for the Marxist, anti-colonialist school. According to Fanon (and others), the imperialists and colonialists had raped the Third World over an extended period of time. They had behaved like war criminals with their deportations, massacres, forced labor, and slavery. All these atrocities had been committed for the sake of profit—to enrich the capitalistic coffers of Western men and Western countries. The capitalist economic system thus bore much of the blame for the destruction of the Third World. To a large extent, Europe's wealth and power derived from the systematic exploitation of the Third World. Gold, raw materials, diamonds, cotton, wood, and humans flowed from the Third World to Europe. In fact, Europe is really the creation of the Third World, brought into existence by the wealth stolen from the underdeveloped reaches of the globe. Even though the imperialists and colonialists are now being forced out, they owe the Third World much and should be required to make restitution.

In the context of the Cold War's heightened tensions, this interpretation confirmed what many in the Third World believed—they were poor because the imperial powers were rich. The West's humanitarian campaign, described as a form of atonement for the damage done to colonial nations, was presented as one more piece of evidence in support of the Marxist interpretation of the Third World's plight.

By the mid-1960s, the Third World had become a hot academic and intellectual topic. Scholars from a variety of fields churned out works that reflected the mood of the era. In many cases, the thesis of the authors was summarized in the titles they chose: "On the Mechanism of Imperialism," *Development and Underdevelopment in Latin America, How Europe Underdeveloped Africa.* Marxist writers found in the Third World a potent vehicle enabling them to challenge the West. Colonialism, aid, development, and foreign investment became symbols of the Third World's impoverishment at the hands of the West. In the charged climate of the 1960s, jargon served as a strong weapon for anti-colonial, pro–Third World advocates. "Imperialist exploitation," "neocolonialism," "core and periphery," "surplus appropriation," "polarization," "dominance-dependence relations," "dependent development," and "subservient development" were the terms of choice employed to denigrate imperialism while advancing the cause of the world's underprivileged peoples.

Historians, sociologists, geographers, and polemicists were drawn into the debate. The variety of views poses a considerable problem for the student who must struggle in many cases with the ideology and political perspective of the authors. Non-Marxist scholars and popular writers responded to the negative interpretation of imperialism. They stressed the altruism of the former colonial powers or the pragmatism of decolonization, and they emphasized that the imperial powers had consciously encouraged the transition from colonial status to independence. In making their case, they belittled the economic significance of imperial possessions. According to writers like Ronald Robinson and John Gallagher, empires were acquired in a fit of absentmindedness. In *Africa and the Victorians: The Official Mind of Imperialism,* they argued that "the partition of tropical Africa might seem impressive on the wall maps of the Foreign Office. Yet it was at the time an empty and theoretical expansion."

Robinson and Gallagher pointed out that before 1900, Great Britain did little or nothing to exploit its African empire. The British held this empire, which had come to them almost by accident, but they virtually ignored it. Certainly commercial or imperial motives did not play an important role in Britain's penetration of Africa. It was only later, well after spheres of influence in Africa had been allotted, that Great Britain began to develop its holdings, and then only to make good on earlier promises of African progress and to buttress its territorial claims. The trader, the planter, and the colonial official did not bring about or accompany the partition of tropical Africa; they only came later.

Thus, the British Empire—at least in Africa—arose not from any conscious desire by capitalists in cooperation with the government to plunder the natives and exploit the land but from minor and at the time not very pressing political considerations.

In the political and international climate in which Robinson and Gallagher developed their thesis, this interpretation stood as a clear challenge to the extreme critics of empire and colonialism. Imperialism, rather than being a deliberate act of will, happened in a haphazard, nonmalicious, nonpernicious, nonavaricious manner, with the participants failing to give serious thought to the implications of their actions. An empire acquired in such a fashion and contributing little to the national treasury could be dismantled as easily as it was put together.

However, this interpretation ignores the concern expressed in Britain, France, and the Netherlands in the 1950s and 1960s about the loss of investments and access to cheap resources. The peaceful retreat by the British from their possessions in Asia reveals the extent of the decline of British power rather than the altruism of the British government and British investors. The reality, clear to Britons at the end of World War II, was that Britain could ill afford to defend or retain its overseas interests. In addition, it should be emphasized that while Britain might have acquired its empire in a fit of absentmindedness, these possessions were held with the assistance of the political and economic elites. Without their support, the empire would have crumbled decades before the decolonization era.

Asia's political elite, swept by the winds of nationalism and buoyed by Japan's success before and during World War II, had matured, and stood ready to advance its interests before those of its colonial masters. Jawaharlal Nehru, cofounder of modern India, underscored the pride and national consciousness of Asians when he recalled Japan's initial victory over the West in the 1904–1905 Russo-Japanese War. L. S. Stavrianos, in *Global Rift: The Third World Comes of Age*, quotes Nehru: "Japanese victories stirred up my enthusiasm. . . . Nationalist ideas filled my mind. I mused of Indian freedom. . . . I dreamed of brave deeds of how, sword in hand, I would fight for India and help in freeing her."

During the last half of the twentieth century, colonialism disappeared, and each former colony groped its way toward a workable political structure. However, all too often bright promises of democratic rule faded, and dictatorships—military or civilian—became the Third World norm. With the global resurgence of the democratic spirit in the 1980s and 1990s, a number of these dictatorships gave way to tentative experiments in democracy. Nevertheless, the political future of Third World countries remains cloudy. For many of these states, the search for political stability promises to be lengthy and arduous, and there is no guarantee that it will end successfully.

In the realm of international relations, most former colonies adopted a policy known as non-alignment. First outlined by Nehru at the 1955 Bandung Conference, non-alignment called for the newly independent countries to maintain strict neutrality in the Cold War. In practice, non-alignment often meant bashing the West while giving the Soviet Union the benefit of the doubt. However, with the end of the Cold War, any leverage the Non-Aligned Movement might have exercised disappeared, thereby forcing many Third World countries to rethink their international position. This reevaluation continues today without any clear unifying doctrine in sight.

Because of the Third World's numerical strength at the United Nations, it tends to view the UN as a vehicle to express its concerns and to achieve its international goals. Several recent UN secretaries general have come from the ranks of Third World diplomats. Nevertheless, because individual states refuse to surrender their national sovereignty to the world body, the Third World–dominated UN is often ignored and the Third World appears impotent on the global stage.

By 1980, the old imperial powers had finally relinquished their political hold over the underdeveloped world. However, the issue of economic growth remained unresolved. The gap between the developed and underdeveloped nations had grown considerably, and the optimism that greeted independence had given way to cynicism and despair. The nations that had supported decolonization, particularly the United States and the Soviet Union, balked at the cost of supporting the Third World's modernization efforts.

At one time or another, most of the Third World found itself enmeshed in Cold War rivalries. Many Third World countries were able to exploit this situation to extract aid from one superpower or the other. However, as the Cold War wound down, both superpowers tended to regard the Third World as a liability rather than an asset, and funds dried up.

As the superpowers retreated from the Third World, the smaller nations of the First World, in conjunction with the nations of the Third, addressed the issue of the north-south divide, or the geographic division between the rich and poor nations. Generally, the rich nations are situated north of the equator and the poor nations are situated south of the equator. In 1985, the Vienna Declaration on Cooperation for Development reiterated the view that the most urgent problem of the second half of the twentieth century was the "conditions of poverty, misery, disease and degradation for two-thirds of the human race." It seemed that very little had changed since 1965 when the United Nations published a very bleak report on the condition of the underdeveloped world. Despite the concerns and lofty ideals expressed by the delegates to the Vienna conference, the Third World moved inexorably toward financial bankruptcy and possibly political irrelevancy.

Imperialism's extraordinary achievement was the creation of a world economy. It stimulated world trade and interdependence on a scale never before known, and in a sense the "world revolution of Westernization" is an appropriate descriptive phrase, stripped of its negative connotations, for the modern era. Although the former imperial powers relinquished their colonial possessions, they continued to exert tremendous control over the world's flow of goods.

Initially, many Third World countries chose to ignore this reality. They rejected capitalism, the foundation of the world economy, and embraced socialism instead. However, whether it was Nehru's version of socialism, Kwame Nkrumah's "African socialism," or a variation of the Soviet or Chinese models, Third World socialism featured a high level of state planning; a large, corrupt, and stultifying bureaucracy; and grandiose plans for development that featured rapid industrialization.

In Asia, however, several former colonies opted for capitalism and have enjoyed remarkable economic growth. Noting the success of Singapore, Taiwan, Malaysia, Hong Kong, and South Korea among others, and shocked by the Soviet Union's collapse, a growing number of Third World leaders have rejected the decades-old interpretation that global capitalism is the cause of their nations' misfortunes. For example, the leaders of Mexico, Argentina, and Brazil, supported by the current generation of intellectuals, stress the liberalization of their economies as the solution to the problem of underdevelopment. Thus, since the 1990s, market competition and international competitiveness have captured the imagination of the Third World's elite, who express confidence in their long-term future.

For a handful of former colonies, especially in the Middle East, lack of wealth has not been a problem. Blessed with large petroleum reserves, they were able to exploit successfully the global reliance on oil. However, questions remain about both the distribution of this fabulous wealth and its use to create a sound economic infrastructure.

In the wake of international trade, cultural imperialism intensified. Western values as expressed in art, film, television, and fashion are so pervasive that the pressing issue before the nations of the Third World continues to be the retention of their identity. In a number of countries such as Iran, the omnipresence of Western styles and forms provoked an important reaction featuring the elevation of indigenous values and the demonization of Western culture.

The achievements of the Third World are noteworthy; yet they are frequently overshadowed by seemingly insoluble problems. Certainly the mere fact of having gained independence is a signal of success. So too is the production of sufficient food supplies—the so-called Green Revolution of which India is a prime example. Nevertheless, the list of problems is legion. Among the more intractable ones, one must include government instability, lack of internal cohesion, overpopulation, grinding poverty, epidemic disease such as AIDS in Africa, destruction of the environment in locales ranging from Brazil to Myanmar, illiteracy, and disregard of human rights.

Nevertheless, the freeing of the Third World from its colonial yoke clearly carries major importance for our world. The long-term impact of imperialism and decolonization was that it forced people to reassess their institutions and their approach to life. Because imperialism highlighted technological and organizational strengths and weaknesses, its effect must be measured in terms of its tremendous psychological impact on the way people perceive themselves and their civilization, be they in the Third World or in the First or Second.

SELECTED BIBLIOGRAPHY

Ansprenger, F. *The Dissolution of Colonial Empires.* New York: Routledge, 1989. The dismantlement of the European empires is handled in a thorough and knowledgeable manner.

Blusse, L., et al., eds. *History and Underdevelopment: Essays on Underdevelopment and European Expansion in Asia and Africa.* Leiden: Centre for the History of European Expansion, 1980. A series of critical essays on a most controversial topic.

Brendan, Piers. *The Decline and Fall of the British Empire, 1781–1997.* London: Jonathan Cape, 2007. Brendan, of Cambridge University, details the long process leading to the end of the British empire. In lucid prose he suggests that because of Britain's theoretical commitment to the liberal views of John Locke and others the oppressive empire contained the seeds of its own destruction.

Bruckner, Pascal. *The Tears of the White Man: Compassion as Contempt.* Translation and introduction by William R. Beer. New York: Free Press, 1986. Critique of the methods employed by the left in France to advance their interpretation of the Third World.

Cambridge History of Africa. 8 vols. Cambridge: Cambridge University Press, 1975–1984. Authoritative analysis of Africa. Information on all aspects of African history.

Chamberlain, M. E. *Decolonization: The Fall of the European Empires.* Oxford, England: Basil Blackwell, 1985. An effective, short summary of the topic.

Clapham, Christopher. *Third World Politics: An Introduction.* London: Croom Helm, 1985. Scholarly treatment of the relevant political, social, and economic issues.

de Soto, Hernando. *The Other Path: The Invisible Revolution in the Third World.* New York: Harper and Row, 1989. A good example of the anti-Marxist interpretation of underdevelopment.

Hall, D. G. E. *A History of South-East Asia.* 4th ed. London: Macmillan Education, 1981. Standard account of events in Southeast Asia.

Hoepli, Nancy L., ed. *Aftermath of Colonialism.* New York: H. W. Wilson, 1973. Survey of the problems and politics of the Third World.

Jupp, J. *Sri Lanka: Third World Democracy.* London: Frank Cass, 1978. Overview of democracy in Sri Lanka in the years following independence.

Kreisky, Bruno, and H. Gauhar, eds. *Decolonisation and After: The Future of the Third World.* London: South Publications, 1987. Summary of the Proceedings of the Decolonisation and After Conference held in Vienna on October 7–8, 1985. Provides a summary of the experiences and aspirations of the Third World and its supporters.

Manor, James, ed. *Rethinking Third World Politics.* New York: Longmans, 1991. Survey of literature on the changing attitudes toward Third World development and aid.

McLeod, John. *Beginning Postcolonialism.* 2nd ed. Manchester: Manchester University Press, 2010. A brief study of the academic discipline called "Postcolonialism" that has arisen since the end of Europe's colonial empires. A clear, organized, and focused introduction.

McLeod, John. *The History of India.* Westport, CT: Greenwood Press, 2002. A well-written survey of both the colonial and post-colonial history of Britain's most important possession.

Mortimer, Robert A. *The Third World Coalition in International Politics.* New York: Praeger, 1980. Covers the political evolution of the nonaligned world.

Nassiter, Bernard D. *Global Struggle for More: Third World Conflicts with the Rich Nations.* New York: Harper and Row, 1986. Excellent summary of the economic problems of the Third World.

Ottaway, David, and Marina Ottaway. *Afrocommunism.* New York: Africana Publishing, 1986. Summary examination of the Marxist regimes in Africa.

Rangel, Carlos. *Third World Ideology and Western Reality: Manufacturing Political Myth.* Foreword by Jean-François Revel. New Brunswick, NJ: Transaction Books, 1986. A stinging indictment of the Marxist interpretation of underdevelopment.

Robinson, Ronald, and John Gallagher. *Africa and the Victorians: The Official Mind of Imperialism.* 2d ed. London: Macmillan, 1981. Asserts that imperialism occurred by accident and not design.

Rodney, Walter. *How Europe Underdeveloped Africa.* London: Howard University Press, 1972. Marxist analysis of European imperialism.

Stavrianos, L. S. *Global Rift: The Third World Comes of Age.* New York: William Morrow, 1981. Outlines the development of Third World consciousness and the evolution of political and economic institutions.

Stora, Benjamin. *Algeria, 1830–2000: A Short History.* Ithaca, NY: Cornell University Press, 2004. Despite the title, Stora's book focuses on the bloody war for independence (1954–1962) and the following period of nation-building (1962–1988). The story encapsulates developments experienced by many former colonial peoples: the struggle for independence followed by the struggle to create a viable state.

Von Laue, Theodore H. The *World Revolution of Westernization: The Twentieth Century in Global Perspective.* Oxford, England: Oxford University Press, 1987. Von Laue, an eminent historian of modernization, explores the disruptive nature of that process.

Wesseling, H. L., ed. *Expansion and Reaction: Essays on European Expansion and Reactions in Asia and Africa.* Leiden, the Netherlands: Leiden University Press, 1978. Another very perceptive series of essays focusing on the Third World experience.

BANDUNG CONFERENCE (1955)

The Bandung Conference was a meeting of 29 Asian and African nations held in Bandung, Indonesia, April 18–24, 1955. The end of World War II fostered increased nationalist fervor in the developing world, which sought liberation from the Western colonial powers. In December 1954, Burma, Ceylon (since 1972, Sri Lanka), India, Indonesia, and Pakistan jointly proposed an Asian-African conference aimed at fostering unity among Asian and African peoples and addressing nationalist sentiments.

The Bandung Conference included the People's Republic of China (PRC), the government of which was eager to augment its status in the Third World. Led by Chinese foreign minister Zhou Enlai, the PRC's delegation played an important role in reinforcing China's ties with Asia and Africa. On the second day of the conference, Zhou advocated the Five Principles of Peaceful Coexistence, which outlined the PRC's foreign policy blueprint. The five principles called for the respect of national sovereignty and territorial integrity, nonaggression, nonintervention in internal affairs, equal and mutual opportunity, and peaceful coexistence. Zhou specifically indicted the United States for hindering peaceful coexistence, citing the United States's "aggressive" actions in the ongoing Taiwan Strait Crisis. His principles were well received, and they successfully cemented Chinese leadership in the developing world.

The conference concluded on April 24, 1955, with a 10-point declaration on the promotion of world peace and cooperation, which all participants adopted. The declaration advocated closer political, economic, and cultural ties among the signatories, mutual opposition to imperialism and colonialism, and the promotion of world peace and friendship. These tenets, collectively known as the Bandung Spirit, helped guide politics in the developing world for many years.

The Bandung Conference also eased tensions in the Taiwan Strait. On April 23, 1955, Zhou declared that the PRC was prepared to discuss Asian matters with the United States, including resolution of the First Taiwan Strait Crisis. To show its good faith, the PRC stopped shelling the contested offshore islands, which effectively ended the crisis. This led ultimately to the Sino-American Ambassadorial Talks, first convened in Warsaw, Poland, on August 1, 1955, that provided the first direct channel for Sino-American communications since the PRC's birth in October 1949.

LAW YUK-FUN

FRANTZ FANON (1925–1961)

Frantz Omar Fanon was a leading ideologist of the anti-colonial and Black Power movements of the 1950s and 1960s. In addition to his intellectual contributions to colonial liberation movements around the world, he also worked with the Algerian National Liberation Front (FLN) during Algeria's struggle for independence.

Fanon was born into a middle-class family on the Caribbean island of Martinique on July 6, 1925, one of eight children. His father was a customs inspector, and his mother ran a small store. At that time, Martinique was a French colony, and Fanon spoke French as his native language. Though his parents were not wealthy, they could afford to send him to a French school on the island, where he was taught by Aimé Césaire, an influential Caribbean intellectual.

In 1943, Fanon enlisted to fight with General Charles de Gaulle's Free French Forces in World War II. He was injured in combat in France and received France's prestigious medal, the *Croix de Guerre*, for bravery. After the war, he went to medical school in Lyon, where he trained as a psychiatrist. While living in France, he married Josi Duble.

During this period, Fanon also published his first book, *Black Skin, White Masks,* an analysis of the alienation felt by blacks living within European and colonial societies. In it, he describes the ways in which European culture inspired feelings of disorientation and inferiority among blacks living in Europe and in the Caribbean. The book was inspired by his childhood in Martinique and his experiences in the army and in France. While at medical school, Fanon became active in leftist politics and edited the student newspaper. He also became associated with several leading leftist intellectuals and was heavily influenced by the French existentialist movement.

In 1953, after finishing his medical training, Fanon found work as a government psychiatrist in the French colony of Algeria. Here, Fanon was placed in charge of the Blida-Joinville psychiatric hospital. The year after he took up this appointment, the FLN, an organization committed to wresting Algerian independence from the French, began its guerrilla campaign against the colony's colonial masters. Fanon was soon responsible for treating many Algerians who had been tortured by the French, as well as many of their torturers. This experience inspired him to resign his position at the hospital in 1956 and commit himself to the cause of Algerian independence.

After his resignation, Fanon moved to Tunisia (a former French territory), where he made contact with FLN operatives and joined their movement. Over the next several years, he wrote essays and articles on behalf of the FLN in several French and underground Algerian journals and newspapers. Many of these were collected and published posthumously in 1964 as *Towards the African Revolution.*

In addition to writing in support of the FLN, Fanon also worked as the organization's ambassador to other African nations. He played an important role in coordinating the supply of military material to the FLN from the West African nation of Ghana. He also saw some action with FLN troops operating along the Moroccan border and was slightly injured in one engagement by a land mine.

While living in Ghana, Fanon was diagnosed with leukemia. In the last year of his life, he wrote his most important and well-known book, *The Wretched of the Earth.* In it, Fanon offered his prescription for the liberation of colonized peoples throughout the world. One aspect of the book's argument that has become controversial was Fanon's discussion of violence, which he maintained is a crucial element of all liberation movements. He argued that violence can help end the cultural domination whites have imposed on blacks and that only through violent resistance can subject black peoples overcome their feelings of inferiority. To Fanon, the liberation of colonized peoples can only come when they begin to see their culture, and themselves, as equal to their oppressors. Fanon also argued that the liberation movements should be led by the peasantry and presciently warned of the danger of revolutions becoming co-opted by petty-bourgeois nationalists.

After finishing the book, Fanon died in a hospital in the United States on December 6, 1961. Although he was one of the most important activists and ambassadors for the FLN, his contribution to Algerian independence has been largely forgotten in that country. His writings, however, have influenced a variety of radical intellectuals, from the proponents of the Black Power movement in the United States during the 1960s to the anti-apartheid activist Stephen Biko during the 1970s to contemporary academics working in the field of postcolonial studies.

ABC-CLIO

MOHANDAS GANDHI (1869–1948)

The leader of modern Indian nationalism, Mohandas Gandhi infused the movement with Hindu spirituality. To Gandhi, moral values always superseded material ones, and the improvement of human souls was a necessary precursor to the improvement of India. He was an apostle of nonviolence and civil disobedience, proving that these ideals could unite diverse peoples and accomplish great progress.

Gandhi was born on October 2, 1869, at Porbandar, a city in British-ruled western India. His father, Karamachand Gandhi, worked as an administrator for the local chief minister. His mother, Putlibai, followed a devout religious life noted for fasting; at a later date, Gandhi claimed his mother's religiosity was the biggest influence on his life. Gandhi learned as a boy to worship the Hindu god Vishnu and to abide by the Jainist teaching of nonviolence. His family's religious beliefs included respect for all living things and required strict vegetarianism.

As a youngster, Gandhi was not a good student. He did not show enthusiasm for either his studies or sports. Furthermore, his schooling suffered disruption when in 1882, at age 13, he was married by arrangement. Like many adolescents, Gandhi went through a rebellious period during which he adopted Western ways, ate meat, smoked, and told lies. Each time he did these things he suffered great guilt, and he soon returned to his Hindu teachings and renounced his irreligious behavior.

In 1887, Gandhi barely passed a matriculation exam and began studying at Samaldas College in Bhavnagar. His family felt he should study law, and although he had some desire to become a doctor, he agreed, partly as a way to get away from Samaldas, which he did not like. Legal studies required that he journey to England, and he did this with dreams that he would live amid a culture of great poets and philosophers. He was dismayed by the prejudice against his Indian background that he found instead.

In 1888, Gandhi entered the Inner Temple, a law college in London. He felt awkward with Western food and practices and focused more on the social issues confronting him than on legal obscurities. His vegetarianism, often criticized, became a source of strength for him in maintaining his Hinduism. He even joined the London Vegetarian Society and wrote articles for its journal. He also began reading the Hindu Bhagavad Gita, which had an increasing influence on him.

Gandhi returned to India and obtained admission to the bar in 1891. He had no enthusiasm for the law, however, and made a miserable appearance in the courtroom. As

Indian pro-independence leader Mohandas Gandhi and 78 of his followers march 240 miles to Dandi in March 1930 to protest the doubling of the salt tax by the British. Gandhi perfected the technique of non-violent protest and civil disobedience that was used so effectively by Martin Luther King during the U.S. civil rights movement. (Library of Congress)

a result, he scratched out a living by preparing petitions for litigants. The next year, he agreed to journey to Natal in South Africa to work as a lawyer for a firm there.

Gandhi's South African experience proved momentous in his personal development and, by extension, in India's history. This British-ruled colony discriminated severely against its Indian residents (as well as its African ones), and as Gandhi traveled, he found his movements restricted. Yet he resisted segregation, refusing in one instance to give up his seat on a stagecoach to a European, a decision that resulted in his being beaten by the white driver. These experiences made Gandhi determined to fight social injustice. Almost overnight he became a dynamic leader, and in 1894, he petitioned the British government to reject a bill that would deny Indians the right to vote. Although his effort failed, he organized the Natal Indian Congress and initiated Indian resistance to injustices. His frequent petitions drew world attention to the discrimination in South Africa. He lived a life of great self-discipline, residing in a self-supporting settlement called Tolstoy Farm.

In 1906, the South African government proposed legislation, enacted the following year, requiring that Indians register and be fingerprinted with the authorities so that their movements could be controlled. Gandhi and most Indians considered that insulting, and he organized an opposition drive that focused on *satyagraha*, meaning "truth force." That strategy stressed weaning the oppressor from his unjust practices through nonviolent protest that would make him see the error of his ways. In this instance, Gandhi did not win the repeal of required registration. In continued protests, Gandhi was arrested, and while in jail, he read Henry David Thoreau's "Civil Disobedience," which influenced him greatly.

In 1914, Gandhi won a compromise settlement for Indians in South Africa. It included an end to the tax on formerly indentured Indian workers, the recognition of Hindu and Muslim marriages as legal, and a prohibition against importing indentured Indian labor. Gandhi then returned to India in 1915, enlightened by the many lessons he had learned in South Africa.

During World War I, Gandhi refrained from any verbal attacks on British rule in India. He even helped Britain recruit Indian soldiers, though he disagreed with British actions injurious to his compatriots. By this time, his Hindu philosophy had developed further, assisted by a spiritual adviser. Gandhi embraced *aparigraha,* requiring a rejection of material possessions that hindered spiritual development (an extension of his belief developed at Tolstoy Farm that life close to the earth was best); and he embraced *samabhava,* requiring that he work his deeds without emotion, without any desire to defeat an enemy. In fact, Gandhi always preferred winning over an opponent to his side rather than conquering one. Furthermore, he adopted a celibate life; sex, he believed, interfered with discovering God, and sexual restraint must be included with restraints in diet, speech, and emotions. He may have been acting from a more practical consideration, too, as his wife, having given birth to four sons, developed physical problems that impaired sexual activity.

When Britain announced new legislation after the war that provided for imprisoning Indians suspected of sedition, Gandhi announced a *satyagraha.* His efforts soon produced alarm when protesters engaged in violence in 1919, and the British retaliated by slaughtering 400 Indians meeting at Amritsar in Punjab state. Gandhi called off the *satyagraha* demonstration, but he soon entered a more activist political phase. In 1920, he entered the Indian National Congress, a political organization with a secular, all-India orientation that had developed a cooperative effort between Hindus and Muslims to get concessions from Britain. Gandhi completely reorganized the group, making it stronger and less elitist. A mass organization evolved, wedded to his methods of *satyagraha.* He called for widespread boycotts of British goods with a turn to self-reliance and material simplicity. Once again, though, he was forced to suspend his efforts when demonstrators turned to violence, this time in 1922. The British arrested Gandhi for his activities, and he served two years in prison until his release in 1924 for health reasons.

After his prison term, Gandhi focused on a *satyagraha* to help the untouchable caste. Long despised in India as the lowest group in the caste system, the untouchables appeared to Gandhi as children of God like all human beings, who deserved the same rights as everyone else. Through Gandhi's efforts, they won the right to use a temple road in a southern state, which enlisted their support for the Congress. Meanwhile, the Congress splintered as Muslims and Hindus went their separate ways with one faction led by Chitta Ranjan Das, a Muslim, and another led by Motilala Nehru, a Hindu. The political situation heated again when in 1928, Britain announced the formation of a commission to study reforms. The commission did not have a single Indian representative, and at that point, Congress, under Gandhi's direction, demanded Indian independence. To support this, Gandhi promoted a *satyagraha* in 1930 that sought to eliminate the tax on salt—a tax that especially harmed India's poor. His efforts led to new discussions with Britain, but these produced only modest results, and the Salt March he led earned him another term in jail.

In 1934, Gandhi resigned completely from Congress, as leader and member. He claimed that the party had abandoned his strategy by supporting nonviolence only as a means rather than a principle. He refocused his efforts to uplift India by encouraging his countrymen to live simply, reject manufactured goods, and develop their own handicrafts. He lived as he preached, residing at Sevagram, a small central Indian village, where he spun cotton and reduced his material possessions to the minimum.

In the mid-1930s, Britain accelerated reforms that Indianized the government. A limited franchise that had been granted Indians years earlier was expanded slightly, and more Indians were brought into the bureaucracy. The Congress won elections in 8 of 11 states, among both Hindus and Muslims. Yet the power they gained on election was limited. To many Indians, the British concessions seemed too slow and too meager, leaving Indians as second-class citizens in their own country.

Gandhi raised considerable controversy during World War II, when he demanded that the British withdraw and grant his country its complete independence—the Quit India movement. Critics accused him of hampering the war effort, but Gandhi was reacting to British delays in transferring power to Indians and British efforts to inflame the differences between Hindus and Muslims. The British reacted harshly; in 1942, they jailed Gandhi and the entire Congress leadership. Gandhi remained in prison until 1944.

The following year, the British Labour Party came to power in Britain and changed the policy toward India. Henceforth, steps would be taken to grant the country its independence. Much to the horror of Gandhi and other Congress leaders, however, the procedure adopted by the British provided for two separate states, with Pakistan to be given its independence as a predominantly Muslim state.

With independence promised for no later than June 1948, Gandhi toured India in 1947 and again the following year, attempting to end the religious fighting. Having always been a figure whose personal convictions could bring unity to the Indian population, he began a fast to convince Hindus they should be nonviolent, even when provoked by Muslims, and declared that he would not end his protest until the violence ceased. The rioting, centered in Delhi, came to an end, but his efforts won him the animosity of many Hindus and Muslim extremists. On January 30, 1948, as Gandhi walked to a platform from which he was to address a prayer meeting, a Hindu fanatic, Nathuram Godse, shot him. Gandhi said, "Oh, God," and died instantly.

In his time, Gandhi had obtained the name "mahatma," meaning great soul. He was the leader of Indian nationalism, but his efforts clearly transcended the political realm. He envisioned a better society, founded on compassion and respect for all, a new moral order for his people and the world.

NEIL HAMILTON

HO CHI MINH (1890–1969)

Despite his frail appearance, Ho Chi Minh possessed an iron will and was singularly determined to liberate his country from foreign colonial powers. He did not live to see the final victory, but his three decades of uncompromising leadership placed Vietnam on the path to national unity under a communist government.

Ho was born Nguyen Sinh Cung in Nghe An Province on May 19, 1890. He was the son of Nguyen Sinh Sac, a mandarin and itinerant teacher. Indochina was then under French colonial supervision and suffering from the effects of that outside domination. Like his father, Ho came to resent colonialism and dedicated his life to ending it in Vietnam. Ho received his formal education in Hue at the Quoc Hoc school. After graduation, he taught school in a number of southern Vietnamese towns, including Saigon.

In 1911, Ho, now called Van Ba, hired on to a French ship as a kitchen helper and traveled to the United States, Africa, and then Europe. While in the United States, he supposedly was interested in the U.S. concepts of political rights outlined in the U.S. Declaration of Independence (1776) and the U.S. Constitution. During his years abroad, Ho held a variety of jobs, working as a gardener, waiter, and snow sweeper before settling on more permanent work as a photographer's assistant. In 1913, he sailed to London and worked as a dishwasher and assistant pastry chef at the Carlton Hotel.

When World War I commenced in 1914, Ho ventured to Paris under the assumed name of Nguyen Ai Quoc (Nguyen the Patriot) to join the French Socialist Party. In 1919, he petitioned the Paris Peace Conference to allow political freedom in his native land, but his request was ignored. Undeterred, he broke with the socialists to help found the French Communist Party in 1920 and embarked on a lengthy quest to eliminate French colonialism. In 1923, Ho ventured to Moscow, where he trained as a Comintern agent. The following year, he was dispatched by the Comintern to China for the purpose of organizing Vietnamese dissidents into communist revolutionaries. When the Chinese Kuomintang (Nationalist Party) under Chiang Kai-shek broke with Moscow in 1926, however, Ho and many followers were either expelled or arrested. He went back to Moscow, where he spent several more years before returning to southern China in 1941 at the height of World War II.

The war had brought chaos to Southeast Asia as Japanese troops invaded and expelled the French troops from their Asian colonies. Ho regarded Japanese colonialism with the same antipathy that he felt toward the French and offered his assistance to the Kuomintang who were fighting the Japanese. The Kuomintang arrested him again, however. Shortly after his release in 1942, he adopted the name Ho Chi Minh ("He Who Enlightens") before returning to Vietnam.

In Vietnam, Ho helped to organize communist sympathizers into an effective guerrilla movement, the Viet Minh, which fought the Japanese. He was helped politically and militarily by the U.S. Office of Strategic Services, which viewed him as a potentially useful ally (as it did all communists who were resisting the Axis powers). Although merciless toward his political rivals, Ho was careful to couch his politics in nationalistic, anticolonial idealism to bring a broad spectrum of dissidents together.

Following the Japanese surrender of 1945, a power vacuum was left by the absence of any imperial power in Vietnam, and only the Viet Minh were sufficiently organized to take charge. On September 2, 1945, Ho declared the creation of the Democratic Republic of Vietnam with himself as president.

Unmoved by the rhetoric of self-determination that the Allies had adopted during World War II, the French were determined to revive their Asian empire and returned in force the following year. Ho offered to share power with the French in some kind of

Born in 1890 in the French colony of Indochina, Ho Chi Minh is known as the father of Vietnamese independence. At various times he fought the Japanese, French, and Americans to achieve his goal but died in 1969 before seeing final victory. (Library of Congress)

commonwealth agreement, but when negotiations failed, open warfare broke out. Ho had correctly gauged the temperament of his adversaries and deduced they would be unwilling or unable to endure a protracted conflict. After eight years of fighting, the Viet Minh decisively defeated the French garrison at Dien Bien Phu, and the French withdrew from Indochina.

Subsequent negotiations at Geneva, Switzerland, in 1954 acknowledged Ho's complete control of the northern half of Vietnam but also recognized the regime of the noncommunist government in the southern half. Reunification of the country was to take place via a national election. Ho was easily the most popular man throughout the country and would have easily won the contest, which is why the Ngo Dinh Diem regime in South Vietnam, backed by the U.S. government, never allowed it to occur.

Ho continued consolidating his power in the North until 1960, when he initiated a concerted guerrilla strategy to give support to the communists in South Vietnam and topple its increasingly unpopular government. In many respects, it was less a war than a terrorist campaign directed against political adversaries. When the U.S. government, unsettled by what it viewed as a communist conquest directed from Moscow against its client state, intervened directly with combat troops in 1965, prospects for the North Vietnamese seemed dim. Like the French, however, U.S. forces underestimated the determination and resilience of Ho's forces.For his part, Ho may have underestimated the millions of deaths and ecological destruction that U.S. technology would inflict on his country before the Americans admitted that they could not win and signed a peace agreement in 1973. He was successful in convincing his countrymen that the very presence of

U.S. forces constituted a new imperialist force that must be defeated. Ho was also skilled at the delicate balancing of politics with the Soviet Union and China, bitter ideological rivals that both provided material and military assistance. Ho did not survive to see the fruits of his labors; he died of a heart ailment on September 2, 1969. When the southern capital of Saigon fell to a final communist onslaught in 1975, it was renamed Ho Chi Minh City in his honor.

JOHN C. FREDRIKSEN

MAU MAU REVOLT (1950s)

The Mau Mau Revolt in 1950s Kenya was one of the most violent independence movements in twentieth-century African history. The Mau Maus sought to drive all white people from their country and to gain freedom. They resented European monopolization of their lands and power. They also were angered by attempts to change their culture, especially attacks on female circumcision. The British were able to defeat the Mau Mau movement at great cost, but they realized that they could not prevent Kenyan independence. They implemented a gradual process that gave independence to Kenya in 1963.

After conquering Kenya in 1900, the British encouraged European and Indian immigration to that country. The capital of Nairobi was a new city designed to be the capital and located in the healthy highlands region. Europeans and Indians dominated the political life of Kenya and took much of the land once owned by natives. By the 1920s, Kenyans began to organize political resistance to the British. The most important group was the Young Kikuyu Association (YKA). The Kikuyu people made up 25% of the native population of Kenya and lived in the areas adjacent to Nairobi. One of the leaders of the YKA formed the Kenya African Union (KAU) in 1944. The president of KAU was Jomo Kenyatta, a Kikuyu, who traveled around Kenya spreading a message of making Kenya an African country run by Africans.

In 1950, the Kikuyu began to organize a secret society known as the Mau Mau. The group's goal was to drive all non-Africans from Kenya. Members underwent ritual initiation and were forced to take solemn oaths not to reveal anything about the Mau Mau. British authorities banned the Mau Mau in late 1950, but it continued to grow. Kikuyu were forced to join the Mau Mau, and chiefs who spoke against it were killed. European settlers demanded government action, but little was done until 1952. In October of that year, the government declared a state of emergency. The British arrested 183 known members of the Mau Mau, including Kenyatta. Kenyatta denied being a member, but he was obviously sympathetic to the goals of the Mau Mau. He was sentenced to six years in prison.

Despite the loss of many of their leaders, the Mau Mau continued their terrorist activities. They continued to intimidate Kikuyu into joining them, but they also began to kill white settlers and burn their farms. Their brutal methods of hacking their victims to death with knives and machetes repulsed many who were otherwise sympathetic to the Mau Mau goals. After March 1953, entire anti–Mau Mau villages were attacked and burned to the ground.

In June 1953, the British began to organize an effective campaign against the Mau Mau. They gave weapons to the Kikuyu Home Guard, so loyal Kikuyu could defend their

Kikuyu women, who previously were Mau Mau adherents, renounce their Mau Mau oath during a cleansing ceremony in Nyeri, Kenya, in 1952. The Mau Mau Revolt of the 1950s was one of the most violent independence movements in twentieth-century African history. Although the movement was eventually suppressed, it succeeded in persuading the United Kingdom to grant Kenya's independence. (Library of Congress)

homes. The British soldiers began sweeps through areas thought to have many Mau Mau sympathizers. In open areas, the soldiers were given the right to stop and question any suspicious persons; in the forests, soldiers could shoot to kill without warning. The British forces totaled about 10,000 regular troops divided between British and King's African Rifle (black troops with white officers) battalions. They also had 21,000 Kenyan policemen and 25,000 Kikuyu Home Guards. The Mau Mau were estimated to have 12,000 guerrilla soldiers and 30,000 sympathizers; they were armed mostly with spears, knives, and homemade gunpowder weapons.

The British were hampered by the terrain, which made their movement difficult. Base camps in very hard-to-reach areas were bombed by aircraft. Those Kikuyu that were suspected of being Mau Mau were rounded up and put in detention camps. Those individuals eventually totaled 100,000 people. Other Kikuyu were forced to live in villages that could be easily defended. The Kikuyu traditionally lived on individual farms, so that step caused great unhappiness. However, the central village concept made defense much easier.

By April 1954, the British had cleared most of the countryside of Mau Mau. At that time, they decided to clear Nairobi, which they believed was a center of the movement.

In Operation Anvil, the British sealed off the city and went house to house looking for Mau Mau. They detained almost half the Kikuyu in the city and added 16,000 to the detention camps. Operation Anvil broke the back of the Mau Mau movement, as the guerrillas depended on aid from the city sympathizers. Special teams were organized to move through the forest, using information from turncoats, to kill the remaining Mau Maus. Dedan Kimathi, the most prominent leader of the Mau Mau, was captured in 1956 and executed in October of that year. His death marked the end of the Mau Mau Revolt.

During the war, 10,500 Mau Mau were killed. They killed 1,800 African and 58 European and Indian civilians. The British army lost 63 British and 534 African soldiers. Although it failed, the Mau Mau Revolt forced the British to grant more political power to the Kenyans. They released Kenyatta from prison in 1961, and he became Kenya's first prime minister. Kenya became completely independent on December 12, 1963.

TIM WATTS

KWAME NKRUMAH (1909–1972)

When Ghana obtained independence in 1957, it continued on a course begun several years earlier by Kwame Nkrumah, one of the most strident and controversial leaders in Africa. Nkrumah, called "the Deliverer" by Ghanaians, advocated strong executive power in advancing his concept of African socialism.

Nkrumah was born on September 21, 1909, into the Nzima tribe. At that time, Ghana was under the rule of the United Kingdom and was called the Gold Coast. Nkrumah's father worked as a goldsmith in Nkroful, a small village in the Western Province. Nkrumah went to mission schools for his elementary education and after high school matriculated at Prince of Wales College at Achimota, where he received training as a teacher. He graduated in 1930 and taught for several years while thinking seriously about becoming a priest.

In 1935, Nkrumah traveled to the United States and studied at Lincoln University in Pennsylvania, where he majored in economics and sociology. He completed the program in 1939 and then received master's degrees from Lincoln and the University of Pennsylvania. While in college, he served aboard ships as a steward to earn money for his education; he also preached in black churches in Pennsylvania and New York.

Nkrumah studied such revolutionaries as Vladimir Lenin, Mohandas Gandhi, and Marcus Garvey and became particularly impressed with Garvey's pan-African ideology. Nkrumah served on the faculty at Lincoln University, where he taught philosophy, black history, and Greek. Yet he exhibited much restlessness, an ambitious striving that in 1945 brought him to England to pursue a law degree. When this proved unsuccessful, he tried earning a doctorate in philosophy—but he abandoned that course as well.

Nkrumah's political interests deepened. In England, he served as general secretary of the West African Secretariat (from 1945 to 1947), an organization committed to establishing a united Africa. He also served as secretary to the Pan-African Congress; edited the official publication of the West African Students' Union, an organization in which he served as vice president; led "The Circle," a group experimenting in revolutionary activism; helped prepare a pamphlet distributed in the Gold Coast titled *New Africa;* and wrote *Towards Colonial Freedom,* which promoted an anticolonial struggle.

Nkrumah committed himself to asserting Africa's black identity, which white Europeans had subjugated, a process evident in his homeland, where Great Britain governed the Gold Coast by dividing it into a "colony" along the littoral and a "protectorate" inland. In the former, the residents possessed British citizenship; in the latter, they did not. There existed a Legislative Council composed mainly of senior colonial officials with a few elected Africans who had little power. The colonial governor exercised the most authority.

By the time Nkrumah reached adulthood, new political organizations had emerged. J. B. Danquah began the Gold Coast Youth Conference that criticized foreign exploitation, calling it "dangerous to the economic stability and permanence of the people of this country." Shortly thereafter, he formed the United Gold Coast Convention (UGCC), which advocated gaining self-government through constitutional procedures.

Nkrumah became general secretary of the UGCC when he returned to the Gold Coast in 1947, but he disliked the largely conservative, elitist nature of the organization. In 1948, he founded the *Accra Evening News* to promote his radical ideology, and in 1949, breaking with the UGCC, he founded the Convention People's Party (CPP), which appealed to younger, poorer persons and quickly gained a mass following.

Many strikes and even a few riots—mainly linked to harsh economic conditions—disrupted the Gold Coast in 1948. The British subsequently arrested and detained several leaders, including Nkrumah. In 1950, he promoted what he called "positive action," meaning nonviolent strikes and protests directed against British rule. Nkrumah's strategy brought the Gold Coast to an economic standstill and stirred crowds to chant "Self-government now!" After more rioting and violence, the British again arrested Nkrumah, along with other CPP leaders. These arrests, however, created a "cult of martyrdom," as it was called, and in the 1951 general elections, the CPP won 35 of 38 legislative seats, a landslide victory that meant it would direct the struggle for independence, now recognized as virtually certain to occur.

Released from jail so he could serve in the legislature, Nkrumah made sweeping promises that expanded support for the CPP. He pledged jobs for all, industrialization, free primary education, a national health service, and even free public transportation under a socialist state. He called for power to be given to the masses and for immediate self-government. On March 5, 1952, Nkrumah became prime minister, although much power remained with the British government and its colonial governor. Nkrumah promoted a review of the existing constitution and in July 1953 introduced his "Motion of Destiny" in the legislature, calling for the British to grant independence; it carried unanimously, and the following year, Britain approved a constitutional change allowing the Gold Coast internal self-government but stopping short of complete independence.

In the remarkably short time of three years since the CPP had come to power, Nkrumah had led his homeland to the brink of nationhood. This progress resulted partly from the nature of Gold Coast society, with its relative homogeneity and mature economic development. It also resulted, however, from the attributes that made Nkrumah a strong leader: his near total commitment to politics, his appeal to youth, his appeal to women as a political force, and his knowledge of the Gold Coast's traditional authority structures and how to use them.

Yet in 1954, Nkrumah faced serious challenges to his power from emerging sectional, ethnic, and religious parties, particularly the National Liberation Movement (NLM), an Asante-based group. The NLM advocated more Asante power before nationhood, and it resorted to violence, which caused Britain to hesitate in proceeding toward independence.

After a series of conferences, Nkrumah accepted the British recommendation of establishing regional assemblies alongside a central government, providing for some Asante autonomy. The NLM, however, rejected this proposal, whereupon Britain, to Nkrumah's chagrin, insisted on elections in 1956 to determine popular support for both the proposal and nationhood. The CPP won the vote handily, and the legislature again called for independence. In September 1956, Britain agreed, and on March 6, 1957, the Gold Coast became the nation of Ghana.

Nkrumah moved quickly to consolidate his power. He pushed constitutional changes that discontinued the regional assemblies and established a deportation act, allowing the exile of those persons threatening public welfare. Thereafter, political opposition was increasingly risky. On July 1, 1960, Ghana became a republic under a new constitution, and in a rigged election, the enormously popular Nkrumah became president. The 1960 constitution consolidated his power over the legislature, the judiciary, and the CPP.

Nkrumah reorganized the CPP to establish his African socialism and a welfare state. After massive labor unrest and a general strike in 1961, he further harassed his remaining political opponents, frightening people into silence. His repression resulted in two assassination attempts against him, one in 1962, the other in 1964. After the first attempt, he allied with Marxist extremists, became more reclusive, and encouraged a personality cult labeled "Nkrumaism." After the second attempt, he officially made Ghana a one-party state through a plebiscite, with himself president for life. Despite his affinity for Marxism, the Soviet Union did not offer Nkrumah the support he desired. In practice, his socialism was greatly tempered by his cooperation with businesspeople and the country's economic dependence on Western nations.

Nkrumah stridently supported pan-Africanism and pushed for a union with other nearby states to avoid what he feared would be the Balkanization of Africa. However, the other African nations had just won their independence and wanted to preserve it. Furthermore, Nkrumah's goals and procedures suffered from poor planning and nebulous ideas, leading many African leaders to deride his union plan. Only a few radical states, such as Tanzania, supported him, and in 1964, even this backing evaporated.

As Ghana's economy deteriorated with shortages of foodstuffs and other items and as Nkrumah moved to break relations with Britain over the failure of the former colonial power to act forcefully against the white supremacist government in Rhodesia, Ghana's army launched a coup d'état on February 24, 1966, while the president was in Beijing as part of a peace mission concerning Vietnam. Nkrumah subsequently lived in exile in Guinea. While there, he continued to advocate black nationalism and claimed that an important link existed between Africa's revolutionary struggle and Marxism. He wrote books and articles describing oppression in Africa and advocating activation of the masses in a class struggle. While in a Bucharest hospital on April 27, 1972, Nkrumah died from cancer.

Although Nkrumah left Ghana with enormous debts totaling billions of dollars, he also left many improvements in his nation's infrastructure, a rich political literature, and a revolutionary consciousness. Furthermore, his legacy of black nationalism and black pride stirred sub-Saharan Africa toward new accomplishments.

NEIL HAMILTON

DOCUMENT: EXCERPT FROM KWAME NKRUMAH'S *I SPEAK OF FREEDOM* (1961)

The first president of the independent country of Ghana in Africa, Kwame Nkrumah was one of the most influential figures in the emergence of modern Africa after decolonization. He proved one of the most vocal champions of pan-Africanism and widely promoted the common interests of black Africans regardless of national borders. Within Ghana, he became a controversial figure, particularly for his vigorous suppression of all dissent toward his rule. In 1961, he published his book I Speak of Freedom, *an excerpt of which appears here. It was a manifesto for unity among African peoples.*

For centuries, Europeans dominated the African continent. The white man arrogated to himself the right to rule and to be obeyed by the non-white; his mission, he claimed, was to "civilise" Africa. Under this cloak, the Europeans robbed the continent of vast riches and inflicted unimaginable suffering on the African people. . . .

It is clear that we must find an African solution to our problems, and that this can only be found in African unity. Divided we are weak; united, Africa could become one of the greatest forces for good in the world.

Although most Africans are poor, our continent is potentially extremely rich. Our mineral resources, which are being exploited with foreign capital only to enrich foreign investors, range from gold and diamonds to uranium and petroleum. Our forests contain some of the finest woods to be grown anywhere. Our cash crops include cocoa, coffee, rubber, tobacco and cotton. As for power, which is an important factor in any economic development, Africa contains over 40% of the potential water power of the world, as compared with about 10% in Europe and 13% in North America. Yet so far, less than 1% has been developed. This is one of the reasons why we have in Africa the paradox of poverty in the midst of plenty, and scarcity in the midst of abundance.

Never before have a people had within their grasp so great an opportunity for developing a continent endowed with so much wealth. Individually, the independent states of Africa, some of them potentially rich, others poor, can do little for their people. Together, by mutual help, they can achieve much. But the economic development of the continent must be planned and pursued as a whole. A loose confederation designed only for economic co-operation would not provide the necessary unity of purpose. Only a strong political union can bring about full and effective development of our natural resources for the benefit of our people.

The political situation in Africa today is heartening and at the same time disturbing. It is heartening to see so many new flags hoisted in place of the old; it is disturbing to see so many countries of varying sizes and at different levels of development, weak and, in some cases, almost helpless. If this terrible state of fragmentation is allowed to continue it may well be disastrous for us all. . . .

We have to prove that greatness is not to be measured in stock piles of atom bombs. I believe strongly and sincerely that with the deep-rooted wisdom and dignity, the innate respect for human lives, the intense humanity that is our heritage, the African race, united under one federal government, will emerge not as just another world bloc to flaunt its wealth and strength, but as a Great Power whose greatness is indestructible because it is built not on fear, envy and suspicion, nor won at the expense of others, but founded on hope, trust, friendship and directed to the good of all mankind.

The emergence of such a mighty stabilising force in this strife-worn world should be regarded not as the shadowy dream of a visionary, but as a practical proposition, which the peoples of Africa can, and should, translate into reality. There is a tide in the affairs of every people when the moment strikes for political action. Such was the moment in the history of the United States of America when the Founding Fathers saw beyond the petty wranglings of the separate states and created a Union. This is our chance. We must act now. Tomorrow may be too late and the opportunity will have passed, and with it the hope of free Africa's survival.

8

The Cold War, c. 1946–1991

INTRODUCTION

The Cold War dominated international relations during the latter half of the twentieth century. It featured an intense and unrelenting rivalry between the United States and its allies on one hand and the Soviet Union and its supporters on the other. Cold War competition touched every facet of human activity. The Cold War influenced and in many instances drove politics, economics, diplomacy, culture, and technology. Despite several near misses, the animosity between the two prime antagonists never escalated into an armed clash, hence the term "Cold War."

The origins of the Cold War remain a source of great controversy. Before World War II, many Western leaders viewed the Marxist regime in Russia with a mixture of fear and hatred. Conversely, the Soviet Union of Vladimir Lenin and Joseph Stalin regarded the capitalistic West as its mortal enemy. Although the West and East eventually allied during World War II in a successful military struggle against Nazi Germany, in many ways the wartime experience served to confirm rather than allay prewar suspicions. Almost immediately after the Nazis surrendered in May 1945, the alliance began to break apart. Increasing Soviet domination of Poland—the country Great Britain and France originally went to war to defend—disturbed the West; U.S. president Harry Truman's unexpected decision in May 1945 to end Lend-Lease aid to the USSR upset the Soviets. An acrimonious quarrel soon developed.

Initially the Cold War focused on war-torn Europe. It was there that sides were first chosen and a set of ground rules for the conflict emerged. A major point of disagreement was how to handle defeated and occupied Germany. The issue of reparations presented a serious problem. The Soviets, citing the extensive damage done to their country by the invading German armies, demanded that much of Germany's industrial infrastructure be dismantled and shipped to the USSR. The West, not wanting to support an economically destroyed Germany and fearing that the Soviets wished to cripple the German economy to bring about a communist takeover, refused. In short order, the joint administration of occupied Germany broke down and each side began to formulate its own plan for Germany's future.

Meanwhile, the Soviet Union continued to integrate formerly independent countries such as Estonia, Latvia, and Lithuania into the USSR, and steadily consolidated its hold over Poland, Czechoslovakia, Hungary, Romania, and Bulgaria, countries its Red Army had recently liberated. These actions, together with its German policy and Stalin's belligerent February 1946 speech citing the threat capitalism posed to Soviet security, caused former British prime minister Winston Churchill to declare in a March 1946 speech, "From Stettin in the Baltic to Trieste in the Adriatic, an iron curtain has descended across the continent."

The pivotal year 1947 opened with Great Britain informing the United States that it could no longer continue to support either Turkey or the conservative Greek government that was then fighting a communist insurgency. The implication was clear: Britain was abandoning its position in the eastern Mediterranean. Without much hesitation, the United States moved into the vacuum, replacing Britain as chief supplier to the Turks and the embattled Greeks. On March 12, 1947, Truman delivered a speech to the U.S. Congress in which he enunciated what became known as the Truman Doctrine. The U.S. promised to "support free peoples who are resisting attempted subjugation by armed minorities or outside pressures." The Truman Doctrine became a cornerstone of U.S. policy during the Cold War.

The Truman Doctrine was greatly influenced by the work of American diplomat George F. Kennan and several other American statesmen who at this time formulated the policy of "containment." Containment postulated that the best response to perceived communist expansionism was to strengthen existing Western institutions to deny communism an opportunity to take root, to oppose (chiefly by economic measures) communist attempts to threaten the West's vital interests, and to wait patiently yet vigilantly until the insecure Soviet regime changed for the better or, as eventually happened, collapsed under the weight of its own shortcomings.

Implementation of the containment policy also led to the Marshall Plan, named for U.S. Secretary of State George C. Marshall, which followed quickly on the heels of the Truman Doctrine. Offering exceptional amounts of American aid to devastated Europe, the Marshall Plan proved instrumental in rebuilding the shattered economies of Western Europe. However, Stalin and his allies denounced the Marshall Plan as an insidious American trick to gain economic hegemony over Europe. The USSR refused to participate in the plan and ordered its satellites to do likewise. To secure congressional approval of the Marshall Plan, the Truman administration portrayed it as an effective way to combat communist expansion in Europe.

In the wake of the Marshall Plan, in September 1947 the Soviets established the Communist Information Bureau, or Cominform, which, like the prewar Communist International (Comintern), served to bring the global communist movement under Moscow's close control and to turn that movement aggressively against the West. Following the Soviet lead, communist parties in western Europe, particularly France and Italy, railed against the Marshall Plan and used their influence, especially with the working class, to try to disrupt normal life.

In February 1948, the communists masterminded a coup d'état in Czechoslovakia that replaced a coalition government with one completely subservient to Moscow. Angered by events in Czechoslovakia, the West took steps to create a military alliance and also signaled its intention to form an independent West German state. Stalin retaliated by initiating the Berlin Blockade, one of the most dangerous crises of the Cold War. In June, Stalin cut off Western access to Berlin, the divided German capital located deep within the Soviet zone of occupation. Through something of a logistical miracle, the West managed to supply its portion of Berlin by air for almost a year. Stalin called off the blockade in May 1949, but by that time the West had already committed itself to the

A worker shovels rubble during the rebuilding of West Berlin in front of a building adorned with a sign supporting the Marshall Plan. This massive U.S. financial aid program greatly assisted in the rebuilding of Western Europe after World War II. (National Archives)

establishment of a German state closely allied to the West and to the North Atlantic Treaty Organization (NATO), a military alliance aimed against the USSR. Stalin responded by establishing an East German state tied to the Soviet Union and an opposing military alliance, the Warsaw Pact.

Although initially centered on Europe, the Cold War soon became global in nature. As early as 1946, the United States and the USSR squabbled over the latter's claims to share control over the entrance to the Black Sea with Turkey and to establish a sphere of influence in northern Iran. On both issues the Americans took a tough stance. However, the USSR scored what appeared to be a major victory in 1949 when the Chinese communists under Mao Zedong defeated the American client Chiang Kai-shek and gained control over the most populous country in the world. It was almost universally assumed that Mao would do the Soviet Union's bidding.

In the following year, the Cold War actually heated up. On June 25, 1950, the communist government of North Korea under Kim Il-sung invaded South Korea. Responding to this invasion, the United Nations, the site of seemingly interminable East-West wrangling since its inception, became involved. Taking advantage of the Soviet delegation's boycott of the UN Security Council, the United States managed to have the UN brand North Korea as the aggressor and to enter the conflict on the side of South Korea. Three years later the parties to the Korean War signed a truce, but not before China had joined the fray on the side of North Korea and some American commanders had unsuccessfully urged the use of nuclear weapons.

With the truce in Korea and the death of Stalin in 1953, the Cold War's intensity slackened a bit, and East-West relations entered a phase of alternating periods of rapprochement and crisis that prevailed until the end of the struggle. The Cold War had become institutionalized.

By 1955, Nikita Khrushchev had emerged as Stalin's successor in the USSR, and he embarked on a policy of "peaceful coexistence" whereby East and West were to continue their competition but in a less confrontational manner. Propaganda blasts were interspersed with periodic summit meetings during which Soviet and U.S. leaders sometimes amicably discussed the international situation. Positive steps such as the 1955 Austrian State Treaty, which provided for the end of Austria's occupation and the establishment of a sovereign but neutral Austrian state, were matched by negative steps such as a series of nerve-racking crises over Berlin, culminating in the 1961 construction of the Berlin Wall, which physically divided the already politically divided former German capital.

A truly terrifying arms race was another central feature of the Cold War. Both the United States and the USSR amassed huge arsenals of the most destructive thermonuclear weapons. Moreover, the two rivals also developed myriad systems including intercontinental ballistic missiles with which to rain down a nuclear holocaust upon each other. In this respect, the sides appeared to be evenly matched, leading to a stalemate sometimes described as "the balance of terror." Both sides subscribed to the MAD doctrine (Mutual Assured Destruction), and in a macabre way MAD served to restrain the competing superpowers. In fact, from the early 1960s onward, a growing realization of the dangerous nature of the arms race led to a series of nuclear arms agreements.

This realization was hastened by the 1962 Cuban Missile Crisis, which almost exploded into nuclear conflict. Disturbed by the behavior of Fidel Castro, the successful Cuban revolutionary who identified with Marxism, in 1961 the United States backed an invasion of Cuba by anti-Castro elements that ended in disaster. The failed Bay of Pigs invasion prompted Castro to move clearly into the Soviet orbit. Eighteen months later, upon discovering that the USSR was placing missiles in Cuba that could easily reach the United States, President John F. Kennedy issued an ultimatum to Khrushchev to remove the missiles or face dire consequences. Although Castro was ready for a nuclear showdown, Khrushchev was not. The Soviets removed their missiles, and a nuclear war was narrowly averted.

Beginning in the 1970s, the policy of detente appeared to offer a possible end to the Cold War. Detente seemed an unlikely development at the time. The United States was still mired in Vietnam, fighting what it believed was a Moscow-inspired attempt to spread communism. The Soviet Union had only recently brutally repressed Czechoslovakia's attempt to achieve "socialism with a human face," a move that gave rise to the Brezhnev Doctrine in which the Soviet leader, Leonid Brezhnev, claimed for the Soviet Union the right to intervene in any "socialist" country to preserve socialism. Nevertheless, under detente the United States, led by President Richard Nixon and his chief foreign policy advisor, Henry Kissinger, and Brezhnev's USSR tried to relax tensions in their relationship and to find common ground on a number of issues of mutual interest. High points of detente included the 1972 Strategic Arms Limitation Agreement (SALT I), which set limits on the number of offensive weapons the United States and the Soviet Union could produce and restricted each country's antiballistic missile defense system. In 1975, 35 nations including the United States and the USSR signed the Helsinki Agreements, a set of international accords that legitimized the post–World War II boundaries in Europe and also committed the signatories to honor their citizens' human rights and to expand cultural and trade relations.

Detente, however, was short-lived. In the West, numerous critics attacked detente as little more than thinly veiled appeasement. Their criticism appeared well founded when the USSR cracked down on Soviet dissidents despite a pledge at Helsinki to respect human rights and expanded its military might at an alarming rate. When the Soviets invaded Afghanistan in December 1979 and crushed the independent Polish trade union known as Solidarity two years later, detente was dead. In 1980, Ronald Reagan, a strident anticommunist, was elected U.S. president. Within months of his inauguration, Reagan was publicly denouncing the Soviet Union as an "evil empire." The coldest days of the Cold War had returned.

The Cold War also saw both the United States and the USSR attract and retain clients who frequently served as surrogates for the superpowers. This was particularly true of the Third World, or those countries that emerged from colonialism after the end of World War II. Quite often these clients had nothing to commend themselves to their masters other than a willingness to be bought. More dangerous was the fact that some clients tended to subvert or ignore their master's wishes, pursuing independent and sometimes perilous courses. Many Third World leaders became adept at playing off one superpower against the other to further their own aims.

In 1985, Mikhail Gorbachev came to power in the Soviet Union, and, unexpectedly, the Cold War began to wind down. Realizing that the USSR faced massive economic problems, Gorbachev initiated a policy of reform known by the code words *glasnost* (openness) and *perestroika* (restructuring). He also sought better relations with the West. Real achievements in lessening East-West tensions were soon overshadowed as the reform process within the USSR spun out of control. When the Soviet Union officially disintegrated in December 1991, the Cold War was over.

INTERPRETIVE ESSAY

THOMAS PHILIP WOLF

When World War II ended, optimism prevailed. Allied forces had triumphed over fascism in Japan and Germany, the brutality of which, including the near annihilation of European Jewry, had shocked the world. The victors agreed to punish the guilty and created an organization to address international problems, a successor to the League of Nations called the United Nations. Member states could now concentrate on creating a better world, one in which Allied promises of prosperity and freedom would be realized. That rosy outlook soon dissolved.

No single factor explains the emergence of the Cold War. In part it was due to Soviet actions; in part it was due to Western, particularly U.S., responses to those actions. Mutual mistrust was a compelling factor. Even before the war ended in the Pacific, signs of a troublesome peace emerged. At the Potsdam Conference in July 1945, the new U.S. president, Harry Truman, and the British prime minister, Clement Attlee, who had recently succeeded Winston Churchill, encountered the demanding and inflexible Soviet head of state, Joseph Stalin. Soviet attitudes, reflected in Stalin's behavior, had diverse roots. Although most Americans were unaware of it, the Soviets endured by far the heaviest losses in the war. Conservative estimates put the Soviet death toll at 20 million. In Soviet eyes, these losses were aggravated by the British and American delay in mounting a second front in Western Europe to alleviate German military pressure on the Soviet Union. Soviet leaders were also skeptical of U.S. intentions because the U.S. government had earlier intervened in the Russian civil war on the side of the anticommunist forces and had refused to grant the USSR diplomatic recognition until 1933. When one adds to these factors traditional Russian paranoia, derived from centuries of invasion by their Western neighbors, it is understandable that the Soviets sought a buffer zone on their western border. Soviet expansionism could also be viewed as a continuation of the historic Russian desire to extend the nation's borders to the Pacific and to control a warm water outlet such as the Bosporus Strait. Another element of Soviet conduct greatly contributed to Western distrust. Communist Party commissars accompanied Soviet armies as they moved west, turning back the German forces. Following Stalin's orders, these commissars established regimes abjectly subservient to Moscow.

Largely ignorant of Russian history and Soviet sacrifices during the war, most Americans attributed Soviet expansionism to a worldwide communist conspiracy rather than Russian nationalism. Although West Europeans were less convinced of the conspiracy interpretation, in the aftermath of the war, they had little choice but to accept American leadership. Nevertheless, the conspiracy view had merit. In addition to territory they had directly conquered, in Eastern Europe the Soviets used the threat of military intervention to compel noncommunist leaders to yield to indigenous communists. They also sought an enhanced presence in Western Europe and in the Far East, where they had played only a minor role in the war effort, and they aided communist movements seeking to gain control by force, as in China. Soviet propaganda, disseminated worldwide by radio and print, heightened Western suspicions and reinforced the West's belief in the existence of an international communist conspiracy.

How should the United States respond to this situation? If it followed the precedent of the 1920s, it would promptly disarm and disengage from Europe. Initially it demobilized much of its military capacity and turned inward, but soon a policy known as containment evolved.

President Truman, a student of history, was acutely sensitive not only to the transgressions of recent dictators but also to those of others over the centuries. For his generation, the primary lesson of World War II was that it could have been prevented if the democracies had opposed Hitler sooner. In particular, the outcome of the 1938 Munich Conference was widely accepted as reason for democratic nations to defend their collective security. Many concluded that at the end of World War II, one expansionist totalitarian foe had been replaced by another, and Truman saw no choice but to oppose this new threat. Moreover, the weapons developed during the war, notably the atomic bomb, were so destructive that the United States could not wait until future hostilities began to rearm. To do so would ensure defeat.

Truman's secretaries of state, General George C. Marshall and Dean Acheson, concurred in his assessment. With their economies in disrepair, Western European nations needed American economic aid if they were to resist the communist threat. And, along with many American businessmen, the Truman administration concluded that the nation's economy would not prosper unless world markets, particularly in Europe, were revived.

Especially in Europe, the Cold War fomented espionage and counterespionage on a large scale. Berlin became a notable site for these activities. The United States created its first peacetime intelligence agency, the Central Intelligence Agency (CIA), a successor to the wartime Office of Strategic Services (OSS). The need for this apparatus was confirmed by the defections to the Soviet Union of Guy Burgess and Donald Maclean, British foreign office officials and longtime spies for the Soviets.

Soviet espionage agencies produced more comprehensive information than did their Western counterparts because Soviet agents operated in open societies in which information was relatively easy to obtain. Comparable data were off limits even to citizens of the communist nations. Realizing that it lacked full information, the CIA and other Western intelligence entities assumed that the communist nations were more formidable than they actually were. However, if communism endangered the very existence of Western civilization, it behooved the West to err on the side of caution. To do otherwise was irresponsible.

To implement the multifaceted containment policy, Truman had to overstate the magnitude of the Soviet challenge; otherwise the U.S. Congress would not have provided the funds to build and maintain the most expensive military force in the history of the world or to help Western Europe reconstruct its economy. Persuading the American people to approve this policy was more difficult than persuading Congress. It was desirable that public support be created without producing hysteria; yet the public had to be convinced to accept the burdens of world leadership indefinitely. The effort to achieve a balance between avoiding anticommunist paranoia and obtaining long-term commitment was only partially successful. For example, the American public never fully endorsed foreign aid, but the Truman administration adopted that policy, and subsequent presidents continued it.

The specter of Soviet expansion had a marked impact on the American public, whose reaction was often emotional, based as it was on both incomplete facts and faulty assessment of them. Politicians eager to exploit the communist threat also impaired the public's ability to understand the situation.

Anxiety about communism fanned suspicions about Soviet agents infiltrating the U.S. government. That anxiety was used to promote political careers. Republican Congressman Richard Nixon of California grabbed headlines as a member of a congressional committee investigating allegations that a key ex–State Department official was a Soviet spy. In September 1949, the startling announcement that the Soviets had created an atomic bomb deepened concern about the Soviet threat. In 1951, American courts found Julius and Ethel Rosenberg guilty of transmitting nuclear secrets to the Soviets. The Rosenbergs were subsequently executed.

The most prominent politician to play upon American fears of communist infiltration was Republican senator Joseph McCarthy of Wisconsin. McCarthy and others of his ilk launched a number of congressional investigations. The advent of television magnified the impact of these exercises. Although these hearings were not judicial proceedings, statements by witnesses could be used in subsequent trials, and witnesses could be found in contempt of Congress. With McCarthy encouraging public condemnation of witnesses, the constitutional safeguard of the Fifth Amendment that protects one from self-incrimination was frequently invoked but largely ineffective in persuading the public that a witness was not guilty. Eventually McCarthy overstepped his bounds, and his Senate colleagues censured him in 1954.

Individuals were fired from government agencies, universities, and the entertainment industry. Others were blacklisted or never told why they were dismissed or not hired. Some employers consulted with persons or organizations that maintained lists of persons whose patriotism was deemed questionable. In addition to the U.S. attorney general's list of suspect organizations, others circulated covertly. Generally, the alleged act of disloyalty was membership in an organization in the 1930s or early 1940s when that group was legal and reputable.

Unquestionably, Soviet agents were active in the United States, but anticommunist hysteria in the postwar decade exaggerated the actual threat and appeared ready to sacrifice the liberties that distinguish constitutional governments from authoritarian ones. The underlying consequence of McCarthyism, red-baiting, and other emotional responses to "godless communism" was to place in jeopardy the fundamental principles of a free society. In particular, freedom of speech and freedom of association were in danger of being sacrificed to combat communism on the home front. Thus a subtheme of the Cold War was the struggle to avoid diluting constitutional principles while maintaining national security.

Not all Americans accepted the proposition that containment was the proper response to the Soviet Union. Former Vice President Henry A. Wallace headed a Progressive Party in 1948 that urged a less hostile posture toward the USSR, but his candidacy failed badly at the polls. A few scholars, entertainers, and others continued to advocate a moderate approach toward the Soviets, but their view never appealed to more than a small minority in the United States.

Preoccupation with the communist threat dominated presidential election campaigns throughout the next four decades. For example, in the 1960 campaign, two prominent issues were the commitment of the United States to protect two islands occupied by Chinese nationalist troops off the shore of mainland China, and John F. Kennedy's charge that there was a "missile gap" in favor of the USSR. After the election, the Kennedy administration announced that it had discovered there was no missile gap, and the offshore islands were never heard of again. The elections of 1960 and 1964 brought Democrats to the White House. Because Republican candidates were generally judged to be more anticommunist than their Democratic opponents, the successful Democrats— John Kennedy and Lyndon Johnson—were determined not to appear weak when confronted with a communist challenge.

Initially, international events seemed to confirm the fear of an imminent communist seizure of the world. A pattern of provocation and reaction developed as illustrated by the 1948 Soviet blockade of Berlin. The Soviets would mount deliberate actions to provoke the Western powers, who in turn would respond without using military force. This scenario was repeated on several occasions, including the East Berlin uprising of 1953 and the Hungarian Revolution of 1956. As long as neither side employed military power against the other, a "cold war," as presidential advisor Bernard Baruch termed it in 1947, existed.

Sometimes the West made the first move in this game of international chess. Six years after the United States initiated the North Atlantic Treaty Organization (NATO), the Soviet bloc nations created its mirror image in the Warsaw Pact. The Soviet response to the Marshall Plan was the Council for Mutual Economic Assistance (Comecon), an organization originally composed of the USSR and five other communist nations within the Soviet sphere whose economies were dominated by Moscow.

Diplomatically, one side would offer a proposal, and the other side would make a counterproposal. The communists offered the Rapacki Plan to create a weapons-free zone in Europe, and President Dwight D. Eisenhower suggested an "open skies" policy in which each side would permit a limited number of flights over its sovereign territories to ensure that no sneak attack was being prepared. Western objections torpedoed the Rapacki Plan, and the Soviet Union rejected "open skies."

Domestic pressure dictated that the United States deny the existence, at least diplomatically, of some communist governments. For the most devoted anticommunists, any normal contact with communist regimes was immoral. This explains the U.S. policy toward the People's Republic of China for nearly a quarter of a century. Influenced by outspoken members of Congress who were unstinting in their support of the deposed Generalissimo Chiang Kai-shek, the United States refused to extend diplomatic recognition to the world's most populous nation. Critics of the Truman administration claimed that it had "lost China," which presumed that somehow the United States had possessed, or at least had been able to control, that nation until it fell to the communists. The Soviets also used the nonrecognition tactic, for instance with Israel between 1967 and 1991 and the Republic of South Africa between 1956 and 1992.

Why didn't the Cold War continue as it had under Truman and Stalin? There were several reasons, the most dramatic being Stalin's death in 1953. After that, the Soviet Union showed signs of greater flexibility, both internally and externally. Although there was not steady progress toward less rigidity, changes occurred that were inconceivable under Stalin.

Among other notable events were Nikita Khrushchev's denunciation of Stalin at the Twentieth Congress of the Communist Party of the Soviet Union (1956); the release of *The New Class* by the Yugoslav Milovan Djilas, in which he claimed that communism had merely replaced one exploitive group with another (1957); and the writings of Boris Pasternak, Alexander Solzhenitsyn, and Yevgeny Yevtushenko, dissidents who publicly criticized the Soviet hard line. In contrast to Stalinist practice, none of these Russian authors was imprisoned or executed for his publications.

Cultural and diplomatic exchanges also brought warmer relations. In 1959, the visit of Vice President Richard Nixon to the USSR and Khrushchev's tour of the United States mitigated the view of the superpowers as ogres. The rhetoric was still inflammatory, but threats to break diplomatic ties or declare war disappeared. In the arts and sports, personal interactions increased awareness on each side of the other's lifestyle and created lasting friendships.

Gradually, the United States perceived that some communist states did not take orders from Moscow. Yugoslavia, Albania, and, most important, China demonstrated their independence of Soviet directives. And there were other signs, although not as clear-cut, that the Iron Curtain nations did not agree on all issues. After 1968, the communist parties of Western Europe tended to move away from Moscow, a development called Eurocommunism.

American leaders saw the cost of the arms race escalating. President Eisenhower responded by placing greater reliance on nuclear weapons than conventional military forces, a strategy that required developing more powerful bombs and long-range delivery systems. However, weapons research also created new health hazards, which led to Soviet-U.S. treaties to control that danger. Eventually, both sides admitted the impracticality of nuclear war and sought ways to avoid either accidental or intentional hostilities.

The economic impact of the Cold War was considerable. For four decades, the United States was locked in an arms race that challenged its economic vitality but also provided many jobs in the military, defense industries, and research activities at universities and think tanks. Major contractors such as Boeing, Martin-Marietta, General Electric, and General Motors were awarded defense contracts on a "cost plus fixed profit" basis, which meant that those firms could not lose money. They were assured of a profit even if contract costs ran over budget, as they often did. One could contend that the Cold War justified a kind of welfare system for American industry, including smaller enterprises that received subcontracts from major corporations.

American communities vied with one another to be the sites of defense plants and military bases. Military installations brought employment not only on site, but in the surrounding communities that provided services and goods for military personnel. Public schools near military bases were awarded federal funds to cover the additional costs of teaching the children of military personnel. The total indirect economic benefits of wartime readiness were diffuse and difficult to track, but significant.

Major research universities received billions of federal government dollars to conduct research across a vast spectrum of topics. Independent research institutes appeared as well. The upshot was an expansion of higher education and intellectual activity to an unprecedented level.

The 1957 Soviet launch of the first space satellite, Sputnik, shocked the United States, which until then believed that Soviet technological breakthroughs resulted from stealing the West's secrets; however, Sputnik could not be explained in this way, because the free world did not yet have the ability to put objects into space. The United States now regrouped to put greater emphasis on science and engineering education, although the National Defense Education Act provided support for college students in other fields as well.

Sputnik had profound military implications. If a satellite could orbit the earth, it could be used for global reconnaissance. More important, it could deliver bombs from long distances. This prospect stirred American presidents to shift space and missile research into high gear, culminating in the moon landing of 1969.

Although the prospect of nuclear war was ominous, not everyone thought it was hopeless. Henry Kissinger, a Harvard political scientist, contended in his book *Nuclear Weapons and Foreign Policy* that nuclear warfare, at least on a limited scale, was not unthinkable but rational. Meanwhile, American school children learned drills to follow in case of nuclear attack, and in the early 1960s, civil defense preparations expanded.

At first glance, this response seemed reasonable, but it came to reflect a profound misunderstanding of the key security link between the two superpowers: Mutual Assured Destruction (MAD). MAD assumed that a nuclear attack by either the United States or the USSR would result in a response that would leave both nations destroyed. U.S. civil defense measures and community shelters such as subways in the USSR were potential abrogations of MAD. Even more significant was President Ronald Reagan's Strategic Defense Initiative ("Star Wars"). If one side could perfect a foolproof defense, it could then attack the other without forfeiting its own safety.

The Cold War mentality tended to impose misleading interpretations on events. Three examples illustrate this proclivity to misinterpret and oversimplify. First is the charge that at the February 1945 Yalta Conference Franklin Roosevelt surrendered the nations of east-central Europe to the Soviets. Actually, the USSR had conquered that territory as it repelled the German military. Only by employing comparable force, a clearly unacceptable option, could the United States have dislodged the Soviets.

A second case is the Korean War. For Americans, that war, although unpopular, demonstrated that military might could halt communist aggression. It also reinforced the view of an international communist conspiracy. This reasoning ignored three fundamental factors: first, that independent of communist ideology, China could not tolerate hostile military forces on its border; second, that East Asia was the obvious primary sphere of influence for China, the largest and most dominant Asian nation for centuries; and third, that many Asians saw the U.S. military in the Far East as another instance of Western imperialism, justifying China's armed response.

Similarly, construction of the Berlin Wall in 1961, separating West Berlin from East Berlin, was widely condemned in the West as a cruel provocation. For East Germany, the Wall stopped the loss of highly educated scientists and engineers, who were fleeing to the West through West Berlin. Although the Wall was a personal tragedy for many, it halted the "brain drain" from East Germany and stabilized that country. The most talented and ambitious East Germans now had to make the best of life in that country.

Without the cooperation of governments in Western Europe, American efforts to make that region a bulwark against communism would fail. Support for U.S. policy was diverse. The British Labour Party, despite a faltering economy and a tradition of pacifism until 1939, committed itself to the burden of rearmament under the forceful leadership of Foreign Secretary Ernest Bevin. Robert Schuman, a frequent member of France's coalition cabinets, was a preeminent spokesman for European integration, an explicit principle of U.S. economic aid. Chancellor Konrad Adenauer of West Germany was a fervent anticommunist and devotee of the multinational response to the Soviet threat.

Adenauer, a devout Catholic, was also a leading figure in Europe's Christian Democracy, which was staunchly anticommunist. In France, Christian Democracy was represented first by the Popular Republicans (MRP), a fixture in the cabinets of the Fourth Republic, and later by the Gaullists. Italy's Christian Democrats were automatic cabinet leaders for five decades. Paradoxically, Italy and France, the most Catholic nations in Western Europe, also had the two largest communist parties in the free world.

Although the initial focus of the Cold War was Europe, it assumed global dimensions, spreading to Latin America, the Middle East, and, most violently, Asia. Both blocs—that led by the Soviets and that led by the Americans—sought to create alliances with Third World nations and to subvert those friendly to the other side.

Cold War considerations drove the global policies of both the United States and the Soviet Union. For many years, the United States regarded any nation not critical of the

Soviets as unfriendly and saw any nation, no matter how corrupt, that was anticommunist as deserving of American favor. The Soviet views were the opposite of these. As a result, both Soviet and U.S. foreign aid often had a greater military component than an economic one, as the protagonists worked to keep their clients in power. Arms sales became a major offshoot of the Cold War. The two superpowers became the major purveyors of arms worldwide, sales that were supplemented by those of their respective allies such as Czechoslovakia and France.

If deemed necessary, the United States used direct military power to intervene in Third World nations that appeared to be succumbing to Marxism. At other times the CIA orchestrated the overthrow of popularly endorsed governments, as it did in Iran and Guatemala in the 1950s and in Chile in the 1970s.

The United Nations, intended to be a forum for resolving international problems, became another Cold War arena. The United States and the Soviet Union were at odds on nearly every major issue. Ordinarily, each labored diligently to line up backers, especially in the General Assembly. Early on, the United States had the upper hand, but gradually, as more Third World nations joined, the membership majority assumed a more independent posture, reflecting its detachment from the Great Power struggle and its concentration on issues of direct concern to its members.

The drive for self-determination within the Cold War context presented the United States, and often Great Britain and France, with a dilemma. How could these governments that proclaimed popular sovereignty oppose independence? But the Soviets and Chinese supported Third World independence movements. Whether in Africa, Asia, or Latin America, the typical leaders of independence movements were labeled communists and in fact often received aid from communist regimes. U.S. administrations were reluctant to endorse independence movements because strident anticommunist domestic foes would condemn this.

In Vietnam, the twin forces of containment and anticolonialism clashed. Why did containment fail in Southeast Asia? Unlike Europe and Korea, the anticommunist regime in Vietnam did not maintain popular backing. Its cruelty and corruption were compounded by the fact that its members were largely Catholic in a society that was overwhelmingly Buddhist. For the first time, television brought the brutality of warfare into American homes daily. European allies that endorsed U.S. policy confronted vocal domestic opposition. Young American adults increasingly opposed the war. The Vietnam struggle also underscored the American public's reluctance to support containment indefinitely if that involved heavy loss of American lives.

By the late 1950s, Western Europe was reassessing its Cold War posture for several reasons. First, Soviet nuclear warheads could readily reach European targets but were not a direct threat to the United States. This proximate danger became a concern for Western Europe. Second, although they had no choice in the late 1940s but to follow American leadership, their economies were now strong enough to permit more independence from the United States. Third, by the 1960s, young adults in Europe had little memory of World War II and the birth of the Cold War. Those events were remote for them, but the prospect of military service and televised reports from Southeast Asia were not.

In Britain, efforts to modify U.S. policy arose from the left and the right. The members of a grassroots movement, the Campaign for Nuclear Disarmament (CND), would rather "be Red than dead," preferring unilateral disarmament. This issue split the Labour Party for decades. Even British politicians committed to American leadership sought to mediate between the two superpowers. Prime Minister Harold Macmillan worked for years to arrange a summit conference but met with failure when the 1960 Paris conference was canceled in the aftermath of the downed American U-2 spy flight over Soviet territory.

Reaction to the Vietnam War brought sit-ins, demonstrations, and bombings across Western Europe. These movements were joined to other causes that threatened the stability of democratic governments, notably the May 1968 student demonstrations in France.

Independence from American leadership in the Cold War was also manifested by European statesmen, particularly Charles de Gaulle. As France's president, he endorsed the American position on the U-2 overflights but later pulled all French forces from NATO and frequently criticized U.S. policy in Southeast Asia.

It is easy to forget that even in its early years, containment was flexible. For example, despite the common view of communism as an international monolith, the United States aided Yugoslavia in 1948 so that that state could remain beyond the Soviet orbit. Yet for many, especially in the United States, the Cold War simplified the world. The "good guys," the United States and its allies, confronted the "bad guys," the Soviets and their "stooges," both foreign and domestic. However, this vision became increasingly obsolete. Of many examples, one stands out: Richard Nixon's 1972 visit to China. This U.S. president, who had made his reputation as a relentless foe of communism, added de facto recognition of Red China to his previous approval of grain sales to the Soviet Union. Perhaps his China visit was motivated partially by reelection considerations, but it was the key step in abandoning the myth that Chiang Kai-shek's Taiwan represented China.

The Cold War ended unexpectedly. Two structural factors hastened the collapse of the Soviet Union. One was heavy Soviet expenditures for national defense, which drew massive resources away from the consumer sector. According to one estimate for the mid-1980s, the Soviets were allocating 15 percent of their gross domestic product to military purposes, and about 2 percent of their workforce was under arms, compared to U.S. figures of 7 percent and 1 percent, respectively. A second factor was the increased awareness of the relative opulence of noncommunist nations. Much of this perception filtered through East Germany and other Iron Curtain nations that received television broadcasts from West Germany. This broadcasting, which was not part of any special Western propaganda effort but rather the same fare that Europeans received, expanded in the 1980s as efforts to jam those broadcasts decreased.

As important as these factors were, they probably would have been insufficient to end the Cold War had the Soviet leadership continued in its Stalinist pattern. Certainly, the Soviet economy was no worse than in 1945–1946. The crucial figure was Mikhail Gorbachev. With more formal education than his predecessors, he represented a new generation seeking to free the Soviet people from the economic stagnation generated by an inefficient system of production and distribution, as well as inordinate defense expenditures. Putting his supporters in key posts, Gorbachev transformed the top levels of Soviet decision making while reassuring the West that his changes were genuine. By the late 1980s, his power was slipping, because he had underestimated the impact of the trends he had unleashed. Before he was pushed aside, however, he pressured the governments of east-central European nations to moderate their oppressive rule. The most dramatic event occurred when East Germany opened the Berlin Wall in November 1989, an act that symbolically marked the beginning of the end of the Cold War.

For the United States, the Cold War had extensive consequences. Reaction to the Vietnam War, especially antiwar demonstrations, tore at the very fabric of American society, while the more general threat of confrontation with the Soviet Union justified a larger and more intrusive role for the government. The Cold War also had a marked economic effect. From 1965 to 1990, U.S. Department of Defense expenditures totaled 5 to 8 percent of gross national product, with the military establishment employing a similar portion of the labor force. In the mid-1980s, more than 30,000 companies were involved in military production. Combined with the challenge presented by such international competitors as Japan, the United States faced a wrenching adjustment of its economy as it drew down its Cold War arsenal.

Some results of the Cold War must be speculative. Without it, it is highly unlikely that the United States would have been as devoted to rebuilding the German and Japanese economies. It probably would have adopted a more self-interested, isolationist posture, as it did after World War I. It is also unlikely that the United States and the Soviet Union would have pursued space research as actively as they did, and without the emphasis on space, it is inconceivable that its scientific offshoots, such as miniaturization, would have been achieved as quickly. Even with the Cold War, once the moon landing was accomplished, the American public showed declining interest in financing space programs.

The Cold War's impact on Europe is also speculative. One might assume that the Christian Democrats' doctrinaire anticommunism enabled them to dominate some Western European governments for decades. Undoubtedly the Cold War greatly enhanced U.S. influence in Western Europe. It also generated a sense of urgency among Western Europeans that otherwise they might not have felt, and this sense of urgency furthered the cause of European unification.

What is certain is that the end of the Soviet-U.S. struggle left a far more fragmented, complex world than that which had prevailed for nearly half a century. The breakup of the Soviet empire and its collateral nations, such as Yugoslavia, unleashed nationalistic aspirations that communist leaders had suppressed. Of course, these efforts to combine ethnic identity with national sovereignty probably would have erupted decades before if not suppressed by communist rule.

Despite decades of indoctrination, ideology retained little importance in the former Iron Curtain regimes. Nationalism held a higher priority than ideology, as it did in noncommunist nations. Arguably, anticommunist ideology in the United States proved more durable than Marxist-Leninist instruction in the European communist regimes.

As much as anything, the Cold War suggests the primacy of leadership. Stalin and Truman in the 1940s and Gorbachev later shaped the world to fit their vision. Differences in governmental institutions are important, but individuals can have a monumental impact, as the career of F. W. de Klerk in South Africa demonstrates.

With the end of the Cold War, there will be many postmortems, but it is evident that despite some setbacks, containment was effective in defeating the communist challenge.

It did not, of course, resolve the underlying problems that have beset humankind throughout history: hunger, disease, poverty, and ethnic animosity.

SELECTED BIBLIOGRAPHY

Beschloss, Michael R., and Stuart Talbott. *At the Highest Levels: The Inside Story of the End of the Cold War.* Boston: Little, Brown, 1993. This work traces the final days of the Cold War.

Brinkley, Douglas. *Dean Acheson: The Cold War Years, 1953–1971.* New Haven, CT: Yale University Press, 1993. This documents the persistence of an architect of the containment policy.

Calvocoressi, Peter. *World Politics since 1945.* 6th ed. London: Longman, 1991. First published in 1968, this book examines the Cold War struggle and its impact in five regions of the world.

Feis, Herbert. *From Trust to Terror: The Onset of the Cold War, 1945–1950.* New York: W. W. Norton, 1970. Close examination of this period, with a useful listing of prominent participants in key events.

Gaddis, John Lewis. *The Cold War: A New History.* New York: Penguin, 2005. Gaddis, the preeminent historian of the Cold War, has distilled a lifetime of research into this informative volume. This is an excellent starting point for those who wish to understand the nature and scope of the conflict that dominated the last half of the twentieth century.

Gaddis, John Lewis. *George F. Kennan: An American Life.* New York: Penguin, 2011. The definitive biography of the man most responsible for the policy of containment on which the United States relied during the Cold War.

Gaddis, John Lewis. *The Long Peace: Inquiries into the History of the Cold War.* New York: Oxford University Press, 1987. Eight essays that explore different dimensions of the Cold War.

Graebner, Norman A., ed. *The Cold War: A Conflict of Ideology and Power.* 2nd ed. Lexington, MA: D. C. Heath, 1976. Fifteen essays, by both supporters and foes of U.S. policy.

Haslam, Jonathan. *Russia's Cold War: From the October Revolution to the Fall of the Wall.* New Haven, CT: Yale University Press, 2011. Haslam, a specialist on international relations, has written a difficult if provocative study of Soviet foreign policy from 1917 onward. Filled with facts, the book details Soviet successes and failures and the rationale behind the Kremlin's actions.

Hyland, William G. *The Cold War: Fifty Years of Conflict.* Originally published as *The Cold War Is Over.* New York: Random House, 1991. The author argues that the Cold War began with the Molotov-Ribbentrop Nonaggression Pact of 1939.

Isaacson, Walter, and Evan Thomas. *The Wise Men: Six Friends and the World They Made.* New York: Simon & Schuster, 1986. Detailed account of the backgrounds and roles of several American officials who fashioned post–World War II U.S. foreign and defense policy.

Kofsky, Frank. *Harry S. Truman and the War Scare of 1948: A Successful Campaign to Deceive the Nation.* New York: St. Martin's Press, 1993. A negative assessment of Truman, George C. Marshall, and others who advocated a strong military posture toward the USSR.

LaFeber, Walter. *America, Russia, and the Cold War, 1945–1990.* 10th ed. New York: McGraw-Hill, 2006. This is a standard treatment of the key events in the Cold War.

Lukacs, John. *A New History of the Cold War.* 3rd ed. Garden City, NY: Doubleday, 1966. Useful account of the first twenty years of the Cold War and its origins.

Maddox, Robert James. *The New Left and the Origins of the Cold War.* Princeton, NJ: Princeton University Press, 1974. Seven prominent scholarly dissenters critique American Cold War policy.

Maier, Charles S., ed. *The Cold War in Europe: Era of a Divided Continent.* Rev. ed. Princeton, NJ: Markus Weiner, 1993. Set of essays addressing the major issues and figures in the Cold War.

May, Ernest R, ed. *American Cold War Strategy: Interpreting NSC 68*. New York: Bedford Books, 1993. Includes the text of the document that formally stated U.S. containment policy.

McClellan, David S. *The Cold War in Transition*. New York: Macmillan, 1966. An analytic rather than historical examination that notes the dilemma that military intervention in Southeast Asia presented to the United States.

Purifoy, Lewis McCarroll. *Harry Truman's China Policy: McCarthyism and the Diplomacy of Hysteria, 1947–1951*. New York: Franklin Watts, 1976. Critical of U.S. policy in the Far East, this book blames McCarthyism for those errors.

Rees, David. *The Age of Containment: The Cold War, 1945–1965*. New York: St. Martin's Press, 1968. A British scholar looks at the Cold War from the differing perspectives of U.S. containment and Marxist support of revolutionary efforts around the world.

Spanier, John W. *American Foreign Policy since World War II*. 11th ed. Washington, DC: Congressional Quarterly Press, 1988. An excellent synthesis of events, motives, and forces in the Cold War years.

Thompson, Kenneth W. *Cold War Theories*. Vol. 1: *World Polarization, 1943–1953*. Baton Rouge: Louisiana State University Press, 1981. This is an excellent examination and commentary on the background and early years of the Cold War.

Thompson, Kenneth W. *Interpreters and Critics of the Cold War*. Washington, DC: University Press of America, 1978. Examines the views of Reinhold Niebuhr, Hans Morgenthau, George Kennan, Walter Lippmann, and others.

Westad, Odd Arne. *The Global Cold War*. Cambridge: Cambridge University Press, 2005. Westad details a sometimes overlooked feature of the Cold War—the involvement of the superpowers in Third World countries. He concludes that the attention of the superpowers cost these Asian, African, and Latin American countries quite a bit in terms of independence and development.

Young, John W. *The Longman Companion to Cold War and Detente, 1941–1991*. London: Longman, 1993. Detailed chronology, brief biographies of major figures, and an extensive bibliography are features of this reference source.

JOHN F. KENNEDY (1917–1963)

The presidential administration of John F. Kennedy, famous for its youth and style, ushered in a period of hope, vigor, and commitment for the United States that was cruelly cut short by Kennedy's assassination and more critically evaluated with the passage of time.

John Fitzgerald Kennedy was born on May 29, 1917, in Brookline, Massachusetts, into a large, Irish Catholic family. His father, Joseph Kennedy, stressed self-improvement and public service in a spirit of competition and victory. Kennedy spent much of his childhood sick in bed surrounded by books, suffering from a variety of illnesses. After illness forced him to drop out of the London School of Economics and Princeton University, he graduated from Harvard University in 1940. His senior essay, *While England Slept*, briefly became a best-selling book.

Kennedy tried to enlist in the army in 1941, but he was rejected because of a back injury he had sustained while playing football at Harvard. As a result of his father's influence, he managed to enlist in the navy. In 1943, after the PT boat he was commanding was sunk by a Japanese destroyer, he heroically saved the life of one of his crew members. In the process, however, he aggravated his back ailment and contracted—and

U.S. President John F. Kennedy held a summit meeting with Soviet premier Nikita S. Khrushchev at Vienna on June 3–4, 1961. Khrushchev concluded that the ill and ill-prepared Kennedy was weak and inexperienced, thereby leading the Soviet leader to pursue several risky policies over the next few years. (John F. Kennedy Library)

almost died from—malaria. Painful complications from his war injuries plagued him for the rest of his life.

In 1946, Kennedy was elected as a Massachusetts Democrat to his first of three terms in the U.S. House of Representatives. In 1952, as a result of diligent campaigning and his father's money, Kennedy defeated the incumbent, Henry Cabot Lodge, for a seat in the U.S. Senate. The next year, he married the Washington socialite Jacqueline Lee Bouvier and, while recuperating from back surgery, wrote *Profiles in Courage,* a book of political sketches that won the Pulitzer Prize.

After an unsuccessful attempt to become Adlai Stevenson's vice presidential running mate in 1956, Kennedy's political career was buoyed by an exceptionally wide victory margin in his reelection to the Senate in 1958. Kennedy decided to seek the U.S. Democratic Party nomination for president in 1960. After defeating Hubert H. Humphrey in the primaries and Lyndon B. Johnson and Stevenson at the convention, Kennedy was nominated to run against Richard Nixon. During the campaign, Kennedy faced the challenges of his young age (he was 43) and his Roman Catholic religion by openly confronting the concerns of voters in speeches and during four televised debates. He was narrowly elected by a margin of 118,550 popular votes out of 68.3 million votes cast.

Kennedy brought a refreshing vigor, intelligence, and style to the presidency. In his inaugural speech, he inspired Americans to public service with the famous line, "Ask not what your country can do for you, ask what you can do for your country." As president, he projected an image of a leader directly involved in formulating national and international policy.

Kennedy's rhetoric did not always match his actions. He promised a new American attitude toward Latin America based on trust and partnership through the Alliance for Progress, a program of U.S. aid calling for development and democracy. His efforts, however, were undermined by the disastrous U.S.-sponsored invasion of Cuba in the Bay of Pigs in 1961 to bring about the downfall of Fidel Castro. He opposed the use of American combat troops in Southeast Asia, yet he gradually increased the U.S. presence there until, by the end of 1963, there were 16,732 military advisers in South Vietnam.

Relations with the Soviet Union were complicated by Kennedy's decision to increase defense spending for both conventional weapons and intercontinental ballistic missile development. Soviet leader Nikita Khrushchev misunderstood Kennedy's failure to ensure the success of the Bay of Pigs invasion as weakness and precipitated confrontations in Berlin and Cuba.

Khrushchev had been threatening to sign a separate peace treaty with East Germany, and when he ordered East Germany to build a wall in 1961 to cut off contact between East and West Berlin, Kennedy responded by calling up military reserve units and increasing defense spending. Khrushchev did not sign a treaty, and the crisis cooled. In 1962, American intelligence discovered sites in Cuba being prepared for the installation of Soviet intermediate-range ballistic missiles. Kennedy informed Khrushchev that the United States would not allow the missile sites to become operational and announced a naval arms blockade of Cuba. For 13 days, the world waited for Khrushchev's reaction as Soviet ships loaded with missiles steamed toward the island. Finally, the Soviet ships began to turn around; on October 27, Kennedy and Khrushchev reached an acceptable compromise. The United States promised not to support any further invasions of Cuba and to remove some intermediate-range missiles in Turkey, and the Soviet Union agreed to dismantle the missile sites.

The Cuban Missile Crisis, once regarded as Kennedy's "finest hour," has led to sharp criticism by some historians in recent years of Kennedy's willingness to risk war. Both Khrushchev and Kennedy seemed to have been humbled by the crisis. This led in 1963 to the first thaw in the Cold War, when the United Kingdom and the Soviet Union joined the United States in banning nuclear tests in the atmosphere, in outer space, and underwater. But Kennedy's foreign policy idealism is perhaps best remembered for his creation of the Peace Corps and his decision to commit the United States to a race with the Soviet Union to put a man on the moon by 1970.

Domestic politics were dominated by the economy and the civil rights movement. Kennedy endorsed the use of tax cuts and increases in government spending to stimulate the economy. By 1964, the unemployment rate had dropped from 8.1 percent to 5.2 percent. Because Congress was dominated by a coalition of conservative southern Democrats and Republicans, Kennedy's initial civil rights focus was on executive rather than legislative action. His principal ally was his brother, Attorney General Robert F. Kennedy. Beginning in 1962 with the desegregation of the University of Mississippi, their efforts included an executive order ending discrimination in federally funded housing, the establishment of the President's Committee on Equal Employment Opportunity, the extension of the right to vote for African Americans, the appointment of an unprecedented number of African Americans to public office, and the filing of proposals for more complete civil rights legislation. It should be noted, however, that some contemporary historians now view Kennedy's civil rights efforts as halfhearted and vacillating.

On November 22, 1963, while riding in a motorcade in Dallas, Texas, Kennedy was shot and killed by Lee Harvey Oswald. The magnitude of the tragedy and the speed with which the Warren Commission (headed by Supreme Court Chief Justice Earl Warren) worked in determining the reasons behind the assassination have led people ever since to doubt the commission's conclusion that Oswald acted alone.

ABC-CLIO

NIKITA KHRUSHCHEV (1894–1971)

A reform-minded leader and champion of "peaceful coexistence," Nikita Khrushchev was an initiator of political and social change during his term as leader of the Communist Party of the Soviet Union from 1953 to 1964. As premier, he led the Soviet Union through some of the most tense years of the Cold War and instituted liberal changes that his successors were hard put to alter.

Khrushchev was born in the village of Kalinovka, near Kursk, on April 17, 1894. Unlike other Soviet leaders, who had middle-class backgrounds, Khrushchev was the son of a miner, and he began working as a pipe fitter at the age of 15. Because of his employment, he was not drafted in the tsarist army during World War I, but he joined the Communist Party in 1918 after the Russian Revolution of 1917. He joined the Russian Red Army in 1919 and served as a junior political commissar in the campaigns against the Russian White Army (anti-Bolshevik forces during the Russian Civil War) and invading Polish armies. Afterward, he received a secondary education at a Soviet worker's school in Yuzovka, where he was appointed secretary of the Communist Party Committee. His wife, Galina, died in 1920, and he married his second wife, Nina Petrovna, a schoolteacher, in 1924.

Khrushchev went into full-time party work in 1925 as party secretary of the Petrovsko-Mariinsk district of Yuzovka. His hard work and knowledge of mine and factory conditions came to the attention of Lazar M. Kaganovich, secretary-general of the Ukrainian Party Central Committee and a close friend of Stalin's. Khrushchev accompanied Kaganovich to the 14th Party Congress in Moscow and was active as a party organizer for the next four years.

Khrushchev was assigned by the Communist Party to take courses at the Industrial Academy of Moscow in 1929, and he rose quickly through the party ranks, becoming second secretary of the Moscow Regional Committee in 1933. He supervised the completion of the Moscow subway, for which he received the Order of Lenin, and in 1935, he became the first secretary of the Moscow party organization—in effect, the mayor of

Shown here with Chinese leader Mao Zedong during a 1958 visit to Beijing, Nikita S. Khrushchev led the Soviet Union from shortly after the death of Joseph Stalin in 1953 until his ouster in October 1964. Khrushchev relaxed Stalin's iron grip on the Soviet population; however, both his foreign and domestic policies were marked by impulsive and sometimes counterproductive behavior. (Library of Congress)

Moscow. A zealous supporter of Joseph Stalin, Khrushchev survived the purges of party leadership and was made a member of the Foreign Affairs Commission of the Supreme Soviet in 1937. A year later, he was sent to Kiev as first secretary of the Ukrainian party organization.

As first secretary of the party in the Ukraine during World War II, Khrushchev played an important part in the defense of the republic from the Nazi invasion, evacuating as much of the Ukraine's industry as possible to the east and stimulating the resistance of the civilian population. After the Ukraine was liberated in 1944, he worked to restore civil administration and to bring the country back to a subsistence level. During the worst famine in Ukraine's history in 1946, Khrushchev fought to restore grain production and distribute food supplies, learning firsthand the problems of Soviet agricultural scarcity and planning. He was called back to Moscow in 1949 and resumed his post as head of the Moscow City Party, where he worked more and more with agriculture, developing his schemes for the *agrogorod* (farming town) and large state farms.

Months after Stalin's death in March 1953, Khrushchev took the position of first secretary of the party, making him the most powerful person in the Soviet Union. He took his first trip outside the Soviet Union in May 1955, traveling first to Yugoslavia and later to Switzerland, Afghanistan, and India, where he began to exhibit the brash, outgoing personality for which he became known. Khrushchev's extroverted personal diplomacy, pleasant humor, and attacks on world capitalism were a far cry from the dour image of previous Soviet public figures.

In early 1956, Khrushchev began what became known as the de-Stalinization movement. In his "secret speech" delivered during the 20th Party Congress in Moscow on February 24–25, Khrushchev attacked Stalin's "intolerance, his brutality, his abuse of power" and decried the excesses of his one-man rule. The effects of the speech were far-reaching. Poland and Hungary revolted against their governments in fall 1956. Khrushchev flew to Warsaw in October and granted Poland additional freedoms but crushed the Hungarian Revolution of 1956 by force. The "thaw" in the Soviet Union, the result of Khrushchev's speech, gave new freedom to the European communist parties. After a near overthrow in June 1957, Khrushchev assumed the premiership of the Soviet Union in March 1958.

As premier, Khrushchev widely asserted his doctrine of peaceful coexistence, stating that "war is not fatalistically inevitable." He toured the United States in 1959 and conferred with President Dwight D. Eisenhower at Camp David, bringing about a short-lived improvement in Soviet-American relations. A planned 1960 summit with Eisenhower was aborted, however, after a U-2 American reconnaissance plane was shot down while flying over Soviet territory on May 1, intensifying Cold War tensions. U.S. officials conceded that the flight had been part of an espionage mission, but Eisenhower refused to apologize to Khrushchev at the Paris meeting, and Khrushchev stormed out. A 1961 meeting with President John F. Kennedy was equally futile, and the Berlin Wall was built shortly thereafter.

Soviet success in launching the world's first space satellite in 1957 had resulted in increased missile buildups, and in 1962, Khrushchev attempted to place intermediate-range ballistic missiles in Cuba, just 90 miles off the coast of Florida, leading to the Cuban Missile Crisis. U.S. intelligence discovered the sites, and Kennedy informed Khrushchev that the United States would not allow them to become operational and announced a naval arms blockade of Cuba. For 13 days, the world waited for Khrushchev's reaction as Soviet ships loaded with missiles steamed toward the island. Finally, the Soviet ships began to turn around, and on October 27, Kennedy and Khrushchev reached an acceptable compromise. The United States promised not to support any further invasions of Cuba and to remove some intermediate-range missiles in Turkey, and the Soviet Union agreed to dismantle the missile sites. The Soviet Union was attacked by the Chinese communists for the settlement, and Chinese-Soviet relations were further chilled by Khrushchev's refusal to assist the Chinese nuclear weapons buildup and the Nuclear Test Ban Treaty (1963) with the United States.

Increasingly breaking with the traditions of the Stalin dictatorship, Khrushchev found himself at odds with those in the Soviet Union who pushed for greater freedoms. He struggled to find a balance between popular pressures toward a consumer-oriented society and agitated intellectuals who wanted more freedom of expression. Khrushchev was inconsistent with the intellectuals, repressing Boris Pasternak's *Doctor Zhivago* within the Soviet Union and refusing to allow Pasternak to accept the Nobel Prize in 1958, but permitting the 1962 publication of Aleksandr Solzhenitsyn's *One Day in the Life of*

Ivan Denisovich, a denunciation of Stalinist repression. At the same time, Khrushchev for the first time allowed Soviet tourists to go overseas and seemed open to widening exchanges with socialist and capitalist countries. Within the Soviet bureaucracy, however, there was a fear that the reforms would get out of hand.

Those fears, compounded by Khrushchev's failure to correct the Soviet Union's agricultural problems and the tensions with China, were the major factors in Khrushchev's downfall. On October 14, 1964, the Central Committee accepted his request to retire as the Communist Party's first secretary and chairman of the Council of Ministers of the Soviet Union because of "advanced age and poor health." Khrushchev retired to Moscow and his country dacha and, during the next seven years, appeared in public only to vote in Soviet elections. His memoirs were published in the United States and Europe in 1970, but not in the Soviet Union.

Khrushchev died on September 11, 1971. Almost 48 hours passed before his death was announced to the Soviet public, and he was denied a state funeral and interment in the Kremlin wall, a testimony to official Soviet concern over his increasing public popularity and the belief that the basic changes in Soviet life made under Khrushchev's regime could result in changes in the pattern of Soviet society.

ABC-CLIO

DOCUMENT: WINSTON CHURCHILL'S "IRON CURTAIN" SPEECH (1946)

In a commencement address titled "The Sinews of Peace" delivered at Westminster College in Fulton, Missouri, on March 5, 1946, former British prime minister Winston Churchill painted a picture of the post–World War II world and the emerging struggle between democracy and communism. Describing the birth of the Cold War, Churchill proclaimed that an "iron curtain" had descended across Europe, behind which the Soviet Union exercised unlimited control with no regard for basic human rights. Churchill's phrase caught the public's imagination, and the speech was widely publicized throughout the Western world. The iron curtain metaphor remained in prominent use throughout the Cold War.

President McCluer, ladies and gentlemen, and last, but certainly not least, the President of the United States of America:

I am very glad indeed to come to Westminster College this afternoon, and I am complimented that you should give me a degree from an institution whose reputation has been so solidly established. The name "Westminster" somehow or other seems familiar to me. I feel as if I have heard of it before. Indeed now that I come to think of it, it was at Westminster that I received a very large part of my education in politics, dialectic, rhetoric, and one or two other things. In fact we have both been educated at the same, or similar, or, at any rate, kindred establishments.

It is also an honor, ladies and gentlemen, perhaps almost unique, for a private visitor to be introduced to an academic audience by the President of the United States. Amid his heavy burdens, duties, and responsibilities—unsought but not recoiled from—the President has traveled a thousand miles to dignify and magnify our meeting here to-day and to give me an opportunity of addressing this kindred nation, as well as my own countrymen across the ocean, and perhaps some other countries too. The President has told you that it is his wish, as I am sure it is yours, that I should have full liberty to give my true and faithful counsel in these anxious and baffling times. I shall certainly avail myself of this freedom, and feel the more right to do so because any private ambitions I may have cherished in my younger days have been satisfied beyond my wildest dreams. Let me however make it clear that I have no official mission or status of any kind, and that I speak only for myself. There is nothing here but what you see.

I can therefore allow my mind, with the experience of a lifetime, to play over the problems which beset us on the morrow of our absolute victory in arms, and to try to make sure with what strength I have that what has been gained with so much sacrifice and suffering shall be preserved for the future glory and safety of mankind.

Ladies and gentlemen, the United States stands at this time at the pinnacle of world power. It is a solemn moment for the American Democracy. For with primacy in power is also joined an awe-inspiring accountability to the future. If you look around you, you must feel not only the sense of duty done but also you must feel anxiety lest you fall below the level of achievement. Opportunity is here and now, clear and shining for both our countries. To reject it or ignore it or fritter it away will bring upon us all the long reproaches of the after-time. It is necessary that the constancy of mind, persistency of purpose, and the grand simplicity of decision shall rule and guide the conduct of the English-speaking peoples in peace as they did in war. We must, and I believe we shall, prove ourselves equal to this severe requirement.

President McCluer, when American military men approach some serious situation they are wont to write at the head of their directive the words "over-all strategic concept." There is wisdom in this, as it leads to clarity of thought. What then is the over-all strategic concept which we should inscribe to-day? It is nothing less than the safety and welfare, the freedom and progress, of all the homes and families of all the men and women in all the lands. And here I speak particularly of the myriad cottage or apartment homes where the wage-earner strives amid the accidents and difficulties of life to guard his wife and children from privation and bring the family up in the fear of the Lord, or upon ethical conceptions which often play their potent part.

To give security to these countless homes, they must be shielded from two gaunt marauders, war and tyranny. We al know the frightful disturbance in which the ordinary family is plunged when the curse of war swoops down upon the bread-winner and those for whom he works and contrives. The awful ruin of Europe, with all its vanished glories, and of large parts of Asia glares us in the eyes. When the designs of wicked men or the aggressive urge of mighty States dissolve over large areas the frame of civilized society, humble folk are confronted with difficulties with which they cannot cope. For them is all distorted, all is broken, all is even ground to pulp.

When I stand here this quiet afternoon I shudder to visualize what is actually happening to millions now and what is going to happen in this period when famine stalks the earth. None can compute what has been called "the unestimated sum of human pain." Our supreme task and duty is to guard the homes of the common people from the horrors and miseries of another war. We are all agreed on that.

Our American military colleagues, after having proclaimed their "over-all strategic concept" and computed available resources, always proceed to the next step—namely, the method. Here again there is widespread agreement. A world organization has already been erected for the prime purpose of preventing war. UNO, the successor of the League of Nations, with the decisive addition of the United States and all that that means, is already at work. We must make sure that its work is fruitful, that it is a reality and not a sham, that it is a force for action, and not merely a frothing of words, that it is a true temple of peace in which the shields of many nations can some day be hung up, and not merely a cockpit in a Tower of Babel. Before we cast away the solid assurances of national armaments for self-preservation we must be certain that our temple is built, not upon shifting sands or quagmires, but upon a rock. Anyone can see with his eyes open that our path will be difficult and also long, but if we persevere together as we did in the two world wars—though not, alas, in the interval between them—I cannot doubt that we shall achieve our common purpose in the end.

I have, however, a definite and practical proposal to make for action. Courts and magistrates may be set up but they cannot function without sheriffs and constables. The United Nations Organization must immediately begin to be equipped with an international armed force. In such a matter we can only go step by step, but we must begin now. I propose that each of the Powers and States should be invited to dedicate a certain number of air squadrons to the service of the world organization. These squadrons would be trained and prepared in their own countries, but would move around in rotation from one country to another. They would wear the uniforms of their own countries but with different badges. They would not be required to act against their own nation, but in other respects they would be directed by the world organization. This might be started on a modest scale and it would grow as confidence grew. I wished to see this done after the first world war, and I devoutly trust that it may be done forthwith.

It would nevertheless, ladies and gentlemen, be wrong and imprudent to entrust the secret knowledge or experience of the atomic bomb, which the United States, great Britain, and Canada now share, to the world organization, while still in its infancy. It would be criminal madness to cast it adrift in this still agitated and un-united world. No one country has slept less well in their beds because this knowledge and the method and the raw materials to apply it, are present largely retained in American hands. I do not believe we should all have slept so soundly had the positions been reversed and some Communist or neo-Fascist State monopolized for the time being these dread agencies. The fear of them alone might easily have been used to enforce totalitarian systems upon the free democratic world, with consequences appalling to human imagination. God has willed that this shall not be and we have at least a breathing space to set our world house in order before this peril has to be encountered: and even then, if no effort is spared, we should still possess so formidable a superiority as to impose effective deterrents upon its employment, or threat of employment, by others. Ultimately, when the essential brotherhood of man is truly embodied and expressed in a world organization with all the necessary practical safeguards to make it effective, these powers would naturally be confided to that world organizations.

Now I come to the second of the two marauders, to the second danger which threatens the cottage homes, and the ordinary people—namely, tyranny. We cannot be blind to the fact that the liberties enjoyed by individual citizens throughout the United States and throughout the British Empire are not valid in a considerable number of countries, some of which are very powerful. In these States control is enforced upon the common people by various kinds of all-embracing police governments to a degree which is overwhelming and contrary to every principle of democracy. The power of the State is exercised without restraint, either by dictators or by compact oligarchies operating through a privileged party and a political police. It is not our duty at this time when difficulties are so numerous to interfere forcibly in the internal affairs of countries which we have not conquered in war, but we must never cease to proclaim in fearless tones the great principles of freedom and the rights of man which are the joint inheritance of the English-speaking world and which through Magna Carta, the Bill of Rights, the Habeas Corpus, trial by jury, and the English common law find their most famous expression in the American Declaration of Independence.

All this means that the people of any country have the right, and should have the power by constitutional action, by free unfettered elections, with secret ballot, to choose or change the character or form of government under which they dwell; that freedom of speech and thought should reign; that courts of justice, independent of the executive, unbiased by any party, should administer laws which have received the broad assent of large majorities or are consecrated by time and custom. Here are the title deeds of freedom which should lie in every cottage home. Here is the message of the British and American peoples to mankind. Let us preach what we practice—let us practice what we preach.

Though I have now stated the two great dangers which menace the home of the people, War and Tyranny, I have not yet spoken of poverty and privation which are in many cases the prevailing anxiety. But if the dangers of war and tyranny are removed, there is no doubt that science and cooperation can bring in the next few years, certainly in the next few decades, to the world, newly taught in the sharpening school of war, an expansion of material well-being beyond anything that has yet occurred in human experience.

Now, at this sad and breathless moment, we are plunged in the hunger and distress which are the aftermath of our stupendous struggle; but this will pass and may pass quickly, and there is no reason except human folly or sub-human crime which should deny to all the nations the inauguration and enjoyment of an age of plenty. I have often used words which I learned fifty years ago from a great Irish-American orator, a friend of mine, Mr. Bourke Cockran, "There is enough for all. The earth is a generous mother; she will provide in plentiful abundance food for all her children if they will but cultivate her soil in justice and peace." So far I feel that we are in full agreement.

Now, while still pursing the method—the method of realizing our over-all strategic concept, I come to the crux of what I have traveled here to say. Neither the sure prevention of war, nor the continuous rise of world organization will be gained without what I have called the fraternal association of the English-speaking peoples. This means a special relationship between the British Commonwealth and Empire and the United States of America. Ladies and gentlemen, this is no time for generality, and I will venture to the precise. Fraternal association requires not only the growing friendship and mutual understanding between our two vast but kindred systems of society, but the continuance of the intimate relations between our military advisers, leading to common study of potential dangers, the similarity of weapons and manuals of instructions, and to the interchange of officers and cadets at technical colleges. It should carry with it the continuance of the present facilities for mutual security by the joint use of all Naval and Air Force bases in the possession of either country all over the world. This would perhaps double the mobility of the American Navy and Air Force. It would greatly expand that of the British Empire forces and it might well lead, if and as the world calms down, to important financial savings. Already we use together a large number of islands; more may well be entrusted to our joint care in the near future.

The United States has already a Permanent Defense Agreement with the Dominion of Canada, which is so devotedly attached to the British Commonwealth and the Empire. This Agreement is more effective than many of those which have been made under formal alliances. This principle should be extended to all the British Commonwealths with full reciprocity. Thus, whatever happens, and thus only, shall we be secure ourselves and able to work together for the high and simple causes that are dear to us and bode no ill to any. Eventually there may come—I feel eventually there will come—the principle of common citizenship, but that we may be content to leave to destiny, whose outstretched arm many of us can already clearly see.

There is however an important question we must ask ourselves. Would a special relationship between the United States and the British Commonwealth be inconsistent with our over-riding loyalties to the World Organization? I reply that, on the contrary, it is probably the only means by which that organization will achieve its full stature and strength. There are already the special United States relations with Canada that I have just mentioned, and there are the relations between the United States and the South American Republics. We British have also our twenty years Treaty of Collaboration and Mutual Assistance with Soviet Russia. I agree with Mr. Bevin, the Foreign Secretary of Great Britain, that it might well be a fifty years treaty so far as we are concerned. We aim at nothing but mutual assistance and collaboration with Russia. The British have an alliance with Portugal unbroken since the year 1384, and which produced fruitful results at a critical moment in the recent war. None of these clash with the general interest of a world agreement, or a world organization; on the contrary, they help it. "In my father's house are many mansions." Special associations between members of the United Nations which have no aggressive point against any other country, which harbor no design incompatible with the Charter of the United Nations, far from being harmful, are beneficial and, as I believe, indispensable.

I spoke earlier, ladies and gentlemen, of the Temple of Peace. Workmen from all countries must build that temple. If two of the workmen know each other particularly well and are old friends, if their families are intermingled, if they have "faith in each other's purpose, hope in each other's future and charity towards each other's shortcomings"—to quote some good words I read here the other day—why cannot they work together at the common task as friends and partners? Why can they not share their tools and thus increase each other's working powers? Indeed they must do so or else the temple may not be built, or, being built, it may collapse, and we should all be proved again unteachable and have to go and try to learn again for a third time in a school of war incomparably more rigorous than that from which we have just been released. The dark ages may return, the Stone Age may return on the gleaming wings of science, and what might now shower immeasurable material blessings upon mankind, may even bring about its total destruction. Beware, I say; time may be short. Do not let us take the course of allowing events to drift along until it is too late. If there is to be a fraternal association of the kind I have described, with all the strength and security which both our countries can derive from it, let us make sure that that great fact is known to the world, and that it plays its part in steadying and stabilizing the foundations of peace. There is the path of wisdom. Prevention is better than the cure.

A shadow has fallen upon the scenes so lately lit by the Allied victory. Nobody knows what Soviet Russia and its Communist international organization intends to do in the immediate future, or what are the limits, if any, to their expansive and proselytizing tendencies. I have a strong admiration and regard for the valiant Russian people and for my wartime comrade, Marshall Stalin. There is deep sympathy and goodwill in Britain— and I doubt not here also—towards the peoples of all the Russias and a resolve to persevere through many differences and rebuffs in establishing lasting friendships. We understand the Russian need to be secure on her western frontiers by the removal of all possibility of German aggression. We welcome Russia to her rightful place among the leading nations of the world. We welcome her flag upon the seas. Above all, we welcome, or should welcome, constant, frequent and growing contacts between the Russian people and our own people on both sides of the Atlantic. It is my duty however, for I am sure you would wish me to state the facts as I see them to you. It is my duty to place before you certain facts about the present position in Europe.

From Stettin in the Baltic to Trieste in the Adriatic an iron curtain has descended across the Continent. Behind that line lie all the capitals of the ancient states of Central and Eastern Europe. Warsaw, Berlin, Prague, Vienna, Budapest, Belgrade, Bucharest and Sofia, all these famous cities and the populations around them lie in what I must call the Soviet sphere, and all are subject in one form or another, not only to Soviet influence but to a very high and, in some cases, increasing measure of control from Moscow. Athens alone—Greece with its immortal glories—is free to decide its future at an election under British, American and French observation. The Russian-dominated Polish Government has been encouraged to make enormous and wrongful inroads upon Germany, and mass expulsions of millions of Germans on a scale grievous and undreamed-of are now taking place. The Communist parties, which were very small in all these Eastern States of Europe, have been raised to pre-eminence and power far beyond their numbers and are seeking everywhere to obtain totalitarian control. Police governments are prevailing in nearly every case, and so far, except in Czechoslovakia, there is no true democracy.

Turkey and Persia are both profoundly alarmed and disturbed at the claims which are being made upon them and at the pressure being exerted by the Moscow Government. An attempt is being made by the Russians in Berlin to build up a quasi-Communist party in their zone of occupied Germany by showing special favors to groups of left-wing German leaders. At the end of the fighting last June, the American and British Armies withdrew westward, in accordance with an earlier agreement, to a depth at some points of 150 miles upon a front of nearly four hundred miles, in order to allow our Russian allies to occupy this vast expanse of territory which the Western Democracies had conquered.

If now the Soviet Government tries, by separate action, to build up a pro-Communist Germany in their areas, this will cause new serious difficulties in the American and British zones, and will give the defeated Germans the power of putting themselves up to auction between the Soviets and the Western Democracies. Whatever conclusions may be drawn from these facts—and facts they are—this is certainly not the Liberated Europe we fought to build up. Nor is it one which contains the essentials of permanent peace.

The safety of the world, ladies and gentlemen, requires a new unity in Europe, from which no nation should be permanently outcast. It is from the quarrels of the strong parent races in Europe that the world wars we have witnessed, or which occurred in former times, have sprung. Twice in our own lifetime we have seen the United States, against their wishes and their traditions, against arguments, the force of which it is impossible not to comprehend, twice we have seen them drawn by irresistible forces, into these wars in time to secure the victory of the good cause, but only after frightful slaughter and devastation have occurred. Twice the United States has had to send several millions of its young men across the Atlantic to find the war; but now war can find any nation, wherever it may dwell between dusk and dawn. Surely we should work with conscious purpose for a grand pacification of Europe, within the structure of the United Nations and in accordance with our Charter. That I feel opens a course of policy of very great importance.

In front of the iron curtain which lies across Europe are other causes for anxiety. In Italy the Communist Party is seriously hampered by having to support the Communist-trained Marshal Tito's claims to former Italian territory at the head of the Adriatic. Nevertheless the future of Italy hangs in the balance. Again one cannot imagine a regenerated Europe without a strong France. All my public life I never lost faith in her destiny, even in the darkest hours. I will not lose faith now. However, in a great number of countries, far from the Russian frontiers and throughout the world, Communist fifth columns are established and work in complete unity and absolute obedience to the directions they receive from the Communist center. Except in the British Commonwealth and in the United States where Communism is in its infancy, the Communist parties or fifth columns constitute a growing challenge and peril to Christian civilization. These are somber facts for anyone to have recite on the morrow of a victory gained by so much splendid comradeship in arms and in the cause of freedom and democracy; but we should be most unwise not to face them squarely while time remains.

The outlook is also anxious in the Far East and especially in Manchuria. The Agreement which was made at Yalta, to which I was a party, was extremely favorable to Soviet Russia, but it was made at a time when no one could say that the German war might not extend all through the summer and autumn of 1945 and when the Japanese war was expected by the best judges to last for a further 18 months from the end of the German war. In this country you [are] all so well-informed about the Far East, and such devoted friends of China, that I do not need to expatiate on the situation there.

I have, however, felt bound to portray the shadow which, alike in the west and in the east, falls upon the world. I was a minister at the time of the Versailles treaty and a close friend of Mr. Lloyd-George, who was the head of the British delegation at Versailles. I did not myself agree with many things that were done, but I have a very strong impression in my mind of that situation, and I find it painful to contrast it with that which prevails now. In those days there were high hopes and unbounded confidence that the wars were over and that the League of Nations would become all-powerful. I do not see or feel that same confidence or even the same hopes in the haggard world at the present time.

On the other hand, ladies and gentlemen, I repulse the idea that a new war is inevitable; still more that it is imminent. It is because I am sure that our fortunes are still in our own hands and that we hold the power to save the future, that I feel the duty to speak out now that I have the occasion and the opportunity to do so. I do not believe that Soviet Russia desires war. What they desire is the fruits of war and the indefinite expansion of their power and doctrines. But what we have to consider here today while time remains, is the permanent prevention of war and the establishment of conditions of freedom and democracy as rapidly as possible in all countries. Our difficulties and dangers will not be removed by closing our eyes to them. They will not be removed by mere waiting to see what happens; nor will they be removed by a policy of appeasement. What is needed is a settlement, and the longer this is delayed, the more difficult it will be and the greater our dangers will become.

From what I have seen of our Russian friends and Allies during the war, I am convinced that there is nothing for which they have less respect than for weakness, especially military weakness. For that reason the old doctrine of a balance of power is unsound. We cannot afford, if we can help it, to work on narrow margins, offering temptations to a trial of strength. If the Western Democracies stand together, strict adherence to the principles will be immense and no one is likely to molest them. If however they become divided or falter in their duty and if these all-important years are allowed to slip away then indeed catastrophe may overwhelm us all.

Last time I saw it all coming and I cried aloud to my own fellow-countrymen and to the world, but no one paid any attention. Up till the year 1933 or even 1935, Germany might have been saved from the awful fate which has overtaken her and we might all have been spared the miseries Hitler let loose upon mankind. There never was a war in history easier to prevent by timely action than the one which has just desolated such great areas of the globe. It could have been prevented in my belief without the firing of a single shot, and Germany might be powerful, prosperous and honored today; but no one would listen and one by one we were all sucked into the awful whirlpool. We surely, ladies and gentlemen, I put it to you, surely, we must not let it happen again. This can only be achieved by reaching now, in 1946, by reaching a good understanding on all points with Russia under the general authority of the United Nations Organization and by the maintenance of that good understanding through many peaceful years, by the whole strength of the English-speaking world and all its connections. There is the solution which I respectfully offer to you in this Address to which I have given the title, "The Sinews of Peace."

Let no man underrate the abiding power of the British Empire and Commonwealth. Because you see the 46 millions in our island harassed about their food supply, of which they only grow one half, even in war-time, or because we have difficulty in restarting our industries and export trade after six years of passionate war effort, do not suppose we shall not come through these dark years of privation as we have come through the glorious years of agony. Do not suppose that half a century from now you will not see 70 or 80 millions of Britons spread about the world united in defense of our traditions, and our way of life, and of the world causes which you and we espouse. If the population of the English-speaking Commonwealths be added to that of the United States with all that such co-operation implies in the air, on the sea, all over the globe and in science and in industry, and in moral force, there will be no quivering, precarious balance of power to offer its temptation to ambition or adventure. On the contrary there will be an over-whelming assurance of security. If we adhere faithfully to the Charter of the United Nations and walk forward in sedate and sober strength seeking no one's land or treasure, seeking to lay no arbitrary control upon the thoughts of men; if all British moral and material forces and convictions are joined with your own in fraternal association, the highroads of the future will be clear, not only for our time, but for a century to come.

DOCUMENT: MARSHALL PLAN (1947)

On June 5, 1947, in a speech for the commencement ceremony at Harvard College, an excerpt of which appears here, U.S. secretary of state George C. Marshall proposed that the United States grant financial aid to countries in need to prevent them from succumbing to communism. U.S. president Harry Truman later dubbed the proposal the Marshall Plan, and it came to form the basis of U.S. international policy during the Cold War. Congress debated the Marshall Plan throughout 1948 and eventually enacted a series of laws to put the plan into action.

I need not tell you gentlemen that the world situation is very serious. That must be apparent to all intelligent people. I think one difficulty is that the problem is one of such enormous complexity that the very mass of facts presented to the public by press and radio make it exceedingly difficult for the man in the street to reach a clear appraisement of the situation. Furthermore, the people of this country are distant from the troubled areas of the earth and it is hard for them to comprehend the plight and consequent reaction of the long-suffering peoples, and the effect of those reactions on their governments in connection with our efforts to promote peace in the world.

In considering the requirements for the rehabilitation of Europe the physical loss of life, the visible destruction of cities, factories, mines, and railroads was correctly estimated, but it has become obvious during recent months that this visible destruction was probably less serious than the dislocation of the entire fabric of European economy. For the past 10 years conditions have been highly abnormal. The feverish maintenance of the war effort engulfed all aspects of national economics. Machinery has fallen into disrepair or is entirely obsolete. Under the arbitrary and destructive Nazi rule, virtually every possible enterprise was geared into the German war machine. Long-standing commercial ties, private institutions, banks, insurance companies and shipping companies disappeared, through the loss of capital, absorption through nationalization or by simple destruction. In many countries, confidence in the local currency has been severely shaken. The breakdown of the business structure of Europe during the war was complete. Recovery has been seriously retarded by the fact that 2 years after the close of hostilities a peace settlement with Germany and Austria has not been agreed upon. But even given a more prompt solution of these difficult problems, the rehabilitation of the economic structure of Europe quite evidently will require a much longer time and greater effort than had been foreseen.

There is a phase of this matter which is both interesting and serious. The farmer has always produced the foodstuffs to exchange with the city dweller for the other necessities of life. This division of labor is the basis of modern civilization. At the present time it is threatened with breakdown. The town and city industries are not producing adequate goods to exchange with the food-producing farmer. Raw materials and fuel are in short supply.

Machinery is lacking or worn out. The farmer or the peasant cannot find the goods for sale which he desires to purchase. So the sale of his farm produce for money which he cannot use seems to him unprofitable transaction. He, therefore, has withdrawn many fields from crop cultivation and is using them for grazing. He feeds more grain to stock and finds for himself and his family an ample supply of food, however short he may be on clothing and the other ordinary gadgets of civilization. Meanwhile people in the cities are short of food and fuel. So the governments are forced to use their foreign money and credits to procure these necessities abroad. This process exhausts funds which are urgently needed for reconstruction. Thus a very serious situation is rapidly developing which bodes no good for the world. The modern system of the division of labor upon which the exchange of products is based is in danger of breaking down.

The truth of the matter is that Europe's requirements for the next 3 or 4 years of foreign food and other essential products—principally from America—are so much greater than her present ability to pay that she must have substantial additional help, or face economic, social, and political deterioration of a very grave character.

The remedy lies in breaking the vicious circle and restoring the confidence of the European people in the economic future of their own countries and of Europe as a whole. The manufacturer and the farmer throughout wide areas must be able and willing to exchange their products for currencies the continuing value of which is not open to question.

Aside from the demoralizing effect on the world at large and the possibilities of disturbances arising as a result of the desperation of the people concerned, the consequences to the economy of the United States should be apparent to all. It is logical that the United States should do whatever it is able to do to assist in the return of normal economic health in the world, without which there can be no political stability and no assured peace. Our policy is directed not against any country or doctrine but against hunger, poverty, desperation, and chaos. Its purpose should be the revival of working economy in the world so as to permit the emergence of political and social conditions in which free institutions can exist. Such assistance, I am convinced, must not be on a piecemeal basis as various crises develop. Any assistance that this Government may render in the future should provide a cure rather than a mere palliative. Any government that is willing to assist in the task of recovery will find full cooperation, I am sure, on the part of the United States Government. Any government which maneuvers to block the recovery of other countries cannot expect help from us. Furthermore, governments, political parties, or groups which seek to perpetuate human misery in order to profit therefrom politically or otherwise will encounter the opposition of the United States.

It is already evident that, before the United States Government can proceed much further in its efforts to alleviate the situation and help start the European world on its way to recovery, there must be some agreement among the countries of Europe as to the requirements of the situation and the part those countries themselves will take in order to give proper effect to whatever action might be undertaken by this Government. It would be neither fitting nor efficacious for this Government to undertake to draw up unilaterally a program designed to place Europe on its feet economically. This is the business of the Europeans. The initiative, I think, must come from Europe. The role of this country should consist of friendly aid in the drafting of a European program so far as it may be practical for us to do so. The program should be a joint one, agreed to by a number, if not all European nations.

An essential part of any successful action on the part of the United States is an understanding on the part of the people of America of the character of the problem and the remedies to be applied. Political passion and prejudice should have no part. With foresight, and a willingness on the part of our people to face up to the vast responsibilities which history has clearly placed upon our country, the difficulties I have outlined can and will be overcome.

DOCUMENT: FIDEL CASTRO'S SECOND DECLARATION OF HAVANA (1962)

On February 4, 1962, Cuban communist leader Fidel Castro delivered this address, which became known as the Second Declaration of Havana. In it, he stated his goal of creating a communist society in Cuba based on the ideology of Marxism-Leninism, with its principles of spreading communist revolution around the globe. Such a goal ensured that Cuba openly challenged U.S.-based notions of democracy and capitalism. Castro was motivated to make such a strong statement in part because the U.S. government had already launched several covert operations in Cuba in an attempt to overthrow his government.

What is Cuba's history but that of Latin America? What is the history of Latin America but the history of Asia, Africa, and Oceania? And what is the history of all these peoples but the history of the cruelest exploitation of the world by imperialism?

At the end of the last century and the beginning of the present, a handful of economically developed nations had divided the world among themselves subjecting two thirds of humanity to their economic and political domination. Humanity was forced to work for the dominating classes of the group of nations which had a developed capitalist economy.

The historic circumstances which permitted certain European countries and the United States of North America to attain a high industrial development level put them in a position which enabled them to subject and exploit the rest of the world.

What motives lay behind this expansion of the industrial powers? Were they moral, "civilizing" reasons, as they claimed? No. Their motives were economic.

The discovery of America sent the European conquerors across the seas to occupy and to exploit the lands and peoples of other continents; the lust for riches was the basic motivation for their conduct. America's discovery took place in the search for shorter ways to the Orient, whose products Europe valued highly.

A new social class, the merchants and the producers of articles manufactured for commerce, arose from the feudal society of lords and serfs in the latter part of the Middle Ages.

The lust for gold promoted the efforts of the new class. The lust for profit was the incentive of their behavior throughout its history. As industry and trade developed, the social influence of the new class grew. The new productive forces maturing in the midst of the feudal society increasingly clashed with feudalism and its serfdom, its laws, its institutions, its philosophy, its morals, its art, and its political ideology. . . .

Since the end of the Second World War, the Latin American nations are becoming pauperized constantly. The value of their capita income falls. The dreadful percentages of child death rate do not decrease, the number of illiterates grows higher, the peoples lack employment, land, adequate housing, schools, hospitals, communication systems and the means of subsistence. On the other hand, North America investments exceed 10 billion dollars. Latin America, moreover, supplies cheap raw materials and pays high prices for manufactured articles. Like the first Spanish conquerors, who exchanged mirrors and trinkets with the Indians for silver and gold, so the United States trades with Latin America. To hold on to this torrent of wealth, to take greater possession of America's resources and to exploit its long-suffering peoples: this is what is hidden behind the military pacts, the military missions and Washington's diplomatic lobbying. . . .

Wherever roads are closed to the peoples, where repression of workers and peasants is fierce, where the domination of Yankee monopolies is strongest, the first and most important lesson is to understand that it is neither just nor correct to divert the peoples with the vain and fanciful illusion that the dominant classes can be uprooted by legal means which do not and will not exist. The ruling classes are entrenched in all positions of state power. They monopolize the teaching field. They dominate all means of mass communication. They have infinite financial resources. Theirs is a power which the monopolies and the ruling few will defend by blood and fire with the strength of their police and their armies.

The duty of every revolutionary is to make revolution. We know that in America and throughout the world the revolution will be victorious. But revolutionaries cannot sit in the doorways of their homes to watch the corpse of imperialism pass by. The role of Job does not behoove a revolutionary. Each year by which America's liberation may be hastened will mean millions of children rescued from death, millions of minds freed for learning, infinitudes of sorrow spared the peoples. Even though the Yankee imperialists are preparing a bloodbath for America they will not succeed in drowning the people's struggle. They will evoke universal hatred against themselves. This will be the last act of their rapacious and cave-man system.

9

European Unification, c. 1947–Present

INTRODUCTION

The vision of a unified Europe is neither new nor novel. During the Middle Ages, western, or Latin, Christianity served as a conscious unifying force for much of Europe. However, the sixteenth-century Reformation, which fractured western Christianity, and the development of the nation-state during the Renaissance ushered in a new era. After the Reformation, Christianity was no longer the unifying force it had once been, and the nation-state's rigid commitment to unimpeded national sovereignty struck at the heart of European unity. For the past four centuries, European unification seemed possible only at the hands of aggressive conquerors such as Napoleon or Hitler. However, their efforts always failed, if for no other reason than that the European peoples resisted them. Nevertheless, a small handful of Europeans never abandoned the dream of a voluntarily unified Europe.

The savagery and carnage of World Wars I and II made European unity seem more attractive. These catastrophic conflicts called into question the legitimacy of the nation-state. Many reasoned that if the nation-state had brought such misery to Europe, perhaps it would be in Europe's best interest to jettison the nation-state and replace it with a unified Europe. Furthermore, the wartime destruction itself was so overwhelming that many Europeans concluded that recovery was possible only in a cooperative, noncompetitive atmosphere. This, in turn, required the subordination of the nation-state to supranational institutions. Finally, many credible leaders of wartime resistance movements demanded that a "united states of Europe" replace the nation-state system.

However, if integration was to occur after World War II, it would not be on a European-wide basis; the Cold War was rapidly dividing Europe into two camps. Eventually, the USSR unified Eastern Europe forcibly, creating for itself a large but restive empire. Politically, the individual nation-states of Eastern Europe retained a facade of independence, but real power rested with Moscow, which exercised its authority through puppet leaders and subservient communist parties. The USSR in 1949 created the Council for Mutual Economic Assistance (CMEA, or Comecon), an economic union of Eastern European countries that bolstered the Soviet economy for many years. Militarily, the Soviet Union consolidated its hold over Eastern Europe with the establishment in 1955 of the Warsaw Treaty Organization, or Warsaw Pact, which placed the armies of Eastern

Europe at Soviet disposal. In international affairs, as in every other sphere, the Eastern European countries were expected to march in lockstep with the USSR. Important deviations from the Soviet norm were not tolerated. When Hungary in 1956 and Czechoslovakia in 1968 strayed too far from the Soviet course, the USSR invaded. All this, of course, was not the voluntary unification many Europeans envisioned, but rather a variation on the theme of unification by conquest. The flawed nature of this kind of European unification revealed itself in 1989 when the Soviet empire collapsed and the USSR itself moved to the brink of its ultimate dissolution.

Compared with Eastern Europe after World War II, Western Europe—although greatly influenced by the United States—was much freer to pursue its own goals. Nevertheless, driven by Cold War fears, the United States initiated several major programs that promoted Western European unification. On June 5, 1947, at a speech at Harvard University, Secretary of State George C. Marshall announced that the United States would provide massive aid for Europe's economic reconstruction. Several months later, the U.S. Congress appropriated $13 billion for the European Recovery Program, or the Marshall Plan, as it was popularly known. One of the Marshall Plan's provisions required its European recipients to cooperate with each other in planning the most effective way to employ American aid. The result was the Organization for European Economic Cooperation (OEEC), a European planning and coordinating body. The Marshall Plan was a great success in many ways, not the least being the establishment of organs of European economic cooperation.

In the military sphere, the North Atlantic Treaty Organization (NATO) matched the Marshall Plan. Once again driven by fears of Soviet expansionism, the United States joined with several Western European states to form a defensive military alliance. Beginning with the 1948 Brussels Treaty, which committed Great Britain, France, Belgium, the Netherlands, and Luxembourg to a common defense, the United States, together with Canada, the signatories to the Brussels Treaty, and Denmark, Norway, Italy, Iceland, and Portugal, established NATO in April 1949.

The Europeans took additional steps on their own initiative to reinforce the impetus toward European unification that the Marshall Plan and NATO provided. In 1948, Belgium, the Netherlands, and Luxembourg formed Benelux, a customs union or free trade zone. A year later, several European countries, including Great Britain, France, and the Benelux countries, established the Council of Europe, a parliamentary body that met at Strasbourg, France. Although the Council of Europe was a tangible sign of progress toward European unity, it nevertheless revealed many of the problems that European unionists faced. Members of the Council represented their countries' legislative bodies and were not elected by nor responsible to European voters. Moreover, although the representatives could debate and pass motions, they lacked legislative authority because no state was willing to surrender its sovereignty to the supranational Council. Consequently, the Council proved to be little more than a high-powered debating society.

When the move toward political unity foundered on the rock of national sovereignty, those who favored further European integration looked in a different direction. Under the leadership of Jean Monnet, a dedicated French Europeanist, economic integration advanced rapidly. Sympathetic political leaders including Robert Schuman of France, Alcide de Gasperi of Italy, Konrad Adenauer of the emerging West German state, and Paul-Henri Spaak of Belgium supported Monnet's vision. In May 1950, Schuman presented a proposal calling for the integration of Western Europe's coal and steel industries. Although Monnet devised the proposal, it was named the Schuman Plan. It resulted in the European Coal and Steel Community (ECSC), which began to operate in 1952. Comprised of France, West Germany, Italy, and the Benelux countries, ECSC not only assured each country access to coal and steel resources but also coordinated the development of heavy industry for the member countries and established a viable administrative structure headed by a High Authority that wielded extensive supranational powers.

ECSC's success paved the way for another step toward European economic integration. With Monnet once again providing the vision, on March 25, 1957, the ECSC members signed the Treaty of Rome which created the European Economic Community (EEC or Common Market) with its headquarters in Brussels. The EEC sought to eliminate all tariffs between member states, to formulate a common tariff policy applicable to nonmember states, and to facilitate the unimpeded movement of both labor and capital among the six member states. At the same time, the EEC states also created the European Atomic Community (Euratom) to conduct peaceful nuclear research. The member states also erected a supranational administrative structure comprised chiefly of technological experts committed to the idea of European unity. The EEC embraced 175 million Europeans, forming one of the largest trading blocs and one of the largest free trade zones in the world. The only sour note came when Great Britain rejected membership in the EEC.

Although Western Europe made important strides toward economic integration, the drive for greater unity also encountered difficulties. The Council of Europe continued to languish, and an attempt to create a supranational European army, the European Defense Community, failed in 1954. When Charles de Gaulle became president of France in 1958, the quest for European unification became more difficult. De Gaulle's objectives continue to generate debate among scholars, but it seems that the French president supported the concept of a unified Europe as long as this Europe was led by France and worked to further French national interests above all else. One thing was certain: de Gaulle resented the loose control that the United States exercised over Western Europe and wanted to oust American influence from the Continent. To this end, he removed French troops from NATO in 1966 and created a nuclear arsenal for France, the so-called *force de frappe*. Although these steps certainly undercut U.S. authority, they also harmed the chances for European unification.

De Gaulle also turned his attention to the EEC, where he twice vetoed Britain's belated application for membership (1963, 1967) because he believed that Britain was acting as a Trojan horse for the United States and, perhaps more important, because he feared that Great Britain's presence in the Common Market would diminish his and France's importance. He also insisted that the EEC bend to the wishes of France, and when he could not get his way he was willing to bring EEC activity to a halt, as he did in 1965. De Gaulle resisted attempts to transform the EEC into a vehicle for the political unification of Europe and attacked the already existing supranational nature of the organization. Demanding that national interests take precedence over supranational ones, he carried the day with the Luxembourg Agreement (1966), which gave each member state of the Common Market the right to veto EEC decisions whenever it felt that its national interests were at stake.

After de Gaulle, the EEC was not quite the force for European unity that Monnet had envisioned. Rather than serving as the embryo for European political union, it more than ever became an economic coordinating and planning body in which the individual European states voiced their concerns and tried—sometimes successfully and sometimes not—to balance their competing interests. Behind the Common Market's supranational facade, national sovereignty or national self-interest prevailed. This is not to say that the Common Market's member states abandoned it. In fact, the member states were well aware that the EEC was a major reason for Europe's economic prosperity and they were not about to dismantle it. However, they would not surrender their sovereignty to it.

Despite these setbacks, the EEC experienced some significant gains between 1967 and the mid-1980s. In 1967, the EEC consolidated its numerous supranational bodies into a single organization, the European Community, or EC. In 1968, the last internal tariffs disappeared, three to six years ahead of schedule. More countries also joined. After de Gaulle resigned as French president in 1969, Great Britain joined the EC in 1973. Ireland and Denmark entered at the same time. In 1981, Greece joined the EC, and Spain and Portugal followed in 1985. Thanks to the collection of external tariffs and a 1 percent value-added tax (VAT) levied in all member states, after 1975 the EC enjoyed its own source of income and the greater independence such funds provided. In 1978, the EC created the European Monetary System. Although the system did not provide for a single European currency, it was an important step in that direction. One year later, the European Parliament—consisting of the assemblies of ECSC, EEC, and Euratom, and acting as something of a successor to the moribund Council of Europe—gained the right to elect its membership directly. Henceforth, individual Europeans would vote for representatives to the Parliament rather than having the governments of the member states choose the representatives.

While the EC enjoyed great success, especially in the economic realm, many problems continued to plague the organization. In attempting to balance conflicting national interests, EC regulations grew more complex and less rational. For example, the EC's less than coherent agricultural policy led to "mountains of butter and lakes of wine" in costly storage facilities. Furthermore, with the addition of six new members in 12 years, the EC lost some of its cohesion. This was particularly true with the admission of Ireland and the three Mediterranean states, the economies of which were more agrarian and less advanced than the prevailing EC norm. Margaret Thatcher, British prime minister from 1979 to 1990, proved to be as obstinate as de Gaulle had been. Moreover, despite the elimination of tariffs, other national bureaucratic and administrative practices impeded free trade. Most discouraging, perhaps, the 1973 oil embargo and the subsequent severe economic downturn revealed the fragility of European union. Faced with rising unemployment and declining production, the European countries tended to act independently of each other. This "every man for himself" attitude dealt a severe blow to the cause of European unification.

In the mid-1980s, the EC's member states took steps to revitalize the institution. Spurred on by the need to compete more effectively with the United States and Japan, and fearful of falling behind technologically, the EC member states recommitted themselves to Monnet's original ideas about European unification. In July 1987, they adopted the Single European Act. Hoping to create a "single Europe" by 1992, the act called for an integrated market completely free of exchange controls and barriers to the movement of capital and labor. It also provided for more coordinated industrial and agrarian policies, and it bestowed greater power on the European Parliament. Most important, perhaps, it ended the veto power that individual member states had exercised since the de Gaulle era. Henceforth, binding decisions would require only a majority vote of the EC members.

However, during the early 1990s, the renewed drive toward greater unification encountered some serious problems. The Treaty on European Union, the so-called Maastricht Treaty, designed to advance the Single Act of European Union, was rejected by Danish voters in 1992. Fortunately for the cause of European Union, the Danes reversed their decision the following year when all the other EC countries ratified the Maastricht Treaty. For some, however, the ratification process proved difficult. Maastricht's provisions called for "an ever-closer union among the peoples of Europe" and created a new, 12-nation "European Union." The treaty also enhanced the powers of the European Parliament; increased cooperation among the member states on a wide range of issues including crime, the environment, and immigration; urged greater integration of foreign and security policy with an eye toward eventually creating common defense and foreign policies; and called for a single European currency by 1999.

In fact, the single European currency, the Euro, began to circulate commonly in 2002 when it replaced 12 national currencies. Currently, 17 major European states use the Euro. Nevertheless, some European countries, including Great Britain, have rejected it and continue to use their traditional national currencies.

The trend toward European unification received another boost in 1995 with the Schengen Agreement that ended border controls for a number of countries within the European Union. In 2008, the Schengen Agreement was expanded, and it is now possible for the vast majority of Europeans to move freely within the European Union.

However, since 2000 the drive for European unification has suffered some setbacks. An attempt to create a constitution for Europe failed in 2005 when voters in France and the Netherlands rejected the proposed document. Opinion polls showed voters in other European Union countries would probably follow suit, most likely because they feared surrendering their national sovereignty and because the document was too complex and unwieldy. More recently, a fiscal crisis of major proportions has shaken the European Union as Greece, Ireland, Italy, Portugal, and Spain have teetered on the brink of bankruptcy because of unwise and, perhaps, unethical financial dealings.

Nevertheless, the European Union has continued to grow. Countries that were formerly part of the Soviet Union or under its control have joined or rejoined Europe. Today the European Union has 27 member states with several more nations classified as "candidate countries."

INTERPRETIVE ESSAY

RICHARD A. LEIBY

The twentieth century gave birth to some bold political experiments. Communism, fascism, and the European unity movement all sought to destroy the status quo and replace it with new social and political realities. Yet, despite this basic commonality, these experiments could not have been more different. For communism and fascism, change was not achievable without violence. Both movements tended to resort to warfare or revolution in their efforts to remake Europe. In stark contrast, the raison d'être of the European unity movement was to persuade nations to cooperate with each other and thereby make armed conflict impossible. It is no accident that the European unity movement is the only one of the three experiments to have succeeded. Since the end of World War II, the nations of Europe have slowly but steadily opted to set aside their national self-interests in search of a common European "good." It hasn't always been a smooth process, but today Europe is the world's largest political and economic superpower by population. It is united by common institutions, a single currency, and laws that are binding on all member nations. On a continent that was once dominated by fiercely competitive states, war is suddenly no longer conceivable. How did this transition occur?

In 1945, Europe lay in ruins. Six years of war had destroyed Europe's cities, wrecked its economy, and killed millions of its citizens. For many, this was sufficient evidence that some measure of unity was not only desirable but necessary if the Continent was to recover. Interestingly, the first furtive steps toward unity came from the United States. In the immediate postwar political vacuum, only the United States possessed the requisite moral and material resources to initiate the process. It had good reasons to start the ball rolling. The new enemy was now the Soviet Union, and Western Europe needed to be secure from the growing threat of communist expansion. Consequently, the administration of U.S. President Harry Truman welcomed any arrangement that helped stabilize and strengthen its European allies. European integration was therefore one approach to collective security.

It is somewhat counterintuitive, then, that the initial attempts at institutionalized European integration were undertaken for economic, not political, reasons. The first U.S. grants and loans, allocated in the first two years after the war's end, were used to pay for Europe's more basic food and energy requirements and not for infrastructure. As might be expected, economic hardships continued despite the aid, prompting many Americans to wonder if their money had been "thrown down a rat hole." Consequently, when the Marshall Plan was introduced in 1947, the U.S. government made the loans and grants conditional on the creation of a European organization to oversee their distribution. The resulting Organization for European Economic Cooperation (OEEC) is often touted as the first step toward European unity, but in reality that overstates its impact. The OEEC was incapable of achieving any political or economic integration because it neither contained an embryonic European government nor did it wield any supranational powers. Its recommendations were subject to unanimous agreement, and if a nation abstained from voting on a new regulation, it would be exempted from complying with it. Indeed, the very fact that the United States was itself a member brings into question any notion that "Europe" began with the OEEC. Although Europeans themselves decided which nations received grants and how money would be used, in the final analysis the United States retained control over the delivery of the funds.

As the OEEC worked to rationalize Europe's economic base, attempts to forge political unity proceeded through other venues. Despite the creation of a Council of Europe in 1949, movement toward political cooperation proved very difficult. In part, the lack of progress can be attributed to two divergent views of integration. Some advocates of integration saw it as a means to destroy national barriers and create "Europe." Others saw it only as a device to bring about a common economic and political revival while preserving national autonomy. For the latter group, "Europe" was more an abstraction than a definite goal, and although some were willing to consider a "federation" of independent states, they were not about to support legislation that would impinge on a nation's right to self-determination. Clearly, many Europeans were reluctant to surrender sovereignty so soon after having paid such a high price to regain it.

In those early years it would have been very easy to give up on integration. Instead of surrendering to the prevailing pessimism, some Europeans, including Jean Monnet and Robert Schuman, adopted a gradualist strategy. Monnet, the son of a wine merchant, had made a name for himself as a champion of cooperation during his years as deputy secretary of the League of Nations and later as France's wartime emissary to Great Britain and the United States. He postulated that a more cautious approach, emphasizing limited integration in certain key economic sectors, would be a more appropriate way to begin. Working behind the scenes, Monnet devised plans to pool German and French coal and steel resources. In the belief that someone with more political clout than he should sponsor his plan, Monnet picked Robert Schuman, the French foreign minister, to present his ideas to the public. The choice of Schuman proved not only practically but also symbolically effective. Born in Lorraine, a province that had changed hands between France and Germany on four occasions between 1871 and 1945, Schuman had seen firsthand how national antagonisms can lead to confrontation. On May 1, 1950, the two men unveiled the Schuman Plan, a blueprint for the European Coal and Steel Community (ECSC). Six nations signed on (West Germany, France, Belgium, Netherlands, Luxembourg, and Italy), and Europe took its first true step toward unity.

At first glance, coal and steel do not seem a good choice for a pilot integration project. They were older industries, and because of their links to armaments production, they were always considered essential to national security. But if the ultimate goal of integration was to make war not only unthinkable but materially impossible, then success in these sectors would carry an enormous psychological impact. In addition, the arrangement made good economic sense. Germany's abundant coal supplies, when coupled with French iron, meant more efficient production and lower costs. Furthermore, because steel has many applications, the advantages of integration might spill over into other economic sectors. The scheme also offered a chance to manipulate the steel market, which in the early 1950s was suffering from overproduction and lack of demand. The formation of a community interest could legally rationalize distribution and oversee production before private firms could cartelize and accomplish the same thing illegally.

The Schuman Plan was basically an economic arrangement, but political cooperation was also a key component. The plan entrusted decision making to the High Authority comprising nine members (two each from France and Germany; one each from Belgium, the Netherlands, Luxembourg, and Italy; and one at-large member). The High Authority's job was to make and execute "laws," including production and distribution quotas, taxes on production, and fines for noncompliance. In addition, everyone understood that a rationalization of two such labor-intensive industries as coal and steel would lead to some worker layoffs in the less productive plants and mines. To address the social costs of integration, the Schuman Plan empowered the High Authority to levy and collect a surtax on production. This money could then be used to provide assistance to dislocated workers and to retrain those who lost jobs permanently. The High Authority also committed the community to social reforms intended to bring about uniform standards and practices in the workplace. Considering the power they held, the delegates to the High Authority wielded considerable clout. They were chosen not only for their special expertise, but also for their interest in the common good. Once named, the delegates were no longer responsible to their national governments. Europe had its first real supranational institution.

No one doubts that the ECSC played a major role in Europe's economic revival. The elimination of coal and steel tariffs and the effective restriction of cartelization were clear successes. That the member states were sufficiently encouraged to proceed with further integration is an indication, albeit indirect, that the treaty was (if nothing else) perceived as a success. However, if one looks to production figures to corroborate this perception, distinct conclusions are elusive. Steel production did increase markedly throughout the 1950s and into the 1960s. Even though many historians have linked this dramatic increase in production to the treaty, such a conclusion is presumptuous because it is impossible to "replay" history and compare what production would have been without the ECSC. With no claim for cause and effect, it is still safe to say that steel became cheaper and more profitable to produce and that demand was stimulated. However, such accomplishments fell short for the many supporters of supranationalism, whose hopes for a dramatic increase in production and trade weren't realized.

The ECSC's lasting legacy was not its economic productivity but its political boldness. The treaty was a milestone in the history of international affairs, marking the first instance when national authority was willingly transferred to a supranational body. But this achievement was a far cry from unification. Integration was still confined to only one sector, and it was still uncertain whether the much hoped for spillover effect would actually occur. Indeed, although coal and steel moved toward increased integration, economic particularism continued unabated in other areas, including the key sectors of agriculture and transportation. Many nations clung desperately to their national product standards, labor mobility laws, and tariff schedules as ways of protecting their industry and farming. The Coal and Steel Community failed to address, let alone dismantle, such economic barriers to integration. It is best to regard the ECSC as a bold but limited political experiment. It showed that international cooperation was not only possible but also potentially lucrative. As a first step on the path to complete integration, it was an important one, and it provided a good foundation on which to build.

In 1955, delegates of the ECSC member nations gathered at Messina to begin negotiations for a larger union. Again, external events added impetus to the drive for increased integration. Egypt's seizure of the Suez Canal and the West's subsequent failure to recapture it awakened many Europeans to their dependence on Middle Eastern oil. In addition, the Soviet Union's crackdown on Hungary in 1956 further exacerbated East-West tensions and revived the old theme of Europe's impotence in world affairs. In this tense diplomatic atmosphere, the delegates of the Six (that is, the six original ECSC member nations), emboldened by ECSC success, worked to expand economic cooperation by creating a single market similar to the one already established between Belgium, Luxembourg, and the Netherlands. The Treaty of Rome was the result.

The European Economic Community (EEC or Common Market) went into operation on January 1, 1958. Its goal was to free all other commodities of customs duties and tariffs within 12 years. The agreement created a large free trade area and established a common tariff policy on goods imported from nonmember states. Its supranational institutions mirrored those of the ECSC with the important addition that decisions could be reached only by a "qualified majority"—that is, both a majority of votes *and* a majority of nations had to agree, thereby protecting the interests of the smaller states. The treaty also established a European Social Fund, financed with production surcharges, to continue the ECSC's mandate to retrain and, if necessary, resettle displaced workers. A newly created European Investment Bank provided seed capital to the community's underdeveloped regions.

The Common Market's successes are clearly discernible. Industrial trade barriers disappeared by 1962, and the remaining tariff barriers were all but eliminated by 1968, well ahead of schedule. Intramarket trade rose 73 percent during the treaty's first three years, and the European gross national product increased 21 percent. Standards of living within the Six reached new highs during the 1960s, but it would be erroneous to conclude that such success was easily achieved. One sector that posed particularly thorny integration problems was agriculture. For years, Europe's farmers enjoyed the benefits of national subsidies and tariff restrictions. Although government intervention helped Europe's food producers, the resulting high prices gave farmers little or no incentive to modernize or avoid overproduction. To solve these problems, France (Europe's major producer of foodstuffs and perennial "victim" of protectionism) led negotiations to rationalize agricultural production. It took round-the-clock negotiations to reach a workable consensus, but on January 14, 1962, a Common Agricultural Policy (CAP) emerged. The CAP agreement guaranteed all farmers a fixed price for their produce and community-wide tariffs to bring the price of imported foodstuffs to at least the minimum commodity price.

The CAP points out both the positive and negative nature of European integration. Although CAP was a clear victory for French agriculture, its significance lies in West Germany's willingness to compromise, even at the expense of its own farmers—an action that boded well for supranationalism. On the other hand, the compromise was also a good example of "negative integration." The CAP did not eliminate agricultural tariffs, it consolidated them. Henceforth, the tariff burdens were simply shifted to nonmember states. Consequently, Europe's farmers still had no incentive to modernize production, and food prices remained unusually high compared with world markets.

Despite the EEC's economic success, the movement for political unity encountered further difficulty. Again, the accidents of history played a major role. When the Fourth French Republic collapsed in 1958, Charles de Gaulle, France's war hero, catapulted to power as president of the newly created Fifth Republic. De Gaulle had his own opinions about European unity, preferring a federal approach that would allow France to preserve its national interests. De Gaulle's intransigent nationalism had a number of unfortunate by-products. His opposition to Great Britain's application for membership prevented the EEC from bringing a major economy into the organization. In addition, his steadfast refusal to grant the Common Market's Commission the expanded powers it needed to enforce the vast array of economic and social agreements nearly destroyed supranationalism. In 1966, France partially withdrew from a number of Common Market institutions. This "Empty Chair Crisis" led to the Luxembourg Agreement, which stipulated that any nation could override the Commission if it felt its vital interests were threatened. This humiliation undermined the unity movement and demonstrated that political unity would not be achieved in the foreseeable future.

De Gaulle's retirement from politics in 1969 not only relieved the political impasse, it also helped bring about the most active and productive period of EEC expansion. A new cadre of French politicians (notably Georges Pompidou and Valéry Giscard d'Estaing) led the way in breaking the stalemate of the 1960s. Great Britain was finally accepted for community membership, and by becoming a member it tacitly accepted that its future lay not with its former empire but with continental Europe. Encouraged by Great Britain's entry, the Common Market member nations boldly declared their intent to form a deeper union. In a series of conferences beginning with the Hague meeting of 1969 and culminating at the Paris conference of 1972, the delegates set out to create institutions to achieve this goal. Two major efforts emerged. The boldest move was the creation of a system to keep the exchange rates of Europe's currencies relatively stable. The scheme, called "the snake in the tunnel," stipulated that the values of European currencies would not be allowed to fluctuate more than 2.25 percent vis-à-vis each other and that they would remain within 4.5 percent of the U.S. dollar despite the fluctuations of demand in the world currency market. Although "the snake" was essentially an attempt to end the currency devaluations of the late 1960s, many advocates of union interpreted it as the first step toward creation of a single European currency. In addition, a European Parliament was fashioned from older ECSC and Common Market institutions. For the first time in many years, it looked as though the political side of the European unity movement was back on track. Few could have foreseen that events beyond Europe's control once again would derail the process, this time for 15 years.

In 1973, war between Israel and the Arab states caused the Organization of Petroleum Exporting Countries (OPEC) to cut production, resulting in a quadrupling of the price of oil. The action sent economic shock waves throughout the world but particularly through Western Europe, where many nations were entirely dependent on foreign sources of energy. In this hour of mutual need, the ideals of unity were suddenly and decisively shoved aside. Rather than work in concert, the EEC member governments scurried about individually in an attempt to secure special concessions from OPEC. When a second oil crisis struck in 1979, the malaise of the 1970s continued into the 1980s. Economic statistics tell a harsh tale. Between 1980 and 1983, the combined gross national product of the EC countries grew less than 1 percent each year. Unemployment levels in 1982 were nearly double those of 1978. These statistics may be shocking, but they are comparable with figures recorded at that time in the United States and other industrialized countries. For Europe, however, the oil crisis had an additional, devastating effect; it probably did more than any other single event to retard the cause of unity. It underscored the lack of a common energy policy and tested the will of the members to share bad as well as good times. The recession also destroyed some of the EC's economic institutions. The "snake" died as national governments withdrew their currencies from the scheme, and with it died all hopes of creating a single currency in the near future.

Paradoxically, economic stagnation spurred political progress. Europe's ineffective response to OPEC revealed the need for a concerted foreign policy. The result was the

European Political Cooperation agreement (EPC), a mechanism whereby Europe's governments could confer and reach joint decisions in foreign affairs. This was an important step forward, considering that foreign policy had always been the nation-state's most jealously guarded prerogative. The initiative began modestly as regularly scheduled summit conferences, but those meetings soon changed into a more formal arrangement known as the European Council. The Council, together with the new European Parliament, held out the hope that a truly supranational government was in the offing. In one of its first actions (1974), the Council reiterated that monetary union was vital to the future of European unity and, given the prevailing economic difficulties, all the more important a goal. Eventually, the European Monetary System (1979) emerged, featuring a revival of the "snake" concept called the Exchange Rate Mechanism (ERM). The reform's centerpiece was the creation of the European Currency Unit (ECU), with a value based on a set proportion of each member nation's currency.

The 1970s also saw movement toward realizing the Treaty of Rome's goals for equal employment opportunities for men and women. On February 10, 1975, the EC began what was called "Positive Action," a program to eliminate gender bias in the workplace. Positive Action outlawed sex discrimination in salaries and forbade gender bias in hiring. A recommendation in the following year augmented the program, suggesting equal treatment for men and women in matters of promotion, training, and social security. Unfortunately, social legislation proved difficult to enforce. Most of the directives were optional and compliance was at best sporadic. Nevertheless, as the Community pulled out of its economic malaise, it had at least the trappings of a unified social framework.

After the economic downturn of the early 1980s, the march toward integration could again move forward. The passage of the Single European Act (SEA) in 1985 enhanced the process. The SEA was revolutionary in that it allowed for majority decisions, and thereby provided for a more democratic method of decision making and precluded any single country from blocking or ignoring legislation (à la the Luxembourg Accord). Additionally, it gave the European Parliament de facto veto power over the Council, which could be overridden only by a unanimous Council vote. With a new decision-making apparatus in effect, the EC embarked upon the Single Market Act (also known as "Project 1992")—a push to eliminate unnecessary border controls, divergent national product standards, differing rates of Value Added Taxation (VAT), and some remaining nationally protected markets. The ultimate goal was to eliminate all remaining nontariff barriers to trade by January 1, 1993.

The centerpiece of the new integration effort was the Maastricht Treaty, an agreement that committed Europe to the path of unity and expanded EC supranational authority. With one piece of legislation, barriers to the movement of citizens were lifted. Europeans now could move anywhere they chose and work wherever they wished and travel abroad with a common European Community passport. Getting the Maastricht Treaty passed by the member nations was no easy feat; the debate over the Treaty showed that the acrimony over supranationalism was far from dead. In Great Britain, Prime Minister Margaret Thatcher resigned in 1991 rather than agree to further limitations on British sovereignty. Two years later, that very same government under John Major became the last EC member to approve the treaty. It is ironic but fitting, given the history of the European unity movement, that the British Parliament ratified the Maastricht

Treaty on the same day that economic pressures on the French franc led to a collapse of the ERM. Once again, progress and setback seemed inextricably intertwined.

The collapse of the ERM was just the latest in a series of impediments that kept hindering efforts to create a single currency. Before the collapse, there was reason for optimism that the ECU might become Europe's official legal tender. It was an established commodity on the world's financial and trade markets, and was the vehicle of choice to transmit community aid to nonmember nations. Despite the setback, European monetary authorities continued with plans to create a new currency and put it in circulation by the end of the century. Thus was born the "Euro," Europe's first true currency, which was officially launched in 1999 for commercial transactions. Three years later, the Euro replaced the national currencies of the member states and immediately became one of the world's most sought after currencies. As the participating nations switched over to the new Euro, the older national currencies lost their values to all but collectors. As prices and wages settled in to the new system, the Euro-zone became one huge marketplace. One of the most coveted goals of the unity movement was now a reality.

With the dawn of the new century, the European Union's political role has widened both at home and with its neighbors. In 2003, European troops took part in a peacekeeping mission in Bosnia which saw German troops operating outside the borders of Germany for the first time since World War II. Internally, the process of increased democratization has continued. Although a 2004 attempt to create a European constitution failed, the 2007 Treaty of Lisbon incorporated most of its provisions as the need to adapt the EU's political structures to meet the needs of an ever expanding Europe was recognized. This agreement promises to make the union ever more responsive to the needs of its citizens by strengthening the powers of the European Parliament and streamlining decision making among the member nations. Socially, it reinforces the rights of all Europeans to enjoy basic political and economic freedoms. And, in this age of terrorist threat, it establishes the precedent that an attack on one member nation is an attack on them all.

"Europe" has come a long way since its beginnings in the 1940s. The history of the European unity movement reveals that progress came not in a steady stream of accomplishments but in fits and starts. Economic integration often came as a response to political turmoil and, conversely, progress toward political unification often occurred during economic downturns. That dynamic may seem a bit convoluted, but there is an inner logic to it. Because one sector or another is always making progress toward continued integration, the movement is never totally at rest. Indeed, despite numerous trials and setbacks, the EU's progress has made the question of its survival irrelevant. Europe, and its powerhouse economy, is here to stay. Although member nations are allowed to "opt out" of the union, even the biggest skeptics acknowledge that doing so would be tantamount to committing economic suicide.

Total political unity, on the other hand, is still an open question. Despite the presence of international political parties and Europe-wide elections, national interests still play a large role in the politics of Europe. Is complete integration realistic? Some observers assert that total union is not and never will be the EU's goal. As evidence, they cite the Draft Treaty for Union (1985) and other documents that affirm that the purpose of political integration is not to destroy the nation-state but to enhance it. In other words, the unity movement aims to create not a monolithic super-state but a mixed government in which power is shared between national and supranational authorities. Such an interpretation must disappoint those purists who still believe in complete and total union, but it strikes the neutral observer as a pragmatic attempt to bridge the hopes for continued integration with present political realities. European integration no longer aims for unity but for "an ever closer union."

Social unification has proved a more difficult task. If goods, services, ideas, and even people are to traverse national borders freely, then the quality of the workplace must be ensured and employee rights must be safeguarded the same way in all localities. Many social goals, including gender-neutral pay equalization, industrial hygiene, and safety research, are still not fully realized. Although social integration has even proved difficult for the advanced members of the EU, it poses a greater problem for the recently admitted nations such as Cyprus, and the Balkan and eastern European states, who must struggle to bring their laws in line with EU regulations. It is understandably difficult to bring the social standards of the twenty-first century to countries where enclaves still languish in the twentieth if not the nineteenth.

Although the task seems monumental, there is reason for optimism. The European Social Fund has done much to support underdeveloped areas despite the social prejudices that endure. Conquering those prejudices will remain the Community's biggest project for the twenty-first century. The logic behind gender-neutral hiring practices and environmental protection laws may escape the farmers of Slovenia or the fishermen of Estonia, but without a uniformity of protections, a single community can hardly be forged. Consequently, the EU has had to be patient with its newer partners and allow them time to bring their national social standards up to Union standards. This has slowed the tempo of integration markedly, but it is the price that must be paid for continued expansion.

The movement for political unification has also advanced during the past 20 years. European political parties now represent transnational interests. Their members can seek direct election to the European Parliament, which has become a working legislature complete with lawmaking and taxation powers gleaned from the nation-states. Nevertheless, the Community's political institutions will never function successfully unless they command the respect of the citizens they govern. Hence, the EU's most formidable political task is an intellectual one. It must work to create a "European" identity that can command the allegiance of its people. This will be no mean accomplishment because national loyalties have been around for nearly four centuries and regional or ethnic loyalties even longer.

This begs the question: are there limits to European supranationalism? Nationalism is a double-edged sword. It can be used to stress either the similarities uniting peoples or the differences separating them. Twentieth-century nationalism stressed the latter, as examples from Belfast to Bosnia will attest. But nationalism need not be negative; it can be the same unifying force that brought together the German and Italian peoples, among others, in the nineteenth century. Europe's challenge is to overcome the differences that separate its populations and to emphasize what they all hold in common. It is no accident that the model for integration has always been countries (such as the United States or Switzerland) that have somehow earned the allegiances of their disparate ethnic and religious minorities. "Europe" can emerge only if the member nations accept each other's ethnic and linguistic individuality and realize the strengths of a multiethnic, multicultural society. The EU must somehow redirect Europe's nationalistic urges toward the geographical and historical uniqueness of the continent as a whole, and away from the divisive ideology of the nation-state. In the final analysis, the extent to which "Europe" exists will depend on the hearts of the people themselves. Will future generations of Germans, French, and Italians identify themselves first as "Europeans," or will their ethnic loyalties trump their transnational identities? That answer will be the true measure of the success or failure of the European unity movement.

If Europe succeeds, it has much to gain. The new Europe has already become the world's largest single trading bloc, comprising 27 nations with a total population of more than 500 million people. A politically united Europe, economically on par with the United States and China, and with a common foreign policy, would be a potent world force. Other supranational trading blocs based on the European model have emerged (for example, the North American Free Trade Area, or NAFTA) in the hopes of mimicking Europe's economic and political success. Is it possible that we are witnessing the dawn of a new age of international diplomacy, when geopolitical power blocs supplant the nation-states as the world's power brokers? If so, Europe has been the vanguard of that movement.

Such speculative questions are perhaps best left to the political theorists, but it is safe to conclude that the European unity movement has forever altered traditional assumptions about international relations. Its very existence signals a rejection of the past when international rivalry, competition, and national self-interest formed the status quo. Although born out of the ravages of war, the European unity movement is now a grand experiment in peace, one that (with luck) may set a tone of international cooperation and prosperity for the remainder of the twenty-first century.

SELECTED BIBLIOGRAPHY

Baun, Michael J. *An Imperfect Union: The Maastricht Treaty and the New Politics of European Integration.* Boulder, CO: Westview Press, 1996. Puts the Maastricht Treaty in the larger context of international diplomacy.

Blair, Alasdair. *The European Union since 1945.* New York: Pearson-Longman, 2005. A strong introduction to the history of the EU.

Desmond, Dinan. *Europe Recast: A History of European Union.* Boulder, CO: Lynne Rienner Publishers, 2004. An excellent survey of the history of the unity movement.

Fennell, Rosemary. *The Common Agricultural Policy: Continuity and Change.* Oxford: Oxford University Press, 1997. Possibly the definitive history of European agricultural policy from its beginnings.

Gillingham, John. *Coal, Steel and the Rebirth of Europe, 1945–1955.* New York: Cambridge University Press, 1991. Among the best scholarship on the ECSC's earliest years.

Hackett, Clifford. *Cautious Revolution: The European Community Arrives.* New York: Praeger, 1990. A look at early beginnings of the EU through the lens of the EC institutions and the problems confronting them.

Hix, Simon. *The Political System of the European Union.* 3rd ed. London: Palgrave, Macmillan, 2011. A look at the institutions of the Union from a political scientist's perspective.

Hösli, Madeline O. *The Euro: A Concise Introduction to European Monetary Integration.* Boulder, CO: Lynne Rienner Publishers, 2005. Best and most current look at European monetary developments.

Ludlow, Peter. *The Making of the European Monetary System: A Case Study of the Politics of the European Community.* London: Butterworth Scientific, 1982. Explores the confluence of politics and money policy; part of Butterworth's European Studies series.

Mayne, Richard. *The Community of Europe: Past, Present and Future.* New York: W. W. Norton, 1962. Dated but valuable insider's account of the genesis of the Common Market.

Mayne, Richard. *The Recovery of Europe.* New York: Doubleday Books, 1973. A more in-depth account of the early postwar years.

McNeill, Donald. *New Europe: Imagined Spaces.* Oxford: Hodder Education, 2004. An interdisciplinary approach to the role of the nation-state that postulates how well the idea of a "Europe" can attract the allegiances of its people.

Monnet, Jean. *Memoirs.* Introduction by George Ball. Translated by Richard Mayne. New York: Doubleday, 1978. The reminiscences of the "Father of Europe."

Schmitt, Hans A. *The Path to European Union: From the Marshall Plan to the Common Market.* Baton Rouge: Louisiana State University Press, 1962. Dated, but perhaps still the best scholarly account of the process leading to the EEC's formation, with a particularly valuable account of the ECSC.

Tipton, Frank B., and Robert Aldrich. *An Economic and Social History of Europe from 1939 to the Present.* Baltimore: Johns Hopkins University Press, 1987. As the title indicates, this survey is strong on economic and social developments.

Tsoukalis, Loukas. *The European Community: Past, Present, and Future.* Oxford: Basil Blackwell, 1983. A collection of occasional papers dealing with aspects of integration in the early 1980s.

Urwin, Derek. *The Community of Europe: A History of European Integration since 1945.* New York: Pearson Longman Publishers, 2009. First published in 1991, a valuable survey.

KONRAD ADENAUER (1876–1967)

Konrad Adenauer supervised the creation of the Federal Republic of Germany (West Germany) after World War II and served as its first chancellor. Under his leadership, West Germany emerged from devastation and defeat to become a major economic power and an integral part of the Western effort to contain Soviet communism.

Konrad was born on January 5, 1876, in the Rhineland city of Cologne, Germany, to Konrad and Helene Scharfenberg Adenauer, devout Roman Catholics. His father, as a retired member of the Prussian army and minor civil servant, had little money. With the help of frugality, a scholarship, and a small inheritance left by a boarder the family had taken in to avoid poverty, Konrad was able to study law and economics at the University of Freiburg and later at the universities of Munich and Bonn. He married the well-connected Emma Weyer in 1904.

While practicing law in Cologne, Adenauer made friends in banking and in the Zentrum (German Center Party), a political organization united more by Catholicism than political ideology. He became deputy mayor on the city council in 1906. The period before Adenauer's 1917 election to Cologne's highest mayoral post, a position he held until 1933, was bleak. His wife died, leaving him with three young children, and his political popularity was not widespread. A limousine in which he was riding collided at high speed with a tram-train, nearly killing him. Surgeons reconstructed his face, leaving him with an unusual appearance and lifelong insomnia.

The political support of his clerical and banking friends eased his return to politics. As mayor, Adenauer developed a reputation for efficiency and political wile. Despite his distaste for socialism, he refused to fire on protesting workers in 1918, when postwar unrest following the German defeat in World War I led to violence in other German cities. Adenauer expressed sympathy for Rhineland separatism as a means to avoid socialist rule in Germany, but when the socialists gained constitutional control of the national government, he deferred.

When the Nazi Party took power in 1933, Adenauer was forced out of office. His homes were seized and in 1934 he was arrested. Later, he was given an allowance to build a villa on the Rhine River provided he avoid politics. He said of that time, "I became a very good gardener." Possibly knowing of—but not participating in—a plot to assassinate Adolf Hitler led to Adenauer's arrest in 1944. He avoided deportation to the Buchenwald concentration camp only with the help of a communist fellow prisoner and by faking a heart attack. His second wife, Gussie Zinsser, with whom he had had four children, was jailed for knowing his whereabouts after his escape, and both of them were imprisoned. His wife was poorly treated by both jailer and inmates, and contracted a blood disease that eventually killed her.

After the war, the occupying Allied forces returned control of war-torn Cologne to Adenauer. However, he frequently disagreed with his British supervisors, who fired him in October 1945. Although this event led Adenauer to pursue politics beyond Cologne and thus to the chancellorship of Germany, his animosity toward the British remained, in part because they limited his visits to his hospitalized wife. Later, this bitterness toward the British caused him to ally closely with France and to distrust the British-allied Americans after the death of his friend John Foster Dulles, U.S. president Dwight D. Eisenhower's secretary of state.

Because of the influence of his Protestant associate and later financial adviser, banker Robert Pferdmenges, as well as his own observations, Adenauer believed that a democratic conservative government required cooperation between Catholics and Protestants. He joined the emerging Christian Democratic Union and became its chair in the British-occupied zone of Germany in 1946. With the strong support of big business and eventually the United States, Adenauer's stature grew and he participated in the drafting of the preliminary constitution that established the Federal Republic of Germany from that part of Germany not occupied by the Soviet Union. In August 1949, the Christian Democrats surprisingly defeated the Social Democrats in national elections. The new West German parliament elected the 73-year-old Adenauer chancellor by one vote, his own. Reelected in 1953, 1957, and 1961, he served as German head of state for 14 years.

Motivated by anticommunist sentiment, Adenauer made West Germany an indispensable member of the Western alliance. Serving as his own foreign minister during 1951–1955, Adenauer brought his country into such key organizations as the International Monetary Fund and the World Health Organization. West Germany began to contribute soldiers to the North Atlantic Treaty Organization and joined the European Economic Community, the Council of Europe, and the West European Union.

Adenauer's close ties with the industrial nations of the West contributed to his greatest achievement, often called an economic miracle. With advice from Pferdmenges, Adenauer and Economics Minister Ludwig Erhard took advantage of favorable economic conditions worldwide to transform a ruined economy with no currency into a prosperous industrial power by encouraging the development of private industry in Germany.

Between 1950 and 1963, industrial production nearly tripled. A sign of the rapidly rising standard of living, brandy consumption doubled in the country.

Adenauer did not, however, lack critics. Many Germans believed that he cared more for Europe than for Germany and accused him of neglecting West Berliners when communist East Germany erected the Berlin Wall in August 1961 and attempted to cut off food supplies to West Berlin. Others criticized his tolerance for former Nazis in high positions. His vague support of claims to former German lands now incorporated into postwar Poland—rhetoric designed to pander to the right wing of his conservative political party—irritated some. Other critics also cited his perceived subservience to French president Charles de Gaulle, with whom he signed the Franco-German Cooperation Treaty (Elysée Treaty) on January 22, 1963. Concern mounted about Adenauer's authoritarian tactics, particularly his disrespect for judicial independence, which commentators viewed as a danger to the young democracy. Because of his age, longevity in politics, and strong but strict paternal oversight of the new West German state, he earned the nickname "Der Alte" (the Old One).

Under heavy pressure from his own party, Adenauer resigned in 1963 at age 87. He remained in parliament, although his influence quickly waned, and the Christian Democrats suffered major losses in the 1966 election. Adenauer died on April 19, 1967, from the effects of coronary thrombosis and bronchitis. He told his children there was "no reason to weep."

ABC-CLIO

CHARLES DE GAULLE (1890–1970)

In 1958, Charles de Gaulle, the egotistical, strongly nationalistic World War II hero, established the French Fifth Republic. Leading France in the independent direction he thought appropriate to a great nation's destiny, de Gaulle often infuriated people, including the leaders of allied countries. He was, however, the most prominent French leader of the twentieth century.

De Gaulle was born in Lille on November 22, 1890, and grew up in Paris, where his father worked as a teacher at a Jesuit school, the College of the Immaculate Conception. De Gaulle developed a desire for a military career at age 13, and after attending secondary school in Paris, he entered St. Cyr, the French military school from which he graduated in 1911 with a commission as a second lieutenant. He then served under Colonel Henri Pétain in the 33rd Infantry Regiment.

De Gaulle fought in World War I and earned a reputation for valor. He was wounded three times and in 1916 was captured by the Germans at Verdun. After the war, he joined with other French volunteers to help the Poles fight the Soviet Red Army.

After the Polish army defeated the Russians in 1921, de Gaulle returned to Paris and attended the War College. He promoted controversial military tactics that called for more flexibility in the heat of battle, especially in the use of tanks, than his superiors thought best. They also considered him too conceited and unwilling to accept criticism; hence, they assigned him a low grade. However, Pétain, by then a general, supported de Gaulle, appointed him to his own staff, and had him give lectures at the War College. From 1929 to 1931, de Gaulle headed French military operations in Syria, Egypt, Iraq,

Charles de Gaulle was a French army general, head of the French government-in-exile in World War II, provisional president of the Fourth Republic from 1944 to 1946, and president of the Fifth Republic from 1958 to 1969. Under de Gaulle's leadership, France regained its status as an important power in European and global affairs. (Library of Congress)

and Iran. When he returned home, he gained appointment as secretary-general of the Higher Council of National Defense and was promoted to lieutenant colonel. He was assigned to prepare a study on the mobilization of France during a war crisis.

Many observers believe that de Gaulle exhibited great military insight in the 1930s when he warned about developments in Europe. In his 1940 book *The Army of the Future,* he criticized France's reliance on the Maginot Line for defense against Germany and called for the formation of mechanized armored columns. He asserted that "any defender who limited himself to static resistance by old-fashioned elements would be doomed to disaster." His advice went largely unheeded, and in June 1940, German forces easily invaded and defeated France.

De Gaulle was promoted that year to brigadier general and in a tank operation momentarily turned back the Germans at Laon and Abbeville. He was named undersecretary of national defense and war and went to London for discussions with the British prime minister, Winston Churchill. He refused to accept the truce that the French government worked out with the Germans in the spring of 1940, and later that year announced the formation of a French government-in-exile headquartered in London. He became president of Free France, and the British recognized him as commander of the Free French Forces.

Back in Paris, the collaborationist Vichy government pronounced a death sentence against de Gaulle. On August 7, 1940, he signed an agreement with Churchill in which the British promised to help France regain its independence. Within the Free French Forces, de Gaulle had competition from General Henri Honoré Giraud. The American president, Franklin D. Roosevelt, had close relations with Giraud and favored him to lead the French action in North Africa. In 1943, de Gaulle and Giraud met at Casablanca, and shortly thereafter they agreed to cooperate in forming the French Committee of National Liberation with the two men serving as co-chairs. In a series of maneuvers with Giraud and the Allies, however, de Gaulle soon gained command of the committee and in May 1944 emerged as the overall leader and president of the newly reorganized provisional government of the French Republic.

After the Allies began to drive the Germans out of France, de Gaulle returned to Paris in August 1944. He continued as president of the provisional government and guided France through its writing of a new constitution. He desired a strong executive branch and a weak legislature, and when opposition to his views prevailed in early 1946, he resigned the presidency. In October, the French people approved the constitution for the Fourth Republic.

De Gaulle, meanwhile, said it would not work and organized the Rally of the French People (RPF) to compete in elections and fight for change. In 1947, voters made the RPF the most popular party in France, but in 1953, it suffered a severe loss in municipal elections and de Gaulle resigned the party presidency and retired from politics to begin writing his memoirs.

In 1958, failure to quell a revolt in the French-held African colony of Algeria along with inflation and financial instability within France shattered the Fourth Republic. The nation stood ready for yet another transformation. De Gaulle announced that if the people desired, he would end his retirement and lead France. Many army officers supported him, for they believed that as a fellow military man he would buttress the French presence in Algeria, which at that time was precarious.

In May 1958, the French president asked de Gaulle to form a government. He did so after parliament approved his ascension to the prime ministry. De Gaulle then pushed for a new constitution to shift most power from the legislature to the executive and thereby create a strong presidency rather than a parliamentary government. In a plebiscite, the French approved such a document, and the Fifth Republic was born with de Gaulle chosen president in an election on December 21.

De Gaulle had enormous powers, but although enemies called him a dictator he always fought to maintain the republic and resisted pressure to alter the constitution. As a strong nationalist, he sought to strengthen his country financially and militarily. The economy moved ahead with inflation under control. At the same time, de Gaulle proceeded with the development of nuclear weapons. To do this, he pushed aside objections from the United States and asserted that France needed nuclear capability to be truly independent against both American and Soviet power.

De Gaulle believed that French security and the safety of Europe required a balance between the United States and the Soviet Union, and in his view America had become too powerful. Hence, he withdrew French forces from the North Atlantic Treaty Organization, the American-dominated alliance designed to protect Western Europe from Soviet expansion. He also twice vetoed the entry of the pro-American United Kingdom into the European Common Market, the customs union shared by most Continental countries.

To the surprise of many in the French military, de Gaulle opposed a continued French presence in Algeria, an involvement that he felt was weakening his nation, and sought to extricate France from its existing colonial system. In 1958, he accomplished the latter by forming the French Community, an arrangement that gave the colonies internal autonomy. (With regard to Algeria, French settlers in that country complicated his plans and engaged in vicious fighting until that country gained its independence in 1962.)

De Gaulle frequently antagonized the United States with such independent moves as establishing diplomatic relations with communist China. He considered France to be the leader of continental Europe and bristled at American efforts to "run the show." Although many French criticized his heavy-handed manner, they supported his efforts to restore French prestige. He visited the United States on several occasions, including a meeting with President John F. Kennedy in 1961, during which he displayed his perceptive analysis of international affairs in warning against an increased American involvement in Vietnam—an involvement, he claimed, that would turn into "an endless process," as he knew from the French failures there.

In 1968, violent demonstrations by university students rocked de Gaulle's government. The protesters in the Paris Protests of 1968 demanded not only changes in the college curriculum but also in French society. They rebelled against de Gaulle's authoritarianism and the inequities in wealth and employment in France. Clashes occurred with the police, and in March, many industrial workers joined the students, paralyzing France with a general strike. The Fifth Republic tottered, but de Gaulle moved troops toward Paris to restore order, advocated reform, and called for new elections. He expressed his desire to see more participation by labor in economic decisions. His tactics worked; the student uprising quickly collapsed when a huge demonstration occurred supporting de Gaulle and when French voters, fearful that the disorder would lead to a communist takeover, provided him with a sizable election victory.

Yet the rebellion underscored deep political and economic differences in French society and showed the limits to de Gaulle's administration. Discontent resurfaced, fueled by serious governmental financial problems. Criticism of de Gaulle increased, and when he lost a referendum on a reform proposal, he resigned the presidency in 1969. De Gaulle retired to Colombey-les-Deux-Eglises, where he resumed writing his memoirs. He died from a heart attack on November 9, 1970. The Fifth Republic, however, continued—the result of de Gaulle's leadership in a trying postwar Europe.

NEIL HAMILTON

JEAN MONNET (1888–1979)

The father of the European Economic Community, the precursor of the European Union, Jean Monnet was a twentieth-century French political economist. After working on international economic matters during and after World War I, he was appropriately placed to effect economic cooperation among Allied nations during World War II and to rebuild the European economy after the war ended. The modern French and European economic systems are largely based on innovations introduced by Monnet in the immediate postwar era.

Monnet was born on November 9, 1888, in Cognac, France. He was the son of businessman Jean-Gabriel Monnet, a member of a brandy-making family. Monnet attended the College of Cognac. He married Silvia de Bondini on November 13, 1934; they had two children, Anna and Mariane.

During World War I, from 1914 to 1918, Monnet served as a French representative on the Inter-Allied Maritime Commission. He was deputy secretary-general of the League of Nations from 1919 to 1923, working on the financial redevelopment of Austria in 1923. He left the league in 1923 to return to his family business in Cognac. Having reorganized that enterprise, he became the European partner of a New York investment bank in 1925. In 1932, he participated in the reorganization of Chinese railroads. In the late 1930s, he counseled several nations on their economic development.

In 1940, Monnet became a member of the British Supply Council in Washington, D.C., and helped organize the communal defense portion of President Franklin D. Roosevelt's Victory Program. After suggesting a union between France and the United Kingdom to Winston Churchill, he was made chairman of the Franco-British Economic Coordination Committee. He also helped with the liberation of Algiers in 1943 as a commissioner of armaments.

Monnet did his best-known work after the end of World War II when he reconstructed the economy of France and then did the same for Western Europe as a whole. In fact, the French economy today is still based on Monnet's system. At the end of the war, Monnet was made head of a committee that planned the rehabilitation of the French economy. The Monnet Plan, implemented during 1946–1951, was adopted by the French government on January 11, 1947. Monnet was appointed commissioner-general of the National Planning Board.

Monnet's plan attempted to create a depoliticized, open-ended technocracy in which each economic participant, whether union, industrial trade association, or foreign ministry of finance, sought its own corporate self-interest. Monnet was especially skilled at appealing to his compatriots above the squabbles of petty politics. Though the nationalized sector of the economy was required to comply with the plan and the private sector was strongly encouraged to do so, Monnet made the planning process voluntary, avoiding the appearance of strong-arm tactics. Representatives from each industry met and drew up their own production targets. That approach harmonized well with the political agenda of President Charles de Gaulle.

The Monnet Plan was spectacularly successful, meeting almost all of its goals, though it did receive considerable financial assistance from the Marshall Plan. Its methods gave the French private sector the confidence to break away from traditionalism and invest in risky, growth-oriented ventures. Brilliantly, Monnet managed to convince private businesses that their tax dollars actually benefited them and that the state was providing an excellent business infrastructure at a very reasonable price.

In 1950, Monnet and French foreign minister Robert Schuman suggested applying the principles of the Monnet Plan to the establishment of a common European market for coal and steel. France, Luxembourg, Belgium, and West Germany shared a large ferrous metals zone, and Monnet encouraged those countries to submit their coal and steel industries to a common authority. In 1951, France, West Germany, Italy, Belgium, the Netherlands, and Luxembourg all signed a treaty that created the European Coal and Steel Community (ECSC). Monnet served as president of the ECSC's High Authority between 1952 and 1955.

That organization in turn led to the creation in 1957 of the European Economic Community, or Common Market, whose principles were outlined in the Rome Treaty (1957). Monnet continued to place enlightened economic self-interest above political concerns and deftly managed to convince member states to rise above nationalist rivalries and develop solidarity in the collective pursuit and management of wealth. All parties benefited when they stopped squabbling over borders and cooperated to increase output.

Monnet received many honors and international prizes and headed up other international committees. From 1955 to 1975, he organized and led the Action Committee for the United States in Europe. In 1976, he was named a Citizen of Europe by the nine Common Market governments. He wrote his *Mémoires* in 1976. Monnet died on March 16, 1979, in Houjarray, France.

AMY BLACKWELL

ROBERT SCHUMAN (1886–1963)

Robert Schuman was a post–World War II French statesman who worked to create a lasting European peace. As France's foreign minister in the late 1940s, he assisted in the creation of the North Atlantic Treaty Organization (NATO) and the European Coal and Steel Community (ECSC), laying the basis for the modern European Union.

Schuman was born in the Grand Duchy of Luxembourg on June 29, 1886. As a child, he returned with his family to their native Lorraine, which had been annexed by Germany as a result of France's defeat in the Franco-Prussian War of 1870–1871. Alsace and Lorraine had been at the crossroads of European conquest since the time of Charlemagne, and consequently, the residents of this area possessed a unique culture with elements of France and Germany. Schuman's primary language was French, but with the unique German accent of the Lorraine region.

Schuman was educated at the University of Bonn, the University of Berlin, the University of Munich, and the University of Strasbourg, where he was awarded a doctorate in law. During World War I, he served in the German army but not on active duty. After the war, when Alsace and Lorraine were returned to France, he served as deputy mayor of Metz. From 1919 through 1940, he served as a Christian Democrat in the French Chamber of Deputies, the lower house of the French legislature. There he gained a reputation as an expert in public finances and served as chair of the finance committee.

In 1940, Schuman voted with the majority to confirm Marshal Philippe Pétain as the leader of the Vichy government. Despite this act (which was seen as a betrayal of democracy in France), he was shortly thereafter arrested by the Gestapo and imprisoned. After being released, he worked in the French underground from 1942 until the liberation of France. Following the war, he was a member of the Popular Republican Movement and served in a variety of capacities in the French Fourth Republic, including finance minister, minister of justice, prime minister, and foreign minister. From 1948 through 1953, he served as the minister of foreign affairs in 10 governments, where he advocated the need for a strong France in the context of an economically united Europe.

As foreign minister, Schuman took up the call for the integration of the European economy as a means of encouraging national cooperation. The idea of fostering political cooperation through economic integration was not a new one. Jean Monnet had urged the idea as a means of fostering political cooperation and preventing European wars.

Schuman convinced the French government that economic integration would strengthen French industry and prevent a resurgence of German militarism. One early test of the idea came in the form of the Organization for European Economic Cooperation, which Schuman helped found as the means of distributing Marshall Plan aid. In the last part of the 1940s, Schuman also attempted to forge a French economic union, first with the Netherlands, Belgium, and Luxembourg, and later with Italy. These attempts failed, as nationalism remained strong.

Two events changed European attitudes regarding integration. The first was the Cold War, which saw the creation of NATO as part of an effort to contain the spread of Soviet communism. Schuman signed the North Atlantic Treaty (1949) for France, which planned to rearm Germany, a move that frightened some European nations in light of the previous war. In this context, Schuman recognized the need for French-German cooperation, despite his distrust of the latter.

The second event came in 1950 with the emergence of Schuman, Konrad Adenauer, and Alcide de Gasperi as leaders of France, Germany, and Italy. For the first time, individuals committed to a united Europe were in control of their government's foreign policies. Schuman was not the author of what became known as the Schuman Plan (that distinction went to Adenauer, Gasperi, and Monnet), but it took his name when Schuman advocated it to the French government. The Schuman Plan laid the foundation for what became known in April 1951 as the ECSC, which evolved into the European Economic Community, or Common Market, in 1958.

Although successful in promoting European economic cooperation, Schuman failed to win French support for the European Defense Community agreement in 1953 because of the inclusion of German forces in the military force and British refusal to participate. With Charles de Gaulle's rise to power and the founding of the French Fifth Republic, he concentrated more on furthering European unity. From 1958 to 1963, Schuman served as a member of the European Parliamentary Assembly and from 1958 through 1960, as its president. Schuman died on September 4, 1963, having seen the basis of the modern-day European Union and his dream of a political and economic union of the European nations become a reality.

ABC-CLIO

MARGARET THATCHER (1925–)

The first woman prime minister of the United Kingdom, Margaret Thatcher won three consecutive general elections, making her one of the longest-serving prime ministers in modern British history. Holding office for 11 years in a row, Thatcher was a towering figure who dominated British politics in the 1980s. Controversial throughout her ministry, she sought to restore British economic performance by relying on the free market and implementing a strict monetarist policy. At the same time, she stressed the importance of morality and individual responsibility in building a healthy community.

Thatcher was born Margaret Hilda Roberts on October 13, 1925, in Grantham, England, the daughter of Alfred (a grocer and town councilman) and Beatrice Roberts. A widely respected but hardly wealthy man, Alfred was nevertheless serious about providing his daughter with the best education possible. At age 11, Thatcher obtained a scholarship to Kesteven and Grantham Girls' School. In 1943, her high marks on a qualifying examination won her financial support to attend Somerville College at Oxford University. She studied chemistry and became a prominent member of the Oxford University Conservative Association.

After completing bachelor's and master's degrees in chemistry in 1947, Thatcher joined BX Plastics as a chemist at the same time that she became involved in British Conservative Party politics. After working at BX Plastics for three years, she finally decided to pursue a political career in earnest. In 1950, she took a new job with the food research laboratories at J. Lyons and Company and moved to Dartford so she could stand as a Conservative Party candidate for the parliamentary seat there. She failed to win in either the general election of 1950 or the one in 1951, and decided to study law in London instead. In 1951, she married Denis Thatcher, a successful businessman.

Passing her bar examination in 1953, Thatcher entered Lincoln's Inn where she worked on tax law. She did not give up her interest in politics and finally, in 1959, was elected to the British Parliament by the London constituency of Finchley. Thatcher won a great deal of attention, partly because women were still a rarity in the House of Commons and partly because of her keen abilities in managing government affairs. In October 1961, Conservative prime minister Harold Macmillan appointed her joint parliamentary secretary to the minister of pensions and national insurance.

After the conservatives lost the general election of 1964, Thatcher became the party's spokesperson on housing and land. After another Conservative Party defeat in 1966, she became its spokesperson on the treasury and economic affairs. Her mastery of facts and her mental sharpness made her a dangerous debater in Parliament. In 1967, she became a member of the Shadow Cabinet (the members of Parliament whom the opposition intends to install in the cabinet once it wins a general election), obtaining the shadow ministry of fuel and power. A year later, she became shadow minister of transportation, and in 1969, she became shadow minister of education. In this position, she waged a prominent attack on the British Labour Party government's scheme of amalgamating all secondary and grammar schools into "comprehensive" schools, thus abolishing Britain's two-tiered education system. Thatcher believed that large "factory-like" comprehensives would level the quality of education to a uniform mediocrity.

After the conservatives won the general election of 1970, Thatcher became minister of education. Because the government felt compelled to implement budget cuts, Thatcher believed she had to concentrate limited resources on specific priorities and end a variety of programs. She focused the government's effort on primary education and shut down programs that dispensed free milk and meals to poor students. She fought to preserve direct government grants to high-quality (private) grammar schools. She continued to oppose the development of large comprehensive (public) schools. These policies won her much unpopularity, especially among university students and much of the education establishment.

After the Conservatives lost the general election of 1974, Thatcher became assistant to the shadow chancellor of the exchequer. In this position, she made an impressive showing with her sharp criticisms of the Labour Party's fiscal policies in government. In 1975, dissatisfied with the party leadership provided by Edward Heath, rank-and-file Conservatives forced a contest for the leadership of the party. Thatcher announced her candidacy and won the party's top leadership position. Most of those who voted for her were not so much enamored with Thatcher but disgusted with Heath.

In 1979, a general election resulted in a Conservative Party victory and Thatcher became prime minister. When Thatcher took office, Britain was in the midst of what she saw as an economic and moral crisis. Unemployment was high and inflation rising. Many social critics described British society as permissive and "ungovernable." Seeking to lower inflation, Thatcher curtailed the money supply. This strict monetarist policy produced a severe depression and won her tremendous unpopularity. Nevertheless, she succeeded in bringing inflation down, forcing many to concede that she had handled the situation well. Her popularity was further buoyed in 1982, after Argentina seized Britain's Falkland Islands in the South Atlantic. Thatcher roused public opinion against the Argentines and managed the successful military campaign to recapture the islands in the short Falkland Islands War. Basking in the glow of this success, the Conservative Party maintained its control of the government in the general election of 1983.

Throughout the 1980s, Thatcher sought to enhance Britain's economic performance by unleashing the free market, thus reversing several decades of increasing government control of business designed to create a more comprehensive welfare state. She privatized public corporations and attempted to reduce the size of the public sector; she streamlined welfare and education; she cut taxes; she made war on the labor unions, particularly the miners' union, in an attempt to reduce the costs of the labor market. Thatcher constantly exhorted the British public to practice self-reliance and stop expecting the British government to solve their problems. Irritated with the interventionist pro-labor policies of local town and county councils, however, she tended to concentrate authority in the central government. At the same time, Thatcher sought to restore order in what she saw as a permissive society and inject a moralistic tone in national discussions about social problems. She strengthened the police, criminal laws, and the justice system.

Abroad, Thatcher proved a steady ally of the United States in the Cold War, enjoying a particularly close relationship with U.S. president Ronald Reagan that brought Britain back to an influential position in foreign affairs after several decades of declining importance. Her relations with Premier Mikhail Gorbachev of the disintegrating Soviet Union were warm and proved particularly useful in facilitating the end of the Cold War. At the same time, she proved suspicious of European integration and somewhat hostile to German reunification, although in both cases she was powerless to change opinions in Europe. Her position, in fact, vexed European leaders. She supported British cooperation with Europe for as long as it seemed that such cooperation would mean the extension of free enterprise across Europe, but she adamantly opposed the suggested monetary union which would create a single European currency.

The conservatives handily won a general election in 1987. Nevertheless, Thatcher's days as prime minister were numbered. Her somewhat authoritarian style antagonized a number of her ministers and Conservative Party leaders, earning her the nickname the "Iron Lady." Moreover, many within the party had never been convinced of the soundness of her policies, rejecting her plans for privatization and the dissolution of the welfare state in Britain. On top of this, the government faced unpopularity due to rising unemployment and its plans to implement a poll tax (a flat-rate charge on every adult member of a community to defray the costs of local government). In 1990, believing that they would have to drop her in order to win the next general election, Conservative Party leaders turned against Thatcher and mounted a contest for the party leadership. When it became clear that she would lose the contest, she threw her support to John Major, who eventually succeeded her.

Thatcher's legacy is complex and ambiguous. During her ministry, Britain clearly lurched rightward toward her brand of conservatism. Even after Thatcher's political demise, Major successfully continued many of her policies. The Labour Party, trounced in four straight elections (Major won another general election for the conservatives in 1992), eventually realized it had to move to the right before it finally succeeded in gaining control of the government from the Conservative Party in 1996. Thatcher's determined leadership caused many to question the soundness of the British welfare state, which politicians had been erecting in Britain since the end of World War II.

Thatcher continues to exert an indirect influence on politics in Britain. Elevated to the House of Lords as the Baroness of Kevesten shortly after her resignation as party leader, both the press and the public continue to look to her for guidance on the important issues of the day. She became in the 1990s Britain's foremost elder statesman, although declining health in recent years has silenced her voice.

ABC-CLIO

DOCUMENT: ELYSÉE TREATY (1963)

Negotiated by French president Charles de Gaulle and German chancellor Konrad Adenauer, the Elysée Treaty (also known as the Franco-German Cooperation Treaty) ended years of conflict and pledged an accord of friendship between the two European countries when it was signed on January 22, 1963. In the century prior to the treaty, France and Germany had been on opposite sides in three wars: the Franco-Prussian War, World War I, and World War II. Together with the Rome Treaty (1957), the Elysée Treaty helped facilitate the establishment of the European Union.

TREATY BETWEEN THE REPUBLIC AND THE FEDERAL REPUBLIC OF GERMANY ON FRENCH-GERMAN COOPERATION

Following the Common Declaration of the President of the French Republic and the Chancellor of the Federal Republic of Germany, dated January 22, 1963, on the organization and the principles of the cooperation between the two States, the following provisions have been agreed upon:

I. Organization

1. The Heads of State and Government will give whenever required the necessary directives and will follow regularly the implementation of the program set hereinunder. They will meet for this purpose whenever this is necessary and, in principle, at least twice a year.

2. The Ministers of Foreign Affairs will see to the implementation of the program as a whole. They will meet at least once every three months. Without prejudice to the contacts normally established through the channels of the embassies, high officials of the two Ministries of Foreign Affairs, responsible respectively for political, economic and cultural affairs, will meet each month in Paris and Bonn alternately to survey current problems and to prepare the Ministers' meeting. In addition, the diplomatic missions and the consulates of the two countries, and also the permanent missions to the international organizations, will make all the necessary contacts on the problems of common interest.

3. Regular meetings will take place between the responsible authorities of the two countries in the fields of defense, education and youth. These meetings will not in any way affect the functioning of the already existing bodies—French-German Cultural Commission, Permanent General Staff Group—whose activities will on the contrary be extended. Both the Ministers of Foreign Affairs will be represented at these meetings in order to ensure the overall coordination of the cooperation.

(a) The Ministers of the Armed Forces or of Defense will meet at least once every three months. Similarly, the French Minister of National Education will meet, at the same intervals, with the person who will be designated by Germany to follow up the program of cooperation on the cultural level.

(b) The Chiefs of Staff of the two countries will meet at least once every two months; in the event of their being unable to meet, they will be replaced by their responsible representatives.

(c) The French High Commissioner for Youth and Sports will meet, at least once every two months, with the Federal Minister for Family and Youth Affairs or his representative.

4. In each of the countries, an interministerial commission will be charged with following problems of cooperation. It will be presided over by a high Foreign Ministry official and it will include representatives of all the administrations concerned. Its role will be to coordinate the action of the Ministries concerned and to report periodically to its Government on the state of French-German cooperation. It will also have the task of presenting all useful suggestions with a view to implementing the program of cooperation and to its ultimate extension to new domains.

II. Program

A. Foreign Affairs

1. The two Governments will consult each other, prior to any decision, on all important questions of foreign policy, and in the first place on questions of common interest, with a view to arriving, insofar as possible, at a similar position.

This consultation will cover, among other subjects, the following:

—Problems relative to the European Communities and to European political cooperation;

—East-West relations, both on the political and economic levels;

—Subjects dealt with in the North Atlantic Treaty Organization and the various international organizations in which the two Governments are interested, notably the Council of Europe, Western European Union, the Organization for Economic Cooperation and Development, the United Nations and its specialized agencies.

2. The cooperation already established in the area of information will be continued and developed between the services concerned in Paris and Bonn and between the diplomatic missions in other countries.

3. With regard to aid to the emergent countries, both Governments will systematically compare their programs with a view to maintaining close cooperation. They will study the possibility of engaging in joint undertakings. Since several Ministerial departments are responsible for these matters in both France and Germany, it will be the duty of the two Ministries of Foreign Affairs to determine together the practical bases for this cooperation.

4. The two Governments will study together the means for strengthening their cooperation in other important sectors of economic policy, such as agricultural and forest policy; energy policy; communications and transportation problems and industrial development, within the framework of the Common Market; as well as export credits policy.

B. Defense

1. The following objectives will be pursued in this domain:

(a) On the level of strategy and tactics, the competent authorities of both countries will endeavor to harmonize their doctrines with a view to arriving at mutual concepts. French-German institutes for operational research will be created.

(b) Exchanges of personnel between the armed forces will be increased. These particularly concern professors and students from the general staff schools. They may include temporary detachments of entire units. In order to facilitate these exchanges, an effort will be made on both sides to give the trainees practical language instruction.

(c) With regard to armaments, both Governments will endeavor to organize a joint program from the time of drafting appropriate armaments projects and formulating financing plans.

To this end, joint committees will study the research being conducted on these projects in both countries and will carry out a comparative study. They will submit proposals to the Ministers, who will examine them during their quarterly meetings and will give the necessary directives for implementation.

C. Education and Youth

With regard to education and youth, the proposals contained in the French and German memoranda of September 19 and November 8, 1962 will be studied, in accordance with the procedures indicated hereinabove.

1. In the field of education, the effort will chiefly concern the following points:

(a) Language instruction:

The two Government recognize the essential importance that the knowledge in each of the two countries of the other's language holds for French-German cooperation. They will endeavor, to this end, to take concrete measures with a view to increasing the number of German students learning the French language and that of French students learning the German language.

The Federal Government will examine, with the governments of the Laender competent in this matter, how it is possible to introduce regulations making it possible to achieve this objective.

In all the establishments for higher education, practical courses in French will be organized in Germany and practical courses in German will be organized in France, which will be open to all students.

(b) The problem of equivalences:

The competent authorities of both countries will be asked to accelerate the adoption of provisions concerning the equivalence of academic periods, examinations and university degrees and diplomas.

(c) Cooperation in scientific research:

Research bodies and scientific institutes will increase their contacts, beginning with more extensive reciprocal information. Concerted research programs will be established in the areas in which it will appear possible.

2. All opportunities will be offered to the young people of both countries in order to draw closer the ties that unite them and to strengthen their mutual cooperation. Collective exchanges, particularly, will be increased.

A body whose purpose will develop these possibilities and promote exchanges will be created by the two countries with an autonomous administrative council at its head. This body will have at its disposal a joint French-German fund for the exchanges between the two countries of pupils, students, young artists and workers.

III. Final Provisions

1. The necessary directives will be given in each country for the immediate enactment of the preceding. The Minister of Foreign Affairs will examine the progress made at each of their meetings.

2. The two Governments will keep the Governments of the member States of the European Communities informed on the development of French-German cooperation.

3. With the exception of the provisions concerning defense, the present Treaty will also be applied to the Land of Berlin, barring a contrary declaration made by the Government of the federal Republic of Germany or the government of the French Republic in the three months following the entry into force of the present Treaty.

4. The two Governments may make any improvements which might appear desirable for the implementation of the present Treaty.

5. The present treaty will enter into force as soon as each of the two Governments will have made known to the other that, on the domestic level, the necessary conditions for its implementation have been fulfilled.

Done at Paris on the twenty-second day of January in the year one thousand nine hundred and sixty-three, in both the French and German languages, both texts being equally authentic.

The President of the French Republic: Charles de Gaulle

The French Premier: Georges Pompidou

The French Minister of Foreign Affairs: Maurice Couve de Murville

The Federal Minister of Foreign Affairs, of the Federal Republic of Germany: Gerhard Schroeder

10

The Arab-Israeli Conflict, 1948–Present

INTRODUCTION

Conflict in the area commonly known as Palestine, and now occupied by both Israel and the Palestine Authority, dates back to biblical times, when Isaac, son of Abraham, set up a Jewish state, and Ishmael, an early symbolic leader to the Arabs, established an Arab presence in the same territory at the eastern end of the Mediterranean. At the end of World War I, the British received a mandate to govern Palestine, and many European Jews, influenced by the Zionist movement promoting Jewish nationalism, immigrated to Palestine in the face of growing anti-Semitism in Germany and other parts of Europe. As a result, Jewish population in Palestine rose from 56,000 in 1920 to 650,000 in 1948. When armed conflict broke out, British forces withdrew, and the United Nations (UN) created the state of Israel in 1948 over Arab objections.

The Israelis won the war that followed, as well as three subsequent ones, and acquired a significant amount of territory that the Palestinians had occupied, including Gaza, on the border with Egypt, and the West Bank (of the Jordan River), which had been attached to the nation of Jordan. These territorial acquisitions did nothing to ease hostility in the region, and the conflict continues into the twenty-first century.

One vexing diplomatic question that arises from this situation concerns the status of the Palestinians. In the mid-1990s, the Palestinians were given a degree of autonomy over Gaza and the West Bank and established the Palestine National Authority to govern these areas. Some 100 nations recognize Palestine as an "independent" nation, whereas others, including the United States, do not but accept the notion that there eventually will be an independent Palestine. There has been some movement in that direction. The Palestine National Authority became a nonvoting member of the UN General Assembly in 1998 but does not have the level of recognition necessary to sell bonds or buy weapons openly in the global market. In contrast, Israel was widely recognized at the time of its independence in 1948, which allowed it to buy the arms necessary to prevail in the war against its Arab neighbors in 1949.

The diplomatic process that led to the creation of the nation of Israel began in 1917 with the so-called Balfour Declaration, named for Arthur James Balfour, then the British foreign secretary. The declaration came in the form of a letter, dated November 3, 1917, to Lord Rothschild, the chair of the British Zionist federation. Balfour's letter indicated that the British favored a Jewish national homeland in Palestine.

After the Balfour Declaration, Arab-Jewish conflict over Palestine sharpened. Jewish settlements were attacked as early as February 1920, and 46 Jews were killed in Arab riots in Hebron and Jerusalem in April of that year. More serious riots took place in August 1928, following the spread of false rumors that the Jews were planning to build a temple at the Wailing Wall in Jerusalem, a site equally venerated by Jews and Muslims. As World War II approached in the late 1930s, Axis powers funded a new wave of Arab riots in Palestine in which 5,000 Arabs and several hundred Jews were killed.

The horrors of the Holocaust convinced Jews and their supporters that unless Jews had a homeland of their own, another Holocaust could happen. The British, frustrated by Arab-Jewish rivalry in Palestine, returned their mandate to the UN, which approved the UN Partition Resolution in November, based on the report of a Special Committee on Palestine (UNSCOP) that recommended the partition of Palestine between Arabs and Jews and making Jerusalem an international city. Arab governments rejected the plan, and more riots and bombings in and around Jerusalem ensued. On May 15, 1948, after months of preparation, the British left Palestine, and Israel officially became an independent state. The United States and the Soviet Union announced their diplomatic recognition, but most Arab nations, including Saudi Arabia, Lebanon, Jordan, Egypt, Syria, and Iraq, declared war on the new state. After about a year of intermittent fighting broken by truces, both sides, in separate agreements, consented to an armistice that left Israel with considerably more territory than the original UN resolution had granted it. One consequence of this was that the region was left with about 860,000 Palestinian refugees.

The decade of the 1950s in the region was highlighted by a 1952 revolt in Egypt against British rule, the deposition of King Farouk, and the rise to power of the charismatic Gamal Abdel Nasser in 1954. In 1956, Nasser, facing economic sanctions and hostility from the United States, France, and Great Britain, nationalized the Suez Canal. In this affair, which soon became known as the Suez crisis, Israel invaded the Sinai Peninsula for several months, with the tacit support of the major Western powers. The occupation ended with the arrival of a UN peacekeeping force, and the canal reopened in May 1957. Later that year, Fatah (a word that in Arabic means "conquest"), was informally organized as a group dedicated to Israel's destruction. In May 1964, the Palestine Liberation Organization (PLO), a more formal organization than Fatah but one also bent on the destruction of Israel, was formed, with Yasser Arafat as its leader.

In 1967, the Six-Day War took place. Israel's military forces easily overran those of Egypt and Syria in this short war, leading to Israeli occupation of the Golan Heights on the Syrian border and a large portion of the Sinai Peninsula between Egypt and Israel, as well as parts of the West Bank (then under Jordanian control), along the Jordan River. Israel's assumption of territorial control in these areas created thousands of Palestinian refugees, and also a new wave of Palestinian nationalism and a hardening of attitudes between Israel and the Palestinians. In the wake of the war, the PLO became recognized as the legitimate representative of the Palestinian people.

Following years of tension and arms buildup, another war broke out in October 1973, when Egypt and Syria launched a surprise attack on Israel during the Jewish religious holiday known as Yom Kippur. Fighting lasted about two weeks before each side agreed to a UN Security Council ceasefire. Following the ceasefire, a major diplomatic initiative featuring U.S. Secretary of State Henry Kissinger got underway. Kissinger,

This photograph shows the proclamation of the state of Israel in May 1948, following years of Jewish migration to the region and conflict with neighboring Arabs. Although most Western nations gave diplomatic recognition to Israel rather quickly, Arab nations did not, and what is known as the Arab-Israeli conflict has continued into the 21st century. (AFP/Getty Images)

engaging in what became known as "shuttle diplomacy," failed to bring about a permanent peace in the region, but he was able to restore U.S.-Egyptian relations and increase the amount of foreign aid to Egypt. Upset by Egypt's move toward better relations with the United States, other Arab leaders organized an oil embargo against the United States, Western Europe, and Japan from November 1973 to March 1974.

U.S. diplomacy in the region remained active after 1974, and in 1978, President Jimmy Carter brought both Israeli Prime Minister Menachem Begin and Egyptian President Anwar Sadat to the presidential retreat known as Camp David not far from Washington, D.C. What resulted from three days of intensive negotiation between the two adversaries, with Carter acting as a mediator, was known as the Camp David Accords. These included a framework for peace between Egypt and Israel and another for a more broadly based Middle East settlement. The official state of war between Israel and Egypt was ended, diplomatic relations were resumed, and Israel agreed to return much of the Sinai Peninsula that it had taken in 1967. Although these talks represented a high point in Carter's presidency, the accords failed to bring about a lasting Middle East peace.

Despite the failure to achieve peace in the Middle East, the Camp David Accords, especially the Egypt-Israel Peace Treaty, did produce a new, more cordial relationship between Egypt and Israel. Israel did evacuate the Sinai Peninsula, and Israeli ships began passing through the Suez Canal. Israeli tourists came to Egypt to see the pyramids and other well-known sites, a smaller number of Egyptians visited Israel, and the Egyptian press relaxed its criticism of Israel. But Prime Minister Begin accelerated the construction of residences for Jews in Judea and Samaria, feeling that it was necessary for the maintenance of peace and justifiable compensation for the return of Sinai. This move worried President Carter, who voiced his concern about the impact on long-term peace in the region.

The assassination of Anwar Sadat in October 1981 changed the tone of Egyptian-Israeli relations. Hosni Mubarak, Sadat's successor, maintained the façade of cordiality, but a chill in official relations encouraged rising anti-Israeli sentiment in the media. Meanwhile, the new U.S. president, Ronald Reagan, sold AWACS surveillance planes to Saudi Arabia, a move that Israel regarded as threatening. As a consequence, Israel attacked PLO forces in Lebanon preemptively and in June 1982 launched an invasion of Lebanon that forced the PLO to evacuate to Tunisia.

After the expulsion of the PLO to Tunisia, Israeli troops continued their occupation of Lebanon. During this time, the newly elected Lebanese president, Bashir Gemayel, was assassinated, and an Israeli-sponsored atrocity resulted in the deaths of more than 700 unarmed Palestinians in refugee camps. An official investigation placed the blame on Israel, bringing about Begin's resignation in September 1983. In that same month, more than 240 U.S. Marines were killed when a suicide bomber drove an explosive-laden truck into their Beirut compound. The Marines had been part of a peacekeeping operation that had replaced Israeli forces in Lebanon several months earlier. President Reagan withdrew the remaining U.S. forces in February 1984.

After a few years of relative calm, violence came again with what is called the First Intifada. In October 1987, Palestinians rose up in protest against Israel's continuing occupation, and Israeli military forces responded by killing perhaps 1,000 Palestinians and arresting many others. The increasing hostility led to the formation of the anti-Israel organization known as the Hamas Muslim Brotherhood (or simply Hamas) in January 1988 and the declaration of Palestinian independence by the PLO the following November.

In September 1993, a peace conference in Oslo, Norway, resulted in the Oslo Declaration of Principles in which Israel and Palestine agreed to recognize each other diplomatically, and the PLO was allowed to return to Gaza. For its part, the PLO agreed to remove those parts of its charter referring to the destruction of the state of Israel. Other parts of the declaration altered the conditions of Israel's occupation of Palestinian territory.

Not all Israelis were happy with the Oslo agreement, and one disgruntled settler shot and killed 29 Muslims praying at a mosque in Hebron. This provoked retaliation in the form of a number of deadly Hamas suicide bombings directed at Israeli buses in 1994. In November 1995, Prime Minister Yitzhak Rabin, whose conciliatory policies angered ultra-conservatives, was assassinated by one of them.

Meanwhile, Israeli-Palestinian violence continued. In January 1996, Israeli operatives assassinated a leading Palestinian terrorist, who became an instant martyr, and a month later, a new wave of Hamas suicide bomber attacks broke out. The high level of violence may have spurred the election of Benjamin Netanyahu, leader of the conservative Likud party, to the post of prime minister in June 1996.

The year 2000 saw the beginning of the Second Intifada, a new wave of violence, this time linked to Fatah, another strongly anti-Israel organization. As usual, Israel responded with force, and over the next few years, more than 1,000 Israelis and nearly 5,000 Palestinians were killed. Various efforts at peace talks sponsored by Mubarak of Egypt and by George Mitchell, the Clinton administration's envoy to the Middle East, were largely unsuccessful.

During the first decade of the twenty-first century, little progress was made in solving the Israeli-Palestinian dispute. In January 2002, President George W. Bush called for Israel's withdrawal from occupied Palestinian territory and the creation of a Palestinian state. But his insistence that current Palestinian leaders be replaced scuttled the agreement. The apparent U.S. tilt toward Palestine, moreover, caused Israel to strengthen its position in occupied Palestine by encouraging Israeli settlers to move into occupied areas and by beginning to build a security fence.

A hopeful sign came in May 2005 when President Bush hosted Palestinian leader Mahmoud Abbas at the White House. The United States promised Abbas some $50 million in aid and suggested a settlement based on the borders drawn after the 1949 war. Israel responded by releasing 400 Palestinian prisoners and promising to withdraw from certain areas of the West Bank. But acts of violence continued on both sides, along with varying degrees of Israeli occupation of the West Bank and Gaza. During the remainder of the Bush administration, the same patterns continued. Incidents of Hamas violence, Israeli retaliation, and abortive peace conferences accomplished nothing of consequence.

With Barack Obama's election as president in November 2008, many observers, especially in the Arab world, hoped for significant change in U.S. policy, but violence involving rocket attacks from Gaza into the neighboring Israeli countryside and consequent Israeli air strikes into Gaza indicated a high level of continuing violence. President Obama's speech in Cairo in June 2009 seemed to offer hope for peace when he called for an end to Israel's residential construction program in occupied areas and Arab recognition of Israel, but as of 2011, the dispute was as intractable as ever.

INTERPRETIVE ESSAY

TIMOTHY K. WELLIVER

The dispute between Israel and the Arabs is over a parcel of land smaller than Massachusetts. Yet it is one of the most significant confrontations in modern history. The death toll in the wars has been estimated in the vicinity of 100,000, over a period of more than 60 years. In terms of casualties, this puts the conflict far down in the rankings of late-twentieth- and early-twenty-first-century wars, behind the conflicts in Korea, Vietnam, Cambodia, southern Sudan, the Congo, and Afghanistan, to name a few. But the Arab-Israeli conflict has had widespread and enduring political, economic, religious and emotional consequences. In part this is the result of its duration; practically no other armed conflict in the modern era has lasted this long. The fight has taken place in a strategically important part of the world, astride major sea lanes and close to the largest oil fields on earth. Furthermore, it involves issues of national identity and religion that concern a large portion of the world's population.

ISRAEL AND THE PALESTINIANS

The two peoples most affected by the conflict—Israeli Jews and Palestinians—harbor a great deal of bitterness toward each other. Much of the bitterness of the conflict is a result of the suffering of civilians from communal violence, political violence, terrorist attacks, reprisals, and dispossessions. Communal violence, starting as riots directed at Jews, broke out in the early years of the British mandate. The 1936–1939 Arab revolt saw the first guerilla activity. In the 1940s, radical Zionist groups used terrorist tactics against both the British and Arabs in their drive to create an independent Jewish state. During the 1948–1949 war, Jewish and Arab civilians were killed deliberately by both guerilla groups and regular armies.

But the human cost of the Arab-Israeli conflict goes well beyond the number of casualties. Huge numbers of people were displaced in the 1948–1949 war. Some 860,000 refugees fled their homes in what became Israel to Gaza, the West Bank, and surrounding Arab states. By 2010, they, with their descendants, numbered close to five million, 1.4 million of whom lived in refugee camps, cared for by the United Nations Relief and Works Agency (UNRWA) at a cost of more than $600 million per year. Simultaneously, a nearly equivalent number of Jews were emigrating from Arab and Muslim countries, although this process was spread over three decades. They were encouraged to come by the Israeli government and by persecution in many Arab states. For both populations, the wrenching move meant leaving behind their homes and livelihoods. In Israel, immigrants from Arab and other Muslim countries (known as Mizrahi Jews) faced a difficult assimilation process, discrimination and lower living standards than Jews whose roots were in Russia and the West. Meanwhile, those Arabs who remained in Israel during the war were granted Israeli citizenship, constituting around 20 percent of the population today. Arabs and Jews in Israel in theory have equal legal and political rights, but Arab Israelis face discrimination in many situations.

Palestinians in the Gaza Strip and the West Bank were in a quite different situation. When Israel captured these territories in 1967, the residents found themselves under military occupation. Israel encouraged Jews to settle in these territories, especially the West Bank. At first this activity was relatively restricted, but once the right-wing Likud gained power in the government in 1977, the settlement activity accelerated dramatically. As of 1987, there were 60,000 Jewish settlers in dozens of settlements in the West Bank. By 2010, this number had grown to about half a million, including Jews living in East Jerusalem, which Israel unilaterally annexed. Arab residents in the occupied territories have been, at various times, subject to onerous restrictions. Curfews, school and university closings, detentions without trial, and limitations on movement have all been used by Israeli authorities to control the population. During the first Intifada, which erupted in 1987, Israeli Defense Forces (IDF) used shootings, beatings, arrests, and the bulldozing of homes to try to quell the stone-throwing youths. More than 1,000 Palestinians were killed. Conditions did not necessarily improve with the signing of the 1993 Oslo Accords. While the new Palestinian Authority began to administer some parts of the West Bank and Gaza, the settlements remained, and IDF checkpoints limited Palestinian movement. When the second Intifada began in 2000, the occupied territories experienced even worse violence. This time Palestinians used firearms and suicide bombings to attack Israelis, who retaliated with air strikes against the Palestinians. More than 6,000 Palestinians and 1,000 Israelis died. For the most part, the peace process died as well.

In 2003, the Israeli government, under Prime Minister Ariel Sharon, began to build a "separation" barrier to control all movement between the West Bank and Israel. Sharon's plan was to improve Israeli security—in the absence of any progress in peace negotiations—by disentangling the Jewish and Arab populations in the occupied territories. As of 2011, this has further increased the hardships of Palestinians, many of whom have found themselves separated from their jobs, their fields, or their schools. On the other hand, the wave of terrorist attacks in Israel has for the most part ended. In 2005, Sharon unilaterally withdrew 9,000 Jewish settlers from the Gaza Strip and then pulled the IDF back as well, effectively giving local control to the Palestinian Authority. But the radical Hamas party seized control of the territory in 2007. The Israelis, with the support of Egypt, Europe, and the United States, imposed a stringent blockade on the territory. This was intended not only to prevent military supplies from reaching the militants, who were firing rockets into Israel but also to punish the civilian population for having supported Hamas. The blockade reduced imports to one-fourth their previous level. Despite some smuggling through tunnels from Egypt, the result has been severe poverty for the people in the territory. In 2010, Israel and Egypt began easing the blockade, allowing more consumer goods to enter.

THE REFUGEES, TERRORISM, AND PALESTINIAN STRUGGLE

For Palestinians living outside Israel and the occupied territories, the situation was completely different. For most refugees, decades of living in refugee camps lay ahead. Aside from those in Jordan, refugees were not granted citizenship rights in the host country. For example, Palestinian refugees in Lebanon were (with the exception of the Christians among them) not granted citizenship, and it was illegal for them to hold jobs. On the other hand, Palestinians have clung fiercely to their identity and to their dream of returning to their homes one day: they have not been particularly interested in assuming a Lebanese or Jordanian identity.

In the 1950s and 1960s, various groups of Arab fighters, known as *fedayeen*, continued to attack Israelis from neighboring territories. In two decades, they caused several hundred Israeli deaths, some of them civilian. Israel frequently launched reprisal raids, sometimes also killing civilians. In the aftermath of the devastating Arab defeat in the Six-Day War of 1967, various *fedayeen* factions—such as al-Fatah, Popular Front for the Liberation of Palestine and Democratic Front for the Liberation of Palestine—were brought under the umbrella of the recently created Palestine Liberation Organization (PLO). Yasser Arafat, the head of al-Fatah, the largest faction in the PLO, became chairman in 1969. It was at this point as well that *fedayeen* groups began to internationalize the conflict. Hijacking commercial aircraft proved to be an effective way to draw attention to the cause. The most dramatic hijacking occurred in 1970 when the Popular Front for the Liberation of Palestine simultaneously hijacked four airliners, dramatically blowing three of them up on an airstrip in Jordan, after removing the passengers. This incident, and the real threat that *fedayeen* groups posed to his reign, led King Hussein of Jordan to attack the camps with his army and expel the PLO leadership. In this battle, known to the Palestinians as "Black September," at least 3,000 Palestinians perished, including untold numbers of civilians. The PLO and many of its fighters then established themselves in Lebanon.

While *fedayeen* attacks continued in Israel itself, the field of *fedayeen* operations became global in the early 1970s. In 1972, a group calling itself Black September tried to take members of the Israeli Olympic team hostage in Munich. The incident, broadcast on worldwide television, ended with 11 Israelis dead. In 1976, a team of Palestinian and German radicals hijacked an Air France passenger jet and forced it to fly to Entebbe airport in Uganda. The crew and Jewish passengers, more than 100 in all, were held hostage until most were dramatically rescued by Israeli commandos. Although they provoked international condemnation, such operations were successful in attracting attention to the grievances of the Palestinians. The PLO was granted observer status in the United Nations in 1974, and recognized as the sole representative of the Palestinian people.

Nevertheless, such attention did not translate into tangible progress in achieving the aims of the PLO and other Palestinian factions. Indeed, with the Egypt-Israel peace treaty (1979), and the 1982 removal of the PLO leadership to Tunisia, the achievement of the PLO's aims seemed more remote than ever. Thus during the 1980s and 1990s, Yasser Arafat and the PLO gradually took steps to renounce the use of terrorist tactics, recognize the state of Israel, and amend its charter to remove clauses denying the legitimacy of Israel and calling for armed struggle against it. The United States and Israel insisted that these moves be taken as preconditions to negotiating openly with the PLO, and they ultimately resulted in the Oslo Accords and subsequent agreements between the PLO and Israel.

But if the PLO was moving away from terrorism, other groups were more than happy to take its place. In Lebanon, the Israeli invasion of 1982 triggered the emergence of Hezbollah, a militant Islamic movement based among the Shiite population in southern Lebanon. Supported by Iran and Syria, Hezbollah soon became the most active faction in attacking Israeli forces in southern Lebanon. Israel launched major offensives in 1993, 1996, and 2000 to try to root out Hezbollah guerillas. In each case, Israeli forces attacked civilian infrastructure in Lebanon that caused numerous civilian casualties but failed to defeat Hezbollah.

Ironically, the Oslo peace process in the 1990s helped trigger a renewed outbreak of violence and terrorism, this time by rejectionists opposed to the emerging two-state solution to the conflict. Much of this opposition was articulated in religious rhetoric. Extremist Jews were responsible for the killings of 29 Muslim worshippers in Hebron in 1994 and the assassination of Israeli Prime Minister Yitzhak Rabin in 1995. Meanwhile Palestinian extremist groups—the Islamic Resistance Movement (Hamas) and Palestinian Islamic Jihad—increasingly resorted to suicide bombings in attacking Israeli targets. In many ways, the extremists succeeded. Israeli willingness to transfer power and land to Arafat's new Palestinian Authority nearly evaporated. Peace negotiations broke down, and the second Intifada erupted.

Hamas and Hezbollah have employed missiles to attack Israel, often killing or injuring civilians. In contrast to the international terrorists of the 1970s, however, these groups rarely undertake operations outside Israel, Lebanon, and the occupied territories. The Israelis, for their part, have attacked civilian targets in their battles against these groups. In Israel's 2006 invasion of Lebanon, directed against Hezbollah, Israeli forces attacked bridges and infrastructure, schools and hospitals, and even put the Beirut airport out of commission. More than 1,000 Lebanese civilians were killed—at least twice the combatant death toll. Similarly, in its attack on the Hamas-controlled Gaza Strip in 2008–2009, Israeli forces killed many hundreds of civilians.

The rise of Hamas and Hezbollah in the 1980s underscores a clear trend in the Arab-Israeli conflict: that opposition to Israel is more and more expressed in religious terms. The secular Palestinian al-Fatah movement has lost much of its influence to the Islamist Hamas movement, losing the 2006 election for the Palestinian National Authority, and subsequently losing control over the Gaza Strip. Opposition to Israel figures prominently in the rhetoric of al-Qaeda, and the Islamic Republic of Iran has provided aid to both Hamas and Hezbollah. Iran's implacable stance against Israel is a key motivation in attempts by the United States and its allies to block Iran from acquiring nuclear weapons. The fear is that a state or a terrorist organization that is driven by religious zealotry could not be deterred from using such weapons against Israel, even under threat of retaliation.

ISRAEL

This long history of military threats and terrorism has had profound effects on Israel. Israel has spent its entire existence in a state of war with some or all of its neighbors. Although for most of this period, there was no active fighting, three of the five states that fought Israel in 1948 have not signed peace treaties with the Jewish state. And although Israel is the dominant military power in the region, this does not seem to alleviate the existential fears of the Israeli public, fears that are easily exploited by politicians. The Arab states cannot be said to pose a military threat to Israel, but fear of guerilla operations and terrorist attacks is a constant presence in Israeli life. Israel's very identity is intertwined with a narrative of survival in the face of implacable foes bent on the destruction of the Jewish State. Central to this narrative, of course, is the legacy of the Holocaust. This powerful discourse has profound effects on Israeli culture, politics, and interactions with the outside world. It was hardly alleviated by the peace treaties with Jordan and Egypt or the creation of a Palestinian Authority under the Oslo process. Yasser Arafat was never trusted, even by left-wing Israelis, and new enemies—Hamas, Hezbollah, and Iran, with their fierce rhetoric of destruction—took the place of Arab states in the nightmares of the Israeli public.

Israelis cite security concerns (along with biblical interpretations and Zionist ideology) to justify the expansion of settlements in occupied territories. They justify the human rights violations of the occupation. Obsession with security means that Israel's enemies have always paid a heavy price for Jewish lives, as demonstrated by the violent invasions of Lebanon in 2006 and Gaza in 2009. And it means that critics of the government's policies are accused of weakening Israel's security or even desiring its destruction. Most of the world—with the exception of the United States—is assumed to be antagonistic to Israel. Israelis see the United Nations (UN), in particular, as consistently hostile. In 1975, the General Assembly famously passed a resolution declaring Zionism to be a form of racism. The UN rescinded the resolution in 1991 so that Israel would agree to participate in that year's Madrid peace conference. Over the decades, dozens of other General Assembly resolutions have criticized Israeli policies. The United States has usually vetoed similar condemnations in the Security Council. Israel's diplomatic isolation contributes to its refusal to alter policies in response to international criticism, which in turn elicits more international hostility.

Although normally presenting a united front toward the outside world, the Israeli public and its leaders have long been divided over how to approach territorial and security questions. Because of his participation in the Oslo peace process, Prime Minister Yitzhak Rabin lost his life to an assassin's bullets in 1995. Fortunately, Israel's fractious politics are rarely so violent, but they can be unpredictable at times. In 2005, Israel's largest right-wing party, Likud, split over policies toward the Palestinians. The moderate wing of the party, led by Prime Minister Ariel Sharon, formed the new Kadima party in 2005 when Likud refused to support his "unilateral disengagement plan" in the Gaza Strip. When joined by supporters from the old Labor party, the centrist Kadima soon became the largest party in the Knesset. In the 2009 elections, the once-dominant Labor Party won less than 10 percent of the vote, and in 2011, it suffered a split, sinking it into near irrelevance.

THE ARAB WORLD

The conflict over Israel/Palestine has had an immeasurable impact on the Arab world, particularly those countries that have participated in the wars. In the first place, the conflict has directly undermined their political stability. The humiliating defeat of the Arabs in the 1948–1949 war contributed to the fall of at least three Arab leaders. It brought about the first of a series of military coups in Syria. It also contributed to the eventual overthrow of King Farouk of Egypt in a military coup, resulting in Gamal Abdel Nasser's rise to power. Both Syria and Egypt have spent the better part of the past 60 years under authoritarian rule by military officers. King Abdullah I of Jordan, viewed as a traitor by many Palestinians, was assassinated in 1951. His grandson Hussein, who was at his side when he was killed, assumed the throne in 1952. Hussein continued Abdullah's moderate stance toward Israel, maintained close relations with the United States, and sought to maintain Jordanian control over the West Bank. For this he faced many assassination attempts during his long reign.

Not surprisingly, support for the Palestinian cause has been strongest among Arab states, and hostility toward Israel was often one of the few things most Arabs could agree on. The Arab League officially began an economic and diplomatic boycott of Israel in 1948. In its heyday from the 1940s to the 1970s, the economic boycott not only shut off trade between Israel and the Arab world but also sought to prevent companies from other countries from doing business with Israel. If a company, such as Coca-Cola, sold its products in Israel, it was banned from the Arab market. Thus for many years Pepsi Cola was ubiquitous in Arab countries while its principal rival was unavailable. Similarly, McDonald's chose to do business in the Arab world and did not have franchises in Israel until 1993. Although the boycott did make life more difficult for Israel, it did not have the desired result of undermining American and European support for their ally. In theory, the boycott remains in force, but most Arab states observe it only when convenient. Many of these states relaxed their policies after the signing of the Oslo Accords in 1993.

Indeed the much-vaunted dream of Arab unity has been in decline for some time. The Arab scholar Fouad Ajami points to the shattering Arab defeat in the 1967 Six-Day War as the turning point. It was then, he says, that the "grimness" came to Arab politics. Military dictators ruled with an iron fist. Lebanon was plunged into civil war when the arrival of PLO fighters from Jordan tipped the delicate ethnic balance in Lebanon's political structure. The Lebanese civil war raged from 1975 to 1990, pitted Arab against Arab, and may have cost more than 200,000 lives. In a bid to destroy the PLO bases in Lebanon, Israel invaded the country in 1978 and again in 1982. Israeli forces overran all of southern Lebanon and forced the evacuation of PLO leaders and fighters. Soon thereafter, the Israelis allowed Lebanese Christian militia to attack the refugee camps of Sabra and Shatila, where they killed many hundreds, and possibly thousands, of Palestinian civilians. Three years later, the same refugee camps came under attack by the Lebanese Amal militia, with a death toll in the thousands.

Perhaps the greatest blow to the myth of Arab unity came in 1979 when Anwar Sadat signed a peace treaty with Israel, as part of the Camp David Accords. Egypt was quickly suspended from the Arab League, which moved its headquarters out of Cairo. Egypt's suspension lasted for 10 years. Sadat was assassinated in 1981 by a group of Egyptian soldiers belonging to a radical Islamist group that later evolved into the Egyptian Islamic Jihad, which then merged with al-Qaeda. The same group later attempted to assassinate Sadat's successor, Hosni Mubarak. Nonetheless, Egypt held to its treaty with Israel, maintaining correct if not warm diplomatic relations. After the 1993 Oslo Accords, Jordan signed a similar peace treaty with Israel. Morocco and three Gulf states also recognized Israel but later broke off ties in protest of Israeli policies.

Superpower rivalries exploited and exacerbated divisions in the Arab world. During the Cold War, the Soviet Union took advantage of the growing American support for Israel by expanding its influence among Arab states. Soviet weapons, along with advisors, provided the backbone of the Syrian, Egyptian, and Iraqi armies. Superpower machinations played a role in the outbreak of both the 1956 Suez Crisis and the 1967 Six-Day War. The 1973 Yom Kippur War threatened to escalate into a dangerous confrontation between the United States and the Soviet Union. The states most hostile toward Israel at various times—Syria, Iraq under Saddam Hussein, Egypt under Nasser, Libya under Qaddafi—also had closer ties to the Soviet Union. On the other hand, the more moderate Arab states, such as the Gulf States, Jordan, and Egypt since Sadat, tended to have warmer relations with the United States and Western Europe. But long after the Cold War ended, many of these divisions remained. As of 2011, Syria represents the most inflexible stance toward Israel, while Jordan has remained (out of necessity) the most accommodating.

THE WIDER WORLD

The Arab-Israeli conflict has long been of primary concern to peoples and governments far beyond Israel and the Arab states. For example, the conflict has on occasion had huge repercussions for the world economy. During the Suez Crisis of 1956, Egypt blocked the entrance to the canal, resulting in a 10 percent reduction in world oil supply. In Europe, people queued for gasoline, businesses closed, and heat was cut. World trade dropped, perhaps contributing to the recession of 1957–1958. Egypt again cut off the canal in the 1967 Six-Day War. For eight years, shipping was forced to take the long route around Africa, costing the world some $8 billion in increased shipping expenses and reducing the economic growth of South Asian countries. It also created the first of several "oil shocks" in Europe.

During the October (Yom Kippur) War of 1973, in reaction to American shipments of military supplies to Israel, the Organization of Petroleum Exporting Countries implemented a total embargo on sales to the United States and the Netherlands, and reduced supplies and raised prices for oil shipments to other European countries and Japan. Crude oil prices quadrupled on world markets. In the United States, price controls and lower speed limits were imposed, but gasoline supplies remained tight. With the Israeli withdrawal from the Suez Canal the embargo was lifted. Although the embargo was short-lived, it dealt a severe blow to the world economy, which was already in recession. Since that time, Arab producers have shied away from using oil as a political weapon in this way.

For the most part, the Muslim world has shown sympathy for the Palestinian cause, and recognition of Israel by Muslim states was slow in coming. The largest predominantly Muslim states in Asia—Indonesia, Pakistan, and Bangladesh—have never established diplomatic ties. There have been exceptions, however. Iran and Turkey both recognized Israel within a few years of its creation. Iran under Shah Muhammad Reza Pahlavi cemented close ties to Israel and provided the country with most of its oil. Iran broke relations with Israel after its revolution in 1979 and has since become Israel's most vocal antagonist. Israel's relations with Turkey, involving military cooperation and sales of Israeli weapons, have remained quite close until recently. This relationship, however, was seriously damaged in 2009 and 2010, mainly over Israel's deadly policies toward the Gaza Strip and its attack, in international waters, on the "Gaza Freedom Flotilla," a convoy of ships bringing humanitarian aid to Gaza. Israeli commandos killed eight Turkish citizens, sinking relations between the two states to an all-time low.

Outside the Arab world, countries have had to tread carefully if they wished to maintain friendly relations with both Arab states and Israel. The European states most responsible for creating the conflict in the first place (albeit in different ways)—Britain, France, and Germany—have on the whole managed to do this. Israel has signed a number of cooperative agreements with the European Union, and some observers have speculated that Israel might join that organization. On the other hand, support for Israel in Europe is not as enthusiastic as in the United States, and European states are more often openly critical of Israel. Europe is much more dependent than the United States on Arab oil supplies.

For several decades, there was intense competition between Israel and the Arab states over relations with Latin America and with newly independent countries in Africa and Asia. Some Arab states have used oil, or the wealth generated by oil, to promote warmer relations with these states. Israel has been able to offer advanced technology, weapons, and some development aid. On the whole, Israel has been able to prevent the diplomatic isolation that the Arab states had hoped it would suffer. Most countries maintain normal relations with Israel, but at least a dozen non-Arab states either do not recognize Israel or have broken off diplomatic ties. These tend to be either Muslim states like Indonesia or states with leftist governments, such as Bolivia and Cuba.

Since the Suez Crisis of 1956, no outside power has been as intricately involved in the Arab-Israeli conflict as the United States. The United States provides aid and weapons to both Israel and some Arab states, it shares intelligence with Israel, it protects Israel in the United Nations, and it insists on being involved in any efforts to negotiate a settlement of the conflict. Debates over policy toward Israel and toward the Arab world have played an important role in American politics ever since the creation of Israel. President Harry S. Truman's decision to recognize Israel was made in part because of the importance of securing the Jewish vote in the 1948 presidential election. While the United States was not particularly supportive of Israel in the early decades, the overall trend has been greater and greater devotion to Israel.

Driving American support for Israel has been a confluence of political forces: the influential pro-Israel lobby and a growing Christian Zionist movement among fundamentalists and evangelicals. The most important pro-Israel lobby group in Washington is the American Israel Public Affairs Committee. There are also dozens of political action committees supporting pro-Israel candidates. And support for Israel is not limited to Jewish Americans, many of whom have long financially supported the Zionist cause. There has been growing support for Israel among Christians on the religious right. This peculiarly American phenomenon is grounded in an interpretation of modern events that equates modern Israel with the biblical Israel and views its success as the fulfillment of prophecy. These ideas were popularized by televangelists Pat Robertson and the late Jerry Falwell. Such Christian Zionists tend to support the expansion of settlements in the occupied territories and oppose the peace process. The result has been that whereas 50 years ago support for Israel was more likely to be found on the political left, today it is conservatives who are among its most vocal supporters.

The United States supports Israel with financial aid, weapons, intelligence, and diplomatic support. Nowadays official American criticism of Israel is extremely rare. This unwavering support frequently produces tensions with the rest of the world, even with allies. It also has hindered the achievement of other American goals in the region, such as assuring the flow of oil, preventing nuclear proliferation (Israel long ago developed nuclear weapons), preventing terrorism, and promoting political stability in the region. And it has frequently resulted in the diplomatic isolation of the United States, starkly illustrated when it wields its veto in the UN Security Council. More than 40 vetoes—nearly half of the total cast by the United States—have been used to block resolutions critical of Israel for its policies in the occupied territories, including its settlement activity, and for its attacks on neighboring countries. Usually the U.S. government justifies its vetoes on the grounds that the resolution is not balanced; that it is critical of Israeli behavior but not of the behavior of Arab states or organizations. But the awkward result is that the United States is seen to be defending Israeli violations of international law.

The wars, the monetary costs, the political violence—these are things that are tangible, that are easy to measure. Less visible, but perhaps more important, has been the psychological impact these events have had on Israelis and Palestinians. Researchers have found high levels of posttraumatic stress disorder in Israel and even higher levels in the occupied territories. In both communities, a culture of victimization has long existed, a mind-set in which each sees itself as the victim of the other. The list of griev-ances goes back generations, and the pain that is felt is real. Any threat is seen as an existential threat, and one's enemies can only be deterred by maximum force and eter-nal vigilance. It is this deep emotional condition that not only justifies atrocities but also prevents trust from developing. And without at least a minimal trust, no end to the conflict is in sight.

SELECTED BIBLIOGRAPHY

Caplan, Neil. *The Israel-Palestine Conflict: Contested Histories.* Malden, MA: Wiley-Blackwell, 2009. The focus of this work is the competing narratives that have developed over the conflict. Caplan strives for a detached approach in assessing the conflicting Arab and Zionist histories. While providing an excellent overview of the historiography of the struggle, Caplan's work also serves as an introduction—and a reasonably concise one—to the history of the conflict as a whole.

Carter, Jimmy. *Palestine: Peace Not Apartheid.* New York: Simon & Schuster, 2006. Carter's argu-ment is that the Israeli government has been the main obstacle to a two-state solution to the conflict. This is not a work of history, nor is it "balanced." It is a polemic, with a deliberately provocative title, and it caused an outcry upon its publication. Aside from his personal experi-ence and insights, Carter presents little that is original here; the prominence of the author is what makes this an important work.

Karsh, Efraim. *Palestine Betrayed.* New Haven, CT: Yale University Press, 2010. Karsh takes on the "New Historians" (see Morris and Shlaim below) from the traditional Zionist perspective. The Palestinians have always sought to destroy Israel, and they are responsible for their own pre-dicament. Israel has always been open to a peaceful settlement, which has been prevented by Arab intransigence. Commentators on the political right welcomed this book enthusiastically. It is not a book recommended as an example of clear-headed scholarship but rather as a good example of how polarized the writing of history can become.

Khalidi, Rashid. *The Iron Cage: The Story of the Palestinian Struggle for Statehood.* Boston: Bea-con Press, 2006. Khalidi reflects on the situation of the Palestinians over the past century and to what extent they have been responsible for their own situation: whether they were simply victims of Zionism or they had some control over their destiny. Khalidi outlines the narrow and unsatisfactory choices presented to Palestinian leaders over the decades but also how some of the bars in the "iron cage" were of their own making.

Morris, Benny. *Righteous Victims: A History of the Zionist-Arab Conflict, 1881–2001.* New York: Vintage, 2001. Morris is at the same time enfant terrible and one of the leading New Historians of Israel, who in the 1980s challenged the accepted Zionist narrative of Israel's relationship with the Palestinians. Although he is best known for his detailed studies based on primary sources, this book is an admirable survey of the political and military history of the conflict. Unlike many authors of books destined for classroom use, Morris does not hold back on his opinions.

Schneer, Jonathan. *The Balfour Declaration: The Origins of the Arab-Israeli Conflict.* New York: Random House, 2010. The 1917 Balfour Declaration is the great turning point for the early Zionist movement and hence lies at the root of the state of Israel and the Israeli-Palestinian conflict. Relying mostly on Foreign Office records, Schneer examines the complex political and diplomatic context of Britain's carefully worded commitment to a "national home" for the Jews in Palestine. His study is an instructive reminder of the contingency of history: how often seemingly trivial decisions can have a massive impact on the world.

Shlaim, Avi. *The Iron Wall: Israel and the Arab World.* New York: W. W. Norton, 2001. Like Benny Morris, Shlaim is considered one of the New Historians. This book concentrates on Israeli foreign policy since its founding and the internal debates over policies to be pursued with the Arabs. Shlaim argues that Israel's leaders, despite their differences, all carried on some form of the "iron wall" approach to the Arabs: the stringent use of force against an implacable foe. Although it was successful in creating a strong, independent Israel, Shlaim argues that the time has come to move beyond this policy.

Smith, Charles D. *Palestine and the Arab-Israeli Conflict: A History with Documents.* 7th ed. Boston and New York: Bedford/St. Martin's, 2010. This is the standard textbook on the history of the conflict, but it is by no means a bland, sterile treatment of the subject. Smith is lucid and forceful in his language and can be delightfully scathing about certain individuals and their decisions.

Tessler, Mark. *A History of the Israeli-Palestinian Conflict.* 2nd ed. Bloomington: Indiana University Press, 2009. This weighty volume is the most comprehensive history of the conflict in a single volume; and is also the longest, running to more than 1,000 pages. Tessler attempts to maintain a scrupulous "objectivity," which is not always a welcome approach, but it is understandable in this politically charged field.

Tolan, Sandy. *The Lemon Tree: An Arab, a Jew, and the Heart of the Middle East.* New York: Bloomsbury, 2006. Tolan tells the story of Israel/Palestine through the lives of two people: a Jewish Bulgarian-Israeli woman and a Palestinian Arab man, whose family, before 1948, owned and resided in the house in which the Israeli later grew up. This personal, novelistic approach is a useful supplement, and antidote, to the detached, sweeping historical surveys.

MENACHEM BEGIN (1913–1992)

Menachem Begin was the prime minister of Israel from June 1977 to October 1983. He is best remembered for negotiating the Camp David Accords (1978) with Egyptian president Anwar Sadat, an achievement that earned them the Nobel Peace Prize.

Menachem Wolfovitch Begin was born on August 16, 1913, in Brest-Litovsk, Russia (present-day Belarus). He attended the Mizrachi Hebrew School before earning a law degree from the University of Warsaw in Poland in 1935. An active participant in the Zionist movement throughout his early life, Begin joined the Polish branch of Betar—a youth organization that advocated the establishment of an independent Jewish state in the Middle East—in the 1930s and rose to become its leader. He fled to Lithuania when the Germans invaded Poland during World War II, but he was subsequently arrested by Soviet authorities and deported to a Siberian labor camp in 1940. Upon his release the following year, Begin joined the Polish army in exile and was sent to the British mandate of Palestine in 1942.

Following his discharge from the army, Begin served as leader of Irgun Zvai Leumi from 1943 to 1948. Irgun was a Jewish underground movement determined to undermine British control in Palestine and create a Jewish state in the territory east and west of the Jordan River by any means necessary. Under Begin's watch, the group carried out numerous violent acts, including the bombing of the King David Hotel in Jerusalem in July 1946 and the execution of two British officers in 1947. The Irgun insurgency proved effective; the British eventually surrendered the Palestine mandate in September 1947 and withdrew the following spring. On May 14, 1948, the state of Israel was proclaimed at Tel Aviv under a United Nations mandate.

With Israel's independence achieved, Begin founded the Herut Party and served as its head in the Knesset (Israeli parliament) until 1967. In that year, a national unity

Young Jews celebrate the proclamation of the new state of Israel, Tel Aviv, May 14, 1948. (AFP/Getty Images)

government was formed and Begin was appointed minister without portfolio, a position he held until 1970. In 1973, he became joint chair of Likud, a Herut-Liberal Party coalition that was formed to challenge the politically dominant Israeli Labor Party. Likud won the national elections in May 1977, and Begin took office as the first non-Labor prime minister of Israel on June 21. Although Ashkenazic Jews had traditionally dominated Israeli politics, Begin's election marked the rise of the more conservative Sephardic Jews as a political power in Israel.

As prime minister, Begin took an uncompromising stand on retaining the West Bank and the Gaza Strip, territories that Israel had occupied in the Six-Day War of 1967. During his administration, the number of Israeli settlements established in the West Bank increased significantly. Despite Begin's hardline stance on Arab-Israeli relations, he took steps toward establishing peace in the Middle East by entering into negotiations with Egyptian president Anwar Sadat.

The Israeli government had long been unwilling to speak to leaders of Arab states directly, but on the invitation of U.S. president Jimmy Carter, Begin agreed to meet with Sadat in 1978 at Camp David, the presidential retreat near Washington, D.C. After 13 days of intense negotiations, a formal peace agreement known as the Camp David Accords was signed on September 17, 1978. Begin and Sadat were jointly awarded the 1978 Nobel Peace Prize for that historic achievement, which ultimately led to the signing of the Camp David Peace Treaty between Israel and Egypt on March 26, 1979. Under the terms of the treaty, the Sinai Peninsula—occupied by Israel during the Six-Day War—was returned to Egypt, and in return the Egyptian government formally recognized the existence of the state of Israel.

Begin was reelected in 1980. Despite having made some concessions in his negotiations with Egypt, the prime minister was still defiant against the founding of an independent Palestinian state in the Gaza Strip and West Bank. That firm stance prompted the Palestine Liberation Organization (PLO) to continue its guerrilla attacks against Israel from its bases in Lebanon. In June 1982, Begin's government invaded Lebanon to oust the PLO and put a stop to the attacks. Israeli forces penetrated deep into the country and were successful in driving the PLO from their headquarters in the Lebanese capital of Beirut, but the large number of civilian casualties that resulted from the fighting caused a harsh backlash in world opinion. That negative reaction was compounded when Israeli troops stood by as Christian militants attacked the Sabra and Shatila refugee camps in September, killing an estimated 1,000 Palestinian civilians. International pressure ultimately compelled Begin's government to withdraw Israeli forces from Lebanon, leaving behind only a small security force along the southern border.

Suffering from ill health and deeply affected by the death of his wife, Begin resigned from office in October 1983 and retired from public life. He died from a heart attack on March 9, 1992, in Tel Aviv. Begin wrote several books, including *The Revolt* (1951), which details the Irgun's struggle against British rule in Palestine; and *White Nights* (1957), a depiction of his experiences in Europe during World War II.

ABC-CLIO

MUHAMMAD DAHLAN (1961–)

A Palestinian politician and important figure in both Fatah and the Palestinian Authority (PA), Muhammad Dahlan was born on September 29, 1961, in the Khan Yunis Refugee Camp in the Gaza Strip. His family had fled from Hammama, Palestine (now Nitzanim, Israel). Dahlan became politically active as a teenager in Khan Yunis, recruiting other youngsters for civic projects. He earned a degree in business administration from the Islamic University of Gaza, where he was also a student leader and founded an organization that became known as the Fatah Youth Movement (Fatah Shabiba) that distributed food and medicine to the needy, as well as Palestinian nationalist propaganda.

By the time he was 25 years old, Dahlan had been arrested by the Israeli authorities on 11 separate occasions. Altogether he spent six years in Israeli prisons, becoming fluent in Hebrew in the process. One of the leaders of the First Intifada (1987–1994) in which the Fatah Youth Movement was very much involved, he was again arrested by the Israeli authorities in 1988 and deported to Jordan. He then went to Tunis, where he worked with the leaders of the Palestine Liberation Organization (PLO).

A protégé of PLO chairman Yasser Arafat, Dahlan returned to Gaza with Arafat in July 1994. Arafat appointed him to head the Preventive Security Service (PSS) for the Gaza Strip, a PLO security force, and to be Fatah's leader in Gaza. The two posts made Dahlan one of the most powerful figures in the new Palestinian Authority. With a police force of 20,000 men, Dahlan also became the most powerful figure in Gaza, which some came to refer to as Dahlanistan. To enforce his authority, Dahlan's associates reportedly used strong-arm methods, including torture. As with many other Fatah leaders, he became wealthy through PLO monopolies such as oil and cement and kickbacks on building contracts. The fact that he had been born in a refugee camp and been imprisoned by the Israelis and had the loyalty of other such prisoners helped shield him from some Palestinian criticism, however.

As head of the PSS in Gaza, Dahlan was responsible for ensuring support from all members of Hamas for the 1993 Oslo Accords. He apparently met regularly with Israeli security officials and U.S. Central Intelligence Agency representatives to coordinate security issues. In 1995, following a number of Hamas suicide attacks, Dahlan, reportedly on the orders of Arafat, ordered the PSS to crack down on Hamas militants and some 2,000 were arrested. The PSS also raided Islamic charities, schools, and mosques. Dahlan was able to succeed in such activities in large part because of the initial Palestinian support for the Oslo Accords and his tough methods. Because the Likud government of Prime Minister Benjamin Netanyahu in Israel was obstructionist toward the peace process, however, the PA crackdown on militants soon lost support, and Dahlan himself backed off from it.

Dahlan was a regular member of negotiations with Israeli government officials on a variety of issues. He was also a participant in the Wye River negotiations (1998), the Camp David Summit (2000), and the Taba negotiations (2001). Dahlan's relationship with Israeli authorities cooled considerably with the beginning of the Second (al-Aqsa) Intifada in September 2000. Although he claimed that he remained committed to the peace process, Israeli officials blamed him for some of the violence in the Gaza Strip; in particular, he was suspected of being involved in a November 2000 attack on an Israeli school bus. In May 2001, his motorcade came under attack from the Israel Defense Forces in Gaza, and four of his bodyguards were wounded. Israeli prime minister Ariel Sharon denied that Dahlan was deliberately targeted and expressed regret for what the Israeli government later called an unfortunate mistake.

Dahlan reportedly offered to resign from the PSS in November 2001 in protest of the PA's policy of arresting Popular Front for the Liberation of Palestine and the Palestinian Islamic Jihad members. Arafat supposedly refused the resignation. Anticipating that Arafat would be forced to unify his security forces, Dahlan began to expand his authority among low-level commanders in the West Bank PSS, seeking to undermine the authority of its commander Jibril Rajob. Reportedly enjoying the support of U.S. president George W. Bush's administration, Dahlan also began to see himself as the possible successor to Arafat. Expecting to be named to head the unified security service, Dahlan resigned as head of the PSS. Arafat, however, resisted U.S. pressure to unify the security services. Although in July 2002 Arafat appointed Dahlan his national security adviser, the position was devoid of any real power and did not include control of security services.

When Arafat was pressured into naming Mahmoud Abbas as the PA's first prime minister in February 2003, Abbas sought to name Dahlan the minister of the interior. Arafat opposed this, and after considerable turmoil within the PA leadership Arafat agreed in April that Abbas would retain that post as well as the prime ministership, while Dahlan would become minister of state for security affairs. Abbas then authorized Dahlan to restructure the PA's Ministry of the Interior with a view toward cracking down on militants opposed to the peace process. In effect, Dahlan controlled some 20,000 security personnel but without having the title of interior minister. It proved an impossible situation, with a Likud government in Israel and Hamas militants both opposing the U.S.-sponsored road map to peace. Dahlan instead proposed negotiations with Hamas to achieve a cease-fire, which was reached in July 2004. The cease-fire collapsed soon thereafter following the Israeli assassinations of Hamas and Islamic Jihad leaders.

Abbas resigned on September 6, 2003. The new prime minister, Ahmed Qurei, dropped Dahlan from his cabinet. This decision led to demonstrations in Gaza in support of Dahlan, and to Dahlan's posturing as a reformer when he called for elections in Fatah organizations that would bring in new leadership. Dahlan was seen as a prime mover in a wave of intra-Palestinian violence in Gaza during the summer of 2004 between his supporters and those favoring the Fatah old guard. In January 2005, after Arafat's death, Abbas was elected president of the Palestinian Authority and appointed Dahlan minister for civil affairs. Dahlan worked with Israeli minister of defense Shaul Mofaz to bring about the Israeli pullout from Gaza. In January 2006, Dahlan narrowly won election to the Palestinian Legislative Council in the general elections as a representative of Khan Yunis.

In March 2007, over Hamas objections, Palestinian president Mahmoud Abbas named Dahlan to head the newly reestablished Palestinian National Security Council, which controlled all security services in the Palestinian territories. Dahlan resigned from this post in July 2007, but the National Security Council had already been dissolved following the Hamas takeover of Gaza in mid-June. Many in Fatah held Dahlan responsible for that easy Hamas victory, during which time he and key lieutenants were absent from Gaza. In the course of the fighting, Dahlan's Gaza residence—which many Palestinians had come to view as a symbol of Fatah corruption—was seized by Hamas militants and demolished.

SPENCER C. TUCKER

LEVI ESHKOL (1895–1969)

Levi Eshkol was the third prime minister of Israel. He is noted for bringing water and economic development to Israel, but his term as prime minister is best remembered for the Six-Day War of 1967.

Eshkol was born to a wealthy family in Oratov, Ukraine, on October 25, 1895. His father, Yoseph Shkolnik, was Lithuanian, and his mother, Devorah, came from a Hasidic Jewish family. They had nine sons and one daughter, and Eshkol was only the second of four boys to survive. He grew up on a farm, where he gained experience in agriculture and finance as his family operated flower mills and traded cattle. Eshkol received a traditional Jewish Talmud education and had tutors for secular subjects. Restrictions on Jews did not allow Eshkol to enter the local high school, so at age 16, he entered a Hebrew high school in Vilnius, where he became involved in Zionism. He joined Tzeirei Tzion (Youth of Zion), and was inspired by Yoseph Shprinzak, who later became the first speaker of the Knesset.

In 1914, motivated by the Second Aliyah (a mass emigration of Jews to Palestine), Eshkol moved to Erez, Palestine, which was part of the Ottoman Empire. He refused money from his parents and became an agricultural laborer. He explained, "Only if I come empty-handed will these hands be ready to work."

In 1918, during World War I, Eshkol volunteered for the Jewish Legion of the British army and served until 1920. He then joined a group that founded the kibbutz Degania Beth in Palestine. In Erez, he became involved in agricultural, financial, and political affairs, and he established the Histadrut (General Federation of Labor) and worked to promote cooperative agricultural development. In 1921, he was elected to the defense committee of the Histadrut, and in 1922, he was arrested while purchasing arms in Vienna for the group.

Eshkol went to work in the Palestine Office in Berlin in 1934 to help with settlement problems in Palestine. He worked with the German government, now under Adolf Hitler, to allow German Jews who were emigrating to Palestine to take their personal property with them. In 1937, Eshkol helped establish the Mekorot Water Company and became the company's chief executive. In 1940, during World War II, Eshkol helped establish a Jewish Zionist underground military organization known as the Haganah. He managed the organization's finances and helped procure arms for it. He also gained influence in the Mapai (Labor Party) and became the party's secretary for the remainder of the war.

After the war, Eshkol remained active in politics. In 1947, he began recruitment for the Israel Defense Forces. The following year, a provisional government of Israel proclaimed the Israeli Declaration of Independence, and Eshkol became the first director of the ministry of defense. Eshkol's political and financial skills were essential to supplying Israeli troops for the subsequent Arab-Israeli War. In late 1948, Eshkol also became treasurer and head of the settlement department for the World Zionist Organization, a position he held until 1963.

In 1951, Eshkol was elected to the Knesset as a member of the Mapai and appointed minister of agriculture. As a consequence, he resigned as chief executive of Mekorot. His term at Mekorot is noted for his development of the National Water Carrier project, which provided water for intensive irrigated farming throughout the nation. The massive project, which went into operation in 1964, is credited with bringing economic and agricultural growth to Israel.

Eshkol became minister of finance in 1952, a position that he held until 1963. During that time, Israel's gross national product increased by an average of 10 percent annually, and his policies helped the country's economic development and ability to absorb massive immigration.

In June 1963, after the resignation of David Ben-Gurion, Eshkol became prime minister and minister of defense.. Eshkol established formal diplomatic relations with West Germany in 1965 and improved relations with the United States. He became the first Israeli prime minister to visit the White House and signed agreements with U.S. president Lyndon B. Johnson for a joint water desalinization project and for the development of nuclear energy. Eshkol also visited various African countries and worked to improve Israeli relations with the Soviet Union, which resulted in increased immigration of Soviet Jews to Israel.

During the mid-1960s, after France stopped sending military supplies to Israel, Eshkol was able to obtain military supplies from the United States that proved invaluable to Israel during and after the Six-Day War. Arab-Israeli relations were tense throughout the 1960s, and when Egyptian president Gamal Abdel Nasser moved his troops into positions abandoned by United Nations troops and proclaimed an Arab blockade against Israeli shipping through the Gulf of Aqaba, Israel interpreted that move as preparation for war. To ensure political and public support for the impending conflict, Eshkol established a Government of National Unity by unifying the three labor parties of Israel into the Israeli Labor Party. He then brought Menachem Begin into his cabinet, and after much pressure, appointed war hero Moshe Dayan as minister of defense.

The Six-Day War began when Israel launched a preemptive strike against Egypt and Syria, defeated an attack from Jordan, and emerged in possession of Jordan's West Bank, Arab East Jerusalem, and Syria's Golan Heights. Although Israeli leaders had no plan to deal with occupied areas, Eshkol was adamant that Israel should retain the captured land until there was a solution to the entire Arab-Israeli conflict. After the war, he concluded further arms agreements with the United States for more sophisticated weaponry and began talks with Palestinian leaders in the occupied areas in an attempt to avert further violence. He died from a heart attack on February 26, 1969, while still in office.

ABC-CLIO

GAMAL ABDEL NASSER (1918–1970)

From the time he became president of Egypt in 1954 until well after his death in 1970, Gamal Abdel Nasser was the hero of Arab nationalists. Determined to bring Egypt into the modern age and overcome the colonialist influence of British rule, Nasser was wildly popular not only among Egyptians but also throughout the Arab world. The first Egyptian to rule Egypt in a millennium, the charismatic Nasser brought dignity to his people, although he failed to fulfill his goal of uniting the Arab world.

Nasser was born on January 15, 1918, in a mud brick house, typical of lower-middle-class dwellings in Alexandria. His father, Abdul Nasser Hussein, worked in the government bureaucracy as head of the local post office. Later he was transferred to al-Khatatibah, a poor village in the Egyptian delta. Nasser first attended school there before being sent to Cairo to live with an uncle.

Although Egypt received its independence from the United Kingdom in the 1930s and was officially ruled by King Farouk, the British continued to occupy the Suez Canal Zone and retained influence in the Egyptian Parliament and the higher echelons of the military. Nasser led student protests against British rule in 1934, in an early display of his organizational abilities. He continued to protest the lingering effects of colonialism after entering the Royal Military Academy. After joining the Egyptian Third Rifle Brigade and becoming a platoon commander, his discontent showed when he complained of the incompetence of his senior officers and led some junior officers in a protest.

Nasser saw duty as a lieutenant in Alexandria and then served in the Sudan. It was in the Sudan that Nasser made friends with three other officers, with whom he formed a secret organization. Zakaria Mohieddine, Abdel Hakim Amer, and Anwar Sadat—all of whom would be important in Nasser's future—came into this organization called the Free Officers with the goal of overthrowing the Egyptian monarchy and ousting the British from the Canal Zone. Nasser so structured the Free Officers that only he knew its full membership.

In 1948, the Egyptian army participated with other Arab armies in the Israeli War. As an officer, Nasser suffered the humiliation of being surrounded and pinned down by Israeli forces for more than three weeks. His overall experience in this conflict left a

As premier (1954–1956) and then president of Egypt, Gamal Abdel Nasser was a staunch nationalist and subsequent champion of Arab unity who led Egypt until his death in 1970. (AP/ Wide World Photos)

deep impression on him. First, the formation of Israel with British help assaulted his sensibilities as an Arab and furthered his dislike for Britain; second, the poor training received by the Egyptian troops and the shabby equipment provided them convinced him of the need to modernize the armed forces.

For the next four years, Nasser and other members of the Free Officers—perhaps numbering 700—infiltrated the government and worked against King Farouk. They soon gained hold of the military high command, and on July 23, 1952, a coup d'état occurred that led to the fall of the monarchy. Nasser's Revolutionary Council took control of the nation. Nasser, however, did not publicly emerge as Egypt's leader. Because he and other members of the Free Officers believed that their youth and inexperience would be rejected by the Egyptian people, he selected Major General Mohammad Naguib, a respected war hero, as head of state and made himself deputy prime minister. In 1954, however, Nasser deposed Naguib—whom he suspected of plotting against him—and became prime minister.

That same year, Nasser wrote *The Philosophy of Revolution,* explaining his belief that Egypt faced the challenge of undergoing two revolutions at the same time: a political one and a social one. Although Nasser was sincerely interested in improving the conditions in which the majority of Egyptians lived, he was not interested in democratic government. His policies were issued with little public discussion, and he met political opposition with repression, particularly when it came from Muslim groups and communists who enjoyed considerable popular support. Early in 1953, the government dissolved all opposing political parties, and only the Liberation Rally, a group supportive of Nasser, could function legally. Nasser filled scores of government positions with military officers he felt he could trust and imprisoned large numbers of trade unionists, intellectuals, and students who criticized him. His regime ruled as a police state.

Nasser's initial foreign-policy accomplishments won him the adoration of many Egyptians, for he seemed finally to have restored the dignity of his nation. In 1954, he reached an agreement with the United Kingdom for the removal of British forces two years later, thus ending foreign occupation. He voiced support for the Algerian revolution against France, signed a major Czech-Russian arms deal in 1955, and in 1956 nationalized the Suez Canal. This last move provoked retaliation from the British, who conspired with France and Israel to attack Egypt. The Israelis marched into the Sinai Peninsula, and the Egyptian Air Force was destroyed. Yet diplomatic pressure brought the invaders' withdrawal and victory for Nasser in successfully portraying his enemies as aggressors grasping for imperialistic power.

With the nationalization of the canal, Nasser became the most prominent leader of the pan-Arabic movement and sought to place Egypt in the forefront of advancing Arab unity. He had already emerged as a leader of the Non-Aligned Movement with his appearance at the Bandung Conference of Asian and African nations in 1955. He viewed Egypt as the epicenter of three great circles enclosing Arabs, Muslims, and Africans and envisioned the day when he might lead all Arabs and Muslims. Toward this end, he signed a pact in 1958 that brought Syria and Egypt together as the United Arab Republic (UAR) with himself as president. In 1961, however, the UAR collapsed when Syria withdrew, primarily because of economic policies that angered Syrian interests and Nasser's attempt to dominate the union.

Within Egypt, Nasser remained a popular hero, buoyed by the widespread approval of his domestic policies. Early in his regime he broke the power of the landed oligarchy with a land reform law. Although this law recognized the right to private property, it limited the size of landholdings to 208 acres (later modified downward). Under Nasser, a new middle class of Egyptians began to form in the cities to replace the foreigners who had filled those positions for decades, and women were accorded more rights than many would have thought possible.

The centerpiece of Nasser's modernization program, however, was the construction of the Aswan High Dam. Because he had accepted the help of the Soviet Union on this project, the United States had withdrawn its support in the early 1950s, inspiring the nationalization of the Suez Canal to raise revenue. An audacious project designed to regulate the flow of the Nile River, Egypt's historic source of life, the dam aided agriculture through irrigation and reduced flooding while it generated hydroelectric power for industry. This and similar projects brought twentieth-century life into many villages.

Under Nasser, industry became the fastest-growing part of the Egyptian economy (while agricultural production increased a significant 2 percent per year). In 1961, Nasser nationalized banks, insurance companies, and other firms; companies handling light industry had to turn more than 50 percent of their capital to the government. Industrial growth, however, did not reach the levels envisioned by Nasser, the peasants received few economic benefits, and by 1967, the economy hit bottom as the nation's hard currency reserves nearly evaporated. Despite his mixed economic performance, the Egyptian masses retained faith in Nasser and continued to do so even in military defeat.

Responding to erroneous Soviet intelligence that Israel was planning an invasion in 1967, Nasser requested the withdrawal of United Nations troops from the Gaza Strip and Sharm ash-Shaykh, where they had been placed after the 1956 conflict. He also announced the closing of the Gulf of Aqaba to Israeli shipping. In the process, he heightened the anti-Israeli vehemence of the Egyptian people. In response to these measures, the Israeli government decided that a preemptive strike was necessary to save their country.

The ensuing 1967 war proved a disaster for the Egyptians. Within six days of the invasion, the Israeli forces destroyed Egypt's Air Force and routed the army. Poor planning, inept leadership, and overconfidence doomed the Egyptians. Although his friend Field Marshal Abdel Hakim Amer had actually commanded the troops, Nasser accepted full responsibility for the fiasco of the Six-Day War and on June 9 resigned as premier. At that point, however, massive street demonstrations broke out as the Egyptian people pleaded with their leader to remain in office. Crowds shouted, "Nasser, do not leave us, we need you!" and he responded by resuming his rule. The Soviets eventually replaced all of Egypt's destroyed military hardware and even placed surface-to-air missiles along the Suez Canal.

In 1970, Nasser unexpectedly accepted a plan initiated by the United States that would begin peace talks with Israel. By then, however, the Egyptian leader was in bad health. Diabetes took its toll along with circulatory problems and a serious heart condition, and on September 28, 1970, while at his villa outside of Cairo, he died from a heart attack.

NEIL HAMILTON

ABD AL-AZIZ RANTISI (1947–2004)

A Palestinian political leader and head of operations for Hamas in the Gaza Strip, Abd al-Aziz Rantisi was born on October 23, 1947, in Yabna (Jibna), a town near Ashdod (Isdud) and Jaffa, Palestine. His family fled their home for Khan Yunis in the Gaza Strip in 1948 during the Arab-Israeli War (1948–1949). Following Israel's independence in May 1948, Egypt administered the Gaza Strip until its occupation by Israel in the aftermath of the Six-Day War in 1967.

Rantisi excelled in school, and upon graduating from secondary school in 1965, he was admitted to Alexandria University in Egypt to study medicine. He graduated with a bachelor's degree in medicine in 1972 and returned to Gaza for two years before resuming his studies in Egypt and obtaining a master's degree in pediatrics in 1976. It was during his nine years in Egypt that he became exposed to the ideals of Islamic fundamentalism espoused by the Muslim Brotherhood, an organization with a long history and numerous affiliates throughout the Muslim world. These same ideals lay at the heart of Hamas, which is, in addition, also a nationalist organization.

Upon returning to Gaza in 1976, Rantisi worked as a resident physician at the government-run Nasser Hospital in the city of Khan Yunis until 1986. He also busied himself with posts in several organizations dedicated to public works, including service as a board member of the Islamic Complex, as a member of the Arab Medical Society in Gaza, and as a member of the Palestinian Red Crescent (the Islamic counterpart to the Red Cross). In 1978, he was promoted to the post of chief pediatrician in the Khan Yunis hospital and joined the faculty of science at the Islamic University of Gaza in its inaugural year.

Rantisi's political convictions first landed him in trouble in 1983, when he was arrested for refusing to pay taxes to Israel. However, his political involvement with the organization that came to be known as Hamas first became widely known in 1987. The triggering event was the killing of four Palestinians after an Israel Defense Forces truck ran into a group of residents of the Jabalya refugee camp in the Gaza Strip on December 8, 1987. Rantisi has claimed that he and six other associates—Sheikh Ahmed Yassin foremost among them—on the following day helped to channel the seething discontent of Palestinians into the civilian uprising that spread like wildfire across the occupied territories. This was the origin of what came to be known as the first Palestinian Intifada. Hamas emerged after its outbreak.

Rantisi was arrested twice in 1988. The first time he was held for 21 days, and the second time he was held for a year and a half. His release in September 1990 was short-lived, for he was arrested again in December 1990 and held in detention for a year. On December 15, 1992, he was expelled to Marj Al-Zuhur, in southern Lebanon, along with 415 other Hamas and Islamic Jihad activists. The expellees were not permitted by the Lebanese government to leave the area where they were dropped off by Israeli air transport, and with no rights or supplies, they attracted international attention.

Rantisi then became a leading spokesperson for the expelled Palestinians. Allowed to return to the Gaza Strip in September 1993 with other expellees, he was frequently imprisoned by the Palestinian Authority (PA) for his open criticism of it and Palestine Liberation Organization (PLO) chairman Yasser Arafat.

Following the signing of the Declaration of Principles on Interim Self-Government Arrangements (1993), better known as the Oslo Accords, which Hamas opposed, the organization staged several knife attacks on soldiers and settlers in the occupied territories. However, following the massacre of 29 Palestinians by Israeli settler Baruch Goldstein in the Cave of the Patriarchs (Hebron Mosque Massacre) on February 25, 1994, Hamas and other organizations and unaffiliated individuals embarked on a campaign of suicide bombings. Although peaking in the years 2001 and 2002, Hamas continued these bombings with occasional breaks.

Upon the return of Sheikh Ahmed Yassin to Gaza in 1997, Rantisi worked with him to reconstitute Hamas's Gaza leadership. In mid-1999, following Rantisi's release from a PA prison, Rantisi became Yassin's right-hand man and the public spokesperson for Hamas in the Gaza Strip, in part because of his fluent English.

Despite Hamas's attempts to portray its political leadership as separate from its military wing (known as the Izz al-Din al-Qassam Brigades), Israel recognized no such separation and targeted the political department of Hamas for assassination. Rantisi narrowly avoided such a fate on June 10, 2003, when a helicopter rocket attack on his car missed its mark.

Within Hamas, Rantisi was always considered a hard-liner who never missed an opportunity to use his rhetorical skills to further inflame any situation. He vehemently denied the Holocaust engineered by Nazi Germany, and he was uncompromising in his call for an Islamic Palestine—in contrast to the PLO, which is secular and includes many Christian Palestinians—and refused to recognize Israel's right to exist. Following the March 2004 assassination by Israeli forces of Sheikh Yassin, Rantisi took the opportunity of Yassin's funeral to seize the leadership of Hamas in the Gaza Strip, having himself proclaimed Yassin's appointed heir during the accompanying protest rally. Rantisi was recognized as Hamas's Gaza leader by Khaled Mashal, whom Rantisi recognized in return as the leader of Hamas in the West Bank. (Mashal was operating in exile in Damascus, Syria.) Not surprisingly, Rantisi, who had already been targeted for assassination by Israel once, was again targeted, and on April 17, 2004, only hours after Hamas had claimed responsibility for the assassination of an Israeli soldier, an Israeli helicopter gunship fired a missile at his car, killing Rantisi, his 27-year-old son, and a bodyguard.

SPENCER C. TUCKER

YOM KIPPUR WAR (1973)

The Yom Kippur War took place in 1973, one in a series of Arab-Israeli conflicts. Planned by Egyptian president Anwar Sadat, the war ended inconclusively but served as a pretext to force the issue of peace talks between Egypt and Israel.

Sadat began building up the Egyptian military and planning an attack on Israel in hopes of occupying so much territory that Israel would be forced to negotiate. Sadat wished not only to regain territory lost in the 1967 Six-Day War but to resolve diplomatic issues that had been festering for years because no peace agreement had followed the 1967 war. Sadat persuaded Syrian President Hafez Assad to invade the disputed Golan Heights area to Israel's north in order to split the Israeli defense forces. Israeli intelligence failed to take seriously signs of activity on the part of Syria and Egypt, insisting until it was too late that there would be no war.

The Arab forces made their move on October 6, 1973, at the start of the Jewish holy day of atonement, Yom Kippur. Egypt and Syria were aided by nine Arab nations in a variety of capacities. The Israeli army had little advance warning of the attack and was taken almost entirely by surprise. Through the next day, divisions of the Egyptian Second and Third Armies streamed across the Suez Canal with 500 tanks. Simultaneously, Syrian forces moved on Israeli positions in the Golan Heights. The Egyptians in particular were initially very successful, inflicting heavy losses on Israel's defense forces, especially its powerful air force. Though outnumbered, the Israelis managed to hold back the Egyptians and the Syrians, now joined by Jordanian army divisions. By October 9, both sides were seeking aid from allies; the Israelis from the United States and the Arabs from the Soviet Union. Over the next week, both superpowers airlifted supplies to the warring Middle Eastern nations and put their own military forces on alert. By October 19, despite a serious threat posed by the Egyptian forces, the Israelis had gained the upper hand, driving the Syrians from the Golan and pushing the Egyptians back almost as far as the Gulf of Suez.

An initial cease-fire, backed by the United Nations, was reached on October 22. The actual end to hostilities would not come until the following year, however, with Israel and Egypt signing an agreement in January 1974 that stipulated an Israeli withdrawal to the eastern bank of the Suez Canal. Syria, however, began a war of attrition, bombarding Israeli territory in hopes of gaining back control of the Golan Heights. An agreement was not reached between the two countries until May, with Israel conceding small portions of land captured in 1967 and 1973.

Despite Israel's impressive showing on the battlefield, the war was considered a failure, in no small part because of the inability of military intelligence to foresee the attack

In October 1973, an uneasy quiet in the Middle East was shattered when Egypt and Syria attacked Israel without warning. Although initially successful, both the Egyptian and Syrian armies were soundly defeated within a few weeks. The war is also noteworthy in that it brought each side's "protector" (the United States for Israel and the Soviet Union for the two Arab states) close to war. (Corel)

and the loss of 2,688 soldiers, with 7,500 wounded and 530 captured. Egypt, on the other hand, while losing in the field (Egyptian casualties numbered some 15,000 dead, 30,000 wounded, and 9,000 captured; Syria suffered similar losses with an estimated 3,500 killed, 21,000 wounded, and 370 captured), claimed a moral victory.

ABC-CLIO

DOCUMENT: CAMP DAVID PEACE TREATY (1979)

The Camp David Peace Treaty, also known as the Egyptian-Israeli Peace Treaty, was signed in 1979 as an outcome of the Camp David meeting that brought leaders from Israel and Egypt to U.S. president Jimmy Carter's Camp David retreat. During the 13-day conference, a framework for peace between Israel and Egypt was negotiated and formally agreed on in this document. Following are excerpts of the document and summaries of three appendices.

PREAMBLE

"The Government of the Arab Republic of Egypt and the Government of the State of Israel;

Convinced of the urgent necessity of the establishment of a just, comprehensive and lasting peace in the Middle East in accordance with Security Council Resolution 242 and Resolution 338;

Reaffirming their adherence to the 'Framework for Peace in the Middle East Agreed at Camp David,' dated September 17, 1978. . . .

Agree to the following provisions:

ARTICLE I

1. The state of war between the Parties will be terminated and peace will be established between them upon the exchange of instruments of ratification of this Treaty.

2. Israel will withdraw all its armed forces and civilians from the Sinai behind the international boundary between Egypt and mandated Palestine . . . and Egypt will resume the exercise of its full sovereignty over the Sinai.

3. Upon completion of the interim withdrawal . . . the Parties will establish normal and friendly relations. . . .

ARTICLE II

The permanent boundary between Egypt and Israel is the recognized international boundary between Egypt and the former mandated territory of Palestine . . . without prejudice to the issue of the Gaza Strip. . . .

ARTICLE IV

1. In order to provide maximum security for both Parties on the basis of reciprocity, agreed security arrangements will be established including limited force zones in Egyptian and Israeli territory, and United Nations forces and observers . . . and other security arrangements the Parties may agree upon. . . .

ARTICLE V

1. Ships of Israel, and cargoes destined for or coming from Israel, shall enjoy the right of free passage through the Suez Canal and its approaches through the Gulf of Suez and the Mediterranean Sea. . . . Israeli nationals, vessels and cargoes, as well as persons, vessels and cargoes destined for or coming from Israel, shall be accorded nondiscriminatory treatment in all matters connected with usage of the canal.

2. The Parties consider the Strait of Tiran and the Gulf of Aqaba to be international waterways open to all nations for unimpeded and nonsuspendable freedom of navigation and overflight. The Parties will respect each other's right to navigation and overflight for access to either country through the Strait of Tiran and the Gulf of Aqaba."

Annex I describes the details of Israeli withdrawal from the Sinai Peninsula over a three-year period. It also establishes several zones in the Sinai and surrounding territory in Egypt and Israel and the restricted distribution of military forces in these areas, including United Nations forces.

Annex II is a map of the Sinai Peninsula and the agreed-upon boundary between Egypt and Israel.

Annex III sets the terms for the normalization of relations between Egypt and Israel in regard to diplomacy, economics and trade, culture, the freedom of movement of the citizens of each nation, transportation and communication, human rights, and the mutual right of passage through each nation's territorial seas.

11

Computers and the Age of Hi-Tech, 1976–Present

INTRODUCTION

Since the 1980s, computers and their many applications have played an ever-increasing part in the daily life of hundreds of millions of people around the world. The ancestry of computers dates back some 275 years or so, but beginning in the late 1940s, soon after World War II, when computers began to be used for sophisticated scientific research, the development of more compact and more powerful computers has proceeded at a pace that is perhaps unrivaled by any other invention in world history.

In the 1720s, Basile Bouchon, of France, used a system of punched cards that a calculating machine could read. In 1835, an Englishman named Charles Babbage invented what he called an "Analytical Engine," which operated on the same principles as modern digital computing does. Babbage's Analytical Engine was conceived to perform any kind of mathematical calculation that could be programmed by punched cards. It would have had a memory in which to store numbers as well. Unfortunately, it would have been the size of a locomotive, and Babbage was never able to get the financial support from the British government that would have enabled him to make a working machine. An American, Herman Hollerith, developed the basic punch-card system of data collecting and sorting while working for the U.S. Census, which by 1880 was incredibly bogged down in trying to analyze the results of the decennial census. This was important because Congress needed the information for legislative purposes. By 1889, Hollerith had developed a complicated electronic sorting and tabulating machine that included a punching device, a tabulating machine with counters, and an electrically controlled sorting box for grouping the punch cards based on the arrangement of the holes punched in them. Hollerith's machine was successfully used in the 1890 census, cutting the time for data analysis by two-thirds, and it was quickly adapted for use by a number of other countries. Most historians agree that Hollerith's machine marks the beginning of modern data processing.

In the first decade of the twentieth century, Hollerith developed a new style of punch card that contained 80 columns and could be used with a simpler kind of key punch and a more efficient card-sorter and tabulator. These new punch cards were found to have multiple applications and were even used by U.S. forces in Europe during World War I. In 1911, Hollerith started a business, the Computing-Tabulating-Recording Company

(CTR), and the following year, he sold his patents and became a highly paid consultant. Thomas Watson, Sr., became head of CTR in 1914 and focused his efforts on manufacturing punch card machines that CTR leased to its business clients. These machines, which used only punch cards that CTR made and sold, were very profitable. In 1924, Watson changed the name of the company to International Business Machines (IBM). Four years later, IBM introduced an 80-column punch card that became the industry standard for the rest of the century.

The years between the wars saw a number of new applications based on punch card computing technology. In 1932, a machine based on punch cards could reproduce music, and the following year, the technology was applied at race tracks with the introduction of the "Totalizor," or tote-machine, which could rapidly calculate odds based on the amount of money wagered on each horse and then determine how much winning bettors would make from their bets. In 1938, an application enabled direct dialing in telephone communication, and in 1940, the first machine was built that could serve more than one terminal and that could be used from a remote location. Other important developments had less visibility. In 1936, an American, Paul Eisler, created the first circuit board. The concept of electronic circuits found application during World War II and, after the war, the printed circuit board transformed the electronics industry. By the 1960s, the use of silicon chips as semiconductors became feasible, leading to the great miniaturization of circuit boards and their use in computer microprocessors.

In 1946, ENIAC was unveiled as the first electronic digital computer after years of development at the University of Pennsylvania. It occupied a 30- by 50-foot room, utilized 18,000 vacuum tubes, and weighed 30 tons. ENIAC remained operational until 1955 and was used primarily for military and atomic energy calculations. Interestingly, a 1974 court decision transferred the honor of inventing the first electronic computer to John Vincent Atanasoff and Clifford Berry, who had developed a similar computer in 1942 but had never made it operational.

More significant for our story, perhaps, was Univac I, which Remington Rand introduced in 1951 as the first commercially available computer, and the first to attract public attention. It was used by the U.S. Census Bureau and put to work in the 1952 presidential election where it correctly forecast the results on CBS television, based on its analysis of public opinion polls. The same year, LEO I was introduced. It was the first business use computer, one that could perform various business transactions, such as payroll and tax calculations, far more quickly than an accountant could by hand. But, like ENIAC, Univac, LEO I, and other early computers were huge machines that consumed vast amounts of electricity and gave off tremendous amounts of heat. It was not long, however, before important developments in electronic technology made the smaller and cooler computer possible.

In 1947, the transistor was invented at the Bell Laboratories in New Jersey. It was a semiconductor that was very small and shortened the path of the electronic impulse that circulated data into the computer. Several transistors were combined in a printed circuit that took care of all of a computer's functions and greatly reduced its size. In 1958, an engineer named Jack Kilby invented the integrated circuit at Texas Instruments. In this device, individual transistors and their connectors were eliminated, and thousands of tiny transistors and capacitors could be accommodated in a small device, further reducing the size of a computer and leading to the introduction of the personal or desktop computer after the invention of the microprocessor in 1971. The microprocessor is a kind of an integrated circuit that encompasses all of the computer's functions together in an even smaller space.

The shrinking size of computers signaled the end of punch-card viability. Punch cards began to be phased out when operating systems were created that could fulfill the same purpose. In the 1950s, as computers became faster and more complex, the human time commitment involved in loading punch cards and setting up tapes for each separate job became a major problem. By the early 1980s, however, "batch" operating systems were coming into use. These performed multiple and varied tasks with much less human involvement and provided results very rapidly. Perhaps the best known of these systems was OS/360, for use in an IBM computer, which allowed the computer to perform varied tasks in minutes rather than hours. At about the same time, researchers at the Massachusetts Institute of Technology successfully implemented CTSS (Compatible Time-Sharing System) that permitted many users to access a central computer from their own terminals, with each user seeming to have the full power of the computer available just as quickly as if each were using the computer alone.

As the technology behind computers advanced, so too did their applications and the manner in which people could use them. Many of the applications developed around what is called "software" (in contrast to "hardware," which refers to the actual computer, keyboard, monitor, and other peripherals). Early software was developed around programming languages, that is, programs actually written for the computer. Research on this began at the end of World War II by Konrad Zuse of Germany, although his language, Plankalkul, was never put to use. FORTRAN (Formula Translation) came along in 1957 as the first widely used computer-programming language that could be used for many applications. In 1958, an international group of researchers developed IAL (International Algebraic Language), also known as Algol, which led to a new wave of programming language work. One of the results of this work was COBOL (Common Business-Oriented Language), which employed words and phrases in its commands instead of mathematical symbols and was therefore easier to learn and use. ASCII (American Standard Code for Information Interchange) came along in 1962 and enabled computers from different manufacturers to talk to each other. In the 1960s and 1970s, work began on languages that would work in "embedded" computers (in which a computer is incorporated into a device with other equipment) and in interactive computer systems (in which users can access a computer from a remote site). The most important of these was Basic, first implemented in 1964 and used for more than 20 years. By 1980, there were many new languages under development or in use with specific applications, such as civil engineering or in classroom settings.

In 1962, the first university departments of computer science were established at Stanford and Purdue, and the first computer game, "Space War," was launched, which enabled players to shoot at each other's spaceships and avoid being sucked into a black hole.

More important, IBM introduced word processing in 1964; it worked by recording words on a magnetic tape in such a way that revision and repetitions were possible. Printing was possible on crude machines that produced words that looked vaguely as if they had been typed, but that situation improved with IBM's laser printer, first available in 1971. The evident usefulness of word processing was probably an important factor in the launch of the first desktop computer in 1965, manufactured by Digital Equipment Corporation and sold for $18,000. The same year saw the appearance of floppy disks on which to store documents for later use. At first, these were 8 inches in diameter, but the size was soon reduced to 5.25 inches, and then to 3.5 inches in a non-floppy diskette. By the early 1980s, desktop computers had become small enough (they actually fit on a desktop) and cheap enough that many people could afford them and schools and universities could make them available to students. Apple brought out its first desktop computers in 1976, followed a year later by Tandy's TRS-80 "microcomputer," making these two companies the early leaders in the industry. But IBM brought out its first IBM PC in 1981 and intensified the competition in the desktop marketplace.

Today, we all look at the Internet as a standard feature of daily life, and we spend a great deal of time utilizing its many features. It's hard to imagine a time when there was no Internet, but its birth dates to 1968, when a Department of Defense research network known as ARPAnet (Advanced Research Projects Agency Network) sponsored this system, which was designed to support data communication among those engaged in different military research projects. In time, other networks, such as NSFnet (National Science Foundation), were organized and added to ARPAnet, and the name Internet was adopted. In simple terms, the Internet is a network of networks linked by various protocols under the name of Internet Protocol (IP) that sends digital information to an array of other networks and media sources in a timely and efficient manner. In this way, users are connected on media systems, such as telephone and cable television, as well as on local area computer networks (LAN) and wide area networks. Clearly the two most important real life applications are electronic mail (e-mail) and the World Wide Web (WWW).

E-mail was developed in the 1990s as a way of transferring a message from one user to another over a computer network. Originally, it was possible only for multiple users of a single computer to leave messages for one another, but the technology rapidly developed so that a message could be sent from one computer to another (or to many others), and e-mail has become the most frequently used form of written communication in the world.

The World Wide Web was born in 1989 as a concept of CERN, a European particle physics laboratory on the border between France and Switzerland. Credit for the WWW is given to Tim Berners-Lee, who, with colleagues, designed HTML (hypertext markup language), HTTP (hypertext transfer protocol, and URL (universal resource locator), the technical processes that enable the WWW to function. Since the early 1990s, the Web has exploded, both in the number of users (more than 1 billion) and in the number and variety of applications (everything from individual home pages to e-commerce to Web search engines such as Google to social networking sites such as Facebook and YouTube.

INTERPRETIVE ESSAY

MARK RICE

Every so often, the world goes through such a fundamental shift in people's ways of life that the societies that emerge from the change bear little similarity to their predecessors.

The advent of civilization in ancient times, and the several changes in agricultural technology and practices are some of the most striking examples of these shifts. Although these shifts can often be disruptive and harmful, they usually produce advances in the structure of societies that ultimately benefit their citizens. Thus, they can be difficult to live through, but those societies that take advantage of the changes can profit greatly by them, both economically and socially. These periods of change are often separated by hundreds or even thousands of years, yet happen often enough that we can recognize some of their patterns and consequences.

The twenty-first century has opened in the midst of one of those transformations, which we may call the High-Tech Revolution. The development of computers and their many applications during the second half of the twentieth century created a world that looked very different from the world of the first half of the century. Now, in the twenty-first century, it is a world that is increasingly interconnected, and where the flow of information plays an increasing importance in both everyday life and in the great events around the world. The world is now moving into a digital age, one dominated by the binary code of the computing world, and one increasingly connected by the microchips in computers, consumer electronics, communication devices, and just about any other type of electronic device imaginable.

Despite the wide range of products that this high-tech revolution has brought us, at its core it is an information revolution. As the amount of information transferred from person to person and from place to place increased dramatically in the final decades of the twentieth century, the value of information has increased even more dramatically. An information economy now drives the wider economy, and many observers point to the development of an Information Age replacing the Industrial Age. Through the reductions in costs of transferring information over long distances, the increase in the ability to store and process that information electronically, and the ability of almost every person worldwide to gain access to that information, the information revolution has changed the way that people think, interact, learn, and communicate, and its effects continue to reverberate across societies.

The last time the world went through a transformation as fundamental as the Information Revolution was at the beginning of the nineteenth century, when large-scale industrialization in Great Britain, western Europe, and North America created a new economic system based on large-scale manufacturing. Industrialization brought major changes to national production, demographics, social structures, and political systems. It gave the Western world significant advantages over other societies, opening a new stage of imperialism that brought much of the world under European economic and political domination. It mechanized war and enabled the massive devastation of the two World Wars of the early twentieth century, culminating in the destructive power of nuclear weapons. Perhaps most important, however, it transformed daily lives for millions of people, drawing them into new forms of work and play and new relationships with employers and political leaders.

The Industrial Revolution was built on the development of new technologies at the end of the eighteenth century. Inventions such as the water frame, spinning jenny, and power loom increased the potential for each worker to produce more with less effort and less cost. But the real start of the Industrial Revolution came when these devices were combined with steam power in new factories. The development of steam power—

first for pumping water out of mine shafts, then for powering factory machinery, and finally for locomotion—drove the Industrial Revolution. Factory production was much more efficient than previous forms of manufacturing, allowing producers to reduce costs and increase supply. Once combined with steam-powered railroads and ships, manufactured goods could be moved to markets more quickly and cheaply. By the mid-nineteenth century, Great Britain was leading the world in industrial output, making the British economy the envy of the world.

The Information Revolution was also driven by an influx of new technologies, although their implementation took longer to have a significant impact on society. Inventions such as the transistor and the integrated microchip opened new possibilities for information storage and processing, but like the early inventions of the Industrial Revolution, they needed to be combined with a central technology to have a real impact. For the Information Revolution, that central technology was the computer. When transistors and microchips became the core elements of computing technology, the cost of computing decreased quickly while the capabilities of computers increased even more quickly. The result was an explosion in high technology that began to bring noticeable changes to society by the 1980s.

The first mechanical computers date back to ideas developed in the eighteenth and nineteenth centuries, but it was not until after World War II that computers began to gain broad use. The sheer amount of material, especially encrypted material, that intelligence operations during the war were bringing in required new methods to process the information, quickly leading to the development of mechanical, and soon electronic, aids. The first machines were essentially reverse-engineered copies of Germany's Enigma encrypting device, designed to allow Allied cryptographers to run potential decryptions of German messages. However, as the Germans made the Enigma machines more complicated, it became more difficult for the cryptographers at Bletchley Park (the location outside of Oxford where Allied decryption efforts were concentrated) to decrypt the messages. Under the direction of British mathematician Allan Turing, the Allies built an electro-mechanical computer, called a *bombes*, which could run through many more possible combinations of letters to decrypt the Enigma messages. Despite the development of larger and more powerful *bombes* throughout the war, the machines were little more than Enigma machines linked together to increase the speed of decryption. They could not be programmed nor did they have much potential to function outside the context of cryptanalysis.

Still, the work done on the *bombes* opened the door to the use of electronic devices to analyze encrypted messages. In 1943, the British began work on an electronic machine that would store incoming material in an internal memory system to use that data to compare with encrypted messages intercepted from earlier German communications. By the end of the year, researchers had designed and built the first electronic computer, the Colossus, and by early 1944, it was in operation in Bletchley Park. Using vacuum tubes, the Colossus could be programmed to look for certain variables in messages and compare them with stored data to determine the validity of the new data. By the end of the war, the Allies had 10 Colossus machines in operation. Although the British decided for security reasons to destroy most of the machines, along with their designs, and to classify all material related to them, the Colossus machines showed the possibility of building programmable electronic digital computers that would have many applications.

During the decade after World War II, computing technology advanced along the lines set down by Colossus. The ENIAC computer, built at the University of Pennsylvania between 1943 and 1946 was, like Colossus, an electronic computer using vacuum tubes. But unlike Colossus, ENIAC's design was not focused on a specific task like decryption but allowed the computer to be programmed to analyze many different kinds of mathematic functions. Further enhancements of the design continued, and soon computers were moving from government use to commercial use. Companies such as Remington Rand (builder of the first large-scale commercial computer, the UNIVAC) and International Business Machines (IBM) were soon designing and selling computers to companies to manage payroll and do other accounting tasks and automate many of the basic computational jobs that large organizations needed done on a regular basis.

These mainframe computers, however, were large and complex machines that required dozens of people to operate and hundreds of square feet of office space. They were prone to frequent breakdowns, often due to the failure of vacuum tubes. Thus, the invention of the transistor as a replacement for vacuum tubes brought in a new generation of computers by the 1960s. These computers did not differ much in the functions that they carried out and still required large amounts of space and manpower. But they were smaller, more powerful, and more reliable than the first generation of computers, and early second-generation computers, like IBM's 1401, soon dominated the market. Later in the 1960s, researchers found a way to increase the number of transistors, reduce their size, and imbed them on a microchip, a process that further reduced the cost of a computer.

By the mid-1970s, affordable computers began to enter the consumer market. Work on microchip development had continued through the 1960s, and by the early 1970s, it was possible to put all the components of a computer's central processing unit (CPU) onto a single microchip, called a microprocessor. The first widely used microprocessor, Intel's 8080, was released in 1974, and soon both corporate and amateur computer builders were designing new machines around it. One of those amateur machines, the Altair 8800, was the first microcomputer sold, mainly to computer hobbyists gathering in small clubs across the country. The Altair was a build-it-yourself kit sold in electronics stores and through computer magazines, and it formed the basis for the personal computer industry. For example, Bill Gates and Paul Allen used the Altair to write their new operating system in the BASIC computer language, an operating system they would later market as MS-DOS through their company, Microsoft.

Two members of one of the larger computer hobby clubs (the Homebrew Computer Club near Stanford University in California), Steve Jobs and Steve Wozniak, also saw the potential for the microprocessor-based microcomputer. In 1976, working out of their garages, they assembled a computer kit that was simpler than the Altair, needing only a television set and a keyboard, and called it the Apple I. A year later, in 1977, they built a more sophisticated computer that incorporated all the necessary processing components on a motherboard, and included a monitor and a keyboard. This was the Apple II, the first mass-produced personal computer. The Apple II was a huge success, with sales reaching 50,000 units by October 1979. With this, the personal computer market was created.

Other companies were quick to jump into this market. IBM popularized the term "personal computer" with the release of the IBM PC in 1981, and, along with the Apple II and its successor, the Apple Macintosh, the PC became the basis for the spread of computing from the corporate level to the personal level. Processing power continued to increase, while the cost of new microprocessors decreased, making personal computers more practical and more affordable. These personal computers added disk drives and internal hard drives for data storage, color monitors for better display, and printers for hard copy output. Graphical user interfaces like Apple's Mac OS and Microsoft's Windows made using computers much easier for ordinary people, and by the early 1990s, many families owned an Apple computer or an IBM PC or a PC clone made by Hewlett-Packard, Compaq, or Dell. However, most personal computing was limited to word processing, personal financial management, or playing games. Some computers were connected to modems that allowed them to communicate with other computers, but most of the communicating was done on bulletin board systems that were enclosed networks.

The idea of networking computers together turned the computing revolution into the Information Revolution. Just as steam power had driven the early years of the Industrial Revolution, powering factories and increasing output, the development of computers drove the early years of the Information Revolution. But what made the Industrial Revolution more than a localized change in economic and social norms and into an important shaper of global events was the connection of steam power to locomotion in the form of railroads. The railroad building boom that started in the 1830s connected communities and created regional economies. These economies grew as railroad networks expanded and led to the creation of national and, eventually, international markets. Along with the development of steamships to bridge the world's oceans faster, it was now possible to integrate the manufacturing of Europe and North America with the resources and markets of the rest of the world. Combined with the new wave of political imperialism in the late nineteenth century, the newly integrated markets put the Industrial Revolution on a truly worldwide scale.

A similar phenomenon occurred in the Information Revolution. Computers formed the basis of the new economy, but their use was still limited to individual operators, or at best, small businesses. Although computers could connect with each other over telephone lines by the 1980s, this communication was largely confined to personal interactions between individual users. Two developments, one started before the rise of the personal computer and one started after, brought computers together into an integrated worldwide network that transformed the global economy and society.

The first of these developments was the Internet, a wide-scale connection between multiple computers for the sharing of information. The idea for the Internet originated in the Department of Defense in the 1960s. The concept for a network of computers was not new, and theorists had written about it as early as the 1940s, but it remained largely in the realm of science fiction. In 1966, several researchers in the Advanced Research Projects Agency (ARPA), created for defense research and development, began work on what became ARPAnet, the first true computer network. Working with colleagues at the Massachusetts Institute of Technology (MIT), they wired together four mainframe computers at the University of California at Los Angeles, the Stanford Research Institute, the University of California at Santa Barbara, and the University of Utah (the Pentagon and MIT would soon be added to the network as well), using intermediary computer terminals they called Interface Message Processors (IMPs), which translated the various computer languages each mainframe used. The goal of the network was to allow researchers working in different locations to share information and data. The technical application of that goal was not as simple.

One of ARPAnet's main innovations that allowed for the fast, long-distance sharing of information was the use of "packet switching" technology to transmit data over telephone lines. Packet switching involves the breaking down of data into discrete bundles, sending each bundle—often in multiple copies to reduce the risk of data loss—over the lines, and then reassembling the data at the receiving end. Packet switching allowed multiple streams of data to be sent along the same transmission line without causing interference. In October 1969, the first two nodes of the ARPAnet, at Stanford and at UCLA, were connected, and the first message exchanged. By December 1966, all four original nodes were up and running, and ARPAnet was established.

By 1971, ARPA researchers built ARPAnet up to 15 nodes by 1971. They also began working with other network researchers, including a group at the University of Hawaii that developed a method for packet switching on radio networks, and another in Southern California that operated out of mobile vans. As the network expanded, users found new ways to share data. Starting in 1972, users could send direct messages to each other using what became known as electronic mail, or e-mail. Although not originally part of ARPAnet's intentions, e-mail communication soon dominated ARPAnet traffic. ARPAnet's other major innovation was the development of a communications protocol, TCP/IP, which allowed computers from different networks, many of which were springing up in government agencies and universities around the country, to communicate with each other without additional hardware. TCP/IP became the backbone of the burgeoning system of networks, and became the backbone of the Internet by the end of the century.

By the end of the 1980s, ARPAnet and other networks—quickly coming to be known as the Internet—included more than 100,000 different hosts, most of which were either connected to government agencies or academic institutions. By that time, ARPAnet had moved away from its defense-related origins, and much of the Internet was run through the National Science Foundation's NSFnet. Commercial organizations could connect to the Internet, and companies like America Online (AOL), CompuServe, and Prodigy provided networking access for individuals on their PCs. However, these services were their own networks, and they were not connected to the larger Internet. Still, they showed that connecting personal computers to a network could be a viable money-making operation, and this concept provided a rationale for the commercialization of the Internet.

In the early 1990s, the second development leading to the worldwide Internet appeared. In 1989, Tim Berners-Lee, an employee at the European Organization for Nuclear Research (CERN), proposed a new system to make it easier for researchers from different countries and laboratories to exchange data. He wrote the software for the system, which he called the World Wide Web (WWW) and implemented it within CERN the next year. In 1991, CERN launched the WWW software without cost to users, and within four years, it was the most popular method for navigating the Internet.

The key feature of the WWW was the method of connecting, or linking, different sections, or pages, of the network together. Berners-Lee wrote the WWW software in a new language, called Hypertext Markup Language (HTML), which allowed him to develop a dynamic interface for the network. Rather than linking the network sequentially, WWW software allowed users to highlight a phrase (link) and select it to bring up the material from that part of the network, so that the pages were connected in a lattice-like web. Each page would have its own address, defined by a Universal Resource Locator (URL) that would make navigating the Web simpler and more direct. Finally Berners-Lee developed a new protocol for the clients (the computer terminals) and the servers so that the data (i.e., the text and graphics) would be displayed in the same form regardless of which computer the user was accessing it from. Although the World Wide Web was not by itself a major technical breakthrough, by bringing together these various elements in a simple format, Berners-Lee was able to make the Internet much more accessible for all users.

However, the WWW still needed some experience to navigate, because it was largely text-based. Not long after the WWW entered the Internet and began to take it over, a group of computer science students at the University of Illinois, Champaign, developed a piece of software to display graphically Web content to the user. This browser, first called Mosaic and later renamed Netscape Navigator, made it possible for computers to display HTML graphically and made it more intuitive for users to navigate the pages, especially in a Graphical User Interface (GUI) like Mac OS or Windows. By giving away their browser to anyone using it for personal use (they licensed it to companies for a fee), Mosaic/Netscape made the Internet fully accessible at just the time when the network moved from a government/academic service to a commercial service. In 1992, Congress passed an amendment to the National Science Foundation Act of 1950 that opened the door to the commercial use of the Internet. Now those companies that had functioned only within their own networks could access the wider Internet, and the Internet itself became more useful to general users looking to communicate with the rest of the world.

By the mid-1990s, the combination of personal computers and the WWW-powered Internet transformed people's relationship with information technology. Computers were no longer machines that existed at the periphery of people's lives, useful for some tasks but generally not important on a daily basis. With access to the whole world of information available through their home computers, people could now make use of computers in new ways—from research to communication to shopping—and, in the developed world, computers moved to the center of most people's daily lives. As commercial opportunities expanded, driven by companies such as AOL, Amazon.com, eBay, and Yahoo!, the Internet's economic importance grew dramatically, and soon it was at the center of a new information economy. Just as steam-powered trains and ships had enabled people to move across countries and around the world more easily, so too did the Internet now allow people to communicate across the world much more easily. And just as industrialization and steam locomotion had allowed markets to develop on national and international scales, so too did the Internet allow markets to develop on a truly global scale.

This shift to a new global economy was the last major impact that the Information Revolution had. During the Industrial Revolution, the economy transformed from a locally based, small-scale system of production to a nationally based, large-scale system. New centers of production emerged, and new networks of trade and commerce developed, tying national economies closer together. This new system had a profound effect not only on the economy but also on society and politics. Similarly, the Information Revolution transformed the global economy from one centered around manufacturing to one centered around information transmission. And again, the new system's effects went beyond the economy to society and politics.

During the Industrial Revolution, the focus of economic activity shifted from market towns to factory towns. Cities such as Manchester, England, Cologne, Germany, and Pittsburgh came to exemplify this new industrial existence: built around new factories that employed large numbers of unskilled laborers and produced manufactured goods in unprecedented quantities. Connected by railroads to the resources they needed for manufacturing and to the markets where they could sell their finished product, industrial cities across Western Europe and North America rapidly grew in population and became the driving force behind national economic growth and technological innovation in the late 1800s. These new workers lived in densely populated neighborhoods and labored under often brutal conditions. Over time, new social and political forces brought a better quality of life to the working class, even as the products of industrialization brought prosperity to the "better" class.

Activity in the Information Revolution likewise clustered around new centers. In the 1940s, Stanford University opened the Stanford Research Institute near its campus in Palo Alto, California, as a center to promote innovation and economic development in the region. Soon Stanford itself was a focus for the study of computer science, and Stanford Research Institute was one of the first connected to ARPAnet. New technology companies, including Hewlett-Packard and Fairchild Semiconductor (which spawned Intel), began to cluster around the greater San Francisco area.

By the 1970s, the region was coming to be known by a new moniker, Silicon Valley. Here the Stanford Homebrew Computer Club made the Altair computer, and here Apple got its start (Jobs and Wozniak established Apple in nearby Cupertino). In 1970, the Xerox Corporation opened the Palo Alto Research Center (PARC), to promote uninhibited research into new technology and innovation. Early on, PARC played a major role in the development of the PC and later pursued other innovations, such as Graphical User Interface, laser printing, and Ethernet networking.

Silicon Valley was a center of the Information Revolution not just because of its large number of engineers and computer scientists, but also because it attracted investors to underwrite the creation of new companies based on the innovations coming out of the labs. Starting in 1957, Arthur Rock, a New York investment banker, began investing in new technology companies, such as Fairchild Semiconductor and Intel, providing them with their initial startup capital. Out of this came a new funding model, now called venture capital, where investors supplied critical startup capital to new technology companies that had limited access to standard resources in return for a portion of the company's ownership and management. This model soon became standard in Silicon Valley, and dozens of new venture capital firms formed in the area in the 1970s and 1980s. The convergence of innovators and capital in Silicon Valley made the region the dominant locale for high technology well into the twenty-first century.

Another aspect of the effect of the Information Revolution has been the declining importance of physical location for business success. The increased ease and lower cost of communication around the world has made it easier for companies anywhere in the world to gain access to resources and markets anywhere they see fit. In its broadest sense, this phenomenon is known as globalization, and it has had a profound effect on society in the late twentieth and twenty-first centuries. For information technology, it has allowed companies to benefit from various advantages that different locations offer around the world. For example, whereas Silicon Valley remains the center of the Information Revolution, new centers in places such as Bangalore, India, and Dalian, China, have sprung up to take advantage of the large number of engineering graduates coming out of Indian and Chinese universities. Although these cities are best known for housing outsourced services such as technical customer support and basic manufacturing, they are increasingly becoming centers of innovation in their own right.

These shifts in the centers of economic activity have brought both positive and negative changes to economies and societies. The relatively open atmosphere of Silicon Valley created the twenty-first-century workplace where employees of technology companies enjoyed good working conditions and generous benefits, often including stock ownership in the company. Workers are not tied to the time clock as their predecessors were during the Industrial Revolution. Ideas such as time-shifting, working from home, and outsourcing work during off hours have helped liberate workers from standard office practices. Yet information technology has also increasingly tied them to their work during their off hours through the Internet and mobile communications technology.

Similarly, the globalization of information technology has offered new opportunities for educated Indians and Chinese, among others, to find well-paying and rewarding work, spurring a burgeoning middle class that enjoys improved standards of living. At the same time, however, the movement of manufacturing and, increasingly, service jobs from Europe and North America to Latin America and Asia as a result of the Information Revolution and globalization has brought new unemployment and other jarring economic shifts to developed economies. Nor have those new jobs in Latin America and Asia always assured workers there of prosperity, and there are concerns about poor working conditions, low wages, and strict labor rules in high-technology companies in the developing world. Although not reaching the level of the worker abuse during the Industrial Revolution, labor issues related to the Information Revolution need to be monitored in order to maximize stability and prosperity to the areas where it is having an impact.

One of the most interesting aspects of the Information Revolution has been the quickened pace of innovation and change that the technologies, especially the Internet, have brought on. By the late 1980s, the Internet had begun to enter the consumer world, through personal computers and the early Internet service providers. Once it became available beyond government and academic institutions through the development of the WWW and removal of barriers to commercial activity in the early 1990s, use of the Internet exploded, and by the middle 1990s, it had become a daily part of many people's lives. By the end of the 1990s, the Information Revolution was experiencing its first speculative boom, the "dot.com" boom between 1995 and 2000 that pushed Internet company stocks to unprecedented levels.

Although this boom soon collapsed, the Internet continued to grow after 2000, and by 2005, it was achieving new success through concepts such as Web 2.0, in which individual users provided content through blog posts, commentary, and other interaction with each other. By 2010, the Internet was expanding into new areas, and new models such as social networking, exemplified by Facebook, became dominant both in the information economy and in society at large. Computers themselves continue to be made smaller, faster, and less expensive, and the development of mobile computers and smartphones makes it easier for people to access the Internet from virtually any location.

It is not possible to predict what direction the Information Revolution will take in the twenty-first century nor what effects it will continue to have on the economy, society, and politics. The revolutions in the Middle East beginning in 2011 have shown some hints of how the freer flow of information might turn the Information Revolution into a true revolution, but the outcomes of the uprisings might prove incomplete in this regard. Similarly, although technology continues to advance at a rapid pace, the next stage of the Information Revolution is still unclear, as is who, if anyone, might control the direction that it takes. Yet in barely half a century, the Information Revolution has changed everyday lives, created new economic opportunities, and brought a wealth of new information and tools for sharing and exploiting that information to much of the world's population.

SELECTED BIBLIOGRAPHY

Benkler, Yochai. *The Wealth of Networks: How Social Production Transforms Markets and Freedom.* New Haven, CT: Yale University Press, 2006. A provocative look at the conflicts between rapidly developing technology (and its largely positive effects on society) and the regulatory regimes in place to deal with the issues behind that technology.

Bodanis, David. *Electric Universe: The Shocking True Story of Electricity.* New York: Crown Publishers, 2005. A somewhat quirky but easy to understand overview of the history and science of electricity, ranging from its discovery to how it affects present-day society, biology, and culture.

Burman, Edward. *Shift!: The Unfolding Internet: Hype, Hope and History.* Hoboken, NJ: Wiley, 2003. Using Thomas Kuhn's famous concept of the paradigm shift, Burman argues that the Internet represents the next stage in scientific development and thus is more than just a new commercial tool.

Friedman, Thomas L. *The World Is Flat: A Brief History of the Twenty-First Century.* Further updated and expanded hardcover ed. New York: Farrar, Straus & Giroux, 2007. Perhaps the quintessential promotional text for late-twentieth-century globalization. Friedman argues that technology and communications are making the world "flat" by making global interaction faster and easier.

Gleick, James. *The Information: A History, a Theory, a Flood.* New York: Pantheon Books, 2011. A broad look at the place of information in human society, going back to prehistoric times. A largely theoretical examination of the development of information technology and the understanding of information itself.

Kaplan, Fred M. *1959: The Year That Changed Everything.* Hoboken, NJ: Wiley & Sons, 2009. A narrow case study of a single year in science, music, art, foreign relations, and other elements of society. Although the focus is largely American, Kaplan does expand that view in arguing for the significance of 1959 in the twentieth century.

Morozov, Evgeny. *Net Delusion: The Dark Side of Internet Freedom.* New York: Public Affairs, 2011. A cautionary look at the effects of the Internet on foreign relations, the spread of freedom, and the interactions between people and their governments. Largely aimed at persuading government officials to take care when promoting the use of the Internet in their foreign policies, the book's argument has been somewhat undermined by events in the Middle East when it was published.

Naughton, John. *A Brief History of the Future: From Radio Days to Internet Years in a Lifetime.* Woodstock, NY: Overlook Press, 2000. An overview of the history of the Internet, reaching back to its earliest conceptions, focusing on the communications aspects of technology, and highlighting the roles of specific individuals like Tim Berners-Lee.

Norman, Jeremy M. *From Gutenberg to the Internet: A Sourcebook on the History of Information Technology.* Novato, CA: Historyofscience.com, 2005. A collection of various articles on various aspects of the computing, networking, and other information technology. Although focused on twentieth-century developments, many articles deal with pre-twentieth-century technologies reaching back to the invention of moveable type in Europe in the fifteenth century.

Okin, J. R. *The Information Revolution: The Not-for-Dummies Guide to the History, Technology, and Use of the World Wide Web.* Winter Harbor, ME: Ironbound Press, 2005. A reference guide of common information technology terms, concepts, and ideas. The book explains these concepts in clear and readable language but with enough detail that it is useful for a more specialized audience.

Poole, Hilary W., Laura Lambert, Chris Woodford, and Christos J. P. Moschovitis. *The Internet: A Historical Encyclopedia.* Santa Barbara, CA: ABC-CLIO, 2005. A biographical, chronological, and issues-based reference book of the history of the Internet.

Ryan, Johnny. *A History of the Internet and the Digital Future.* London: Reaktion Books, 2010. A history of the Internet with a focus on where that history is going in the future. Argues about the effect that the Internet has had on opening up communications and freeing exchanges of ideas and explores the likelihood of further advancements.

Segaller, Stephen. *Nerds 2.0.1: A Brief History of the Internet.* New York: TV Books, 1998. A fast-paced and interesting look at the development of the Internet from its early theoretical beginnings to its explosion in the 1990s.

Wu, Tim. *The Master Switch: The Rise and Fall of Information Empires.* New York: Alfred A. Knopf, 2010. Argues that new information technologies usually start out open and available to all but soon fall under the monopoly control of a single corporation or group of corporations, often with support from government regulators.

APPLE COMPUTER

Based in Cupertino, California, Apple Computer Inc., the maker of the popular Macintosh line, revolutionized the personal computer industry during the late 1970s and early 1980s. The mid-1990s, however, saw Apple's market share erode to just 4 percent and brought serious concerns about the viability of the company and its products. Despite that, Apple maintained a strong presence in the education and graphics fields. In addition to personal computers, Apple also produces peripheral equipment and operating and applications software for use with its computers.

Apple began in California's Santa Clara Valley in 1976, when two college dropouts, Steve Jobs and Steve Wozniak, began selling microcomputers that they built in Jobs's garage. Both had worked in the electronics field in the Silicon Valley; Wozniak worked for Hewlett-Packard (HP), and Jobs had worked first for Atari and then HP, where the two met. They went on to develop the Apple I, which they introduced at the Homebrew Computer Club in Palo Alto. At an initial cost of $666.66, the computer did not get much traction in the marketplace. When the Apple II was introduced in 1977, it was met with a more positive response and nearly 130,000 units had been sold by the time the company went public in 1980.

The Apple Computer Company was established in 1976 and introduced one of the first personal computers the following year. This picture shows co-founders Steve Jobs (left) and Steve Wozniak (right), along with Apple president John Sculley, introducing the Apple IIc computer in 1984. When Jobs died in 2011, he was hailed as one of the industry's giants. (UPI-Bettmann/Corbis)

The company introduced the high-priced Apple III in March 1980 with little result. At the same time, Jobs began the development of a personal computer named "Lisa" along with other Apple engineers. It was the first personal computer (designed for business) to use a graphical user interface (GUI); however, at $9,995, not many businesses took the risk and bought the computer. The technology and innovation of Lisa was not wasted, and Jobs used it to develop the Macintosh personal computer. The Macintosh was slated to be an affordable $500; however, Jobs wanted to enter the personal computing market with much more. As a result, the Macintosh included a new, faster Motorola chip, was the first to use a mouse as an input device, and had a floppy drive that took 400KB 3.5-inch disks. The Macintosh debuted with much fanfare in January 1984 with the now-legendary Super Bowl commercial directed by Ridley Scott aptly named "1984" in homage to George Orwell's book of the same name. (The commercial also set a new standard in the advertising industry and marked the advent of "event" marketing and the phenomenon of Super Bowl commercials.) With a price tag of $2,495, the Macintosh was an instant success, and the company rebounded from the failure of the Apple III. That rebound was short-lived, and by the end of the year, sales dipped as problems with the computer became known.

Wozniak had left the company in 1983 following an accident. Jobs became the chair of the company, and two years later, he left after a bitter power struggle with chief executive officer (CEO) John Sculley. In 1986, the company resumed its success with the introduction of the Mac Plus and the LaserWriter printer. Those new tools made the production of high-quality documents easy and initiated the desktop-publishing revolution. Apple entered into important new partnerships and began developing software and hardware with IBM in 1991, worked with Sony to introduce the Macintosh Power-Book laptop computer that same year, and began an alliance with Sharp to produce the Newton, a new personal digital assistant, or electronic notebook. The Macintosh Power PC, which was capable of running both DOS and Windows applications, was launched in 1994.

Apple's net sales were sluggish during the mid-1990s, prompting a 1997 alliance with rival Microsoft Corporation and the return of Jobs to help get the company back on track. That alliance guaranteed that Microsoft would continue to produce such Apple-compatible products as the popular Microsoft Office. Microsoft also invested in a large number of nonvoting shares in Apple, which gave the company a much-needed finan-cial boost. In return, all Apple computers would carry Microsoft's Internet Explorer, which allowed Microsoft to corner that area of the market.

In addition to the deal with Microsoft in the summer of 1997, Apple announced a series of changes to the company intended to revitalize its flagging sales and reverse unhealthy losses. Jobs returned as interim CEO and brought back the basic ideas that made the company such a success in the 1970s and 1980s (user-friendly products and a relaxed corporate attitude that demanded excellence from its employees). A new board of directors was appointed in August 1997 to assist him. The changes in personnel were accompanied by efforts to streamline production and management costs. By late 1997, losses were less than expected, although the company was still in the red.

In 1998, Apple introduced a new personal computer designed to be even more user-friendly than the Macintosh. The iMac also featured a new look—Apple departed from traditional beige tones to give it a turquoise monitor. The company shipped 278,000 iMacs in the product's first six weeks, making iMac the fastest-selling Macintosh and the best-selling computer in the nation for most of the fall. That gave Apple its first prof-itable fiscal year in three years with earnings of $106 million.

In July 1999, Jobs introduced the iBook notebook computer and the PowerMac G4, a professional desktop computer. Stock in the company rose to an all-time high in the fall. In 2000, Jobs became the permanent CEO of Apple, but also that year, a massive slowdown occurred in the technology industry. Apple responded in January 2001 by introducing a new line of PowerMacs with disk drives that could read and write both CDs and DVDs, and Apple built Mac-only applications for such personal electronic devices as CD players, MP3 players, digital cameras, and DVD players. In 2001, Apple opened retail stores nationwide to sell Apple computers and various brands of digital products.

In October of that same year, Apple introduced the iPod, a MP3 digital music player, which met with tremendous success; the little white case and headphones have become a ubiquitous sight around the world. Soon, Apple owned the digital music marketplace with the introduction of iTunes, a music download service introduced in April 2003. Against the backdrop of the international music piracy/file sharing controversy, Apple managed to create partnerships with the major music labels for digital access rights to thousands of albums.

In subsequent years, Apple introduced the new G5 computer as well as the latest versions of its digital music player to further acclaim: iPod shuffle, iPod nano, and iPod video. At the 2006 Macworld Expo, Jobs announced the new MacBook Pro computers built with the Intel Core Duo chip, which is a chip most often used in Microsoft Windows-based computers. Up to four times faster than previous generations, the new generation of Apple computers was met with great critical accolades, ensuring their dominant position in the niche, high-end consumer electronics market. In 2007, Apple introduced its cell phone, the iPhone, which supports third-party applications using the Safari search engine. Hundreds of customers lined up at Apple Stores nationwide to buy the device. Then, in April 2010, Apple introduced a line of tablet computers known as the iPad.

ABC-CLIO

TIM BERNERS-LEE (1955–)

The inventor of the World Wide Web (WWW, or simply the Web), Tim Berners-Lee is largely responsible for the exploding popularity of Internet communication during the 1990s. A quiet, unassuming English physicist and computer scientist, Berners-Lee created the WWW in the hope that it would facilitate communication around the world, much as its name describes.

Born on June 8, 1955, in London, England, Timothy Berners-Lee is the son of two mathematicians, both of whom participated in the early development of computers. From 1969 to 1973, Berners-Lee attended the prestigious Emanuel School in London, where he developed an interest in electronics. From there, he went on to Queen's College at Oxford University and earned a bachelor's degree with honors in physics. His love for electronics remained strong during his time at Oxford, and while there, he assembled his own primitive personal computer system from a variety of spare parts. After graduating from Oxford in 1976, Berners-Lee took a position working on communications systems for Plessey Telecommunications Ltd. in Dorset. By 1978, he had switched jobs to join D. G. Nash Ltd., also in Dorset, where he continued to work on communication systems and computer programming. From June to December 1980, Berners-Lee served as a consultant for the European Particle Physics Laboratory of the European Organization for Nuclear Research (CERN) in Geneva, Switzerland. While at CERN, he wrote a communications software program that he dubbed "Enquire" (a nickname for a nineteenth-century book titled *Enquire Within upon Everything*). Although he did not share the program with others, it served as an important precursor for his later development of the WWW.

Between 1981 and 1984, Berners-Lee worked for another computer company called Image Computer Systems, Ltd., where he continued to develop his computer skills. In 1984, he returned to Geneva to take up a permanent position at CERN. CERN's computer needs were challenging for the young scientist.

With physicists located all over the world, CERN needed a means to facilitate communication among them so that they could share research and ideas. Building on the worldwide Internet network that already existed for scientists in 1989, Berners-Lee designed a set of software programs to enhance the Internet that would allow CERN's physicists to access easily the research of other scientists and distribute their own research to others regardless of its form—text, images, programs, or anything else available as a digital file. In anticipation of the success and availability of that program, he called it the World Wide Web.

Tim Berners-Lee invented the World Wide Web in 1990, along with the software necessary to store and transmit the data placed on the Web. (AP/Wide World Photos)

Choosing to design the WWW to work as a part of the already-thriving Internet was a stroke of genius. Often called a network of networks, the Internet links computers at any location with any other participating computer anywhere in the world and allows the transfer of information from one computer to another. The Internet had been growing increasingly popular since its development in the 1960s, when the Advanced Research Projects Agency, an agency under the U.S. Department of Defense, created ARPAnet, a means to link scientists' computers at the Stanford Research Institute, the University of California at Los Angeles, the University of California at Santa Barbara, and the University of Utah with each other. By the late 1980s, the Internet had spread to many major scientific research institutions. Because it was primarily a form of standardized communication, however, the Internet provided little help for the actual users. Also, learning to use it was extremely difficult and required a large investment of time and resources for everyone involved.

The software program Berners-Lee designed simplified the Internet by making it friendlier and more accessible for users. Essentially, the WWW is a set of programs and standards that allows users to present information in a concise but user-friendly fashion. It has three main components: URLs (uniform resource locators), HTTP (hypertext transfer protocol), and HTML (hypertext markup language).

Each URL is an address that is unique throughout the world and that fully describes where material is located—that is, which computer server it is on, which directory (similar to a multilevel index) it is in within the server, and what its unique filename is within the directory, which is usually, but not always, a Web page.

HTTP is a standard protocol that defines how two URLs can be associated so that each URL knows exactly where the other is located, which allows users to jump quickly from Web page to Web page. The association is called a hyperlink and is usually identified by the "http://" in the front of an address.

HTML is a standard that was derived from the SGML (Standard Generalized Markup Language) standard used extensively in the publishing business for large and complex documents containing several forms of information (text, tables, images, and others). It is based on using document markup techniques to support a hypertext link. Hypertext had existed for some time when Berners-Lee created the WWW, but HTML provides functions that are embedded in a file of textual and graphic information so that it can be transmitted on the Internet and displayed on a computer screen in a coherent and consistent fashion.

By December 1990, Berners-Lee had made the Web available to the scientists working for CERN. It proved so incredibly popular that by the following summer, it had spread to users outside of CERN. Despite several lucrative offers to sell the WWW technology, Berners-Lee chose instead to make the Web available to everyone at no cost. Being both free and popular, the Web swept throughout the world in a matter of months and fueled the demands of millions of people for Internet access. For the next three years, Berners-Lee worked on refining the Web and managing the incredible explosion of interest in his invention.

In September 1994, Berners-Lee left CERN to join the Laboratory for Computer Science at the Massachusetts Institute of Technology (MIT).As of 2011, he remains at MIT, heading up the World Wide Web Consortium (W3C), a nonprofit group dedicated to establishing standards for the Web. W3C has nearly 400 members, including several large corporations that wish to see the Web become more stable and thus a more reliable place to conduct business. Berners-Lee maintains that W3C only suggests standards; it does not enact mandates or have the power to enforce mandates regarding the Web's use. Instead, W3C forwards suggested standards to its members, who in turn consider introducing such standards into their Web businesses. As the group's membership includes such powerhouses as International Business Machines, Sun Microsystems, and the Oracle Corporation, those suggestions command a great deal of influence, but they are suggestions nonetheless. In that manner, Berners-Lee continues to exercise tremendous input regarding the use of the Web, as he struggles with some of the complex issues that have emerged from that technological revolution. Some of those issues include the conflict between centralized control of the network and almost no control of it, aggressive competition among browser producers, concerns regarding privacy and security, the benefits and drawbacks of government regulation, and the general transformation of society as the Web and the Internet become part of millions of people's daily lives.

In 1999, *Time* magazine named Berners-Lee one of the top 100 minds of the twentieth century. On December 31, 2003, Buckingham Palace announced that it would dub Berners-Lee a Knight Commander of the Order of the British Empire for his contributions to the development of the Internet.

ABC-CLIO

BILL GATES (1955-)

As of 2011, one of the wealthiest people in the world, Bill Gates is cofounder of the multibillion-dollar Microsoft Corporation, the world's leading computer software company. He is the youngest person ever to become a billionaire, and he topped *Forbes* magazine's list of the World's Wealthiest People from 1998 to 2010. A 1983 profile in *People* magazine said Bill Gates "is to software what Edison was to the light bulb."

William Henry Gates III was born in Seattle, Washington on October 28, 1955, the second oldest of three children. His father was a well-known lawyer, and his mother was a school teacher, a member of the University of Washington's board of regents as well as several corporate boards. Gates attended Lakeside School, a local private school renowned for its tough academic standards. At age 13, he began his lifelong affair with computers when the Lakeside Mothers Club used money they had made from rummage sales to buy a digital training terminal for the school. His father later recalled that Gates became "completely engrossed" in using the terminal and that he and several school friends (including Paul Allen, with whom Gates would later found Microsoft) often cut classes to spend hours with the machine. Entranced by the new technology and the possibilities it represented, the boys established the Lakeside Programming Group. One of Gates's first successful programs created a schedule that put him in classes with all the school's prettiest girls. He earned $4,200 that summer for arranging everyone's classes.

Gates's first professional job came soon after he and his computer friends wrote *The Problem Report Book,* a 300-page manual they compiled after going through the garbage bins of Seattle's Computer Center Corporation (CCC) and finding all the programmers' errors. CCC officials were so impressed with the boys that they gave them jobs. Shortly after that, Gates got into trouble at another job at the Control Data Corporation, when he figured out how to cause the company's CYBERNET computer system to crash and successfully carried out a plan to do so. After a formal reprimand from the company, Gates swore off computers. With so much free time all of a sudden, Gates turned his energies to school activities, including acting in school plays. Teachers recalled that he was amazingly fast at memorizing his lines.

After a year, Gates was unable to stick to his ban on computers and rejoined his friends in the Lakeside Programming Group. In his absence, the club had been taking real jobs to help pay for time in the computer lab. Some of their projects included creating a computerized payroll system for Lakeside School and using a computer to count the holes punched in cards by highway traffic-monitoring machines. Two years later, the group founded a new company called "Traf-O-Data" to sell their traffic-counting program, with Gates serving as president of the new company. Within a year, the company folded because its customers had learned that Traf-O-Data was run by teenagers, but not before it had earned $20,000.

Gates took another break from computers during the summer of 1972 to be a congressional page. In Washington, he again demonstrated his entrepreneurial streak when he and a friend bought 5,000 George McGovern-Thomas Eagleton campaign buttons for five cents each after the Democrats dropped Eagleton from the ticket. They were soon making a small fortune from people who paid up to $25 per button to have them as collector's items. Gates graduated from Lakeside in 1973 after scoring a perfect 800 on the math portion of the Scholastic Aptitude Test. He began attending Harvard University in the fall of 1973 and enrolled as a prelaw major.

During his sophomore year, Gates's old friend Paul Allen called him with news of the Altair 8800, the world's first commercially available microcomputer, made by a New Mexico company called MITS. Immediately recognizing the potential of the microcomputer, Gates and Allen contacted the president of MITS and told him they had already completed a program for the Altair. Panic set in when the president asked to see the program, which they had not even begun. Gates and Allen started working 24 hours a day in Gates's dormitory room, using simulated 8800 software they created at Harvard's computer lab because they had never seen the actual microcomputer. Using a book that described the machine, Gates and Allen adapted BASIC computer language to write an ambitious program that would fit into the Altair's tiny 256-byte memory. As soon as they finished, Allen dashed off to New Mexico with the program to present it to Altair. When Allen called Gates to say their program had worked on the first try, Gates "knew that people in schools everywhere would have these computers." For the next six years, the BASIC language that Gates and Allen wrote for the Altair was the industry standard and dominated the software market.

Encouraged by such success, Gates dropped out of Harvard when he finished his sophomore year in 1975 to concentrate on his new business full time. Despite his parents' disapproval, he and Allen moved to Albuquerque and established a company called Microsoft. They quickly gained many customers, including the brand-new computer companies Commodore and Apple Computer. By 1977, Microsoft had earned about $300,000, making it a small but successful business. Their success and fame continued to grow with such ventures as creating software for the Tandy Corporation's Radio Shack computers. In 1979, Gates and Allen moved Microsoft to Bellevue, a suburb of Seattle.

In 1980, Microsoft's big break came when International Business Machines (IBM) asked Gates to develop an operating system for its new personal computer. Gates initially declined the offer, not sure Microsoft could meet IBM's deadline, but he eventually reconsidered and accepted. To meet the IBM deadline, Gates paid $50,000 for the rights to a rudimentary operating system called "Q-DOS" ("quick and dirty operating system") designed by a Seattle programmer. Gates and his team made some adjustments to the system and added some new features, renaming the result MS-DOS (after Microsoft). He sold the system to IBM and then persuaded the business giant to release its design specifications so software makers could create software for it more easily. IBM agreed, and soon, more than 100 companies had bought licenses to use MS-DOS so that their products would be IBM-compatible. The phenomenon that would make Gates's fortune had been put into motion—his operating system had become the industry standard and the basis for future software development. Within a year, Microsoft's staff and profits had grown exponentially.

In the mid-1980s, Gates started developing applications software, the programs that tell a computer how to perform a specific task such as word processing. That type of software represents the largest portion of the software business. By the end of the decade, Microsoft dominated the field, surging past all competitors. That progress came despite Allen's diagnosis of cancer in 1983, which forced virtually the entire burden of leadership onto Gates's already overloaded shoulders. He hired a number of new executive recruits to help out and distinguished himself from most other company owners by delegating numerous responsibilities to others. In 1986, by which time Allen's cancer had gone into remission, Microsoft moved to new headquarters in Redmond, Washington, with room for its more than 1,200 employees. At the same time, Microsoft stock went public. The company's stocks went on sale on March 13, 1986, for $21 a share, and when they hit $90.75 a year later, the 32-year-old Gates became the world's youngest billionaire. Because Microsoft had been offering stock options to its employees for years, the conversion to public stock also made many Microsoft employees, from executives to secretaries, millionaires.

Nonplussed by his enormous wealth, Gates started to realize that MS-DOS was insufficient to carry out the more-complex tasks he knew personal computer users would soon demand. In 1987, Microsoft introduced OS/2, a new, more powerful operating system that could execute several functions simultaneously. His next innovations made computers more efficient and easier to use. The combination of Microsoft Word (a word-processing program that became popular in the late 1980s) and Windows (an operating system based on icons that went on the market in 1992) simplified basic computing and dramatically expanded the number of computer users worldwide.

With his huge success, Gates came under increasing scrutiny and criticism for his voracious business practices. His agreements with hardware manufacturers often served to prevent the success of rival products even when they were already on the market and Microsoft versions had yet to be completed. In 1995, the development of Windows 95, a revolutionary operating system, drove hardware manufacturers to produce computers with more memory and more hard disk space. Microsoft thus effectively compelled the entire computer industry to follow its lead. Such practices involved Gates and Microsoft in legal struggles over alleged anticompetitive practices and copyright infringement throughout the 1990s.

In 1999, the U.S. Justice Department found that Microsoft had indeed overstepped the bounds of legal competition, and a breakup of the company was threatened. In June 2000, District Judge Thomas Penfield Jackson said he was ordering the breakup because the company was unwilling to admit that it had violated federal antitrust law and had shown no willingness to modify its business conduct. However, a federal appeals court overturned the breakup of Microsoft in June 2001, allowing the corporation to remain intact.

In 1995, Gates coauthored *The Road Ahead,* a book illustrating his thoughts about how computers will affect society over the long run. *The Road Ahead* quickly became a best-seller and was followed by *Business @ the Speed of Thought* (1999), which outlined his ideas on how business problems could be solved digitally. With an estimated personal wealth of almost $40 billion in 1997, Gates became increasingly active in philanthropy.

In 2000, Gates began reducing his responsibilities at Microsoft. Steve Ballmer replaced Gates as the company's chief executive officer, although Gates remained chairman and head software architect. In the same year, he and his wife, Melinda, consolidated three family foundations into the Bill and Melinda Gates Foundation, the philanthropic goals of which they based on the work of Andrew Carnegie and the Rockefeller family. The foundation's chief focus is on the eradication of global health problems, including AIDS, malaria, and tuberculosis. In June 2006, Gates announced that he would step down from the day-to-day management of Microsoft in July 2008 to devote more time to charitable work. Also in June 2006, the Bill and Melinda Gates Foundation received an endowment of more than $31 billion from Berkshire-Hathaway chair and longtime friend, Warren Buffet, with the stipulation that the money be used to match donations from the Gates Foundation's assets. In 2010, Gates and Buffet jointly announced plans to give to charity at least half of their wealth over time and urged other billionaires to do the same.

ABC-CLIO

ADA KING, COUNTESS OF LOVELACE (1815–1852)

Ada King, the countess of Lovelace, was a mathematician considered by some to be the first computer programmer. While an associate of Charles Babbage, an English mathematician who spent most of his life trying to design a computing machine, Lovelace's ideas about computing came to fruition.

Lovelace was born Augusta Ada Byron on December 10, 1815, in London to George Gordon, better known as Lord Byron, the famous poet and the sixth Baron Byron, and his wife, Anne Isabella Milbanke. On April 21, 1816, Byron signed a deed of separation, dissolving his marriage. Lady Byron obtained sole custody of Lovelace. Meanwhile, Byron soon left England for the Continent and never returned to see his only child.

During the early nineteenth century, British noblewomen who studied science were sometimes tolerated, but in general, they were not supposed to take part in such intellectual activities. Despite those social expectations, Lovelace studied mathematics and science. Her mother, who was interested in mathematics, encouraged her daughter's interest in science so that she would grow up without any of the influences of Romanticism, which had been her father's passion. Lovelace received her education in science, mathematics, and music from a variety of tutors. She excelled in her studies, but as a child her favorite subject was geography. To refocus her mind on arithmetic, her mother added more mathematics and less geography to her daughter's curriculum. Lovelace was rewarded when she did well, but she also received a variety of punishments that included writing apologies, lying motionless, or sitting in solitary confinement when she did not meet expectations.

In 1828, the 13-year-old Lovelace devised a plan for a flying machine. Five years later, she met Charles Babbage, a mathematics professor at Cambridge, and heard his ideas for an analytical engine. Babbage wished to design a machine that would calculate numbers rapidly and could act on foresight. Lovelace was intrigued by his ideas.

When she was 18, Lovelace met Mary Somerville, another scientifically-minded woman, who supported Lovelace in her studies. Somerville and Lovelace became friends, and together they attended scientific and mathematics demonstrations, as well as musical concerts. In 1835, Lovelace married William King, and they became the earl and countess of Lovelace in 1838; they had three children, Annabella, Byron, and Ralph Gordon.

In 1842, an Italian scholar, Luigi Federico Menabrea, wrote *Elements of Charles Babbage's Analytical Machine,* detailing Babbage's analytical engine. The work was written in French, and for nine months, between 1842 and 1843, Lovelace translated the article, attaching her own annotations to it. Her notes, combined with the translation, resulted in a work that was three times the length of Menebrea's original.

Lovelace's notes appeared in Richard Taylor's 1843 *Scientific Memoirs* (Volume 3), although she used her initials, A. A. L., as her pseudonym. In her article on the engine, Lovelace predicted that the device could be used for both practical and scientific uses. She also thought that it could be used to create graphics as well as compose music. Some scholars believe that Lovelace's ideas foreshadowed the uses of the personal computer.

Lovelace considered herself to be a metaphysician and an analyst. In a written explanation, she suggested that Babbage's engine could be used to calculate Bernoulli numbers—a system of numbers named after Jakob Bernoulli, a seventeenth-century Swiss mathematician who created the principles of the calculus of variation. Some scholars contend that Lovelace's suggestion to Babbage was the first computer program.

Lovelace socialized with many famous intellectuals, including Sir David Brewster, who invented the kaleidoscope; author Charles Dickens; and physicists Michael Faraday and Charles Wheatstone. Lovelace had not grown up to be entirely scientifically minded; her mathematical descriptions often contained poetic metaphors. She also enjoyed drinking, music, horses, and gambling. At the time of her death, Lovelace owed around £2,000 in gambling debts.

On November 29, 1852, Lovelace died of uterine cancer in London. At her request, she was buried next to her father in the Byron family vault in the Church of Saint Mary Magdalene in Hucknall, a town outside Nottingham, England. In the late 1970s, a U.S. Department of Defense software programming language was named ADA in honor of Lovelace.

ABC-CLIO

ALAN TURING (1912–1954)

British mathematician Alan Turing was a pioneer in the theory of computers. In 1936, he described a theoretical machine that contained elements of what would become the modern computer. He helped crack German codes for Great Britain during World War II and went on to design some of the world's first computers.

Alan Mathison Turing was born on June 23, 1912, in London, England, to an upper-middle-class family. His father, a high official in England's colonial administration, was usually away in India, so Turing and his brother were raised mostly by relatives. When he was old enough, Turing was sent to private boarding schools, where he excelled in math-

Alan Turing, an English scientist, worked during World War II to help decipher the German Enigma codes and then went on to develop one of the earliest stored-program computers. (Time & Life Pictures/Getty Images)

ematics and science but had little interest in other academic subjects. He studied the emerging field of quantum physics and Albert Einstein's work in physics all on his own.

In 1931, Turing won a scholarship to King's College of Cambridge University, where he soon distinguished himself as a mathematics scholar. He graduated with a master's degree in 1934. His 1935 paper "On Gaussian Error Function" earned him the 1936 Smith's Prize for mathematics. Turing was awarded a year-long fellowship to Princeton University in New Jersey, where he met Alonzo Church, a professor working on some of the same problems Turing discussed in his paper.

Turing researched binary numbers, Boolean logic, and cyphers. His most famous and important paper, "On Computable Numbers," was written in 1937. In it, he tackled an important topic in mathematical logic—which mathematical procedures could be conducted entirely by a machine. It was a theoretical machine, now called the "Turing Machine," but in many ways, it laid out the concept for a computer program. He stayed on at Princeton for three years to work on his doctoral dissertation on ordinal logic under Church's direction. After Turing was awarded his doctorate, Princeton officials invited him to stay on, but instead, he opted to accept a fellowship at Cambridge.

In 1938, Turing returned to England. When Great Britain was pulled into World War II, he joined the government's top-secret Code and Cypher School in Bletchley, near Oxford. The group's prime goal was to break German communication codes that had been encrypted by machine. Turing's work with the Code and Cypher School was instrumental in developing the machines and techniques to crack Germany's secret codes, as he had extensive experience in connecting complex logical and mathematical theory with actual physical machines. Many of the details of his contribution to Great

Britain's decoding machines are still classified. Turing was awarded the prestigious Order of the British Empire in 1946.

Turing gained much experience in electronics and calculating equipment. That experience helped him gain a position at the National Physical Laboratory (NLP) in Teddington, England. There, he developed the Automatic Computing Engine (ACE), which ran programs and stored information for the government. A smaller version of his ACE, called the Pilot ACE, was finished in 1950. Among other things, the Pilot ACE was used to facilitate aircraft design for many years.

Although his work at the NLP was successful, the slow-moving bureaucratic structure frustrated Turing. He moved on to Manchester University, where the Royal Society Computing Laboratory was working on the Mark I, a new larger computer. As chief programmer, Turing wrote stored computer programs that enabled the Mark I to do math, perform encryption and language analysis, and play chess. It was a great leap forward to make a computer do things other than compute. His work had a deep impact on the computer designs of several companies in the 1950s, including English Electric and Bendix.

Enthralled by the idea of artificial intelligence, Turing also invented the "Turing Test," a series of criteria to judge whether a computer is actually thinking. He published papers refuting arguments why a machine could not be intelligent and postulated that scientists would make more progress in artificial intelligence through programming instead of designing robots. His 1950 paper "Computing Machinery and Intelligence" was widely read. However, Turing found himself between worlds—he had been away from straight mathematics for so long that he was no longer a cutting-edge mathematician, but he was not quite an electronic engineer, either.

Turing was a homosexual, which was illegal in Great Britain at the time. He had begun having an affair with a seedy young man, one of whose associates burgled Turing's home. When the police came to investigate the crime, Turing did nothing to hide his relationship with the young man. He was convicted in 1952 of publicly practicing homosexuality. Instead of imposing a jail term, the court sentenced Turing to chemotherapy with the female hormone estrogen (intended to reduce libido) for one year. After that experience, he became terribly depressed. Turing's death on June 7, 1954, in Wilmslow, England, was ruled a suicide. Just 41 years old, he had laced an apple with cyanide.

ABC-CLIO

12

China's Rise to Global Importance, 1978–Present

INTRODUCTION

As unimaginable as it might seem today, barely 100 years ago the ancient Chinese state lay prostrate at the feet of Europe's imperial nations and Japan, its Pacific rival. Beginning early in the nineteenth century, modernity in the form of European imperialism increasingly encroached on Chinese territory and sovereignty. The pace accelerated toward the end of that century as a modernizing but belligerent and aggressive Japan joined China's European tormentors, reaching a climax with the 1894–1895 Sino-Japanese War that revealed China's utter helplessness in the face of its predators.

Alarmed by this perilous condition, some Chinese leaders and intellectuals urged a thorough reform to counter the clear and present danger presented by the more advanced foreigners. However, Chinese conservatives undermined numerous reform initiatives. Simultaneously, there arose a grassroots movement aimed at the hated foreigners. The Righteous and Harmonious Fists, better known as the Boxers, attacked foreign interests and, especially, Chinese converts to Christianity. The Boxer Rebellion peaked in 1900 when the rebels murdered the German ambassador and besieged the foreign diplomatic corps in its Beijing compound.

The Boxer Rebellion provoked a harsh response. A multinational force numbering 20,000 soldiers under the command of German field marshal Alfred von Waldersee scattered the Boxers, forced the dowager empress and her government to flee, and occupied the capital's Forbidden City. Among other punishments, the victorious foreigners imposed an indemnity of 450 million taels, or almost twice China's annual income. One would think that China had reached its lowest point; however, things got worse. Over the next several decades, a seemingly endless orgy of war, revolution, civil war, chaos, and ideological extremism claimed the lives of uncounted millions of Chinese.

In 1911, Dr. Sun Yat-sen entered on the stage of history. Chinese by birth, Sun was a British-trained medical doctor who had travelled extensively outside of China. More important, he was a revolutionary who sought to both modernize China and drive out the hated foreign imperialists. In 1911, a revolt at Wuchang army garrison gave Sun's revolutionary movement, later known as the Kuomintang (KMT) or Chinese Nationalists, an opportunity that it seized. The decrepit Manchu dynasty virtually disappeared overnight, replaced by a republic led by Sun. However, Sun and the KMT lacked the necessary "muscle" to rule over all of China in an orderly fashion. In many provinces local leaders known as warlords successfully defied the central government's authority. Moreover, with the founding of the Chinese Communist Party (CCP) in 1921, the KMT faced yet another challenger for control of the country. Meanwhile, the tough and unbending Chiang Kai-shek assumed leadership of the KMT after Sun's death in 1925. A low-grade civil war pitting the KMT against the CCP convulsed the country for decades before dramatically intensifying after the close of World War II in 1945.

Even though World War I and the Bolshevik Revolution in Russia provided China some relief from its European adversaries, the same could not be said of Japan, which steadily moved to expand its considerable role in China. During the course of the war, Japan issued its Twenty-One Demands that clearly challenged China's sovereignty and provoked a decidedly anti-Japanese reaction among many Chinese students. Although China managed to deflect the harshest of the demands, Japan remained adamant. In 1931, it seized the rich Chinese province of Manchuria, setting up a puppet regime under Pu Yi, the last emperor. Then, in 1937, it launched an undeclared but full-scale attack against China proper, thereby igniting the Asian phase of World War II. The war, which featured horrifying Japanese atrocities against civilian Chinese, ravaged China until its conclusion in 1945.

With the defeat of Japan, the KMT and CCP resumed their civil war with much greater intensity. The conflict ended in 1949 with the victory of the CCP under the leadership of Mao Zedong and the declaration of the People's Republic of China (PRC). In December, the remnants of the KMT fled to the island of Taiwan (Formosa) where they maintained the fiction that they were the legitimate rulers of China.

From 1949 onward, the CCP ruled China with an iron fist and Mao, although sometimes challenged by his comrades, ruled the CCP until his death in 1976. Even today, Mao remains a controversial figure; however, a good case can be made that he and the CCP enjoyed significant success in their relations with the outside world. Most important, after 1949 outside or imperial forces from either Europe, or Asia, or North America, never again seriously threatened China. Despite involvement in the Korean War (1950–1953) that saw the People's Liberation Army (PLA) clash with U.S. forces and serious skirmishes in 1969 between the PLA and Soviet Red Army troops along the Chinese-Soviet border, Mao and the CCP restored and maintained the integrity of the Chinese state. The long era of imperialist aggression against China had come to an end.

Moreover, China began to assert itself in world affairs. With the help of the USSR, its ally during the 1950s, China exploded an atomic bomb in 1964, thereby joining the very exclusive club of those countries possessing nuclear weapons. At about the same time, the CCP threw off Soviet tutelage and, surprisingly, mounted a serious challenge to Moscow for leadership of the world's Marxist movement.

Perhaps the most consequential indications of China's revitalization and emergence as a state of global importance occurred in the early 1970s. In 1971, Mao's PRC replaced Chiang Kai-shek's Taiwanese government as China's official representative at the United Nations. In doing so, the PRC claimed one of the five permanent seats on the United Nations Security Council. A few months later, in February 1972, the most powerful man in the world, U.S. president Richard M. Nixon, traveled to Beijing to meet Mao and to sign the Shanghai Communiqué that began to restore normal diplomatic relations between the two countries.

View of fireworks launched over the National Stadium, known as the Birds' Nest, during the opening ceremony for the Beijing 2008 Olympic Games in Beijing. The Chinese viewed their hosting of the Olympic Games as validation of their rise to global prominence. (Guimahky/Dreamstime.com)

Although Mao's PRC achieved impressive triumphs in the world of international affairs, its domestic policies left much to be desired. It is true that the task of revitalizing China and restructuring it according to Marxist principles proved a monumental one; nevertheless, some serious errors with major negative repercussions hindered China's development. During the first few years of its reign, the CCP attempted to strengthen its grip on power, resuscitate Chinese economic life, create a sense of national unity, and impose a set of radical concepts on a traditional society oriented much more toward Confucius than Marx. On the whole, the CCP was fairly successful in achieving its goals. Yet the cost was staggering. Millions of lives were lost to starvation, disease, exposure, and gradual but inexorable class warfare featuring executions and forced labor in brutal "rehabilitation" camps. Chinese agriculture was progressively collectivized and private industry was nationalized. The standard of living rose somewhat, the population was successfully indoctrinated, and formal opposition to the CCP dictatorship disappeared.

When unrelenting pressure from the CCP provoked a backlash, in 1957, Mao introduced the Hundred Flowers campaign which encouraged the Chinese people—but especially intellectuals—to speak their minds freely. However, when too many availed themselves of this opportunity, Mao cut short the campaign and the CCP wreaked havoc on those who had dared to open their mouths. The hare-brained scheme known as the Great Leap Forward was even more disastrous and demoralizing. Initiated in the late 1950s, the Great Leap Forward called for massive forced collectivization of agriculture and rapid industrialization including more than a million "backyard steel furnaces." The results were nothing short of devastating. The industrialization drive collapsed amid mismanagement, lack of quality control, and the absence of effective coordination. Even worse, the peasant communes failed completely. A catastrophic famine followed, bringing death by starvation to an estimated 30 million Chinese before the Great Leap Forward campaign was called off.

These failures prompted a challenge to Mao's preeminent position in the CCP that he warded off with some difficulty. Having managed to hang on to power, in 1966 Mao embarked on a new drive, the Great Proletarian Cultural Revolution that consequently plunged China into total chaos. For reasons that had much more to do with cementing his grip on power than promoting the well-being of the Chinese people, Mao enlisted his allies in the PLA to purge the CCP of not only those who opposed him and his policies but also those who had urged caution and orderliness in the wake of the Great Leap Forward fiasco. Mao selected the youth of China, whom he designated as the Red Guards, as the vehicle to achieve his goals and urged them forward in what turned out to be an orgy of denunciations, purges, and humiliations directed against respected party members, administrators, intellectuals, and virtually anyone else who got in the way of the Red Guards as they ran amok. The result was utter chaos. As paralysis crept over the country, Mao moved to wind down the Cultural Revolution, but the damage that had been done set back China for years.

The 1976 deaths of both foreign minister Zhou Enlai and Mao himself signaled a changing of the guard. Nevertheless, two years elapsed as a succession struggle convulsed China. By late 1978, 74-year old Deng Xiaoping, a longtime CCP dignitary who had been purged during the Cultural Revolution and then rehabilitated, emerged as China's new leader. Surprisingly, Deng immediately placed China on the path of a major economic reform that also carried significant social and cultural connotations.

Amazingly enough, the old communist Deng called for China's economic modernization through an infusion of capitalism! He declared that "to get rich is glorious." Under the slogan "socialism with Chinese characteristics," Deng introduced a form of modified market capitalism sometimes referred to as a socialist market economy. By unleashing the creative spirit of the Chinese population, Deng was also inaugurating one of the most spectacular economic booms in recorded history. Yearly growth rates of 10 percent became common, and references to Marx and the class struggle faded into the background. The Chinese leadership placed great emphasis on the advancement of technology. To hasten this process, China opened itself to Western scholars, entrepreneurs, and tourists while actively seeking capital and additional expertise. Simultaneously, China sent its best and brightest students to North America and Europe for advanced training in technical fields such as physics, engineering, computer science, and electronics.

The results were impressive to say the least, with more than a few observers likening China's progress to that of the Meiji Restoration of late-nineteenth-century Japan. One could produce several weighty tomes cataloguing the economic advances made by China over the past few decades; however, a few statistics should serve to make the point. Between 1976 and 2006, China's population increased by about 40 percent to 1.3 billion people. At the same time, its gross domestic product increased by 7,000 percent;

its household consumption increased by 8,000 percent; and its exports increased by a mind-boggling 14,000 percent. Once an importer of capital, China now regularly buys U.S. Treasury instruments, invests in far-flung enterprises from Africa to the Middle East to South America, and plays an increasingly key role in such global economic and financial bodies as the International Monetary Fund and the G-20.

Throughout all this change, the one constant has been the CCP's unassailable political supremacy. This point was graphically demonstrated in 1989 when PLA forces mercilessly crushed a large pro-democracy protest movement that had set up camp in Beijing's Tiananmen Square. Hundreds, perhaps thousands, of protestors died in the square, and countless more innocent bystanders suffered a similar fate. A few days later, Deng effusively praised the PLA and condemned the protesters—most of whom were students—as the "dregs of society" intent on counterrevolution.

Although Deng died in 1997, his successors, including current premier Wen Jiabao and Hu Jintao, president and head of the CCP, continued to broaden and deepen the reform policies that he initiated—especially those of an economic nature—with great success. With an annual 2010 GDP of $4.9 trillion, China's economy is more than 90 times larger than when Deng assumed control. It has overtaken the United States as the world's largest auto market and eclipsed Germany as the world's largest exporter of manufactured goods. In the summer of 2010, it surpassed Japan as the world's second largest economy, and most experts predict that it will catch up to and outstrip the U.S. economy within 10 to 20 years.

Perhaps the most obvious indication of China's arrival as a modern, powerful, respected, and prosperous state occurred in 2008 when it hosted the XXIX Summer Olympic Games. Athletes from throughout the world flocked to Beijing, tens of thousands of spectators descended on the Chinese capital, and countless millions took in the spectacle via television. The games went off without a major hitch, thereby seeming to give some credence to those who claim that the 21st century will indeed belong to China.

INTERPRETIVE ESSAY

YUXIN MA

One of the four oldest river valley civilizations with a history of almost 4,000 years, China was known as a densely populated country with reasonable political stability throughout most of its existence. Historical China, or China proper, was bounded by the Great Wall and included the watersheds of the Yellow and Yangtze Rivers. It enjoyed a mild climate, fertile soil, and water resources, thus nurturing a sophisticated agrarian economy that supported a large population. For most of the time from 221 BCE to 1911, China was a unified and centralized bureaucratic state governed by an authoritarian ruler—the emperor. The ancient political theory known as the Mandate of Heaven legitimized the emperor's authority in the eyes of his subjects, and the rational government recruiting system—the Civil Service Exam—singled out the best-educated Confucian scholars to serve the state as bureaucrats. The standardized educational curriculum of Confucian classics and the highly competitive Civil Service Exam produced a like-minded

Chinese elite who oversaw taxation, administration, and judicial matters. It buttressed the state rather than opposing it. In times of dynastic transition, the consensus in favor of unification, centralization, and rational bureaucracy contributed to the desired stability and institutional continuity.

Because of its extensive territory, brilliant administration, and visible opulence, China often influenced its neighbors in east, central, and southeast Asia. When China controlled the Silk Road and southeast Asian sea routes, it imposed a tributary system on its neighbors whose rulers gave China gifts and recognition. Under this system, China had the moral obligation to provide military protection to tributary states and to guarantee regional peace.

Premodern China was a manufacturing center for the finest goods—tea, silk, lacquerware, porcelain, fine furniture, and domestic ornaments. Most of its products were for domestic consumption. In the second millennium, a growing population led to pressure on the land. In turn, this fueled a major economic transformation. By the sixteenth century, commercialization and urbanization had produced a monetized market economy. Commerce accelerated the trend toward regional specialization and increased merchant activity. To meet a rising demand, both close-by and far-flung markets developed. Food staples as well as luxury goods became a commodity as some peasants switched to cash crops for profit.

A Sino-centric and self-sufficient China did not see the need to develop trade with the Europeans. Nevertheless, from the sixteenth century on, China was a desirable destination for European missionaries and traders who sought either to convert the vast Chinese population or to develop trade with China. China reserved one port—Canton—for limited and supervised foreign trade and remained largely closed to Europeans until the British administered a humiliating defeat in the Opium War of 1840. Over the next several decades, Western powers imposed unequal treaties upon China and forced it to open its coast for trade. Protected by the privilege of extraterritoriality, foreign sailors, traders, missionaries, and explorers landed in China's treaty ports with diverse agendas. By their presence and their endeavors, the foreigners challenged the sovereignty of the last imperial dynasty—the Qing state. They shook the vulnerable Chinese economy by exposing it to the global market and provoked both reforms and rebellions. Under such pressure, the 1911 revolution brought the imperial system to its end.

From 1911 to 1949, politicians with different agendas and ideologies strove to build their vision of modern China, but their efforts were diluted and undermined by conservatives, warlords, subversive forces, the Japanese invasion of 1931–1945, and the civil war of 1946–1949. The Chinese Communist Party (CCP) won the civil war through its peasant revolution and forced the Nationalist regime to flee to Taiwan in 1949. Yet the CCP alienated many people. Its blind imitation of the Soviet economic model of collectivization and state "commandism" challenged the deeply ingrained peasant values of private property, household economy, and market activities. Peasants had neither the incentive nor the morale to produce effectively. After three decades of Communist rule, China was still a country in poverty and isolation. With a quarter of the world's population, in 1978 China generated less than 0.5 percent of the global economic output.

Great changes have taken place in China since the economic reform launched by Deng Xiaoping in 1978. Today, China has the world's second largest economy. It is growing at a rate three times faster than that of the United States. Moreover, China is the biggest investor in the United States and accounts for 10 percent of the global economic output. China's rapid industrialization and urbanization over the past three decades has produced close to 200 cities with populations of more than one million. Furthermore, it has generated better-educated young citizens, a disciplined labor force, and an improved livelihood for its people. More than 400 million Chinese have been lifted above the poverty line of $1 a day; Chinese citizens increasingly work, live, and travel where they want; and a significant portion of enterprising Chinese have become owners of businesses, houses, cars, and stocks. Accompanying its economic takeoff, China has gained global economic, political, and military standing. This is particularly true in the realm of technology where China has surpassed the technologies of some mature industrial states, completed construction of a cutting-edge infrastructure, and explored space with its own rockets. Today, China's needs for energy, resources, jobs, and markets have affected even far-off nations and societies. Over the past three decades, the millions of Chinese who have chosen to migrate to the Western world have built bridges between China and the developed world. Many overseas Chinese are successful professionals who are fully integrated into Western societies yet keep familial, economic, and emotional ties with their birth country.

What has happened in China since the late 1970s? What of the decision-making and policy-implementing logic that has produced the fastest and most unthinkable changes in such a short period of time? How did the CCP successfully transform its planned economy dictated by state "commandism" into a profit-seeking market economy fully integrated into the global, capitalist world? What has enabled the Chinese economy to maintain an average growth rate of more than 9.5 percent?

Since the economic reform in 1978, the CCP has shifted its focus from ideological dogma to economic development. It has decentralized its control over the economy and transferred greater power and responsibility in economic activities to local governments and individuals. Thus, with the freedom to make their own economic decisions, local governments and individuals have stronger incentives and greater opportunity to do their best. The initial changes took place in the early 1980s when the government de-collectivized the rural economy and implemented the household responsibility system that let individual peasant families make their own economic decisions and adapt their productive activities to maximize personal profit. Soon the state introduced the market into the socialist economy, allowing peasants to enrich themselves through commercial activities. Peasants diversified their economic activities by selling their products, engaging in handicrafts and processing, and investing in rural industries.

The household responsibility system had both positive and negative effects on villagers' lives. On the positive side, as their lives improved, some courageous peasants explored the freedom and mobility newly available to them and migrated to cities or economically developed areas to earn additional wage income. They reinforced bonds with rural villages by sending their income home, and through their seasonal migration they brought back to their villages urban culture, values, and fashion, as well as new ideas and lifestyles. On the negative side, because of de-collectivization, village culture (political meetings, sports events, mutual assistance, and group activities), which was cultivated by the socialist state, has gradually declined. Minimal welfare (education and health care) at the village level evaporated and local order deteriorated. By the late 1990s, many corrupt village leaders fleeced peasants to enrich themselves and relied on despotic measures to reinforce local order, which increased the peasantry's burdens and suffering. Fully aware of the corruption at the local level, the Chinese government has made major efforts to improve peasants' lives in recent years: in 2006, it abolished the land tax; in 2007, it reinforced the commitment to nine years of free, compulsory education by extending national subsidies to rural schools.

In the urban areas, the Chinese government has diversified the economic structure by encouraging industrial investments from foreign, local, and individual capital. At the same time, it gave more freedom to managers of the state-owned enterprises, letting them be fully responsible for the economic outcome of their units. In this manner, it was hoped that state-owned enterprises would become more efficient and less dependent on state assistance. Factory managers were pushed to improve their productivity in the most efficient way, even if it meant laying off surplus workers from overstaffed production lines. They had to handle millions of employees at highly inefficient state enterprises with great caution to avert potential social unrest arising out of economic desperation. In the 1980s, collective enterprises owned by villages and town governments were freed from encumbrances that hampered state-owned enterprises and did much better than the latter.

Privately owned industries in the early 1990s were tied to collective industries through subcontracting arrangements. By the late 1990s, this sector of the economy had grown much larger, stronger, and more independent. Gradually it came to dominate the urban economy. In contrast, during the period of economic reform, state-owned industries did poorly. The number of workers employed at state-owned firms shrank from 112 million workers in 1995 to 65 million by 2005. Those laid-off workers turned to market activities or other sectors of the economy to eke out a living. Most of them were reintegrated into the urban economy after some trying times.

At the beginning of the economic reform, the Chinese government designated Special Economic Zones (SEZs) along its southeast coast at locations strategically chosen to attract overseas investments (mainly from Hong Kong and Taiwan) by providing favorable tax rates and land use terms. Taking advantage of the cheap and abundant Chinese labor and the financial incentives, foreign enterprises flocked to the SEZs. They manufacture goods mainly for export—clothes, toys, and electronics, for example. The rapid growth of export-oriented enterprises not only drew more labor and capital into the SEZs but also served to speed up the integration of Chinese labor and markets into the global capitalist economy. In providing jobs for migrant labor, many factories in the SEZs maximized their profits by requiring long hours of work for low wages with little in the way of benefits and welfare. The economic growth in the SEZs sometimes was achieved at great human cost; some factories violated the regulations on working conditions, thereby jeopardizing workers' health and causing permanent injury to some.

The development of investment-led exports and energy-intensive heavy industry at state enterprises in the SEZ had some negative results. It aggravated income inequality among the Chinese, undermined workers' employment gains, and heightened people's discontent with the government. Corruption has been rampant since the economic reform. Many business entrepreneurs colluded with government officials, and some officials bought and sold offices, which led to the criminalization of the state. Yet corruption, discontent, and social dislocation neither undercut economic growth nor significantly undermined the CCP. The economic reform brought uneven and unbalanced changes to

China. It created a new regional hierarchy—the well-off southeast coastal area and the backwater of inland provinces—and a new social hierarchy based on economic standing. The wealthy people are officials, private businessmen, or real estate developers. The middle class own their private apartments and even automobiles (private ownership of automobiles became legal in the mid-1990s; China is now the second largest market for motor vehicles). Life for the large working class has improved and workers are treated relatively well as full members of the urban society.

As rural migrants flocked to the cities for work, the Chinese population underwent an unprecedented urbanization. Today, more than half the population lives in urban areas. Among the 200 to 300 million rural migrant laborers, many have managed to settle permanently in urban areas with their families. Nevertheless, many still carve out a marginal living characterized by poor housing, substandard working conditions, and a lack of social services, including health care. Moreover, some urban folk hold them in contempt or discriminate against them.

Economic reform has brought greater political tolerance and cultural diversity to the once closed People's Republic of China. As the state no longer monopolizes the means of communication, Chinese people have greater freedom and access to newspapers, magazines, books, radio, TV, "hotlines," and the Internet. Moreover, greater mobility has enabled Chinese citizens to evade state surveillance more easily. Some Chinese have employed uncensored forms of expressions (tabloid literature, satirical oral culture, and the Internet) to express their different opinions and discontent; others have turned to the commercial culture, which caters to popular taste for pleasure and spiritual enrichment. Popular culture in contemporary China has become an important venue for citizens to express their feelings, aspirations, and resignations. It has shaped the direction of economic and political change. Rock music and contemporary art satirize China's lack of freedom and democracy, criticize the corruption of the party and state, and challenge the official culture of the CCP. Western culture has entered China in the form of music, film, consumerism, and cosmopolitan lifestyles, helping to build a new identity for the new middle class in urban China. Many urban youth, who have grown up in material comfort as the single child of their families, happily embrace the global consumer culture and sail through life seeking individual fulfillment, self-expression, and success. They relentlessly explore new opportunities to make big money and follow commercial advertisements on how to live a cosmopolitan, middle-class lifestyle faithfully. As more Chinese students study abroad, they encounter new ideas and behaviors beyond the norms in China. When they return home, there is the potential that they might become subversive influences.

Trade tension between China and other countries has increased because Chinese economic growth has relied heavily on exports. Moreover, China's favorable investing environment has caused manufacturers from many advanced countries to relocate to China. For example, Americans are unhappy at the manufacturing jobs they have lost to the Chinese. Some U.S. factories have moved to China, and others have closed because they cannot compete with their Chinese rivals. Furthermore, China is growing at the expense of other European, Asian, and Latin American countries. China has taken over the manufacture of electronic equipment from Japan, silk from Italy, and Christmas ornaments from Germany. However, one should note that although the cost of labor in China is low by American standards, it is not lower than that in many other developing countries. What distinguishes China is that it is efficient as a supplier, provides the relative stability that global capital desires, and has a reliable, docile, and capable industrial workforce.

Western consumers have benefited from the low price of products manufactured in China. The "Made in China" label can be found everywhere: clothes, shoes, toys, and even furniture. Almost half of the furniture on the American market is "Made in China." Chinese manufacturers produce goods that cater to quintessential American and European tastes more effectively and less expensively than their Western competitors. "Made in China" has a growing presence in the technological field as China has become the largest maker of consumer electronics such as TVs, DVD players, and cell phones. China is moving into biotech and computer manufacturing and even makes parts for the Boeing 757.

The Western world has also benefited from China's investment and market for Western goods and services. As an engine of global economic growth, Beijing holds the largest amount of foreign currency reserves, totaling $1.8 trillion as of May 2008. Much of it has been used to buy U.S. treasury bonds, which helped the United States to finance public spending, pay for its war in Iraq, and keep interest rates low. China is the biggest market for the United States, and Chinese are happy customers of Citibank, Disney, GE, and Microsoft. The newly rich in China are consumers of fashion and luxury items produced by Western countries; chic boutiques in the fashion capitals of Milan, New York, and Paris have expanded to Shanghai and Beijing.

China plays an increasingly important role in stabilizing the regional economy in the Pacific Rim and poses a new challenge to America's role as the guarantor of security in Asia. To promote regional identity and solidarity, China has developed infrastructural ties (roads, railways, and pipelines) with nations throughout Asia. China and India, another growing global force, have improved their relationship based on common economic, developmental, and trade interests. China carefully balances its economic relations with India and its strategic relations with Pakistan, India's rival. China has tolerated trade deficits with East Asian countries and increased both its economic cooperation and trade with the ten member states of the Association of Southeast Asian Nations (ASEAN). In 2005, China's trade with ASEAN exceeded $130 billion, which was a third more than that of one year earlier. Japan and South Korea count China as their largest trade partner. Australia exports iron ore, aluminum, natural gas, and other resources and commodities to China.

Overall, China has made a positive contribution to Africa's local economies and infrastructure. In looking for energy and resources, China has increased its investments in and trading relations with African countries rich in energy and resources but lacking manufacturing. From 2003 to 2006, trade between China and Africa tripled, creating a boom that brought African economic growth in 2005 to its highest level in 30 years. African nations prefer China's attitude of respect, equality, and partnership in its economic outreach to the perceived condescension of the West's "charity" and "help." Nevertheless, there is a backlash within Africa against low-grade Chinese goods supplanting African goods in local markets, Chinese labor being used for infrastructural projects, Chinese investors' disinterest in local environmental standards, and Chinese extraction of resources rather than investment in industry.

China has bought oil fields throughout the globe and imported the world's scrap metal and steel for industrial production. In competing for global resources, China has developed economic and military ties with countries that the West has tried to isolate. China's relationship with Sudan, Uzbekistan, Iran, and North Korea has given it a critical role in global security issues. Despite the casualties in the civil war between Muslims and Christians in Sudan, China has provided the Sudanese government with Chinese-made arms such as tanks, fighter planes, bombers, helicopters, machine guns, and rocket-propelled grenades. In turn, Sudan has furnished China with 10 percent of its total oil imports. Such transactions greatly disturbed the regional peace and gave new impetus to the civil war. China National Petroleum owns 50 percent of the Greater Nile Petroleum Operating Company in Sudan, and Sinopec, China's second largest oil firm, has erected a pipeline to Port Sudan where China's Petroleum Engineering Construction Group is building a tanker terminal. In 2005, the Uzbek army killed hundreds of civilian protesters. This did not stop China from forming an economic partnership with that country. The Uzbek president's visit to Beijing brought a $600 million deal that allowed China National Petroleum to access 23 Uzbek oil fields. China has developed a warm relationship with Iran, which has supplied 11 percent of China's oil imports. Sinopec has implemented an oil and natural gas agreement worth $70 billion with Tehran.

As China's economic development has transformed it from an isolated bystander to an active player in many important global matters, there is a need for a constructive realignment of global economic leadership that incorporates China. Yet the geopolitics of scarcity and the fierce competition for resources and energy have brought China into strategic and diplomatic conflict with the United States. By virtue of her economic weight, China can pose a threat to both the United States and world stability. It is challenging the U.S.-dominated political and economic systems and upsetting some of the key ground rules on which American postwar supremacy has been based. China has replaced the United States as the dominant country in attracting foreign money and industrial capital, and much global investment now flows to China from all directions. From Washington's perspective, China is a strategic and military rival of the United States and its allies in Asia and elsewhere, and China has pursued energy and resources at the expense of its international reputation. China's appearance and subsequent influence in Africa, the Middle East, and South America, and its increasingly dominant position in East Asia serve to create anxiety in Washington.

As a permanent, veto-wielding member of the United Nations Security Council, China has the status and authority to influence the critical international challenges facing the world. Yet China is still an authoritarian state ruled by a single Communist Party that has fostered a vibrant capitalist economy that outshines the United States in some ways. Although China's political evolution is not moving toward a Western form of participatory government, it nevertheless provides an alternative to Western democracies as a model for developing states. China's engagement with the world is invaluable in addressing global problems such as global warming, HIV/AIDS, and energy security. The United States and China should coordinate on issues of mutual interest such as trade, monetary policy, energy, and foreign assistance. The United States should aid China in the construction of its legal system and implementation of the rule of the law. Westerners need to learn to understand Chinese values and perspectives.

Recently, China has begun efforts to shift from investment and export-led development to domestic consumption to continue its strong economic growth. Because trade and industry count for more than one-third of China's economy and more than half of its trade is controlled by foreign firms, China's economic development is vulnerable to Western protectionism. In the face of their own domestic difficulties, it is conceivable that the United States and Europe would respond to China's economic growth by restricting the shipment of capital, expertise, and technology to China, and by limiting China's access to foreign markets. Such economic restrictions could be justified by citing the Chinese system of governance and China's restrictions on human rights.

By shifting from trade and export to meeting the consumer demands of its increasingly wealthy population, China hopes to create a stable and reliable domestic market to underpin its economy. Currently, China's economy rests on energy-intensive heavy industry and exports, which contributes to serious energy and environmental problems as well as less optimal growth and employment outcomes. The shift to an emphasis on the domestic market will bring rapid job creation, more equal distribution of income, a reduction in the increase of energy consumption and environmental degradation, and a drop in the country's excessive trade surpluses. But the government's policies in the fiscal, pricing, and exchange rate domains are faulty. For example, key elements of the economy such as energy, interest rates, and the exchange rate are mispriced. The result is inflation. In recent years, many Chinese have felt the impact of this inflation as the cost of living has moved steadily upward.

Although China has pursued peaceful development and its foreign policy is defensive in nature, its potential military power and the modernization of its People's Liberation Army (PLA) have aroused concern. The PLA has improved its operational and institutional capacities through the development, acquisition, and deploying of new weapons systems. It has carried out institutional and systemic reforms and developed new strategic doctrines. Although the modernization of the PLA is said to be strictly for peaceful purposes, a more capable PLA has the potential to alter significantly the strategic balance in Asia. Undoubtedly, it will have a noteworthy impact on Asian countries as well as the United States.

Besides its economic and military power, China wields considerable soft power as evidenced by the attraction of traditional Chinese culture. As the state loosened its ideological control, the Communist political culture in China gave way to the revival of traditional Chinese culture. Confucianism, Buddhism, Daoism, and classical literature and art have found their way back to mainland China via Hong Kong and Taiwan. Traditional Chinese cultural values, codes, and maxims, particularly those associated with Confucianism, are among the more fundamental and universal cultural contributions that China has promoted in recent years. Moreover, China has provided substantial overseas financial and infrastructural assistance, sent its doctors and teachers abroad, funded education opportunities in China for foreign nationals, encouraged the spread of traditional Chinese medicines, and promoted the study of the Chinese language abroad by building more than 200 Confucius Institutes around the world. China's economy and its culture have attracted an increasing number of foreigners to visit China as students, businessmen, and tourists. Experiencing China firsthand has corrected some Western misconceptions about China.

China's rise has increased the bargaining power of peripheral manufacturers in the global supply chain and shaped the world toward a multipolar interstate system amid rising geopolitical tensions. Although its relationship with the United States has been vital for China's economic development, China has also strengthened its economic ties with other countries. The common goal of constraining U.S. power has brought China and Russia close. Russia is China's leading source of advanced military equipment and technology, and both countries are permanent members of the UN Security Council. They have successfully blocked sanctions against Iran, Burma, and Zimbabwe, and opposed U.S. deployment of a missile defense as destabilizing and contemptuous of their respective national interests. China, Russia, and the Central Asian countries have formed the Shanghai Cooperation Organization for the purpose of multilateral military exercises. Today, the Middle East provides half of China's oil and Africa another one-third. China's trade with the Persian Gulf alone has doubled since 2000 to $240 billion annually. China has also increased trade in commodities and resources (oil, minerals, soy) with Latin America, reaching a figure of $100 billion in 2007. But China faces competition with the manufacturing industries of Mexico, Brazil, and other low-wage Latin American countries. China's relations with Europe have deteriorated. Europe dislikes China's violations of intellectual property rights, lack of product safety concerns, and the loss of low-tech manufacturing industries to China. From Europe's perspective, China's unconditional aid policy in Africa has been harmful to their efforts in promoting human rights, good governance, and environmental health on that continent.

In summary, China's economic reform over the past three decades has not only improved its citizens' material lives in general, but it has also given them greater freedom and mobility. Despite its authoritarian political structure, China nonetheless has produced a vibrant capitalist economy that challenges U.S. economic dominance and provides an alternative model to Western democracy for developing states. China's rise to prominence and its integration into the global capitalist system has enabled it to play an important economic, strategic, and diplomatic role on the world stage, thereby moving the globe toward a multipolar interstate system. The Western world must now deal with the challenges posed by China in a variety of fields: economic, geopolitical, and military. Simultaneously, China is the Western world's largest potential market and investor. Consequently, some tension is almost inevitable. Nevertheless, despite these strains, China's future seems to be bright.

SELECTED BIBLIOGRAPHY

Benewick, Robert, and Stephanie Donald. *The State of China Atlas: Mapping the World's Fastest-Growing Economy.* Berkeley: University of California Press, 2009. This study provides a visual survey of the profound economic, political, and social changes taking place in China as well as their implications for the world at large.

Bergsten, C. Fred, Charles Freeman, Nicholas R. Lardy, and Derek J. Mitchell, eds. *China's Rise: Challenges and Opportunities.* Washington, DC: Peterson Institute for International Economics, 2009. This recent work analyzes China's economic development, foreign and domestic policy, national security issues, and domestic challenges.

Denoon, David, ed. *China: Contemporary Political, Economic, and International Affairs.* New York: New York University Press, 2007. This anthology deals with many issues concerning contemporary China: foreign policy, national security, economic policy, social disruption, domestic politics and governance, military power, de-communization, growing economic strength, nationalism, and the prospects for democracy.

Dittmer, Lowell. *China's Deep Reform: Domestic Politics in Transition*. Lanham, MD: Rowman & Littlefield, 2006. This work provides a comprehensive assessment of domestic politics in China and explores the origin, content, and significance of its post–1989 development.

Fishman, Ted C. *China, Inc: How the Rise of the Next Superpower Challenges America and the World*. New York: Scribner, 2005. This popular study examines China's economic transformation from Mao to Deng and the challenges China's rise poses for the world.

Gamer, Robert E., ed. *Understanding Contemporary China*. 3rd ed. Boulder, CO: Lynne Rienner, 2008. This collection focuses on economic, political, social, cultural, geographic, literary, environmental, and historical aspects of China.

Gries, Peter, and Stanley Rosen. *Chinese Politics: State, Society, and the Market*. London: Routledge, 2010. An interesting look at some of the destabilizing aspects of China's economic development including social protests over corruption, land seizures, and environmental concerns.

Hung, Ho-Fung, ed. *China and the Transformation of Global Capitalism*. Baltimore: John Hopkins University Press, 2009. This scholarly volume assesses how China's economic rise and liberalization reshape the structure and dynamics of global capitalism in terms of income distribution, geo-economic integration, and access to raw materials and labor.

Kynge, James. *China Shakes the World: A Titan's Rise and Troubled Future—and the Challenge for America*. New York: Houghton Mifflin, 2006. Kynge utilizes labor costs and modern production technology to evaluate China's socioeconomic transformation. He points out China's weaknesses such as a shortage of arable land, serious environmental problems, systemic corruption, and a dearth of resources.

Lampton, David M. *The Three Faces of Chinese Power: Might, Money, and Minds*. Berkeley: University of California Press, 2008. The author investigates the military, economic, and intellectual dimensions of China's growing influence.

McGregor, James. *One Billion Customers: Lessons from the Front Lines of Doing Business in China*. New York: Wall Street Journal Books, 2007. This lively study probes the promises and perils that Western businesses face in China's huge but chaotic market, pointing out problems such as overbearing Communist officials, corrupt bureaucrats, irrational regulations, and personal and family ties.

Murphy, Michael. *China Rises: City of Dreams* (TV documentary series). Silver Springs, MD: Discovery Channel School, 2006. This documentary records how economic development has enabled many people in Shanghai to experience an improved lifestyle.

Murphy, Michael. *China Rises: Food Is Heaven* (TV documentary series). Silver Springs, MD: Discovery Channel School, 2006. A companion piece to the above documentary, this study examines how China has transformed its economy and risen to prominence on the world stage but also notes that dwindling water supplies threaten China's ability to feed its people.

Plafker, Ted. *Doing Business in China: How to Profit in the World's Fastest Growing Market*. New York: Hachette Book Group, 2007. Plafker, *The Economist*'s correspondent in Beijing, gives tips and insights on China's rules and regulations, cultural differences, and sales and marketing strategies, all of which differ greatly from the rest of the world.

Shambaugh, David. *Modernizing China's Military: Progress, Problems, and Prospects*. Berkeley: University of California Press, 2004. This study addresses important questions about Chinese strategic intentions and military capabilities.

Shambaugh, David, ed. *Power Shift: China and Asia's New Dynamics*. Berkeley: University of California Press, 2006. The contributors explore the various dimensions of China's rise, its influence on the region, the consequences for the United States, and alternative models of the evolving Asian order.

Shirk, Susan L. *China: Fragile Superpower.* Oxford: Oxford University Press, 2008. This fascinating study analyzes the paradox of China's leaders—the more developed and prosperous the country becomes, the more insecure and threatened they feel. The author depicts a fragile Communist regime desperate to survive in a society turned upside down by miraculous economic growth and a stunning new openness to the greater world.

Steinfeld, Edward S. *Playing Our Game: Why China's Rise Doesn't Threaten the West.* Oxford: Oxford University Press, 2010. The author argues that in its modernization process China has integrated itself into the Western economic order and is "playing the game" by Western rules, thereby reinforcing the dominance of U.S. companies and regulatory institutions.

Sutter, Robert G. *Chinese Foreign Relations: Power and Policy since the Cold War.* Lanham, MD: Rowman & Littlefield, 2009. In discussing China's increasingly complex role on the international stage, Sutter also examines its numerous bilateral relationships.

Wasserstrom, Jeffery N. *China in the 21st Century: What Everyone Needs to Know.* Oxford: Oxford University Press, 2010. Wasserstrom, one of America's leading scholars of things Chinese, charts the historical legacies—Western and Japanese imperialism, the Mao era, and the Tiananmen Square massacre—that largely define China's present-day trajectory. He introduces the reader to such varied topics as the Chinese Communist Party, the building boom in Shanghai, and the environmental consequences of rapid Chinese industrialization.

Womack, Brantly, ed. *China's Rise in Historical Perspective.* Lanham, MD: Rowman & Littlefield, 2010. A group of renowned historians, economists, and political scientists discuss the internal dynamic of China's rise from traditional to contemporary times.

DENG XIAOPING (1904–1997)

The life of Deng Xiaoping is closely entwined with the history of Communist China. Born at the beginning of the century and reaching adulthood as the Qing dynasty crumbled, Deng participated in all stages of the Chinese Communist Revolution, eventually becoming the dominant figure in Chinese politics from 1978 until his retirement in 1989.

Deng was born in Sichuan Province, China, in 1904. He was the son of a landowner and county sheriff who named him Deng Xixian, meaning "first saint." Deng attended school within the province and later continued his studies in France. There, he joined the Chinese Socialist Youth League and then the Chinese Communist Party.

Deng returned to China in 1926, after Chiang Kai-shek had become head of the Kuomintang, the government party originally organized by Sun Yat-sen that Chiang shaped into a more conservative nationalist force. Deng took a position as an instructor of political science at the Xian Military and Political Academy but was removed from his post a year later because of his Communist affiliations as Chiang worked to destroy the Communist Party. It was during those struggles between the Communists and the Kuomintang Nationalists in 1927 that Deng took the name Deng Xiaoping, meaning "little peace." In the long years of retreat, civil war, and war with Japan that followed, Deng was often at the side of Mao Zedong. He helped to organize the People's Liberation Army (PLA), worked as the army commissar, and edited a PLA journal.

When the Communist Party and the PLA finally defeated the Kuomintang and declared the People's Republic of China in 1949, Deng retained considerable prestige. He was entrusted with the invasion of Tibet in 1950, which he accomplished according to the goals of the party. Deng was appointed vice premier in 1952 and, by 1956, became secretary-general of the Communist Party.

The mid-1950s in China were the setting for the Great Leap Forward, a phrase Mao coined to describe his program for accelerated development and the solidification of socialism in China. In the opinion of Deng (and many other people), Mao's goals for the Great Leap were too high, causing many dislocations in the countryside as peasants struggled to adapt to radical new demands. Deng tried to introduce reforms to Mao's programs to ease conditions for farmers and stabilize the food supply. In 1960, he uttered the trademark statement, "It doesn't matter whether the cat is black or white, as long as it catches mice." In other words, feed the people, no matter what it takes.

By the mid-1960s, however, Mao and his most radical supporters began to crack down on such criticism. A new era called the Cultural Revolution was ushered in beginning in 1966, as Mao worked to purify the Chinese government and the Communist Party of anyone believed to entertain capitalist thoughts or practices. During that process, not only was Deng forced out of government office, but also all of China was plunged into chaos and terror as Mao turned the zeal of young people in the army against the bureaucracy and cultural and intellectual figures.

In 1973, Deng was recalled by the government to assist Zhou Enlai in checking the power of the People's Liberation Army, the national military force grown overzealous during the Cultural Revolution. Both Zhou and Mao died in 1976, and Deng's power increased as he sought ways to restore some sort of equilibrium to his country. In July 1977, he was reinstated as vice premier and emphasized the need to understand the messages of the revered Mao as an integral whole (rather than concentrating on any single one of the more extreme positions of his later years). Deng insisted that the basic task was to concentrate on building a strong, modernized, socialist country.

Deng and his moderate allies led China on a course of more open political and economic relations with the world after the early 1980s. Deng's policy was one of promoting China's economic growth, even at the compromise of some principles of communist economics. He was one of the architects of the Four Modernizations program, which set a course of improving agriculture, industry, science and technology, and the military. The goal of that national program was to have China achieve the status of a world economic power by 2000.

More cordial relations with other nations were instituted as Deng himself traveled to foreign capitals, visiting U.S. president Jimmy Carter in 1979. In 1984, he received President Ronald Reagan in China. Although encouraging greater opportunities for economic exchange, Deng was not willing to overlook all strategic differences. He objected to U.S. support for Taiwan, which he defined as an "unsinkable aircraft carrier of the United States."

By 1989, Deng was facing unforeseen consequences of his more open policies. On the one hand, he was expecting a visit from Soviet leader Mikhail Gorbachev, which would mean the first step toward healing the rift between the two huge Communist powers. At the same time, however, Beijing was occupied with thousands of students who were making overtures to the government for more political openness. Although there were men in the government who were willing to begin a conversation with the students (as the students had anticipated), Deng was not one of them. When the students refused to disperse after strongly worded announcements of the government's position, Deng took a hardline approach.

Deng recalled some of the country's most elite fighting forces from around China, and on the night of June 3, 1989, they struck. By that time, the students had been joined by professors and workers. The army units not only converged on Tiananmen Square in Beijing, the ceremonial center of Chinese government for centuries and the principal location of the student demonstrations, they pursued the fleeing students and workers to other parts of the city. The violence and killing lasted all night. Deng later described the demonstrators as the "dregs of society," but it was clear that the government had reached yet another impasse that would require its ideological reformulation.

Resigning from government in 1989, Deng remained influential. His legacy was not to lead a united nation as he had hoped, however. Rather, he continued to believe that radical economic reforms could be accomplished without any attention to the cultural and political effects those would have. On March 12, 1992, the Communist Party Politburo approved a strategy outlined by Deng for a campaign of quick economic liberalization centered on free-market reform. The event was perceived as a huge victory of the senior leader over more conservative hardline elements in the government, but it was not clear whether the party could summon the new ideas necessary to preserve its hold on government.

Deng died on February 19, 1997, from Parkinson's disease and complications from a lung infection.

ABC-CLIO

HU YAOBANG (1915–1989)

A steadfast follower of Deng Xiaoping, Hu Yaobang emerged in the 1980s as a powerful voice of reform in the People's Republic of China only to be forced to resign by his own mentor. His death in the spring of 1989 sparked the student demonstrations in Beijing that led to the Tiananmen Square massacre in June that year.

Born in Liuyang, Hunan, in 1915, Hu was the son of poor peasant farmers. He was involved in the quickly squelched Autumn Harvest Uprising organized by Mao Zedong in 1927, worked with youths in the Jiangxi Soviet that Mao established with the support of the veterans of the earlier uprising, and participated in the Long March during 1934–1935.

At the end of the Long March, Hu took over the Communist Youth League's organization department, a position to which he returned in the 1950s and 1960s. The most crucial assignment of Hu's early career was his association with the Second Field army as head of the political department in early 1949. There, he became a close associate of Deng, who headed military operations during the communist conquest of Sichuan province. In 1952, both Deng and Hu moved to Beijing and took up posts there.

Along with Deng, Hu fell out of favor during the Cultural Revolution that began in 1966 and was stripped of his responsibilities in 1967. Still with Deng, however, Hu reappeared on the political scene in 1972 and assisted his mentor with his famous Four Modernizations plan in 1975. Although demonstrations in the wake of the death of Zhou Enlai in 1976 led to Deng's—and hence Hu's—temporary eclipse, the death of Mao

Hu Yaobang was a close associate of Deng Xiaoping, rising to Party General Secretary in the 1980s. However, he was deposed for his reformist agenda, considered too extreme by his political foes. The Tiananmen Square student protests arose out of public demonstrations at the time of his death and funeral in 1989. (AFP/Getty Images)

Zedong later that year permitted the pair to return to political leadership. Thanks to Hua Guofeng, with whom Hu had been friendly for a decade, Hu was appointed head of the Central Party School, and in the following years worked to erase the ideological mistakes of the Cultural Revolution. Late in 1978, he was named to the Politburo.

In February 1980, Hu took on the responsibilities of party general secretary, replacing Hua. From June 1981 to September 1982, he served as chairman of the Chinese Communist Party, a post whose historical prominence meant little at a time when Deng was running the party from behind the scenes. In any case, the position was formally abolished at the end of that period, and Hu instead became the party's general secretary.

During this period, Hu had a characteristic role in the changing relations between the Chinese Communist Party and the Dalai Lama (Tenzin Gyatso) who had fled Tibet in 1959 after the Chinese conquest of that country and remained in self-imposed exile in India. In 1980, Hu traveled to Tibet as part of a study group and was shocked by the conditions he observed there. Not only did Tibetans live in markedly worse conditions than the Han Chinese in other parts of the People's Republic of China, but their traditional culture had by no means recovered from the chaos of the Cultural Revolution. Hu immediately made a series of recommendations for improving conditions in Tibet, including allowing Tibetan autonomy within the republican structure of the Chinese state, exempting the area from taxes, opening more schools, permitting limited private trade, and encouraging Han Chinese living in Tibet to learn the Tibetan language. Many of these suggestions were acted on.

The following year, Hu met with the Dalai Lama's brother, Gyalo Thondrup, in an attempt to bring about some rapprochement between China and the Dalai Lama. Ultimately, though, these overtures were doomed, because the Communist leadership (principally Deng) would not discuss the issue of independence, and the Dalai Lama feared that he might appear to be coopted by the Chinese leaders if he returned to Chinese-occupied Tibet. Nonetheless, in a letter of March 23, 1981, the Dalai Lama singled out Hu for praise and acknowledged the efforts he had made to improve conditions in Tibet.

In the spring of 1986, Hu initiated a series of reform programs aimed at emancipating thought, increasing the number of elected governmental positions, and separating state and party. By September, however, the reforms had been rescinded because of the opposition of other government leaders. Student protests had sprung up in Shanghai and then Beijing, however, and the unrest drove hardliners in Beijing to call for an immediate clampdown. Such well-known advocates of liberalization as astrophysicist Fang Lizhi and journalist Liu Binyan were purged from Communist Party rolls. Hu followed them, the principal scapegoat, fingered by Deng himself. Jonathan Spence wrote that "Hu's outspokenness on the need for rapid reform and his almost open contempt of Maoist excesses had made him a controversial leader of the party." Hu's resignation as general secretary was announced in January 1987.

From that time until his death on April 15, 1989, Hu remained a political nonentity, but he was remembered by many. Two days after his death, thousands of students from Beijing's universities gathered in Tiananmen Square to commemorate the death of a leader who had filled them with hope for real change. Less than two months and more than 1,000 deaths later, the Communist Party reaffirmed its opposition to that change.

ABC-CLIO

JIANG ZEMIN (1926–)

As president of China from March 1993 to March 2003, Jiang Zemin represented the change in leadership of the Chinese Communist Party (CCP) after the Tiananmen Square massacre in 1989. He retained his influential role as the chair of the Central Military Commission until September 2004. He ceded the powerful post of secretary-general of the CCP to Hu Jintao—leader of the younger "fourth-generation" of leaders—at the 16th CCP Congress in November 2002. Jiang then handed Hu the presidency on March 15, 2003, when Hu was confirmed as president by the National People's Congress. In September 2004, Jiang officially retired from the government by resigning his role as military chairperson, placing China's military in Hu's hands.

Born in Yangshou, China, on August 17, 1926, Jiang was the third of five children of a prolific writer and electrician father, Jiang Shijun, and a peasant mother, Wu Yueqing. He received a traditional Chinese education based on four arts: music, chess, literature, and calligraphy of the complex pre-1949 characters. As part of that discipline, Jiang Shijun made his young son recite an article of Chinese literature each day. Advanced abilities in reading and writing earned Jiang a place in the prestigious Dongguan Primary School, where for six years he enjoyed a happy environment of songs and games. His appreciation for music, both Chinese and Western, took root during those early days. Life inside the walls of Dongguan revealed none of the hardships associated with the incursions of Japan into China in the years before the Sino-Japanese War of 1937–1945.

The transition from Dongguan Primary to Yangshou Middle School was a challenge even for the precocious Jiang because the competition was so intense. The year Jiang applied, only 10 percent of the 3,000 students who sat for the entrance examination were accepted. Classes came to a halt during Japanese occupation after 1937, however, and did not resume for another two years. "Those were the days when the Chinese nation was ridden with disaster," wrote Jiang, as World War II was followed by civil war in 1945.

Believing that twentieth-century engineering science could provide "the food of the people," Jiang enrolled in Nanjing Central University's industrial technology and electrical machinery program. It was there that he joined the CCP in 1946. He spent the last two school years at the Jianotong University of Shanghai. With a degree in engineering in hand, Jiang elected to remain in Shanghai, though it was rife with tension between the Nationalist Party (Kuomintang) and the CCP until the Communist victory in 1949.

In December 1949, Jiang married Wang Yeping, described by one writer as "introverted, accommodating, kind, and hospitable." Their first child, son Mianheng, was born in 1952. Two years later, son Miankang joined the family unit.

The first order of business for the new leadership of the People's Republic was to shore up the economy by utilizing the technological skills among its citizens. CCP leader Mao Zedong lamented the absence of Chinese industries capable of producing "a single car, plane, tank, or tractor." As a loyal party member with technical skills, Jiang was summoned to Beijing to help draw up the blueprints for the first Machine-Building Ministry. Known as the Great Leap Forward, that period of massive and frenetic industrialization bore catastrophic results, as agriculture suffered and famine threatened. By 1961, party leaders attempted to mitigate the results of the Great Leap Forward by pulling the economy back from near collapse.

The next great movement was the Cultural Revolution that began in the late 1960s. That period saw the destruction or demotion of many intellectuals and bureaucrats, including Jiang, who found himself sidelined until 1970, when he was recalled to Beijing and appointed to the Foreign Affairs Bureau. Since his graduation from the university, he had held positions in factories and research institutes but never in government. His linguistic skills and earlier trips to Moscow to observe technological advances, however, now made him a good candidate for the diplomatic positions in the Foreign Office. In the 1970s, he became the director of the Foreign Affairs Bureau in the Ministry of Industry.

After Deng Xiaoping came to power in 1979 and restored order to the tumult of Chinese revolutionary politics, Jiang's political fortune rose steadily. Beginning as vice minister of the state Commission on Imports and Exports in 1980, Jiang next served as vice minister and then minister of the Electronics Industry until 1985. "I tried to develop our country's electronics industry, but it was not accomplished in line with my original hopes," Jiang admitted. He had also ascended to the Central Committee of the CCP in 1982. When he was offered the position of mayor of Shanghai, he happily accepted and officially took office in June 1985, promising "less empty talk and more concrete actions" in modernizing the sprawling city. By 1987, he joined the Politburo, one of the most powerful branches of the CCP.

Deng launched his economic reform program without any intention of allowing a corresponding liberalization of social or cultural practice. Nevertheless, students believing in the need for greater democratization protested and demanded a dialogue with government in 1989. In Shanghai, Jiang was able to quell local protests without using force. From May to June 1989, he demonstrated restraint in handling major demonstrations in Shanghai, although he supported the use of force against the students and workers in Beijing's Tiananmen Square. That support put him in favor with Deng, who selected Jiang to succeed the deposed Zhao Ziyang as general secretary of the CCP in June 1989. Although not the strongest man in the CCP, Jiang was a good compromise choice because he endorsed a continuation of Deng's free-market reforms but was also committed to preserving the CCP's control of political power.

Jiang succeeded Deng as chairman of the Central Military Commission in 1989 and in 1993 became president of the National People's Congress, the ceremonial head of the Chinese state. With the death of Deng in February 1997, the Jiang era began.

During Jiang's presidency, China's economy flourished, and China became a member of the World Trade Organization. Jiang introduced his theory of the Three Represents, his political philosophy that stressed the CCP's role in representing production forces, culture, and the basic interests of the people. In November 2002, at the 16th Communist Party Congress, Jiang stepped down from his party position, and the CCP chose Vice President Hu Jintao as its new general secretary. Hu then succeeded Jiang as president in March 2003. In an effort to retain oversight over the new generation of leaders, Jiang held onto his position as head of the powerful Central Military Commission. However, on September 19, 2004, Jiang relinquished that post to Hu Jintao and announced his retirement.

ABC-CLIO

LI PENG (1928–)

Li Peng became president of the National People's Congress of China in March 1998 after he served the legal limit of two five-year terms as prime minister. Li remains regarded by many as the "butcher of Beijing" for his role in the Tiananmen Square massacre.

Li was born in Chengdu, Szechwan Province, on October 20, 1928. He was the son of the writer Li Shouxun, who was executed by the Kuomintang; that led to his being taken in by the wife of Zhou Enlai, and, in an unofficial sense, adopted by the family. Li was schooled at the Moscow Power Institute; that training prepared him for such diverse utilities posts as electric power and industry minister from 1981 to 1982 and water conservancy and electric power deputy minister from 1982 to 1985.

As a loyalist of the Chinese Communist Party, Li rose through the ranks and became a member of the Central Committee in 1982. A trusted adherent to Chinese Communist Party policy and a member of the party's Standing Committee, Li was appointed acting prime minister in 1987, and the next year succeeded the disgraced liberal Zhao Ziyang as prime minister.

Li's prime ministership was marked by his declaration of martial law, which served to facilitate the government's brutal suppression of pro-democracy protests in Tiananmen Square in 1989. He also conducted highly unusual diplomatic trips to Asian and Middle Eastern countries in 1990 and 1991 that led to a slight warming of traditionally cool diplomatic relations. In June 1991, Li announced that the Chinese government was at last willing to sign the 1968 international Nuclear Nonproliferation Treaty. Despite a heart attack in 1993, Li continued to foster economic growth in China. However, he remained unpopular with many Chinese because of the Tiananmen Square massacre.

Li's administration was also characterized by its continued refusal to address the country's human rights crisis. He also balked at demands made by the United Kingdom to implement greater democratic and capitalist safeguards in Hong Kong before the reversion of the colony to the PRC in 1997. Li did work to foster closer ties with two of China's neighbors, Russia and Japan, and sponsored better communication and trade with both countries. At the end of his second term as premier in 1998, he was named head of the Chinese Parliament. In November 2002, Li announced his retirement from the Chinese Politburo, and in March 2003, he announced his retirement from Chinese politics in a speech during the annual National People's Congress.

ABC-CLIO

ZHAO ZIYANG (1919–2005)

Zhao Ziyang was one of the leading economic reformers in the 1970s in the People's Republic of China (PRC). He rose rapidly through the ranks of the Chinese Communist Party (CCP) and became premier and party general secretary in the 1980s. However, he was dismissed from office following his very public opposition to the crackdown in 1989 that resulted in the Tiananmen Square massacre.

Zhao was born as Zhao Xiusheng in Huaxian County, Henan Province, in 1919. His father was a local landlord. He attended primary school in his native town and middle schools in Kaifeng and Wuhan. He joined the Communist Youth League in 1932 and the CCP in 1938. By 1940, Zhao was the party secretary of the third Special District in the Hebei-Shandong Border Region. After the end of World War II, he occupied himself with rural reform work in the Hebei-Shandong-Henan Border Region. He also served as the party secretary of Luoyang District in Henan from 1948 to 1949.

After the establishment of the PRC, Zhao served in numerous positions in Guangdong Province. He was elected a member of the People's Council of Guangdong in 1955, was appointed secretary of the Guangdong Province Communist Party in 1957, and rose to the position of provincial first party secretary in 1965. He played an instrumental role in consolidating CCP control and implementing land reform policies.

During the Cultural Revolution, Zhao was accused of being a follower of such unpopular figures as Tao Zhu and Liu Shaoqi. During the late 1960s, he was denounced publicly, forced from office, and paraded through the streets of Guangzhou (Canton) in a dunce cap. In 1971, he was sent to what amounted to internal exile as a party secretary in Inner Mongolia.

In the dying days of the Cultural Revolution, Zhao was rehabilitated by Zhou Enlai and assigned as provincial first party secretary in Sichuan Province in 1976. He proceeded to address the province's economic stagnation that resulted from the Cultural Revolution. He allowed up to 15 percent of land in communes to be worked privately. He also permitted both farmers and workers to engage in a wide range of small-scale private economic activities. The results were impressive; grain production grew by 24 percent, and industrial production rose by 80 percent during 1976–1979.

Because of his success in Sichuan, Zhao was promoted rapidly by China's paramount leader Deng Xiaoping. Zhao was appointed alternate member of the Politburo in 1977, a full member of the Politburo in 1979, a member of the Politburo's Standing Committee in 1980, and vice premier in the same year. Six months later, he replaced Hua Guofeng as premier. He was appointed to the post of CCP general secretary in January 1987.

In positions of nationwide power and influence, Zhao continued to advocate market-style reforms and a more open policy toward the outside world, particularly the West. He also implemented measures to streamline the bloated bureaucracy and called for the gradual separation of the CCP from both government administration and industrial management. Although many of his reforms were praised, his economic liberalization program was blamed for the rising inflation of the late 1980s.

Zhao's most important moment and his political downfall came with the student protests in Tiananmen Square in May and June 1989. Many of the student demonstrators felt that Zhao would be more sympathetic to their demands for reform than many of Zhao's more hardline colleagues. That belief was borne out in secret meetings of China's top leaders, where Zhao consistently opposed the use of force against the demonstrators. When Deng declared, "I have the army behind me" in a tumultuous May 17, 1989 Politburo meeting, Zhao reportedly retorted, "But I have the people behind me. You have nothing." However, as the students, emboldened by worldwide media coverage and joined by over 1 million residents in Beijing, became increasingly strident in their criticism of the government, averting the ultimate repression of the demonstrations proved impossible.

Zhao's personal visit to Tiananmen Square to urge students to end their hunger strike had no effect; "I came too late; I came too late," he lamented to student leaders. After the declaration of martial law and the bloody clearing of Tiananmen Square by military troops, Zhao was removed from office and replaced by Jiang Zemin. Zhao was placed under house arrest. He remained a member of the CCP but disappeared from public life. No charges were ever officially brought against him.

Eight years after the Tiananmen Square massacre, an unsigned letter was sent to the CCP urging Zhao's rehabilitation. The letter argued that eight years of virtual house arrest were "abnormally long" for the then 77-year-old Zhao. The plea, however, fell on deaf ears. In later years, he was allowed to make excursions; however, he had to receive permission from the highest government levels. Zhao managed to maintain a media presence albeit only outside of China. When U.S. president Bill Clinton visited China in 1998, Zhao was able to issue an open letter calling for a reassessment of the Tiananmen Square massacre. It made the news throughout the world, but Zhao's letter was banned in his homeland.

On January 14, 2005, Zhao fell into a coma after suffering a series of strokes. He died on January 17.

ABC-CLIO

DOCUMENT: "THE TRUTH ABOUT THE BEIJING TURMOIL" (1990)

In June 1989, large masses of students gathered in Tiananmen Square, Beijing, to protest the repressive policies of the Chinese communist government.

The government responded by ordering the Chinese army, led by a battalion of tanks, to break up the demonstration. Many people were subsequently killed as the army moved in. The world responded with outrage to this most recent demonstration of the Chinese government's apparent disregard for the rights of its citizens. In response, the Chinese government issued a statement titled "The Truth about the Beijing Turmoil" in 1990. An excerpt appears here. The statement did little, however, to change worldwide opinion regarding the low status of human rights in China.

INTRODUCTION

In 1989 when spring was passing to summer, a shocking turmoil happened in Beijing, which has attracted the close attention of people at home and abroad. Influenced by foreign media, people have many questions, guesses and misunderstandings. What really happened in China? What is the situation now like in Beijing? This album, with its abundant pictures, will help our readers understand the whole story of and truth about the turmoil and the present situation in Beijing.

This turmoil was not a chance occurrence. It was a political turmoil incited by a very small number of political careerists after a few years of plotting and scheming. It was aimed at subverting the socialist People's Republic. By making use of some failings in the work of the Chinese government and the temporary economic difficulties, they spread far and wide many views against the Constitution, the leadership of the Chinese Communist Party and the People's Government, preparing the ground for the turmoil ideologically, organizationally and in public opinion. The former general secretary of the Central Committee of the Chinese Communist Party Zhao Ziyang supported the turmoil and thus has unshirkable responsibility for its formation and development. The various political forces and reactionary organizations abroad had a hand in the turmoil from the very beginning. Some newspapers, magazines and broadcasting stations, especially the Voice of America, fabricated rumors to mislead people, thus adding fuel to the flames.

When Hu Yaobang suddenly died on April 15, a handful of people, thinking that their time had come, stirred up a student upheaval on the pretext of "mourning" for Hu Yaobang. The student unrest had been taken advantage of by the organizers of the turmoil from the very beginning. In violation of the Constitution, laws and regulations, some people put up big-character posters everywhere on the college campuses, preaching bourgeois liberalization and calling for the overthrow of the Communist Party and the legal government. They held many rallies, made speeches, boycotted classes and organized demonstrations, all without permission; they stormed the seat of the Party Central Committee and the State Council; they forcibly occupied the Tiananmen Square on many occasions and organized various illegal organizations without registration for approval. In Changsha, Xi'an and other cities, some people engaged in grave criminal activities such as beating, smashing, looting and burning stores, and even broke into the compounds of provincial government seats and set fire to the motor vehicles there.

In view of this turmoil, the *People's Daily* issued, on April 26, an editorial exposing the nature of the turmoil. Even under this circumstance, the Party and the government exercised great restraint towards the students' extremist slogans and actions and had all along given due recognition to the students' patriotic enthusiasm and reasonable demands. At the same time, the Party and the government warned the students not to be made use of by a handful of people and expressed the hope for solving the problems through dialogues and by normal, democratic and legal procedures. However, on May 13, the illegal student organization started a general hunger strike involving over 3,000 people and lasting for seven days. Party and government leaders, on the one hand, went to see the fasting students at Tiananmen Square and met with students' representatives on many occasions, asking them to value their lives and stop the hunger strike, and on the other hand, they lost no time in organizing on-the-spot rescue teams and providing all kinds of materials so as to relieve the suffering of the fasting students. Thanks to efforts of the government and other quarters. not a single student died in the hunger strike. But all this failed to win active response.

On the contrary, some media, taking the cue from a small number of people, wrongly guided the public opinion, escalating the turmoil and throwing Beijing and even the whole country in a serious anarchic situation, something that cannot be tolerated in any other country. In Beijing, demonstrations were held continuously, slogans insulting and attacking leaders and openly calling for overthrowing the government could be heard and seen everywhere. The traffic was seriously congested and difficulties were created for Beijing's production and daily supplies. The police were unable to keep normal social order. Gorbachev's schedules in China were also seriously hampered. The small handful of people attempted to take the chaos as an opportunity to seize political power and threatened to "set up a new government in three days."

On May 19, the Party Central Committee held a meeting attended by cadres from the Party, government and military institutions in Beijing. At the meeting, Premier Li Peng and President of the People's Republic of China Yang Shangkun announced the decision to adopt resolute measures to stop the turmoil. But Zhao Ziyang, then general secretary of the Party Central Committee, refused to attend this important meeting.

On May 20, Li Peng signed a martial law order as empowered by Clause 16 of Article 89 of the Constitution of the People's Republic of China. The martial law was to be enforced at 10 a.m. on the same day in parts of Beijing. The small handful of people took fright and coerced those residents who were in the dark about the truth to set up roadblocks at major crossroads to stop the advance of army vehicles and prevent the martial law enforcement troops from getting to designated places according to plan. Besides, they threatened to mobilize 200,000 people to occupy Tiananmen Square and organize a nation-wide general strike. Using the funds provided by reactionary forces at home and abroad, they installed sophisticated communication facilities and illegally purchased weapons. They gathered together hooligans and ruffians to set up terrorist organizations such as the "Dare-to-Die Corps" and the "Flying Tiger Team," and threatened to kidnap or put Party and government leaders under house arrest. They offered high prices in recruiting thugs and fabricated rumors to deceive people.

All the facts proved that, no matter how tolerant and restrained the government was, such people would not give up their wild scheme; on the contrary they threatened to "fight to the end" against the government.

On the evening of June 2, a handful of people bent upon inciting a riot used a traffic accident to spread rumors and mislead people, lighting the fuse of a rebellion. In the small hours of June 3, rioters set up roadblocks at every crossroad, beat up soldiers and armed police, seized weapons, ammunition and other military materials. Mobs also assaulted the Great Hall of the People, the Central Propaganda Department, the Ministry of Public Security, the Ministry of Radio, Film and Television and the west and south gates of Zhongnanhai. the seat of the Party Central Committee and the State Council. At about 5 p.m., the illegal organizations distributed kitchen knives, daggers and iron bars, to the crowd on Tiananmen Square and incited them to "take up weapons and overthrow the government." A group of ruffians banded together about 1,000 people to push down the wall of a construction site near Xidan and seized large quantities of tools, reinforcing bars and bricks, ready for street fighting. They planned to incite people to take to the streets the next day, a Sunday, to stage a violent rebellion in an attempt to overthrow the government and seize power at one stroke.

At this critical juncture, the martial law troops were ordered to move in by force to quell the anti-government rebellion. At 6:30 p.m., on June 3, the Beijing municipal government and the headquarters of the martial law enforcement troops issued an emergency announcement, asking all citizens to keep off the streets and stay at home. The announcement was broadcast over and over again. At about 10 p.m., the martial law troops headed for Beijing proper from various directions. The rioters, taking advantage of the soldiers' restraint, blocked military and other kinds of vehicles before they smashed and burned them. They also seized guns, ammunitions and transceivers. Several rioters seized an armored car and fired guns as they drove it along the street. Rioters also assaulted civilian installations and public buildings. Several rioters even drove a public bus loaded with gasoline drums towards the Tiananmen gate tower in an attempt to set fire to it. At the same time, rioters savagely beat up, kidnapped and killed soldiers and officers. On the Chang'an Avenue, when a military vehicle suddenly broke down, rioters surrounded it and ferociously crushed the driver with bricks. At Fuchengmen, a soldier's body was hung heel over head on the overpass balustrade after he had been savagely killed. At Chongwenmen, another soldier was thrown down from the flyover and burned alive. Near a cinema, an officer was beaten to death, disembowelled and his eyes gouged out. His body was then strung up on a burning bus.

Over 1,280 vehicles were burned or damaged in the rebellion, including over 1,000 military trucks, more than 60 armored cars, over 30 police cars, over 120 public buses and trolley buses and over 70 motor vehicles of other kinds. More than 6,000 martial law officers and soldiers were injured and scores of them killed.

Such heavy losses are eloquent testimony to the restraint and tolerance shown by the martial law enforcement troops. For fear of injuring civilians by accident, they would rather endure humiliation and meet their death unflinchingly, although they had weapons in their hands. It can be said that there is no other army in the world that can exercise restraint to such an extent.

The martial law troops, having suffered heavy casualties and been driven beyond forbearance, were forced to fire into the air to clear the way forward. During the counter-attack, some rioters were killed, some onlookers were hit by stray bullets and some wounded or killed by armed ruffians. According to reliable statistics, more than 3,000 civilians were wounded and over 200, including 36 college students, were killed.

At 1:30 a.m. on June 4, the Beijing municipal government and the martial law headquarters issued an emergency notice asking all students and other citizens to leave Tiananmen Square. The notice was broadcast repeatedly for well over three hours over loudspeakers. The students on Tiananmen Square, after discussion among themselves, sent representatives to the troops to express their willingness to withdraw from the square and this was approved by the troops. Then at about 5 a.m., several thousand students left the square in an orderly manner through a wide corridor in the southeastern part of the square vacated by the troops, carrying their own banners and streamers. Those who refused to leave were forced to leave by the soldiers. By 5:30 a.m., the clearing operation of the square had been completed.

During the whole operation not a single person was killed. The allegations that "Tiananmen Square was plunged into a bloodbath" and "thousands of people were killed in the square" are sheer rumors, and the true state of affairs will eventually be clear to the public.

After the decisive victory in quelling the riot, order in the capital was basically restored to normal and the situation throughout China soon became stable. The measures adopted by the Chinese government to stop the turmoil and put down the rebellion have not only won the acclaim and support of the Chinese people, but they have also won the understanding and support of the governments and people of many other countries. The Chinese government has announced that it will unswervingly carry on the policy of reform and opening to the outside world, the policy of developing friendly cooperation with different countries of the world on the basis of the five principles of peaceful coexistence, and the policy towards Hong Kong, Macao and Taiwan. We will continue to strive for the realization of the socialist modernization. We are fully confident of our future.

13

The Collapse of the Soviet Union, 1985–1991

INTRODUCTION

On November 10, 1982, Radio Moscow took to the airwaves with a steady stream of dirges and somber classical music, the traditional signal that an important Soviet personage had passed from the scene. And in fact, Leonid Brezhnev, general secretary of the Communist Party of the Soviet Union (CPSU) and leader of the USSR since he ousted Nikita Khrushchev in 1964, had died. At the time of Brezhnev's death, the Soviet Union was a mighty state, universally acknowledged as one of the world's two superpowers. However, beneath this glistening facade a number of serious problems challenged the Soviet leadership.

The Soviet economic model, little changed since Joseph Stalin created it in the 1930s, was increasingly unable to meet the demands of a modern society. Untouched by market forces, which were virtually outlawed in the USSR, the Soviet Union's economy continued to produce outmoded and shoddy products more appropriate for the early stages of the Industrial Revolution than for a high-tech world. Moreover, the gigantic Soviet military establishment had first call on whatever resources the state possessed. The result was a curious anomaly in which the Soviets could project their military might across the globe and send their cosmonauts into space for long periods of time but could neither feed their population without large and expensive grain imports nor house them properly.

In addition to the critical question of economic stagnation, other difficulties confronted the USSR. At the end of World War II, the Soviet Union had established its control over Eastern Europe. However, the Soviet satellite empire was a restive one. Poles, Czechs, Hungarians, and others chafed under Soviet domination and yearned to break free. The ethnic minorities within the Soviet Union itself, who had never fully reconciled themselves to Soviet power, were potentially even more troublesome. Although these ethnic minorities were outwardly quiescent, events soon demonstrated that the spirit of nationalism had put down deep roots among the more than 100 ethnic groups that comprised the USSR.

At the time of Brezhnev's death, the Soviet Union also found itself seriously overextended in its pursuit of a vigorous global foreign policy. Under the leadership of Ronald Reagan, the United States, the USSR's old rival, evinced both a renewed purposefulness and a willingness to spend billions on new armaments. At the same time, the Soviet Union was increasingly bogged down in a guerrilla war in Afghanistan that not only siphoned off money and manpower but also estranged the Soviets from the Islamic world. Finally, dozens of client states in the Third World casually squandered Soviet aid and then demanded more.

Facing such an array of difficulties, it seemed unlikely that the old men who led the Soviet Union at the time of Brezhnev's death could muster the imagination and initiative to find solutions. And they couldn't. Although Yuri Andropov, Brezhnev's immediate successor, was unusually bright and sophisticated for a Soviet leader, he was already fatally ill when he came to power, and his plans for reform never got off the drawing board. Andropov's successor, Konstantin Chernenko, was a doddering old timeserver who accomplished virtually nothing from the time he was named general secretary in February 1984 until his death in March 1985.

With Chernenko's death, the CPSU finally turned to a younger person to lead the Party and the state: Mikhail Gorbachev, a 54-year-old Communist Party functionary from the Stavropol region of southern Russia. The son of a collective farmer, Gorbachev had risen rapidly through the party ranks, gaining admittance to the Politburo, or inner council of the Party, in 1979.

After being named general secretary, Gorbachev moved to establish his control over the Communist Party. Older Soviet leaders died, retired, or were removed from positions of authority. Their replacements, like Gorbachev himself, were younger, better educated, and committed to reforming the system. Among those pushed out was Andrei Gromyko, longtime Soviet foreign minister and subsequently president of the USSR, who relinquished the latter post to Gorbachev; among those brought into the inner circle was Boris Yeltsin, an outspoken communist reformer from western Siberia.

The leadership vacuum of the previous few years had allowed the great difficulties confronting the Soviet Union to intensify. The domestic economy had slowed to almost a standstill as the rate of growth of the Soviet Union's gross national product dipped to less than 1.5 percent per year in the mid-1980s. A number of factors accounted for this precipitous decline: antiquated factories, a startling absence of high technology, costly and inefficient state and collective farms, a significant drop in oil production which supplied the USSR with badly needed hard currency, and the diversion of badly needed resources for dubious military purposes. The *apparat*, the cumbersome, hidebound, venal, and incompetent bureaucracy that oversaw every aspect of life in the Soviet Union, greatly aggravated the situation.

Economic woes led to a decline in the already low Soviet standard of living. For a long time, a lack of good housing and an absence of decent consumer goods had plagued the average Soviet citizen. Now these conditions worsened. Furthermore, the health care system showed signs of collapse as the rate of infant mortality increased while life expectancy declined—demographic trends that were truly astonishing for an industrialized country. The amount of resources devoted to education decreased as well, and pollution in every imaginable form threatened to engulf the entire country. The Soviet population exhibited signs of serious demoralization. The divorce rate climbed, and corruption, a hallmark characteristic of both Russian and Soviet life, intensified. Alcoholism, a long-standing social problem, worsened and brought with it increased absenteeism, thereby further weakening the country's economic performance. The Soviet

Angry Soviet demonstrators using cranes pull down a statue of Felix Dzerzhinsky, founder of the KGB security police, outside its Lubyanka headquarters on August 22, 1991. (Anatoly Sapronenkov/AFP/Getty Images)

media's repeated references to the USSR's superpower status brought little consolation to a worn-out people.

However, even the Soviet Union's global position was in growing jeopardy. The war in Afghanistan dragged on, with mounting Soviet casualties. As always, the Eastern European peoples chafed under Soviet domination. Relations with the United States and its Western allies were less than cordial. And Third World client states drained limited Soviet resources without providing much in return.

Acutely aware of the problems confronting the USSR and determined to sweep away the preceding decades' stagnation, Gorbachev initiated the policy of *perestroika*, or renewal/reconstruction. At the heart of perestroika was a determination to reform, but not replace, the existing Soviet system. Perestroika called for extensive decentralization of the rigidly controlled Soviet economy. Both industry and agriculture were to have greater freedom in the form of self-management, and the role of the *apparat* would be significantly reduced.

To make perestroika work, Gorbachev coupled it with the policy of *glasnost*, or openness. Glasnost allowed, even encouraged, a frank and open examination of not only the problems confronting the Soviet economy but virtually all aspects of Soviet life. Gorbachev apparently launched glasnost to win over public opinion and to undercut any opposition from entrenched interests threatened by perestroika.

Although never as clearly articulated as perestroika and glasnost, Gorbachev also determined to reassess the USSR's global position. He concluded that perestroika's success required better relations with the capitalist West and a reduced commitment to global activism.

Perestroika proved more difficult to implement than Gorbachev had imagined, and glasnost brought a tidal wave of criticism that challenged the Soviet state's very foundations. Sailing into uncharted waters, Gorbachev either introduced or permitted such radical (for the Soviet Union) concepts as economic decentralization, the profit motive, individual enterprise, a socialist or regulated market economy, and cost accounting. The role of the bureaucracy in general, but especially Gosplan, the omnipotent state planning agency, was curtailed. State subsidies for industries were reduced, and plans to transform the collective and state farms into private holdings were considered.

The perestroika reforms failed to achieve their objective. Deeply entrenched vested interests, including the *apparat*, factory and farm managers, much of the Party hierarchy, and some of the army opposed perestroika and successfully worked to undermine it. They were aided by the bumbling and inconsistent manner in which the naive and inexperienced Gorbachev approached his task. Industrial and agricultural production declined. Store shelves were stripped bare. Inflation skyrocketed. Economic chaos and confusion set in, and the Soviet economy began to collapse.

Glasnost also led to unanticipated and, for Gorbachev, unpleasant results. Discontent with Soviet life, repressed for decades, now burst into full view. Open criticism of leaders, policies, and institutions—at one time unthinkable in the Soviet Union—now became commonplace. Ad hoc groups that originally formed to discuss current issues began to appear more and more like rival political parties in the making. Atheism, the official policy of the USSR, was rejected, and the various religions of the Soviet people, especially Russian Orthodoxy, enjoyed renewed popularity. Even the heretofore sacrosanct KGB, or secret police, was publicly taken to task.

Most ominous for the Soviet leadership, glasnost permitted ethnic or national feelings, long condemned by the class-conscious Soviet leadership as reflective of a petit bourgeois mentality, to bubble to the surface. The Soviet Union was a multiethnic state. Of the approximately 285 million Soviet citizens, only about one-half were Russians. Nevertheless, Russians clearly dominated the USSR, a condition that the numerous ethnic minorities greatly resented. With glasnost, these minorities now had the opportunity to vent their frustration. If the cry of "Russians Out!" was not yet heard on the streets, it was at least beginning to form in many minds.

As pressure mounted on Gorbachev, events rapidly spun out of control. Astoundingly, the Soviet empire in Eastern Europe collapsed. Taking advantage of Gorbachev's new course, the Eastern Europeans broke free of Moscow's embrace. Acts of defiance toward Moscow and the puppet Marxist rulers it had installed increased in frequency until a tidal wave of revolution rolled over the Soviet bloc in 1989. Poland withdrew from the Moscow-sponsored Warsaw Treaty Organization and the Council for Mutual Economic Assistance (Comecon, or CMEA); Czechoslovakia underwent its "velvet Revolution"; and on November 9 the Berlin Wall, symbol of the Soviet Union's domination of Eastern Europe, came crashing down. The overthrow and execution of Nicolai Ceausescu, the Stalinist dictator of Romania, on Christmas Day, punctuated the complete collapse of the Soviet Union's position.

Meanwhile, the Soviet economy came perilously close to total collapse itself. Although Gorbachev's incomplete and sometimes ill-conceived reforms caused growing chaos, the entrenched elite mounted a determined opposition to his policies. Consequently, Soviet agrarian and industrial production slowed dramatically. Supplies of food, fuel, and other necessities dwindled, and a rash of crippling strikes occurred. By 1991, inflation was running at more than 250 percent annually and the Soviet Union could no longer service its multibillion-dollar foreign debt.

Emboldened by glasnost and spurred on by the Eastern European example, the economically hard-pressed ethnic minorities within the Soviet Union itself began to contemplate secession. The Baltic peoples (the Estonians, Latvians, and Lithuanians), who had been forcibly incorporated into the USSR in 1940, led the way. They were soon joined by the nations of the Caucasus (the Georgians, Armenians, and Azerbaijanis). Neither threats of repression (and in the case of Lithuania the spilling of blood) nor promises of better treatment dampened the growing sentiment for independence. The emergence of a strong nationalist movement (Rukh) in Ukraine, the Soviet Union's second largest republic, seemed to call into question the USSR's continued viability.

Overwhelmed by events, Gorbachev turned to political solutions. In particular, he determined to break the CPSU's political monopoly and move the Soviet Union closer to the Western, liberal-democratic model in the hope that this would assure perestroika's success. To that end, in March 1989 he presided over elections to the Soviet Congress of People's Deputies that were remarkably free and open by Soviet standards. Although the CPSU and its allies exercised their right to appoint 750 delegates, the Soviet people elected 1,500 delegates. Many of the elected delegates opposed the CPSU's privileged position, and some criticized Gorbachev for failing to push his reforms ardently enough. Andrei Sakharov, a leading Soviet dissident and winner of the Nobel Peace Prize, and Boris Yeltsin, maverick communist who had once supported Gorbachev but now broke with him, led the charge against the CPSU and the USSR's military-industrial complex.

Stunned by the rising tide of popular sentiment that demanded further and more rapid reform, Gorbachev offered additional political concessions. In February 1990, the Supreme Soviet, the executive body of the Soviet Congress of People's Deputies, abandoned Article 6 of the Soviet constitution, which had given the CPSU a monopoly over all political power in the USSR. Shortly thereafter, Gorbachev permitted the USSR's individual republics to hold parliamentary elections. The largest republic, the Russian Republic, elected a majority of delegates favorable to Yeltsin, who now emerged as a rival to Gorbachev for power.

Although Yeltsin, who was overwhelmingly elected president of the Russian Republic in June 1991, pushed Gorbachev to quicken the pace of reform, Gorbachev's opponents within the party and the crumbling power structure were not idle. With increased frequency and boldness, they objected to the entire program of reform and urged a return to traditional policies and methods. Buffeted from both sides, Gorbachev vacillated, first trying to placate his conservative opponents and then abruptly returning to the path of reform.

When Eduard Shevardnadze, the Soviet Union's foreign minister, resigned in December 1990, Gorbachev chose to ignore his warning of an imminent attack from the threatened hard-liners. However, several months later Gorbachev's conservative opponents attempted a coup d'état. With Gorbachev on vacation in the Crimea, a conspiratorial group of disgruntled party chieftains, disaffected military officers, and KGB officials tried to seize power on August 19, 1991. Gorbachev was placed under arrest;

but the coup failed when Yeltsin rallied his forces at the Moscow White House, the parliament building of the Russian Republic, and the Red Army refused to support the conspirators.

Although Gorbachev was freed and returned to Moscow, he was a spent force. The new man of the hour was Boris Yeltsin. The Soviet Union itself, already under attack on several fronts, was also a victim of the failed coup. Within Russia, Yeltsin proceeded rapidly to destroy the Communist Party and to lay the groundwork for Russia's secession from the USSR. As the CPSU disintegrated, other member states of the USSR moved toward independence, beginning with Ukraine, which declared its independence on August 24. Other republics followed suit, and when a Ukrainian referendum on December 1 resoundingly confirmed the decision to secede, the Soviet Union was dead. On December 25, the Soviet flag, the hammer and sickle, was lowered from atop the Kremlin, and on December 31, 1991, the USSR officially ceased to exist.

INTERPRETIVE ESSAY

CHARLES E. ZIEGLER

From its birth in the Revolution of 1917 to its demise at the end of 1991, the Soviet Union stood as the chief political, ideological, and military adversary of the Western democratic world. The Western democracies were constitutionally based systems embodying the concept of representative government, holding regular competitive elections for political office, respecting (in general) the rights and freedoms of the individual citizen, and promoting market economies with extensive private enterprise. By contrast, the Soviet Union and its East European colonies rejected the principles of "bourgeois democracy" as a sham, promoting instead the Marxist concept that the industrial working class should exercise political power without regard for the niceties of democratic procedure. The supposedly transitional phase of the "dictatorship of the proletariat" gradually solidified into a centralized, repressive dictatorship in which every facet of life—political, cultural, and economic—was regulated by the Communist Party and state bureaucracy.

Under the energetic direction of Vladimir Lenin, founder of the Communist Party of the Soviet Union (CPSU, originally called the Bolshevik Party), all competing political forces in revolutionary Russia were either discredited as insufficiently radical, or militarily defeated in the Civil War (1918–1921). After Lenin died early in 1924, Joseph Stalin, an ethnic Georgian born Josef Djugashvili, utilized his position as general secretary of the Communist Party to gradually eliminate his rivals in the Soviet leadership, most notably Leon Trotsky, cofounder of the Soviet state.

In 1928, Stalin, his political position now secure, launched an ambitious program to transform the Soviet Union from a backward peasant economy into a highly industrialized modern system. The more relaxed period of the 1920s, which permitted small private businesses and private farming in a market economy (the New Economic Policy, or NEP), was jettisoned in favor of a series of Five Year Plans that demanded ever-increasing quotas of steel, coal, cement, and other heavy industrial goods from state enterprises. During the 1930s, all private farms were forcibly consolidated into enormous collective and state farms *(kolkhozes* and *sovkhozes).* Millions of peasants died during this period; they were shot for resisting collectivization, or simply starved to death as a result of excessive government requisitions of grain. Millions left the countryside to work in the new urban factories. Underlying these monumental transformations of Soviet society was what Robert Conquest has called the Great Terror, Stalin's paranoid, determined attempt to root out all possible forms of opposition to his absolute control. When the archives were finally opened after the collapse of the Soviet Union, estimates of those who had perished in the huge labor camp system (the Gulag Archipelago) or were shot outright ranged in the millions.

Stalin established the central elements of the totalitarian Soviet state: a Communist Party headed by the general secretary acting as the absolute political authority; an intrusive government bureaucracy that controlled every facet of society and the economy; the use of force and intimidation to achieve full compliance of the population; state censorship and manipulation of information through the mass media and the educational system; and state ownership of the entire economy (industry, agriculture, and services), with minimal attention to consumer needs and fulfillment of production quotas as the primary goal.

Following the trauma of World War II, in which the Soviet Union lost some 20 million people, Stalin extended the Soviet model to the newly occupied countries of Eastern Europe, thus creating the first communist empire. Soviet control of Eastern Europe was thorough but not absolute, and weakened considerably after Stalin's death in 1953. Yugoslavia had defected from the Soviet bloc as early as 1948; Hungary and Poland challenged Soviet control in 1956. Albania threw in its lot with China after the Sino-Soviet split in 1961, and a Czechoslovak reform program that foreshadowed Gorbachev's was repressed with Soviet tanks in August 1968. Nicolai Ceausescu had promoted an independent-minded brand of Romanian national communism from his accession to power in 1965. Poland proved a constant irritant—demonstrations in 1968, 1970, and 1976 were followed by the emergence of the broad-based Solidarity movement, which challenged the Polish Communist Party's monopoly on power from August 1980 to December 1981. Soviet attempts to organize its allies into economic (Council for Mutual Economic Assistance) and military (Warsaw Treaty Organization) alliances were only partially successful, because these pacts were not based on sovereign consent or shared interests.

The first indications of the economic problems that would eventually lead to Gorbachev's reforms surfaced during Nikita Khrushchev's tenure as general secretary from 1953 to 1964. Khrushchev's ill-fated attempts at reform alienated much of the party and government bureaucracy, who deposed him in a bloodless Kremlin coup in October 1964. His successors—Leonid Brezhnev, who served as general secretary from 1964 to 1982, and Aleksei Kosygin, premier of the Soviet government from 1964 until his death in 1980—merely tinkered with the Stalinist structure of centralized political control and economic planning. A period of bureaucratic lethargy, what Gorbachev and the reformers would later call the "time of stagnation," supplanted Stalin's terroristic oppression and Khrushchev's amateurish experiments. Problems became more acute and obvious to younger, reform-minded Soviet leaders as the industrial economy could not keep up with the dynamic computer- and information-driven economies of Europe, the United States, and East Asia.

The Soviet economy had provided the population with a modestly improving standard of living ever since Stalin's death, but it could not match rising consumer expectations. Much of Soviet investment went to feed the huge military machine, which absorbed 25 percent or more of total gross domestic product. As the United States retreated from international commitments following the Vietnam debacle, the Brezhnev regime increasingly resorted to military threats, and occasionally the direct exercise of military power, to achieve its foreign policy goals. In the latter half of the 1970s, Soviet officials confidently asserted that the "correlation of forces" in world affairs had shifted in favor of socialism and against the capitalist states. By the time of Brezhnev's death in November 1982, however, the Soviet Union confronted stubborn guerrilla resistance in Afghanistan (which the Soviets had invaded in 1979), a restive population in Poland (where the Solidarity movement had openly defied the government during 1980–1981), and a conservative administration in Washington determined to rebuild America's military strength and confront the Soviet Union around the globe. And few members of the Third World any longer admired the USSR as a model of development, preferring instead the example of newly industrializing and increasingly wealthy capitalist nations.

In sum, the early 1980s found an aging and unimaginative Soviet leadership facing intractable domestic problems and an increasingly difficult international environment. As the old guard died off or retired, a new generation of leaders, influenced more by Khrushchev's thaw than by Stalin's terror, moved into the highest echelons of power.

The dramatic changes that led to the collapse of the Soviet Union and its communist empire cannot be attributed to any one individual or factor. Certainly Mikhail Gorbachev, the relatively young party official from Stavropol who was appointed general secretary in March 1985, deserves much of the credit for initiating the reform process. Gorbachev is not the entire story, however. Nor is it accurate to assert, as have some prominent American conservatives, that President Ronald Reagan's confrontational policies and accelerated defense spending led to the collapse of the USSR. These factors played a role, but they were overshadowed by the critical importance of internal motivations. So many domestic problems had accumulated under Brezhnev—economic stagnation, technological backwardness, corruption, environmental pollution, growing cynicism and alienation, simmering discontent among the various nationalities—that the need for reform was apparent to all but the most obdurate ideologues.

From the perspective of Gorbachev and the reformers, the economy was the greatest weakness of the system. Top-heavy central planning, with its focus on generating ever larger quotas of heavy industrial products, was clearly out of sync with the modern electronic age. Pressure for economic reform had been building since the 1960s, but the oil price shocks of 1973 and 1979 greatly increased the value of the Soviet Union's chief exports (oil and natural gas), providing windfall revenues that allowed Kremlin decision makers to import foodstuffs and other consumer goods, pay for an expensive war in Afghanistan, and postpone hard decisions on reform. However, in 1985, Saudi Arabia ramped up oil production, and oil prices declined dramatically. Still, Gorbachev's political situation was not strong enough to enact the necessary reforms (abandoning the East European empire, pulling out of Afghanistan, and/or curtailing food imports) until 1989, at which point the government was reduced to massive international borrowing. By then, it was too late.

Shortly after Brezhnev died, the country's top social scientists had been charged with developing a set of recommendations for economic and social reform. Gorbachev was assigned to head this task force. Many reform proposals looked back to the limited capitalism of the NEP, whereas others suggested adopting ideas from the Hungarian, East German, or Chinese experiments. Occasionally these internal debates spilled into the pages of mass circulation journals and newspapers. One of the most prominent voices of reform, the sociologist Tatiana Zaslavskaia, argued that rigid authoritarian methods of production established under Stalin were no longer appropriate for an educated urban work force. The recent example of Poland and instances of worker dissatisfaction throughout the USSR and Eastern Europe suggested that alienation, a Marxist concept applied until now only to capitalist systems, was a very real problem in the "workers' paradise."

When Brezhnev's simpleminded protégé Konstantin Chernenko died in March 1985, Gorbachev assumed office with literally hundreds of proposals for reform in hand. Of course, there were still conservatives in the Soviet leadership who resisted significant change, so Gorbachev had to proceed cautiously until he could develop a stronger base of support in the Kremlin. Through a series of adroit maneuvers, Gorbachev demoted or retired many of the older generation of policy makers, replacing them with younger, more reform-minded officials. By the middle of 1987, he had solidified his political position and had managed to put his ideas for change—most notably, perestroika and glasnost—at the top of the Soviet agenda. It should be emphasized, however, that neither Gorbachev nor his reformist allies had a grand strategy for change. They were experimenting, trying to reshape a moribund system and yet preserve most of the central elements of that system. It was a strategy that could not succeed.

Perestroika, broadly defined as the restructuring of the Soviet economy, was at the heart of Gorbachev's reform program, as outlined in his book of the same title. Gorbachev, who never abandoned his belief in the inherent superiority of socialism, initially sought to modernize the Soviet economy by correcting some of its more egregious failures while leaving the basic structure intact. For the first two years, Gorbachev stressed the importance of "accelerating" economic performance, improving worker discipline, and attacking alcoholism (which seriously impaired productivity). These measures had been proposed during the brief tenure of Yuri Andropov (1982–1984), who had been a cautious voice for reform and one of Gorbachev's patrons in the leadership. Such palliatives did not get at the root of the problem, however. By mid-1987 it was increasingly apparent that more was needed than simply adjusting the Soviet system of central planning.

The second major principle of Gorbachev's reform program, glasnost, was supposed to provide the conditions for more effective economic restructuring. Usually translated as "openness" or "publicity," glasnost was meant to expose the full extent of mismanagement, corruption, and falsification in the economic system, holding both management and workers up to the glare of public opinion. Given the long Soviet (and Russian) tradition of secrecy, most Soviet leaders, Gorbachev included, did not envision completely abolishing the government's control over information. It proved difficult to apply glasnost selectively, however. When Reactor Number 4 at the Chernobyl nuclear power station in Ukraine exploded on April 26, 1986, the Kremlin's treatment of this disaster tested the limits of glasnost. Although the Soviet government withheld information on the true extent of the damage, domestic and international concern forced a public investigation unprecedented in Soviet history.

Chernobyl encouraged a frightened Soviet populace to demand from their government more honest reporting on a wide range of social, economic, and political issues—environmental pollution, disease, crime, official corruption, accidents, and natural disasters. As censorship weakened, the official Soviet press became increasingly critical of government actions, and subjects open for public discussion expanded to include nationality relations, military issues, foreign policy, and even the private lives of top Soviet leaders. Encouraged by Gorbachev, the media attempted to fill in the "blank spots" in Soviet history, events that had been ignored or blatantly falsified in order to portray the Soviet system in a more flattering light. Stalin's bloody dictatorship was reappraised, and such prominent "enemies of the state" as Leon Trotsky, Nikolai Bukharin (the party's chief theoretician in the 1920s and an outspoken advocate of the liberal policies of that period), and Alexander Solzhenitsyn, the famous dissident novelist and historian of the prison camps, were reevaluated. By the end of the 1980s, even Lenin, who had been virtually deified after his death as a prophet of Marxism and a supposedly infallible ruler, was condemned for having planted the seeds of dictatorship.

Ever since Lenin had convinced other party leaders to ban opposing "factions" at the Tenth Party Congress in 1921, political opposition had been punished as a crime against the state. Not only were competing parties illegal; all social and cultural organizations from churches to chess clubs were tightly controlled and monitored by the Communist Party. As perestroika and glasnost evolved, political controls were relaxed and independent groups began to organize and articulate their demands. Ecology was one prominent issue that captured a great deal of attention, especially after Chernobyl, and many of the earliest "informal" groups organized to combat local environmental problems. The Soviet government's abysmal record on the environment, due to careless practices in agriculture, industry, nuclear power, and defense, contributed significantly to the crisis in Soviet health care. Environmental destruction also helped stimulate greater militancy among the Soviet Union's national minorities, who shared the belief that the Soviet government had, in classic colonial style, deliberately located heavily polluting industries in their homelands.

Of course, ecology problems were only one in a long list of resentments held by the national minorities. The elaborate federal structure of Soviet government theoretically gave the republics, autonomous republics, autonomous regions, and national areas a certain measure of self-determination. In reality, the national aspirations of most minorities were frustrated by centralized party control and persistent efforts at Russification. Gorbachev and many of the reformers did not realize the strength of nationalism in the Soviet Union. By 1989–1990, "National Front" movements in the Baltic states, Ukraine, Belarus, and the Caucasus were demanding from Moscow sovereign control over their internal affairs; soon Lithuania would declare its outright independence from the USSR.

The Soviet government's willingness to accept social and political pluralism late in the 1980s also extended to Eastern Europe. Gorbachev encouraged Eastern European communist leaders to emulate his reforms, although the "new thinking" in foreign policy, as it was called, rejected the use of coercion as a tool to ensure compliance with

Soviet practice. Moscow now abandoned its claim to be the only true defender of communist orthodoxy. As Foreign Ministry spokesman Gennadi Gerasimov explained, the Brezhnev Doctrine of limited sovereignty enunciated after the Czechoslovak invasion had been supplanted by the "Sinatra Doctrine," letting the East European states "do it their way."

As it became clear that Soviet military forces would no longer intervene to prop up unpopular communist governments, demands for change in Eastern Europe intensified. Cautious reforms were begun in Hungary and Poland, traditionally the most liberal of the communist regimes, but leaders in Czechoslovakia, Romania, Bulgaria, and East Germany resisted ceding political power. Between October and December 1989, however, a wave of revolution swept over Eastern Europe, as communist regimes fell and the Berlin Wall was torn down. The summary execution of Romania's Nicolai Ceausescu and his wife on Christmas Day marked the end of communism in Eastern Europe.

Eastern Europe's liberation provided further encouragement to the movements for greater autonomy in the 15 union republics that comprised the Soviet Union. The Soviet constitution promised "self-determination" for Ukrainians, Armenians, Uzbeks, Lithuanians, and other major ethnic groups but did not adequately satisfy aspirations of the various nationalities. Although some cultural autonomy was permitted, and education in native languages was available, the Communist Party exercised tight central control from Moscow over the republics' affairs. Efforts to promote a unifying Soviet identity became a thinly disguised policy of Russification, antagonizing the 49 percent of the population that was not ethnic Russian. The end of the Soviet empire in Eastern Europe raised the possibility of independence for the "internal empire" as well, accelerating demands for sovereignty and in some cases complete independence.

Beyond Eastern Europe, Gorbachev's new thinking in foreign policy led to major improvements in relations with the United States, China, and Western Europe, and reversed decades of support for radical Third World causes. Successful domestic reform, Gorbachev realized, could not be achieved in an atmosphere of international hostility. Before 1985, no Soviet leader had ever admitted that aggressive Soviet behavior might be responsible for the poor state of East-West relations or for the Sino-Soviet split. New thinking acknowledged that confrontational Soviet foreign policies, based on Lenin's ideas of class struggle, had often proved ineffective or even counterproductive to Soviet national interests. Gorbachev and the Kremlin reformers now spoke of "universal human values" and a "common European home," promised an end to the "enemy image" that had characterized Moscow's portrayal of the West, and pledged a reduction of military forces to a level sufficient for an adequate national defense.

Despite initial skepticism in the West, new thinking produced a sea change in Soviet foreign policy. The first breakthrough—the December 1987 Intermediate Nuclear Forces (INF) Treaty signed by the United States and the USSR—eliminated an entire class of highly destabilizing nuclear weapons. In 1988, Gorbachev announced that all Soviet troops would be withdrawn from Afghanistan within a year, and at a May 1989 summit meeting in Beijing, China and the Soviet Union put an end to 30 years of bitter confrontation. A major treaty requiring the Soviet Union to undertake asymmetrical cuts in conventional forces in Europe was signed in 1990 (the CFE Treaty), and in 1991 an unprecedented agreement significantly reducing strategic arms (the START Treaty) was signed between the United States and the Soviet Union.

Although these remarkable developments in foreign policy created the relaxed international climate necessary for perestroika, many influential voices in the Soviet Union were critical of Gorbachev's "extravagant" concessions to the West and disturbed by the loss of the Soviet empire. These same conservatives were also disturbed by the increasing disorder and confusion in Soviet society, and resisted efforts to develop private enterprise and a market-oriented economy. As the 1980s drew to a close, political forces in the USSR split between the supporters and the critics of reform.

Radical changes in Soviet political and economic life had polarized opinions, with elites divided between such conservatives as Politburo member Yegor Ligachev and supporters of more rapid reform, led by former Moscow Communist Party Secretary Boris Yeltsin. Gorbachev sought to occupy the middle ground, but it was a difficult balancing act. The Nineteenth Party Conference of June 1988, which illustrated the strength of conservative opposition to reform within the Communist Party, marked a watershed in political reform. Gorbachev was convinced that perestroika could not succeed without a shift of political power from the authoritarian CPSU to elected governmental institutions. Popular pressure expressed through the electoral process, he reasoned, would compel reluctant officials to support his reform program. This was the beginning of a cautious and incomplete democratization.

The elections to a new Congress of People's Deputies, held in March 1989, were relatively free by Soviet standards. Voters could now choose among candidates and, although the outcome was biased in favor of conservative forces, roughly one-fifth of the elected deputies were ardent reformers. Unaccustomed to democracy, deputies to the Congress haggled over procedural issues and traded accusations, all of which was broadcast on national television to a fascinated Soviet audience. As might be expected, this new Congress could not immediately provide effective governance. Its emergence, however, helped legitimize the concept of representative democracy among an important segment of the population. It also marked the beginning of the end of the Communist Party's monopoly over political power.

Much of the problem in trying to effect reform stemmed from the pervasive influence of the CPSU in Soviet political life. The party had succeeded, albeit at tremendous cost, in constructing the rudiments of a modern industrial society—an urbanized population base, factories, transportation and communications infrastructure, mass education, and science. As a consequence, Soviet society and the economy had experienced major transformations since the revolution. The moribund political system, however, had great difficulty adapting to the changing conditions of the late twentieth century. The Communist Party's obsession with secrecy clashed with the demands of the information age, its myopic focus on expanding industrial output ignored the worldwide trend toward quality and efficiency, and its centralized approach to political issues could not meet the challenge of creating community out of an increasingly diverse society. Before Gorbachev, the party had resisted granting the population a larger role in governing. Lacking flexibility, the Soviet state maintained the appearance of exercising effective authority right up to the point when the system began to collapse.

As Samuel Huntington pointed out in his classic *Political Order in Changing Societies*, a political system with several powerful institutions is more likely to adapt to change than a system with only one significant institution. If one institution suffers a loss of legitimacy, the others can assume some of the weakened institution's functions.

Soviet reformers, however, faced the daunting task of creating entirely new political institutions—a functioning legislature, independent courts, a responsible executive, and genuine federalism—virtually overnight, to replace a rapidly disintegrating Communist Party. As might be expected, there was considerable disagreement over the precise form these new governing institutions would assume.

More important, it takes time for new institutions to acquire legitimacy. Recall that in the United States a bloody civil war was fought over federal power versus states' rights more than 70 years after the Constitution was first enacted. It would be unrealistic to assume that new institutions could be designed, staffed, and functioning smoothly within a few years, especially in the context of exponentially increasing demands from the population. Again, drawing on Huntington's study of transitional societies, political instability in the Soviet Union resulted from the rapid expansion of political participation, coupled with the inability of reformers to organize and institutionalize the means of reconciling conflicting demands. In other words, political change could not keep up with social and economic change.

The most potent source of new demands from the population was ethnic and national disaffection. Contrary to Marxian predictions, nationalism, not class, was the basis for revolution in the Soviet context. Few Soviet reformers, Gorbachev included, understood the strength of national feeling among the hundred-odd ethnic groups that comprised the USSR. Soviet leaders actually seemed to believe their own propaganda, that the tsarist "prison of nations" had been supplanted by a "family of nations" under communism. For 70 years, the pressures of ideological conformity and the threat of physical force had constrained national aspirations. There were occasional glimpses of discontent bubbling beneath the surface, as in 1978 when Georgian students took to the streets of Tbilisi to protest plans to drop their native language from the republic's constitution. But few could anticipate the tremendous surge of nationalism that accompanied the relaxation of political controls between 1987 and 1991.

Revelations about official corruption and mismanagement and the obvious failure of Gorbachev's economic reform policies undermined the credibility of central authorities and inspired calls for greater autonomy in the provinces. Toward the end of 1990, Soviet leaders began to reevaluate the sham federalism that had promised cultural autonomy while ensuring centralized Communist Party control over the various national republics. Plans were drawn up for a new Union Treaty to replace the one that had created the Union of Soviet Socialist Republics in 1922. Gorbachev and the reformers were finally willing to draw up a new constitution that would grant significant self-governing powers to the republics. But conservatives, who saw their influence expand in late 1990 and early 1991, argued that the establishment of genuine federalism would undermine the basis of the Soviet communist system. Ironically, the movement toward political autonomy in the republics had progressed so far that even a decentralized system patterned on the U.S. or Canadian constitution would not satisfy the demands for sovereignty or independence.

These conflicting pressures continued to mount through 1991, culminating in the coup by hard-liners opposed to the new Union Treaty on August 19–22. Reactions to the attempted takeover illustrated the highly fragmented character of public opinion toward the changes taking place in the USSR. Many courageous individuals rallied to support Russian president Boris Yeltsin at the parliament building. The demoralized Soviet army was divided—some officers ignored orders to march on Moscow and St.

Petersburg, and others commanded tanks in the streets of the capital. A few regional leaders condemned the coup; most cautiously waited for the situation to clarify before committing themselves.

For the minority republics, the conservatives' bid for power, and Gorbachev's apparent inability to grasp the significance of the August events following the coup, confirmed their worst fears. In this climate full independence seemed the best guarantee against Moscow reestablishing centralized political control. Gorbachev attempted to hold the USSR together in a looser arrangement, but his authority and credibility had been so tarnished that he was doomed to fail. Starting with the three Baltic states, each of the republics declared its independence from the Soviet Union. The death blow came with Ukraine's December 1 referendum in favor of independence. Gorbachev's resignation on Christmas Day signaled the end of the Soviet experiment.

Many factors played a role in the collapse of the Soviet Union. The most important seem to have been internal, although international pressures, many linked to Moscow's inept foreign policies, also deserved some credit for the collapse. Domestic factors include the increasingly poor economic performance of the centrally planned economy, technological backwardness, a stifling and repressive political system that discouraged creativity, excessive military spending, incredible bureaucratic inefficiency, a catastrophic ecology record, and insensitivity to the national interests of the Soviet Union's diverse minorities. A spiritual vacuum, alienation, and corruption eroded social cohesion. Confrontational foreign policies, influenced by the ideology of class struggle, estranged many Soviet allies and brought the capitalist world together in an effort to contain the perceived communist threat.

The accretion of domestic problems and international pressures coincided with a major generational change in the Soviet leadership. Gorbachev was central in planning and promoting reform, but it should be remembered that he was supported by younger officials for whom the terror of the Stalin era was only a vague memory. This generation was better educated and more critical of Soviet "achievements" than were the Brezhnevs, the Suslovs, and the Gromykos, whose careers were built over the graves of the old Bolsheviks. And lastly, we should not forget the Soviet people, who were disillusioned and impatient with a corrupt, repressive system that refused to acknowledge their humanity. The revolution that brought about the collapse of the Soviet Union may have started with the party elite, but it ended with an extraordinary display of public affirmation that dictatorship was no longer an acceptable form of government.

SELECTED BIBLIOGRAPHY

Aron, Leon. *Yeltsin: A Revolutionary Life*. New York: St. Martin's Press, 2000. Massive biography of post-communist Russia's first president has a wealth of detail on the late Soviet era.

Banac, Ivo, ed. *Eastern Europe in Revolution*. Ithaca, NY: Cornell University Press, 1992. Historians and sociologists discuss the collapse of communism in Eastern Europe.

Brzezinski, Zbigniew. *The Grand Failure: The Birth and Death of Communism in the Twentieth Century*. New York: Collier Books, 1990. A sweeping discussion of the critical weaknesses of communism in the Soviet Union, Eastern Europe, and China.

Dawisha, Karen. *Eastern Europe, Gorbachev, and Reform: The Great Challenge*. 2nd ed. Cambridge, England: Cambridge University Press, 1990. Analyzes Soviet intentions and interests in Eastern Europe.

Feshbach, Murray, and Alfred Friendly, Jr. *Ecocide in the USSR: Health and Nature under Siege.* New York: Basic Books, 1992. A very thorough, albeit depressing, chronicle of abuse of the natural environment and the related issue of neglect in Soviet health care.

Gaidar, Yegor. *Collapse of an Empire: Lessons for Modern Russia.* Washington, DC: Brookings Institution Press, 2007. Insider, reformer, and (briefly) acting prime minister, Gaidar places the Soviet case in the trajectory of the rise and decline of empires.

Gorbachev, Mikhail. *Memoirs.* New York: Doubleday, 1996. Autobiography of the former general secretary.

Gorbachev, Mikhail. *Perestroika: New Thinking for Our Country and the World.* New York: Harper and Row, 1987. The general secretary's explanation of his plans for reform.

Hasegawa, Tsuyoshi, and Alex Pravda, eds. *Perestroika: Soviet Domestic and Foreign Policies.* London: Sage, 1990. Assesses the links between Soviet domestic reforms and changes in foreign policy.

Hewett, Ed A. *Reforming the Soviet Economy: Equality Versus Efficiency.* Washington, DC: Brookings Institution, 1988. A superb review of the Soviet economic structure and its operation.

Hosking, Geoffrey. *The Awakening of the Soviet Union.* Cambridge, MA: Harvard University Press, 1990. An analysis of the social and cultural factors underlying the transformations of the late 1980s.

Kagarlitsky, Boris. *The Disintegration of the Monolith.* Translated by Renfrey Clarke. London: Verso, 1992. A critical look at the political forces that emerged during the reforms by a Russian observer.

Kotkin, Stephen. *Armageddon Averted: The Soviet Collapse 1970–2000.* Updated edition, Oxford: Oxford University Press, 2008. Princeton University scholar Kotkin focuses on elites and structural conditions as he provides a historical and geopolitical analysis of the last two decades of the Soviet Union and the first decade of transition.

Lewin, Moshe. *The Gorbachev Phenomenon: A Historical Interpretation.* Expanded ed. Berkeley: University of California Press, 1991. Lewin, a leading economic historian, places Gorbachev's reforms in the context of the major socioeconomic transformations that took place in the USSR.

Marples, David R. *The Collapse of the Soviet Union, 1985–1991.* White Plains, NY: Longman, 2004. Marples, a Canadian history professor, focuses on the nationality issues, economic problems, and power struggles among the leadership.

Matlock, Jack. *Autopsy on an Empire: The American Ambassador's Account of the Collapse of the Soviet Union.* New York: Random House, 1995. Perceptive account by the last U.S. Ambassador to the USSR.

Matlock, Jack. *Reagan and Gorbachev: How the Cold War Ended.* New York: Random House, 2005. Insider's account of the interactions of the two leaders and their top advisers.

McAuley, Mary. *Soviet Politics 1917–1991.* Oxford: Oxford University Press, 1992. This slim volume cogently analyzes the political factors that formed and transformed the Soviet state.

Remnick, David. *Lenin's Tomb: The Last Days of the Soviet Empire.* New York: Random House, 1993. Former Moscow correspondent for the *Washington Post* delivers a penetrating portrait of Soviet life during the reform period.

Sakwa, Richard. *Gorbachev and His Reforms: 1985–1990.* New York: Prentice Hall, 1991. Examines the interactions of the principal individuals, institutions, and ideas that dominated the reform period.

Sebestyen, Victor. *Revolution 1989: The Fall of the Soviet Empire.* New York: Pantheon Books, 2009. Very readable interpretation of the collapse by a Hungarian-born British journalist.

Smith, Hedrick. *The New Russians.* New York: Random House, 1991. A perceptive survey of the impact of Gorbachev's economic, social, and political reforms on the Soviet people by one of the West's leading journalists.

Strayer, Robert W. *Why Did the Soviet Union Collapse? Understanding Historical Change*. Armonk, NY: M. E. Sharpe, 1998. Short and readable text on various interpretations of the Soviet collapse.

White, Stephen. *After Gorbachev*. Cambridge: Cambridge University Press, 1993. A sophisticated analysis of the reform process under Gorbachev by a leading British scholar.

Yeltsin, Boris. *Against the Grain: An Autobiography*. Translated by Michael Glenny. New York: Summit Books, 1990. Russia's controversial president chronicles his career.

Yurchak, Alexei. *Everything Was Forever, Until It Was No More: The Last Soviet Generation*. Princeton, NJ: Princeton University Press, 2006. A postmodernist examination of the late-Soviet period focusing on discourse, ideology, and identity of the people, and how they came to terms with socialism and its collapse.

Ziegler, Charles E. *The History of Russia*, 2nd ed. Santa Barbara, CA: ABC-CLIO/Greenwood Press, 2009. Survey of Russian history with emphasis on the late twentieth century.

Zubok, Vladislav. *A Failed Empire: The Soviet Union in the Cold War from Stalin to Gorbachev*. Chapel Hill: University of North Carolina Press, 2007. A revisionist history of Soviet foreign policy during the Cold War.

YURI ANDROPOV (1914–1984)

Yuri Andropov was an important Soviet political figure who assumed leadership of the Soviet Union after Leonid Brezhnev's death in 1982. Reputed to be a reformer, his tenure as leader proved to be a short one, however, as he ruled the Soviet Union for only 15 months before his death. Ill during most of that time, Andropov was unable to reverse the Soviet Union's decline.

Born on June 15, 1914, Andropov was the son of a railway worker. Just three years old when the communists took over in Russia following the Russian Revolution, Andropov became active in the socialist movement at an early age. At the age of 16, he joined the Komsomol, the only officially recognized political organization for young people in the Soviet Union. Andropov rose quickly through the ranks of the Komsomol as he established himself as a rising star in the political system. He held a variety of jobs during that time, working as a telegraph operator, a film projectionist, and a boatman before attending Petrozavodsk University.

Andropov benefitted greatly from the Great Purge that Joseph Stalin initiated to eliminate all real and potential opposition within the Communist Party to his dictatorship. As many of the old veterans of the communist revolution of 1917 were unmasked as "enemies of the people," young party members like Andropov rose to take their place.

During World War II, Andropov served as leader of the Komsomol in Karelia, that part of Finland seized by the USSR in the 1939–1940 "Winter War." Later he helped to organize resistance against Germany and rose to second in command in the Karelo-Finnish region in the late 1940s. He advanced quickly through the party ranks by showing his loyalty to Stalin, which was the only key to survival and a successful career. By 1951, Andropov had been transferred to Moscow, where he worked for the Central Committee of the Communist Party of the Soviet Union.

From 1954 to 1957, Andropov served as ambassador to Hungary. While there, he played an important part in organizing the Soviet suppression of the Hungarian Revolution of 1956. After the Soviets crushed the revolt, Andropov was appointed head of the

Yuri Andropov, a former head of the KGB, the Soviet Union's spy agency, succeeded Leonid Brezhnev as leader of the USSR in 1982. However, he was terminally ill at the time and died early in 1984. He acted as mentor to Mikhail Gorbachev. (Getty Images)

Central Committee's bureau that dealt with "socialist" countries. In 1961, he was elected to the Central Committee, another significant step to power in the Soviet Union.

By 1967, Andropov headed the Soviet secret police (the KGB), a position of great power. Andropov distinguished himself in the position, and in 1973, he was elected to the country's highest ruling body, the Politburo. He was referred to within party circles as the "party's sword" against "internal and external enemies."

While head of the KGB from 1967 to 1982, Andropov changed the role of the organization in both the Soviet Union and abroad, increasing the KGB's importance dramatically. During his 15 years as chairman of the organization, Andropov led the suppression of the dissident movement in the Soviet Union and expanded the KGB's espionage activities abroad. In addition, Andropov turned the position into a stepping stone to party leadership. The KGB became synonymous with power in the Soviet Union, and under Andropov the organization came to lead the party as much as serve the party.

Andropov became general secretary of the party and premier of the Soviet Union after the death of Leonid Brezhnev in November 1982. Initially, there were hopes in the United States and the West that Andropov would be more liberal and therefore more conciliatory to the West than Brezhnev had been, but those hopes quickly dissipated. Andropov continued to pursue the Soviets' war in Afghanistan and increased the repression of Soviet dissidents.

During his short tenure as premier, Andropov attacked the corruption that had infiltrated and become rooted in the massive Soviet bureaucratic system of government. Andropov's attempts to weed out corrupt and incompetent officials were only marginally successful, however, and his actions did little to help stimulate the stagnant Soviet economy.

In August 1983, Andropov became fatally ill and was never seen in public again. He died on February 9, 1984.

ABC-CLIO

MIKHAIL GORBACHEV (1931–)

As general secretary of the Communist Party of the Soviet Union, Mikhail Gorbachev stunned Westerners throughout the 1980s. Never before had a communist leader seemed so outgoing, intellectual, and committed to reforms viewed favorably by the West. Gorbachev set out to change and strengthen both the Soviet Union and the Communist Party. His reforms led to unanticipated results, however, and caused both his personal downfall and the disintegration of the Soviet Union.

Gorbachev was born on March 2, 1931, in Privolnoye, a village in the northern Caucasus region of the Soviet Union. Gorbachev's parents were peasants, and as a child he endured many hardships. Possessing little money, he had to combine schooling with farm work. At age 10, he witnessed German troops invade his homeland during World War II. His father fought against the Germans, an action Gorbachev referred to proudly in future years. The war brought devastation, however. Gorbachev excelled at the challenge of rebuilding, however, and in 1949 earned the Order of the Red Banner for his contribution to that year's harvest. At the same time, he did well in school, earning a silver medal for his work, and in 1950, he entered law school at the Soviet Union's prestigious Moscow State University.

Although law was not a glamorous field at the time, Gorbachev found his first professional outlet in the Komsomol, or Communist Youth League, in which he became active as an organizer. In 1952, he joined the Communist Party. Gorbachev graduated from law school in 1955 and then advanced rapidly and impressively. He served as first secretary of the Komsomol in Stavropol from 1956 to 1958, and in the latter year became the organization's first secretary for the entire Stavropol region. He then shifted his efforts to the Communist Party and in 1962 worked as an organizer for the collective farm administration, thus returning to his rural background. At the same time, he attended Stavropol Agricultural Institute, where he studied agronomy. In 1966, he became first secretary for Stavropol and, the following year, obtained his agronomy degree. Just three years later, he was the party's first secretary for the Stavropol region and in 1971 was named a member of the Central Committee of the Communist Party—a young man in a politically powerful body dominated by older leaders.

During his tenure in Stavropol, Gorbachev gained a substantial following among workers on the collectives. He introduced reforms that allowed farmers more power in making decisions and encouraged larger private plots where they could grow food for the open market. Gorbachev's good standing with influential men was evident in the 1970s when party officials sent him overseas on three occasions, including in 1976 as head of a delegation visiting Paris.

Gorbachev's career progressed again in 1978 when Agriculture Secretary Fyodor Kulakov died. The party chose Gorbachev to fill Kulakov's position—once more unusual

U.S. president Ronald Reagan meets with Soviet leader Mikhail Gorbachev during the Geneva Summit in Switzerland on November 19, 1985. (Ronald Reagan Library)

for a man so young. The following year, while still serving as agriculture secretary, he gained appointment to the Politburo, the party's inner circle, as a nonvoting member. In this position, he applied his law background and, as requested by the party leadership, proposed new rules for the Supreme Court and the Prosecutor's Office. In 1978, he backed the Soviet invasion of Afghanistan in support of the communist regime fighting a rebellion.

Yuri Andropov, who had often served as Gorbachev's mentor, became the new general secretary of the Communist Party after the death of Leonid Brezhnev in 1982. Gorbachev's power subsequently increased, and he ranked as one of only three men who held both a Politburo position and a position as a national party secretary. Gorbachev helped Andropov carry out a purge of corrupt officials—considered necessary as the economy worsened and the party stagnated—and the general secretary revived Gorbachev's plan to increase agricultural production through incentives.

As Andropov's health worsened throughout 1983, Gorbachev assumed more duties, making important speeches and leading a delegation to Canada. Many observers believed that Gorbachev would succeed Andropov, but when the leader died the party chose Konstantin Chernenko. Gorbachev supported Chernenko while taking charge of ideology and economics. In 1984, he added to his duties when he became chairman of the Foreign Affairs Committee of the Supreme Soviet (the national legislature), a development that displayed his diverse expertise and confirmed his importance beyond agricultural matters.

When Chernenko died in 1985, it was not clear that Gorbachev would become the new general secretary. Several in the party's old guard opposed him, but in the end the Politburo elevated him. Gorbachev set about changing the personnel and structure of the Soviet system, making appointments to the Politburo and bringing fresh blood into prominent positions. Perhaps nothing so symbolized the need for reform as the catastrophic meltdown at the Chernobyl nuclear power plant in 1986—a disaster stemming from shoddy procedures and one whose initial cover-up resulted in additional casualties.

As Gorbachev faced enormous internal challenges, he pursued an easing of tensions with the United States. He met several times with U.S. president Ronald Reagan and negotiated arms control measures. In all, Soviet-American relations improved considerably.

Within the Soviet Union, Gorbachev announced his policies of glasnost (openness) and perestroika (restructuring). With glasnost, Gorbachev allowed intellectual and political debate. Books previously banned in the Soviet Union were now allowed, including critical works by prominent Russian dissidents. Newspapers displayed editorials questioning government policies and people gathered at meetings where they freely debated issues.

With perestroika, Gorbachev pursued extensive political and economic change. In 1989, he initiated competitive elections for a new Congress of People's Deputies, which had the responsibility of electing the more powerful Supreme Soviet. Furthermore, whereas in the past the Supreme Soviet seldom met—the Politburo within the Communist Party approved all major decisions—it now was to convene regularly. The same year, Gorbachev added to his duties that of chairman of the Supreme Soviet, meaning he served as the legislature's speaker. More important, in 1990, the Supreme Soviet created the office of national president as a powerful position and made it elective—a crucial development in weakening the Politburo. Initially, Gorbachev was elected to the presidency by the Congress of People's Deputies, but subsequent elections were to be by popular vote.

Gorbachev also promoted an increased role for leaders from the republics that made up the Soviet Union. They represented different ethnic groups, and Gorbachev intended to calm their secessionist desires. In the economy, Gorbachev lessened the state's role and developed plans to introduce free-market practices. He moved cautiously, however, ever fearful that reforms such as the end to price controls and guaranteed jobs would lead to inflation and unemployment, and consequently social unrest.

Overall, glasnost encouraged criticism. Certainly it failed to calm separatist desires in the outlying republics. Rather, it allowed an intensification of ethnic pride and nationalism. Perestroika produced economic dislocation and angered both conservatives, who detected an assault against communism, and liberals, who believed the economy needed quicker, more extensive change—a "shock treatment." Gorbachev seemed unable to advance beyond his communist outlook, his belief that the system in which he advanced his career should not be totally dismantled. Furthermore, by 1990, his effort to subordinate the military to other interests produced rumblings of discontent from powerful generals.

Amid these developments, the Soviet domination of Eastern Europe collapsed. Forces similar to those in the Soviet Union had been at work there, and such nations as Poland, Hungary, and Czechoslovakia ended their Communist regimes and claimed their independence. As promoter of glasnost and beset with internal difficulties, Gorbachev, for the most part, let these nations go their own way, even agreeing to the reunification of Germany. He took a firmer stand toward the Baltic republics, where many ethnic Russians lived, but these nations also gained their independence.

At home, Gorbachev faced an uprising in the Russian Republic, the largest of the Soviet republics, when its leader, Boris Yeltsin, demanded more radical reform. Then on August 18, 1991, conservative communists tried to overthrow Gorbachev. They isolated him while he was away from Moscow and cut his communications. Yeltsin, however, rallied the Russian people, promoting a general strike and huge demonstrations. His supporters surrounded and fortified the Parliament building to protect it. On August 21, the Soviet coup attempt collapsed and Gorbachev resumed his presidency. Within days, he resigned as general secretary, and the government suspended all Communist Party activities. Meanwhile, several republics declared their independence, including Russia, Ukraine, and Kazakhstan, and others prepared to do the same.

Yeltsin, not Gorbachev, emerged the hero. His courageous stand and call for democracy and a market economy won him an enormous following. At the same time, the coup attempt was the death blow to the Soviet Union, which formally dissolved in December 1991. Gorbachev and Yeltsin cooperated in forming the Commonwealth of Independent States, a loose confederation consisting of Russia and 10 other former Soviet republics. With the Soviet Union defunct and Yeltsin as Russia's leader, Gorbachev retired from the political scene. His reputation in shambles among the Russian people, he stayed out of the public eye for the next several years but reemerged to participate in the June 1996 presidential elections. He won only one-half of 1 percent of the national vote.

In 2001, Gorbachev cofounded the Russian United Social Democratic Party in an attempt to steer a course between capitalist and communist economic extremes. He led the party until May 22, 2004, when he resigned citing dissatisfaction with the party's direction under coleader Konstantin Titov.

NEIL HAMILTON

GOVERNORS ISLAND MEETING (1988)

The Governors Island Meeting was the final meeting between Soviet general secretary Mikhail Gorbachev and U.S. president Ronald Reagan (December 7, 1988). By 1988, Soviet-U.S. relations had improved dramatically from a deep chill in relations in 1983 (Reagan's "evil empire" speech, the KAL 007 incident, and placement of Pershing II missiles in Western Europe) as evidenced by the Soviet withdrawal from Afghanistan, the Intermediate-Range Nuclear Forces (INF) Treaty, and Reagan's visit to Moscow (May 1988). Ignoring political opposition and economic difficulties at home as he continued his push for perestroika and glasnost, Gorbachev came to New York in early December to announce perhaps his most dramatic international initiative at the United Nations General Assembly. In his address, Gorbachev declared it impossible to maintain "closed" societies in the face of globalization, emphasizing his support for human rights, the need to free international relations from ideological constraints and to decrease the threat of the use of force, and freedom of choice for all nations. He then announced a unilateral ten percent reduction of total Soviet armed forces, nearly half a million men, including

10,000 tanks, 8,500 artillery systems, and 800 combat aircraft, mostly stationed in Eastern Europe. In so doing, Gorbachev sought to give credibility to the idea that the Soviet Union had undertaken a fundamental change in the way it looked and dealt with the world.

Following his UN speech, Gorbachev traveled to Governors Island in New York Harbor to say farewell to Reagan and to prepare a working relationship with president-elect George Bush. Gorbachev and Reagan greeted each other warmly but Bush would only meet with the Soviet leader as vice president, not as president-elect. Gorbachev hoped to gain a commitment from Bush to build on his relationship with Reagan, but Bush remained aloof throughout the meeting. When Reagan announced his full support for Gorbachev's troop reduction initiative, Bush merely stated, "I support what the president said." Gorbachev, hoping to draw Bush out of his shell, replied, "That's one of the best answers of the year." During the luncheon, Gorbachev directed most of his remarks toward Bush, trying to assure the vice president that he could trust the Soviet leader, that he would not try to undermine or take advantage of Bush, and that his policies represented "real politics" that were necessary because Gorbachev had started a revolution in the Soviet Union. Bush only asked Gorbachev what his reforms might produce in the Soviet Union over the next five years, to which Gorbachev replied, "Even Jesus Christ couldn't answer that one." Some discussion occurred regarding chemical weapons but U.S. officials, fearful of any surprises, refused to engage in any serious negotiations. In a gracious climax to their relationship, Reagan presented Gorbachev with a picture of their first walk at Geneva, stating that the two leaders had come a long way together to clear a path for peace. He then offered a toast to the Soviet leader celebrating what they had accomplished and expressing his hope that such progress would continue once Bush assumed the presidency. Gorbachev, raising his glass toward Bush, declared, "This is our first agreement." As the luncheon ended, Bush told Gorbachev that he looked forward to working with him "at the appropriate time." The three men then posed for pictures with the Statue of Liberty as a backdrop.

Reagan viewed the meeting as a tremendous success, writing in his diary that he believed Gorbachev viewed the United States as "a partner seeking to make a better world." Gorbachev had to rush home, canceling trips to Havana and London, to deal with an earthquake in Armenia that killed 25,000 and left another half-million people homeless. This crisis became a symbol of the domestic problems that preoccupied Gorbachev until his removal from power in December 1991. Such difficulties made it impossible for Gorbachev to undertake any new international initiatives and influenced his decision not to interfere when Moscow's Eastern European allies broke loose from their allegiance to the Soviet Union in 1989. After assuming the presidency, Bush abandoned his initial caution in dealing with Gorbachev, making agreements that increased Soviet-U.S. trade, reduced chemical weapons, reduced conventional forces in Europe, and achieved further cuts in Soviet and U.S. nuclear arsenals with the START-1 Accord (1991).

DEAN FAFOUTIS

VLADIMIR PUTIN (1952–)

The hand-picked successor of Russia's then-president Boris Yeltsin, Vladimir Putin was transformed within a few short months from a political unknown to a prime minister, a

Vladimir Putin, president of Russia, speaks at the Kremlin in Moscow. Putin, a former KGB agent, dominated Russian life during the early years of the 21st century. He brought a degree of stability and prosperity to Russia; however, he opposed democratic reform and reestablished authoritarian rule. (Presidential Press and Information Office)

top presidential candidate, and then president of Russia. In contrast to the unpopularity of his ailing predecessor, Putin appealed to a Russian public that had grown increasingly tired of years of clumsy leadership and widespread corruption. He took over the presidency following Yeltsin's December 31, 1999, resignation and was elected to the permanent post in March 26, 2000, national elections. After serving two terms, Putin stepped down to make way for his successor, Dmitry Medvedev, who appointed Putin to the post of prime minister immediately upon taking office in May 2008. In 2011, Putin announced that he would once again run for president. In March 2012, Putin won the election. However, he did so against a backdrop of large urban protests against him and the almost universal corruption and stifling of civil liberties that he seemed to embody.

Putin was born on October 7, 1952, in the city of Leningrad, which is now known as St. Petersburg. He graduated with a law degree from Leningrad State University in 1975 and then joined the foreign intelligence directorate of the KGB, the Russian security police, with which he served until 1990. Little information has been made public regarding the details of Putin's KGB career other than that he spent some time during the Cold War in East Germany monitoring the political climate there. However, speculation about his intelligence career has flourished as his name has become internationally known, with claims that he was involved in economic espionage in Western Europe competing for legitimacy with rumors that he was a low-level domestic spy. Although international sources have raised concerns over his background as an officer of one of history's most brutal police organizations, Putin's KGB career has done little to detract from his popularity among Russians since his rise to power.

Returning to St. Petersburg after retiring from the KGB with the rank of colonel in 1990, Putin began his political career in the early 1990s under the wing of Anatoly Sobchak, then the mayor of St. Petersburg. As Sobchak was known as a liberal democrat, Putin's role in his administration provides some of the few clues to his political orientation, which at the time of his later appointment to the federal government was not evident. Putin himself became deputy mayor of St. Petersburg in 1994 and proved himself a capable administrator. With just two years of politics under his belt, he was brought to the Kremlin in 1996 to serve on Yeltsin's presidential staff. From there, he was appointed by Yeltsin to head the KGB's main successor organization, the Federal Security Service (FSB), in 1998; to manage the network of all intelligence agencies and ministries in March 1999; and to head the government as prime minister in August 1999.

As Yeltsin's fifth prime minister in less than two years, Putin quickly accomplished the improbable task of gaining the confidence of a wary Russian public. He was swift and stern in his response to an Islamic insurgency in Dagestan that was threatening to erupt into war in Chechnya by the time of his confirmation as premier. He earned a reputation among Russians as a pragmatist for his tough-minded conduct of a government invasion of Dagestan in the wake of a string of terrorist bombings that struck the heart of Moscow. Although Yeltsin's early resignation from the Russian presidency on New Year's Eve 1999 came as a shock to many, his appointment of Putin as acting president was a surprise to few. Yeltsin had publicly endorsed Putin as his preferred successor since naming him premier in August. Drawing speculation that a deal had been struck between the two, Putin, in his first official move as acting head of state, signed a decree granting Yeltsin, among other perks, full immunity from criminal prosecution as well as a lifetime pension.

Although Putin did not win the March 2000 presidential elections by as large of a margin as analysts had predicted, he easily defeated his closest challenger, Communist Party leader Gennady Zyuganov, by some 20 percentage points. The vote evidenced what experts and pollsters described as a profound shift in Russian public opinion, which for the first time in a decade rallied around one candidate—a newcomer to politics—who constructed a significant support base from formerly split constituencies and disparate parties. Putin was inaugurated in May 2000 in the first democratic transfer of power in Russia's 1,100-year history.

Putin was reelected in March 2004 with more than 70 percent of the vote. The result was never truly in doubt, as few sought to oppose him and those that did were unable to pierce the media blockade imposed on his critics. In consequence, both European and U.S. election observers criticized both the media coverage and polling irregularities. In response, Putin said, "In many so-called developed democracies there are also many problems with their own democratic and voting procedures," a veiled reference to U.S. president George W. Bush's questionable victory over Al Gore in the election of 2000.

Stepping down from office in accordance with constitutional limits at the end of his second term, Putin remained enormously popular at home, despite rankling many in the international community by using Russia's gas resources as a political leveraging tool and vehemently opposing a proposed missile-defense system in Eastern Europe. Moreover, Russia's bitter political feuds with such former Soviet states as Georgia and Latvia irritated some Russians. Putin's own domestic popularity, however, virtually ensured the victory of his chosen successor, former Gazprom chair Dmitry Medvedev. Upon taking office on May 7, 2008, Medvedev immediately nominated his predecessor to the post of prime minister, and Putin was confirmed by the legislature the following day. Prior to Medvedev's election, Putin, who had previously espoused no party affiliation, joined the United Russia Party to secure a seat in the legislature allowing him to be nominated for prime minister. Putin now also serves as chair of the United Russia Party.

In late 2011, Putin's planned return to the presidency hit a snag when discontented Russian voters took to the streets to protest rigged elections held under Putin's and Medvedev's auspices. Discontent with rampant corruption also fueled the protests. Putin initially reacted by ridiculing the demonstrators and strongly suggesting that they were pawns of foreign forces determined to cause trouble for Russia. In a few days, however, he changed his tune, noting that reforms might be necessary but insisting that they must come from above rather than below. Despite the protests, Putin was easily elected to the presidency in March 2012. Nevertheless, it is apparent that his popularity has waned and it remains to be seen if he can govern effectively.

ABC-CLIO

SOVIET COUP OF 1991

On August 18, 1991, Mikhail Gorbachev, the leader of the Soviet Union, was placed under house arrest when eight high-ranking government officials tried to take control of the Kremlin to allow the Soviet Communist Party to implement necessary procedures to block any changes to the government.

During the 1980s, the Soviet Union began struggling economically, which prompted younger members of the Communist Party to explore the possibilities of reform. On March 11, 1985, Gorbachev became general secretary of the Communist Party and ruler of the Soviet Union. Realizing the need for change, he initiated a policy of political openness known as glasnost and economic restructuring known as perestroika. Within the Soviet Union, those changes resulted in free elections in 1989, and reformist politicians won many of the seats in the Soviet Congress. Eastern European nations took advantage of those developments, and by 1990 many of them had asserted their independence from their Moscow-based communist overlords.

Even as the tide of reform grew within the country, change remained slow and reformers grew restless. The leaders of the various Soviet republics fought for a greater share of power, which forced Gorbachev to draft a treaty of alliance that would alter the power structure within the central government. Gorbachev was warned of a possible coup attempt by hard-line Communist officials who opposed the measure because they

Boris Yeltsin, president of the Russian Federation, makes a speech from atop a tank in front of the Russian parliament building in Moscow on August 19, 1991. Yeltsin called on the Russian people to resist the communist hard-liners in the Soviet coup. (AP/Wide World Photos)

feared the loss of their jobs and political power. However, he proceeded with his plans to vacation in the Crimea before meeting with the leaders of the republics, including Boris Yeltsin, the president of Russia.

On Sunday, August 18, 1991, Yuri Plekhanov, a high-level KGB official, knocked on the door of Gorbachev's home. When an aide informed him who was there, Gorbachev attempted to call Moscow, but the lines were dead. Plekhanov and one of Gorbachev's top aides, Valery Boldin, informed Gorbachev that the State Committee of Emergency had instructed them to demand that he sign a declaration of emergency that would allow the Communist Party to implement necessary procedures to block any changes to the government. When Gorbachev refused, he was placed under house arrest and the rest of the world was told that he had serious health problems.

The eight conspirators—who included Gennady Yanayev, vice president; Vladimir Kryuchkov, head of the KGB; Dimitri Yazov, defense minister; Valentin Pavlov, prime minister; Oleg Baklanov, Soviet Defense Council member; Vasily Starodubtsev, member of the Soviet Parliament; Alexander Tizyakov, president of state enterprises, industrial construction, transport, and communications; and Boris Pugo, interior minister—then ordered thousands of troops into Moscow. However, they failed to arrest Yeltsin, who proceeded to lead a resistance movement from the Russian White House.

When tanks entered the city, Yeltsin mobilized the citizens, climbed atop a tank in front of 20,000 protesters, and declared the coup unconstitutional. He then ordered a general strike and proclaimed himself the "Guardian of Democracy." When the troops threw their support behind Yeltsin, the members of the so-called Gang of Eight realized that their efforts had failed. They tried to arrange a meeting with Gorbachev, but he refused to talk with them.

The attempted coup lasted three days. By the end of August, Yeltsin issued a decree that suspended the activities of the Communist Party, and the government seized all party records. Within the next few months, negotiations continued over the transfer of power from the Soviet Union to the republics. On December 21, 1991, the collapse of the Soviet Union was complete. Four days later, on Christmas Day 1991, Gorbachev, the last leader of the Soviet Union, resigned from office, and the former Soviet Union formed a new 11-member Commonwealth of Independent States.

ABC-CLIO

BORIS YELTSIN (1931-2007)

Boris Yeltsin was the first democratically elected president of Russia, and although his power and position were challenged various times after he took office in 1991, he maintained the presidency until his resignation on the last day of 1999. During his eight years in office, Yeltsin tried to steer Russia toward capitalism with great determination, despite a faltering economy and his own health problems.

Boris Nikolayevich Yeltsin was born on February 1, 1931, in Sverdlovsk province. Shortly thereafter, he and his family relocated to the Perm region. He grew up in dire circumstances but excelled in school and became a strong athlete, especially in volleyball. He trained as an engineer at the Ural State Polytechnic Institute in Sverdlovsk and worked in construction from 1955 to 1968.

Yeltsin joined the Communist Party of the Soviet Union in 1961 and became first secretary of the Sverdlovsk District Central Committee in 1976. While in Sverdlovsk, he became acquainted with Mikhail Gorbachev, then first secretary in the city of Stavropol. After Gorbachev came to power as Soviet president, he appointed Yeltsin secretary of the Construction Department of the Communist Party of the Soviet Union's Central Committee in 1985. In December of that year, Yeltsin became the first secretary of the Moscow City Communist Party Committee, a post equivalent to that of a mayor in Western cities. He moved to institute several reforms, especially regarding the city's bureaucracy, which was mired in several unnecessary layers. Gorbachev elevated him (as a nonvoting member) to the Politburo in 1986.

Yeltsin was discredited while serving in the Politburo because he wanted more extensive political and economic reforms than even Gorbachev was implementing. He criticized the slow pace of reform at party meetings and even criticized Gorbachev himself. As a result, Yeltsin was forced to resign in disgrace from the party leadership in 1987 and from the Politburo in 1988. He was demoted to a deputy minister for construction.

Russian president Boris Yeltsin laughs during a speech at the Franklin D. Roosevelt Library in Hyde Park, New York, in 1995. Then-president Bill Clinton stands next to Yeltsin. (National Archives)

Yeltsin's dismissal corresponded with several changes in the Soviet government, specifically Gorbachev's creation of the Congress of People's Deputies, a national parliamentary group with a coinciding congress in each republic. Elections to each congress were held in 1989, the first time Soviet voters were presented with a choice of candidates; some were even noncommunists. It was within that atmosphere of change that Yeltsin staged a remarkable comeback. His popularity among Soviet voters as an advocate of democracy and economic reform was such that he won a seat to the national congress in March 1989 in a landslide election.

In July 1989, Yeltsin founded an independent "interregional group" that vowed to speed up perestroika (restructuring reforms) and fight the hard-line communist elements within the legislature. He was elected president of the Supreme Soviet of the Russian Federation on May 30, 1990, against Gorbachev's wishes, and began taking steps to reduce the power of the Soviet government and increase the power of the Russian government. He declared himself in favor of a market-oriented economy and a multiparty political system, and in July 1990 he quit the Communist Party.

In 1991, the changes begun with the creation of the congresses culminated when the post of president of the Russian Federation was created to head the executive branch of government and to be nominated by popular vote. Receiving 61 percent of the vote, Yeltsin won the presidency in May to become Russia's first democratically elected leader.

Yeltsin was a key figure in the collapse of the Soviet Union after the failed August 18, 1991 Soviet coup in which Communist Party hard-liners tried to reverse the trend of reform that Yeltsin and Gorbachev had been promoting. Yeltsin played an important role in mobilizing opposition to the coup; he even jumped on top of a Soviet tank outside the Russian legislature to call on the people of the Soviet Union to resist the hard-liners. He became increasingly powerful after the failed coup, and on December 7, 1991, he met with presidents Leonid Kravchuk of Ukraine and Stanislav Shushkevich of Belarus and declared that the Soviet Union no longer existed and had been replaced by a Commonwealth of Independent States. The coup had led to the collapse of most Soviet government organizations, abolished the Communist Party's leading role in government, and dissolved the party itself.

Yeltsin encountered numerous obstacles in his campaign to reform Russian society and the economy, notably from hard-liners, former communists, and nationalists. Despite crushing an October 1993 insurrection by Soviet-era parliamentarians, Yeltsin continued to face resistance from a legislature whose hard-line majority reflected a growing public anxiety over the disorganization, lawlessness, and financial insecurity that plagued Russia. Nevertheless, he was reelected to a second term in 1996, defeating nine challengers. Largely perceived as a weak ruler by a society historically cynical about politics in general and thoroughly accustomed to authoritarian leadership, Yeltsin remained unable to fill the void left by the demise of the Communist Party and the central authority it once enforced. His declining health caused considerable speculation about his ability to control Russia's volatile political and economic situation, and he announced in September 1997 that he would not seek another term in the elections of 2000. He then surprised Russia and the world on December 31, 1999, by announcing that he would step down from the presidency that day.

In his farewell speech, Yeltsin apologized for not achieving all of his goals for Russia: "I want to ask you for forgiveness, because many of our hopes have not come true, because what we thought would be easy turned out to be painfully difficult. I ask you to forgive me for not fulfilling some hopes of those people who believed that we would be able to jump from the gray, stagnating, totalitarian past into a bright, rich and civilized future in one go." He then designated Prime Minister Vladimir Putin as his chosen successor to serve as acting president until the March 2000 national elections. One of Putin's first moves was to sign a grant of immunity to Yeltsin for any wrongdoing or lack of success, an act that raised questions as to whether Yeltsin was forced from office. Just days after the resignation, *Newsweek* magazine reported that Yeltsin was linked to a Russian money-laundering operation under investigation by authorities in Switzerland. Nonetheless, world leaders praised Yeltsin for stabilizing democracy in Russia and setting the country on a path to a brighter future.

Following his resignation, Yeltsin largely kept out of Russian politics, although he famously voiced protest over Putin's 2004 electoral reforms which abolished regional gubernatorial and presidential elections and provided the president with the power to handpick politicians for those posts. After years of battling recurring medical problems, Yeltsin died in Moscow of heart failure on April 23, 2007.

ABC-CLIO

DOCUMENT: BORIS YELTSIN'S SPEECH FOLLOWING A HARD-LINE REVOLT (1993)

President of Russia throughout most of the 1990s, Boris Yeltsin came to power following a failed coup by hardline Communists against Soviet premier Mikhail Gorbachev in August 1991. Yeltsin led the popular movement against the Communists and was subsequently elected president of the new Russian state. Following is a speech he delivered to the Russian people on October 4, 1993, after he had suppressed yet another hardline Communist coup attempt against his government.

Dear compatriots:

I am turning to you at this difficult moment.

Shots are thundering in Russia's capital and blood has been spilled.

Fighters who have been brought from the whole country and have been incited by the White House leaders are sowing death and destruction.

I know that it was a sleepless night for many of you. I know that you have understood everything.

This troubled and tragic night has taught us a lot. We did not prepare for a war. We hoped that we could reach an agreement and preserve peace in the capital.

Those who moved against the peaceful city and unleashed the bloody massacre are criminals. But it was not just a crime committed by individual bandits and vandals. Everything that happened and is happening in Moscow—it was an armed revolt planned in advance. It was organized by communists seeking revenge, by fascist leaders and some of the former [parliament] deputies—representatives of the Soviets. . . .

Those waving red flags have once again covered Russia with blood.

They hoped to use surprise to sow fear and confusion with their impudence and unprecedented ruthlessness.

They hoped that the military would stay away calmly and watch defenseless Muscovites be persecuted and a bloody dictatorship be established in our country. . . .

For them and for those who gave them orders, there can be no forgiveness, because they lifted their hand against peaceful people, against Moscow, against Russia, against women, children, and old people.

The armed revolt is doomed. Troops are entering Moscow to restore order, peace, and quiet. . . .

I am asking you, dear Muscovites, to give your moral support to boost the spirits of the Russian soldiers and officers. They belong to our national army and police. They have one task today: To defend our children, to defend our mothers and fathers, to stop and neutralize the rioters and murderers. Moscow and Russia are awaiting your courage and decisive action.

The public organizations that took part in mass disorders and other unlawful actions are banned on the entire territory of Russia. . . .

I appeal to all political forces in Russia. For the sake of those whose lives have already ended, for the sake of those whose innocent blood has already been spilled, I appeal to you to forget your internal disputes that seemed important yesterday.

14

September 11 and the War on Terror, 2001–Present

INTRODUCTION

The infamous attack of September 11, 2001 (9/11) represents both a turning point in global history and the culmination of a stream of increasingly violent and deadly assaults against the United States, its interests, and its friends and allies dating back to at least the early 1990s. As is well known, the devastatingly destructive attacks of 9/11 were carried out by a terrorist organization called al-Qaeda ("the base" in English) under the leadership of Osama bin Laden, a religious fanatic from Saudi Arabia whose family was rich and powerful. What is more difficult to define is al-Qaeda's precise nature. Most experts believe al-Qaeda can be traced to the guerilla war in Afghanistan (as discussed subsequently) where it established itself in the late 1980s. Since then, al-Qaeda has gone by many names and appeared in many places, but especially throughout the Muslim world. In turn, this has led observers to conclude that al-Qaeda is not a monolithic body. Rather, it is seen as simply the most prominent and most deadly of many Islamic terrorist organizations that comprise a global movement. These organizations are loosely connected and maintain a degree of contact with each other, but there is no supreme leadership, discernible formal structure, or overt support from any state.

Nevertheless, all branches of the radical Islamic terrorist network hold to certain ideals and objectives. There is universal agreement on the need to expel non-Muslims—but especially a Western physical presence—from the lands of Islam. Moreover, there is a determination to eradicate Western cultural influences such as music, movies, and Coke, which are seen as debasing the purity of Islamic culture. Interestingly enough, Western technology such as computers, cell phones, and plastic explosives are not only accepted but even desired. Sometimes overlooked is the fact that the radicals want to destroy any number of governing regimes in the Islamic world in the conviction that they are not only propped up by Western interests but, even more important, also defile Islam by their actions and policies. This hatred is particularly strong for Saudi Arabia, the home of Islam's holiest sites, where the rulers are charged with protecting Islam above all else. In destroying these regimes, al-Qaeda and its friends hope to replace them with pious Islamic states resting on a pure, unadulterated version of Mohammed's word as interpreted by the devout leadership of the radical movement. A particular bête noir for the terrorists is the state of Israel, which they see as a cancer on their lands.

According to the radicals, Israel must be annihilated, and Western countries, but especially the United States, which is seen as Israel's patron and protector, must pay a large price for their support of the Jewish state. Finally, just as Christianity is divided among Roman Catholicism, Protestantism, and Orthodoxy, Islam is divided between Sunni and Shia. Al-Qaeda and its ilk are almost exclusively Sunni; however, Shia Islam also has its religious radicals including Hezbollah and the current Iranian leadership. There is no love lost between Sunni and Shia. Their respective zealots hold each other in utter contempt and have no problem unleashing their deadly fury on what they consider to be unworthy heretics.

There is little argument that the Islamic terrorists responsible for 9/11 are religious fanatics wedded to an almost medieval form of Sunni Islam. The modern origins of this ultra-conservative interpretation of Islam can be traced back to at least the eighteenth century and the appearance of the Wahhabi movement in the Arabian Peninsula. Based on the words and deeds of Muhammad ibn Abd-al-Wahhab, an Islamic scholar, Wahhabism seeks to cleanse Islam of accumulated deviations to restore the religion to its original purity. The Wahhabi version of Islam eventually gained the support of the Saud family who, in turn, came to rule modern Saudi Arabia where Wahhabism is now the norm. It is the alleged failure of Saudi Arabia's current and recent Saud rulers to maintain strict Wahhabi rules that infuriated Bin Laden.

In the middle of the twentieth century, the rise of the Muslim Brotherhood in Egypt bolstered reactionary Islam. The Brotherhood rejected modernity as contrary to Islam's principles and advocated a return to the simplicity of traditional Islam. While gaining popularity in Egypt, the Brotherhood also earned the enmity of the secular Egyptian government, which outlawed the Brotherhood and imprisoned and executed its leaders. Nevertheless, the Brotherhood and the ideas that it stood for gained adherents throughout the Islamic world but especially among the Arabs of the Middle East.

The catalyst that gave rise to a radical, reactionary Islam willing to engage in terrorism was the Soviet Union's 1979 invasion of Afghanistan, a very backward but very devout Muslim country. A state in little more than name only, by the late 1970s Afghanistan had come under the control of indigenous Marxists who were increasingly close to Moscow. For a variety of reasons, a growing number of Afghans expressed unhappiness with this leadership. Because of this, a fearful Soviet Union decided to send troops to Afghanistan to bolster its Marxist allies. This decision provoked a guerrilla insurgency.

Consequently, more and more devout Muslims gravitated to Afghanistan to aid the local Afghans in their quest to oust the infidels and their puppet government. Many of these holy warriors, or mujahideen, were Arabs even though none of the tribal entities comprising the Afghan state is ethnically Arab. The religiously conservative lands of Saudi Arabia supplied the bulk of the Arab mujahideen including Osama bin Laden. In a scenario reminiscent of the Vietnam War, the ragtag but immensely popular mujahideen fought the mighty Red Army to a standstill, inflicting a steadily growing number of casualties. Not only was the Soviet Union losing soldiers, it was also hemorrhaging money in what proved to be a futile attempt to defeat the insurgency. Mirroring the role that Soviet Russia played in the Vietnam War, the United States supplied money and armaments to the mujahideen including the forces led by Osama bin Laden.

However, the Islamic radicals fighting in Afghanistan despised the Americans as much as they did the Russians. When the mujahideen finally toppled the puppet Afghan

The two towers of the World Trade Center burn after being struck by airliners piloted by terrorists on September 11, 2001. (http://www.bigfoto.com)

government and forced the Soviets to withdraw, internal conflict ensued until the Taliban, perhaps the most religiously fanatical of all the mujahideen, gained power. The Taliban leadership esteemed Bin Laden, and after he spent some time in Sudan, he and al-Qaeda set up camp in Afghanistan under the protection of the Taliban government.

It should come as no surprise that the Arabian Peninsula not only bred Osama but also supplied 15 of the 19 suicidal Islamic fanatics that carried out the 9/11 attacks. (There were to be 20 hijackers; however, apparently one could not secure a U.S. visa.) From its establishment in 1932 with the immeasurable help of Great Britain's imperial-minded foreign office, the modern Saudi Arabian state has embraced Wahhabism. Saudi Arabia's rulers, drawn from the tribal house of Saud, early on realized that their interests demanded cooperation with Wahhabism rather than confrontation. To that end, Saudi Arabia enforced—and continues to enforce—the strict Islamic code that is Wahhabism's trademark. To maintain a more secure grip on power, Saudi Arabia's rulers rather cleverly helped to channel Islamic fundamentalist wrath in an outward direction while providing a safe haven for the Wahhabists as long as they did not challenge the house of Saud. However, even that was not enough to please the truest of the true believers such as Osama bin Laden.

Osama, the man behind 9/11, despised the Saudi rulers as impure and impious because of their alleged failure to protect the holy shrines of Islam, and he wanted those rulers gone. His unhappiness turned to outrage when the Saudis, in close cooperation with their U.S. backers, allowed U.S. troops to be stationed in Saudi Arabia. The fact that the United States had aided the mujahideen in Afghanistan cut no ice with Bin Laden.

What followed was a series of attacks increasingly directed against the United States, the country that not only provided indispensable support for the Saudi monarchy but also buttressed hated Israel and had the greatest presence and left the largest footprint in the Muslim world. Bin Laden's al-Qaeda opened its campaign with a bang—quite literally. In late February 1993, it exploded a large bomb in one of New York City's World Trade Center's garages, killing six people and wounding more than 1,000. While some question al-Qaeda's direct involvement in this attack, it is worth noting that the terrorist's chief operative, Ramzi Yousef, is a nephew of Khaled Sheikh Mohammed, an al-Qaeda chieftain and the mastermind behind 9/11, and that he had resided in an al-Qaeda safehouse both before and after the attack.

A few months later, U.S. forces in the lawless country of Somalia were attacked. In the "Black Hawk Down" episode, two U.S. helicopters were downed and eighteen U.S. soldiers subsequently killed by Somali militants allegedly trained by al-Qaeda. Shortly thereafter, the United States left Somalia. Bin Laden praised those who had killed the American servicemen and claimed victory for the Islamic movement over the infidels. In the meantime, al-Qaeda or its allies hatched plots to assassinate U.S. President Bill Clinton and Pope John Paul II. They also planned to blow up several airliners simultaneously as they flew across the Pacific Ocean and successfully destroyed a major Shiite shrine in Iran.

In June 1996, a truck-bomb detonated at Khobar Towers in Saudi Arabia killing 19 U.S. service personnel living there. More than 400 were wounded. Responsibility for the blast was attributed to al-Qaeda, although suspicion remains that Iran, a Shiite country that loathes the Sunni-dominated al-Qaeda but also regards the United States as its greatest enemy, was behind this attack. Bin Laden did not claim direct responsibility but declared his pleasure with the carnage.

After a period of relative quiet during which Bin Laden relocated his operation from Sudan to Afghanistan, al-Qaeda launched a spectacular attack in the summer of 1998. Earlier that year, Bin Laden had issued a fatwa, or a religious opinion offered up by one supposedly knowledgeable about Islamic law and tradition, calling on the devout to murder Americans whenever and wherever the opportunity presented itself. Then, in August, al-Qaeda suicide bombers attacked the U.S. embassies in the East African nations of Kenya and Tanzania. Detonating trucks laden with explosives, the bombers killed more than 220 including 12 Americans. However, most of the dead were Africans, and more than a few were Muslims. In retaliation, the Clinton administration ordered missile attacks on al-Qaeda bases in Sudan and Afghanistan.

After the embassy bombings, a period of relative quiet once again ensued. However, with the approach of the millennium (the beginning of the year 2000 according to the Christian calendar), terrorist activity picked up again. Jordanian authorities disrupted an al-Qaeda plot to launch a series of attacks in that country and the United States detained a potential suicide bomber who intended to blow up Los Angeles International Airport.

Undeterred, al-Qaeda struck again. In October 2000, it sent suicide bombers against the USS *Cole* at anchor in Yemen's port city of Aden. The *Cole*, a very expensive vessel equipped with the most highly sophisticated intelligence-gathering equipment in the

U.S. force, sustained major damage and came close to sinking. Seventeen U.S. sailors were killed in the attack and dozens more were wounded.

All of this was prelude to the September 11, 2001, attack on the U.S. homeland. At the direction of Bin Laden and his associates, over the course of several months a number of al-Qaeda "foot soldiers" made their way to the United States with the ultimate intention of wreaking as much death and destruction as possible on their perceived enemy.

Early on the morning of September 11, 19 young Middle Eastern men made their way to airports in Boston, Newark, and Washington, D.C., where they boarded four planes headed for California. Once the flights took off, these men seized control of the airplanes. In three of the four cases, there was no known resistance on the part of the passengers or crew because standard operating procedure for hijackings—as these appeared to be—called for the passengers and crew to remain calm, wait until the plane was finally landed at the hijackers' destination of choice, and continue to remain calm until the situation was finally resolved, at which time the grossly inconvenienced but safe passengers and crew would be allowed to disembark and return safely to their point of origin. Although the terrorists apparently acted in a violent manner, in three of the four airplanes, no one had a clue that they were suicidal. In the one exception, United Airlines Flight 93 from Newark to San Francisco, the passengers learned of their hijackers' intentions through mobile phone conversations with relatives and rose to challenge the terrorists rather than passively accept their fate. They failed as Flight 93 crashed in rural Pennsylvania; however, they did thwart the hijackers' intentions of crashing the airplane into a Washington, D.C. building. Many think that the intended target was the Pentagon, the U.S. military's headquarters located in suburban Washington, D.C.; others suspect that the target was the U.S. Congress building or the White House.

Meanwhile, the terrorists successfully crashed American Airlines Flight 77 into the Pentagon and, most spectacularly, crashed American Airlines Flight 11 and United Airlines Flight 175 into the North and South Towers, respectively, of New York City's World Trade Center. Thanks to an abundance of aviation fuel, the crashes ignited both towers. Despite the fact that the Twin Towers were well constructed, the burning infernos exposed design flaws in the buildings—something al-Qaeda could not possibly have known beforehand—and shortly after 10:00 a.m. the structures collapsed.

A precise death toll is quite impossible to determine, especially in light of the fact that people—but especially first responders—are still dying today as a consequence of injury and disease arising from the collapse of the Twin Towers. Nevertheless, there seems to be no question that approximately 3,000 blameless people lost their lives on that September morning. They included men, women, and children; whites, blacks, yellows, browns, and reds; young and old; rich and poor; and Christians, Jews, Buddhists, Hindus, and a fair number of innocent Muslims.

INTERPRETIVE ESSAY

CLIFFORD L. STATEN

In 1996, Khaled Sheikh Mohammed, the uncle of Ramzi Yousef who was responsible for the bombing of the World Trade Center in 1993, met with Osama bin Laden at his camp in the caves of Tora Bora, Afghanistan. Mohammed presented a number of proposals to Bin Laden about how to attack the United States. One idea was to train pilots to fly airplanes into buildings. During the fall of 1999, Bin Laden transformed this idea into a workable plan that was designed to strike terror into the American homeland. The terrorist attacks of September 11, 2001, or what is now simply called 9/11, shocked the U.S. public and the world. Yet the attacks should not have come as a surprise. For almost a decade before 9/11, Islamist terrorist groups had been waging a war against the United States. In 1993, a Yousef-led group exploded a truck full of explosives in the basement of the World Trade Center in an attempt to collapse the building. In the same year, Omar Abdel Rahman staged a failed attempt to blow up the Holland and Lincoln Tunnels. In 1995, authorities discovered a plot by Yousef to blow up American passenger planes over the Pacific, and a year later, a truck bomb destroyed the Khobar Towers apartment complex in Dhahran, Saudi Arabia. Nineteen U.S. soldiers died and hundreds were wounded.

In 1996, Bin Laden declared war against the United States, citing American occupation of Islam's holiest places—in particular Saudi Arabia—and U.S. aggression against Muslims. In 1998, he specifically stated that his goal was to kill Americans. That same year, al-Qaeda launched simultaneous truck-bomb attacks against U.S. embassies in Nairobi, Kenya and Dar es Salaam, Tanzania. More than 220 people were killed, and thousands were wounded. The next year, Ahmed Ressam was caught trying to smuggle explosives into the United States for an attack on Los Angeles International Airport, and in 2000, an al-Qaeda group almost sank the USS *Cole* near Aden, Yemen, with a motorboat laden with explosives. The stage was set for the airliner that flew into the North Tower of the World Trade Center at 8:46 a.m.; the airliner that flew into the South Tower of the World Trade Center at 9:03 a.m.; the third airliner that crashed into the Pentagon at 9:37 a.m.; and the airliner that crashed in southwestern Pennsylvania at 10:03 a.m. on that fateful day in September of 2001. One month later, Bin Laden stated that the world was divided into believers and infidels; almost simultaneously, President George W. Bush declared, "We are in a conflict between good and evil."

9/11 and the subsequent war on terror brought dramatic changes to the United States and the world. These events unleashed a wave of anger, discrimination, and hate crimes toward Muslim Americans, while the civil liberties of all Americans were restricted in the name of national security. A Director of National Intelligence (DNI) and the Department of Homeland Security were created. The purpose of this major government reorganization was to prevent another 9/11-like intelligence failure. President Bush saw the war on terror through the eyes of a missionary as he righteously stated that "Either you are with us or you are with the terrorists." By the end of 2001, the United States had ousted the Taliban government in Afghanistan, run al-Qaeda out of the caves of Tora Bora, and set its sights on Iraq. The president insisted that the war on terror was unlike any previous war, and he reinterpreted both national and international law to make use of interrogation techniques that in the past would have been considered torture and illegal.

The United States adopted a global war on terror based on a strategy of preemption. President Bush defined the new policy in his address to the graduating class of the United States Military Academy on June 1, 2002: "If we wait for threats to fully materialize, we will have waited too long." Based on "irrefutable" evidence of weapons of mass destruction, the United States invaded Iraq as part of its war on terror on March 19, 2003. Although there was a global consensus and support for U.S. efforts against al-Qaeda in Afghanistan, there was much less support for its preemptive invasion and subsequent occupation of Iraq. Traditional allies on the European continent, Muslim countries, and other nations opposed U.S. policies. Public opinion outside the United States condemned the so-called unilateral policies of the Bush administration and its use of torture. The prolonged occupation of Iraq coupled with the growing death toll of U.S. military personnel and a seemingly never-ending, violent sectarian war in Iraq turned U.S. public opinion against the president; it also led to a Democratic sweep of the congressional midterm elections in 2006 and the election of Barack Obama two years later with the promise of a new foreign policy.

One of the major consequences of 9/11 was the increase in prejudice, mistrust, and hate crimes against Muslim Americans and the religion of Islam. The Pew Research Center, the most trusted public opinion survey center in the United States, has run numerous public opinion surveys on attitudes toward Muslims before and since 9/11. These surveys consistently indicate a strong anti-Muslim bias among non-Muslim Americans, and most indicate that they do not understand Islam. More than one-third of Americans have an unfavorable view of Islam, question the loyalty of Muslim Americans, and believe that Islam encourages violence more than other religions. Negative views of Islam and Muslim Americans are highest among evangelical Protestants, the less educated, the elderly, and conservative Republicans. David Schanzer, director of the Triangle Center on Terrorism and Homeland Security, finds that hate crimes against Muslim Americans increased dramatically from 28 recorded incidents in 2000 to 481 recorded incidents in 2001 with current levels at about five times the 2000 level.

A national controversy erupted in 2010 in the wake of a decision allowing construction of a Muslim cultural center in New York City near "Ground Zero." Opposition to existing mosques and the construction of mosques or Islamic cultural centers also surfaced in Iowa, Wisconsin, Tennessee, and California. When a small church in Gainesville, Florida, threatened a "Burn a Koran Day" on the anniversary of 9/11 in 2010, national decision makers became involved. In February 2011, Muslim American children and their parents in Yorba Linda, California, who were attending a fundraiser for a woman's shelter, were subjected to screams, jeers, and taunts as they were called terrorists and wife beaters and were told to "go home" by demonstrators, local government officials, and two members of Congress. In March 2011, Congress started McCarthyesque hearings on what is perceived to be the radicalization of America's Muslim community. Ironically, the committee is chaired by Republican Representative Peter King, an avowed supporter of the Irish Republican army, an acknowledged terrorist organization.

This growing divide between non-Muslim and Muslim Americans has occurred despite evidence, lectures, statements, educational programs, and pleas to the contrary from prominent American political leaders, educators, journalists, and Christian, Jewish, and Muslim American leaders and organizations. President Bush was among the first who told Americans six days after 9/11 that "The faith of terror is not the true faith of Islam." This divide has also occurred despite the fact that there are relatively few instances of Muslim Americans having become radicalized. It has occurred despite the fact that most Americans admit that they have never met a Muslim and that the estimated Muslim population is only 2.35 million—less than 1 percent of the total U.S.

population. The divide continues despite the fact that the Pew Research Center's Global Attitudes Project finds that the vast majority of Muslims throughout the world reject the extremism of al-Qaeda.

In response to 9/11, President Bush and Congress created the Department of Homeland Security in November 2002. Agencies that focus on border and internal security and protection were put together under one department. The purpose was to centralize these security agencies to improve cooperation, coordination, and communication. A National Counterterrorism Center was established within Homeland Security. Critics of the governmental reorganization point out that the Federal Bureau of Investigation (FBI) and the Central Intelligence Agency (CIA) are not part of the Department of Homeland Security. They argue that this defeats the purpose of centralizing all the agencies that focus on homeland security. In 2004, the National Commission on Terrorist Attacks upon the United States, chaired by former New Jersey governor Thomas Kean and former Indiana Congressman Lee Hamilton, released its report and recommendations to President Bush. The report cited several missed opportunities to discover and possibly prevent 9/11. It found that intelligence was not shared among all the intelligence-gathering agencies. Bureaucratic rivalries prevented an overall assessment of what the intelligence community actually knew about al-Qaeda. From 1995 through 9/11, there were no national intelligence estimates on terrorism. Joint operations that included the FBI, CIA, the State Department, and the Department of Defense (DOD) did not take place. In response to the commission's report, President Bush and the Congress reorganized the intelligence agencies by creating a DNI or "intelligence czar." The DNI coordinates all the activities of the various intelligence agencies and advises the president, the National Security Council, and the Homeland Security Council. Critics point out that the DOD and its intelligence agencies do not report to the DNI and that this runs contrary to the goal of coordinating and centralizing the vast intelligence community.

According to John Lewis Gaddis, noted historian of the Cold War, President Bush's post-9/11 foreign policy was the most sweeping remake since the end of World War II. It began to take shape with the emergence of the United States from the Cold War as the only remaining superpower, or what Charles Krauthammer, conservative columnist and founding father of and articulate spokesman for neoconservatism, called the "unipolar moment." The idea was that the United States now had the opportunity and unparalleled power to reshape global values and norms unilaterally and to remake the global political system to its advantage. The policy began to develop following the first Gulf War because of the growing influence of other neoconservatives such as Paul Wolfowitz, Richard Perl, Douglas Feith, Donald Rumsfeld, William Kristol, Condoleezza Rice, and Dick Cheney associated with what came to be called the Project for a New American Century. As early as 1992, Wolfowitz made the case to use American military forces in a preemptive, unilateral manner to achieve a "new American Century." Throughout the 1990s, this group publicly stated that the United States should invade Iraq and topple Saddam Hussein. Almost all of these individuals became part of the Bush foreign policy team in 2001. The terrorist attack of 9/11 provided the raison d'être for the full development and implementation of what came to be identified as the Bush Doctrine. The President stated that:

The United States will not seek security through the more modest realist strategy of operating within a global system of power balancing, nor will it pursue a liberal strategy in which institutions, democracy, and integrated markets reduce the importance of power politics altogether. America will be so much more powerful than other major states that strategic rivalries and security competition among the great powers will disappear, leaving everyone—not just the United States—better off.

Princeton professor G. John Ickenberry described the policy in this manner:

America is to be less bound to its partners and to global rules and institutions while it steps forward to play a more unilateral and anticipatory role in attacking terrorist threats and confronting rogue states seeking weapons of mass destruction. The United States will use its unrivaled military power to manage [and remake] the global order. The new policy projected an unrivaled military might without apology, claiming to be pursuing a moral mission

Although some advisers wanted to move immediately on Iraq after 9/11, it was decided that the initial strategy should be to find and defeat al-Qaeda in Afghanistan. Buoyed by overwhelming domestic and international support, the Bush administration received an authorization from the Congress to use force against those responsible for attacking the United States. Bush demanded that the Taliban government turn over the al-Qaeda leadership to the United States or face destruction. U.S. and British forces working with anti-Taliban groups within Afghanistan began the attack against both the Taliban and al-Qaeda on October 7, 2001. Coalition forces took the capital city of Kabul by November. The following month, Afghan forces led the assault on the immense complex of caves at Tora Bora, the headquarters of al-Qaeda. Although more than 200 al-Qaeda fighters were killed, Bin Laden and several leaders escaped to Pakistan. In the same month, the Taliban gave up its final stronghold in Kandahar, and Hamid Karzai was sworn in as the leader of an interim power-sharing government. At the Virginia Military Institute in April 2002, Bush spoke of the successful rebuilding of Europe after World War II led by former Secretary of State and Virginia Military Institute graduate George C. Marshall. Bush committed the United States, North Atlantic Treaty Organization (NATO) forces, and civilian experts from the United Nations (UN) to a process of rebuilding the government and nation of Afghanistan in a Marshall Plan–like manner. A democratic Afghanistan became the new goal. Yet in the month before this speech, military and intelligence resources were diverted away from Afghanistan to Iraq, the next phase of the war on terror.

Although Hussein had few admirers in the Arab and Muslim worlds, most viewed secular Iraq as the only country capable of countering the greatest threat to the region—Iran. U.S. policy before the Bush administration focused on dual containment of both Iraq and Iran with each country serving as a check on the power of the other. In his State of the Union Address in January 2002, Bush focused on Iraq and emphasized that the United States would act preemptively against any country with weapons of mass destruction. In August 2002, the Bush administration began a public relations campaign which used intelligence estimates and questionable testimony of exiled Iraqis concerning weapons of mass destruction to build public support for a preemptive war on Iraq. The administration effectively tied Iraq to 9/11 and al-Qaeda. Although none of the 9/11 perpetrators were from Iraq and there was no credible evidence to link al-Qaeda and Iraq, the Bush administration argued time and time again that Iraq was a clear threat to the region and the United States because of the presence of weapons of mass destruction and its support for terrorism.

None of the intelligence used to frame the debate could be challenged by the vast majority of Congress, the public, and the media. Within the intelligence community, many disagreed with the administration. Their views were found in the intelligence reports but were never reported publicly. For example, many CIA analysts and scientists rejected the administration's statements in September 2002 that aluminum tubes imported by Iraq were irrefutable evidence of a nuclear weapons program. These objections were never made public. So-called evidence of mobile chemical weapons labs and weapons of mass destruction sites was deemed unreliable by CIA analysts, yet Secretary of State Colin Powell reported this as fact in January 2003. That same month, the National Intelligence Council prepared an analysis predicting that toppling Hussein would trigger broad support for Islamic fundamentalism among Iraqis and other Arabs and that there was a real possibility of a coordinated insurgency and guerrilla warfare aimed at Americans. This profoundly prophetic estimate was never shared with the public. No later than January 2003, and most likely at a much earlier date, Bush had fully committed to wage a preemptive war against Iraq.

The entire public relations campaign was cast within a package of fear that was very effective in the aftermath of 9/11. Orchestrated daily discussions occurred throughout the fall of 2002 on radio and television and in key newspapers through sympathetic writers, some of whom were paid by the administration. For example, Fox News hammered away at the existence of weapons of mass destruction in Iraq. The administration controlled the debate so extensively that a public discussion of dual containment as an alternative to preemption in Iraq never took place. In October, the Congress voted to authorize the administration to use any means appropriate to enforce UN Security Council resolutions on Iraq. In November, the UN Security Council passed Resolution 1441 which warned Iraq of serious consequences unless it submitted to unrestricted weapons inspections. That same month, UN weapons inspectors entered Iraq. There was no substantive public discussion of the success of the embargo against Iraq and the fact that UN weapons inspectors and the International Atomic Energy Agency found no evidence of weapons of mass destruction. On March 17, 2003, Bush ordered Hussein to leave Iraq or face military attack. The U.S. attack began on March 19 over the objection of many allies including France, Germany, Canada, and Mexico who argued that UN Security Council Resolution 1441 did not authorize such an action. Turkey refused to grant the United States permission to use its territory as a base of operations. Anti-U.S. demonstrations broke out throughout the Muslim world.

The war on terror brought about a dramatic erosion of individual liberties in the United States. Security at airports increased as passenger inspections became more invasive and complete. Greater restrictions were placed on the ability to carry items on airplanes. Security checks became more extensive at borders, national parks, monuments, and museums. Most Americans tolerated these changes in the name of security and the war on terror; nevertheless, the American public did not welcome many restrictions on individual liberties. Within weeks after 9/11, hundreds of U.S. citizens who fit the profile of the 19 attackers were held and detained administratively without charge. On October 26, 2001, President Bush signed the Patriot Act, which gave the government unprecedented power in the use of enhanced surveillance of e-mail, electronic address books, and computers. It allowed the FBI almost complete access to personal records such as library records, book-buying habits, medical, marriage counseling or psychiatric files, business records, internet habits, and credit reports. The person, organization, or business turning over these data was not allowed to inform the person they had done so under threat of prosecution. The FBI was now able to search a home or business without the permission or knowledge of the occupant. It allowed for nationwide search warrants and the indefinite detention of immigrants. Within weeks of 9/11, President Bush signed an order that allowed the National Security Agency to eavesdrop on U.S. citizens without a court order. This was a violation of the Federal Intelligence Surveillance Act (FISA). Four years later, the president unapologetically admitted that he had violated the FISA by approving warrantless surveillance and illegal monitoring.

In February 2002, President Bush declared American citizens Jose Padilla and Yaser Esam Hamdi, both Muslims and terrorist suspects, to be enemy combatants and therefore concluded they had no right to either a trial or habeas corpus—rights guaranteed under the U.S. Constitution. Both were sent to Guantanamo Bay with other enemy combatants from the war on terror. Two years later, their denial to the right of trial and habeas corpus was declared unconstitutional by the U.S. Supreme Court in *Hamdi v. Rumsfeld*. That same year, hundreds of other enemy combatants were given access to legal counsel through the Supreme Court decision *Rasul v. Bush*.

In January 2002, legal counselors to President Bush argued that detainees from the war on terror were not covered under the protections guaranteed to prisoners of war under the Geneva Conventions. The Geneva Conventions had been an established part of international law which the United States had accepted for more than 50 years. The Conventions had provided protection during conflicts in Korea, Vietnam, Panama, Bosnia, Haiti, and Somalia. The Third Geneva Convention states that "no physical or mental torture, nor any other form of coercion, may be inflicted on prisoners of war to secure from them information of any kind whatever." The Fourth Geneva Convention prohibits the torture of civilians. In February, President Bush, under advice from legal counsel, declared the detainees from the war on terror to be enemy combatants rather than prisoners of war or civilians. None were granted protections under the Geneva Conventions.

In August, White House legal advisers argued in a secret memo, the so-called Torture Memo, that there should be an extremely narrow interpretation of the definition of torture in the U.S. Anti-Torture Act. The Torture Memo narrowly defined torture as a situation in which the detainee experiences "intense pain or suffering of the kind that is equivalent to the pain that would be associated with serious physical injury so severe that death, organ failure or permanent damage resulting in the loss of significant body function will likely result." This opened the door for the use of interrogation techniques that had previously been defined as torture and were prohibited by the U.S. Anti-Torture Act, the U.S. Uniform Code of Military Justice, and the Geneva Conventions. These techniques included routine beatings of the detainee, forcing the detainee to stand for more than 40 hours, forcing the detainee to stand naked in a cell at a temperature of 50 degrees Fahrenheit or less while being doused with cold water for hours and hours, forcing the detainee to assume very painful stress positions for hours, causing the detainee to endure sleep deprivation, using ferocious dogs to induce fear into the detainee, forcing the detainee to remain nude, forcing detainees to perform sex acts, inducing sensory deprivation in the detainee through extended periods without sound or light, and waterboarding the detainees.

The Torture Memo was accepted without input from the Judge Advocate General (JAG) Corps or the State Department. In December 2002, when Secretary of Defense Donald Rumsfeld authorized these various techniques, the JAG Corps objected, arguing that they were inconsistent with military treatment of detainees. That same month, two detainees at Bagram detention facility in Afghanistan died while being interrogated by members of the 519th Military Intelligence Battalion. Military physicians ruled that the deaths were due to homicide caused by "blunt force injuries to lower extremities." One had been hit in the legs so many times that the tissue was "falling apart" and "basically had been pulpified." Were it not for the Torture Memo finally being leaked to the public, it would never have fallen under scrutiny by those outside the president's circle of closest advisers. As a result of enormous public outrage and criticism, it was eventually withdrawn and revised. The revisions supposedly ended the practice of waterboarding. Detainee Manadel el-Jamadi was turned over to the CIA at Abu Ghraib, a notorious detention center near Baghdad, in the early morning of November 4, 2003. Within a few hours, he was pronounced dead as a result of the position in which he was hung. According to one medical examiner, "Asphyxia is what he died from—as in crucifixion." Those that continued to interrogate detainees at Abu Ghraib, Bagram, and Kandahar detention centers in Afghanistan, Guantanamo Bay, and other secret or black sites continued to use these so-called enhanced interrogation techniques.

In April 2004, photographs were published that showed U.S. military guards at Abu Ghraib abusing the detainees through these enhanced interrogation techniques. Pictures of U.S. troops subjecting detainees to mock executions, sexual humiliation, and beatings were shown to a global audience. It was also at this time that stories documenting the terribly harsh conditions and the use of enhanced interrogation techniques on the detainees at Guantanamo were made public. Public and international opinion turned against the Bush administration. The U.S. Congress began investigating the use of the enhanced interrogation techniques. In December 2004, President Bush signed a law that prohibited "cruel, inhuman, or degrading treatment" of detainees. The president then stated that he had the right to determine how to apply it, and in February 2005 Attorney General Alberto Gonzales endorsed another secret memo that allowed the CIA to "barrage detainees with a combination of painful physical and psychological tactics including head slaps, simulated drowning, and frigid temperatures."

Rendition is the practice of illegally seizing and then taking an individual to another country. The United States had engaged in rendition for many years, but until 9/11 the seized individual was brought back to the United States to stand trial and given the rights afforded U.S. citizens. Until 9/11, the FBI reported the instances of rendition that were committed by the United States. In 1994, the United States signed the UN Convention against Torture, which banned the transfer of a prisoner to another country where there is the possibility that he would face torture. The first case of so-called extraordinary rendition occurred in 1995 under President Bill Clinton when a terrorist suspect was captured in Croatia by the United States and flown to Cairo for interrogation. He was later executed by Egyptian authorities. In 1996, the United States passed the War Crimes Act, which allows federal courts to prosecute those found guilty of war crimes such as torture, inhuman treatment, unlawful deportation or transfer, and violations of the Geneva Conventions. In late 2001, Ibn al-Sheikh al-Libi, a top al-Qaeda official, was captured and taken to a CIA secret interrogation site in Cairo. CIA extraordinary renditions to Guantanamo Bay, Abu Ghraib, Afghanistan, Pakistan, Morocco, Thailand, Uzbekistan, Syria, Jordan, Ethiopia, Macedonia, Gambia, and Poland became common during the war on terror. These activities did not require presidential approval, and by September 2007, it was estimated that about 150 suspected terrorists were rendered to countries with significant human rights problems. Enhanced interrogation techniques were the norm at these facilities.

The Iraqi regime collapsed quickly under the "shock and awe" of the U.S. invasion, and the president declared "mission accomplished" in May 2003. Despite this bravado, the war was really just beginning, and the Bush administration was not ready for it. Just as predicted by the CIA before the U.S. invasion, an insurgency against U.S. troops was growing with many Iraqi groups opposing the occupation. These included remnants of Hussein's paramilitary forces, the minority Sunni Muslims who had dominated Iraq under Hussein and feared the long-oppressed majority Shia Muslims, and radical Shia Muslims led by Moqtada al-Sadr who opposed a long U.S. occupation. The Shia and Sunnis also turned against each other. For the first time, al-Qaeda fighters from all over the Muslim world led by Abu Musab al-Zarqawi began to appear in Iraq in 2004. There was near global condemnation of the U.S. treatment of detainees, and the Bush administration was embarrassed that no weapons of mass destruction were found. Despite being reelected in 2004, Bush's policy in Iraq was in trouble. A full-scale civil war between Sunni and Shia Muslims had broken out with U.S. troops caught in the middle. With mounting American casualties and retired generals speaking out against the occupation, the 2006 U.S. midterm elections ended in a sweep for the Democrats. In January 2007, Bush reluctantly agreed to a new policy in Iraq, the so-called "surge." Bush sent 30,000 more U.S. troops to Iraq, and the United States promised Sunni groups that it would not allow the majority Shia to completely dominate the new government. The United States paid these Sunni groups to turn against the al-Qaeda fighters. Although the violence began to decline by the middle of 2007, the damage was done. A Democrat, Barack Obama, was elected president in 2008.

At the end of the Cold War, the military, economic, and technological superiority of the United States, or what some call its hard power, was unequaled. The United States was also at the center of a global communications network that accentuated American values, ideals, culture, music, and films. Its education system attracted people from all over the world. Journalist Mark Hertsgaard stated that the United States was admired as "an exciting, inspiring place that combines personal freedom and economic abundance with invigorating energy and inventiveness." Zbigniew Brzezinski, former U.S. national security advisor during the Carter administration, argued that the United States enjoyed "an appeal that is unrivaled, especially among the world's youth." Charles Kegley and Gregory Raymond, authors of *Global Future: A Brief Introduction to World Politics,* argued that this so-called soft power enabled the United States to "entice others to do what [it] wants through the attractiveness of its culture and ideals rather than by threatening coercion or inducing them with payments." Countries and people from across the world were attracted to the United States because of its democratic practices, values, norms, and its use of international institutions to promote orderly change.

The Bush Doctrine as implemented in Iraq and elsewhere undermined the very values that attracted so many people to the United States. This policy as applied in Iraq was a dramatic rejection of self-prescribed U. S. values and established practices concerning the interpretation of international law, the use of international institutions, consultation with allies, military intervention, the interpretation of U.S. laws, and the use of torture. It effectively undermined U.S. support from its allies and much of the Muslim world. Its arrogant attitude of attempting to remake the world undermined the post–Cold War dominance by the United States. The policy paved the way for the Democrats to win the Congress in 2006 and the election of Obama with the promise of a new foreign policy in 2008.

SELECTED BIBLIOGRAPHY

Brzezinski, Zbigniew. *The Grand Chessboard: American Primacy and Its Geostrategic Imperatives*. New York: Basic Books, 1997. Brzezinski is one of the foremost strategists when it comes to geography and foreign policy. Acknowledging U.S. dominance in the post–Cold War era, he offers suggestions as to how to maintain that dominance.

Burke, Jason. *Al-Qaeda: Casting a Shadow of Terror*. London: I. B. Taurus, 2003. This is one of the best books written on al-Qaeda from its ideological roots, to its birth, to 9/11, and afterwards.

Frontline/World PBS. "Extraordinary Rendition." November 4, 2007. http://www.pbs.org/front lineworld/stories/rendition701 (last accessed 3/2/2011). This well-documented investigative program provides a detailed look at the secret rendition program of the Bush administration's war on terror.

Hertsgaard, Mark. *The Eagle's Shadow: Why America Fascinates and Infuriates the World*. New York: Picador, 2003. Hertsgaard, a journalist, goes a long way in helping Americans to understand why many in the world admire and complain about the United States at the same time.

Ickenberry, G. John. "America's Imperial Ambitions." *Foreign Affairs* 81, no. 5 (September/October 2002): 44–60. The author presents a critique of the Bush Doctrine and how it is radically different from previous foreign policies of the United States. He argues that the Bush Doctrine is better understood as preventative war rather than preemptive war and warns of the dangers of such a policy.

Kegley, Charles W., and Gregory A. Raymond. *After Iraq: The Imperiled American Imperium*. New York: Oxford University Press, 2007. This is perhaps the best critique of the Bush foreign policy. The authors show how the Bush policy harmed the long-term interests of the United States by undermining the moral and legal restraints—which were built over the past century—on when and how states use force. Kegley and Raymond explain how U.S. hard and soft power is crucial in terms of maintaining world leadership and how the Bush policy effectively undermined the very soft power of the United States that is so crucial to its world leadership position.

Krauthammer, Charles. "The Unipolar Moment." *Foreign Affairs* 70, no. 1 (1990/1991): 23–33. This seminal article focuses on the new role of the United States in the post–Cold War era.

Kurzman, Charles. *The Missing Martyrs: Why There Are So Few Muslim Terrorists*. Oxford: Oxford University Press, 2011. This meticulously researched book documents and suggests that terrorist groups are thoroughly marginal in the Muslim world.

Kurzman, Charles. "Muslim-American Terrorism Since 9/11: An Accounting." Published by the Triangle Center on Terrorism and Homeland Security, Duke, UNC, RTI, February 2, 2011. http://sanford.duke.edu/centers/tcths/about/documents/Kurzman_Muslim-American _Terrorism_Since_911_An_Accounting.pdf (last accessed March 2, 2011). Kurzman provides evidence indicating that there are fewer Muslim American terrorists than is commonly perceived.

National Commission on Terrorist Attacks upon the United States chaired by Thomas Kean and Lee H. Hamilton. *The 9/11 Report*. New York: St. Martin's Press, 2004. This is the official government report on 9/11. It discusses what happened on 9/11, why it happened, the lessons learned from 9/11, and recommendations to the Bush administration.

Pew Forum on Religion and Public Life. "Public Remains Conflicted over Islam." Data for this interpretive essay were taken from August 24, 2010. http://pewforum.org/Muslim/Public -Remains-Conflicted-Over-Islam.aspx (last accessed 1/25/10). The Pew Research Center is one of the best polling and research centers in the country. Its forum on religion and public life presents ongoing public opinion on all aspects of religion and public life.

Pillar, Paul. "Intelligence, Policy, and the War in Iraq." *Foreign Affairs* 85, no. 2 (March/April 2006): 15–27. Paul Pillar was in charge of intelligence gathering in Iraq under the Bush administration. He states that the Bush administration selectively "cherry picked" intelligence that would support its prior decision to invade Iraq.

Project for a New American Century website. http://www.newamericancentury.org (last accessed 2/1/11). This is the Web site for the Project for a New American Century chaired by William Kristol. One is able to find the justification for preemptive war and the Bush Doctrine, as well as the neoconservative view of the role of the United States in the post–Cold War era.

Risen, James. *State of War*. New York: Free Press, 2006. This book provides evidence of the abuses of power by the Bush administration under the justification of national security.

Schanzer, David, Charles Kurzman, and Ebrahim Moosa. "Anti-Terror Lessons of Muslim-Americans." Published by the National Institute for Justice, January 6, 2010. http://sanford .duke.edu/centers/tcths/documents/Anti-TerrorLessonsfinal.pdf (last accessed 2/24/10). This study documents the relatively few cases of Muslim American radicalization.

Simon, Steven. "The Price of the Surge." *Foreign Affairs* 87, no. 3 (May/June 2008): 57–76. An excellent article that covers all the aspects of the so-called surge strategy and the possible backlash in terms of the success of the democratic process.

Western, Jon. *Selling Intervention and War*. Baltimore: Johns Hopkins University Press, 2005. The author gives several case studies that illustrate the competition among foreign policy elites in the executive branch and the Congress in gaining the support of public opinion for military intervention. The chapter on Iraq is a must read for those who want to understand how the Bush administration sold the military intervention in Iraq to the American public.

Woodward, Bob. *Plan of Attack*. New York: Simon & Schuster. 2004. This work by journalist Bob Woodward is the best inside look at how the decision to invade Iraq was made.

Wright, Lawrence. *The Looming Tower: Al-Qaeda and the Road to 9/11*. New York: Vintage Books, 2007. This is without a doubt the best book written that explains the events leading up to 9/11. Wright received the Pulitzer Prize and many other awards for this book.

AL-QAEDA

The terrorist organization al-Qaeda is determined to end all U.S. influence in Islamic nations. Al-Qaeda and its founder, Osama bin Laden, are believed to be responsible for many of the worst acts of terrorism of the late twentieth and early twenty-first centuries,

Al-Qaeda, an Islamist terrorist group that Osama bin Laden formed in the late 1980s, is generally held responsible for many of the worst terrorist attacks since the late 1990s. Beginning in 2001, captured al-Qaeda suspects were held in a detention center built at the U.S. base in Guantanamo Bay, Cuba. Here a detainee is being escorted into a cell at Guantanamo in 2003. (U.S. Department of Defense)

including the World Trade Center and Pentagon attacks in the United States which killed nearly 3,000 people.

Bin Laden founded al-Qaeda in his native Saudi Arabia in the late 1980s after he returned from Afghanistan where he fought in the resistance against the Soviet Union's intervention in that country. His initial aim was to use al-Qaeda to overthrow all pro-Western governments in Islamic nations. He was able to recruit many members of the Islamic Alliance of Afghan Mujahideen that fought side by side with him in Afghanistan.

Bin Laden's goal for al-Qaeda began to change during the Persian Gulf War when he became incensed at the presence of U.S. soldiers in Saudi Arabia. He decided to use al-Qaeda to eliminate all U.S. influence in Islamic nations around the world as well as to destroy Israel. In 1991, he was expelled from Saudi Arabia and quickly established al-Qaeda's headquarters in Khartoum, Sudan. Under pressure from Saudi Arabia and the United States, Sudan expelled bin Laden in 1996 and he relocated al-Qaeda's base of operations to Afghanistan.

Under the protection of the ruling Taliban, bin Laden used his extensive personal wealth to help set up several terrorist training camps in Afghanistan. Most estimates suggest that several thousand Islamic militants from such countries as Egypt, Pakistan, and Saudi Arabia trained at those camps and then disappeared into terrorist cells all over the world. Bin Laden issued a declaration of war against the United States in August 1996 and then issued a fatwa (religious decree) in 1998 that proclaimed it the duty of all Muslims to wage jihad (holy war) on the United States and its citizens as well as against all Jews.

Even before bin Laden issued his proclamations, U.S. military forces and citizens were the victims of several terrorist acts believed to be linked to al-Qaeda, including the killing of U.S. soldiers during the Battle of Mogadishu in Somalia in 1993 and the World Trade Center bombing that same year. Al-Qaeda continued to focus on U.S. targets throughout the 1990s, and it is suspected of being involved in the U.S. embassy bombings in Africa in 1998 and the bombing of the USS *Cole* in Yemen in 2000. However, its most notorious act of terrorism, the attack on the World Trade Center and the Pentagon on September 11, 2001, led to an all-out war on terrorism led by the United States with bin Laden and al-Qaeda as the primary targets.

Following the September 11 attacks, the United States used U.S. special forces and an extensive bombing campaign to overthrow the Taliban. It then sent in ground troops to hunt down all suspected terrorists. U.S. forces have killed or captured hundreds of al-Qaeda members in Afghanistan including several top lieutenants. Worldwide, more than 3,000 extremists with suspected ties to al-Qaeda have been arrested in about 90 countries. U.S. officials believe that military committee commander Muhammed Atef was killed during a November 2001 air strike in Afghanistan. In March 2002, Abu Zubaydah, who is reportedly al-Qaeda's top operational commander, was captured in Pakistan. In March 2003, Khalid Sheikh Mohammed, the alleged mastermind behind the September 11 attacks, was captured and has been held at an undisclosed location since that time.

However, U.S. officials admit that there are still potentially thousands of al-Qaeda members hiding in terrorist cells all over the globe. Bin Laden himself evaded capture until he was killed in a May 1, 2011, raid by U.S. forces at the compound in Pakistan where he was hiding. Still at large is one of bin Laden's most trusted advisers, Ayman al-Zawahiri, an upper-class Egyptian doctor who is al-Qaeda's theological leader and helps oversee the group's loosely organized network of terrorist cells that operate independently of each other. This autonomy makes it difficult for authorities to capture more than one cell at a time. Abu Musab al-Zarqawi, a Jordanian who fomented much of the anti-U.S. and anti-Shiite insurgency in Iraq after the start of the Iraq War in March 2003, was killed by a U.S. air strike in June 2006.

Al-Qaeda serves as an umbrella organization for a worldwide network of terrorist groups that have similar aims.

DANIEL E. SPECTOR AND JERRY D. MORELOCK

OSAMA BIN LADEN (1957–2011)

Osama bin Laden was perhaps the world's most notorious terrorist. He has been blamed for several terrorist attacks against the United States, including the bombing of U.S. embassies in Kenya and Tanzania and the World Trade Center and Pentagon attacks on September 11, 2001. Osama bin Mohammad bin Laden was born in 1957 in Riyadh, Saudi Arabia, the 17th son of the owner of Saudi Arabia's largest construction company. He had more than 50 siblings, but his position made him among the least regarded of

Saudi Arabian Osama bin Laden was undoubtedly the world's most notorious terrorist. He was widely held to be responsible for masterminding the September 11, 2001, terrorist attacks on the United States as well as many other acts of terrorism in the Middle East and elsewhere in the world. Bin Laden was killed in 2011 by U.S. Special Forces (Navy SEALs) who attacked his secured hiding place in Pakistan. (AP/ Wide World Photos)

the clan. Raised as a pious Muslim, bin Laden turned to religion after the death of his father in 1967.

In the 1970s, bin Laden studied management and economics at King Abdul Aziz University, and there he became interested in fundamentalist Islamic groups. He was deeply influenced by a teacher, Sheikh Abdallah Azzam, a Palestinian who had become disillusioned with the Palestine Liberation Organization and felt Islam needed to return to its roots.

In 1979, bin Laden joined many other young Muslims in fighting against the Soviet Union's Afghanistan invasion. The rebels of the Islamic Alliance of Afghan Mujahideen were supported by the U.S. government, then led by President Ronald Reagan. Although it is not entirely clear, bin Laden probably went to Afghanistan and then returned to Saudi Arabia to raise money for the mujahideen, or "freedom fighters." In Pakistan, across the border from Afghanistan, he used his expertise in construction to manage logistics for what was becoming a jihad, or holy war. By the mid-1980s, he was working inside Afghanistan, building roads and hideouts. He also established a base and training camp for the mujahideen.

When the Soviet Union pulled out of Afghanistan in 1989, bin Laden returned to Saudi Arabia a hero, full of religious zealotry, enriched by the family fortune, and well trained by U.S. forces. He was not a supporter of the United States, however. His zeal was reserved for Islam, and he bore some of the resentment common to soldiers returning from a bloody and punishing war. Seeing in Saudi Arabia a nation that catered to the United States and that was moving away from Islamic principles, bin Laden became an outspoken critic of the Saudi royal family. He also established a charitable organization to support veterans of the Afghan war, many of whom went on to fight in other wars in Chechnya, Somalia, and Bosnia.

In 1990, Iraqi troops under Saddam Hussein invaded Kuwait and threatened Saudi Arabia. The Saudi royal family accepted the help of U.S. troops to defend the nation. Bin Laden was infuriated and was vocal in his opposition and criticism of the royal family. In response, his citizenship was revoked. Bin Laden left Saudi Arabia in April 1991 and made his way to Sudan.

Working from Khartoum, bin Laden established terrorist training camps where he passed on the skills and techniques he had learned from American troops to religious zealots who would conduct a jihad against the United States. Although he refrained from publicly calling for attacks on the United States, the U.S. government identified him as a major financier of terrorist organizations. Cut off from his family in 1994, bin Laden nonetheless had a fortune estimated at $400 million.

In February 1993, two terrorists bombed the World Trade Center in New York City. The suspects were connected to the Maktab-al-Khidamat, a sort of recruiting office originally established to support the Afghan mujahideen and connected to bin Laden. Also in 1993, 18 American soldiers were killed in Mogadishu, Somalia. Bin Laden claimed responsibility. Two years later, a bomb in Riyadh, Saudi Arabia killed five U.S. soldiers. Nineteen more were killed when a bomb exploded at a military barracks in Dhahran.

In 1996, under pressure from the United States and Saudi Arabia, Sudan forced bin Laden to leave the country. He moved to Afghanistan where his quiet opposition to the United States became defiant and loud. On August 23, 1996, bin Laden issued a fatwa, a religious decree, calling for jihad against the United States.

Two years later, bin Laden convened a meeting of terrorist leaders and called for attacks on American interests anywhere in the world. The response was quick and severe. In August 1998, on the anniversary of U.S. involvement in the Persian Gulf War, two bombs exploded at American embassies in Tanzania and Kenya. Although no conclusive evidence was found to link bin Laden to either bombing, the U.S. government openly pointed the finger at him.

In 2001, the U.S. government accused bin Laden of orchestrating the September 11 attacks on the World Trade Center and the Pentagon, the most destructive acts of terrorism in history. Claiming finally to have evidence that implicated bin Laden, the United States, along with the support of the United Kingdom and many other countries, declared a war on terrorism and launched an attack on Afghanistan on October 7. U.S. officials claim that from his base there bin Laden led a loose confederacy of terrorist groups known as al-Qaeda, although some critics question whether he could manage the movements of terrorist cells a world away from an isolated outpost in an undeveloped, war-torn country.

The massive bombing campaign by the United States in Afghanistan decimated the Taliban and al-Qaeda forces, and enabled the anti-Taliban Northern Alliance to regain control of most of the country. The United States, believing that bin Laden was hiding in caves in the mountains near Kandahar, used special forces and marines on the ground to hunt him down. However, this operation failed and bin Laden eluded his American pursuers.

President Barack Obama and Vice President Joe Biden, along with members of the national security team, receive an update on the mission against Osama bin Laden in the Situation Room of the White House, May 1, 2011. (The Illustrated London News Picture Library)

After the 9-11 attacks on the United States, bin Laden became a portrait of evil to much of the Western world. In many Islamic countries, however, he was more of a folk hero, fighting against unbelievers who would trample on Islam.

Bin Laden's end came on May 1, 2011 (May 2 Pakistan Standard Time) when a group of Navy SEALs stormed his secret compound. Bin Laden was killed in the skirmish, and his body was buried at sea. There were no U.S. casualties.

ABC-CLIO

GEORGE W. BUSH (1946–)

George W. Bush was elected the 43rd president of the United States in November 2000 after a hard-fought campaign, but he was not certified the winner until the U.S. Supreme Court handed down its historic decision in *Bush v. Gore* (2000) in December. He was elected to a second term in 2004 and left office in January 2009. As the governor of Texas during 1995–2000, Bush earned a reputation as a conservative who shaped policy based on the principles of limited government, personal responsibility, strong families, and local control.

George Walker Bush was born on July 6, 1946, in New Haven, Connecticut. His parents are George Herbert Walker Bush and Barbara Bush (née Pierce). He grew up in

George W. Bush, president of the United States from 2001 to 2009, engineered the passage of the Patriot Act and launched wars on terrorism in Afghanistan and Iraq in the wake of the destruction of the World Trade Towers in New York City on September 11, 2001. (White House)

Midland and Houston, Texas. He graduated from Yale University with a bachelor's degree in history in 1968 and from Harvard University with a master's degree in business administration in 1975. During the 1970s, he was a F-102 pilot in the Texas Air National Guard.

In 1975, Bush began his career in the oil and gas business in Midland and was involved in energy exploration throughout the 1980s. He founded and managed Spectrum 7 Energy Corporation in 1975 and worked in the energy business until 1986, when he moved to Washington, D.C., to help in his father's presidential campaign. In 1978, Bush unsuccessfully ran for the U.S. House of Representatives in west Texas. In April 1989, he led a group of partners in purchasing the Texas Rangers baseball team and building their playing field, The Ballpark in Arlington.

On November 8, 1994, Bush was elected governor of Texas with 53.5 percent of the vote. During his first legislative session, he worked with Lieutenant Governor Bob Bullock, Texas House speaker Pete Laney, and members of the legislature to enact substantial reforms and pass a balanced $79.9 billion two-year state budget. Much of the revenue from the no-new-taxes budget went to Texas public schools. The major reforms included curbing lawsuit abuse, providing local control of schools, strengthening juvenile and criminal justice laws, reforming welfare, increasing the state's share of funding for schools, and giving parents more flexibility when choosing schools for their children. In November 1998, Bush was reelected governor of Texas.

Bush's wife, Laura Bush, is a former teacher and librarian who grew up in Midland. The couple has twin daughters, Barbara and Jenna. Laura's main concern as first lady of Texas was highlighting literacy and education, and she continued those efforts as first lady of the United States. She joined the National Governors Association's Governor's Spouse Program to promote breast cancer awareness and women's health issues, and she worked with agencies and volunteer groups to promote child health and safety.

In 1999, Bush announced his candidacy for president of the United States. While the media publicized his past drinking habits and critics noted his tendency to respond vaguely to questions about national policy, many others welcomed his ideology of "compassionate conservatism." In the 2000 primaries, Bush faced a challenge from Arizona senator John McCain, who appealed to many Republicans, moderate Democrats, and independents alike. After several defeats in the Super Tuesday elections, however, McCain suspended his campaign on March 9. In July, Bush selected former defense secretary Dick Cheney to be his running mate. Bush formally accepted his party's nomination in August at the Republican National Convention in Philadelphia, Pennsylvania, where he pledged to cut taxes and improve education.

Although many predicted that the outcome of the 2000 presidential election would be close, no one foresaw how equally the country was divided along Republican and Democratic lines. After a hard-fought campaign in which Bush and rival Vice President Al Gore struggled to highlight their differences, the night of the election, November 7, saw Gore pull ahead in the popular vote and Bush in the electoral vote, with the state of Florida's results too close to call. After the media called the election for Bush, Gore offered his concession, only to withdraw it later when realizing that in Florida, just over 1,000 votes separated the two candidates.

Weeks of legal wrangling followed in which activists leveled charges of ballot irregularities, outdated voting machines, and minority disenfranchisement. With various cases bouncing throughout the Florida court system on behalf of both candidates, it eventually fell to the U.S. Supreme Court to decide whether ballot recounts (which many assumed would give the presidency to Gore) would continue. In a much derided opinion, the Court ruled for Bush on December 12 and called off the recounts. Bush delivered a televised acceptance speech the following day, saying he would work to earn the respect of the nation. He was just the third man in history to have won the Electoral College vote but not the popular vote, only the second son of a former president to win the presidency himself, and the only man to win the presidency based on a decision of the Supreme Court.

Without a popular vote majority with which to enter the White House, it was unknown how Bush's presidency would fare. In the weeks leading up to his inauguration, he continued to stress his campaign themes of compassionate conservatism, changing the "tone" of Washington, D.C., and working with Republicans and Democrats alike in order to accomplish his goals for the nation. During Bush's first months in office, he was faced with a crisis in China when a U.S. surveillance plane crashed there, saw Democrats gain control of the Senate after a Vermont Republican senator, Jim Jeffords, declared himself an independent and managed to pass an enormous tax refund bill before being faced with a major national and international crisis: the World Trade Center and Pentagon attacks of September 11, 2001.

The terrorist attacks pushed the United States into war with Afghanistan, where Bush believed al-Qaeda mastermind Osama bin Laden was in hiding. Bush took a hard stand against terrorism and the nations that supported it. This pleased many Americans who felt his stance would curb terrorism but troubled others who feared an escalation of violence instead. In March 2003, a U.S.-led coalition force launched an attack on Iraq, toppling the regime of Saddam Hussein. More than a year later, with American casualties still mounting in the unfinished Iraq War and the Abu Ghraib prison scandal making headlines, Bush experienced low approval ratings—dipping below 50 percent—just months before the election of 2004. In a narrow race, Bush won the November 2, 2004, presidential election over Democrat John Kerry.

Declaring that he had won a mandate in the election, Bush moved forward with his war on terror and the Iraq War, which was increasingly unpopular. His second term was soon faced with a disaster when Hurricane Katrina devastated the Gulf Coast in August 2005. The administration came under fire for the federal government's response because the Federal Emergency Management Agency, under Bush appointee Michael Brown, was slow to respond to the crisis. In the 2006 midterm elections, Democrats won control of both the U.S. Senate and House of Representatives in what many saw as a rebuke of the Bush administration's policies, particularly the handling of the Iraq War. Following the election, Bush announced that Secretary of Defense Donald Rumsfeld, one of the key architects of the war, would resign. Soon after, in early 2007, it was revealed that U.S. veterans of the Iraq War and conflict in Afghanistan were living in substandard conditions and often receiving substandard care. With a change in leadership at the Department of Veterans Affairs, Bush declared that veterans would receive the best care available.

Although a troop surge in Iraq appeared to be having a positive effect, Bush's approval ratings declined throughout the final years of his presidency, reaching an all-time low in October 2008, when they hit 23 percent. His approval ratings improved slightly over the next several months, with a *Washington Post*/ABC news poll putting them at 33 percent as he left office. Although this was the lowest approval rating recorded for an outgoing president in the previous 70 years, Bush had also had the highest approval rating following the September 11, 2001, attacks. He was succeeded in office by Barack Obama. On May 1, 2011, President Obama announced that Osama bin Laden had been killed in Pakistan by U.S. Navy SEALs, nearly a decade after the September 11 attacks.

TRACI HEITSCHMIDT

IRAQ WAR (2003)

The Iraq War of 2003 pitted a coalition led by the United States and the United Kingdom against the government of Iraqi president Saddam Hussein and his Arab Baath Socialist Party. Hostilities commenced with U.S.-led attacks on March 20, 2003—without the approval of the United Nations (UN)—following months of U.S. and British assertions that Hussein was harboring weapons of mass destruction (WMDs).

The war had much longer-lasting effects in the Middle East and the international community than the Persian Gulf War of 1990–1991. Sparking a great deal of controversy,

In the wake of the 9/11 attacks, the United States rushed to war against Iraq on the basis of false intelligence. While in Iraq, U.S. forces suffered more than 4,000 casualties and billions of dollars were expended before the United States withdrew at the end of 2011. (Department of Defense)

the war triggered arguments among UN member states regarding the appropriate action to take and spurred millions of people around the world to march in protest of the military action. In addition, a great deal of suspicion arose regarding the U.S.-led coalition's motives behind the war, with pundits suggesting that the coalition desired more to control Iraq's great oil reserves than to liberate a people long oppressed by Hussein.

Following the Persian Gulf War, the UN imposed sanctions on Iraq calling for Hussein to destroy the country's arsenal of WMDs. Over the next decade, however, Hussein repeatedly evaded attempts by UN weapons inspectors to ensure that the sanctions were enforced. Upon assuming the U.S. presidency in January 2001, George W. Bush and his administration immediately began calling for renewed efforts toward ridding Iraq of WMDs—an endeavor that greatly intensified after the September 11, 2001, World Trade Center and Pentagon attacks.

In Bush's 2002 State of the Union message, he castigated Iraq for continuing to "flaunt its hostility toward America and to support terror" and called the Middle Eastern nation part of "an axis of evil, arming to threaten the peace of the world." In the months that followed, he increasingly spoke of taking military action in Iraq. Bush found an ally in British prime minister Tony Blair, but pressure from citizens of both countries pushed the two leaders to take the issue before the UN Security Council in the form of UN Resolution 1441 which called for UN weapons inspectors, led by Hans Blix, to return to Iraq and issue a report on their findings.

On November 8, 2002, the 15-member Security Council unanimously passed the resolution and weapons inspectors began work on November 27. On December 7, Iraq delivered a 12,000-page declaration of its weapons program, an insufficient accounting according to Blix, and a month later Bush stated: "If Saddam Hussein does not fully disarm, we will lead a coalition to disarm him." Bush and Blair actively sought the support of the international community, but their announcement that they would circumvent the UN if necessary ruffled many nations' feathers, most notably drawing the ire of France, Germany, and Russia, all of which pushed for further inspections. Spain joined with the United Kingdom and the United States to propose a second UN resolution declaring Iraq to be in "material breach" of Resolution 1441. Although a small number of other nations pledged their support for military action in Iraq, only Australia committed troops to fight alongside British and U.S. forces.

Blair in particular incurred negative reaction from his country's citizens, and reports indicated he might lose his job. As a result, Blair pushed for a compromise that would give weapons inspectors a little more time to inspect Iraq. However, Blair's proposal failed to gain support and was withdrawn. Undeterred by that set of events as well as the Turkish government's refusal to allow coalition troops to use Turkey as a platform for a northern invasion of Iraq and increasing protestations by antiwar groups around the world, on March 17 Bush issued an ultimatum to Hussein that he leave Iraq within 48 hours or face military action. Hours before the deadline was to expire, Bush received intelligence information that Hussein and several top officials in the Iraqi government were sleeping in an underground facility in Baghdad. Bush ordered a "decapitation strike" aimed at killing Hussein, and on March 20, around 2:30 a.m. local time, three dozen Tomahawk missiles with 1,000-pound warheads were launched from warships in the Persian Gulf and Red Sea. Three hours later, they hit their targets in Baghdad and were followed immediately by 2,000-pound bunker-busters. The war had started.

Although intelligence reports suggested that Hussein was carried from the facility on a stretcher, it became clear in the coming weeks that the decapitation strike had failed and Hussein was still alive. U.S.-led coalition troops crossed the border from Kuwait into Iraq on March 20. Armed with new technology that included stealth bombers and smart bombs—which constituted 80 percent of the coalition arsenal, as opposed to 10 percent during the Persian Gulf War—the coalition commenced its "shock and awe" campaign, designed to stun and demoralize the Iraqi army so it would quickly surrender.

Iraqi soldiers did not surrender with the same celerity as in the Persian Gulf War, but within a matter of days the coalition had overtaken Iraq's second-largest city of Basra, the port city of Umm Qasr, and Nasiriya. The coalition also destroyed Hussein's government buildings and palaces on the Tigris River in Baghdad, symbolizing the end of the Iraqi regime. Nearly 10,000 Iraqi troops surrendered to coalition forces during those first days. Still, the coalition troops were caught unprepared by some of the Iraqis' guerrilla tactics, including faking surrenders and ambushing troops from the rear. Throughout the fighting, news reporters and camera crews "embedded" in military units brought live action to television viewers worldwide.

After securing southern Iraq and its oil fields, coalition soldiers began moving toward Baghdad; they secured an airfield in western Iraq and Hussein International Airport (immediately renamed Baghdad International Airport) with little difficulty. On

April 5, coalition forces entered Baghdad, and six days later, the United States declared the end of Hussein's regime. One last hurdle remained, and by April 14, coalition forces accomplished it by capturing Hussein's hometown of Tikrit. Formal military action ceased, with fewer than 200 confirmed coalition deaths.

In the weeks after the Battle of Tikrit, coalition forces began searching for WMDs, Hussein, and other top Iraqi officials. Although there was a degree of success in the latter endeavor, the troops were unable to find WMDs or Hussein (though he was eventually captured by U.S. soldiers on December 13, 2003). Those failures drew criticism from many who already questioned the coalition presence in Iraq, as did the looting of historic treasures from Iraqi museums, which the coalition failed to protect. In addition, though many Iraqi citizens and neighboring countries were very happy to see Hussein's regime toppled, many others protested the continued presence of coalition forces and the influence they, particularly the United States, would have in the new Iraqi government.

Bush appointed L. Paul Bremer to govern Iraq through the Coalition Provisional Authority, whose stated aim was to reconstruct Iraq as a liberal, pluralist democratic state. However, the occupation was plagued by violent resistance which greatly hampered the economic and political reconstruction of the country, preventing international aid organizations from working in Iraq and discouraging badly needed capital investment. An interim constitution was signed in March 2004, and on June 28, 2004, sovereignty was transferred to the Iraqi people. On January 30, 2005, Iraq held its first open election in half a century, selecting a 275-member transitional National Assembly. Despite the withdrawal of several Sunni parties from the poll and threats of election day violence from insurgents, turnout was high. After two months of deadlock, on April 6 the new legislature elected Kurdish leader Jalal Talabani as president and Ibrahim al-Jaafari as prime minister. In April 2006, Talabani was reelected and Nouri al-Maliki was selected to succeed al-Jaafari as prime minister. Nevertheless, the country continues to be racked by sectarian violence as the disparate parties, warring factions, religious groups, and ethnic minorities remain bitterly divided.

Although Bush declared major combat operations over on May 1, 2003, deadly guerrilla attacks against U.S. troops continued and increased. In addition, major violence broke out between Shiite and Sunni insurgents, causing many observers to begin calling the conflict a civil war. By late 2008, the U.S. public's support for the Iraq War had plummeted. The U.S. and Iraqi governments signed a status of forces agreement that required U.S. combat troops to leave Iraqi urban areas by the end of June 2009 and to leave the country entirely by the end of 2011. Soon after taking office in early 2009, President Barack Obama announced that most U.S. troops would exit from Iraq by the end of August 2010, with a smaller transitional force remaining until the end of 2011. The last U.S. troops left Iraq on December 17, 2011.

ABC-CLIO

ABU MUSAB AL-ZARQAWI (1966–2006)

As the leader of al-Qaeda in Iraq and the mastermind of numerous violent attacks on civilians in Iraq and Jordan, Abu Musab al-Zarqawi was one of the world's most wanted terrorists until his death in June 2006 in a U.S. air strike in Iraq. Although some people questioned his very existence and others believed that his role may have been overstated to add legitimacy to the United States' presence in Iraq, the U.S. government had maintained a $25 million bounty on his head, and video and audio recordings released by Zarqawi had confirmed his influence and position in al-Qaeda.

Zarqawi, whose given name may have been Ahmad Fadeel al-Nazal al-Khalayleh, was born on October 20, 1966, in Zarqa, Jordan. ("Zarqawi" means "man from Zarqa.") Although little is known about his childhood, he was believed to have dropped out of school when he was 17 years old. After serving a short time in prison for petty crimes, he traveled to Afghanistan in 1989 to participate in the fight against the country's occupation by the Soviet Union. He remained there only briefly, as the decade-long Soviet presence was nearing its end by the time of his arrival, but it is suspected that during this time Zarqawi became acquainted with al-Qaeda founder Osama bin Laden.

Zarqawi returned to Jordan, where in 1992 he was imprisoned for plotting to replace the monarchy with an Islamic regime. After his release in 1999, he again traveled from his homeland, spending time in Europe in addition to the Middle East and South Asia. While traveling, Zarqawi reportedly raised funds and gathered members for a new organization—the Tawhid and Jihad group—aimed at establishing an Islamic caliphate in Jordan. Although some reports indicate that he may have received $200,000 from bin Laden in support of the group, captured members reportedly told German government officials that the organization was designed for militants who were looking for an alternative to al-Qaeda. It was at this time that Zarqawi was charged in absentia in Jordan for his role in a plot to use explosives at the Radisson Hotel, a popular hotel for U.S. and Israeli tourists in the Jordanian capital, Amman. The judge hearing the charges sentenced Zarqawi to death.

In Afghanistan, Zarqawi was believed to have established a militant training camp near the Iranian border and may have reconnected with bin Laden. Following the September 11, 2001, World Trade Center and Pentagon attacks on the United States and subsequent U.S. attacks on Afghanistan, Zarqawi may have fled to Iraq due to a missile strike on the camp. Once in Iraq, he joined with a militant Kurdish group in the northern part of the country where he reportedly continued to mastermind attacks in his Jordanian homeland in addition to plotting violence in Morocco, Turkey, and Iraq. The October 2002 assassination of Laurence Foley, a U.S. Agency for International Development official who worked in Amman, was attributed to Zarqawi by the U.S. government. Again Zarqawi was charged in absentia in Jordan and again he was sentenced to death.

Zarqawi attained notoriety in the United States in February 2003 when U.S. secretary of state Colin Powell claimed that Zarqawi's presence (and possible medical treatment for injuries sustained in the missile attack in Afghanistan) in Iraq was evidence of Saddam Hussein's connection to al-Qaeda. This terrorist connection was considered by some to be justification for the U.S. invasion of Iraq and subsequent Iraq War.

After the Iraq War's start in March 2003, Zarqawi instigated a variety of attacks on U.S. targets and was the first proponent of widespread sectarian conflict in the country—by the time of his death in June 2006, Shiite civilians in Iraq were his Sunni supporters' primary target. Over a period of time, the United States accused him of more than 700 killings, the U.S. State Department named him as the person primarily responsible for the bombing of a United Nations hotel in August 2003, and the U.S. Central Intelligence

Agency claimed that he was the man who beheaded American communications worker Nicholas Berg in a videotape released in May 2004. Indicative of the contradictory accounts that surrounded Zarqawi, many reports had claimed that he lost a leg in the Afghan missile attack though the videotape proved that claim to be false. Although Zarqawi was accused of planning a series of bombings in November 2005 that killed 70 people in Amman, a Shiite cleric in Iraq went so far as to claim that Zarqawi himself was fictitious and possibly a creation of U.S. propagandists.

Although possibly captured by Iraqi forces in 2004 and released because of Iraqi officials' failure to recognize him (a claim that the United States never confirmed but acknowledged as possible), Zarqawi remained hidden until his June 2006 death. Despite an April 2006 report that he had resigned as the leader of a coalition of Iraqi militant groups, it was believed that he still led al-Qaeda in Iraq, which was established in 2004 when his Tawhid and Jihad organization merged with bin Laden's al-Qaeda. Zarqawi was considered the number two man in al-Qaeda, and the United States' offer of $25 million for information leading to his capture was the same amount that the U.S. government offered for bin Laden until his death in 2011. Zarqawi was killed on June 7, 2006, by the U.S. Air Force, which discovered his whereabouts and bombed a safe house north of Baghdad where he was attending a meeting.

ABC-CLIO

DOCUMENT: PRESIDENT BARACK OBAMA ANNOUNCES THE DEATH OF OSAMA BIN LADEN (2011)

On the evening of May 1, 2011, President Barack Obama announced in the following speech that a team of U.S. navy SEALs had found and killed Osama bin Laden in a compound in Pakistan. The announcement led to eruption of spontaneous celebrations outside the White House and elsewhere in the United States.

THE PRESIDENT: Good evening. Tonight, I can report to the American people and to the world that the United States has conducted an operation that killed Osama bin Laden, the leader of al Qaeda, and a terrorist who's responsible for the murder of thousands of innocent men, women, and children.

It was nearly 10 years ago that a bright September day was darkened by the worst attack on the American people in our history. The images of 9/11 are seared into our national memory—hijacked planes cutting through a cloudless September sky; the Twin Towers collapsing to the ground; black smoke billowing up from the Pentagon; the wreckage of Flight 93 in Shanksville, Pennsylvania, where the actions of heroic citizens saved even more heartbreak and destruction.

And yet we know that the worst images are those that were unseen to the world. The empty seat at the dinner table. Children who were forced to grow up without their mother or their father. Parents who would never know the feeling of their child's embrace. Nearly 3,000 citizens taken from us, leaving a gaping hole in our hearts.

On September 11, 2001, in our time of grief, the American people came together. We offered our neighbors a hand, and we offered the wounded our blood. We reaffirmed our ties to each other, and our love of community and country. On that day, no matter where we came from, what God we prayed to, or what race or ethnicity we were, we were united as one American family.

We were also united in our resolve to protect our nation and to bring those who committed this vicious attack to justice. We quickly learned that the 9/11 attacks were carried out by al Qaeda—an organization headed by Osama bin Laden, which had openly declared war on the United States and was committed to killing innocents in our country and around the globe. And so we went to war against al Qaeda to protect our citizens, our friends, and our allies.

Over the last 10 years, thanks to the tireless and heroic work of our military and our counterterrorism professionals, we've made great strides in that effort. We've disrupted terrorist attacks and strengthened our homeland defense. In Afghanistan, we removed the Taliban government, which had given bin Laden and al Qaeda safe haven and support. And around the globe, we worked with our friends and allies to capture or kill scores of al Qaeda terrorists, including several who were a part of the 9/11 plot.

Yet Osama bin Laden avoided capture and escaped across the Afghan border into Pakistan. Meanwhile, al Qaeda continued to operate from along that border and operate through its affiliates across the world.

And so shortly after taking office, I directed Leon Panetta, the director of the CIA, to make the killing or capture of bin Laden the top priority of our war against al Qaeda, even as we continued our broader efforts to disrupt, dismantle, and defeat his network.

Then, last August, after years of painstaking work by our intelligence community, I was briefed on a possible lead to bin Laden. It was far from certain, and it took many months to run this thread to ground. I met repeatedly with my national security team as we developed more information about the possibility that we had located bin Laden hiding within a compound deep inside of Pakistan. And finally, last week, I determined that we had enough intelligence to take action, and authorized an operation to get Osama bin Laden and bring him to justice.

Today, at my direction, the United States launched a targeted operation against that compound in Abbottabad, Pakistan. A small team of Americans carried out the operation with extraordinary courage and capability. No Americans were harmed. They took care to avoid civilian casualties. After a firefight, they killed Osama bin Laden and took custody of his body.

For over two decades, bin Laden has been al Qaeda's leader and symbol, and has continued to plot attacks against our country and our friends and allies. The death of bin Laden marks the most significant achievement to date in our nation's effort to defeat al Qaeda.

Yet his death does not mark the end of our effort. There's no doubt that al Qaeda will continue to pursue attacks against us. We must—and we will—remain vigilant at home and abroad.

As we do, we must also reaffirm that the United States is not—and never will be—at war with Islam. I've made clear, just as President Bush did shortly after 9/11, that our war is not against Islam. Bin Laden was not a Muslim leader; he was a mass murderer of

Muslims. Indeed, al Qaeda has slaughtered scores of Muslims in many countries, including our own. So his demise should be welcomed by all who believe in peace and human dignity.

Over the years, I've repeatedly made clear that we would take action within Pakistan if we knew where bin Laden was. That is what we've done. But it's important to note that our counterterrorism cooperation with Pakistan helped lead us to bin Laden and the compound where he was hiding. Indeed, bin Laden had declared war against Pakistan as well, and ordered attacks against the Pakistani people.

Tonight, I called President Zardari, and my team has also spoken with their Pakistani counterparts. They agree that this is a good and historic day for both of our nations. And going forward, it is essential that Pakistan continue to join us in the fight against al Qaeda and its affiliates.

The American people did not choose this fight. It came to our shores, and started with the senseless slaughter of our citizens. After nearly 10 years of service, struggle, and sacrifice, we know well the costs of war. These efforts weigh on me every time I, as Commander-in-Chief, have to sign a letter to a family that has lost a loved one, or look into the eyes of a service member who's been gravely wounded.

So Americans understand the costs of war. Yet as a country, we will never tolerate our security being threatened, nor stand idly by when our people have been killed. We will be relentless in defense of our citizens and our friends and allies. We will be true to the values that make us who we are. And on nights like this one, we can say to those families who have lost loved ones to al Qaeda's terror: Justice has been done.

Tonight, we give thanks to the countless intelligence and counterterrorism professionals who've worked tirelessly to achieve this outcome. The American people do not see their work, nor know their names. But tonight, they feel the satisfaction of their work and the result of their pursuit of justice.

We give thanks for the men who carried out this operation, for they exemplify the professionalism, patriotism, and unparalleled courage of those who serve our country. And they are part of a generation that has borne the heaviest share of the burden since that September day.

Finally, let me say to the families who lost loved ones on 9/11 that we have never forgotten your loss, nor wavered in our commitment to see that we do whatever it takes to prevent another attack on our shores.

And tonight, let us think back to the sense of unity that prevailed on 9/11. I know that it has, at times, frayed. Yet today's achievement is a testament to the greatness of our country and the determination of the American people.

The cause of securing our country is not complete. But tonight, we are once again reminded that America can do whatever we set our mind to. That is the story of our history, whether it's the pursuit of prosperity for our people, or the struggle for equality for all our citizens; our commitment to stand up for our values abroad, and our sacrifices to make the world a safer place.

Let us remember that we can do these things not just because of wealth or power, but because of who we are: one nation, under God, indivisible, with liberty and justice for all.

Thank you. May God bless you. And may God bless the United States of America.

APPENDIX A: GLOSSARY OF TERMS AND PEOPLE

Abbas, Mahmoud (b. 1935). The chairman of the Palestine Liberation Organization since 2004 and of the Palestinian National Authority since 2005, Abbas has been active in Palestinian affairs since the mid-1950s. He signed the Oslo Declaration of Principles in 1993.

Armistice. An armistice is a cessation of hostilities preliminary to the signing of a peace treaty. At the end of World War I, an armistice stopping the war was put into effect on November 11, 1918.

ARPAnet. The earliest forerunner to the Internet. ARPAnet was created at MIT and the Defense Advanced Research Projects Agency, which wanted a linked system of communication. It was launched in 1969.

Atlantic Charter. This statement, approved by Franklin D. Roosevelt and Winston Churchill at a conference in 1941, outlined the principles that should guide the Allies in World War II. It endorsed self-determination and access for all to raw materials and suggested a postwar organization to guarantee peace. The United States and Great Britain also abjured territorial gain as a result of the war.

Bandung Conference. Held in Ceylon in 1955, the Bandung Conference brought together representatives from a number of Asian and African countries. The conference laid the groundwork for Third World cooperation at the United Nations and stimulated the formation and growth of the Non-Aligned Movement.

Beer Hall Putsch. In November 1923, Adolf Hitler joined with the former World War I general Erich Ludendorff in an attempt to overthrow the German (Weimar) Republic. Based in Munich, the coup attempt, or putsch, failed. It was called the Beer Hall Putsch because the conspiracy was hatched in the back rooms of Munich's taverns.

Begin, Menachem (1913–1992). Active in Israeli politics since 1948, Begin was a founder of the conservative Likud Party in Israel in 1973 and served as prime minister of Israel from 1977 to 1983, when he resigned after the controversial invasion and occupation of Lebanon.

Berlin Wall. Constructed in August 1961 to halt the exodus of people from East Germany, the Berlin Wall separated East Berlin from West Berlin. The wall came to represent the post–World War II division of Europe in general and Germany specifically. A continual source of irritation between East and West, the Berlin Wall was destroyed in November 1989, thereby signaling the end of the communist regime in East Germany and clearing the way for German reunification.

Berners-Lee, Tim (b. 1955). A British physicist and computer scientist who teaches at MIT, Berners-Lee is credited with proposing the World Wide Web in 1989 and implementing it the following year by successfully using HTTP (Hyper-Text Transfer Protocol) between a server and a client.

Boxer Revolt. The Boxers were a secret society in China that launched a terrorist campaign against foreigners in 1900 with the tacit support of the government. A multinational military force relieved the besieged diplomatic community in Peking, and diplomatic pressure finally resulted in the suppression of the Boxers.

Catholic Popolari. The Catholic Popolari was an Italian political party founded in 1919. Sometimes called the Christian Democrat Party, the Catholic Popolari enjoyed widespread support among Roman Catholics opposed to the anticlericalists who had governed Italy since its founding in 1860. Beyond support for Roman Catholicism, the Catholic Popolari had no coherent or unifying philosophy.

COBOL. Acronym for Common Business-Oriented Language. COBOL was developed in 1959 as one of the first computer languages that was not specifically meant for scientific purposes.

Comintern. Officially known as the Third International or Communist International, the Comintern was formed in Moscow in 1919. Firmly under the control of the Bolsheviks, the Comintern attacked less radical socialists, promoted world revolution, and served the interests of the Soviet state. Joseph Stalin abolished the Comintern in 1943 as a concession to his wartime allies, the United States and Great Britain.

Commonwealth. Formerly known as the British Commonwealth of Nations, the Commonwealth of Nations or Commonwealth is an organization consisting of the United Kingdom and many of its former colonies that have gained independence. It is a consultative body pulling together a diverse group of nations from all corners of the globe.

Confucianism. Confucianism is a philosophy based on the writings of Kongfuzi (Confucius), who lived in the sixth and fifth centuries BCE. Confucianism placed great emphasis on righteousness and restraint for people to achieve harmony with nature. For centuries, Confucianism provided the philosophy by which the Chinese lived.

Cultural Revolution. The Cultural Revolution was a radical movement in Mao Zedong's China between 1966 and 1976. It was disruptive in the extreme, causing serious political, economic, and social instability in its drive to create a state of "permanent revolution."

Darwin, Charles (1809–1882). Charles Darwin was a British naturalist who developed the theory of evolution by natural selection and survival of the fittest. Under Social Darwinism, some of his followers applied his ideas to individual humans, nations, and/or races.

Doughboy. Doughboy was a nickname given to American infantrymen during World War I.

Dow Jones Industrial Average. The Dow Jones Industrial Average is an index of the New York stock market performance based on the value of the stock of 30 leading industrial corporations. The "average" is calculated by means of a mathematical formula that is periodically adjusted in such a way as to make comparisons of past and present performance meaningful.

Dzerzhinsky, Felix (1877–1926). Born into a Polish noble family, Felix Dzerzhinsky became a revolutionary in tsarist Russia. He is best known for establishing the first Bolshevik secret police, the Cheka.

Entente. A French term meaning a friendly understanding or agreement, entente also came to designate the cordial relationship among Great Britain, France, and Russia on the eve of World War I. At the outbreak of the war, this relationship solidified into a formal alliance.

"Flanders' Fields." Flanders' Fields refers to the area of northern France and western Belgium bordering the North Sea. During World War I, several ferocious battles were fought there resulting in a staggering number of casualties.

FORTRAN. A computer language with applications for mathematical computing. FORTRAN was developed in the 1950s and, after many upgrades, is still used for sophisticated scientific purposes.

Fox News. A cable and satellite television news outlet overseen by media tycoon Rupert Murdoch and Roger Ailes, a one-time political operative for Presidents Richard Nixon and Ronald Reagan. Purporting to be "fair and balanced," most media observers regard Fox News as a conscious mouthpiece for conservative Republican causes.

Freud, Sigmund (1856–1939). A Viennese physician turned psychologist, Sigmund Freud is universally regarded as the father of psychoanalysis. In 1900, he published *On the Interpretation of Dreams* and ultimately suggested that human behavior is rooted in the irrational rather than the rational.

Great Leap Forward. Between 1958 and 1961, Mao Zedong attempted to stimulate China's economy. The Great Leap Forward featured a sustained propaganda barrage, collectivization of the peasants, and decentralization of industry. The Great Leap Forward was a disaster as economic production declined and famine stalked the land.

Hamas. A Palestinian Islamist political party that governs Gaza. It was founded in 1987 out of Egypt's Muslim Brotherhood and won a majority in the Palestinian parliament in 2006, defeating the Palestine Liberation Organization. Its rocket attacks into neighboring Israeli territory generated much controversy between 2008 and 2011.

Hollerith, Herman (1860–1929). Although he was trained as a mining engineer, Hollerith developed the original punch-card system of sorting, counting, and storing data. His device was first used in the 1890 U.S. census, and he went on to build machines called tabulators that did these functions. His company, along with others, eventually became IBM.

Mandate of Heaven. A traditional Chinese belief that Heaven has selected a certain dynasty to rule because of its fitness in Confucian terms. Deviation from these terms would displease Heaven. Thus, any change in ruling dynasty is—ex post facto—conclusive evidence that the former dynasty has displeased Heaven and lost the Mandate. Conversely, the new dynasty had pleased Heaven and, consequently, gained the Mandate.

Marianne. Marianne is the personification of the French Republic in much the same manner that Uncle Sam is the personification of the United States. Frequently, Marianne is portrayed in flowing robes with a liberty cap and a tricolor cockade.

Marx, Karl (1818–1883). A German publicist, historian, philosopher, and sociologist, Karl Marx is generally regarded as the father of modern socialism. The most cogent synopsis of his ideas is found in his *Communist Manifesto* (1848).

Mau Mau. From 1952 until 1956, the Mau Mau, a secret society of Kenyan natives committed to driving the British imperialists from their homeland, waged a campaign of terror against British settlers. Although the Mau Mau were defeated, the cost was so high that Great Britain decided to grant independence to its East African colonies rather than fight to retain them.

Meiji Restoration. Lasting from 1868 until 1912, the Meiji Restoration or era was a period of intense reform in Japan. To preserve its sovereignty from Western encroachment, Japanese reformers during this era adopted Western technology and ideas to modernize the Japanese state and make it capable of resisting the West.

Mensheviks. The Mensheviks were the non-Leninist faction of the Russian Social Democratic Party. Although sometimes cooperating with Lenin's Bolsheviks, the Mensheviks were less rigid and conspiratorial. In 1922, the Bolsheviks suppressed the Mensheviks.

Nasser, Gamal Abdel (1918–1970). Nasser led the revolution in Egypt in 1952 that removed both the monarchy and British authority. He launched an era of modernization and socialist reform marked by close ties with the Soviet bloc. His nationalization of the Suez Canal escalated into the Suez Crisis in 1956, the year he became president of Egypt. During his 14 years as president, he inspired independence movements and Arab nationalism throughout North Africa and the Middle East.

New Deal. The New Deal refers to the series of socioeconomic reforms inaugurated by U.S. President Franklin D. Roosevelt at the height of the Depression. Among the more permanent reforms were Social Security, federal insurance for bank depositors, and laws limiting the work week, child labor, and discrimination against labor unions.

NKVD. NKVD is the Russian abbreviation for the People's Commissariat of Internal Affairs, the Soviet security force or secret police. A successor to the Cheka, the NKVD later changed its name to become the KGB.

Old Bolsheviks. The term "Old Bolsheviks" applies to those who belonged to Lenin's Bolshevik faction of the Russian Social Democratic Party before the 1917 Russian Revolution that brought the Bolsheviks to power. Joseph Stalin, who always suspected the Old Bolsheviks, eliminated most of them during the purges of the 1930s.

OPEC. This acronym stands for the Organization of Petroleum Exporting Countries, a cartel created by oil-rich nations to regain control over their resources from the various oil companies that had received favorable concessions. In the 1970s, OPEC worked to raise prices and nationalize foreign-owned production facilities.

Palestine Liberation Organization (PLO). A political organization created in 1964 and, since 1974, recognized by the United Nations and more than 100 countries as the legitimate representative of the Palestinian people. In the 1990s, the PLO recognized Israel's right to exist.

Palestinian National Authority. An administrative body that purports to govern the West Bank and Gaza. Formed in 1994 after the Oslo Declaration of Principles, the Palestinian National Authority differs from the PLO, which is a quasi-national government with diplomatic representation.

Paris Peace Conference. The Paris Peace Conference is the official name given to the peace negotiations that concluded World War I. Held in Paris from January to June 1919, the conference's main participants were Woodrow Wilson of the United States, David Lloyd George of Great Britain, Georges Clemenceau of France, and Vittorio Orlando of Italy. In all, 32 nations were represented, with thousands of participants and over sixty commissions dealing with specific problems.

Plebiscite. A plebiscite is a direct vote of the population on a specific issue put to them by the government, or on the government itself, or on the leader of the government.

Pogrom. From the Russian, a pogrom is an organized and usually officially condoned attack on a minority group. Pogroms have most frequently been directed against Jews, especially the Jews of eastern Europe.

Rapprochement. From the French, rapprochement is a term used frequently by diplomats to describe a warming of relations between two countries.

Red Army. Founded by V. I. Lenin in 1918 and built into an effective fighting force by Leon Trotsky, the Red Army defended the Soviet state from its external enemies. After World War II, its name was changed to the Soviet Army.

Reichstag. Reichstag is the name formerly given to the German legislative assembly or parliament.

Reparations. Reparations are payments made by the loser or losers of a war to the victor or victors to "repair" damages done by the former to the latter during the course of the war. At the Paris Peace Conference ending World War I, this definition was stretched to make Germany liable for virtually the entire cost of the war, thereby creating fiscal chaos in Europe until the 1924 Dawes Plan restructured Germany's payment schedule.

Sadat, Anwar (1918–1981). The president of Egypt from 1970 until his assassination in 1981, Sadat was a senior officer in the 1952 revolution that forced King Farouk and Great Britain out of Egypt. He led Egyptian forces during the Yom Kippur War and subsequently won the Nobel Peace Prize for his role in the Camp David Accords.

Silk Road. The Silk Road was not a road. Rather, it was an interconnected group of trading routes linking the eastern Mediterranean with India, China, and the Indonesian archipelago.

Sino-Soviet Split. The Sino-Soviet split was the breakdown in relations that occurred between the Soviet Union and the People's Republic of China during the 1950s and

1960s. By 1969, war appeared imminent, but cooler heads prevailed. Nevertheless, Sino-Soviet relations remained frigid for many years.

Social Darwinism. Derived from Charles Darwin's pioneering nineteenth-century work on evolution, Social Darwinism concluded that the struggle for existence and survival of the fittest applied to man as well as plants and lesser animals. This concept served to justify a number of injustices, including racism, belligerent nationalism, genocide, and monopoly capitalism.

Social Revolutionary Party. Commonly referred to as the SRs, the Social Revolutionary Party was a radical political movement active in Russia in the late nineteenth and early twentieth centuries. The SRs supported collective ownership of the land and enjoyed great support among the Russian peasantry. The SRs were suppressed by the Bolsheviks after the Russian Revolution.

Spanish Civil War. Precipitated by fundamental disagreements over the nature of the Spanish state, the Spanish Civil War, which began in 1936 and ended in 1939, pitted a loose coalition of republicans, socialists, communists, anarchists, and syndicalists against the forces of tradition—clericals, aristocrats, monarchists, big businessmen, army officers, and Falangists or Spanish fascists. Aided by Benito Mussolini and Adolf Hitler, the traditionalists, or nationalists, under the leadership of General Francisco Franco, defeated the loyalists, or republicans, who were aided by Joseph Stalin.

Status quo ante bellum. From the Latin, status quo ante bellum means the existing condition or state of affairs before the outbreak of a war.

Syndicalism. Syndicalism was a radical, working-class movement that was particularly strong in Italy and France in the late nineteenth and early twentieth centuries. It called for direct action such as the general strike to deliver the means of production into the hands of the working class.

The Six. The Six is a common term used to designate the original six members of the European Coal and Steel Community—Belgium, France, Italy, Luxembourg, the Netherlands, and West Germany.

Third Reich. This term was applied by Adolf Hitler to the German state after he came to power. Hitler saw the Third Reich as the legitimate successor to the First Reich, or Holy Roman Empire, and the Second Reich, or Otto von Bismarck's German Empire. Intended to last for a thousand years, the Third Reich disappeared along with Hitler in 1945.

UNIVAC I. Acronym for Universal Automatic Computer. This computer was launched in 1951 by IBM as the first American-made commercial computer. It was enormous and used magnetic metal tape on large reels to store data.

Watson, Thomas, Sr. (1874–1956). Founder of IBM and its president from 1914 to 1956, Watson was responsible for IBM's growth and success through his encouragement of a distinctive corporate culture and his marketing expertise. His son, Thomas Watson, Jr., took over IBM after his father's death.

World Trade Center. The World Trade Center was a seven-building complex located in New York's Lower Manhattan. On September 11, 2001, al-Queda terrorists flew two airliners into the complex's two twin towers—at that time the tallest buildings in the world—destroying them and killing 3,000 people.

APPENDIX B: TIMELINE

1900	World population is estimated at 1.6 billion
	Sigmund Freud publishes *On the Interpretation of Dreams*
	Boxer Rebellion in China
1901	Queen Victoria dies
1902	Alliance between Japan and Great Britain
	Boer War ends
1903	Wright brothers make first powered flight
	United States leases Guantanamo in perpetuity from Cuba
1904	Anglo-French Entente
	New York subway system opens
1904–1905	Russo-Japanese War
1905	Revolution in Russia
	First Moroccan Crisis
	Albert Einstein publishes "On the Electrodynamics of Moving Bodies"
	All-India Muslim League founded
	Norway gains independence from Sweden
1907	Formation of the Triple Entente (Great Britain, France, Russia)
1908	Bosnian Crisis
	Henry Ford initiates production of the Model T
	Boxer Jack Johnson becomes the first black heavyweight champion of the world
1909	Selma O. L. Lagerlof of Sweden is first woman to win Nobel Prize for Literature
1910	Revolution in Mexico
	Establishment of Union of South Africa
	Japan annexes Korea

1911	Chinese Revolution
	Second Moroccan Crisis
1912–1913	Balkan Wars
1914–1918	World War I
1914	Ulster Crisis
	Assassination of Archduke Franz Ferdinand
	First Battle of the Marne
	Battles of Tannenberg and the Masurian Lakes
	Panama Canal completed
1915	Italy enters World War I
1916	Battle of Jutland
	Battle of Verdun
	Battle of the Somme
1917	Russian revolutions; Bolsheviks come to power
	United States enters World War I
	Dada movement influences cultural and intellectual world
	Balfour Declaration indicates British support of a homeland for the Jews in Palestine
1918	Treaty of Brest-Litovsk
	Collapse of Austro-Hungarian, German, and Ottoman Empires
1919	Paris Peace Conference; Treaty of Versailles
	Civil war in Russia
	Establishment of Weimar Republic in Germany
	Revolution in Egypt
	May Fourth Movement in China
	Spanish flu kills 50 to 100 million worldwide
1920	League of Nations founded
	Chinese Communist Party founded
1921	New Economic Policy (NEP) introduced in Russia
1922	Benito Mussolini seizes power in Italy
	USSR established
	Mandate System in the Middle East
1923	Ruhr occupied
	Hyperinflation in Germany
	Turkish Republic founded

	More than 100,000 die as another earthquake strikes Tokyo
1924	First Labour government in Great Britain
	Vladimir Lenin dies
	First Winter Olympics
	Thomas Watson, Sr. founds IBM, pioneer in punch card technology
1925	France begins to construct the Maginot Line
	Sun Yat-sen dies
	Scopes Trial in Tennessee
1926	Claude Monet dies
1927	Charles Lindbergh flies solo across the Atlantic Ocean
1928	Joseph Stalin leads Soviet Union; first Five-Year Plan introduced
	Serious outbreak of Arab-Jewish violence in Palestine
1929	U.S. stock market collapses; beginning of the Great Depression
	Alexander Fleming develops penicillin
	The Roman Catholic Church and Benito Mussolini sign the Lateran Treaty
1930	World population is estimated at 2 billion
	Getulio Vargas comes to power in Brazil
	Astronomers discover Pluto
1931	Manchurian crisis; Japan threatens China
	Credit-Anstalt collapses
	Great Britain abandons the gold standard
	King Alfonso XIII of Spain ousted
1932	Franklin D. Roosevelt elected president of the United States
1933	Adolf Hitler comes to power in Germany
1934	Lazaro Cardenas comes to power in Mexico
1935	Mussolini invades Ethiopia (Abyssinia)
1936	Hitler remilitarizes the Rhineland
	Spanish Civil War begins
	J. M. Keynes publishes *General Theory of Employment, Interest, and Money*
	Purge trials begin in USSR
	Paul Eisler creates first circuit board
1937	Japan seizes Nanking from China
1938	Germany annexes Austria (*Anschluss*)
	Munich Conference

1939   Nazi-Soviet Non-Aggression Pact

Germany invades Poland

USSR invades Poland

"Winter War" between USSR and Finland begins

World's Fair opens in New York City

1940   Germany conquers France

Winston Churchill becomes prime minister in Great Britain

USSR absorbs Estonia, Latvia, and Lithuania

Atlantic Charter

Battle of Britain

1941   Germany invades the Soviet Union

Japan attacks the United States

Mohammed Reza Pahlavi comes to power in Iran

1942   Battle of Stalingrad begins

1943   Battle of Kursk

Italy surrenders

1944   Allies invade Nazi-occupied Europe

1945   Yalta Conference

Roosevelt dies

Mussolini is executed

Hitler commits suicide

Germany surrenders

Potsdam Conference

Labour wins election in Great Britain; Churchill replaced by Clement Attlee

United States drops atomic bombs on Hiroshima and Nagasaki; Japan surrenders

United Nations established

USSR begins to establish empire in Eastern Europe

Cold War begins

1946   Juan Peron comes to power in Argentina

ENIAC, first electronic computer

1947   Truman Doctrine

Marshall Plan

India and Pakistan achieve independence; Jawaharlal Nehru comes to power in India

	Researchers at Bell Laboratories invent the transistor
1948	Communist coup in Czechoslovakia
	Berlin Blockade begins
	Israel established; First Arab-Israeli War
	Stalin feuds with Yugoslavian communist leader Marshal Tito (Josip Broz)
	Organization of American States (OAS) established
	Gandhi assassinated
1949	North Atlantic Treaty Organization (NATO) established
	Dutch are forced to leave Indonesia
	Federal Republic of Germany (West Germany) founded
	German Democratic Republic (East Germany) founded
	Council for Mutual Economic Aid (Comecon or CMEA) established
	Chinese communists win Chinese Civil War
1950	North Korea invades South Korea
1951	European Coal and Steel Community (ECSC) established
	Oil nationalization crisis in Iran
	Libya achieves independence
	Remington Rand introduces Univac I, first commercially available computer
1952	Gamal Abdel Nasser comes to power in Egypt
1953	Stalin dies
	Watson and Crick describe the double helix structure of chromosomes
1954	French are forced to leave Indochina
	Beginning of revolt against French in Algeria
1955	Bandung Conference
	Warsaw Treaty Organization (WTO) established
1956	Nikita Khrushchev denounces Stalin at the Twentieth Congress of the Communist Party of the Soviet Union
	Suez Crisis
	Hungarian Revolution suppressed by USSR
1957	Treaty of Rome establishes the European Economic Community (EEC)
	USSR launches Sputnik (first orbiting satellite)
	Colonialism in black Africa begins to disappear
	FORTRAN, first widely used computer programming language, introduced

	Mao Zedong initiates the "Let One Hundred Flowers Bloom" campaign
1958	Start of the Great Leap Forward in China
	Charles de Gaulle named president of France; establishment of the Fifth French Republic
1959	Cuban Revolution; Fidel Castro comes to power
1960	World population is estimated at 3 billion
1961	Increased U.S. involvement in Vietnam War
	Berlin Wall constructed
	Soviet cosmonaut Yuri Gagarin orbits the earth
1961–1965	Second Vatican Council
1962	Independence for Algeria
	Cuban Missile Crisis
	Sino-Soviet split
	Alexander Solzhenitsyn publishes *One Day in the Life of Ivan Denisovich*
1963	U.S. president John F. Kennedy assassinated
	Organization of African Unity founded
1964	Nehru dies
	Khrushchev ousted; Leonid Brezhnev comes to power
	Military seizes power in Brazil
	China detonates a nuclear device
	The Beatles appear on U.S. television
	IBM introduces word processing
	Palestine Liberation Organization (PLO) founded with Yasser Arafat as leader
1965	First desktop computer made available to public
1966	Beginning of Cultural Revolution in China
1967	Arab-Israeli Six-Day War
	Civil war (Biafran War) in Nigeria
1968	USSR invades Czechoslovakia
	Martin Luther King, Jr., assassinated
	Unrest in major Western countries, including the United States and France
1969	United States lands a man on the moon
	Woodstock music festival
1970	Beginning of détente
1971	People's Republic of China replaces the Republic of China in the United Nations

1972	SALT I agreement
	U.S. President Richard Nixon pays official visit to China
1973	Third Arab-Israeli War (Yom Kippur War)
	Start of Arab oil embargo
	Salvador Allende overthrown in Chile
	Pablo Picasso dies
	Great Britain joins the European Economic Community
1974	Beginning of world economic recession
	Richard Nixon resigns
	Marxist revolution in Ethiopia
	India detonates a nuclear device
1975	End of Vietnam War
	Last European empire in Africa (Portugal) ends
	Helsinki Conference on European Security and Cooperation
	Dmitri Shostakovich dies
1976	Mao Zedong dies
	Apple brings out its first desktop computer
	Chou En-lai dies
1978–1997	Deng Xiaoping leads China
1978	Camp David Peace Accords between Israel and Egypt
1979	Margaret Thatcher becomes prime minister of Great Britain
	USSR invades Afghanistan
	Sandinista revolution in Nicaragua
	Revolution in Iran brings fundamentalist Islamic regime to power
	Saddam Hussein comes to power in Iraq
1980	Solidarity movement in Poland
	Ronald Reagan elected U.S. president
	Iran-Iraq War begins
	United States boycotts Moscow Olympic Games over USSR'S invasion of Afghanistan
1981	Anwar Sadat, Egyptian president, assassinated
	IBM introduces its desktop computer, the IBM PC
1982	Brezhnev dies
	Israel invades Lebanon
1983	Argentina returns to civilian rule

	Suicide bomber attacks U.S. Marine compound in Lebanon; 240 Marines killed
1984	Indira Gandhi assassinated
	Soviet Union and its satellite countries boycott the Los Angeles Olympic Games
1985	Mikhail Gorbachev named to head Soviet Union
	Brazil returns to civilian rule
	Passage of the Single European Act
1986	Chernobyl nuclear power station accident
	Olof Palme, prime minister of Sweden, assassinated
1987	Intermediate Nuclear Forces Treaty (INF) signed
	Montreal Protocol limits substances that deplete the ozone layer
	Start of Palestinian uprising (Intifada)
1988	Hamas, Muslim anti-Israeli organization, founded
1989	China crushes movement for democracy
	Ayatollah Khomeini dies
	Revolutions in Eastern Europe
	Berlin Wall falls
	Japanese emperor Hirohito dies
	World Wide Web (WWW) first comes into use
1990	World population is estimated at 5 billion
1991	Persian Gulf War results in defeat of Iraq
	USSR collapses
	Rajiv Gandhi assassinated
1992	European Community achieves full economic integration
	Yugoslav federation breaks up
1993	Apartheid in South Africa ends
	Israeli-Palestinian peace accords
	North American Free Trade Agreement (NAFTA)
	Maastricht Treaty
	Terrorist bomb exploded in garage of New York's World Trade Center
1994	Nelson Mandela elected president of South Africa
	Yitzhak Rabin, Israeli prime minister, assassinated
1995	Schengen Agreement ends border controls for many European Union countries
1996	Taliban capture Kabul, Afghanistan capital

	Truck bomb kills 19 U.S. service personnel in Saudi Arabia
1997	Deng Xiaoping dies
	Hong Kong returned to China
1998	Suharto, Indonesian dictator, ousted
	Terrorists destroy U.S. embassies in Kenya and Tanzania
2000	World population estimated at 6 billion
	Slobodan Milosevic ousted as leader of Serbia
	U.S. Navy destroyer *Cole* attacked by terrorists
	Second Intifada breaks out; more Israeli-Palestinian violence
2001	9/11 terrorist attacks in the United States
	United States attacks Afghanistan
	U.S. Patriot Act passed and signed into law
2002	Terrorist attack in Bali (Indonesia) kills hundreds
	U.S. Department of Homeland Security created
	The Euro replaces national currencies in much of Europe
2003	United States and allies invade Iraq
2004	Haiti's president, Jean-Bertrand Aristide, overthrown
	NATO admits seven new members
	Beslan school hostage crisis in Russia results in 340 deaths
	More than 200,000 die in Asian tsunami
2005	Pope John Paul II dies
	Mahmoud Ahmadinejad elected president of Iran
	Terrorists strike London transit killing 52
	Kitzmiller v. Dover strikes down teaching of Intelligent Design
2006	North Korea explodes a nuclear device
	Iraqi dictator Saddam Hussein executed
	Israel-Hezbollah conflict in Lebanon
2007	Treaty of Lisbon creates a de facto constitution for Europe
2008	Fidel Castro relinquishes power in Cuba
	Vladimir Putin moves from president to prime minister in Russia
	Georgia and Russia fight short war
	Major terrorist attack in Mumbai (Bombay) kills 170
	Barack Obama is first African American elected president of the United States
	Global economic downturn underway

	Alexander Solzhenitsyn dies
	Summer Olympic Games held in Beijing
2009	Israel launches ground assaults into Gaza
	Rio de Janeiro awarded 2016 Olympic Games
	Treaty of Lisbon goes into effect
2010	Major earthquake devastates Haiti
	Global fiscal crisis continues
	China's economy is world's second largest
2010–2012	Financial difficulties in Greece, Ireland, Italy, Spain, and Portugal shake the EU
2011	Massive earthquake and tsunami strike Japan; nuclear power plants destroyed
	Political unrest convulses the Arab world
	Osama bin Laden killed
	United States withdraws from Iraq
	Steve Jobs dies
2012	Summer Olympic Games held in London

APPENDIX C: POPULATION OF SELECTED COUNTRIES (IN MILLIONS)

Country	1900	1920	1940	1960	1980	2000
Brazil	20	24.5	41.3	68	123	173.3
China	370	400	457.8	670	1027	1268.3
Egypt	10	12.6	16.1	26.1	41.9	70.5
France	38.5	40	41.9	45.7	53.7	61.1
Germany	56.3	60	69.3	72.8	78.3	82.1
India	294	315	365	532	837.1	1029
Indonesia	36	49.5	55.7	92.6	151.8	213.8
Italy	33.6	36	45.3	50.7	57.1	57.7
Japan	45	77	78.2	93.6	116.7	126.1
Mexico	13.6	16	19.4	34.6	71.9	99.9
Nigeria	—	15.1	20.6	34	77.1	123.1
Ottoman Empire/Turkey	26.8	14	17.8	27.8	45.3	65.6
Persia/Iran	9	10	16	20.6	38	63.2
Russia/USSR	104	147	192.6	214.4	262	146.7
United Kingdom	38	45.5	47.1	51.7	55.9	59.5
United States	76	106	131.7	179	226	282.1

APPENDIX D: MEMBER STATES OF THE UNITED NATIONS

Member State	Date of Admission
Afghanistan	1946
Albania	1955
Algeria	1962
Andorra	1993
Angola	1976
Antigua and Barbuda	1981
Argentina	1945
Armenia	1992
Australia	1945
Austria	1955
Azerbaijan	1992
Bahamas	1973
Bahrain	1971
Bangladesh	1974
Barbados	1966
Belarus	1945
Belgium	1945
Belize	1981
Benin	1960
Bhutan	1971
Bolivia	1945
Bosnia and Herzegovina	1992
Botswana	1966
Brazil	1945
Brunei Darussalam	1984
Bulgaria	1955
Burkina Faso	1960

Member State	Date of Admission
Burundi	1962
Cambodia	1955
Cameroon	1960
Canada	1945
Cape Verde	1975
Central African Republic	1960
Chad	1960
Chile	1945
China	1945
Colombia	1945
Comoros	1975
Congo	1960
Costa Rica	1945
Cote D'Ivoire	1960
Croatia	1992
Cuba	1945
Cyprus	1960
Czech Republic	1993
Democratic People's Republic of Korea	1991
Democratic Republic of the Congo	1960
Denmark	1945
Djibouti	1977
Dominica	1978
Dominican Republic	1945
Ecuador	1945
Egypt	1945
El Salvador	1945
Equatorial Guinea	1968
Eritrea	1993
Estonia	1991
Ethiopia	1945
Fiji	1970
Finland	1955
France	1945
Gabon	1960
Gambia	1965
Georgia	1992

Member State	Date of Admission
Germany	1973
Ghana	1957
Greece	1945
Grenada	1974
Guatemala	1945
Guinea	1958
Guinea Bissau	1974
Guyana	1966
Haiti	1945
Honduras	1945
Hungary	1955
Iceland	1946
India	1945
Indonesia	1950
Iran	1945
Iraq	1945
Ireland	1955
Israel	1949
Italy	1955
Jamaica	1962
Japan	1956
Jordan	1955
Kazakhstan	1992
Kenya	1963
Kiribati	1999
Kuwait	1963
Kyrgyzstan	1992
Lao People's Democratic Republic	1955
Latvia	1991
Lebanon	1945
Lesotho	1966
Liberia	1945
Libyan Arab Jamahiriya	1955
Liechtenstein	1990
Lithuania	1991
Luxembourg	1945
Macedonia, Former Yugoslav Republic of	1993

Member State	Date of Admission
Madagascar	1960
Malawi	1964
Malaysia	1957
Maldives	1965
Mali	1960
Malta	1964
Marshall Islands	1991
Mauritania	1961
Mauritius	1968
Mexico	1945
Micronesia, Federated States of	1991
Monaco	1993
Mongolia	1961
Montenegro	2006
Morocco	1956
Mozambique	1975
Myanmar	1948
Namibia	1990
Nauru	1999
Nepal	1955
Netherlands	1945
New Zealand	1945
Nicaragua	1945
Niger	1960
Nigeria	1960
Norway	1945
Oman	1971
Pakistan	1947
Palau	1994
Panama	1945
Papua New Guinea	1975
Paraguay	1945
Peru	1945
Philippines	1945
Poland	1945
Portugal	1955
Qatar	1971

Member State	Date of Admission
Republic of Korea	1991
Republic of Moldova	1992
Romania	1955
Russian Federation	1945
Rwanda	1962
Saint Kitts and Nevis	1983
Saint Lucia	1979
Saint Vincent and the Grenadines	1980
Samoa	1976
San Marino	1992
Sao Tome and Principe	1975
Saudi Arabia	1945
Senegal	1960
Serbia	2000
Seychelles	1976
Sierra Leone	1961
Singapore	1965
Slovakia	1993
Slovenia	1992
Solomon Islands	1978
Somalia	1960
South Africa	1945
Spain	1955
Sri Lanka	1955
Sudan	1956
Suriname	1975
Swaziland	1968
Sweden	1946
Switzerland	2002
Syrian Arab Republic	1945
Tajikistan	1992
Thailand	1946
Timor-Leste	2002
Togo	1960
Tonga	1999
Trinidad and Tobago	1962
Tunisia	1956

Member State	Date of Admission
Turkey	1945
Turkmenistan	1992
Tuvalu	2000
Uganda	1962
Ukraine	1945
United Arab Emirates	1971
United Kingdom of Great Britain and Northern Ireland	1945
United Republic of Tanzania	1961
United States of America	1945
Uruguay	1945
Uzbekistan	1992
Vanuatu	1981
Venezuela, Bolivarian Republic of	1945
Viet Nam	1977
Yemen	1947
Zambia	1964
Zimbabwe	1980

APPENDIX E: MEMBER STATES OF THE EUROPEAN UNION

Member State	Date of Admission
Founding Members	
Belgium	Founder
France	Founder
Germany	Founder
Italy	Founder
Luxembourg	Founder
Netherlands	Founder
Later Admissions in Chronological Order	
Denmark	1973
Ireland	1973
United Kingdom	1973
Greece	1981
Portugal	1986
Spain	1986
Austria	1995
Finland	1995
Sweden	1995
Cyprus	2004
Czech Republic	2004
Estonia	2004
Hungary	2004
Latvia	2004
Lithuania	2004
Malta	2004
Poland	2004
Slovakia	2004
Slovenia	2004
Bulgaria	2007
Romania	2007

APPENDIX F: MEMBER STATES OF THE NORTH ATLANTIC TREATY ORGANIZATION (NATO)

Members Admitted in 1949

Belgium	Luxembourg
Canada	Netherlands
Denmark	Norway
France	Portugal
Iceland	United Kingdom
Italy	United States of America

Later Admissions in Chronological Order

Member State	Date of Admission
Greece	1952
Turkey	1952
Germany	1955
Spain	1982
Czech Republic	1999
Hungary	1999
Poland	1999
Bulgaria	2004
Estonia	2004
Latvia	2004
Lithuania	2004
Romania	2004
Slovakia	2004
Slovenia	2004
Albania	2009
Croatia	2009

ABOUT THE EDITORS AND CONTRIBUTORS

EDITORS

FRANK W. THACKERAY is professor emeritus of history at Indiana University Southeast. A former Fulbright scholar in Poland, he received his PhD from Temple University (1977). Specializing in Russian-Polish relations in the nineteenth and twentieth centuries, he is the author of *Antecedents of Revolution: Alexander I and the Polish Congress Kingdom* (1980). He also edited *Events That Changed Russia Since 1855* (2007) and *Events That Changed Germany* (2004). He is series co-editor of *The Greenwood Histories of the Modern Nations*.

JOHN E. FINDLING is professor emeritus of history at Indiana University Southeast. He earned his PhD from the University of Texas and has pursued research interests in world's fairs and the modern Olympic movement for nearly 30 years. Among his recent publications are *Fair America* (2000), coauthored with Robert Rydell and Kimberly Pelle, and *Encyclopedia of the Modern Olympic Movement* (2004) and *Encyclopedia of World's Fairs and Expositions* (2008), both coedited with Kimberly Pelle. In retirement, he sells stamps and vintage postcards at Collectors' Stamps Ltd., in Louisville, Kentucky.

CONTRIBUTORS

BRUCE F. ADAMS. The late Dr. Adams was professor of history at the University of Louisville. He earned his PhD from the University of Maryland. He is the author of *The Politics of Punishment: Prison Reform in Russia* (1996) and *Tiny Revolutions in Russia: Twentieth-Century Soviet and Russian History in Anecdotes* (2005).

GEORGE P. BLUM is professor emeritus at the University of the Pacific. He received his PhD from the University of Minnesota. He is the author of *The Rise of Fascism in Europe* (1998) and *Coming of Age in War-torn Lithuania and Germany* (2008).

FRANS COETZEE is an independent scholar who has taught at Yale University and George Washington University. He earned his PhD at the University of Chicago. Along with Marilyn Shevin-Coetzee, he is the coeditor of *Authority, Identity, and the Social History of the Great War* (1995) and *The World in Flames: A World War II Sourcebook* (2010).

RICHARD A. LEIBY is associate professor of history at Rosemont College. He received his PhD from the University of Delaware. Dr. Leiby's research concentrates on European developments after World War II. He is the author of *The Unification of Germany, 1989–1990* (1999).

YUXIN MA is associate professor of history at the University of Louisville. She earned her PhD from the University of Minnesota. Recently she published *Women Journalists and Feminism in China, 1898–1937* (2010). Currently she is researching how popular Chinese media under the Japanese occupation (1931–1945) represented gender issues.

MARK RICE currently teaches at Mankato State University. He received his PhD from the Ohio State University. His academic interests include diplomatic and international history with a particular focus on NATO and Berlin during the Cold War.

MARIJAN SALOPEK has taught in the department of history at the University of British Columbia. He received his PhD from Cambridge University. He has contributed to *Statesmen Who Changed the World.*

LOWELL J. SATRE is professor emeritus of history at Youngstown State University. He received his PhD from the University of South Carolina. Professor Satre is the author of *Thomas Burt, Miners' MP, 1837–1922: The Great Conciliator* (1999) and *Chocolate on Trial: Slavery, Politics, and the Ethics of Business* (2005).

MARILYN SHEVIN-COETZEE is an independent scholar who has taught at Yale University and George Washington University. She earned her PhD at the University of Chicago. Along with Frans Coetzee, she is the coeditor of *Authority, Identity, and the Social History of the Great War* (1995) and *The World in Flames: A World War II Sourcebook* (2010).

CLIFFORD L. STATEN is professor of political science and international studies at Indiana University Southeast. He holds a PhD from the University of North Texas and is the author of *The History of Cuba* (2003) and *The History of Nicaragua* (2010).

LARRY THORNTON is professor of history at Hanover College. He received his PhD from the University of Illinois. His current research interests include Mennonite relief efforts to Poland, 1939–1942, and Oxford University student opinion about armed conflict during the interwar years.

JEFFREY N. WASSERSTROM is professor of history at the University of California–Irvine. He earned his PhD at the University of California–Berkeley. He is the author of *China in the 21st Century: What Everyone Needs to Know* (2010) and *Global Shanghai, 1850–2010* (2008).

TIMOTHY K. WELLIVER is associate professor of history at Bellarmine University. He holds a PhD from Northwestern University. His primary research interest is the political economy of Zanzibar. He is the editor of *African Nationalism and Independence* (1993).

THOMAS PHILIP WOLF is professor emeritus of political science at Indiana University Southeast. He received his PhD from Stanford University. He is editor of the

"British Politics Group Newsletter" and coeditor of *Franklin Delano Roosevelt and Congress* (2001).

CHARLES E. ZIEGLER is professor and university scholar in the political science department at the University of Louisville. He received his PhD from the University of Illinois. He is the author of *The History of Russia* (2009), *Foreign Policy and East Asia* (1993), and *Environmental Policy in the USSR* (1987). Dr. Ziegler is coeditor of *The Russian Far East: A Region at Risk* (2002).

INDEX